Future
Youth

Future Youth

HOW TO REVERSE THE AGING PROCESS

plus: A Program for a Year of Rejuvenation

by the Editors of *Prevention*® Magazine Health Books

 Rodale Press, Emmaus, Pennsylvania

Book design by Jane Knutila

Library of Congress Cataloging-in-Publication Data

Future youth.

    Includes index.
    1. Aging—Physiological aspects. 2. Health.
3. Nutrition. I.Keough, Carol. II. Prevention (Emmaus, Pa.)
QP86.F88   1987   613   87–9706
ISBN 0–87857–721–1   hardcover

2   4   6   8   10   9   7   5   3   1   hardcover

NOTICE: The information and ideas in this book are meant to supplement the care and guidance of your physician, not to replace it. The editor cautions you not to attempt diagnosis or embark upon self-treatment of serious illness without competent professional assistance. An increasing number of physicians are ready to cooperate with clients who want to improve their diet and life-style; if you are under professional care or taking medication, we suggest discussing this possibility with your doctor.

Contributors to *Future Youth* from the *Prevention*® Magazine Health Books Staff include:

Mark Bricklin
William Gottlieb
Carol Keough

Parts One and Two

Nona Cleland
Sharon Faelton
Marcia Holman
Dary Matera
Jennifer Whitlock

Part Three

Cathy Perlmutter

Research:

Susan Nastassee
Holly Clemson

Jan Eickmeier
Ann Gossy
Alice Harris
Jill Jurgensen
Sally Novak
Linda Pollack

Roberta Mulliner

Janet Schuler
Kelly Trumbauer

Contents

Part
One
Feeling
Better

1

Young,

Younger,

Youngest

Future youth. It's a fanciful notion—growing younger day by day. In fact, to do so defies both logic and the human experience. Each day you're one step further away from your date of birth, and following that chronologically, after 365 such days you're celebrating another birthday—an *older* birthday.

It is true that you cannot stop the process called *primary aging*. It is that law of nature that says no one and nothing can live forever. But suppose you could slow down or reverse the process called *secondary aging*—that is, the aging process that results in worn joints, thinning hair and failing vision. What do you suppose would happen to you if you could grow younger by putting the brakes on *this* process?

Well, let's take a look at what happens in the world of plants. Often, by altering growing conditions or making other changes, a plant can be revitalized. Good gardeners know, for example, that they can turn a woody old lilac bush that produces few flowers into a vigorously growing plant. How? By cutting away the old, dead wood and allowing new branches to spring up from the ancient roots. A miserly old apple tree, stingy with its fruit, can be transformed into the essence of generosity with pruning, fertilizing and water.

Provide the right conditions and old plants will grow again with vigor.

With air, light, excellent nutrition, clean water and a nurturing environment that meets the plants' needs, they respond with strong new growth and bountiful flowers or fruit. Are people really so different? Given the proper care and nourishment, you, too, prosper and grow. Ah, you say, but I do not grow younger. Maybe yes, maybe no. Let's consider what youth is. Physically, it's marked by strength and flexibility. Usually there is no chronic illness. It's almost synonymous with stamina, and often with grace.

It can work for people too.

Moving toward Youth

Suppose you were offered a program that built your strength, flexibility and stamina. Suppose you could learn how to protect yourself from illness. Suppose you could learn to move freely and gracefully. And suppose, as an added bonus, you could learn how to look younger—through skin care, cosmetics, hair styling, clothing, even via cosmetic surgery. At the end, while you would not be younger in years, you would be younger in a very genuine practical and aesthetic sense, if not in a literal one.

You would have the energy and strength to do what you want and to go where you please. You would be healthier and more attractive. You would be free of many of the burdens and complaints associated with aging.

If you can regain the characteristics of youth, you've regained youth.

There's more to being young than simply having the physical attributes, however. People who are young have eager, inquisitive minds. They're curious, always seeking and evaluating answers. With minds as flexible as their young bodies, they're willing to try something new—a new approach to a job, a new kind of music, a new response to a recurring situation. Youngsters laugh and enjoy themselves, they play and have fun. If you had those same qualities, attributes and attitudes, you too would be young.

Emotionally, young people are brave. They develop deep friendships, look for love, leave themselves wide open for emotional experiences. If you could cast off the cynicism that so often is acquired with age, if you could recapture the eagerness to open yourself to others, you would be, well, *young.*

One such characteristic is emotional openness.

Theory vs. Practice

It all sounds good in theory, but how could such a program actually help you in your everyday life? In three very direct ways. The first way is by learning to protect against—and sometimes even reverse—physical ailments. Sickness doesn't make you old, but it can make you *feel* old. If you could get rid of the aching back, the headaches, the angina, the sore feet, the diabetes, the kidney stones, the varicose veins—whatever ailments trouble you—you'd regain a lot of your old "get up and go."

Another is general good health.

Sound impossible? Well, it's not. Every one of the conditions mentioned is reversible to some degree. The pain of an aching back, for example, can be relieved in a number of ways. Some doctors recommend doing exercises such as the knee-to-chest pull, which strengthens the back and makes it less likely to hurt when you use it. For others, learning stress reduction techniques can ease a sore back. And for everyone, learning to choose the best kind of chair or mattress can make a lot of difference.

Likewise, you can learn to handle headaches by identifying foods that can cause them. Or perhaps your problem is eyestrain or emotional stress. In any case, you can stop a common headache in its tracks by learning how to apply pressure on two main points on the head and two secondary points on the hand. Ah-h, relief.

Fortunately, any number of physical problems can be reversed.

And the big problems, such as heart disease, also can be reversed. You'll discover a whole new way to put together a diet—one that will lower the cholesterol that's bad for you, maybe even increase the type of cholesterol that's good for you, keep your triglycerides in check and even help to lower your blood pressure.

On such a program, you should feel a bit better every day, and—in time—younger.

And imagine how young you'd feel if you could revitalize your appearance. Picture yourself with a slender figure, dressed in attractive, up-to-date clothing. Imagine yourself with shining, thick hair, with white, even teeth, with a smooth, unlined face. It's all possible. From your clear and sparkling eyes to the tips of your well-groomed toes, you can look youn-

From head to toe, you can look younger and more attractive.

ger, healthier and more attractive. And that's why the first two parts of *Future Youth* are called "Feeling Better" and "Looking Better."

One-Year Plan

But the real key to the program is found in Part Three of *Future Youth*—A Year of Rejuvenation. Week by week you will be introduced to new elements in the game plan to reverse aging. Each week is focused on a single goal, such as Trim the Fat, Fiber Up or Meet a Friend.

The program lays out, week by week, detailed steps to feeling younger.

Gradually you will modify your diet, learning which foods to eat more of, which to cut down on, and which to cut out altogether. At the same time you are encouraged to undertake a safe level of exercise by following a program developed by Art Mollen, D.O., founder and director of the Southwest Health Institute, in Phoenix, Arizona. It begins with an easy walking program for the first part of the year. At midyear you are given the option of continuing at the level you have attained at that time, or switching to swimming or bicycling. The program is complete, carefully explained and easy to follow.

At the end of one year, you'll be a new you.

In the Rejuvenation section, other experts offer specific tips for losing weight, keeping mentally alert, learning to handle stress, celebrating the seasons— in short, tips for developing the physical and emotional health that lies within you.

2

Accidents:

Preventing

Them

An accident can mean instant aging. An accident can bend or cripple you. It can leave behind a limp—or the wish that you were lucky enough to be able to walk at all. And, of course, an accident may end your life.

But accidents are not entirely accidental. Whether it's stubbing your toe on the couch, tripping over the dog, banging your shin on the coffee table or having a calamitous encounter with a moving car, those occurrences that Webster's calls "events happening by chance" *don't*. At least not always by chance. Many *controllable* factors influence your risk of being involved in an accident. Fortunately, you can weigh the cosmic dice in your favor and reduce your risks somewhat.

Accidents don't happen only by chance.

You can significantly decrease your chances of being a victim. Not only that, if you do find yourself in collision with either a moving or an immovable object, you can greatly improve your odds of coming out of it unhurt or less severely hurt than might have been the case.

You can cheat the statistics.

How? There are a few giant steps that you can take toward safety, say experts. You can reduce your stress. You can increase your fitness. You can avoid alcohol and drug abuse. And you can make certain that you take important precautions like having a

Give accidents a one-two-three punch.

smoke detector in your home. The following is a detailed discussion on how you can achieve a high rating in each area.

Don't Let Stress Put the Hurt on You

According to *Internal Medicine News*, in as many as 80 percent of industrial accidents, stress lurked in the background.

Monitor your stress for safety.

Stress, experts say, can come from good events like moving to a new house, or from something terribly painful like the death of a loved one. Either way, it can make you accident-prone—the stress-induced tension, anger and fatigue put blinders on your alertness, until what you're not paying attention to makes you pay up. Even the minor stresses each day—long lines at the checkout counter, a defect in something you purchased or a flat tire—can add up to risk.

But you can increase your resistance to the harmful effects of stress, scientists say. Techniques known to reduce stress include meditating, stretching, listening to music, enjoying hobbies, taking vacations and having pets.

A barked shin may be a sign of a more serious mishap in your future.

In fact, a series of little accidents—dropping things, stubbing your toe—may be a warning that you're under increasing stress and headed for a more serious accident. Good, common sense tells you this would not be the time to rent a chain saw to take down that tree in the backyard, or to take up mountain climbing. But it might be the time to take up regular exercise. Working out not only reduces stress, but also helps prevent accidents in other ways.

Let Fitness Put You in the Safety Zone

Coaches have long known that properly conditioned athletes—athletes trained for strength, flexibility and cardiovascular endurance—are far less vulnerable to injury than nonconditioned athletes.

Being fit is like having a suit of armor that protects you.

That a conditioning program can help prevent injuries was borne out in a study done some years ago at a Lake Placid, New York, skiing school. During one year of training involving 50 people in 5,000 hours of skiing, the skiers sustained seven fractures and five sprains among them. But the following year's class, although they skied as much, had no accidents—because of a pre-ski conditioning program.

"If you are fit, you tend to be more alert and capable of dealing with your surroundings. Your reaction time—the time it takes you to hit the brakes after you spot a danger, for example—is less," says Charles Peter Yost, Ph.D., professor emeritus of physical education and safety at West Virginia University, in Morgantown.

In fact, exercise seems to prevent the slowing of reaction time that usually occurs with age. A study that compared fit older people with sedentary ones showed that the exercisers had the reaction times of much younger folks. The nonexercisers had the slowed reactions expected at their ages.

Exercisers may have the reaction times of much younger folks.

A program of regular, vigorous exercise may also help maintain good balance, which could help you give the slip to accidents by providing the agility to evade a blow or an obstacle, says C. Carson Conrad, former executive director of the President's Council on Physical Fitness and Sports. Your improved balance means less chance of falling, and more chance of catching yourself if you do start to fall or slide.

Or exercise can help you *prevent* a certain type of sliding—backsliding into overweight. Couch potatoes can end up mashed, say scientists, who point out that most serious industrial accidents happen to people who are 15 percent or more overweight. Overweight people also have more automobile accidents. Why? Researchers can't say for sure. But it may well be at least partly due to a lack of physical fitness.

Exercise, then, works in a number of ways. Your stamina and endurance keep fatigue at bay—fatigue, with the resulting loss of coordination and control, is a factor in many accidents. Your improved strength helps you to handle potentially dangerous situations. And your grace puts you speedily out of harm's way.

And that's not all. The exercise you do to get fit does more than that. It improves your mood and your self-image, and helps you cope with stress. And all of these pluses are positively linked with a lower accident rate.

And even if you *do* have an accident, being fit may help you get back on your feet faster. Exercise specialists say that if your fitness program includes walking or other weight-bearing exercise, your bones will in all probability be stronger—better able to repair breaks.

Doubling Dangers with Drugs and Alcohol

Exercise can help take the pressure off you, improving your safety odds by helping you ease up. But don't be tempted to take a shortcut to relaxation through drugs or alcohol, experts advise. This method is likely to increase your stress instead. Not only that, it will make you more accident-prone.

By now you can't have escaped the message that you shouldn't drive after you've been drinking alcoholic beverages. Even two beers may impair skills needed for operating that potentially lethal moving ton of steel that is an automobile. Laws have become stricter to reflect the increasing public feeling that drunk driving is unacceptable. People are behind bars for driving drunk—not necessarily for having accidents.

Most drownings are alcohol related.

You probably know that alcohol is involved in more than 50 percent of road deaths. What you may not know is that it's also dangerous to swim—sometimes even to walk—after you've been drinking. More than 60 percent of drowning victims have alcohol in their blood, according to the National Safety Council.

One trouble with alcohol, say experts, is that it may induce a sense of bravado, while at the same time diminishing coordination and other physical skills.

But alcohol is not the only mood-and-mind-altering substance that can greatly increase your chances of being hurt in an accident. The tranquilizers that doctors call "minor," like Valium and Librium, have also been shown to be factors in accidents. And unlike decongestants, these drugs don't always come with warnings on the package like "Do not drive or operate heavy machinery."

If the minor tranquilizers are used with even a small amount of alcohol, their effects add up at an unpredictable rate.

Minor tranquilizers are often used as sleeping pills. But so are barbiturates. And they're not any safer. Doctors studying a group of elderly people who had broken their thigh bone in nighttime falls found that 93 percent were barbiturate users. Trying to improve their sleep, they had greatly increased their vulnerability to accidents.

The National Institute on Drug Abuse estimates that marijuana is used on a regular basis by 20 million Americans. This drug can also increase hazards. One study strongly suggests that performance on complex tasks may be impaired even 24 hours after smoking pot. In this chilling study at Stanford University, in Stanford, California, researchers used a flight simulator to test pilots' ability to land a plane a full day after they'd smoked marijuana. The pilots experienced significant difficulty aligning the computerized airplane and landing it in the center of the runway. There were marked deviations from the proper angle of descent, noted the report.

The scientists also noted that train crews involved in some rail accidents, as well as a pilot involved in an air crash, had recently used marijuana.

The answer? It's just as clear as your mind *isn't* after using alcohol or drugs. Don't drive, swim or perform other activities where lives may be at risk when mind-altering drugs, including alcohol, are in your system. And since these substances impair judgment, you should be prepared to help others. Like the ads say, "Friends don't let friends drive drunk."

Alcohol and tranquilizers combine unpredictably.

Even 24 hours later, pot-smoking pilots have trouble with landing skills.

Safe at Home—and Away

The last step to safety is to take precautions to lower the odds of being accidentally injured. Too many people fail to take precautions because they have a false sense of invincibility. They feel that accidents can't happen to them. But in a recent year, 1 in 27 Americans was injured badly enough in accidents

Home Safety Quiz

Here's a little test that will help you check your home safety knowledge:

1. True or false: A colonial home with a full flight of stairs is safer than a ranch-style home with just a few steps between levels.

2. Which of the following materials is least flammable and hence the best choice for a couch?
a. Cotton b. Wool c. Rayon d. Nylon

3. What's the best temperature for hot tap water?
a. 100°F b. 120°F c. 130°F d. 150°F

4. If you come home to, or wake up in the morning to, a flooded basement, what should you do?
a. Turn on your sump pump if you've got one. b. Quickly check appliances to see if they've been damaged. c. Call your electric company to have your power turned off before you do anything.

5. True or false: In high-traffic areas, it's best to keep electrical cords under rugs so people can't trip.

6. True or false: It's O.K. for a cat to sleep on an electric blanket.

7. If you don't know the correct wattage to choose when replacing a light bulb, which of the following should you choose?
a. A 50-watt bulb. b. A 100-watt bulb. c. A 60-watt bulb. d. Leave it empty.

Answers:

1. True. People tend to be more aware of steps when there are a lot of them. One or two steps tend to get overlooked more easily.

2. b. Wool.

3. b. 120°F. That's the best compromise for most people (though by going lower you can save even more energy). The danger in going warmer than 120° is that you can scald yourself. Exposure to water

to be considered "disabled." In 1984, there were almost 9 million disabling injuries, with 92,000 of them resulting in death.

Accidents are the fourth leading cause of death in the United States. They're the number one cause of death for people under 38. No wonder that when the Louis Harris organization quizzed 103 top health experts for their advice on the most important things

Feeling invulnerable may be hazardous to your health.

140° or hotter can cause a severe burn within seconds. Run the tap for two minutes, then take a temperature reading with a candy thermometer. If a change is needed, adjust the setting on the water heater accordingly.

4. c. Call your electric company. If enough water has accumulated to short-circuit any wires or appliances in your basement, you're looking at a wading pool chock-full of electrical current.

5. False. Electrical cords under rugs are a fire hazard, because the cords' insulation can be damaged by foot traffic. It's best to keep electrical wires out from underneath both feet and carpets.

6. False. Nothing should rest atop an electric blanket because excessive heat can build up or the blanket's coils can become damaged. For the same reason, the corners of an electric blanket should never be tucked in. There are some new blankets on the market that may eliminate these problems, but pets are a definite no-no with all electric blankets, since claws may rip into insulation surrounding the coils. Be certain to read the manufacturer's instructions carefully.

7. c. A 60-watt bulb. It's your best choice. Fires can be caused by overloading (putting a high-wattage bulb into a low-wattage fixture), but a 60-watt bulb is a safe compromise. Leaving a light fixture with no bulb at all is an invitation for serious electrical shock.

Scoring:
None wrong: Congratulations. You're a home-safety genius.
One to two wrong: You show promise, but still have some things to learn.
Three to five wrong: You've got some heavy-duty homework ahead of you.
More than five wrong: You're an accident about to happen.

people could do to promote longevity, 6 of the top 12 tips were safety precautions.

The number one safety tip was not to smoke in bed. Then the experts wanted you to wear your seat belt, not to drive after drinking and to drive within the speed limit. Then they wanted you to live in a house with a smoke detector and to take precautions against home accidents.

Home, deadly home.

Home. The word brings to mind warmth, comfort, security. But perhaps it's because home represents safety that people have so many accidents there. Blinded by its comforts, they neglect the very real dangers that abound. There are, in fact, more accidents in the home than on the job.

Survey your space with an eye toward safety and make it a priority to correct any flaws. If there's a coffee table that frequently gets in the way of your shins or toes, move it or get rid of it. A throw rug that slips a bit when you pass over it? Even though you may land safe and sound, visiting Aunt Matilda may not be so lucky. Get double-sided tape to anchor it or give it to Bowser for a bed.

Falling down is funny when a clown does it. It can even be funny when it happens to you—once you discover that the only thing injured is your dignity. But it can be painfully serious when it bends your arm at some place other than the elbow, fractures a bone, or does some other serious injury. Those folks who don't earn their living with a round rubber nose in the middle of their face would prefer to avoid falling.

Other than motor vehicle accidents, falls are the leading cause of accidental death. For every four people who are killed on roads and highways, one dies in a fall.

Don't be a fall guy (or gal).

Stairs, decks and walkways are frequent culprits. If you're smart, you keep your stairs clear and don't use them as a storage area. You have a sturdy handrail beside the stairs. The bathtub is also a site of frequent falls. A grab bar that will withstand your full, falling weight—not just a towel rack or a soap dish—is a key safety feature there. And, of course, the bottom of the tub should have a no-slip surface or mat. Try to remove any hazards between your bed and the bathroom. The reports say the bedroom—because of nighttime trips—is the most hazardous in the home.

Watch out for the power of distraction. Distraction is a bigger cause of accidental falls than tripping over objects, say experts. For example, people let their concentration wander from the stairs they are climbing or descending.

Dr. Yost maintains that another frequent factor

in accidents is haste. "Someone is rushing to do something, and decides to use a rickety chair rather than going for the stepladder."

Haste makes accidents.

If small children live in or visit your home, you should childproof cabinets containing medicines, paints and cleaning compounds. Upper story windows should have childguards such as stairs or sturdy gates.

Getting There in One Piece

Leaving home can be unsafe too—particularly if you leave by the garage. But there are ways to steer clear of mishaps. Starting with your radio.

If you play your car radio or tape deck at a high volume, you compound your risk of having an accident. The sound may do more than just obscure horns and other warning noises—it could interfere with your ability to *see*, research has suggested.

Blinded by a wall of sound?

If you've formed the habit of wearing your seat belt, you won't be a victim of the myth that being thrown free of your vehicle could save your life. If you are thrown out of your car, you're 25 times *more* likely to die.

Another old drivers' tale about seat belts: You don't need them in low speed accidents. The truth is that an unbelted driver in a head-on crash between two vehicles moving at 30 miles per hour hits the windshield and dashboard with as much impact as a person hitting the ground after diving out of a third floor window. The body has only a hundredth of a second to stop.

"Click!" is the sound of safety.

And if you don't buckle up for short trips near home because you feel safe, you're also making a mistake. That's where 75 percent of all accidents occur, and at speeds of less than 40 miles per hour.

What if you fear being trapped by your seat belt in a burning or submerged car after an accident? Safety experts who've studied the records say you have a better chance of escaping if you were wearing a belt. The protection it gives you leaves you in better shape to deal with your situation.

If you don't wear your belt because it seems too loose to help in an accident, don't be fooled. That "play" has been engineered into modern belts for comfort. But in an accident, belts lock instantly. If you're skeptical, try hitting your brakes hard sometime in safe circumstances.

Or do you use the excuse that wearing a belt is too fatalistic? The grim truth is that statistically the average driver can expect to be in a traffic accident at least once every ten years. Seat belts are one precaution you can take that can make a significant difference in your risk of being injured.

As for smoking, it not only harms your health, it could also increase your chance of having an accident if you light up while driving, researchers have found. Food, on the other hand, can help most people stay alert for driving. Stopping and eating a small snack every two hours should do the trick. And that's about how often you should stop to rest, experts say.

Speeders die young.

And you should never get behind the wheel when you are troubled or upset, says Dr. Yost. "Sometimes people who are depressed try to release it by getting into the car. But that's very dangerous because they are distracted and cannot give their full attention to driving," he says.

Don't try to be a superhuman driver. Too many hours behind the wheel will put anyone's head in a fog, says safety scholar Yost.

And keep to the speed limit—don't be in a hurry to get to eternity. You'll live to enjoy your fitness, serenity and safe environment.

3

Arthritis:

Overcoming It

T here's no way around it. Arthritis means suffering. And if you're afflicted in middle age or later, you might as well just look back with fondness on the years that have already passed. You certainly won't have any good years in your future.

What? That's hogwash.

If you reply this way instead of thinking "poor me," you'll be a lot better off. Because common as this negative sentiment about arthritis might be, it's simply not valid.

Sure, most arthritis is incurable. But then, so is the annual birthday. And sure, most arthritis is unpredictable—you never know when it will change. But that's how the weather is. You don't let your birthdays or the weather rule your life. And you don't have to let arthritis dominate you, either.

Inflammation, tenderness, stiffness—a whole list of symptoms go along with the various types of arthritis. Self-confidence, exercise, good nutrition, wise medical advice, support from others—these are just some of the tools used to fight these symptoms.

With a program that's well thought out, you can reduce pain and inflammation, prevent damage to joints, aid in limiting deformities before they occur and keep your joints flexible. In other words, you can learn to live well in spite of the problems.

Help Yourself

Only one thing is necessary to make maximum use of these tools to minimize the effects of arthritis. You. Arthritis is one illness that's very responsive to self-help. And the first step in helping yourself is learning what you're dealing with.

You are the primary tool needed to minimize arthritis—and keep feeling young.

"You've got to understand arthritis if you have it. Because if you understand what is happening in your body, where the pain is from, and what is likely to happen in the future, you'll have less fear of the disease. Understanding what is happening, or might happen, takes away your stress—and thus your suffering," says Frances Mason, who has arthritis, and works as self-help coordinator of the New York Arthritis Foundation.

Start with a definition. While arthritis encompasses many different types of disease, here is a simple explanation of what it is. "Arthritis is a degenerative process of the joints, which may have inflammation. If the joint is beginning to degenerate, you may have inflammation. By definition, then, you have arthritis," says Edward A. Abraham, M.D., assistant clinical professor of orthopedics at the University of California at Irvine. Most types of arthritis can strike at any age, but others are more prevalent as people get older. And no one is exempt, says Dr. Abraham: "Arthritis is a universal problem. Everyone experiences it to some degree as they age."

That prediction doesn't mean that you'll suffer debilitating arthritis, with swollen joints and excruciating pain. These symptoms are more in line with rheumatoid and other types of arthritis that aren't necessarily a result of aging, though they often do strike older people. Rather, it means that you, and everyone else, will experience joint deterioration as the years add up. This condition is called degenerative (or osteo-) arthritis. Although degenerative arthritis is often felt only as a mild ache when you move, it can be very severe.

The first step is to learn what you are dealing with.

The medical experts agree: "Education is important," says Dr. Abraham. "In the case of degenerative arthritis, you've got to learn what happens clinically with the aging process. You've got to find out just how your body works."

The symptoms usually begin slowly, perhaps with pain or stiffness in just one or two joints. Degenerative arthritis most commonly strikes the fingers, hips, knees, and the spine, though it can occur in any joint and the pain can be felt in large areas around the afflicted joint—or even elsewhere in the body. Although there is no cure for degenerative arthritis, it can be controlled. It needn't be a major factor in your life as you get older. There are ways to minimize its impact.

There is no cure for arthritis, but it can be controlled.

"A major step towards coping with degenerative arthritis is to accept the aging process," says Dr. Abraham. "And this is often a very difficult hurdle for people to overcome."

It helps to look at your joints as parts of your body subject to stress, just like your eyes, hair and skin. "You lose elasticity as you age," says Dr. Abraham. "The tissue becomes less elastic." This shows up on the outside of a person's body as gray hair and looser skin—and nobody is too surprised. But people are surprised when their joints begin to hurt. "What you need to understand," says Dr. Abraham, "is that the same tissue degeneration occurs inside your joints. You just can't see it."

To add to this general decrease in flexibility, you inflict trauma on your joints every day of your life. Though you may not know it, each movement you make contributes to microtrauma—tiny cracks in the joint—that is a major component of degenerative arthritis. This microtrauma eventually leads to joint changes later in life. Everyone experiences this to some degree.

Keep Moving for Comfort

But not everyone needs to suffer. Certain lifestyles actually promote healthier, less troublesome joints.

One of the most important requirements of an arthritis-fighting life-style is to keep moving. Exercise won't reverse the degeneration, but it will build up muscles that can compensate for the damaged joint, relieving it of much painful stress. Whereas it's best to begin an exercise program when you are young, because there is some evidence that this will help

How you live influences your arthritis.

prevent debilitating osteoarthritis later, exercising at any age is still the best way to beat arthritis. The exercise you choose depends on your level of fitness, and the extent of your degenerative arthritis.

Valery Lanyi, M.D., associate clinical professor of rehabilitation medicine at the New York University Medical Center, in New York City, says you should definitely have a doctor help you choose your exercises—after you undergo a thorough physical examination. "The doctor will help you devise a program that is suited to you, that puts your muscles through a variety of movements," says Dr. Lanyi. "This will reduce the risk of injury and increase your benefits."

Even with your doctor's help, you should use plenty of common sense. Don't dive in and do more than your body can take. Judge your limits yourself. A good rule of thumb, according to Dr. Lanyi, is that if your muscles still ache two hours after you exercise, you overdid it and should cut back next time.

If you are already an exerciser, adapt your physical activities to your age. "I've seen athletes over 40 who just continue to try to perform as though they were still kids. They try to discount the aging process," says Dr. Abraham. "And what happens is they suffer injury after injury to their bones and joints."

Instead of giving up athletics for the sake of their bones, however, these people should explore the alternatives. A runner, for instance, might find a less punishing endurance sport like swimming, says Dr. Abraham.

Sometimes alternative ways of working out will help.

"A physiatrist, a doctor who specializes in physical rehabilitation, would be a good person to turn to for help in setting up a new exercise program," says Dr. Lanyi.

In addition to sports, many doctors recommend a series of exercises that put the joints through their full range of motion. Dr. Lanyi has her arthritic patients do these exercises—they move the joint in all the ways it can move—with someone to assist them. And when the arthritis is in remission, Dr. Lanyi usually tells her patients how to do their exercises on their own, at home.

The important thing is to do the exercises every day. "Doing the exercises won't necessarily improve your arthritis," says Dr. Lanyi, "but it will ease the burden by toning the muscle and strengthening the bone. And if you don't exercise, the muscles may atrophy and you'll be less able to function than before."

Regular exercise tones muscles and strengthens bone.

Here are some more tips to help you exercise away the pain of various types of arthritis:

• Start slowly and gently, increasing your workout just a little bit each day.
• Perform your exercises twice or more a day.
• Have someone help you if you need it, especially at first.
• Maintain good posture to reduce stress on your joints.

Aquatic Exercise

If you experience times when even the gentlest range of motion exercises are more than you can handle, think *aquatic exercise.* "Water exercise works because the water displaces the body's weight, putting much less stress on the joints," says Dr. Lanyi. Yet the water does offer enough resistance for a serious workout. In addition, the pleasant social atmosphere of a water workout class supports and encourages all your efforts.

Water displaces your body weight but also provides resistance.

A good example of an aquatic exercise class is the one taught by Loyf Green at the 53rd Street YWCA, in New York City. Green is a fit-looking woman who has been gently coaxing people to work out harder in water for most of the last two decades. People come to her classes once a week to keep their arthritis at bay.

The classes are split into different levels—beginner, intermediate and advanced. "Some of the people come in hardly able to walk," says Green. "But I work with them, and they work out, and sooner or later everyone begins to move more easily." Evidence of this was found recently at her Monday afternoon advanced class, cosponsored by the Arthritis Foundation. Most of the people in this class (both men and women are welcome at this YWCA) had been working out in water for two to three years. "We even do it on vacation," said one, "though of course it's never as good when we're away from Loyf."

The class started with the participants spending a few minutes getting used to the water by floating and walking around the shallow pool. There is real camaraderie among the exercisers, who appear to range in age from about 45 years old to much older. They've been encouraging each other to work out for a long time.

One woman swims a bit, and then stops to rub her shoulder. "This shoulder is really hurting today," she says. Another women replies, "I guess that means bad weather tomorrow," and the other aquatic exercisers laugh.

Once the workout begins, it's nothing but stretching muscles and moving joints to maintain or increase their range of motion. Each of the exercises is prefaced with a short stretch. People hold the side of the pool and flutter kick; put floats on their ankles and do leg lifts; do push-ups against the pool wall; and rotate their hands with their arms out from their sides.

You don't have to know how to swim to aqua exercise.

All the while Green is in the pool exercising along with the students. Most of the exercises are done with at least one hand holding onto the side of the pool. And those done standing in shallow water are very simple. It's safe enough so that there's no need to know how to swim. "But we can teach anyone who wants to learn," says Green.

At the end of the class everyone looks exhilarated. "It really makes you feel much better, just the exercise, because it gets your blood pumping," says one woman. "And it makes it so I can move much more freely. It is by far the best thing I do for my arthritis. Working out is a lot better than just taking drugs and complaining. A lot better."

Slenderize

While water exercises work because the liquid takes a lot of the stress off your bones and joints, there's a way to take some of that stress off on land, too. It's no big revelation, but it is a sure way to lessen the pain of arthritis.

"I advocate that people who are overweight lose the extra pounds as part of their treatment," says Ellen Ginzler, M.D., associate professor of medicine at the State University of New York Health Science Center, at Brooklyn, New York, and chairman of the Medical and Scientific Committee of the New York Arthritis Foundation. "Weight loss is a good way to treat symptoms, though of course it won't reverse arthritis."

It's not too hard to understand why extra weight can mean extra pain, especially when a person has degenerative arthritis. Imagine loading up a folding table with too many casserole dishes. Pretty soon the table will start to creak, and then the legs might crack or buckle. That's pretty much how your joints react to carrying extra pounds around. The daily pounding of city streets and hard floors is tough enough on your skeleton when there's just one of you. But when extra weight makes it seem like two you's are on the same frame, you'll have trouble.

Extra body weight means extra joint pain.

"Being overweight can change the whole alignment of your body," says Dr. Abraham. "Picture, for example, a line running from the back of your head, to your rear, to the back of your heels. When you add a lot of extra weight to your body, you're going to change this line of gravity. The new strain will mean new pain. So, weight can really be a factor."

Weight Loss Secrets

You probably already know that just being 20 percent above your ideal weight can be harmful to your health. And if you have extra pounds, you've probably tried to lose them. But you found that it was a tough job, or that you lost the weight only to have it come right back. That's a common experience. But there is an alternative.

One of the secrets of successful weight loss has already been discussed. Exercise. Any type of exercise, just as long as you do it regularly, will help you lose weight. Another secret is good all-around nutrition. "I think that people should definitely eat a balanced diet and get good nourishment to keep their overall health up, and to help them lose weight if they need to," says Dr. Ginzler.

A balanced diet might include an emphasis on

**Lose weight gradually
with diet and exercise.**

fresh fruits, grains and vegetables, and replacing saturated (animal) fats with polyunsaturated and monounsaturated (vegetable) fats and eating more fish. This diet would help you lose weight, and some doctors believe it might have a pain-reducing effect as well. A study at Albany Medical College, State University of New York, found that people on a diet high in vegetable fats, supplemented with eicosapentanoic acid (EPA), a factor found in fish oil, experienced a drop in morning stiffness and fewer tender joints than people eating a diet high in animal fats. The researchers say the diet might reduce substances produced in the body (prostaglandins) that cause inflammation. As said, the diet would probably help you lose weight, especially if you combined it with perhaps the most secret weight loss secret of them all—time.

No weight loss plan will have lasting results if you don't give it time to work. "You have to have a reasonable diet," says Dr. Abraham. "One you can live with. That means you shouldn't choose a grapefruit diet, because you'll soon get sick of grapefruits. Or a banana diet, because you'll get very tired of bananas. Don't kid yourself. You've got to find a diet—a nutritionist or your doctor can help you— that is realistic. If you do need to lose weight, do it gradually. And do it under a doctor's supervision. Just remember to give it time."

Time, lonely, isolated time, is one thing many arthritis sufferers feel they have too much of. And few things make a person feel older than too much idle time. So an important part of beating arthritis is maintaining the right attitude.

A poor self-image compounds the problem.

"I have found that many people I speak to through my work at the Arthritis Foundation use the term 'freak' to describe themselves," says Frances Mason. "They feel alone, because they are suffering with this disease that a lot of people don't understand. Well, that self-image can just make the problem worse."

A more realistic attitude can really improve a person's life. Attitude obviously plays an important role in arthritis. A person with a good attitude will function better than a person with a bad attitude," says Dr. Ginzler.

You Can Lead a Horse to Water . . .

But sometimes creating a positive attitude is easier said than done. "Mental attitude is the most important thing, and also the most difficult to develop," says Dr. Abraham. "It's easy to tell a person, 'Don't give in!' But as the saying goes, 'You can lead a horse to water, but you can't make him drink.' You must try to help yourself," says Dr. Abraham. "Others can only teach you so much."

If you do decide you want help developing a more positive attitude, there's plenty available. Just ask Frances Mason. She discovered that positive attitude in herself—despite the extreme difficulties she's had with numerous kinds of arthritis since she was a teenager—and helps others feel better too. One of the main ways she does so is by helping organize self-help groups for people with arthritis, under the auspices of the Arthritis Foundation and the National Self-Help Clearing House. "All meetings are unique, but the meeting I go to has two parts. First, there's a medical education lecture, with a speaker who talks about arthritis. The second part is a psychological education session where we choose a topic related to arthritis—say, depression, poor me, fear, bad attitudes—and talk about it. This releases a lot of tension and lets you know that you aren't alone.

Organize your own self-help group.

"We also share tips on how to cope with different tasks, where to get help and other advice. The groups help a lot because you have a lot of identification." You can find out about self-help groups (in some places they are called arthritis clubs) in your area by calling the Arthritis Foundation.

What's the attitude that works best? According to Mason, the way to win your war against arthritis is not to give up. "There is no cure for arthritis, but you can always hope for the better. You must hope. Giving up will get you nowhere. Moving forward takes a lot of faith in yourself. And remember, if you stay home, the arthritis won't get better, it will get worse, and you'll feel older and more tired. Get out there and do something. Get a job or do volunteer work— even if it is only for one hour a week."

Keep active, keep going, keep hoping.

If you plan ahead, you can avoid getting too fatigued. You have to be flexible when you plan, because it's sometimes difficult to gauge just how you'll be feeling, but schedules will help you minimize the effect arthritis has on your life. Set priorities for your activities, and rank them according to difficulty. Then try to arrange them so the difficult tasks aren't all grouped together in one day. Break up your schedule. And try to leave room to cancel activities you find you aren't able to handle.

Relieving the Pain

Even with the best attitude and a good all-around program against arthritis, you'll probably experience pain once in a while. And when you do, you'll want relief. Here are some tips for getting it:

Moist Heat. Soak a towel in hot water, wring it out, cover it in plastic or dry towels to protect your skin from burns, and apply it to the painful joint.

Cold. Wrap a towel around a bag of ice cubes or frozen peas and apply it to the joint that hurts. Some people find this uncomfortable. Others say it works better than heat.

Use Tools. Try the long grabbers available from the hardware store, for example, or any of a variety of items available to help you prevent pain associated with everyday tasks.

Learn a Relaxation Technique. Pain is often increased by tense muscles, and relaxing them can help.

Use Home Hydrotherapy. With the water between 100° and 102°F, just get in your bathtub and move through as much motion as you can manage. The water will displace much of your body weight—and allow you to move your joints more freely. Or for a really soothing experience, soak in a hot tub where you can swing your arms and legs through their full range of motion.

Try Hot and Cold Therapy. Fill one basin with hot water (110°F) and another with cold water (60°F). Place your hands or feet in the hot water for ten minutes, then in the cold for one minute. Then repeat in the hot water for four minutes, the cold for one minute, for a total of six times. The resulting increased blood flow helps eliminate pain.

Make Love. A doctor at Cook County Hospital, in

Chicago, found that a number of her patients reported that they were free of arthritis pain for several hours following sex. Not in less pain: Free of pain.

Many people find relief from acute and chronic pain with drugs. And some people even find that medicine makes their arthritis go into remission. But, as with any medical treatment, you've got to know what you're doing when you take medicines. Here are some good questions to ask before you start taking drugs.

Choosing the Best Medicines

Do the benefits outweigh the risks? Which drug is most effective? Can it do anything more than simply suppress symptoms? Exactly how does it work?

For one thing, anti-arthritis drugs usually aren't just painkillers or analgesics. They also try to reverse the inflammation, thereby reducing all the arthritis symptoms, including pain, in the process. Good examples of these nonsteroid anti-inflammatory drugs (NSAID) include aspirin and ibuprofen. These substances try to cool inflamed joint tissue, the core symptom of arthritis.

The drug you choose should do more than kill pain.

There's quite a bit of difference between a drug like this and one that's just a painkiller, like Tylenol, Darvon, Demerol, and others. James F. Fries, M.D., director of the Stanford University Arthritis Clinic, in Stanford, California, and author of *Arthritis: A Comprehensive Guide* (Addison-Wesley), says that plain painkillers have little place in arthritis therapy.

"First," he says, "they don't do anything for the arthritis; they just cover it up. Second, they help defeat the pain mechanism that tells you when you are doing something that is injuring your body. Third, the body adjusts to pain medicines, so they aren't very effective over the long term. This phenomenon is called tolerance and develops to some extent with all of the drugs we commonly use. Fourth, painkillers have side effects."

So, you must work with your doctor to balance the dosage for maximum relief with minimum toxicity. You don't want to trade in one problem for another.

Frequently, people with the same type of arthritis demand different drugs. Someone with rheumatoid arthritis may get relief with Motrin; another might not. The same holds true for other types of arthritis and other drugs.

The cheapest and most widely used drug for arthritis is still aspirin. It's recommended by most doctors as the first line of defense against several types of arthritis, including osteoarthritis and rheumatoid arthritis.

Take aspirin with food to minimize the side effects.

Prickly Treatment

What would you do if your doctor told you to take two yucca tablets and call him in the morning?

If you were at the end of your rope trying to find relief for arthritis, you might just do it. And you wouldn't be alone. Several clinics in the United States recommend yucca tablets as a way to treat arthritis.

Unfortunately, the people who visit these clinics might as well be spending their money on sugar pills, according to Floyd Pennington, Ph.D. "There are no data to prove the effectiveness of yucca, so there is no reason to think there would be any benefit from yucca beyond the placebo [fake pill] effect," says Dr. Pennington, who is group vice-president for education at the Arthritis Foundation National Office, in Atlanta. I'm not saying it wouldn't help people, because the placebo effect will work on about 30 percent of them, but yucca is just a folk medicine. These clinics are making an unsubstantiated claim."

The Desert Arthritis Medical Clinic, in Desert Hot Springs, California, claims that yucca contains a high concentration of "steroid saponin, which acts in the intestinal tract to improve circulation and reduce abnormal fat content in the blood." While steroids are used for some very serious types of arthritis, the doses must be closely controlled. "Yucca may have this steroid," says Dr. Pennington, "but it would be hard to get a controlled dose from yucca tablets. And steroids can be very dangerous substances."

The Arthritis Foundation's advice on yucca? "Don't replace your conventional treatment with yucca," says Dr. Pennington.

Osteoarthritis patients may be after the mild analgesic component. Those with rheumatoid arthritis will be given aspirin for the anti-inflammatory response. The effect depends in part on the dosage.

Dr. Fries believes that the strictly analgesic effect of aspirin is maximum after 2 tablets (five grains each) and lasts about four hours. "In contrast," he says, "the anti-inflammatory activity requires high and sustained blood levels of aspirin. A patient must take 12 to 24 tablets (five grains each) each day, and the process must be continued for weeks to obtain the full effect." These high dosages require close medical supervision because of aspirin's side effects, which include peptic ulcer, upset stomach, stomach bleeding, tinnitus (ringing in the ears), hearing loss, liver damage, even interference with the blood's ability to clot. And aspirin is second only to penicillin in causing allergic reactions.

Many doctors recommend that you take aspirin with food, use coated aspirin or use aspirin's almost identical twin. It is called magnesium trisalicylate (Trilisate) and is not to be confused with nonaspirin drugs like Tylenol.

Other nonsteroidal anti-inflammatory drugs include the prescription drugs Motrin, Indocin, Nalfon, Clinoril, Naprosyn, Butazolidin, Tolectin and the over-the-counter drugs, Advil and Nuprin. They all have some analgesic potential, roughly as much anti-inflammatory power as aspirin. They work on the same types of arthritis as aspirin.

And whereas aspirin still seems to be the most recommended drug, these other NSAID have a distinct advantage—dosage. Someone with rheumatoid arthritis might need to take only two Naprosyn tablets a day—instead of 15 aspirin.

NSAID generally have less severe side effects than aspirin alone. But of course, as with any arthritis drug, it's best to get your doctor's approval before self-prescribing.

There are other, much stronger, drugs that also help free people from their arthritis. Corticosteroids, hormones (or their synthetic equivalents) similar to those manufactured by the adrenal gland, can be injected into the body to dramatically reduce inflammation. While they seem to work miracles, they can

Corticosteroids seem to work miracles—but they do have side effects.

also have serious side effects, including ulcers, skin ailments, bone disease and cataracts. Doctors try to avoid these reactions by carefully controlling dosage and duration of treatment of these steroid drugs.

"In certain cases of rheumatoid arthritis, steroids can actually be life-saving," says Sanford H. Roth, M.D., Phoenix rheumatologist and editor of *Handbook of Drug Therapy in Rheumatology* (PSG Publishing). "And low-dose steroids can be useful in select situations. But generally, if we can achieve good results without steroids, we should not use them, because of the many problems common to long-term hormonal therapy."

Another class of drugs knocks out symptoms for a long time, and sometimes even forces the arthritis into remission. The most widely known of these remission-inducing drugs are gold salts, sold by prescription under the trade names Solganal, Myochrysine and Ridaura. About 75 percent of rheumatoid arthritis patients who try them get positive results. It can take weeks for the salts to start working, but once the therapy kicks in, it can last for months.

No one knows why they work, but doctors do know that gold salts extract their payment in side effects. About 30 percent of people who use them will experience difficulties—possibly including skin rashes, jaundice, mouth ulcers, kidney damage, blood disorders and aplastic anemia.

"Because of the potential problems, patients taking gold have to be carefully monitored," says Paul H. Waytz, M.D., a Minneapolis rheumatologist. "They should have periodic urine tests and blood counts. And at the first sign of adverse reactions, the drug should be withdrawn."

That goes double for another drug, called penicillamine. Like gold, this drug is impressively effective, but mysterious. And it has all of gold's side effects—and then some. Gastrointestinal disturbance, autoimmune disease, taste impairment, vomiting and fatal bone marrow disruption are some of the possible hazards of taking penicillamine.

"Penicillamine should be administered in the lowest possible dose that will suppress the signs and symptoms of rheumatoid arthritis," says Dr. Waytz.

Other drugs, called antimalarial compounds, aren't nearly as toxic as gold or penicillamine, but they probably aren't as effective, either. However, whereas it may take three to six months for the drugs to work, their positive effects may last just as long.

Still, these drugs have serious side effects. Deciding whether or not you take any drug is serious business. Be sure to keep the lines of communication open with your doctor.

This partnership is what can make your arthritis beat a hasty retreat. You supply the willingness to help yourself with exercise, nutrition and other self-help tools. Let your doctor advise you and give you the best medical treatments available. Together, you should succeed.

Working in partnership with your doctor is the key to freedom from arthritis.

4

Building a

Better Back

" A *pain-free back in X minutes a day!"* If that promise ballyhooed in hundreds of books and magazines sounds too good to be true, that's probably because it is.

"All that a doctor can do for a person with back pain is offer guidance," says Edward A. Abraham, M.D., an orthopedic surgeon in Santa Ana, California, assistant clinical professor of orthopedics at the University of California at Irvine and author of *Freedom from Back Pain* (Rodale Press). "There is no simple prescription that can cure backache. Often it involves a life-style change. I want my patients to become their own back doctors."

If you're one of those people who have never had to curse your aching back, don't be too smug— you may one day reach for a dropped pencil when— YAA!—your back flares up. A noted researcher estimates that 80 percent of Americans will experience back pain sometime during their lives. To avoid becoming another statistic, you too should pay attention to the advice offered by the experts. By following their suggestions, good back habits will become as automatic as your former bad back habits.

Be your own back doctor.

Exercise for Strength and Flexibility

Even many surgeons who used to pooh-pooh its benefits now agree that exercise can be your spine's salvation.

"Exercise is important for a back problem—whether the problem is muscular in nature, or not," says Willibald Nagler, M.D., a specialist in physical medicine and rehabilitation.

That's just what it is in 90 to 95 percent of cases, according to Dr. Nagler, who is physiatrist-in-chief at New York Hospital-Cornell Medical Center, in New York City. And that's also why back problems increase with age. "Muscles tend to deteriorate with age for most people because they lead sedentary lives," says Dr. Nagler. "Add to that the usual changes that occur in the spine as we get older. We get a little shorter from bone shrinkage, there's a thinning of the disks, and the spine often develops arthritic spurs. But the muscular insufficiencies of the back, stomach and hips usually cause the most pain and immobility. That's why increasing the strength and flexibility of those muscles almost always brings relief."

Since individual bodies have their own muscular idiosyncracies, there is no universal exercise program that will help everyone. A physiatrist (a medical doctor specializing in physical medicine and rehabilitation) can custom-tailor a set of exercises for backache sufferers.

Dr. Nagler prescribes a series that includes knee-to-chest pulls, cat curls and hip rolls. To tighten the stomach, he recommends half sit-ups with knees bent, alternate leg lifts, pelvic tilts and other exercises.

An excellent program incorporating many of these exercises, according to Dr. Nagler, is "The Y's Way to a Healthy Back," offered at some YMCAs. Also, the *American Medical Association Straight-Talk, No-Nonsense Guide to Backcare* (Random) says walking and swimming (except for the breaststroke) may help the back. A word of warning: Rest, not exercise, is best when you are in acute pain. And no exercise should hurt your back.

Acute pain requires rest, not exercise.

Relaxation Eases Pain

Stress is another culprit in the case of the aching back.

"The process of stress begins with our perception that a situation is a challenge," says Dr. Abraham. "This intensity of emotion triggers the release of adrenaline and other stress chemicals into the bloodstream. You can overdose on stress chemicalization the same way you can on any other drug. If not eliminated through physical activity and relaxation, it has serious side effects. It becomes a toxin in the body, resulting in muscle tension. Sustained tension contracts muscles, and continued constriction can easily prove the primary cause of eventual back strain, sprain or spasm."

Once the pain sets in, the stress might be multiplied. "Fear of more pain makes us tense, hindering recovery," says Dr. Abraham. "Since healing can't happen without relaxation, and we can't relax, we become anxious. Anxiety, in turn, adds to both fear and muscle tension. So the pain cycle becomes a self-fulfilling reality for both brain and body."

Being uptight can cramp your back.

Visualization

Relaxation doesn't mean lying in bed and watching reruns of "Gilligan's Island." Dr. Abraham is referring to a deeper, programmed relaxation. Exactly *how* can one achieve such relaxation? *Any* technique that provides a break from stressful activities can help your back, according to Arthur C. Klein and Dava Sobel, medical writers who interviewed 492 backache sufferers for their book *Backache Relief* (Times Books). Survey participants practiced meditation and prayer, but visualization was the most popular.

Visualization, or guided imagery, involves playing out positive images in your mind. The idea is to visualize as many details—sights, sounds, smells and feelings—as you need to create a scene so real that your body becomes convinced it's happening.

"You need to recall a place or an experience in which you felt utterly relaxed, then focus your undivided attention on that place or experience, holding

Picture yourself in a serene environment.

that focus until it becomes so real you're aware of nothing else," says Dr. Abraham. "Don't picture yourself as a figure in that environment—*be* there, experience it as you did when it actually happened."

The mental pictures should be accompanied by physical relaxation. "Ideally, you'll be lying down or resting comfortably in an easy chair," says Dr. Abraham. "Visualization seems to work best with closed eyes and deep breathing. If any muscle groups are tense, focus warmth in those areas."

Yoga

Yoga helped nearly every Klein-Sobel survey participant who tried it—a full 96 percent benefited. That's probably because it combines exercise with relaxation.

A few survey participants learned yoga on their own, but the ones who got started with professional instruction reported better results. But before you enroll in a class, talk to the instructor and make sure he or she will modify the therapy for your particular back problem. A few regular yoga positions could be dangerous.

Yoga can be modified for back problems.

Biofeedback

Some people don't really know whether they're tense or relaxed. Biofeedback machines can teach these people the difference. Once tension is recognized, back sufferers can learn to relax stiff, sore muscles and thus ease the pain. The Klein-Sobel survey revealed that the particular technology and gadgetry are less important than the skill and concern of the therapist. The patient must be an active participant in the therapy as well.

Before deciding to use biofeedback, you'll want to check with your insurance carrier or worker's compensation program to be sure the therapy is covered. An article in the *Back Pain Monitor* newsletter reports that sometimes it is not. A biofeedback session is estimated to cost between $40 and $80 per hour and could be even higher depending on your location.

Everyday Habits for a Pain-Free Back

Standing. Some physicians believe bad posture is a major factor in back pain, while others say, "Nonsense!" But here's one thing that many doctors agree on: The position that may have been taught as "good" posture is actually bad for some backs. This is the posture of attention—chest up, shoulders back, stomach flat and buttocks protruding—and it throws the lower back into an abnormally accentuated arch. Other postures that can cause a swayback are: slumping, so that the shoulders and the lower back sag; bending backwards at the waist with the abdomen protruding; locking the knees, which tilts the pelvis forward. Wearing excessively high heels also can force you to exaggerate the arch in your back.

"Good" posture is bad.

Poor posture can affect the *upper* back too. If your head hangs forward and your shoulders are rounded when you stand, that's going to cause neck and shoulder strain.

Then how *should* one stand? Keep your rear tucked in, tuck in your chin, tighten your abdominal muscles, and keep your knees unlocked—just a little bent. If you have to stand for a long period of time, put one foot up on a stool, chair rung or bar rail. This flattens out any excessive arch you may have in your lower spine. Many back sufferers recommend shifting your weight from one foot to the other every few minutes.

Tuck in your chin, rear and belly, and keep your knees bent a little.

"I recommend taking 30 seconds each hour to bring your joints through a full range of motion," says Susan L. Fish, registered physical therapist, of New York City. "It takes off the strain. To loosen up, try this: sitting down, alternate pulling your knees to your chest, one at a time."

Sitting. Sitting down can rest your weary feet, but it can hurt your aching back.

"Stress on the spine is greater when you're sitting than when you're standing," says Lawrence W. Friedmann, M.D., chairman of the department of physical medicine and rehabilitation at Nassau County Medical Center, in East Meadow, New York.

Dr. Friedmann points out that the muscles automatically exert hundreds of pounds of force when you're standing up—but even more when you're sitting down. And much of that force is directed at the spine, especially if you have the common (but bad) habit of leaning forward while you sit. This force translates into tension and pain.

Don't lean forward when you sit.

One strategy to avoid this posture is to reduce the amount of time you sit. Office workers, for example, can stand up to talk on the phone. And take a stand-up break every hour.

When you *do* sit, use a good chair and a good sitting position to reduce the strain. According to the American Medical Association's *Guide to Backcare*, there is no single type of chair or position that is ideal for everyone all the time. The main criterion in choosing the chair—whether you have a back problem or not—is comfort, and probably the best way of determining that is through trial and error. The authors of *Backache Relief* recommend sitting on a desk chair for 30 to 45 minutes before buying it.

Nevertheless, some general principles are involved: Choose a chair that helps you to sit comfortably erect, not slumped forward. The ideal chair has a tiltable back support and adjustable height so you can sit with your feet flat on the floor and knees slightly higher than or level with your hips. It has a contoured seat pan, not a square cushion, and it's deep enough to support about three-quarters of your thighs—in other words, it doesn't cut into the back of your knees. Try to find a chair with an armrest—that way, your arms can help reduce the spine's load, and it will be easier to get in and out of the chair. Finally, the chair should be roomy enough to let you shift your position from time to time.

Choose a chair carefully.

If your office chair isn't so hot, you can put a small pillow two or three inches thick behind your lower back to avoid slouching. And think of constructive ways to vary your position. If it doesn't violate office etiquette, put your feet on your desk every so often. Or rest them in an open bottom drawer. Or prop them across the top of the wastebasket.

Sleeping. Even sleeping can spell doom for your back if you don't heed the back experts' advice. "All night long as you sleep on a too-soft or too-hard bed, your muscles are working overtime to align your spine," explains Robert G. Addison, M.D., director of the center for pain studies at the Rehabilitation Institute of Chicago.

"No one bed is good for everyone," notes Dr. Addison, who has helped design mattresses for major bedding manufacturers. "However, the ideal mattress should cradle the spine in the same position as if you were standing with good posture."

The mattress should evenly distribute your weight.

Usually that takes a firm mattress. It should distribute body weight evenly and eliminate pressure points so that no part of the body is being pressured more than another.

How, then, should you choose the mattress of your dreams? If your back pain is from a pinched nerve or bad posture, let comfort be your guide—the bed should relieve the pain, says Lionel A. Walpin, M.D., director of the Walpin Physical Medicine and Pain Institute, in Los Angeles. But if your problem is tight joints or muscles, you may *need* to experience some initial discomfort to help realign the tense body parts.

And remember, when it comes to firmness, don't be swayed by manufacturers' labels, such as super-firm, ultra-firm or the very medical-sounding ortho-firm. There are no industry-wide standards when it comes to bedding descriptions, so what you feel is what you get.

Sleep in the fetal position.

Now that you have the right mattress on your bed, don't waste the money you spent on it by sleeping in the wrong position. Lying face down is a bad idea because it increases the arch in the lower back, which can aggravate backache, according to the American Medical Association's *Guide to Backcare*. Instead, if you suffer from low back pain, the book recommends that you sleep in the fetal position—on your side, with hips and knees bent. Or keep that position when lying on your back by piling up pillows under your knees.

Once again, comfort is the guide. Often, people with a healthy back can sleep however they want. And if their sleep position doesn't cause any pain, it probably doesn't hurt their back.

One place to find back-compatible furniture is at a back store. And while you're there, you can check out items such as positioning pillows, automatic massage tables, books and "reachers," which enable users to pick up small objects without bending over. There are about 100 back stores nationwide. Check the yellow pages under furniture, office furniture or orthopedic appliances.

Lifting. According to the participants of the Klein-Sobel survey, it seems safer to bench press 100 pounds than to lift a 20-pound carton of groceries from a car trunk.

When is a carton of groceries heavier than a barbell?

That's because you have to bend over for the groceries. "The force the back muscles must exert is far greater than the weight of the bent-over body and the load on the arms," says Jack R. Tessman, Ph.D., physicist and author of *My Back Doesn't Hurt Anymore* (Quick Fox). "The back muscles are very strong and can usually exert the necessary pull without difficulty. *But*, as a consequence, the lower vertebrae and disks are very strongly compressed; they may be overloaded and cause low back pain," says Dr. Tessman.

For the 120-pound person, lifting a 44-pound weight (the equivalent of a 4- to 6-year-old child) would increase the load on the lower disks from 70 to 154 pounds, according to the research of Alf L. Nachemson, M.D., professor and chairman of the department of orthopaedic surgery at Sahlgren Hospital, University of Göteborg, in Sweden, and a noted scientific researcher of back problems. If you add twisting to the lifting and forward bending, that's the worst position of all, points out Dr. Nachemson, increasing the load by several hundred percent.

To lift something, don't bend forward without support.

This needn't be an excuse to give up lifting once and for all—you merely have to lift differently.

"The only way the back muscles will pull less is to demand less of them," says Dr. Tessman. "The guiding principle thus becomes: Avoid situations that impose large forward-bending torques upon the upper body."

Avoidance means never bending forward to pick up anything—not even a paper clip—unless you support your weight with something, Dr. Tessman explains. You may brace your body by pushing against a chair or table. Or support your back by resting your forearm on your knee. But no freestyle lifting.

Better yet, let your legs do most of the lifting. Squat as close as possible to the object you want to pick up, bending your knees but keeping your back vertical. Grasp the object and hold it against you as you slowly stand up. Your legs get a workout, but your back muscles get time off.

Carry a load behind your back.

Another lifting strategy is to carry things on your back or behind it. "Backward" carrying techniques are far nicer to your back than the usual front-toting method, because front carrying invariably means nasty forward torques.

"It may look funny to the unknowledgeable on-looker who sees you carrying a box behind you instead of in front, as most people do," says Dr. Tessman. "But you can be smug in the knowledge that you are being kind to your disks."

That "beer belly" forces back muscles to counterbalance it.

What about that heavy object many people carry in front of them all the time—the protruding paunch? It's a life-style by-product that begs for back pain. Physicists calculate that if a person had 10 extra pounds of weight on his stomach, centered ten inches in front of his spine, then the back muscles must exert a force of 50 pounds to counterbalance the "beer belly."

Sex and the Bad Back

"Not tonight, I have a backache." That excuse, as much as the traditional headache, is a common reason to veto sexual intercourse.

Sex is a great healing therapy.

It doesn't have to be that way. "Sex is great for your back," says Dr. Abraham, in *Freedom from Back Pain.* "If all the world's orthopedic specialists convened to formulate the best single exercise for releasing muscular constriction, toning back muscles and relaxing the nervous system, making love would be that exercise. It accomplishes all the above and more. And it's not a boring form of exercise.

"Orgasm is the best muscle relaxant around. It has a profound effect on the entire body. Scientifically, it has been demonstrated that orgasm has ten times the effect of Valium. In addition, the deep inhalations and exhalations following the orgasm itself continue the relaxation process of muscles and nerves. For back sufferers, the ten minutes following a sexual climax can be a healing luxury not to be denied."

Yet it often is denied because of pain. And that's too bad because—except in cases of severe pain that requires bed rest—sexual intercourse can be comfortably performed if you use positions least likely to strain the back. The key to avoiding strain is to make sure you don't arch your back or your neck, according to Hamilton Hall, M.D., founder and director of the Canadian Back Institute and author of *The Back Doctor* (Berkley).

Just find a position that doesn't cause pain.

Many backache sufferers think it's best to find out for yourself what you *cannot* do, and leave the rest up to individual preferences and limitations. But the following positions were most popular in the Klein-Sobel survey:

Lying on your side with your knees bent, facing your partner was number one. Another favorite, often recommended by back doctors, is lying front to back, nestled like spoons, with the man behind the woman. The missionary position can be used if the person with the backache is on the bottom with elevated knees and the person on top can support most of his or her own weight.

What to Do for an Acute Attack

"A back attack seems to hit when you least expect it, and, seemingly, for no reason at all," says Edward Tarlov, M.D., neurosurgeon at the Lahey Clinic, in Burlington, Massachusetts (with coauthor David D'Costa) in the book *Back Attack* (Little, Brown and Company). "You do something you've done unthinkingly a thousand times—pick up a paper clip, tie your shoelaces, whatever—and WHAM! *This* time you're absolutely splinted with pain across your lower back."

In the acute phase of a back attack, pain is likely to be a consequence of spasm in your back muscles, which is probably a result of a misspent life, backwise. But never mind that now. Before you turn over a new leaf, you have to reduce that pain.

Bed Rest

Doctors who treat backs may haggle over which are the best treatments. But doctors agree about this—bed rest is necessary for acute back attacks.

If you have an acute back attack, don't get out of bed.

And the "victim" hardly has a choice anyway—it would be painful and difficult to do anything else.

"You have to rest those tissues," says Dr. Abraham. "Your body is telling you, 'You did something to me, you really put me down and now you've got to rest.' There's no choice."

And he means complete bed rest. "Any physical act, even getting up to go to the bathroom, should be kept to a minimum," says Dr. Abraham. For the first day or so, even that may be avoided in favor of a bedpan if the pain is very acute.

And how long should you stay in bed? The answer may depend on the person or the particular doctor dispensing the advice. But depending on the degree of pain it can be from one to ten days.

Medications

Aspirin may relieve pain better than some prescription drugs.

Drugs won't cure your back problems, but they can make you feel better in the acute stage. And relief can be as close as your medicine cabinet— aspirin. It's not addictive, and it relieves pain and reduces inflammation. The Klein-Sobel survey backs this up. Aspirin temporarily relieved pain for 78 percent of the participants who took it, while commonly prescribed drugs such as painkillers, muscle relaxants, or tranquilizers left the patient feeling just as bad or worse, in most cases. If you *do* use a prescription drug, make sure you know about possible side effects.

Hot or Cold Packs

Ice packs deaden nerve perception, so they can be great, according to Dr. Abraham, especially during the first two days of pain. Then again, heat relaxes muscles and increases circulation to facilitate healing, so hot towels, hot packs, hot water bottles or hot tubs (if someone can help you into one) can also spell relief. You can experiment to see which one feels better.

Recuperating Diet

Avoid constipation.

"Just being less active can, and often does, cause constipation, which in turn makes some people's back pain considerably worse," Klein and Sobel found.

Papaya Won't Cure Backaches

When chymopapain was introduced to the United States in 1983, newspaper headlines heralded it as a cheap alternative to surgery for many people suffering from back pain. But now it appears that chymopapain may do more harm than good. Injections of the drug, a derivative of the tropical fruit papaya, are still approved by the Food and Drug Administration (FDA) to dissolve spinal disks and supposedly relieve pain. But neurosurgeon Charles Fager, M.D., says he's going to limit his papaya intake to the breakfast table.

"The whole concept of chymopapain injections is wrong," says Dr. Fager, chairman emeritus of the department of neurosurgery at the Lahey Clinic, in Burlington, Massachusetts. According to Dr. Fager, chymopapain will dissolve an undamaged disk if it's injected into the disk space, but it won't dissolve the ruptured portion of the disk. The catch is that it is the ruptured portion that is pressing on the spinal nerve and causing pain.

In other words, chymopapain is useless as a treatment.

Many doctors used the drug when it was first introduced in this country, but most neurosurgeons have since quit. Those who continue to use it are putting their patients at great risk, according to Dr. Fager, because chymopapain can have many side effects, including shock, paralysis and death. "That's a tragedy," says Dr. Fager.

Why do some doctors still use chymopapain? "They look upon it as a method of treatment that might avoid surgery. Actually, a number of patients who have had chymopapain injections still require surgery anyway," says the doctor. While the FDA still approves of the drug, Dr. Fager and others are working to change that.

Meanwhile, Dr. Fager doesn't recommend that anyone, no matter how much pain he or she is in, let a doctor administer chymopapain injections.

So don't tempt Mother Nature by eating lots of fried foods, fast foods, sugar and salt, because they're harder for the body to digest, says Dr. Abraham. Try to drink at least eight glasses of water or juice a day. And make sure you get plenty of fiber by eating whole-grain foods, fruit and vegetables.

Massage

"In an acute attack's first days, even the thought of being touched can make you cringe," says Dr. Abraham. "A bit later, however, massage is useful as an aid to relaxation, especially if the person giving that massage uses a gentle touch."

Though a professional massage is best, you can let a nonprofessional give it a try if you ask your physical therapist for some guidelines first. Those guidelines will be based on gentle stroking, since kneading can be extremely painful.

Getting Back into Activity

Start moving, even if it hurts a little.

"Your acute attack will be well on the wane within ten days' time," says Dr. Abraham. "But you don't need to wait that long to help recovery begin. No matter how bad the initial pain, you very probably *can* walk, bend or sit to some extent."

And you *should.* Only increased activity alternated with relaxation can diminish physical pain. Some people who fear pain will stay in bed indefinitely because any activity might hurt. So, ironically, these people will hurt the longest.

Remember that if you regularly perform carefully controlled physical activity, and get back into the mainstream of your life, you're on your way to recovery, says Dr. Abraham.

He recommends a program of basic movements such as bending knees, extending arms, turning over, sitting back and moving the head. It's called stretch testing.

"If you haven't had an acute attack, stretch testing may sound deceptively simple," he says. "But for anyone who has suffered an acute attack or who's recovering from one right now, stretch testing may sound very challenging indeed. The point is that doing this kind of controlled exercise gives sufferers the assurance that physical motion is possible, thus encouraging them to make further efforts toward expanding their level of activity."

Seeing the Doctor

Following the aforementioned tips regularly can prevent or relieve most types of backache. "I think

90 percent of back conditions are associated with long-term habit patterns that induce restricted muscular flexibility, culminating eventually in an acute attack of back pain," says Dr. Abraham. "True sciatica (that is, with herniated disks) occurs in less than 10 percent of people."

Danger Signs

So how do you know if you're one of the 10 percent? The American Medical Association's *Guide to Backcare* put together the following danger signs and symptoms of possible back problems that should send you to a physician:

- A backache that persists for more than two weeks. Most backaches, like colds, go away by themselves in a few days or weeks. If a backache lasts longer, it may mean that it is caused by some more serious back problems that should be treated.
- Pain that shoots down your leg toward your foot, or down your arm toward your hand, whether accompanied by backache or not. Such pain may mean that a herniated disk or other diseased tissue is pressing against a nerve in your back or neck.
- Numbness in your leg or foot, or in your arm or hand. It may mean that a nerve carrying sensations from the affected limb back toward your brain is being compressed.
- Muscular weakness in your leg or foot, or in your arm or hand. This can mean that something is pressing upon a nerve carrying messages from your brain to that limb.
- A backache so severe that it wakes you in the night. Most backaches feel better when you lie down. One that does not might be caused by some more serious disease, such as an infection or tumor, that should be treated without delay.
- Inability to control urination or defecation. Again, this is a sign that some diseased tissue may be compressing crucial nerves in your back.

Which Doctor to See

It's not an easy question to answer. Currently there are more than 100 different kinds of practitioners, treatments and self-help therapies out there,

Back sufferers rated their doctors in a survey.

each one claiming to be the ticket to back heaven. What's a backache to do?

You could take the advice of the 492 back-pain sufferers in the Klein-Sobel survey. The average number of practitioners seen by each survey participant was five and the average number of years before effective treatment was found was 12. So listening to them might save you from the same runaround. The following doctors are listed according to frequency seen, *not* according to their effectiveness in helping back patients.

The Orthopedist. An orthopedist (also known as an orthopedic surgeon) is a medical doctor who specializes in disorders of the musculoskeletal system—the bones, joints and related muscles, ligaments and nerves. Although more people in the survey reported seeing orthopedists than any other specialists, the orthopedic track record wasn't good. Relief (either short- or long-term) was provided by only 32 percent of the orthopedists while 61 percent were judged as "ineffective." According to the survey, the more effective orthopedists are less likely to perform surgery and prescribe drugs as a major part of the recovery program, and more likely to spend more time listening to than examining you.

The General Practitioner (Family Doctor). It's a good idea to get checked out by your family doctor to rule out the possibility of a disease or tumor as the cause of your backache. But after that, it's unlikely that your family practitioner is going to be of much service—other than medicating you with pills. Only 34 percent of the GPs provided short- or long-term help, and 54 percent were judged ineffective.

The Osteopath. Osteopaths are akin to regular medical doctors in that they can prescribe drugs and perform surgery, but they differ in that they also practice spinal manipulation, much like chiropractors. Osteopaths didn't make out too well in the survey, providing relief (short- or long-term) for only 43 percent of their patients. They were considered ineffective by 46 percent of their patients.

The Neurosurgeon. "Having your back pain treated by a neurosurgeon is usually a make-or-break proposition," report Klein and Sobel. "Either you'll be eter-

Orthopedists were popular, but not always effective.

A general practitioner can rule out the possibility of a disease.

nally grateful for the wonders of modern surgery, or you'll rue the day the word neurosurgeon was ever mentioned to you." Thirteen percent of neurosurgeons dramatically helped their patients, but 15 percent were reported to make the patient feel worse.

The Neurologist. Despite being immensely knowledgeable regarding the neurological makeup of the human body, neurologists fared worse than any other medical doctor in the survey. Only 8 percent of them were reported to provide relief; fully 76 percent were judged ineffective. Neurologists also were the most likely practitioner to prescribe drugs. "In short, the average back sufferer has no use for a neurologist," Klein and Sobel concluded.

Only 8 percent of neurologists provided relief.

The Physiatrist. The physiatrist (also called doctor of physical medicine, doctor of rehabilitative medicine) was the survey winner, proving to be about three times more effective than orthopedists. There aren't a lot of them around, unfortunately (only about 1,900 in the entire country). But "this exceptional healer is your best bet among all practitioners—medical or nonmedical—for both acute and chronic back problems," Klein and Sobel report. Fully 86 percent of them were reported to successfully provide relief, with only 14 percent not being helpful. The physiatrist's unique combination of being both a medical doctor and someone extensively trained in all aspects of physical rehabilitation appears to be "what the doctor ordered" for effective back-pain relief. (Rarely listed in the yellow pages, physiatrists can be located by writing to the following address: American Academy of Physical Medicine and Rehabilitation, 122 South Michigan, Chicago, IL, 60603-6107.)

The physiatrist was the survey winner.

Practitioners Who Are Not Medical Doctors

The Acupuncturist. Yes, this increasingly popular procedure can work. Fully 68 percent of acupuncturists mentioned in the Klein-Sobel survey helped provide relief, and only 4 percent were reported to make the patient feel worse. More impressive still, some respondents reported that relief from their treatments lasted up to two years.

The Chiropractor. People seeing chiropractors reported relief in some form (either dramatic long-term, moderate long-term or temporary) in 56 percent of all cases. Chiropractors were judged ineffective by 33 percent of their patients, and they made 11 percent feel worse. Some points to be careful about regarding chiropractors:

Chiropractors may help certain backaches.

- They can help you get temporary relief from minor or moderate low back or neck pain. But for severe, chronic low back pain, don't expect miracles.
- They are not advised for the treatment of serious back disorders, such as herniated disks and scoliosis (abnormal curvature of the spine).
- They are more effective if they counsel you on diet, exercise and life-style instead of merely performing spinal manipulation.
- They may need to see you on a regular—and hence fairly costly—basis to be most effective.

The Physical Therapist (Physiotherapist). "By far the most successful nonphysician practitioner for helping patients with almost any kind of back ailment," report Klein and Sobel. The key to the physical therapists' success (73 percent of their patients reported positive results from physiotherapy) appears to be treatment of the whole person: Everything from work habits to sleep habits get analyzed. And an impressive array of rehabilitative techniques are employed: heat, cold, instruction on posture, relaxation therapy, exercise therapy, massage and stimulation of muscles through both electricity and ultrasound.

The physical therapist is the most helpful nonphysician practitioner.

Diagnosing Your Diagnosis

Even if your doctor is trustworthy, his diagnosis could scare you. One reason for this, Dr. Hall points out, is that doctors speak in medical jargon. In his book, *The Back Doctor*, he gives an example of this curious language:

Make the doctor explain the diagnosis in everyday terms.

PATIENT: Doctor, I have something wrong with my neck.
DOCTOR (examining): You have cervical spondylosis.
PATIENT (recoiling): Oh, my God!

" 'Cervical spondylosis' is simply Doctor for 'something wrong with (the spinal portion of) your neck,' " says Dr. Hall. "As you can see, the Doctor language has the power among laymen to make even the most mundane diagnosis sound terribly profound, medically learned and frightening."

And because each medical field has its own perspective and its own terminology, a patient may get a different diagnosis from each doctor. And sometimes they mean the same thing. Dr. Hall points out that both "facet arthritis" and "spinal osteoarthrosis" can refer to the same spinal joint problem.

If the doctor admits that he or she doesn't know the exact cause of the pain, that can be just as scary. The patient may assume that it's the sign of a mysterious, incurable disease. But the truth is, a specific diagnosis is usually not essential to successful treatment. Back-pain sufferers who received no diagnosis often do just as well in the long run as patients who received one or more diagnoses.

What you *do* need is a diagnosis that rules out serious medical conditions. Many diseases or disorders can cause back pain, says the American Medical Association's *Guide to Backcare.*

You need a thorough examination to rule out serious medical conditions.

David Imrie, M.D., head of the Back Care Centre, in Toronto, and author of *Goodbye Backache* (Arco), conducts a thorough examination "to rule out the small percentage of serious diseases that fall into two categories—significant *congenital* disease (which means a disease one is born with, such as congenital scoliosis) or *acquired* disease (under which fall osteoporosis, ankylosing spondylitis, tuberculosis and tumors)." His other concern is to see if his patients have a herniated disk, because this condition, if left untreated, can cause irreversible damage to the nerves and muscles of the legs and feet, he says.

If you are one of the few troubled souls who have a serious disease, this chapter is not for you, though your doctor may recommend the life-style changes after he treats your condition.

What a Doctor Might Do for Your Back

By now it should be painfully obvious that your backache will bow to no miracle cure, and that only *you* can prevent back flare-ups. But that doesn't mean that a doctor can't help you along. Picking a treatment is about as confusing as choosing a doctor, so here is some information on commonly prescribed treatments.

Surgery

A *Time* magazine article described a surgeon with a sinister approach to surgery: "Seated across the desk from a patient, he outlines the exercise routine, then picks up a scalpel and hones it a few times on a small whetstone. 'Remember,' he says, 'if you don't want to be bothered with exercise, I also do surgery.' "

Actually, there's no evidence to suggest that exercises are a substitute for necessary surgery. But it is true that surgery can be avoided.

Most back problems can't be helped by surgery.

"Surgery is the answer to only a fraction of back problems in which a specific mechanical condition exists—a bulging disk pressing against a nerve, for example," says Dr. Imrie. And even then it is only one step in what will be a lifelong process of back care. There was a time when surgery was held to be a panacea for back problems. But the results were so often discouraging that in the last decade it was not uncommon to meet patients who had had two, three or four operations and still suffered backache. Their lack of success at permanently relieving backache has made surgeons much less enthusiastic about operations during recent years. In the United States, surgery fails completely in about 20 percent of cases, and three out of five patients continue to have symptoms despite it."

What's more, surgery might not be necessary, even if your doctor suggests it. For every participant in the Klein-Sobel survey who had disk surgery (the most common type of back surgery), three others were told they probably had disk problems requiring surgery but found successful alternatives. Bed rest, pain medication, physical therapy and a supportive practitioner were important factors in these people's recoveries.

If you see a surgeon and are advised to have an operation, participants in this survey suggest the following:

• Get a second opinion. And a third. See at least one other surgeon and one practitioner who is not a surgeon. Explore the potential benefits of rest and physical therapy if you have a ruptured disk.

• Ask about your chances of success. Specific figures should be available at every medical center. Take your business elsewhere if you get an evasive answer.

• Ask about postoperative care. If your treatment ends with surgery, either change doctors or make other arrangements for postoperative treatment that will restore you to full activity.

Traction

Back traction made more people in the Klein-Sobel survey feel worse than any other widely used form of back treatment. Although the American Medical Association's *Guide to Backcare* cites fracture, herniated disk and spinal injury as main reasons for using this contraption, the most common reason given to the survey participants was to keep antsy patients in bed and assure complete bed rest. But since traction made nearly one-quarter of those who had it prescribed feel worse, and an additional 52 percent feel the same, willpower may be a safer way to ensure bed rest.

Back traction makes more people feel worse than any other widely used form of back treatment.

Braces

Girdles and braces can make you feel good because they do the same things your muscles are supposed to be doing—they hold your belly in and keep your spine in a comfortable position. But that's the same reason why they can be bad—you don't have to use your muscles, so they get weaker and your back gets worse.

"They can be used at first, when your muscles can't do much," says Dr. Abraham. "But your goal is to be free of any apparatus except for your back muscles."

Back braces may feel good, but they shouldn't be a substitute for good muscle tone.

Commit Yourself to Back Relief

"Back pain is not a disease and therefore it has no cure," says Dr. Hall. "But it can be controlled. To make your back better, you need to spend the time, you need to have the patience and you need to accept the responsibility."

Just because your back is your responsibility doesn't mean you don't need help. "Very few people have the discipline and the drive to maintain difficult changes all alone," says David F. Fardon, M.D., orthopedic surgeon, founder of the Knoxville Back Care Center, in Tennessee, and author of *Free Yourself from Back Pain* (Prentice-Hall). "One particularly good way to combine social and personal commitments is to join new group activities that complement your efforts. Athletic associations, swim clubs, track clubs, health spas and dance groups offer exercise programs that combine enjoyable forms of exercise with the stimulation and encouragement of group membership."

5

Bones that

Stay Strong

An often repeated horror movie scene depicts a human skeleton springing to life and running amok, terrifying those in the film and in the audience. You laugh about it afterward, comforting yourself with the secure knowledge that skeletons aren't really alive. They are merely lifeless structures that support the body.

Aren't they?

Au contraire.

Doctors worry more about this misconception than they do the prospect of grinning skeletons invading their waiting rooms. The reason: Your bones are very much alive, and ignoring this fact can lead to problems more frightening than a nightmare inspired by Hollywood.

The misconception probably stems from the feeling that, once you've grown to your full height, your bones have done their job and can retire. People often find it difficult to accept that even after childhood, bones continue to grow, shrink, hunger, hurt and heal, just like the rest of the body. The marrow inside bones manufactures the body's vital blood cells. Once you accept these facts, it becomes easier to comply with the skeleton's simple maintenance demands. Heed them and you will not only keep the structure strong and straight, but also avoid

Bones are living structures.

Stay healthy by giving your bones the care they require.

51

the tragic results of "dead" thinking—osteoporosis, adult rickets (osteomalacia), and fractures caused by brittleness.

Walking Tall

You can prevent the bent-back tragedy of osteoporosis.

One of the most dramatic medical stories of the last quarter-century has been the discovery that calcium may prevent osteoporosis, a crippling bone disease once thought to be an unavoidable part of aging.

In turn, some of the saddest personal stories of this same period are the millions of women who didn't receive or heed the message.

Osteoporosis remains a critical problem affecting as many as 15 to 20 million individuals in the United States. About 12.3 million people over the age of 45 annually suffer fractures as a result of this condition. One-quarter of all women over age 60 and half of those over age 70 have osteoporosis severe enough to cause pain, loss of height, and spinal deformity. Among those who live to age 90, 32 percent of the women and 17 percent of the men suffer a hip fracture, and it's usually caused by osteoporosis. Twenty percent of those will die within the year. The cost of osteoporosis in the United States alone has been estimated at almost $6 billion annually.

All of this may be avoidable. Doctors and researchers around the world are doing everything but hiring town criers to alert not only the most susceptible group, postmenopausal women, but to get a jump on preventing the disease in postpubescent women.

The calcium-robbers in your life-style.

"We think osteoporosis is a life-style condition, not a disease," says Morris Notelovitz, M.D., director of the Center for Climacteric Studies, in Gainesville, Florida. "Osteoporosis is a modern event. We live longer, are more sedentary and have diets low in calcium and high in calcium-robbers such as caffeine and cigarettes. We are not exercising or feeding our bones."

"Education is the best way to help. We have to let women know that the condition exists and that there are ways to prevent it. We should be able to go into old age without osteoporosis. It's not inevitable," Dr. Notelovitz says.

To fully grasp the necessity for preventive measures, a simple explanation of the disease is appropriate. Your skeleton is more than girders to your flesh. The bones actually resemble a silo holding minerals vital to operate your entire life system. When your dietary mineral intake is inadequate, the body robs the bones to bolster the mineral level. Years of calcium deficiency result in brittle and porous bones as the body literally feeds upon itself. The severe medical damage to the structure combines with the aesthetically shocking manifestation of a bent, slumped back.

The body borrows from the bones to make up for inadequate minerals in the diet, leaving them weak and vulnerable.

In men, the bone loss rate begins sometime in their late thirties and proceeds at a rate of .3 percent a year, according to Robert P. Heaney, M.D., a professor at Creighton University School of Medicine, in Omaha, Nebraska. Men usually don't have crippling problems until their eighties.

Women are another story. The loss rate starts earlier, as early as the late twenties, then kicks into overdrive after menopause, when it soars to ten times the rate of men. One of the reasons is the loss of the female hormone estrogen, which works to retard bone loss. Dr. Heaney says the double whammy of estrogen loss and low calcium intake can cause some bones, including those in the lower back, to lose an astounding 8 percent a year. Between the ages of 50 and 70, a woman can lose 30 percent of her bone mass.

The deck is stacked against women, but they still can win.

Other factors tipping the scales to disfavor women include: a smaller body size and bone mass; the strain of pregnancy and breast-feeding upon calcium reserves; more frequent weight loss diets; a longer life span; and a more sedentary life-style.

This staggering gender imbalance can be erased. A few simple tips can stop the erosion or slow it to such a miniscule level that it will have no adverse effects regardless of how long you live.

A Plan to Beat Osteoporosis

In her early twenties, a woman should begin a lifetime program to prevent osteoporosis, says Louis Avioli, M.D., director of the division of bone and

Women should start early if they want to avoid future trouble.

mineral metabolism at Washington University, in St. Louis. If you are beyond that age, don't worry. Starting 10 to 30 years later, you still can do things to minimize the risk or treat the condition.

Here's what to do.

Calcium. Although the current Recommended Dietary Allowance (RDA) for calcium is 800 milligrams (mg) a day for adults, Dr. Avioli believes that all women 20 years old and older should be getting a minimum of 1,000 to 1,500 mg a day. Dr. Notelovitz recommends 1,000 mg for premenopausal women, and 1,400 for postmenopausal. Teenagers and pregnant women should be getting at least 1,200 mg per day. Foods such as milk, yogurt, cheese and sardines are loaded with calcium (see chart), and supplemental calcium can be taken through tablets if you have an irregular diet. Dr. Avioli recommends calcium carbonate tablets along with vitamin D, which aids in calcium absorption. However, Robert R. Recker, M.D., of Creighton University School of Medicine, says a study he performed determined that older people with inadequate stomach acid (achlorhydria) have better results with calcium citrate, a soluble calcium salt.

Be aware that caffeine, tobacco, red meat, soft drinks and fiber-rich foods (if taken at the same time as the calcium) can inhibit calcium absorption. In addition, some doctors recommend taking 250 to 350 mg of magnesium with calcium because they believe it may aid in the absorption of calcium.

Stanton Cohn, Ph.D., professor of medicine at the school of medicine, State University of New York at Stony Brook, and head of the medical physics division of the Brookhaven National Laboratory, in New York, says you can take calcium supplements with meals or at bedtime, but added that it's better to spread out the doses rather than take all the calcium at once. "If you overload, there's a chance that a good bit will be lost through body wastes," Dr. Cohn explained.

Don't try to make up for lost time with megadoses, doctors warn. Taking supplements of more than 2,000 mg per day can, in rare cases, lead to kidney stones and constipation.

If you're a big milk drinker, you probably don't need supplements at all. An eight-ounce glass of

One expert believes all women 20 years old and up should get at least 1,000 to 1,500 milligrams of calcium daily.

Take calcium supplements throughout the day, says this expert.

The Best Food Sources of Calcium

Food	Portion	Calcium (mg)
Yogurt, skim-milk	1 cup	452
Swiss cheese	2 oz	438
Provolone cheese	2 oz	428
Monterey Jack cheese	2 oz	424
Cheddar cheese	2 oz	408
Muenster cheese	2 oz	406
Colby cheese	2 oz	388
Brick cheese	2 oz	382
Sardines, Atlantic, drained solids	3 oz	371
Mozzarella cheese	2 oz	366
American cheese	2 oz	348
Milk, skim	1 cup	302
Buttermilk	1 cup	285
Limburger cheese	2 oz	282
Salmon, sockeye, drained solids	3 oz	274
Broccoli, cooked	1 medium spear	205
Pizza, cheese	⅛ of a 14-in pie	144
Blackstrap molasses	1 tbsp	137
Soy flour, defatted	½ cup	132
Tofu	3 oz	109
Collards, cooked	½ cup	74
Dandelion greens, cooked	½ cup	73
Kale, cooked	½ cup	47

Milk is a major weapon in the fight against osteoporosis.

low-fat milk contains 297 mg of calcium. Four to five glasses a day would do the trick. A study by doctors at Creighton University School of Medicine concluded that calcium obtained through drinking milk was just as beneficial to the body as the calcium obtained through supplements.

Exercise. Physical inactivity is another culprit that can lead to osteoporosis. A study of bedridden patients, for example, showed they can lose up to 1.1 percent of their heel bone mass in only one week. In contrast, Everett Smith, Ph.D., a specialist in the aging process at the University of Wisconsin's department of preventive medicine, performed an extensive, four-year study of women ages 36 to 67 participating in a vigorous exercise program. The activity included 45 minutes of aerobic dancing and jogging three times a week, using arm and ankle weights. According to Dr. Smith, the exercise program reduced bone loss by 80 percent.

Lifting weights is a good way to strengthen your bones.

An additional study by Lee N. Burkett, Ph.D., a biomechanist at Arizona State University, in Tempe, determined that weight lifting reshapes bones into stronger and more flexible configurations while increasing their density, enabling them to withstand more tension and compression before reaching the breaking point. Dr. Burkett says moderate weight training may help prevent fractures in the elderly.

Vitamin D. One of the major factors contributing to osteoporosis is that older people absorb less calcium from their food. Vitamin D is necessary for calcium absorption. Those who are deficient in this vitamin can contract osteomalacia, or adult rickets, a disease that is similar to osteoporosis, but causes a softening of the calcium-starved bones. Even when you are getting enough calcium, osteomalacia can occur, because the body is unable to process it. The problem is easy to correct. Dr. Avioli often prescribes 400 international units (I.U.) of vitamin D per day to increase dietary calcium absorption, especially for women who don't get enough sunlight (the main source of D) during the longer winter seasons or who have sicknesses or injuries that keep them from getting outdoors. Vitamin D-fortified dairy products and oily fish are good dietary sources.

Salt. Experiments performed by Ailsa Goulding, Ph.D, senior research officer of the department of medicine at the University of Otago, in New Zealand, concluded that excess salt bleeds calcium out of the body via the urine. Dr. Goulding calculated that a single teaspoon of salt a day can cause bone mass to decrease by 1.5 percent a year. Osteoporosis, he says, may join the growing list of reasons people should reduce salt.

Alcohol. While men, under normal conditions, don't suffer the damages of osteoporosis until their eighties (which is beyond their current estimated life expectancy), there's evidence that alcoholism could put them in the same boat as women. A study of 96 chronic alcoholic men at the Veterans Administration Hospital, in Hines, Illinois, determined that 47 percent had evidence of bone loss. Even more telling, 31 percent were under 40 years old.

Alcohol can induce severe bone loss and place men in the same risk category as women.

Doctors recommend combining the above suggestions for the best results.

If you go out and buy a bottle of calcium supplements without considering the importance of the other factors, you'll realize some benefit," says Dr. Heaney. "But if you're striving for the maximum results, you must make sure the other pieces of the puzzle are there also."

A common medical technique to combat osteoporosis is prescribing estrogen to make up for the hormone's decrease in a woman's body after menopause. However, estrogen treatments have been linked to uterine cancer, gallstones, high blood pressure and stroke, and have lost favor among some doctors.

Solving the estrogen dilemma.

"Estrogen and calcium retard the loss of bone equally as well," Dr. Avioli says. "So the question for the average physician is, does the patient want a treatment that combines female hormones, which have potential side effects, with a little calcium, or one that uses no female hormones and more calcium?"

James A. Nicotero, M.D., a nephrologist (kidney doctor) and director of the Osteoporosis Diagnostic Center, St. Francis Medical Center, in Pittsburgh, says estrogen treatments may still be the best therapy for some people. These include women who are resistant to vitamin D and therefore have trouble absorbing calcium, along with women who have hypercalciuria, an abnormality that causes excessive calcium loss in the urine.

It's Never Too Late

Osteoporosis was once considered irreversible. Many doctors still feel that way. However, the latest research has determined that innovative medical treatment, improvement of the diet and exercise not only can prevent osteoporosis, but actually can regenerate weak bones.

Lila Wallis, M.D., clinical professor of medicine at Cornell University Medical College, in Ithaca, New York, says both sodium fluoride, the mineral used in water supplies to protect teeth, and the male sex hormone testosterone, can help regenerate bones ravaged by osteoporosis. However, Dr. Wallis warns that there are often complications. Side effects of sodium fluoride include nausea, vomiting, upset stomach and arthritis. If calcium is not taken with the sodium fluoride the bones can become "coarsely serrated"—their surfaces are rough as a rusty knife. Adding estrogen to the sodium fluoride/calcium package improves the regenerative results—but it adds the problems of estrogen therapy mentioned previously. And testosterone, if given in high doses, can cause women to "virilize," with deep voices and/or facial hair. Dr. Wallis says she prevents these problems by prescribing a mix of hormones. "This therapy," she says "helps bone pain, prevents bone loss and is not associated with masculinization or linked to uterine cancer."

Exercise appears to be the safest method of regenerating bones.

Dr. Smith says there is a much safer route. He determined that exercise performed by people in their eighties can actually increase bone mass and repair some of the osteoporosis damage. Dr. Smith designed a series of 30-minute exercise sessions that can be performed even by those confined to a wheelchair. One of his favorites is "walking in place" in a chair by placing your hand on your thighs, and at one pace per second, lifting first one foot, then the other. Other exercises in the program include chair jumping jacks, arm rotations and leg extensions.

Those performing the exercises were able to increase their bone mass by 2.3 percent, while a control group suffered a 3.3 percent loss.

A similar study performed by researchers at West Virginia University, in Morgantown, found that postmenopausal women put on a program of walking or aerobic dancing were able to increase their bone width by 1.6 and 1.3 percent respectively in just six months.

Dr. Smith says it's never too late to start exercising, adding that he once gave the green light to a patient who was 97.

Get in the Swim

To help you ease into an exercise program, authorities recommend starting with one or more of these "soft" exercises.

Soft exercises can ease you into a lifetime exercise program.

Swimming. "Swimming is particularly good for people whose joints have stiffened with age or arthritis," says Zebulon Kendrick, Ph.D., director of the biokinetic lab at Temple University, in Philadelphia. "It helps to loosen up stiff joints."

Walking. Walking is perfect because it's a normal activity that's beneficial to the bones but doesn't seem like work. You shoud walk at least 30 minutes, five times a week, for the exercise to be effective. "Walk with your spouse or a friend," advises Dr. Smith. "It's a wonderful way to socialize and share your thoughts."

Cycling. Tour the countryside outdoors, or visit exotic locations through a book while pumping the pedals on a stationary bike indoors. Either way, the benefits are substantial. Doctors recommend starting slow and easy.

Dancing. Whether you fancy the rumba, polka, twist, ballet, bop, limbo, shimmy, jazzercise, square dancing or folk dancing, the idea is to go, flow, rock, sway, turn, strut, swing and sweep to your favorite tunes. Without even noticing it, you'll give your body and bones an exhilarating workout!

Protect Your Hips

Remember that irritating skeleton song about this bone being connected to that bone? They

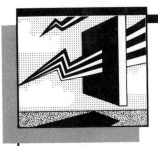

New Developments in Osteoporosis

Scientists and doctors have given an old tool a new application, and the combination has revolutionized the diagnosis and treatment of osteoporosis. The device is called a single-photon densitometer. In a simple, 15-minute office procedure, the instrument can measure the mineral content of the wristbone at two precise locations. The wristbone measurements mirror the mineral content of both the hipbone and the spinal column, the two major osteoporosis trouble spots. The densitometer uses only one-hundredth the radiation of standard forearm x-rays. Despite its space-age name, James A. Nicotero, M.D., director of the Osteoporosis Diagnostic Center, St. Francis Medical Center, in Pittsburgh, says the tool has been around since the late 1960s.

"Conventional x-rays can't detect osteoporosis until 30 to 40 percent of the bone mass is lost, in which case bone loss is so extensive that fractures may occur. At that stage, estrogen is often prescribed. The beauty of the densitometer is that we can detect as little as a 2 percent change in bone mass, which means we can initiate therapies before too much damage is done. This device could also decrease the use of estrogen, because a woman wouldn't be given estrogen if she were found to have excellent bone density at the time of her menopause," Dr. Nicotero says.

Mark P. Ettinger, M.D. medical director of the Osteoporosis-Bone Diagnostic Laboratory, in Stuart, Florida, says that a dual-photon testing system can make an early identification of abnormal bone loss. "With this new technology, we have discovered that women should be tested around menopause for identification of bone problems. Early detection means early treatment that will keep women's bone strength out of the 'fracture zone.' "

should have added an extra verse. "The hip bone is connected to trouble."

Falling and fracturing the brittle hip can be disastrous. Hip fractures are a major cause of death in the elderly. Twenty percent of all the people who have this type of break die within the year.

Most hip fractures can be prevented by preventing osteoporosis. Maintaining a daily calcium and magnesium intake of 1,500 and 250 to 350 mg respectively will help. (Magnesium may aid in the absorption of calcium.) A premenopause prevention strategy can have significant results. Researchers at the National Institute on Aging suggest that such preventive measures can cut the risk of hip fractures in half throughout a woman's life.

Calcium toughens the bones and enables them to withstand accidents that often result in serious fractures.

Additional Strategies

"The first thing I tell people with bad hips is to lose weight," says Robert C. Bartlett, M.D., of Ocala, Florida, author of *Arthritis of the Hip: Yours and Mine* (Arco). "One extra pound is equal to carrying around an extra ton if you walk a mile," he says, calculating the added pressure.

If you are experiencing hip pain, the most important thing to do is see a doctor at once. Like most bone disease, hip problems are progressive and grow worse every day you delay treatment.

Bad Breaks

The hip isn't the only bone that can snap during a routine fall. Weak bones can cave in to stress anywhere in the body. The object is to prevent accidents before they happen.

Environmental boobytraps are thought to be a primary cause of about one-third of all falls. Joseph Melton III, M.D., and Lawrence Riggs, M.D, of the Mayo Medical School, in Rochester, Minnesota, say the leading hazards seem to be slippery floors and loose rugs. Poor lighting on stairways is yet another problem.

Domestic accidents are a common but avoidable cause of broken bones.

The American Society for Bone and Mineral Research, founded by Dr. Avioli, offers these guidelines to make your home fall-proof.

- Get rid of deadly throw rugs.
- Don't wear high heels or unstable shoes.
- Use a walking aid if necessary.
- Remove clutter in your house.
- Install safety rails on stairways and in bathrooms.
- Provide adequate lighting.

Bolstering the Breaks

If you couldn't part with that heirloom throw rug, and it did you in, here are some ways to restore your broken bones once the doctor has set them back in place.

Diet. Research has shown that nitrogen loss is high after fractures, a sign that the body is using vast amounts of protein to rebuild the damage. The researchers found that by doubling the RDA of protein, the fracture patient can catch up with his nitrogen losses more quickly.

Calcium, diet and sleep can speed your recovery from fractures.

Calcium. If the white mineral seems to be dominating this chapter, it's because bones and calcium go together like bricks and cement. Following a fracture, experts say that calcium intake should be increased by diet or supplements to 1,000 to 1,500 mg per day. It's a good idea to maintain that level as a preventative measure afterward.

Sleep. Researchers at the Royal Edinburgh Hospital, in Scotland, say "cell division and protein synthesis (necessary for healing) reach their maximum values during the hours of sleep and are minimal during wakefulness."

Noisy bones are nothing to worry about unless pain is involved.

There are some bone "cracks" that don't require any treatment. These are the noisy "breakfast cereal bones," that snap, crackle and pop. Doctors say unless there is pain or a grinding sensation accompanying those crackling bones, it's probably all normal.

6

Breathe

New Health

into Your Lungs

S tanding on top of a mountain, your chest lifts, your diaphragm contracts and your lungs fill with crisp, clean, pine-scented air. Or you're walking along the seashore on a beautiful summer day, drawing in glorious draughts of salty breezes.

Breathing—that simple, necessary activity that usually takes place without your giving it a conscious thought—can also be one of life's great pleasures.

Surprisingly, a simple breathing test—it's similar to blowing up balloons—is one of the most precise predictors of how long you will live. Doctors analyzing data from the Framingham Study, a 27-year-old medical study of a Massachusetts community, looked at the results of a simple, inexpensive procedure, called a spirometry test, given to each person in the study. The test measures the amount of air expelled from the lungs in one quick deep breath. This is known as "forced vital capacity" (FVC), and it's the standard measure by which doctors gauge the health of your lungs.

Spirometry is most often used to confirm a diagnosis of lung disease, such as emphysema or chronic bronchitis. Doctors at the Mayo Clinic, in Rochester, Minnesota, say it beats a physical exam or x-rays at detecting lung disease, and that smokers age 35 and older should have this test every five years to deter-

Your breathing is an important indicator of your health.

A simple breathing test predicts your life expectancy.

mine if there is lung damage. And the Framingham researchers discovered that the test shows even more. "We found that the lung's forced vital capacity is indirectly related to the rate of all cardiovascular diseases and to overall mortality," says William B. Kannel, M.D., MPH, professor of medicine and chief of preventive medicine and epidemiology at Boston University School of Medicine. "The lower someone's forced vital capacity, the more likely he was to go on to develop heart disease or to die early. In fact, it turns out to be one of the strongest predictors of life expectancy, even competing with major cardiovascular risk factors like smoking or high blood pressure."

Let a Lung Test Save You from Heart Disease

Dr. Kannel also found that a below-normal score on the forced vital capacity test was an especially good early predictor of heart failure in people who showed none of the typical symptoms, like fatigue, swollen ankles . . . and shortness of breath. The test picked up this sign of impending failure even before the patient or doctor was aware of it.

"Most doctors regard this lung test as a useful index of the severity and progression of heart failure once it has begun," Dr. Kannel says. "But they don't realize they could also use it to detect patients with vulnerabilty to heart disease. That's unfortunate, because too often, by the time symptoms become apparent, the heart is too worn out to be saved."

It is true that many people who do poorly on the forced vital capacity test don't have heart disease. They have chronic lung disease caused by smoking, says Robert Hyatt, M.D., director of the Mayo Clinic's pulmonary function laboratory. And the test is underutilized to detect even this, he says. "It could detect lung disease in smokers early enough to do something about it, but most doctors don't use it for that. I'd say the average patient has lost half of his lung function by the time he sees a doctor for shortness of breath."

Used properly, the test can predict disease early enough to do something about it.

For Smokers, Good Reasons to Quit

If you're an ex-smoker, give yourself a pat on the back. You've taken the first major step toward healthy lungs and new stamina.

It's rare for nonsmokers to get lung disease, although ex-smokers have slightly higher risks. Tobacco compromises your ability to use oxygen at every level of the game: Its tars destroy lung cells; its carbon monoxide gets into the bloodstream 26 times faster than can oxygen; its nicotine constricts the capillaries that feed oxygen to the muscles.

Lung capacity declines more rapidly in smokers than in nonsmokers. Smokers who stop halt that rapid decline, although they're unlikely to regain lung capacity. It will always be lower than comparably fit people who never smoked. Whether or not that makes them become short of breath more quickly depends on their level of fitness and the amount of lung damage they had when they stopped smoking, says Robert Hyatt, M.D., director of the Mayo Clinic's pulmonary function laboratory.

But nonsmokers who do poorly on the test or whose test results for lung disease are unclear could get further screening with a heart function test called an echocardiogram, Dr. Kannel says. This painless ultrasound scan can determine the amount of blood that flows through the heart with each beat. It can tell you if your poor lung function is due to a weak heart.

What does the heart have to do with the lungs? If the heart isn't pumping as efficiently as it should, blood begins to back up in the lungs' millions of tiny capillaries, making them stiff and swollen with retained fluid, and reducing their ability to expand and contract. A failing heart also hinders the lungs' ability to oxygenate blood, because fluid buildup around the lungs' tiny cells prevents the close contact between blood and air needed for oxygen to move into the blood. The result is a painful gasping for air that can't be used anyway.

People can perform normally on the forced vital capacity test and have no signs of lung or heart

Do less knitting and more cha-cha-cha.

disease, but still find themselves short-winded. Their problem is too much knitting and not enough cha-cha-cha. They're out of shape.

"And their lungs really have very little to do with their being short of breath," says Bryant Stamford, Ph.D., director of the exercise physiology laboratory at the University of Louisville School of Medicine, in Kentucky. "One of the big misunderstandings about exercise is that when people become winded they are having problems with their lungs. That's just not the case. Healthy lungs have a tremendous excess capacity. They have no problem moving enormous amounts of air or diffusing all the oxygen they can

Check Your Technique

Is how you breathe important, especially while you're engaging in exercise?

It can be, Bryant Stamford, Ph.D., says. "Rapid shallow breathing is extremely unproductive, because you end up moving air back and forth in the 'dead space' between your nose and mouth area and the depths of your lungs where oxygen uptake occurs. No oxygen is absorbed from air in the dead space."

It's best to breathe deeply but not in an unnatural way, Dr. Stamford says. "You don't want to take great big deep breaths, but neither do you want rapid shallow breathing." And remember not to hold your breath while you're exercising, especially when you're lifting weights. It can raise your blood pressure. Some instructors believe it doesn't matter whether you inhale or exhale on the exertion, but others suggest you exhale.

And were you ever warned against exercising outdoors in the winter because of the danger of freezing your lungs? It's nonsense, according to doctors. The air you breathe in has been warmed to above freezing temperature by the time it reaches your bronchial tubes. It may be a little uncomfortable at first, says an exercise physiologist, but that is mostly because cold air is so dry.

But be careful. Extremes in temperature are risk factors for heart attacks. Researchers think that when it's cold out, blood vessels may constrict, cutting off the blood supply to the heart.

hold into the blood stream. They can keep up with any physical activity. It's almost impossible to overload them."

Then why the huff-and-puff schtick? Because there are other links in the oxygen-bearing chain that can slow you down, Dr. Stamford says.

Iron Helps Carry Oxygen

Take the bloodstream, for example. "Can the blood carry enough oxygen? Here you are dependent on the number of red blood cells and the amount of oxygen-carrying hemoglobin they contain," he explains. In this case, the most common problem would be anemia, probably caused by an iron deficiency. Iron is an essential part of hemoglobin. Without it, oxygen can't move through the bloodstream, tissues are deprived and so a feeling of breathlessness occurs, often accompanied by rapid heartbeat. Getting the iron you need is important to your exercise program, because exercise helps to promote a slight increase in both blood volume and the number of red blood cells. Provided enough iron is available, this makes your blood better at carrying oxygen.

Iron and exercise are linked.

And can the heart pump enough blood? "The heart is probably the primary bottleneck in the oxygen delivery system," Dr. Stamford says. "If you are not aerobically trained, the best way for the heart to circulate blood is to beat very often. That's just not very effective, and it stresses the heart."

An aerobically trained heart, on the other hand, begins to pump more blood with each beat, during exercise and at rest. It becomes a more muscular, efficient pump, and is less stressed. It allows you to be more active without running out of breath.

An aerobically trained heart allows you to be active without huffing and puffing.

Let a Workout Pump Up Your Lungs

The muscle tissues are the final link in the oxygen chain. Muscle tissues that aren't getting enough oxygen send a message to the lungs—breathe more! But that doesn't help. The lungs are already providing plenty of oxygen.

What does help is exercise, Dr. Stamford says.

Exercise promotes the development of good capillary channels to the muscle tissues, making sure the blood gets where it's needed. It increases the number and size of tiny energy-producing mitochondria in the muscle cells, making them more effective oxygen users. And it increases the amount of a substance found in the muscles, myoglobin, that escorts oxygen from the bloodstream into the cells.

Endurance Building

So how can you benefit from all these stamina-building goodies? It takes some time, and possibly some perseverance, Dr. Stamford admits. It means you have to exercise strenuously enough to deliberately make yourself short of breath, to create an oxygen demand that reaches all the way down to your muscles.

"You need to do aerobic exercise at least 30 minutes at a time, three or four days a week," Dr. Stamford says. The first few weeks you'll certainly feel your body screaming for the oxygen it can't get, but after several weeks, the links in the chain begin to tighten up, and you'll find yourself gaining stamina, perhaps even enjoying the exercise.

If you're over 30, overweight or become breathless even while inactive, you should see a doctor before beginning an exercise program, Dr. Stamford says. You want to make sure you don't have an undiagnosed heart condition that could be aggravated by exercise.

Can You VO_2?

VO_2 is not a hair tonic.

Although people who are aerobically trained tend to have above-normal vital capacity, the FVC test won't measure your degree of fitness or ability to use oxygen. For that, you need a VO_2 Max test. The VO_2 Max test measures your body's oxygen consumption during exercise. It's not often done, though, except for research purposes or to satisfy the curiosity of super-athletes.

And you don't really need to have it done, doctors say. It might be better, and it's certainly less expensive, to learn to monitor your body's oxygen needs yourself, pushing just a little further each time you exercise. But be careful not to overdo it. You be the judge and back off if you are breathing too hard.

"If a doctor is reasonably sure his patient is simply out of shape, he might put the patient on an exercise program and see if his stamina improves," Dr. Hyatt says. "If it doesn't, it becomes more a diagnostic problem, and the doctor might then go to formal exercise testing, including the VO_2 Max test."

It's true that your lungs' vital capacity and your body's ability to use oxygen decrease as you age. On average, your vital capacity drops about 5 percent with each decade of life, mostly due to loss of lung elasticity. But it drops much faster in people who smoke, and may drop slower in people who get regular aerobic exercise, contends Dr. Kannel.

Lung capacity may last longer in those who exercise.

Maximum oxygen uptake also stays higher in people who exercise.

"In most people who find themselves becoming breathless, it's because of a lack of fitness, not necessarily aging," Dr. Stamford contends. "In our society, it's not difficult to find 30-year-olds who are huffing and puffing."

In fact, a 50-year-old endurance runner can have the stamina of a sit-at-home 18-year-old, although that's not to say the same runner does as well at age 50 as he did at 18.

A 50-year-old runner can have the stamina of a sit-at-home 18-year-old.

"We do know there's something more than exercise involved, although we don't really know what it is," Dr. Stamford says. "Even though our marathoner continues to train, he will see a progressive decline in capacity over the years."

But chances are he won't see a debilitating decline. You don't have to run marathons to stay fit enough to function, Dr. Stamford says. "Even gentle exercise will help older people regain stamina. I think sometimes the best thing to do is walk, and just try to get a little bit farther each day."

Healing with a Breath of Fresh Air

But what about those who can't make it around the block? What about those with a serious lung condition? An estimated 18 million people in this country find themselves gasping and wheezing from asthma, chronic bronchitis or emphysema. Together, these ailments are called chronic obstructive lung disease, or COLD. And at a time when the incidence of heart disease is falling, the COLD rate is rising by 10 percent a year. In fact, lung disease has been called the nation's "most serious health threat" because of its increasing incidence.

Not all of the news about lung disease is bad, however. Pulmonary specialists say that it is easily within your power to prevent chronic bronchitis and emphysema—the two worst forms of COLD—and that more effective treatment of both may eventually be in reach.

It is easily within your power to prevent some of the worst lung diseases.

The causes of chronic bronchitis (an inflammation of the larger airways) and emphysema (the blockage and destruction of the smaller airways) are no longer a mystery. Tobacco smoke is the number-one cause of each of these illnesses, and most lung patients are veteran smokers. Even among coal miners and asbestos workers, those who develop lung disease are usually smokers.

"Without cigarettes, those two lung diseases would be uncommon," says Lawrence Martin, M.D., chief of the pulmonary division at Mt. Sinai Medical Center, in Cleveland, and author of *Breathe Easy: A Guide to Lung and Respiratory Diseases for Patients and Their Families* (Prentice-Hall). "Even in industry, it is the smokers who have the most respiratory illnesses."

"Smoking may not be the whole story," adds Robert Sandhaus, M.D., Ph.D., of the National Jewish Center for Immunology and Respiratory Medicine, in Denver, "because there are a few people who smoke for 60 years and don't get sick. But for most lung patients, cigarette smoking is the common link."

Breath-Building Exercises

If smoking is the common link between those who develop lung disease, then exercise is one of the links between those who fight back most successfully. Even though exercise may be the last thing an emphysema patient feels about to do, it must be done. The reason: Trained muscles need less air than weak ones.

Silent (Snoreless) Night

A log being sawed in two is the cartoon symbol for snoring. But when the volume reaches the level of a jackhammer—as it does in some cases—it's not anybody's idea of a joke.

For some who snore, the old home remedy of a snore ball—a marble or small ball sewn or taped onto the back (lying on the back is the position where most snores start) will work. Humidifiers also often help by keeping upper airway passages clear. Weight loss may be effective, too. A high percentage of snorers are simply too fat.

But chronic, loud snorers may have to resort to more extreme measures, particularly when sleep apnea—a condition in which breathing actually ceases—is also present. Ninety percent of apnea sufferers are also loud snorers. As many as 2 in 100 people are believed to be afflicted with sleep apnea.

Some medical methods developed in recent years offer hope to serious nocturnal noisemakers. They all deal with the actual cause of snoring—difficulty getting air through the upper respiratory passages. One method is the drug protriptyline (Vivactil), which opens passages through stimulation of parts of the central nervous system. It may help as many as 60 percent of snorers, according to Richard Martin, M.D., author of *Cardiorespiratory Disorders during Sleep* (Futura) and director of the cardiorespiratory sleep disorders laboratory at the National Jewish Center for Immunology and Respiratory Medicine, in Denver. New, promising drugs are being developed and tested constantly, he adds.

Then there's the CPAP—short for Continuous Positive Airway Pressure. It's a procedure in which upper airway channels are expanded like balloons with a machine that snoring and apnea sufferers must use while they are sleeping. The CPAP device costs about $900, which may be covered by insurance.

In some cases, a surgical procedure may be recommended. Doctors call it the UPP, for uvulopalatopharyngoplasty. It amounts to a "reaming out" of the upper throat. It works, says Dr. Martin, for about 40 percent of apnea victims.

"Emphysema patients get so out of breath when they walk because their muscles are inefficient for their condition," Dr. Sandhaus explains. "When they do start exercising, they won't necessarily feel 'stronger,' but they'll find that they aren't out of breath so often."

Winter therapy: a walk in a mall.

"Strong muscles require less oxygen because they're more efficient," agrees Pat Peabody, R.N., who works with lung patients in Monterey, California. "A well-tuned car uses less gas, and well-tuned muscles use less oxygen."

"We advise our patients to walk—not jog—a mile every day," Dr. Martin adds, "and in the winter we ask them to walk in shopping malls."

Breathing exercises are just as important as leg exercises. People with chronic respiratory ailments tend to breathe shallowly, Dr. Martin says. They use their shoulder and neck muscles rather than their diaphragm and abdominal muscles. This is only true when they're short of breath and begin to panic.

"Belly breathing" strengthens the diaphragm.

One breathing exercise that might help would be to practice breathing deeply and letting the air out slowly. One technique is called "belly breathing." The idea is to push the stomach out on the inhalations and then to suck it back in on the exhalations. This strengthens the diaphragm, which is the muscle that ideally should expand and contract the lungs.

Another technique is called "pursed lip" breathing. Air has a tendency to be trapped in diseased lungs, and pursed lip breathing helps people exhale more thoroughly. Janice Volk, a physical therapist at Monmouth Medical Center, in New Jersey, says, "When you exhale, purse your lips and breathe out as if you were blowing out a candle. Breathe out twice as long as you breathe in. This helps to keep the airways open longer to rid them of stale air."

Vitamins Advised

Nutrition also plays a major role in the treatment of chronic lung disease. In fact, it is becoming popular among some doctors who doubted its value in the past.

Vitamins C and E may help emphysema patients.

"We are using what is still an unproved theory, which is unusual for us," says Dr. Sandhaus. "We know that the oxidants in cigarette smoke are what damage the lungs. And we know that vitamin C and vitamin E are both antioxidants. That is why we are advising a minimum of 250 milligrams of vitamin C, twice a day, and 800 international units (I.U.) of vitamin E, also twice a day, for all of our emphysema patients." (Note: Dosages of vitamin E in excess of 1,200 I.U. daily should best be taken under a doctor's supervision.)

"We also stress nutrition," says Dr. Martin. "We ask our patients to eat regular meals if they can. Sometimes they can't eat a large meal because a full stomach can press against their diaphragm and make breathing harder. If that is the case, we tell them to eat several small meals instead."

There is also evidence that selenium deficiency weakens the repair mechanism that would normally counteract the damage done to the lungs by cigarette smoke. A study of emphysema patients at the University of Pittsburgh showed that vitamin C, vitamin E and selenium all help protect the lung tissue from oxidants. (Note: No more than 100 micrograms of selenium should be taken as a supplement.)

Drugs are a fact of life for many people with chronic lung disease. Asthma and chronic bronchitis sufferers need bronchodilators to open up their constricted air sacs. Without such drugs, many people would die. But medication often has pitfalls that patients should know about.

Some people, for example, unnecessarily resign themselves to the side effects of their medication. "A lot of people get the shakes, and their appetite vanishes as a result of the drugs," says Peabody. "But they don't tell their doctors. They just say to themselves, 'I must be getting older, that's all.'"

Tell your doctor if you have drug side effects.

Dr. Martin emphasizes that each person must have the patience to find the medication and dosage that is right for himself or herself. There are hundreds of possible drug combinations and dosages, he says. He keeps in "constant contact by phone" with new patients, asking them what side effects they are or aren't encountering.

Of all the drugs used for lung problems, the corticosteroids are the most potent. When all else fails, the steroids are brought in to improve breathing. Physicians don't know exactly how steroids work, but they agree that this class of drugs is for short-term use only. Dr. Martin advises against using oral steroids for more than two weeks at a time.

Reversing the Irreversible

Another major issue in the pulmonary field is the question of reversibility. Among doctors, traditional wisdom dictates that asthma is treatable and reversible, that chronic bronchitis is treatable but not reversible and that emphysema is neither treatable nor reversible. Revising this position, doctors now believe that emphysema patients often suffer to some extent from asthma, and are therefore at least partially treatable.

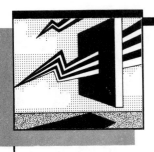

Bright Promise: An End to Emphysema

If you have emphysema, the medical profession should have excellent news for you very soon. Within a year or two, drugs will be available that will stop the disease in its tracks, according to Robert Sandhaus, M.D., Ph.D., senior staff physician at the National Jewish Center for Immunology and Respiratory Medicine, in Denver, and inventor of one of the emphysema-stopping drugs now being tested. Halting the progression of the disease will put an end to its most horrifying feature—the slow, inexorable deterioration.

Dr. Sandhaus also foresees that science may be able to reverse the course of the disease perhaps as soon as a decade from now. This hope rests on research now underway that was quickened by an exciting recent discovery, says Dr. Sandhaus.

Just a few years ago, medical schools taught that babies were born with all the lung tissue they were ever going to have, Dr. Sandhaus explains. Now medicine has learned that lungs continue to form until children are 8 or 9 years old. The research being done is attempting to isolate the factor which causes the lungs to cease generating themselves. Doctors may then be able to counter it and help the lungs regenerate.

But prevention is still better than cure. Not smoking would eliminate 99 out of 100 cases of emphysema, according to Dr. Sandhaus.

"It's rare to find a case of pure emphysema," says Dr. Sandhaus. "There is usually a component of asthma or chronic bronchitis, which is treatable or reversible. We also have medications that reduce the mucus production that's characteristic of bronchitis, and that reduction can lead to better breathing for every patient.

Almost every case of emphysema has a component that is reversible to some extent.

"Just because people have emphysema doesn't mean that they can't breathe better," he adds. "We are even finding out that the lungs might be able to repair the damage caused by emphysema"—though that lies in the future.

Dr. Martin doesn't give up either, even on those emphysema patients who have given up on themselves. "We try not to label people as having 'emphysema' or 'chronic bronchitis,' " he says. "We evaluate people individually. We start from scratch."

"We go for every bit of reversibility we can get. If we see someone who is breathing at only 40 percent of normal capacity, then we try to push them up to 60 percent. That increase can make the difference between someone leading a normal life or not," Dr. Martin says.

People with chronic breathing problems need that kind of morale boost, because depression is a constant hazard for them. "When you can't breathe, you become very alarmed," says Jean Taylor, a 64-year-old bronchitis sufferer in Middlesex County, New Jersey. "Some people become so frightened that they are unable to go on with their lives. So many people become invalids. But once you understand the disease and accept it—the more you become aware—then you can go on with your life."

The best way to avoid this predicament, of course, is to prevent lung damage in the first place. Not smoking is the single most important factor. But paying attention to the early warning signs of lung disease is also critical. The first indications of emphysema and bronchitis may appear years before a person reaches the severe stage of the disease, when he or she needs emergency care.

Know the early warning signs of lung disease.

"I've asked people how long they've been coughing and they say, 'For years—but it's just a smoker's cough,' " Dr. Martin says. "But it isn't normal to cough up sputum every morning."

"Someone else might tell me that she hasn't been able to climb stairs for years. But she'll say, 'It doesn't bother me, I live in a ranch house.' A lot of people ignore the early signs of lung disease," Dr. Martin says.

"People often live with the symptoms of lung disease for 10 to 15 years before they seek medical help," adds Phyllis Krug, a New Jersey physical therapist. "They tell themselves, 'I'm just getting a little short of breath,' or, 'I guess I'm getting old,' or, 'It couldn't happen to me.' Sometimes they would rather not find out that they have emphysema. There's a tremendous amount of denial with lung disease."

Hopefully, as public awareness of lung disease grows, denial will give way to prevention so that someday no one will need to "starve" for want of something as freely available as air.

7

Cancer:

A Life-long

Protection Plan

W hat causes cancer? Judging from the press reports, just about everything. Even the air you breathe and the water you drink is said to contain cancer-causing chemicals (carcinogens). Is it a wonder so many people feel helpless and begin to believe that there is nothing they can do to keep from developing this deadly disease?

Yet such a vulnerable attitude is not only mistaken, it can be fatal. In fact, there is much you can do to protect yourself from cancer. Experts estimate that about 80 percent of cancer cases are tied to lifestyle. "Too few Americans realize the simple truth that cancer is usually caused by the way we live, and its risks can be reduced by the choices we make," former Department of Health and Human Services Secretary Margaret M. Heckler was quoted as saying. Her message was clear: You *can* fight back against the most feared disease.

Margaret Heckler wasn't talking about taking on nuclear power plants or eradicating all pollution, although these things certainly may contribute to cancer and need to be reckoned with. The truth is that you'd be better off worrying about your daily diet than the depletion of ozone from the earth's atmosphere. It has been estimated that 35 percent of all cancers may be related to what people eat or

Eighty percent of all cancers are related to the way people choose to live.

You can help prevent cancer with the right diet.

77

don't eat. According to Vincent T. DeVita, Jr., M.D., director of the National Cancer Institute, researchers are learning that some foods, for example, those high in dietary fat, may promote cancer while others, such as those high in fiber, may inhibit or interfere with the cancer-causing process. So while you may not be able to wipe out all carcinogens, one way you can protect yourself from disease is by using simple weapons like dietary factors. And there are more life-style factors than diet that you can alter to keep you healthy and protect you against cancer. But let's begin with diet.

A Change of Menu

Jon dines on white bread and pork in the city of Copenhagen, Denmark. Across the sea in rural Finland, his friend Jann lunches on potatoes, milk and chewy rye bread. Both men have high fat diets, but with one important difference: Jann's diet, like most Finns', includes plenty of fiber, such as whole-grain rye bread. And according to one study, the fact that Finns eat lots of fiber may be the reason why there is a lower incidence of colon cancer in Finland than in Denmark, where people generally eat less fiber.

Fiber may fend off cancer by quickly escorting toxins out of your body.

Ironic, isn't it? Even as people await the miracle cure, the magic pill, there is something as lowly and common as "roughage" that can be used to help. How does it work? One theory suggests that by increasing the bulk of the stool, fiber can "dilute" cancer-causing bile acids in the intestine. Another theory holds that fiber speeds up the time between bowel movements, hustling out the carcinogens before they can do their damage. What's more, fiber means more fecal output and that may mean estrogen is flushed from the body and not reabsorbed, where it can stimulate the breasts and trigger tumors. Current studies are looking at how phytic acid (present in grain fiber) and uronic acid (in vegetable fiber) may inhibit cancer. Until the results are in, it certainly seems wise to eat a high fiber cereal for breakfast, vegetables for lunch, snack on fresh fruits and include whole grain breads and beans whenever possible.

Forgo the Fat

If you are like most Americans, about 40 percent of the calories you eat come from fat. Sounds impossible, doesn't it. But consider the cream in your coffee, the dressing on your salad, the butter on your toast, the cheese in your quiche, the marbeling in your steak—to say nothing of ice cream, fried chicken, doughnuts, french fries and the like, and it's easy to see how your daily menu becomes loaded with fat. And fat is the enemy not only of your waistline but of the breasts, the prostate and the colon.

The precise mechanism at work is not known. One theory is that by-products of bile acids, which the body produces to break down fat, are cocarcinogenic—that is, while they may not *cause* cancer, they promote its development. There is also evidence that fat upsets the body's hormone balance and increases hormone levels of estrogen, androgen and prolactin. In countries like Japan and Thailand, where low-fat diets are the rule, there are one-fourth the number of breast cancer deaths compared to countries like the United States, where people consume up to twice as much fat.

Fatty foods stimulate bile acids, the by-products of which are potential troublemakers.

Many doctors suggest you adjust your daily diet so that it consists of no more than 25 to 30 percent fat. Probably the easiest way to achieve this goal is to cut down on butter, switch to skim milk and use nonstick pans for fat-free cooking. It's also a good idea to eat less red meat, remove the skin from chicken before you cook it and eat lots of fruits and vegetables. Also eat a limited amount of fried foods which, according to a recent study, may raise your risk of ovarian cancer.

Switch to skim milk, eat less meat and limit fried foods.

Go for the Greens and Yellows

What do sweet potatoes, cantaloupes, carrots and apricots have in common? They all contain beta-carotene, the pigment which gives them their color and which may protect you from cancer. One thing scientists know is that beta-carotene acts as a kind of "shock absorber," protecting the valuable genetic blueprints inside each cell. It seems beta-carotene may prevent the damage caused by "free radicals," which are highly unstable molecules that theoreti-

Beta-carotene may work at a cellular level, protecting genetic "blueprints" against free radical damage.

cally can scramble the genetic information in a cell, starting a chain reaction that can lead to cancer.

In the body, beta-carotene converts to vitamin A, the nutrient that controls epithelial cell differentiation and assures that cells act normally. In vitamin A deficiency, for example, cells that line the lungs do not secrete the mucus needed to keep the linings of the lungs moist. And without mucus, the lungs are left vulnerable to disease. Yet, studies have shown that people who eat plenty of vitamin-A packed, beta-carotene loaded veggies reduce their risk of lung cancer. "We think it is prudent for all apparently healthy adults to include in the daily diet one or two servings of the vegetables or fruits that are rich in beta-carotene," says Richard B. Shekelle, Ph.D., professor of epidemiology at the University of Texas Health Science Center, in Dallas.

Dark green and yellow vegetables contain beta-carotene and vitamin A.

By the way, not all foods high in beta-carotene are orange. Ironically, some are a deep green—such as parsley and spinach.

Don't forget to add the cabbage-type vegetables to your menu, too. Broccoli, brussels sprouts, cauliflower, cabbage, kale, kohlrabi and other so-called "cruciferous" vegetables, studies suggest, may reduce the risk of cancer, particularly of the gastrointestinal and respiratory tracts. Why? Possibly, cruciferous vegetables contain a special cancer-fighting ingredient. One thing is for certain: Cruciferous vegetables are chock-full of the proven champion cancer fighters, including vitamins A, C and fiber.

Vegetables in the cabbage family may protect two major body systems against cancer.

Stay Away from Smoked Foods

Avoid foods that are smoked, salt-cured, pickled or preserved with nitrites or nitrates (like most bacon, hot dogs, and hams). Nitrites interact with other substances, called amines, in the gastrointestinal tract to form nitrosamines—agents which can cause cancer in the esophagus and stomach. That means if you eat a three-ounce portion of nitrite-preserved bacon, for example, your body could be absorbing the same amount of nitrosamines as if you smoked a pack of cigarettes. So check labels and limit your consumption. For extra protection, you also might want to reduce the frequency of grilling,

Eating smoked, cured meat should be made a rare occasion.

charcoal broiling or barbecuing any type of meat. It seems these "high-fire" cooking methods can produce mutagens. And when you do barbecue, wrap meats in foil.

Stock Up on Vitamin C

And you thought vitamin C was just to fight colds! Studies now show that people whose diets are rich in vitamin C are less likely to get cancer, particularly of the stomach and esophagus. Vitamin C also may protect women who are at high risk for cervical cancer.

Vitamin C may stimulate immunity and inhibit the formation of certain cancer-causing substances.

This nutrient appears to stimulate the immune system, and one doctor, John Weisburger, M.D., of the American Health Foundation, believes it can inhibit the formation of certain cancer-causing substances in the stomach. And it's not hard to apply this knowledge in a practical way. If you love bacon, for example, but are afraid to eat it because it has been preserved with nitrates (which can convert to nitrosamines) you'd be better off eating a bacon, lettuce and tomato sandwich than, say, bacon and eggs. Why? Because tomatoes—and lettuce to a lesser extent—contain vitamin C. Dr. Weisburger says, "You would have enough vitamin C in all those foods to counteract the nitrite" and you would be protected from mutagens that may form during digestion. Just be sure they're in the stomach at the same time.

There's also some evidence that vitamin C can prevent tumors from forming after exposure to carcinogens. Researchers at Children's Hospital, in Los Angeles, exposed mouse embryo cells to a carcinogen for 24 hours, removed the carcinogen and then immediately added vitamin C. They found that vitamin C completely prevented cell transformation that normally occurs after exposure to cancer-causing agents. To be on the safe side, eat vitamin C-rich foods daily, including oranges, grapefruit, green peppers, broccoli, tomatoes and potatoes.

Cut Down on Sweets

Your sweet tooth may be to blame for more than a blossoming beltline. A recent study indicates that diets rich in foods that are combinations of sugar and fat (such as cakes, candy and pastry) are associated with the development of colon cancer. And in lands where women consume more sugar, the incidence of breast cancer in older women is also higher. Scientists speculate that too much sugar in the blood produces a sudden overabundance of insulin, a hormone which, under certain circumstances, could act as a mild carcinogen on breast tissue.

Practice Girth Control

Women who are 40 percent or more overweight are twice as likely to develop cancer.

If your scales have been tipped to the heavy side, you may be burdening your health. In one massive study conducted over 12 years by the American Cancer Society, researchers found an increased incidence of cancers of the uterus, gallbladder, breast, colon, kidney and stomach in obese people. The study found that for those people who were 40 percent or more overweight, women were more than twice as likely to get cancer than people of normal weight. Obese men were a third more likely to develop cancer.

Exactly how obesity contributes to cancer is unclear. There does seem to be a link between obesity and higher blood estrogen levels and it is known that excess estrogen can lead to greater vulnerability to cancer. The message is clear, though, says Charles A. LeMaistre, M.D., president of the American Cancer Society. "The long-standing and repeated observation that obesity is correlated with cancer is sufficiently substantiated to take action." That means, lower your calorie intake and increase your exercise, but only after you get the go-ahead from your doctor.

More New Styles for Living

In addition to manipulating diet, you have many additional ways to improve your odds of avoiding cancer. Some are easier to do than others. One of the toughest life-style changes is giving up smoking. It's also the most important.

Become a Quitter

By now, you've heard the bad news about smoking: Cigarette smoking puts you at ten times the risk of getting lung cancer. And it's not just the lungs that are affected. Smoking accounts for approximately 30 percent of all cancer. The pancreas and bladder, for example, are targets for cancers that are the result of smoking. Moreover, male smokers develop kidney cancer while female smokers are prone to cervical cancer.

Quit smoking now and your risk of lung cancer begins to drop almost immediately.

If you smoke and also drink heavily, you are at grave risk of developing cancer of the mouth and throat. And heavy drinkers are at risk of developing cancer of the liver. Now for the good news: *As soon as you quit smoking, you decrease your risk of cancer.* And your odds get better the longer you're off cigarettes.

One British study of more than 18,000 people found that those who had smoked for as long as 20 years but who had been off cigarettes for 10 years or more, had no greater risk of lung cancer than people who had never smoked at all. It seems that cigarette smoke inhalation causes rapid depression of antibody production within lung tissue. And when smoking is discontinued, the body's defenses against tumor growth may be restored. Experts agree that if you are a smoker, the single most effective action you can take against cancer is to stop the habit.

Go Easy on Estrogens

If the Pill is your choice for birth control, make sure you ask for the lowest possible dose of estrogen and progestogen, to be on the safe side. Whether oral contraceptives contribute to breast cancer is still debatable. In 1983, two studies—both funded by the National Institute of Child Health and Human Development—drew completely different conclusions. One study found no correlation between the Pill and breast cancer. The other found that women under 25 who used high-progestogen oral contraceptives for five or more years developed cancer at a rate four times the average. But in 1986, a study that followed a large number of women reported that there seemed to be no increased risk of breast cancer after taking the Pill. If you are worried about developing breast cancer, you could switch to barrier forms of contraception or at least choose a birth control pill with the lowest dose of both hormones.

Make sure your medication contains the lowest possible dose of estrogen.

That's good advice for older women, who are often prescribed estrogen to relieve menopausal hot flashes and to protect against the bone-loss condition known as osteoporosis. The Food and Drug Administration (FDA) has approved a product containing a low dose of estrogen (about half the dose found in birth control pills) to retard further bone loss in post-menopausal women with evidence of loss or deficiency of bone mass. The labeling also states that the estrogen should be used with other measures such as calcium and exercise. Provided that a woman's health allows for the use of estrogen, the therapy seems to be as safe as it is effective. However, some doctors do caution that there is an increased risk of endometrial cancer in women taking post-menopausal estrogen. So take it only under the supervision of your doctor.

Watch Out for Environmental Hazards

Wear a sunscreen when you spend time outdoors.

Every day, the most potent natural carcinogen in the environment rises in the east. To protect yourself from the searing rays of the sun, be sensible: Use a sunscreen with a Sun Protection Factor (SPF) of 15 or more, and cut your risk of harmful radiation by being especially wary of the sun from 11 A.M. to 3 P.M. Remember, too, there is nothing healthy about a tan, so skip the trip to the tanning booth.

When you are x-rayed, make sure the machine has a filter.

Another environmental factor to watch out for is radiation. The next time your dentist or doctor orders x-rays, ask first if they are necessary, and second, if the machine is equipped with yttrium (pronounced it-tree-um) filters. The idea is to protect yourself against overexposure to radiation, which can cause mutation and cancer in a dose-related manner. The organs most sensitive to this change in cells are the lymphoid system, thyroid, female breast and lung.

Test your home for the presence of radon.

Take care to guard against hazards at home, too. If you live in a well-insulated, air-tight home, radon could be a very real bogeyman in your basement. An odorless, colorless gas given off in the decay of uranium, a radioactive ore found in soil and rocks, radon can seep through cracks in basements and become trapped inside energy-efficient homes. A few ways to reduce exposure to the second leading cause of lung cancer are by sealing cracks in your basement floor and allowing for proper ventilation, even during the cold winter months.

Testing kits are now available which allow you to detect the level of radon in your house and then have the results analyzed. One such device, the Track Etch (about $50, including processing), can be obtained by contacting the Terradex Corporation, 460 West Wiget Lane, Walnut Creek, CA 94598. And some state and local agencies buy them in quantity, and provide them to residents at a discount or for free.

Learn to Let Off Steam

Stress doesn't make you sick, but the way you handle it may. Several studies suggest that how you react to stressful events like the death of a loved one or retirement could affect your immune system and leave you more susceptible to diseases, including cancer. At Beth Israel Hospital, in Boston, Steven Locke, M.D., director of the psychoneuroimmunology research project there, reports that people who got very upset over stressful events had only one-third the level of "natural killer T-cell activity" of people who experienced the same stressful events but were able to deal with them psychologically. (T-cells are a type of white blood cell critical to the immune system.)

Anger takes its toll on the immune system.

Other studies indicate that suppressed hostility may be a factor in developing breast disease. "A significantly higher proportion of patients with both benign and malignant tumors stated they had experienced much more anger during the previous year than the 1,100 respondents who did not have disease," reports Marjorie Brooks, Ph.D., of Jefferson Medical College, in Philadelphia. On the other hand, women in normal health were more likely to "blow up" in an anger-provoking situation and then forget about it, redirecting their energies to more pleasant things.

Partner in Prevention

Besides the fact that much of cancer is preventable, the second best news is that much of it can be reversed, claims Robert McKenna, M.D., clinical professor of surgery at the University of Southern California School of Medicine, in Los Angeles, and past president of the American Cancer Society. How? By learning what symptoms to look for, performing self-exams and getting regular checkups. Consider these statistics:

Detecting some cancers early can result in a 90 to 100 percent chance of survival.

• When breast cancer is detected early, women have nearly a 90 percent chance of cure. "There's no reason why that figure can't be 99 percent," says Dr. McKenna.
• If every American over 40 were tested for colorectal cancer (which is second only to lung cancer in incidence), an estimated 40,000 lives could be saved every year.
• Men have nearly a 100 percent survival rate if testicular cancer is detected early.

Recommended Examinations

The power to prevent and control cancer is in your hands, say the experts. The following regular screening and exams are recommended for all people over 40 whether you have suspicious symptoms or not:

Self-examination of the testicles and breasts should be done monthly.

Breasts. Breasts should be examined yearly by a doctor. An x-ray (mammogram) should be taken between the ages of 35 and 40 and used as the standard against which later x-rays are compared. Then, every one to two years, and every year after age 50, a follow-up mammogram should be done. Breast self-exams (BSE) should be performed each month, at about the same point in the menstrual cycle. According to Roger S. Foster, Jr., M.D., director of the Vermont Regional Cancer Center, in Burlington, women who examine their own breasts find tumors at an earlier stage and are more likely to survive the disease.

Here's how to perform BSE:

1. During your shower: Use the flat part of your fingers, and check both breasts for any lump, thickening or hard knot.

2. In front of your mirror: Inspect your breasts, with your arms first at your sides, then raised, then on your hips. Look for changes in the nipples and breast contours and for swelling and dimpling of the skin.
3. While lying down: With your right hand behind your head and a pillow under your right shoulder, place the fingers of your left hand flat on the outermost top of the right breast. Press in circular motions around the breast. Continue circling around the breast, moving an inch toward the nipple each time. Repeat the procedure for your left breast using the fingers of your right hand.

If you feel you need individual instruction, ask your doctor or visit a hospital breast clinic. Such a demonstration can help you distinguish a potentially dangerous lump from the natural lumps (glands and tissues) found in the breast. It's also a good way to reduce your fear and increase your self-assurance, and along the way, make you stick to self-exams.

Female Reproductive System. Be sure to have a yearly pelvic exam. Also schedule a Pap smear test at least every three years following two negative tests 12 months apart. The Pap smear examines cells taken from the cervix for abnormalities. Have a tissue sample taken at menopause if you are at risk for endometrial cancer. Such risks include infertility, obesity, ovulation failure, abnormal bleeding and estrogen therapy.

A Pap smear is needed at least every three years.

Male Reproductive System. A digital rectal exam should be performed periodically by a physician to check the prostate. Testicular self-exams should be performed each month. After showering, gently roll each testicle between the thumbs and fingers of both hands to check for lumps.

Colon. A digital rectal exam should be performed yearly by a physician. A proctological exam should be done every three to five years after age 50 following two negative tests 12 months apart. During this examination, a doctor uses a hollow, lighted tube to inspect the intestinal tract for the presence of cancer or polyps. A blood stool test should be done annually after age 50. This test can be done at home with a kit. Be warned, however, that home kits sometimes give a false negative reading, meaning you could be

Colon test kits allow you to check for blood in the stool at home.

(continued on page 90)

Understanding—and Undermining—the Cancer Cell

Like a street gang terrorizing a neighborhood, cancer cells are the body's delinquents. These cells, say researchers, are wildly out of control; they are immature and confused. The usual medical response to these cellular punks is a vicious counterattack: drugs, surgery or radiation. But the surrounding normal tissue, like innocent bystanders, can get injured in the process. Well, researchers are now not only working to refine established cancer treatments, but are also experimenting with another approach: Don't try to smash the cell, but instead *understand* how it functions and then craftily undermine its ability to do harm. This is a report about the new techniques that use this approach.

Singling Out the Cancer Switches. Scientists have been able to isolate the genes that transform healthy cells to cancerous ones (oncogenes) from the genes that regulate normal cell growth. What's more, investigators are also looking at which genetic switches trip the events that lead to cancer, and studying what substances might prevent these cancer switches from turning on.

Activating the Immune System. The work that really intrigues cancer researchers is that being done to strengthen the immune system with natural cancer-fighters such as interferon and interleukin. Interferon attacks viruses that invade the body and interleukin stimulates the immune system. Transferring this anticancer immune power directly into cancer patients can stimulate the body's natural defense system.

"It's like taking recruits into the army who don't know how to kill until they are trained in boot camp," explains Gregory Curt, M.D., deputy director of the division of cancer treatment, National Cancer Institute. "We take the white cells from the patient and convert them to killer cells using interleukin and interferon."

What's really exciting about immunotherapy research is that it is challenging the long-held theory that as people get older, their immune cells wear out. "What we found," explains Hans Schreiber, M.D., Ph.D., professor of pathology at the University of Chicago Medical School, "is that, in individuals who have cancer, for some reason, certain immune cells don't work. We've found a way to take them out of their environment and regenerate the stimuli which spark the immune cells." So far, early results have been encouraging:

According to Dr. Curt, tumors shrink by greater than 50 percent in nine out of ten patients with kidney cancer, half of those with colon cancer and one-third of those with melanoma.

Dr. Curt predicts the day that a doctor will prepare to transplant immune cells into a cancer patient by "ordering a supply of these white killer cells from the pharmacy, like plasma." But there are a few bugs to be worked out before that happens, says Dr. Schreiber. For one thing, once they get the immune cells working, they have to figure out how to get them to kill just the bad guys—cancer cells—and not destroy the good cells, too. Research is "going full speed ahead" to test this adaptive immunology with clinical trials set to begin at six research facilities.

Cells that Search and Destroy. Scientists are also excited about their newfound ability to produce antibodies that carry drugs to cancerous cells, where they unload them.

"Monoclonal antibodies are like guided missles," explains Dr. Curt. "They home in on a cancerous tumor, identify it and mark it for destruction." What's more, these hybrid antibodies apparently do their duty without disturbing surrounding tissue.

Stunting the Growth. Understanding the way cancer spreads is leading to ways of stopping it before it grows to deadly proportions. "It's not usually the tumor in its original site that kills, but the spread of it [metastasis] to a vital organ," says Carl Pinsky, M.D., chief of the biological resources branch, Biological Response Modifier Program, National Cancer Institute. Researchers are conducting a variety of studies in an effort to discover ways to prevent this metastasis. For example, a separate group of researchers at the National Cancer Institute is studying ways to interfere with laminin, a protein that is found on the lining of blood vessels and to which cancer cells attach themselves and spread.

Educating Wayward Cells. New advances in drugs called differentiation inducers may actually reverse the malignant behavior of tumor cells under experimental, test-tube conditions. How? By re-educating the abnormal cells and forcing them to develop more normally. In preliminary tests, one such drug, called hexamethlene bisacetamide, has been shown to rehabilitate experimental cancer cells originally derived from tumors in animals and man.

bleeding and they don't detect it. Some test kits use a piece of paper or a slide treated with guaiac, which turns blue if blood is in your stool when a developer solution is applied. But if, for example, you take large doses of vitamin C, these tests could fail to detect bleeding.

Eight Signs to Live By

Not every lump, cough, scaly patch or pain signals cancer. Many are false alarms. But you should know the warning signs well, so that you can judge when it's time to see your doctor for further examination. Here's what to watch for:

1. Breathing problems (coughing, chest pain, shortness of breath, blood in sputum).

Know the eight signs that could save your life.

2. Menstrual changes (unusual bleeding or discharge).

3. Throat irritation (hoarseness, difficulty swallowing).

4. Bowel or bladder changes (bleeding from rectum; blood in stool; persistent constipation or diarrhea; abdominal cramps; weak or interrupted urine flow; inability to urinate or difficulty starting; frequent, painful or burning urination; continuing pain in the lower back, pelvis or upper thighs).

5. Skin changes (changes in number, color, shape or size of moles or other pigmented portions of the skin; sores that won't heal; a dry, scaly patch or pimple that persists; an inflamed area with a crusting center; a waxy, pearly nodule; a mole-like growth that ulcerates and bleeds).

6. Mouth sores (raised, irregular warty area; lump or thickening of cheek, gum or tongue).

7. Digestion problems (persistent indigestion, discomfort or mild pain, fullness, slight nausea, heartburn, loss of appetite, belching or regurgitation).

8. Breast changes (lump or thickening, indentation of the skin, retraction of the nipple, discharge from the nipple).

Adapted from *Warning Signs*, by Robert J. McKenna, M.D., as published in *Rx Being Well*, Vol. 3, No. 6. Dr. McKenna is past president of the American Cancer Society.

8

Circulation: High Blood Pressure and Other Problems

H igh blood pressure. Newspapers and magazines print scads of articles about it. Scientists and doctors conduct study after study on it. Airport lounges and malls install coin-operated machines which measure it.

But despite all this hoopla, the average Joe and Josephine don't seem to give it much serious thought. And if they do, that thought might be wrong.

Some people believe, for instance, that high blood pressure is a mild disorder. Or that if it were doing any harm, you'd feel the symptoms. Others figure that since the condition is also known as "hypertension," it must affect only tense, high-strung types. But these people are wrong, and their misconceptions might get them into trouble.

High blood pressure is more serious than many people suspect.

Understanding High Blood Pressure

"To get an idea of what happens in high blood pressure, think of a fireman's hose," says Margaret Chesney, Ph.D., director of the department of behavioral medicine at Stanford Research Institute, in

Menlo Park, California. "If you turn up the water or squeeze the hose, the pressure increases. Your blood flow operates on the same principle—narrowed arteries or extra fluid volume increase blood pressure."

Measuring Blood Pressure at Home

A visit to the doctor may actually *cause* high blood pressure. Temporarily, anyway. Research shows that, apparently, the anxiety some people feel at a doctor's office may make their blood pressure the highest reading of the day. And a false diagnosis may lead to unnecessary treatment for high blood pressure.

The truth is, blood pressure varies tremendously throughout the day in response to feelings, actions and environment. And that may be one reason people take their blood pressure at home—*one* elevated blood pressure reading does not necessarily mean you have hypertension.

A home blood pressure kit can do more than just *detect* consistently elevated blood pressure. It can also *enhance* active participation in its treatment.

If you have high blood pressure, you'll be encouraged by evidence that it's being controlled and you'll be more likely to stay on your treatment program, points out the American Heart Association.

Home tests can help your doctor help you, too. Keeping careful records of home readings (including time, date, your body position and what activities you're doing) helps your doctor to prescribe, evaluate and adjust your treatment program. This is especially important for those trying drugless therapy, or a treatment program that includes nondrug measures, say doctors affiliated with the National High Blood Pressure Education Program, and the National Institutes of Health, in Bethesda, Maryland.

Finally, home measurement may allow hypertensives to make fewer visits to their doctor once the "goal" blood pressure is reached and maintained.

The variety of home blood pressure kits can be confusing. That's why the National Institutes of Health and the American Heart Association (AHA) published statements that give guidelines for purchasing such equipment. This is what they found:

There are three types of sphygmomanometers (blood pressure

Constant high blood pressure can batter the blood vessels, along with the organs they serve. Vessels can even rupture. When that happens in the brain, for instance, it triggers a stroke. The heart, kidneys and eyes also can be harmed by high blood

measuring devices). Each has a cuff that encircles the arm and encloses an inflatable rubber bladder, a gauge to indicate pressure, an inflation bulb that allows air to be pumped into the cuff's bladder and a control valve that adjusts the rate of deflation.

The mercury sphygmomanometer has a gauge that looks like a thermometer. It's considered to be the most accurate and reliable device when properly used. However, it's bulky to carry, and awkward to use, since you have to keep the mercury column upright on a flat surface during measurement.

The aneroid manometer looks basically the same, except its gauge is a small dial. It's easier to carry, somewhat easier to use (since the gauge functions in any position) and relatively inexpensive. But it's more likely to go out of whack. The AHA suggests you have it adjusted for accuracy at least once a year.

If you have impaired hearing or diminished dexterity, both these devices may seem nearly impossible to use. That's because both devices require you to use a stethoscope to listen to sounds of your blood pressure. If juggling a stethoscope sounds like too much work, one of the electronic/digital readout devices may be more your speed. They have a stethoscope built right in. Many of these are fully automated—the push of a button inflates and deflates the cuff. However, they're more expensive and less accurate than the other models. Factors such as body movements and noise can influence the reading, and they should be checked for accuracy more than once a year.

The AHA recommends you purchase your equipment from a medical supply house or pharmacy, where there usually is a person trained to teach you how to use the equipment.

(For more information, write American Heart Association, 7320 Greenville Avenue, Dallas, TX 75231 or High Blood Pressure Information Center 120/80, National Institutes of Health, Bethesda, MD 20892.)

Hypertensives are at greater risk for a stroke, heart attack and other dangerous diseases.

pressure. The destruction happens silently, without severe pain or warning. But if it leads to a more serious condition, the symptoms are all too apparent. People over age 45 who have high blood pressure are three times as likely to have a heart attack and seven times as likely to experience a stroke as those with normal blood pressure, and their lives are shortened by an average of 10 to 20 years.

This disorder is more common than most people think—it affects about two-thirds of those between ages 65 and 74, and three-fourths of those over 75.

"It used to be a common idea that the rise in blood pressure which occurs as people in Western societies age is acceptable, and that older people need that extra pressure to get enough blood to their organs," says Michael D. Cressman, D.O., of the department of heart and hypertension, Cleveland Clinic Foundation. "But now we know that high blood pressure is bad for people of all ages."

High blood pressure is 140/90 or higher.

It's estimated that almost half of those who have hypertension are unaware of their condition. The only way to detect it is to measure your blood pressure. High blood pressure is considered to start at 140/90 mm Hg. (The larger number refers to systolic pressure, which is the maximum pressure put on the arteries, when the heart is pumping. The second number, diastolic pressure, represents the minimum pressure, when the heart is resting between beats. The term "mm Hg" is simply a unit of measurement, which indicates the number of millimeters a column of mercury rises as a result of the pressure.)

Even pressure at 130/85 needs to be lowered.

Even people with pressures *below* the 140/90 threshold may have reason to be concerned. "Research shows that there's a progressive increase in cardiovascular risk as systolic pressure rises above 130 and diastolic pressure goes above 85," says Aram V. Chobanian, M.D., a member of the Joint National Committee on Detection, Evaluation and Treatment of High Blood Pressure and director of the Cardiovascular Institute at Boston University Medical Center. "So even people with diastolic pressures as low as 85 to 89 (the 'high normal' category) should act to bring their pressures under control, especially since a significant percentage of high normals eventually become severe hypertensives."

There is good news. This disorder is the most treatable—and perhaps one of the most preventable—of all chronic ailments.

"Thirty years ago, relatively few people with hypertension could control their blood pressure," says Dr. Chobanian. "But now practically everyone can achieve some degree of control, and most can bring their pressure down to the normal range."

For decades, hypertension researchers have been debunking myths and advancing treatments. And they're still at it. Here's what science is learning about what works—and what doesn't—in controlling America's most widespread cardiovascular health problem.

Drugs and Other Therapies

Do people with high blood pressure need medication? *Some* do. People with moderate to severe hypertension—the 30 percent who have diastolic pressure above 104—have little choice but to take anti-hypertensive drugs to control their disease. Two commonly prescribed drugs are beta blockers and diuretics. Beta blockers can cause depression and impotence, while diuretics in some cases may raise cholesterol levels. For people with a diastolic reading above 104, the potential side effects of such drugs are outweighed by their life-preserving benefits. Few cardiologists *wouldn't* prescribe medication for the hypertensives in this group.

But the 70 percent of all hypertensives whose diastolic pressure falls between 90 and 104 (this range is called "mild" hypertension) have the option of taking the medication or first trying one of the nondrug therapies. And considering the increasing cost of drugs and the possible side effects, it's worth a try.

Older people, in particular, may want to attempt drugless therapy. "Many doctors believe that older people may not tolerate the potential side effects as well," says Dr. Cressman. "That's why the Joint National Committee on Detection, Evaluation and Treatment of High Blood Pressure has recommended that if an elderly person needs hypertension drugs, the doctor should start him or her on half the usual dose."

"There are other methods of blood pressure control besides drug therapy. Weight reduction, salt restriction and stress management through relaxation are receiving increasing attention as possible alternatives. A doctor can monitor you, so if your blood pressure goes down as you reduce sodium intake and lose weight, he or she may gradually reduce the strength of the drug," says Dr. Chesney.

Start Exercising

Exercise might be just what the doctor ordered to help lower high blood pressure. Robert Cade, M.D., a University of Florida professor of medicine and inventor of GatorAde, made this discovery when he got involved in his son's junior high school science project.

The story goes like this: Dr. Cade's son designed a science project called "The Effect of Cardiovascular Response to Exercise in a Fat Old Man." The project called for the "fat old man"—his dad—to run daily for seven weeks and measure his blood pressure at periodic intervals. Dr. Cade went along with this program, and discovered that jogging produced a healthy decline in his mildly elevated blood pressure.

Since then, Dr. Cade has studied the effects of exercise on more than 400 people with high blood pressure, half of whom were taking medication for the disease. Ninety-six percent of them, he says, reduced their blood pressure significantly. Fully 60 percent of those on medication went off it, and the rest reduced their dosage.

Exercise allowed 60 percent of those taking medication to give it up.

Other researchers also have found that exercise may be an effective nondrug method for normalizing mild high blood pressure—although it can take months to produce results. In one study, 9 out of a group of 12 mildly hypertensive Japanese people lowered both their systolic and diastolic pressures with exercise. Ten weeks of thrice-weekly hour-long sessions on exercise bikes dropped their readings an average of 20 and 10 points, respectively. Another ten weeks of workouts brought similar results in 3 more people. This happened even though all the volunteers were taken off their blood pressure medication when the study started.

To reduce blood pressure, it's generally agreed, a workout has to be "aerobic." That is, it has to raise one's pulse to what's called the "target heart rate" for a half hour or so. (To figure your target heart rate, subtract your age from 220, and then take 70 to 85 percent of that.)

An increased heart rate however, doesn't mean that exercise has to be punishing in order to reduce blood pressure. At the Institute for Aerobic Research, in Dallas, a group of 64 men with mild hypertension—their diastolic pressure was between 90 and 104—undertook a program of conservative walk-jogging for 30 to 40 minutes a day, three times a week. Their progress was slow—it took four months—but eventually they reduced their systolic pressure by an average of 12.4 points and their diastolic pressure by nearly 7 points. Dr. Cade has also found that daily walking at a moderate pace lowers high blood pressure in some people.

Even low-intensity exercise can help attain lower blood pressure.

Shed Some Pounds

Compared to drug therapy, exercise can produce much better "side effects"—not the least of which is weight loss. And medical studies have shown that when weight goes down, blood pressure goes down. By the same token, as body weight goes up, so does blood pressure. On the average, a man's blood pressure jumps 6.5 points systolic for every ten pounds of weight gain. A woman's pressure increases about half this amount.

On the average, blood pressure increases 6.5 systolic points for every ten pounds you gain.

"Our data suggest that overweight is one of the most powerful contributors to hypertension," says William B. Kannel, M.D., MPH, professor of medicine and chief of preventive medicine and epidemiology at Boston University School of Medicine. "Our estimate is that as many as 70 percent of the new cases of hypertension in young adults could be directly attributed to weight gain."

The good news is that weight-induced high blood pressure can be reduced dramatically through weight loss—even if ideal weight isn't reached. One estimate is that obese people can decrease their blood pressure an average of 8 to 10 points (systolic or diastolic) by losing 20 to 25 pounds.

Researchers from Stanford's Center for Research in Disease Prevention, in Stanford, California, have found that weight loss through diet alone or exercise alone can reduce blood pressure and improve cholesterol levels, but conclude that a program combining both diet and exercise is the healthiest strategy.

Take It Easy

Some people figure that when they're under stress, their blood pressure shoots up. And they may be right.

Though it's possible to be serene and have hypertension, or not have hypertension and be a nervous wreck, some people do react to stress with at least a temporary rise in blood pressure. Whether stress can cause chronic hypertension, though, isn't yet known, but scientists do suspect that stress plays a role in most cases of high blood pressure. Some doctors believe that continued stress boosts blood pressure by activating the involuntary (autonomic) nervous system (the system that controls the heart muscles, among others), thereby producing a permanent constriction of the arteries.

But the question is, can you lower blood pressure by controlling stress?

For some people the answer is yes. Studies have shown that stress-management techniques (like relaxation, biofeedback, yoga and meditation) can mildly lower blood pressure for up to a full year. A few people may respond even better than that, while others may not respond at all.

Exercise also may help your body bounce back from stressful events, suggests research done at Jackson Veterans Administration and University of Mississippi Medical Centers, in Jackson. The study compared the effects of stressful situations on aerobically trained and untrained men with high blood pressure. The resting blood pressures were about the same in the two groups, but the untrained men experienced a greater rise in diastolic blood pressure with a marginal rise in systolic pressure after feeling stressed.

Coping with stress may be as easy as opening your mouth and talking. That's the conclusion reached by researchers at the University of Michigan

Stress may be a factor in hypertension.

School of Public Health, in Ann Arbor, who studied the blood pressures of people who became angry when unfairly confronted by authority figures. "Those who bottle up their anger have the highest blood pressures, and those who become openly hostile have the second highest pressures. People who take action to resolve their anger have the lowest pressures," the researchers noted. The chief researcher on the project suggests that discussing the problems that cause the angry feelings may release them harmlessly or may even prevent them from welling up in the first place.

"You have to remember that stress-management therapies can get almost anyone's blood pressure down temporarily," says Lyle H. Miller, Ph.D., professor of psychiatry at Boston University School of Medicine. "For such techniques to have a more permanent effect, you have to learn to use them habitually in the everyday world, especially in stressful situations. And to learn the right techniques for you, you have to consult knowledgeable medical professionals."

Stress-management techniques must become habitual in order to work.

"If you suspect stress may be related to your blood pressure, take your blood pressure several times a day in different situations," says Dr. Chesney. "Identify if there is a pattern in blood pressure related to stress. If there is, you can modify your environment (by moving out of a constantly noisy area, for instance) or your response to the environment (with techniques such as deep breathing or relaxation exercises)."

Choose Foods Wisely

Blood pressure is not just a matter of how much food you eat—it's also regulated by what *kinds* of food you do (and do not) eat. So here are some basic guidelines to help you select healthy foods:

Eat Less Salt. It has earned its bad reputation for good reasons. Many studies show that you can raise or lower blood pressure in some people simply by adding or subtracting salt in their diet. Salt is an enemy to hypertensives and a suspicious character for people with normal blood pressure.

Some people may even be able to temporarily discontinue their drugs by restricting sodium. Researchers divided into two groups 496 hypertensives who had successfully controlled their high blood pressure with drugs for some time. During the study, one group continued to take medication while the other stopped. Members of this group were put on a low-salt diet in place of medication. The researchers found that 77.8 percent of the people with mild hypertension who were not overweight successfully controlled their blood pressure for at least a year when they restricted sodium. Before abandoning your high blood pressure medication for a low-salt diet, however, be absolutely sure to get your doctor's approval.

The salt/blood-pressure connection, however, is more dangerous for some people than for others. A few people (the "salt resistant") can consume as much as 15 grams of salt a day (10 grams daily is the American average) without a significant jump in blood pressure. Others (the "salt sensitive") can get a rise in pressure with a much lower amount. And as far as scientists know, one-third to one-half of all adults may be in this sensitive group.

How do you know if you're one of them? Researchers have recently devised tests that can tell you where you stand, but the tests aren't widely available yet. Researchers do know, however, that if high blood pressure runs in your family, there's a good chance you're one of the susceptible people.

But whether you are or not—and regardless of your blood pressure level—cutting back on salt is usually a good idea, say scientists from Boston University School of Medicine. Human beings need only about a teaspoon of salt a day (a little more than 200 milligrams (mg) of sodium). Americans generally get up to 20 times that much. And if you're taking blood-pressure medication (especially diuretics), keeping your salt intake down is crucial. Too much salt can actually undo the drug's pressure-lowering effect, increasing your need for higher doses, and thus raising your risk of side effects.

Among blood-pressure experts, the consensus is that if you're hypertensive, a little salt restriction is usually not enough to bring your pressure down. "The data suggest," says Dr. Chobanian, "that you would need to lower your intake to five grams of salt a day—equivalent to about one teaspoon. This is

Some people are more sensitive to salt than others.

total salt, not just what comes out of a shaker, but the 'hidden salt' in prepared foods as well."

One way to reduce sodium content of food is to rinse the food. In an experiment at Duke University Medical Center, in Durham, North Carolina, chemists drained canned green beans and rinsed them under tap water for one minute. The sodium content of the beans dropped by 41 percent. Rinsing canned tuna for one minute cut sodium content by as much as 79 percent.

Rinsing some foods can remove a substantial amount of salt.

Eat Less Fat. While you're avoiding the saltshaker, you might try snubbing the butter, the bacon and the cheese too.

Some research in Finland suggests that cutting back on the fat in your diet can reduce elevated blood pressure—even when your salt intake and body weight remain unchanged. In one of these studies, 35 healthy middle-aged people switched from their customary diet, in which nearly 40 percent of the calories came from fat, to one that was only 23 percent fat.

Reducing saturated fats can also drive pressure down.

Result: After six weeks, systolic pressures declined by an average of 8.9 points, and diastolic pressures declined by 7.6. When the Finns returned to their customary, (fatty) diet, their blood pressures went back up again.

The researchers also found that a diet low in total fat, with a reduction in saturated fat, was more effective than reducing salt intake for lowering blood pressure.

In fact, research indicates that polyunsaturated and monounsaturated fats, which are usually found in fish, vegetable oils, seeds and nuts, may help lower blood pressure and in effect neutralize the negative effects of saturated fats, which usually turn up in protein-rich foods of animal origin.

Some fats cancel the bad effects of saturated fats.

Which means that if you have to use a fat, just make sure it's unsaturated. So switch from whole to skim milk, go easy on hard cheeses (they contain more saturated fat than soft cheeses) and start using margarine instead of butter. And the American Heart Association recommends using liquid vegetable oils (corn, cottonseed, safflower, sesame, soybean, sunflower) instead of butter in cooking.

Drink Less Alcohol. So far, the medical evidence indicates that throwing down more than three beers,

Moderate drinkers may actually have lower blood pressure than nondrinkers.

three glasses of wine or three mixed drinks (one ounce of alcohol each) per day can indeed raise blood pressure. (Heavy drinking, of course, is also known to be toxic to the heart muscle.) But drinking moderately (at or below this level) doesn't seem to increase blood pressure. In fact, data from the Boston University-Framington Heart Study show that blood pressure is actually lower in moderate drinkers than nondrinkers.

Heavy drinkers, however, risk a pressure increase. What's also clear is that when two-fisted drinkers go on the wagon, there's a good chance that their pressure will drop 10 to 25 points. You have to remember, too, that alcohol is loaded with calories. If you're trying to drop some extra pounds to pull down your blood pressure, drinking is counterproductive.

Eat More Foods with Potassium. Cantaloupe, winter squash, avocados, orange juice, bananas, potatoes, tomatoes and milk are all good choices.

Potassium may reduce blood pressure by booting out sodium and water.

Studies have shown that, while potassium supplements have little effect in people with *normal* blood pressure, they reduce blood pressure *significantly* in hypertensive people. This mineral is especially important to people who are taking diuretics (which are widely prescribed for mild blood pressure) because the drug leaches potassium from the body.

Just how does potassium do its job? No one really knows, but there seems to be a constant battle between sodium and potassium within your body. When sodium is winning, the cells contain more water, and potassium is dumped into the urine for disposal. When potassium is winning, the cells get rid of sodium and water. And if you recall the fireman's hose model of blood pressure, you'll know that too much fluid shoots that pressure up.

To retain potassium— steam, don't boil, vegetables.

For anyone who wants to increase his or her dietary potassium, here's a cooking tip from a group of Swedish scientists: To avoid potassium loss in cooking, steam rather than boil vegetables. When doctors at a Swedish hospital tested the two cooking methods with potatoes, a rich source of potassium, they discovered that boiled potatoes lose 10 to 50 percent of their potassium while steamed potatoes lost only 3 to 6 percent.

Eat Food High in Calcium. You'll find this mineral in dairy products, leafy green vegetables and beans.

In a study involving 20,749 people across the country, calcium was the only one of the 17 nutrients evaluated that differed in the hypertensives. Those people with high blood pressure consumed 18 percent less calcium. And at the University of Oregon, in Eugene, 48 people with high blood pressure were given 1,000 mg of calcium a day for eight weeks. At the end of that time, 21 of them had reduced their blood pressure by 10 points or better. This treatment lowers blood pressure in selected patients with mild to moderate hypertension, the researchers noted.

Calcium works on blood pressure by facilitating sodium excretion and relaxing the blood vessels, says researcher David McCarron, M.D., of the division of nephrology and hypertension at the Oregon Health Sciences University, in Portland. And relaxing the vessels is like letting go of the squeezed fire hose.

"It's the proportions of these minerals in the body that seem to be the most important thing," says Dr. McCarron. "We, of course, consider calcium to be the most important. But if you're not taking in enough sodium, potassium and magnesium, the probability is that you're not getting enough calcium either."

And, not coincidentally, the foods that are abundant in one of these minerals tend to be abundant in the others.

Get More Magnesium. This mineral is found in nuts, brown rice, molasses, milk, wheat germ, bananas, potatoes and soy products.

Inadequate magnesium in the diet has been shown to increase blood pressure in animals and humans. Though the exact mechanism isn't known, there is some indication that magnesium exerts its pressure-lowering effect by regulating the entry and exit of calcium in the smooth muscle cells of the vascular system. Together, the two minerals produce the regular contraction and relaxation of the blood vessels.

Eat More Fish. More specifically, eat ocean fish high in eicosapentanoic acid (EPA), one of the omega-3 fatty acids. (They include haddock, mackerel, sardines, trout and salmon.) Tests in Germany involving 15 volunteers on a mackerel diet provided

Calcium helps rid the body of sodium, which may fight high blood pressure.

An omega-3 fatty acid in certain fish may reduce blood pressure.

some heartening results. After only two weeks, serum triglycerides and total cholesterol dropped significantly, mirrored by "markedly lower" systolic and diastolic blood pressures.

The Germans didn't simply pull mackerel out of their hats. They were attempting to approximate the diet of Greenland Eskimos and Japanese fishermen, who enjoy a very low incidence of cardiovascular disease. The key appears to be the omega-3 fatty acids found in many fish.

Another study tested the effects of cod-liver oil on the Western diet. Cod-liver oil also contains omega-3 fatty acids. A group of volunteers added three tablespoons of cod-liver oil a day to their normal diets and wound up with lower blood pressures.

Eat More Fiber. Be sure to eat plenty of fresh fruit and vegetables, beans and whole-grain breads, as well as bran. There are some early indications that plant fiber can significantly lower blood pressure, though precisely why is still a mystery.

At the Veterans Administration Medical Center, in Lexington, Kentucky, researcher James W. Anderson, M.D., placed 12 diabetic men on a 14-day diet—peculiar in that it contained large amounts of several kinds of foods, including more than three times the dietary fiber of a control diet. Average blood pressures dropped 10 percent. In patients whose blood pressures had been normal, systolic pressures were 8 percent lower and diastolic figures had dropped 10 percent.

The news was even better for the men who had high blood pressure to begin with. Their systolic pressure dropped by 11 percent and diastolic pressure by 10 percent.

Dr. Anderson was pleased with his results, but he's not sure why he got them. "My strongest hunch is that it's related to certain changes in insulin. The patients' insulin needs were low on the high-fiber diet. There's a lot of evidence that insulin contributes to high blood pressure. It's basically a salt-retentive hormone."

What makes the results even more significant is that salt use was not restricted during the diet. "In fact, says Dr. Anderson, "there was a 50 percent increase in sodium intake. But potassium also went up, so the ratio of sodium to potassium stayed the same."

Snuff That Cigarette. There's no question that smoking kills, that it drastically increases your risk of dying of heart disease and other ills—but there's no evidence that it causes chronic hypertension.

"Smoking is not a potent factor in hypertension," Dr. Kannel says. "In fact, smokers generally have lower blood pressures than nonsmokers. When a person lights up, there is a *temporary* effect—blood pressure rises and heart rate speeds up. But smoking doesn't seem to cause any lasting hypertension. The hypertensive smoker, though, can reduce his or her risk of heart attack by 50 percent just by quitting cigarette smoking."

A person with high blood pressure can cut the risk of heart attack in half by giving up smoking.

Other Circulatory Problems

Unfortunately, high blood pressure isn't the only thing that can go wrong with your circulation. What follows is a brief description of a few circulatory maladies and what you can do about them.

Black-and-Blue Marks

Everybody bruises sometimes. A black-and-blue mark appears when a blow to the body has injured blood vessels, causing bleeding beneath the skin.

"Further bleeding is prevented through a process called hemostasis," says Deborah Spitz, M.D. "First, the blood vessels narrow in response to the injury, and the clotting cells, or platelets, are attracted to the areas of blood-vessel damage. The platelets stick to these areas and cause a tight but temporary plug to form. Then proteins called clotting factors are activated, and the plug becomes permanent. This strong structural barrier is what prevents blood loss. If something goes wrong at any point in this chain of events, additional bleeding or bruising may result."

If your bruises are larger than an inch, if you've had no injury that you can recall and if you haven't bruised easily in the past, these black-and-blue marks may be caused by one of several factors known to interfere with hemostasis. And if that's the case, here are some things to do:

Review Any Medications You're Taking. Even common drugs can interfere with the hemostatic process. A single aspirin can reduce platelet function for an entire week. Anti-inflammatory medications, antidepressants, asthma medications, ingredients found in cough remedies and large amounts of alcohol can inhibit platelet action.

Many drugs allow for the formation of bruises.

"If you bruise easily, discontinue unnecessary medication, especially aspirin," recommends Dr. Spitz. Eat a well-balanced diet that includes plenty of folate, vitamin C and B_{12}. "Vitamin C plays a major role in the synthesis of collagen, the main protein in the supporting fibers of the blood-vessel walls," says Dr. Spitz. "If you lack vitamin C, these fibers could weaken, making the blood vessels fragile. It's not certain whether increased doses of vitamin C will cure easy bruising. But it has been shown that vitamin C in doses eight times the Recommended Dietary Allowance of 60 mg speeds wound healing, which also requires the production of collagen."

Eat Sufficient Vitamin B. Deficiencies in vitamin B_{12} and folate may cause a decrease in production of mature platelets and contribute to easy bruising, according to Dr. Spitz. Liver is an especially good source of both B vitamins.

Cold Hands and Feet

The old wives' tale that a new husband gets "cold feet" may be true—literally. When the sympathetic nervous system becomes overactive, which could very well be the case before a wedding, the groom's feet, indeed, may turn cool.

But cold feet (or hands) that last well into the marriage may have two causes: slow circulation and tight blood vessels. So anything that gets your blood moving and your vessels relaxed can help warm your extremities. You could try, for instance, cutting back on cigarettes and coffee or exercising more. If you want to do something that works fast, soak your feet in hot water. It shouldn't take more than two minutes for them to feel toasty.

Sometimes cold hands can be a symptom of Raynaud's disease, a circulatory disorder in which the fingers and toes turn white and then blue when exposed to cold or stress, and switch to red when warmed up. Most of those afflicted are women between the ages of 20 and 40. (If the condition is a secondary symptom of an underlying disease, such as arthritis, it's known as Raynaud's *phenomenon.*)

"Usually, dressing warmly and avoiding the cold may prevent discomfort," says Mark Creager, M.D., director of the Noninvasive Vascular Laboratory at Brigham & Women's Hospital, in Boston, and assistant professor of medicine at Harvard Medical School. "Some people find that medications can be helpful, but it's more effective to keep the whole body warm by dressing appropriately." Also, biofeedback has had positive warming effects, lasting as long as 90 minutes, which is twice as long as any other therapy.

Biofeedback has a positive, warming effect.

Another way to relieve the discomfort of Raynaud's disease is to whirl your arm around like a windmill, suggests Donald R. McIntyre, M.D., who developed this exercise. At the first sign of an attack, swing your arms in a broad circle back and down to one side of your hips, then up in front of the body. Done briskly, at about 80 revolutions per minute, it forces blood into the fingers.

Dr. McIntyre considers his remedy simple, fast and effective. "The maneuver's only complications and adverse side effects thus far," he notes, "have been glancing blows to fingers striking unnoticed ceiling fixtures and also a degree of embarrassment that befalls one in public while waving the arms about."

"Only about 1 percent of those with Raynaud's disease have symptoms that increasingly worsen," says Dr. Creager. "But if you experience severe pain, skin breakdown and ulcers, see a doctor."

Phlebitis

Thrombophlebitis (sometimes called phlebitis for short) is a fancy name for "vein inflammation with blood clot." Veins are the bluish blood vessels that carry blood towards the heart, and their favorite place to get inflamed and clotted is in the calf.

If the vein in question is close to the skin, the

condition is not dangerous, because the clot rarely leaves the vein and therefore does not go to the heart or lungs. The leg will feel increasingly tender and painful, especially during exercise. In time, it may become red, warm and swollen.

This type of phlebitis can be relieved by rest, elevation of the leg, local moist heat and aspirin, says R. Scott Mitchell, M.D., an assistant professor of cardiovascular surgery at Stanford University Medical Center, in Stanford, California. But if a vein deep in the muscle becomes inflamed, that condition can be serious. The clot can create something of a traffic

New Research
May Redeem Chelation

Used as a way to treat metal poisoning, chelation therapy involves administering an agent that binds with metals to form water soluble complexes. These then can be removed from the body during urination. The procedure has been used for treatment of several diseases, including atherosclerosis. But side effects of chelation therapy can be dangerous and there is a lack of convincing evidence from scientific studies that chelation therapy is beneficial. As a result, the treatment fell into disfavor. In fact, several organizations, including the American Heart Association, the National Institutes of Health and the Food and Drug Administration (FDA) all publicly concluded that chelation therapy with the chemical agent ethylenediamine tetracetate (EDTA) is of no proven benefit for the treatment of atherosclerosis.

But in West Germany, at the University of Heidelberg, chelation therapy with EDTA showed surprisingly good results—not in treating atherosclerosis, but in increasing pain-free walking distance in patients with symptoms of intermittent claudication, a circulatory condition. A study performed there on 48 outpatients compared the effectiveness of EDTA therapy with the effectiveness of a European drug, Benzyclan (Fludilardt). Half the patients received one treatment, half the other. Neither the doctors nor the patients knew who was receiving which treatment.

jam in the vessels, and cause fluid to build up in your aching legs. If the clot travels to your heart or lungs, the condition is life-threatening.

"Phlebitis is almost always associated with prolonged bed rest or surgery," says Dr. Creager. "The best way to prevent it is to keep moving. What you should do is move your legs as much as possible if you're confined to bed."

If you suspect you have this disorder, see a doctor immediately, says Dr. Creager. Common treatments include anticoagulant drugs and elevation of the afflicted leg.

Those confined to bed for long periods of time should keep their legs moving to prevent phlebitis.

The effectiveness of the treatment was judged primarily on how much farther the patients could walk before their condition caused them to feel pain. Pain-free walking distance was measured on a treadmill set at a rate of about two miles per hour. Before treatment, some patients could walk only about 66 feet before feeling pain.

Among the group receiving chelation therapy, improvement after four weeks was considerable. Most increased their walking distance anywhere from almost 33 feet to about 164 feet. Four lucky people improved their distance greatly, going from about 656 feet or less to five times that distance.

Most of the group receiving the drug improved as well. In fact, most of them walked a bit further than the chelation group right after the treatment. But when walking distance was remeasured at one month and three months later, most of the chelation group *continued* to improve, while only a few of the drug group did.

In the United States, researchers are planning to study the usefulness of EDTA in the treatment of this sort of circulatory disease, pending FDA approval. "Everyone fully expects this study to be positive, based on the Heidelberg data," says James P. Carter, M.D., chairman and professor of the department of nutrition at the School of Public Health, Tulane University, in New Orleans.

Check with your regular physician before considering such therapy, though.

Intermittent Claudication

"Supposedly, the word 'claudication' comes from Claudius Norman, the Roman emperor who limped," says Dr. Creager. And that's appropriate, because if intermittent claudication hits your legs, you'll be limping too.

Intermittent claudication, which usually hits the calf or thigh, is not a disease, but rather a symptom of atherosclerosis, or hardening of the arteries in the legs. The pain, tightness, fatigue and discomfort in the legs worsen during an activity such as walking, and are often relieved when you stand still.

Leg pain that worsens when walking may be a symptom of atherosclerosis.

"Since atherosclerosis is the cause, smoking, hypertension, cholesterol, obesity and diabetes are risk factors," says Dr. Creager. "To make the leg pain feel better, walking may help. But be sure to stop the exercise before you reach the point of discomfort."

Some doctors also prescribe a drug called pentoxifylline (Trental), which is supposed to restore lost flexibility to rigid blood cells, so they can squeeze more easily through the narrowed vessels.

Getting Back into Circulation

Your eyes allow you to thrill to a great work of art. The ears pipe in a catchy tune. The stomach generates a feeling of warm satisfaction after a good meal. In return, you do what you can to pamper them.

But it's easy to ignore your blood vessels, because they don't provide any obvious pleasure. Exercise may improve cardiovascular fitness, but you have no direct message from your circulatory system that says, "that feels good, do it again."

That's why it's so important to understand what's happening inside your body and how you can improve it. You may not notice what a neglected circulation feels like until some damage has already been done. But hopefully, if you adopt a healthy lifestyle, as discussed in this chapter, you never will have to experience that feeling.

9

Dealing

with Diabetes

T he near 12 million Americans who suffer from diabetes face serious complications due to their blood sugar imbalance—hardening of the arteries, stroke, blindness and kidney damage can be some of the main problems. And older diabetics are much more likely to come down with these and other afflictions than are their nondiabetic friends and neighbors. So it's vital to work to prevent diabetes. And if you have the disease, you must take steps to control it.

While there are two types of diabetes, both are basically the same condition: an excess of sugar, in the form of glucose, in the blood. Type I diabetes, which is the rarest type, and is thought to be genetic, occurs when the pancreas fails to produce adequate amounts of a hormone called insulin. Insulin's job is to see that glucose gets absorbed by cells. In type II diabetes, however (often called maturity-onset diabetes, because it's most commonly contracted later in life), the pancreas produces enough insulin—and sometimes even too much—but the insulin doesn't do its job.

Both types of diabetes are caused by the same thing: too much sugar in the blood.

Preventing Diabetes

Until recently, doctors were having trouble explaining why. Now, however, they can give the rather

111

The most common type of diabetes often can be prevented by staying slim, eating right and exercising.

encouraging response that Type II diabetes is largely due to overweight, inactivity and bad diet. Encouraging? Yes, because these factors are all well within your control. If you reduce these risk factors as you get older, your chances of preventing diabetes may be enhanced. Let's look at obesity first.

A case history reported in the medical journal *Annals of Internal Medicine* paints a picture worth a thousand words. A woman suffering from diabetes came to doctors tipping the scales at 200 pounds—nearly twice her normal weight. But when she dropped down to 130, her diabetes disappeared, totally. In the words of the late Kelly West, M.D., a diabetes specialist associated with the World Health Organization, "If the entire population were lean, the rates of diabetes would be less than half of what they are at present."

The reason?

People who are overweight seem to put out an excess of insulin, an excess which in time can numb cells so that blood sugar isn't absorbed. So the end result is the same as not enough insulin: too much glucose in the blood. Then, too, people who are overweight generally eat the wrong kinds of foods and don't get enough exercise—two more crucial elements in the diabetes story.

Preventive Exercise

Exercise makes tissues more sensitive to insulin, reducing the risk of diabetes.

"Exercise keeps blood sugar levels closer to normal by making tissues more sensitive to insulin," explains Fred Whitehouse, M.D., past president of the American Diabetes Association and head of the division of metabolic diseases at the Henry Ford Hospital, in Detroit. Possible ways this could happen: Exercise might help bring about an increase in the number of receptors on the outer surface of cells, or it could cause changes within the cells, enabling more glucose to get inside and provide energy.

Whatever the precise explanation may be, exercise and this increased sensitivity have been credited with reducing a person's risk of developing diabetes.

Anti-Diabetes Diet

While keeping your weight down and your activity levels up is important for avoiding diabetes, proper diet is important, too. More fiber, less fat and adequate amounts of a trace mineral called chromium are what you should be getting. Less refined sugar wouldn't be a bad idea, either. Here's why.

Fiber, found in fruits, vegetables, nuts and whole grains, slows the rate at which carbohydrates are digested, thus preventing a rush of glucose into the blood in the first place. Less fat in the diet should result in fewer calories and hence less chance of weight gain. Chromium has been shown to bolster the effects of insulin. You can get this mineral in calves' liver, brewer's yeast, potatoes with skin, fresh vegetables, whole grain bread, cheese and chicken legs. And as far as less sugar is concerned, many researchers feel that high sugar diets place demands on the pancreas that eventually wear it out, causing diabetes. So, the next time you hear a call from your sweet tooth, give it a piece of fresh fruit. Fruit has sugar in the form of fructose, which is less demanding on the pancreas. Fruit is also low in calories and high in fiber. And it has chromium to boot.

Fiber can keep blood sugar from raging out of control.

Controlling Diabetes

Diet is also important if you do develop diabetes, despite your attempts to prevent it. While your doctor might want to prescribe insulin and other drugs to provide day-to-day protection, drugs don't offer the kind of long-range protection that diabetics really need. But what you eat can have a big influence on your condition.

That's why more and more diabetics and their doctors are using good diets and even nutrition supplements as therapy for diabetes. A good diet makes sense, for three reasons: Diet control is already the primary form of therapy for the 10.5 million non-insulin-dependent diabetics; nutrition may help prevent heart disease (the real killer in diabetes) and supplements let diabetics stock up on nutrients without violating their special diets.

For every diabetic, avoiding complications means avoiding atherosclerosis, or hardening of the arteries. This is the primary complication, the one that sets the stage for the rest. Diabetics develop this form of heart disease much faster and earlier than the average person, and their risk of heart attack or

A good diet is a primary form of therapy for complications of diabetes.

stroke is roughly double the average. If someone could break the link between atherosclerosis and diabetes, the plight of diabetics would be half solved.

Actually, this is exactly what a pair of researchers think they have done, after years of hard work at the University of Mississippi's atherosclerosis research laboratories, in Jackson. Anthony J. Verlangieri, Ph.D., and John C. Kapeghian, Ph.D., believe that vitamin C can prevent hardening of the arteries in diabetics—and perhaps in everyone else.

"Up until now, there's never been a good explanation of why diabetics develop atherosclerosis so much faster than the rest of the population," says Dr. Verlangieri. "But we think we now have evidence that shows why."

Employing Vitamin C

Sugar molecules and vitamin C molecules, he explains, seem to "compete" with each other as they circulate in the blood. Like two pedestrians flagging down the same taxi, they vie for the same molecular "transport system" that will carry them out of the blood and into the endothelial cells that line every blood vessel.

When the sugar level is high in a diabetic, less vitamin C reaches the endothelial cells. If too little of the vitamin gets through, Dr. Verlangieri says, the "cement" that holds the cells in place on the arterial walls may deteriorate. If that happens, single cells may break off and fly loose. Each missing cell, apparently, can leave behind it a hollow space that quickly provides a toehold for cholesterol. One chunk of cholesterol leads to another, until eventually the arteries are almost choked. The stage is then set for high blood pressure, stroke or heart attack.

Extra vitamin C in the bloodstream protects against gum disease.

In theory, vitamin C supplements can interrupt this process before atherosclerosis sets in. But how much vitamin C does it take? "Our animal studies indicate that two grams (2,000 milligrams) of ascorbic acid is about right for diabetics and about one gram a day is appropriate for healthy people who just want to avoid heart disease," says Dr. Verlangieri, who uses a gram a day himself. (Be sure to get your doctor's approval if you want to try this.) He adds that, as a bonus, extra vitamin C in the bloodstream will protect diabetics from another common complication—periodontal disease. Somehow, the vitamin seems to keep the gums healthy. Dr. Verlangieri thinks that his findings will help lay to rest the notion that vitamin C supplements above the Recommended Dietary Allowance are "wasted."

While Dr. Verlangieri's conclusions about the powers of vitamin C are still controversial, he is not alone in recommending this nutrient to people with high blood sugar. In fact, Stanley Mirsky, M.D., past president of the New York affiliate of the American Diabetes Association and author of the book *Diabetes: Controlling It the Easy Way* (Random), agrees with him.

"We tell our diabetes patients to add 500 milligrams of vitamin C to their daily regimen," Dr. Mirsky says. "It's part of our belief that controlling the diet is the primary goal in preventing diabetic complications. Diet is more important than insulin or other oral agents."

Those diabetics who plan to take an ascorbic acid (vitamin C) supplement must keep one thing in mind, however. Vitamin C can skew the results of certain at-home urine tests. In one of the many test kits marketed to diabetics, vitamin C can trigger a false positive reading, while in another test kit it can produce a false negative reading. "If you seem to be getting unreliable test results, stop the vitamin C for a few days and see if your results are different," Dr. Mirsky says.

Nutrition for Nerves

Dr. Mirsky also has found that good nutrition can soothe neuropathy, another common complication of diabetes. Pain, burning, itching and numbness are typical of this mysterious nervous system disorder, in which symptoms appear and disappear without apparent reason at spots all over the body. It can attack any part of the nervous system without warning. It can even disrupt the nerves of the digestive tract or the bladder, causing constipation, diarrhea or urinary-tract infections.

This nervous system disorder is common in the feet.

The feet, however, seem to be the most common target for neuropathy. Indeed, diabetics have to take exquisite care of their feet, washing them daily, softening them with special creams, checking for any sign of a cut or blister, and seeing a podiatrist often. Poor circulation in the feet means that something as minor as a stubbed toe can lead to an uncontrollable infection. No wonder diabetes accounts for 10,000 foot and leg amputations in the United States each year.

Dr. Mirsky prescribes vitamin B_1, or thiamine, for those of his patients who are kept awake at night by pain or sensitivity in their feet.

"Even though lots of people say that it won't work, I've found that about 80 percent of my patients improve by taking B_1," he says. "I prescribe between 50 and 100 milligrams a day. A week or two after they start taking it they find that their feet don't bother them and they can enjoy their sleep."

Vitamin E supplements can also help the diabetic, Dr. Mirsky says. "I often recommend vitamin E in 400 I.U. [international unit] capsules, three times a day. I don't know exactly how it works, but I think it acts as an antioxidant, which helps prevent harmful peroxide molecules from damaging healthy cells. I prescribe it when I need everything I can get to control the disease."

Harvey Walker, Jr., M.D., Ph.D., of Clayton, Missouri, agrees. "We also use vitamin E in our therapy for diabetic patients who have circulation problems," he says. "Let me explain. There are two pulse sites in each foot. A diabetic patient may lose one or both pulses, which is an indication of reduced circulation in the foot.

"Now, loss of a pulse has always been thought to be irreversible, which of course has serious consequences for the diabetic. But using a year of vitamin E and lecithin supplementation, we have actually restored the pulse at one or both sites in one-third of the 150 patients we've treated this way."

Magnesium for the Eyes

Perhaps the most frightening of all the complications of diabetes is retinopathy. Nine out of ten diabetics who've had the disease for 20 years or more begin to show pinpoint hemorrhages on the retina, the area at the back of the eye that receives incoming light and relays it to the brain for interpretation. The hemorrhages sometimes lead to loss of vision. Diabetic retinopathy, in fact, is the leading cause of blindness in Americans over age 20.

There is some evidence that a deficiency of magnesium might cause or at least aggravate the development of diabetic retinopathy. A study conducted a few years ago in England showed that retinopathy patients had low blood levels of magnesium. Those results suggested the "low concentrations of magnesium may be an additional risk factor" for the eye disease. Since then, there have been a few reports of doctors prescribing magnesium for their diabetic patients. Dr. Mirsky, for example, tells his patients to consume plenty of magnesium-rich foods, like whole grains, nuts and dark green leafy vegetables.

Eye problems associated with diabetes may be aggravated by a diet deficient in magnesium.

Recently researchers in Japan also concluded that a "derangement of magnesium metabolism may have some relationship to the onset and/or development of diabetic retinopathy." Of 109 diabetics studied, those who failed to keep their blood sugar levels under control tended to have low blood levels of magnesium and tended to excrete more of the mineral in their urine. Those with the lowest magnesium levels of all were the patients who suffered from "proliferative" diabetic retinopathy, the most serious stage of the disease.

The Fighting Fibers

A high-carbohydrate, low-fat, high-fiber diet has received the plaudits of some scientists. In one study, conducted at the University of Kentucky, in Lexington, by James W. Anderson, M.D., and Kyleen Ward, R.D., 20 lean men who were on insulin therapy were placed on a weight-maintaining, high-fiber diet for about 16 days. Total calories for the diet consisted of approximately 70 percent carbohydrate, 21 percent protein and 9 percent fat. Carbohydrate foods were a natural combination of carbohydrates and fiber.

They included whole grains or grain cereals and breads; starchy vegetables like corn, beans and peas; and other vegetables and fruits.

Researchers divided the patients into three groups. The first group had been taking 15 to 20 units of insulin daily. Nine of these ten patients were able to discontinue their insulin therapy on the high-fiber diet. Most of them also developed lower fasting and after-meal glucose levels.

Nine out of ten patients could discontinue insulin when on a high-fiber diet.

The second group had been taking between 22 and 34 units of insulin daily. Their insulin was reduced to an average of 12 units a day, and two of the patients were able to discontinue insulin on the high-fiber diet.

The third group consisted of patients requiring between 40 and 57 units of insulin daily. On the high-fiber diet, there was a slight reduction in their insulin doses. Their average blood sugar and urine sugar values also decreased.

Why is a reduction in insulin important? According to a study presented to the American College of Cardiology, high levels of insulin in the blood may be a risk factor for heart disease. A Finnish researcher, Kalevi Pyörälä, examined 1,040 men between the ages of 35 and 64. High insulin levels were associated with a two- to threefold increase in the incidence of heart attacks.

Heart disease can be a serious complication of diabetes, and the high-carbohydrate, low-fat, high-fiber diet may offer diabetics added protection. The Kentucky researchers noted that cholesterol levels also fell while the men were on the diet. That change might be crucial since diabetics are prone to the clogging of blood vessels with fat that can lead to heart disease.

"Our studies suggest that [high-fiber] diets may be the therapy of choice for certain patients with the maturity-onset type of diabetes," the researchers concluded.

While Dr. Anderson's diet has proven to be most effective with adult diabetics, he also treated six juvenile diabetics who were taking more than 40 units of insulin daily. None of them were able to discontinue insulin, but all required less insulin when they switched to the high-fiber diet.

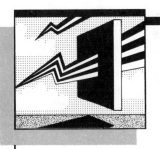

Fiber of the Future

While it's important to stress the prevention of diabetic complications, it would be wrong for a diabetic to forget that controlling the rise and fall of his or her blood sugar level after a meal is the first concern. "The major complications—kidney failure, heart disease, blindness, neuropathy—can all be prevented by keeping blood sugar levels as close to normal as possible all the time," Dr. Mirsky says.

Making sure that there's plenty of fiber in your diet is one excellent way to do that.

While fiber comes in many forms, one type of fiber that has excited researchers lately is guar gum. Extracted from the bean of a plant that grows in India, guar gum has in the past been used as a thickener in foods such as ice cream.

Like other kinds of fiber, guar gum delays the rise in blood sugar that ordinarily follows a carbohydrate-rich meal of, for instance, spaghetti. To demonstrate this effect, researchers in Italy recently fed five diabetics a meal of spaghetti alla carbonara (a pasta dish made with eggs, Parmesan cheese, butter and ham) and later on an identical meal in which the regular pasta was replaced with pasta that was 20 percent guar gum.

Comparing blood samples after each meal, the researchers discovered that sugar levels rose more slowly after the meal made with guar-gum spaghetti. In fact, glucose levels at 60 minutes after the guar-gum meal were roughly equal to the glucose levels at 30 minutes after the meal with ordinary spaghetti. The researchers aren't sure why it happened this way, but they feel confident that guar gum may someday be a valuable tool for the diabetic, either insulin-dependent or not, who wants to control his or her blood sugar while still enjoying high-carbohydrate foods.

Fight Diabetes with Fitness

Another thing that may help diabetics is exercise—regular exercise. It can help as an adjunct to other treatments. Some Type I marathon runners have needed just half their usual number of units of injected insulin on the day of a big race. Many Type II patients have left diabetes behind by dropping some pounds and picking up their activity level. Exercise has also been cited as a way to help lower triglyceride and cholesterol levels and so reduce the risk for cardiovascular crises. And many doctors are fitness fans because of the no-stick effect exercise has on platelets in the blood—platelets are tiny clotting elements that clump together when you cut yourself, but can cluster when they're not supposed to in a diabetic. This clumping may contribute to heart attacks or stroke and may even play a role in tiny eye hemorrhages.

"Most diabetic people know their life span depends upon controlling their blood sugar, and also their weight and blood pressure," says Henry Dolger, M.D., clinical professor emeritus of medicine at Mount Sinai School of Medicine in New York City. "And exercise is an excellent adjunct to caring for all three."

But before you dust off those sneakers, Dr. Dolger says to consult your doctor.

"When my diabetic patients ask me what exercises they can do or what sports they can play, I look at the overall shape they're in," explains Dr. Dolger. "The type and intensity of the exercise depends upon age and any complications the patient may have."

"Heavy exercise can aggravate poorly controlled diabetes, where glucose levels are too high and insulin levels are too low," cautions Dr. Whitehouse. What happens then is that the liver releases high amounts of glucose into the bloodstream and the low levels of insulin can't move the excess glucose into the cells.

On the other hand, an insulin-dependent diabetic can use exercise to enhance the action of injections, and, like the marathon runner, may enjoy a cut in the amount needed. But pushing too hard can cause an insulin reaction. This happens when glucose is absorbed too quickly into the cells, and can cause trembling, sweating and confusion.

Some other facts to be aware of before starting an exercise program: The one-third of older diabetics who have poor circulation must take special care of their feet during a workout. And those people who

Exercise can enhance the effectiveness of insulin.

either have, or are at extreme risk of developing, diabetic retinopathy need to select nonjarring and nonstraining exercises like swimming instead of jumping rope or lifting weights.

The Semi-Tough Approach

One of the leading risk factors for getting Type II diabetes is obesity—fully 80 percent of diabetics fall into this category. Ironically, obese persons need exercise the most, yet they get it the very least.

Getting fit to fight diabetes is like eating lobster—you've got to work to reap the rewards. However, it's not necessary to transform yourself into a Jane Fonda or a Jack LaLanne. And that applies to nonobese diabetics, too. Studies have shown that lowered glucose levels and increased insulin sensitivity results from just three half-hour sweat sessions a week—the time it takes to watch three television sit-coms. Of course, longer or more frequent workouts may result in greater benefits. (Whatever you do, get your physician's approval first.)

Just three exercise sessions a week can lower glucose levels.

Researchers at the University of Vermont College of Medicine, in Burlington, put 18 overweight diabetics on a limited calorie diet for three months. Nine of them did aerobics just three times a week in addition to dieting. Yet that single difference was enough to improve their insulin sensitivity much more than the group who did not exercise.

It doesn't take a miracle to benefit from exercise. Even modest weight loss will improve diabetes. And glucose tolerance returns to normal in 75 percent of obese hyperglycemics who lose weight. More than 100 Type II diabetes patients whose average weight was 212 pounds were studied by researchers at the University of Pittsburgh School of Medicine. The researchers found that keeping even just 15 to 30 pounds off improved the patients' blood glucose levels significantly. The loss also enabled some to decrease their medication.

Losing just 15 to 30 pounds significantly lowers the blood sugar levels of overweight people.

"Because of the difficulty in getting patients to lose large amounts of weight and maintain their losses, these results should encourage patients to persist even if only modest losses are achieved," reports Rena Wing, Ph.D., one of the researchers.

Exercise helps you lose weight. Whether you pedal or paddle, "select an exercise or sport that you enjoy," advises the American Diabetes Association. An activity that registers high on your fun-meter is more likely to become a daily ritual than would something that's spirit-dulling.

"Jogging is a bore for me," admits Dr. Whitehouse, "but I enjoy bicycling. The best exercise is highly individualized.

"However, the exercises or sports that will do the diabetic the most good," he notes, "are isotonics—the 'stamina' or 'aerobic' exercise. Jogging or running, jumping rope, rowing, bicycling, swimming and brisk walking are all excellent for a diabetic in good shape. The 'muscle mass' isometric exercises like weight lifting are fine, too, but they aren't as beneficial as isotonics." Dr. Whitehouse's older patients seem to have the most success with stationary bicycling.

Dr. Dolger frequently asks that those who are able try tennis, join an exercise club, take aerobics classes and even work out to exercise cassettes.

In addition to consulting a physician, the American Diabetes Association says diabetics just beginning to exercise should observe the following guidelines:

• Exercise after a meal, when your blood glucose is rising.
• Start with moderate exercise.
• Exercise regularly, every day if possible.
• If insulin-dependent, adjust food or insulin to accommodate the activity.
• Wear good supporting shoes.
• If overweight, remember that in order to lose one pound of fat it is necessary to burn 3,500 calories.

In addition to changing the diet and following an exercise program, it's important to develop a positive mental attitude. Many people get depressed and bewildered when they first learn they are diabetic—depressed by the fear that it may shorten their life and bewildered by the cautious and complex lifestyle they must adopt. But with proper care, including good nutrition, a diabetic can lead a full, happy, productive life.

10

Digestion:

Smooth

and Easy

I t's 2 A.M. and suddenly you're awakened by strange noises and odd sensations. You realize with a start that the house next door isn't being demolished—those disturbances are coming from *you*! Your abdomen rumbles and gurgles like a draining fish tank. Your stomach churns with syncopated spasms. A fiery pain in your chest makes you choke and gasp for air.

Are the roast pork and chocolate mousse fomenting a rebellion in your gut? Has yesterday's whir of appointments and deadlines come back to spin your innards around? Is this intestinal tumult the start of an ulcer?

You don't appreciate this wakeup call.

Join the crowd. According to Mariam Ratner, director of clinical research of the American Digestive Disease Society, 50 percent of all Americans suffer from occasional digestive distress. These symptoms are the digestive tract signaling how it's working. Learning to read its messages is important, both for self-care and to know when to see a doctor. Let's work our way through the digestive tract, looking at the messages organs send when there's trouble brewing.

Heartburn: How to Spell Relief

Heartburn. It's that uncomfortable, burning sensation behind the breastbone that you may feel after bending, stooping, lying flat or eating. It's so common that an estimated one-third of all Americans have it occasionally or even frequently. Many believe it is a normal part of life and do not seek treatment for it. There are ways to deal with heartburn, however, that will reduce or totally eliminate those unpleasant symptoms.

Many people accept heartburn as a normal part of life, but there are ways to control it.

How Heartburn Happens

At the juncture of the esophagus and the stomach lies a ring of muscle called the lower esophageal sphincter. This muscle continually adjusts to prevent a backward flow of food, acid and enzymes from your stomach to the esophagus. Food is pushed along from your esophagus into the stomach by waves of muscular contraction called peristalsis. If either the peristaltic action or the sphincter (or both) malfunctions, you can get a backward flow or reflux of stomach contents into the esophagus. These contents can be so irritating to the esophagus that they may cause inflammation and even erosion or ulceration of the esophageal wall. Depending on your particular makeup, heartburn may range from severe symptoms with minimal damage of the esophagus to mild or no symptoms with severe damage.

Certain foods and food additives may trigger heartburn symptoms. Peppermint, spearmint, fats and chocolate reduce sphincter pressure, permitting reflux of stomach contents. Citrus juice and tomato products can bring on heartburn symptoms (it's not their acidity but some other as yet undefined characteristic). Coffee, tea, cola and alcohol can initiate heartburn. Foods consumed while very hot may cause spasms of the esophagus and symptoms of heartburn. Cobalt added to beer has been known to produce esophagitis.

Avoid foods that may give you heartburn—for example, coffee, citrus juice, chocolate and alcohol.

Drugs, too, sometimes produce heartburn. Progesterone in oral contraceptives, nicotine in cigarettes, antibiotics like tetracycline, asthma medications like theophylline and certain heart medications are just a few examples. The acidity in ascorbic acid may also cause occasional esophagitis.

Hormonal changes may also trigger heartburn in nonpregnant women. During the later stage of the normal menstrual cycle, the surge in progesterone reduces the lower esophageal sphincter pressure, which can produce heartburn.

Help for Heartburn Sufferers

Here's what you can do to minimize or eliminate heartburn:

• Eat small, more frequent meals instead of a few heavy ones. Eat the last meal several hours before bedtime.
• Avoid irritating foods, drugs and cigarettes. Rinse the esophagus by slowly sipping water.
• Walk around after meals. Don't lie down. Avoid bending and stooping, especially if you are pregnant.
• Elevate the head of your bed eight or more inches with bed blocks. Avoid extra pillows, which fold you in half and aggravate the problem.
• Lose excess weight.
• Avoid tight clothing.

Hiatal Hernia

Hiatal hernia can mimic many internal distresses. It's the Lon Chaney of digestive trouble. It's the condition of a thousand faces—all of them scarier than the real one. On any given day, a stiff, frightening chest pain could send you to the hospital labeled as a possible heart attack victim. (And that's what you might be, so don't take any chances.) But if what you really have is a suddenly apparent, kicking and screaming hiatal hernia, your doctors, at first glance, might think you were having either a coronary, biliary colic, pancreatitis, gastric or duodenal ulcer, disorder of the esophagus, digestive malfunction, angina or any one of many other good but wrong guesses.

It's really a sheep in wolf's clothing, though, and hardly a rare, exotic disease: Estimates as to the number of people who have hiatal (or hiatus) hernias go as high as 78 percent. And most don't even know

It's estimated that 78 percent of people have a hiatal hernia.

they have them. It's a sneaky—and, usually, asymptomatic—little digestive-tract devil. And, more often than not, nothing much to worry about, despite the pain.

What Is a Hiatal Hernia?

Anatomy class is now in session. Would somebody please get the lights? Thank you. In this first slide you see a normal esophagus. As we follow its long, narrow descent from the mouth to the stomach, we see that it must pass through a taut sheet of muscle: the diaphragm, which may be thought of as both the floor of the chest and the ceiling of the abdominal cavity. To get to the stomach, so it can deliver the food that is traveling down it, the esophagus pokes through a teardrop-shaped opening in the diaphragm called the hiatus. It's at this point that the esophagus and stomach join, and where a valve system (the lower esophageal sphincter) keeps the deposited food (and the acid working to digest it) from backing up into the esophagus.

Next slide, please. Here is a hiatal, or hiatus, hernia. As you may notice, the upper part of the stomach has slid up, right through the diaphragmatic hiatus (weakened, perhaps, by age), and into the chest. From 75 to 95 percent of hiatal hernias are of this "sliding" type. These come and go, sliding back and forth, depending on body position (particularly bending forward) and other factors. In another kind, the "rolling" (paraesophageal) hernia, the esophagus-stomach junction stays in its normal location (as opposed to the action of the "sliding" type), but a portion of the large, lower, curved section of the stomach rides up through the hiatus and rolls forward in the chest cavity. These "rolling" hernias can be big problems, and may require surgery. But they're relatively rare.

The hernia itself usually isn't painful.

A hiatal hernia, in and of itself, is not a painful condition. Whereas, for example, a broken arm results in pain, a hiatal hernia results for the most part in nothing except an anatomical deviation. The major difficulty associated with "sliding" hiatal hernias is gastroesophageal reflux, which is a backwash of stomach juices, and in the case of hiatal hernias is probably caused by the stomach's unnaturally altered position. Reflux happens when the esophageal sphincter is weak and allows acidic gastric fluids to travel in the wrong direction. It's important to know that reflux can happen in somebody who doesn't have a hiatal hernia. Just because you have heartburn doesn't mean you have a hiatal hernia, and conversely, just because you have a hiatal hernia doesn't mean you're bound to have heartburn, chest pains, acid backup into the throat or other discomforts associated with reflux. But, then again, you might. A visit to a knowledgeable health professional ought to let you know what your inner story is.

How do hiatal hernias get that way? Scientists aren't sure, and the reason probably varies from case to case. It could be the result of a congenital problem, a side effect of being pregnant or of having given birth or an offshoot of overeating or obesity. Any undue increase in abdominal pressure can do the deed. Some researchers believe that straining during defecation can cause the stomach to be pushed up through a weakened hiatus.

Studies have shown a link between hiatal hernia and gallstones—where you find one, chances are pretty good that you'll find the other—and suggest that lack of fiber in the diet is to blame for both. Lowering animal-fat consumption and increasing fiber, especially in the form of bran, prevents gallstones. At the same time, a high-fiber diet increases the size of stools and eliminates the straining that can cause hiatal hernia. Writes a British researcher, Denis P. Burkitt, M.D., "The hypothesis that fiber-depleted diets are a major factor in the causation of hiatus hernia is consistent with all that is known of the disease."

A diet low in animal fats and high in fiber may help.

The most serious physical effects related to hiatal hernia (or, to be more precise, to gastroesophageal reflux that may or may not be caused by the hernia) have to do with damage to the esophagus. The acidic stomach juices wash back into the esophagus, and normally cause only inflammation and irritation (and, one researcher suggests, asthma attacks). Continued reflux, however, can cause ulceration, scarring and ultimately blockage of the esophagus, requiring surgery. And matters get worse if you use aspirin. The aspirin "may become trapped for extended periods in the esophagi of patients with esophageal hiatus hernia," writes Vernon M. Smith, M.D.; this trapping action allows the aspirin to "injure alkaline mucosa by direct contact." And, in a somewhat ironic twist, by cutting out acidic foods—especially citrus fruits and fruit juices—in order to avoid complications, some reflux/hiatal hernia sufferers have come down with vitamin C deficiencies bordering on scurvy. For these people, vitamin C supplements are probably just what the nutritionist ordered.

Controlling the Problem

The usual treatments and advice have little to do, actually, with fixing the hernia itself, but rather address the issue of keeping the reflux in check. Basically, follow the same steps listed above to control heartburn.

Don't let anybody rush you into surgery for a hiatal hernia, especially the "sliding" type. Only the most severe cases warrant going under the knife. If there is the potential of the herniated stomach pinching off the esophagus, bleeding or danger of lung or heart damage, then an operation is necessary. But only about 5 percent or less of hiatal hernia patients require anything other than good medical advice and a change in habits. Besides its general uselessness, unwarranted hiatal hernia surgery also can be expensive and risky, and may itself produce new symptoms far worse than any associated with the original discomfort. Get a second opinion.

Only 5 percent of those with these hernias require extensive treatment.

For the millions of Americans who suffer from the burning, aches and pains of digestive problems, there are hundreds of products that can bring relief. And they all do it essentially the same way—by neutralizing the stomach acid that's making your life miserable.

Antacids simply help neutralize the contents of the stomach so that the refluxed juices are no longer irritating. They don't neutralize all of the acid, but that really isn't necessary for the relief of pain.

Antacids neutralize the acids that are making your stomach a boiling cauldron.

Antacids have also been shown to increase esophageal sphincter muscle tone, and that action may add to their effectiveness in heartburn relief.

There's no doubt that antacids are truly effective. Ask any heartburn sufferer who's just swallowed an antacid.

Scientists have confirmed their usefulness, too. In one study, 33 heartburn sufferers were given either an antacid or placebo (harmless blank pill) for a period of one month. Twenty-nine of the 33 correctly identified the antacid product, suggesting that the relief offered was not a placebo effect, say the researchers.

Still, all antacids are not created equal, even if the end result is the same. Here's why. Antacid products contain at least one of four primary neutralizing ingredients: sodium bicarbonate, calcium carbonate, magnesium hydroxide and/or aluminum hydroxide, all of which you'll find in a tablet or liquid base. For the most part, they pass through your system quietly, neutralizing the acid and putting a smile back on your face. But depending on how much you take, or what other underlying problems may also be present, there is the possibility of picking up some mild to possibly severe side effects along the way. A closer look at each of the four ingredients is needed to explain it all.

There are four basic types of neutralizing ingredients in antacid products.

Sodium Bicarbonate. Sodium bicarbonate (Alka-Seltzer) is a potent, effective antacid that will relieve your symptoms of indigestion or heartburn. "Taken for occasional digestive discomfort (once a week or less) there's nothing to worry about. But it is definitely *not* recommended for more frequent use or for chronic conditions such as ulcers," says Nicola Giacona, Pharm.D., former supervisor of the Drug Information Center at the University of Utah, in Salt Lake City. Just a look at the name tells you why— *sodium* bicarbonate. "This is ordinary baking soda and it's loaded with sodium. Besides, it's completely soluble in the stomach and readily absorbed into the bloodstream, so it can lead to sodium overload and serious disturbances in the acid base balance of the body.

This type is not for those on a low-salt diet.

"Anyone on a salt-restricted diet (especially for high blood pressure) should forget products with sodium bicarbonate completely," adds Dr. Giacona. For example, a two-tablet dose of Alka-Seltzer contains 592 milligrams (mg) of sodium, enough to upset a salt-restricted diet.

The same is true if you're susceptible to fluid retention, since excessive sodium is usually involved with that problem, too. "Fortunately," says Dr. Giacona, "most brands have taken the sodium out of their products or reduced it drastically."

It's considered effective, economical and safe.

Calcium Carbonate. Calcium carbonate (Tums, Titralac, Alka-Mints) is also an excellent acid neutralizer, besides being fast-acting and inexpensive. Whereas it is safe in small doses, regular or heavy use (more than six doses weekly) of certain products can lead to constipation.

"There is also concern that large amounts of calcium carbonate may cause acid rebound," Dr. Giacona says. "That's when excessive acid is produced several hours after a dose of calcium antacid, setting up a possible vicious circle of acid secretion, antacid, acid, antacid, and so forth."

In one study of 24 patients with chronic duodenal ulcers, taking four to eight grams of calcium carbonate induced excessive acid secretion 3 to 5½ hours later, whereas two to four tablespoons of aluminum hydroxide or four to eight grams of sodium bicarbonate did not. Nevertheless, adds Charles B. Clayman, M.D., formerly of Northwestern University Medical School, in Chicago, "No one has shown that any of this has clinical bearing on the effectiveness of calcium antacids in the treatment of peptic ulcer."

Indeed, even the threat of kidney-stone formation or hypercalcemia (excessive calcium in the blood) has been overplayed, Dr. Giacona says. "The body is designed to compensate for variations of calcium intake. Unless a person has kidney disease, where the mechanisms break down and you can't eliminate the excess amount, those problems are uncommon. In fact, if you are taking a calcium supplement, it probably is calcium carbonate—the same ingredient as the antacid, just without the flavorings that the antacid product has."

Magnesium Hydroxide. Magnesium hydroxide (Phillips Milk of Magnesia) is a little less potent in neutralizing capabilities than the two previous antacids mentioned, but is still very effective. Magnesium is rarely used as the only ingredient in a product, however, because of its well-known laxative effect. Most often it is used in combination with aluminum-containing antacids in order to counteract the constipation that commonly occurs with those products.

Magnesium-containing antacids pose a different threat to people with kidney disease, though. If excess magnesium can't be eliminated from your body, it may accumulate in your blood, causing a condition called hypermagnesemia. When that happens your blood pressure drops, there's nausea, vomiting and, ultimately, coma.

Aluminum Hydroxide. Aluminum hydroxide (ALternaGEL, Amphojel) is the weakest of the acid neutralizers and is rarely used as the sole active ingredient. Most often it is found in combination with magnesium products (Gelusil, Maalox, Mylanta), with sodium bicarbonate (Rolaids), or with calcium and magnesium (Tempo, Camalox).

The aluminum ingredient is not considered risky, but may cause constipation.

Although constipation is the main side effect of aluminum-containing antacids, it is not the one that causes the greatest concern. Doctors used to think that aluminum passed through the body without being absorbed into the bloodstream. Now research has shown that not only is part of it absorbed, but some of it also binds with dietary phosphate and calcium, dragging them out of the body and possibly weakening the bones.

In one study, researchers decided to test the effects on phosphorus and calcium metabolism using small doses of aluminum-containing antacids. Seventeen men participated in the study and were given at least two tablespoons of antacid three times a day for a maximum of 36 days. The doctors also kept a check of each volunteer's dietary calcium and phosphorus intake.

The researchers found that even with small doses of aluminum-containing antacids, there was a significant increase in the amount of calcium and phosphorus excreted from the body.

However, the same study also showed that when calcium intake was approximately 800 mg per day (that's close to the Recommended Dietary Allowance), these antacids did *not* result in a significant increase in calcium excretion, indicating that a diet high in calcium may reduce or counteract the sort of bone loss observed when a person's diet is low in calcium.

If gas reducers work
for you, feel free to use
them.

Simethicone. You may have noticed that some products (Di-gel, Maalox Plus) offer an additional ingredient called simethicone, specifically designed to reduce gas bubbles. The Food and Drug Administration says that simethicone is "safe and effective," but some doctors have their doubts. "The clinical data are scanty," says Dr. Giacona, "but there are some patients who swear by it. So, if it works for you, then use it."

There's no doubt that antacids have made it easy to eliminate heartburn and acid indigestion. Maybe too easy. Occasionally these bouts of indigestion are a symptom of a more serious problem—a symptom that shouldn't be treated offhandedly and forgotten. "Any digestive symptoms that last more than two weeks should be checked out by a physician," advises Dr. Giacona, "since antacids may mask a more serious medical problem. For example, if your heartburn isn't immediately relieved with an antacid, the pain may be from angina, not indigestion—a symptom requiring prompt medical supervision."

Liquid antacids work
faster than tablets, and
both work better on a
full stomach.

For those with simple, occasional acid indigestion, a standard dose of any of the antacids will do the job, say the experts. Liquids work faster because there is more surface area exposed to the acid, but tablets are more convenient. Check the prices—and then pick the least expensive one with the ingredient you can tolerate best, and the taste and form (liquid or tablet) most pleasing to you.

Keep in mind that it's best to take antacids on a full stomach. On an empty stomach, antacids work for only 20 to 40 minutes. Taken one hour after eating, however, they continue to neutralize acid for up to three hours.

Also, antacids interact with certain antibiotics, heart medications and other drugs, so check with your doctor or pharmacist before using them.

And remember, it's still best to try to eliminate the cause of your digestive problem than to accept antacid gobbling as a way of life.

Antacids may have an added bonus of helping ulcers heal, say British researchers. A low dose— about two teaspoons taken for ulcer pain—may heal ulcers in only four weeks. But a higher dose won't speed the process, it will just give you unpleasant side effects, like diarrhea.

There are a whole spectrum of drugs with which your doctor can custom-tailor your treatment. But first you've got to know what an ulcer is. Basically, it's a craterlike sore in the lining of the stomach, esophagus or small intestine caused by excess stomach acid.

Do You Have an Ulcer?

The major symptom of an ulcer in the stomach is a burning, gnawing pain, usually felt throughout the upper part of the abdomen and sometimes in the lower chest. It usually occurs just after eating. The pain can last from half an hour to three hours, and can come and go, with weeks of intermittent pain alternating with short pain-free periods.

Ulcer pain usually occurs just after a meal.

The more common form of peptic ulcer, the duodenal ulcer, is found in the first part of the small intestine, just below the stomach. It produces a gnawing pain that is usually confined to a small area in the upper middle abdomen, but sometimes radiates throughout the area. The pain is often temporarily relieved by eating but then returns one to two hours later and lasts for a couple of hours. It's often worst at night. Awakening with abdominal pain around 1 to 3 A.M. is a strong feature of a duodenal ulcer, although it can also indicate other problems, says Denis McCarthy, M.D., professor of medicine at the University of New Mexico, in Albuquerque.

Mild discomfort that lasts more than two or three days could mean a serious problem, and you should see your doctor if you experience this.

If you hurt for more than two or three days, see your doctor.

Left untreated, ulcers can develop serious complications like bleeding, perforation (when an ulcer eats completely through the stomach wall) or blockage of the upper intestine. Your health-care provider may request an x-ray of your upper gastrointestinal tract. An even better diagnostic tool, called an endoscope, allows the doctor to peer into your stomach and pinpoint ulcers before they progress to a more serious stage.

Here's a simple guide to help you get the best treatment available, once you are diagnosed as having an ulcer.

Ulcer Facts and Fiction

Spicy foods irritate ulcers, so stick with a bland diet.

False. Spicy or fried foods generally don't promote ulcers unless you are particularly sensitive to them. And milk may actually aggravate ulcers because it stimulates acid production. Your best bet is to avoid the known acidic foods like coffee (even decaf), tea, alcohol and highly acidic fruit juices (like orange juice).

A high-fiber diet may protect against developing ulcers.

True. Studies have found that foods rich in fiber (such as fruits, vegetables and whole-grain breads) not only protect against developing ulcers but also promote healing and prevent relapses once ulcers do exist. It is believed that the fiber somehow slows down or buffers the stomach acid.

How you eat may affect ulcer development.

True. Eating slowly and chewing well mean less swallowed air, less food intake and less chance of irritating the stomach lining. Three moderate-sized meals (no eating on the run or late at night) reduce acidity in your stomach.

Ulcers run in families.

True. In fact, if your parents were prone to ulcers, you have a high risk of developing one, too.

There is an ulcer personality.

Maybe. This is controversial. Some believe there may be one personality type that is uniquely prone to ulcers. They think it's related to how people cope. People who internalize their stress and anxiety tend to be more prone to ulcers than those who let out their emotions on a regular and consistent basis.

Whatever the case, it may be wise to learn ways to express your feelings and to include a daily dose of stress management. Progressive relaxation, exercise, deep breathing, massage and biofeedback all may lead you in the right direction.

Crushed aspirin is less irritating to the stomach than whole aspirin.

False. If you are prone to ulcers, avoid aspirin in all forms—even in cold remedies. Be aware that

Learning a stress management technique can be helpful.

other anti-inflammatory drugs and common menstrual medications may also aggravate the stomach lining, advises Janet Elashoff, Ph.D., of the Center for Ulcer Research and Education, in Los Angeles.

If you have an ulcer, avoid aspirin in all its forms.

New drugs can cure ulcers.

False. There's a whole spectrum of drugs with which your doctor can custom-tailor your treatment, ranging from over-the-counter antacids to prescriptions (like Tagamet) that suppress acid production. Most ulcers heal in 8 to 12 weeks if you take the medication as prescribed. Usually the side effects, such as diarrhea and drowsiness, are mild. But healing ulcers is not curing them, says Dr. McCarthy.

Ulcers have a nasty habit of recurring. The best way to keep that from happening to you is to determine which foods cause you problems and to avoid them. Also learn to handle your stress.

Smoking may cause ulcers.

True. Smoking promotes ulcers of the duodenum—the section of the small intestine just below the stomach and the site of most ulcers—and delays their healing. Apparently, smoking inhibits the release of bicarbonate, a natural antacid, from the pancreas to the duodenum. Smoking may also cause the liquid parts of a meal to move out of the stomach and into the duodenum sooner than the solid parts of the same meal.

Smoking may increase your chance of having an ulcer.

Without the solid food to ''buffer'' the liquid food—that is, to neutralize its acidity—it is more likely to burn the duodenum and cause an ulcer.

Pancreatitis

Just behind the lower part of the stomach is the pancreas, a spongy, tapering gland that makes insulin and important digestive juices.

Pancreatitis occurs when cells in the organ rupture, letting enzymes seep into surrounding tissues, explains Roger Soloway, M.D., a professor of medicine at the University of Pennsylvania, in Philadelphia, and a practicing gastroenterologist. An acute attack causes agonizing pain in the middle of your stomach. Chronic pancreatitis produces a dull, cramping pain that is aggravated by food and relieved by sitting up and leaning forward. Diabetes and indigestion may also accompany this condition.

Nine times more men than women develop pancreatitis, usually between ages 35 and 55. It's almost always associated with heavy drinking or gallbladder disease.

"Giving up alcohol is crucial to the control of this disorder," Dr. Soloway says. Cigarette smoking is also strongly associated with pancreatitis, especially in men. Some doctors call for a low-fat diet. And some prescribe supplemental pancreas enzymes, which reduce the organ's activity and relieve pain.

Pancreatitis strikes nine times more men than women.

Irritable Bowel Syndrome

Diane can't remember the last time her lower abdomen felt normal. Often, after a quick meal or during a hectic work assignment, she'll suddenly experience an attack of diarrhea. At other times, she'll be constipated for days. Diane worries that her sharp stomach cramps may mean a serious disease.

Diane is not alone. That worrisome disorder of abdominal pain and alternating diarrhea and constipation is known as irritable bowel syndrome (IBS). It's a condition that affects up to 15 percent of the population. For unknown reasons, twice as many women as men fall victim to it.

IBS is sometimes referred to as spastic colon or spastic colitis. But those terms are less accurate because IBS may involve the *entire* intestinal tract, and inflammation (as implied by the "itis" in colitis) is not a part of the disorder.

Causes and Symptoms

No one really knows what causes IBS. The usual symptoms of abnormal bowel habits and crampy pain appear to occur when electrical activity in the muscles of the intestinal wall produce exaggerated contractions of the intestines. What triggers those symptoms may be infections, colds, weather conditions and psychological stress (although researchers have differed as to the latter's importance).

Most experts today would agree that IBS is a built-in disorder of the natural conveyor-belt mechanism of the bowels that helps move waste products through the body. And it's that conveyor-belt movement that may be stifled by psychological stress.

Probably the most upsetting of all the symptoms of IBS are the recurrent trips to the bathroom and the extreme bowel functions, alternating between diarrhea and constipation.

Rectal bleeding is not usually a symptom of IBS.

The abdominal pain or cramping also associated with IBS is generally mild. Other symptoms of IBS may include bloating, belching and mucus in the stool. Occasionally, rectal bleeding is reported by some sufferers, but it's not considered a part of the IBS syndrome. Rectal bleeding may be associated with hemorrhoids, but in general, rectal bleeding, weight loss or fever suggests the presence of another disorder.

Other conditions with symptoms that mimic IBS include infections, laxative abuse, glandular disease, inflammatory disease of the bowel, disorders of the blood and tumors. Some patients thought to have IBS may be suffering from lactose intolerance, an inability to digest milk sugar.

A doctor usually diagnoses IBS by ruling out these conditions after taking a thorough history and performing a physical exam, along with blood and stool tests. In some cases, your doctor may suggest a sigmoidoscopy (a look at the lining of your colon) and x-rays to be certain of the diagnosis.

Diet May Bring Relief

Most sufferers of IBS find relief by changing their diet. To determine which foods provoke your symptoms, keep a record of everything you eat along with your symptoms. Next, avoid those foods that seem to set off your IBS. For many, that may mean skipping spicy and fried foods, sauces, coffee, tea and alcohol.

Keep a diary to find which foods spur an attack.

The most important dietary changes you can make include:

• Following a high-fiber diet, rich in whole grains, fruits and vegetables. Fiber helps to regulate your bowels. It absorbs water and increases stool bulk, thereby reducing constipation, diarrhea and cramping. The side effects of fiber (gas and bloating) usually subside within a few weeks.

If a diet rich in natural fiber doesn't seem to help, you may try commercial preparations like Metamucil or Konsyl, which are also bowel-bulking agents.

• Avoiding gas-producing foods (if you are sensitive), such as cabbage, carbonated beverages, legumes like peas and beans and sweeteners like sorbitol.

• Steering clear of milk and milk products. Lactose intolerance may accompany IBS or be wholly responsible for your symptoms.

• Changing your life-style to include relaxation techniques, exercise and biofeedback instruction. Those practices can also help to reduce IBS symptoms.

Crohn's Disease

Crohn's disease is a chronic inflammation of the digestive tract. Most often affected is the final section of the small intestine, where it joins the large bowel. Periodic cramps and pain in the lower right abdomen (especially right after eating), diarrhea, and sometimes a slight fever give this disease symptoms very similar to chronic inflamed appendix. Sometimes the patches of inflammation grow and spread, hindering food absorption. Sometimes they heal, but leave scar tissue that can narrow the bowel. Although the disease is uncommon, its occurrence has doubled in the last 20 years. It most often first appears in the late teens or early twenties.

Most doctors rely on anti-inflammatory drugs, painkillers and antidiarrheal medicines to control Crohn's disease. Some, though, see an association between the disease and food sensitivities.

Crohn's disease is usually treated with drugs.

"I find that food restrictions work in some cases with inflammatory-bowel diseases like Crohn's," Barbara Solomon, M.D., a Baltimore, Maryland internist says. "You limit a few foods and many of the symptoms may be less severe. People find they require fewer painkillers to control their symptoms." Food restrictions won't cure the condition, necessarily, Dr. Solomon says, but they can improve it very dramatically.

Diverticulosis

Probably one of the most commonly found intestinal abnormalities is diverticulosis, a condition in which the weakened wall of the lower colon bulges outward into tiny, grapelike pouches. Studies have shown that more than half of those over age 60 have diverticulosis. Most never know it, unless their colon is x-rayed for some other reason. But 10 to 15 percent develop inflammation, a condition that is known as diverticulitis, which causes cramping, bloating, nausea and mild to severe pain in the lower left abdomen.

Diverticulitis can be a serious matter. Most doctors treat it with antibiotics, bed rest and, initially, a low-fiber diet or clear liquids.

But most doctors believe diverticulosis is the result of a low-fiber diet, where the bowel strains to expel small hard feces. They say the best way to avoid the problem in the first place is with a high-fiber diet, plenty of liquids and prompt heeding of nature's call.

To sum up, what do digestive-disease specialists think are the top five best things you can do for your tummy? Each has his or her own favorites, and the list reads like a prescription for overall good health: Eat a high-fiber diet, don't smoke, drink alcohol only in moderation, eat slowly and chew your food well and investigate any changes in bowel habits.

A high fiber diet may help prevent diverticulosis, one of the most common intestinal problems.

11

Energy
for Life

F or 130 working days out of a year Sheila Walker is out of the office and on the road. She's been off organizing the U.S. Olympic Festivals, which are like the Olympic Games only they are held not once, but three times every four years, each time in a different city. Surely her biggest feat is fighting fatigue. "I've been blessed," says Sheila, 43. "I can sleep anywhere, even on concrete, and wake up refreshed." She may owe her second winds to these catnaps. But to permanently fight fatigue, Sheila confesses to having something that keeps her going when she feels she can't go on: judging athletic competitions. Her energy is regenerated by officiating at gymnastic competitions among athletes from 9 years old to college age, which she does between Festivals. "It's distracting; just thinking about it refreshes me like a cup of coffee."

Whenever boredom threatens to steal energy from Californian Roger Minkow, M.D., 40, he gets creative. "I don't give in to negative feelings—I sit down and design." As an emergency physician, artist, musician and photographer, Roger has somehow found the time to design cars, special chairs, exercise equipment and even the entire layout, from carpets to sound systems, for his newly opened BackWorks exercise clinic for clients with back inju-

Creativity unleashes energy.

ries. "For me, creative energy unleashes energy," he says. Rather than depending on professional status to power him, Roger relies on his creative wits. It's taking him far, too. Right now, he's busy designing ways to open up BackWorks studios nationwide.

What does one of the biggest and most respected private eyes in one of the nation's largest, meanest cities do to fight fatigue when he's solving crimes? Drink gallons of coffee from Styrofoam cups? Smoke unfiltered cigarette after cigarette? Drive his motorboat at top speed? Suck on lollipops? "I go for a walk," says Edmond Baccaglini, 51, formerly of the New York City Police Department and now Assistant Director of Investigation for Pinkerton's, Inc. Long walks, short walks, slow walks on the beach, speed walks, walks with his wife, solitary strolls, whatever, Ed finds that walking is just the switch he needs to ward off stress after a day of mulling over murder cases. "Just the pace of New York is enough to kill you," he says. He's also an avid reader of novels, which he keeps handy for whenever his batteries need recharging. The subject? You guessed it—detective stories.

You've watched her on *World News Tonight.* You've seen her covering Ford, Carter and Reagan and listened to her reporting from Capitol Hill. What you probably don't know is that ABC News Correspondent Ann Compton also has four children (all under 7), teaches and is on the speakers circuit. The drowsies are always after her but she manages to escape. Sometimes she slips from the stuffy Senate office and walks several flights downstairs to the basement. Other times she flicks the TV switch from politics to He-Man cartoons. "Breaking stride gives me a breath of fresh air," she says. "The news keeps to a rigid schedule, so it's refreshing to be flexible when I get home, sometimes letting dinnertime slide and the kids stay up."

A change of pace boosts vitality.

A Plan to Fight Fatigue

Without a doubt, these four are high energy people. Were they born with this gift? Perhaps. Yet admittedly these people are not strangers to fatigue. It finds them as it finds you, sneaking up, stealing

Know the enemy and plan your strategy.

energy, leaving its victims drained. "Chronic fatigue may not be an outright killer, but it is among the most disabling of maladies," writes M. F. Graham, M.D., in a popular book on the topic. "As a robber of achievement, a pilferer of potential, it has no peer." But like Sheila, Roger, Ed and Ann, you can fortify yourself against fatigue and activate both internal and external resources to increase your energy level. You can outwit fatigue, and triumph over it.

First you need to know the enemy. Finding the cause of fatigue is like solving a mystery with many suspects. One possible perpetrator is the kind of fatigue that you feel after a round of racquetball, or touring the city on foot. That's a happy kind of "whew" feeling and is easily reversed with a little R and R—rest and refueling. The "Doc-I'm-Always-Tired" type of exhaustion, though, does not feel good. It could mean a cold coming on, or signal an underlying problem connected to any number of diseases or even be a side effect of any number of medications.

Most of the time, however, you're hit with a type of fatigue that not only makes your body feel like it's had a sloth transplant, but also has you *emotionally* worn out: slightly depressed, apathetic, *blah*. This time the prime suspect is stress and tension and the solution isn't as simple as changing a prescription or waiting out a cold. Why is tension fatigue so common in this day and age? Originally, stress was designed to get the body's adrenaline pumping, the heart beating faster, the muscles tightened and the mind poised for action. In ages past, people either ran from beasts or took them on. It's still a jungle out there, but today you have few outlets for the "fight or flight" response. So tension builds up, resulting in chronic fatigue.

You may not be fully able to escape tension, but you can learn to keep from succumbing to the effects of fatigue, to recover stolen energy, to fortify your body and mind and to protect your pep store. Here's how.

Know Your Prime Time

Some people are up and at 'em at the first crow of the cock. Others don't get cookin' until the cows have all come home. It's your internal body clock, your circadian rhythm, that determines the time your energy peaks. For most people, that time is midmorning and sometimes again in late afternoon. For those times, it's wise to schedule activities that require the utmost energy and attention. But what do you do when your body clock gets out of sync, and you feel jet-lagged without ever having left the ground?

You're probably missing certain circadian cues, explains Charles Ehret, Ph.D., senior scientist in neurobehavioral chronobiology at the Argonne National Laboratory, in Argonne, Illinois. "Several things can trigger the body's enzymes for action, including sunlight, high protein meals, strenuous activity, even caffeine. On the other hand, things like carbohydrates help trigger the sleep phase. By paying attention to these circadian cues, you can reset your body clock," he says. In other words, to keep ticking all day, stick to an exercise routine scheduled between 8 A.M. and 5 P.M. rather than later in the evening, plan to eat two-thirds of your daily protein or more at breakfast or lunch instead of at supper and pass up the coffee in the evening. And to unwind at night? Dr. Ehret suggests you try to eat most of your daily carbohydrates for supper.

A high-protein breakfast, sunlight and exercise reset your body clock.

Start the Day with Sex

Why save sex for the last thing at night when all you want to do in bed is sleep? One psychologist says that sex can energize. That may be, but who has the time for it? What with the job, community activities, the workout at the gym, the appointments, the chores—something has got to go. Well, it shouldn't be sex, warns sex therapist Shirley Zussman, Ed.D., who believes that sex should be no less important than your exercise routine.

Put sex at the top of your "to do" list.

She suggests you *schedule* time with your sweetheart, even if it means reordering your priorities. Forgoing the French lessons. Or moving closer to work to cut down on commuting time. Or hiring someone to help clean the house and care for the kids. You may just find that a little romance in the morning will put pep in your step, a smile on your face and give you extra energy all day.

Eat Like a Cow All Day

Eating several small meals rather than three large ones may increase your energy level.

Ever wonder how some people on the go keep going? Probably, they grab a handful of nuts now, a yogurt and fruit then, a salad later. In other words, they've gotten into *grazing*: They nibble on light, nutritious foods in small quantities at several intervals throughout the day. This eating style is portable and even may be healthier than dining on three squares. "There is some evidence that several small meals eaten throughout the day are handled better by the body than three big meals," reports Karen Morgan, Ph.D., associate professor of human nutrition, foods and food systems management at the University of Missouri, in Columbia. For some, grazing helps keep blood sugar levels on an even keel and helps them to resist the temptation to overeat at lunch—one big cause of midday slump.

Good grazing means you need to spread out your calories and select your foods for their nutrient quality. Mix and match complex carbohydrates, protein, vitamins, minerals and fibers, such as hard-cooked eggs, fruits, yogurt, raw vegetables with dipping sauce and cheeses.

Pump Iron into Your Body

Iron helps keep your blood full of oxygen, generating power that lasts.

Your body might look like Arnold Schwarzenegger's on the outside, but inside, your blood cells could be weak and puny. One doctor claims that stress increases your need for nutrients. Moreover, there is an increased withdrawal of minerals from the system when you're under stress. Drained away is your supply of iron, the nutrient that helps the body produce hemoglobin, a protein in red blood cells that makes them oxygen carriers and keeps all systems go. If you are exercising heavily, and are a woman or a vegetarian, you may have an iron shortage. Make sure you have plenty of spinach, sunflower seeds, raisins, beef liver and turkey. And eat them with vitamin C, which helps your body absorb more iron better.

Here's a word to all you who feel dragged out—your diet may be lacking in magnesium and potassium—nutrients that keep the muscles moving along and are key players on the energy metabolism team. To make it to the finish line each day, add magnesium, which is found in wheat germ, whole grain breads and nuts, to your menu lineup. Include potassium foods, too, like potatoes, bananas, oranges, raisins, flounder, milk and lean meats.

Select Your Stimulants Sensibly

Coffee. Where would people be without that jolt of java to get them going? Containing one of the most widely used drugs—caffeine can be a powerful central nervous system stimulant that has been shown to sharpen senses and dispel fatigue—coffee is certainly a favorite of the movers and shakers of the world. The idea, though, is to be a mover, not a shaker. Too much coffee can backfire—unless you know your limits. Nervousness, restlessness, insomnia, frequent trips to the bathroom, headaches, heartburn or a pounding heart are all strong signals that you've had one cup too many. So is reaching for that extra cup when the effects of the last one wear off. If you'd like to cut down, try switching to decaf or mix half decaf with half regular. Or take a brisk walk, or eat a piece of fruit come break time.

Knowing your coffee quotient can help you stay a mover, not a shaker.

Alcohol. When you toss one down the hatch, your energy level may go down the drain. That's because alcohol depresses your blood sugar, the fuel you need for power. To join in the cheer without losing your rah, rah, remember to eat before you drink. Also, choose noncarbonated drinks like chablis rather than champagne, and fruit mixes rather than tonics; those types of drinks are better because they're absorbed less quickly into the bloodstream.

If you want a cocktail, have it after dinner—not before.

Sweets. Can a candy bar boost your energy? The answer is yes—sometimes. If you're halfway up the trail or midway through the marathon, a shot of sugar may help you make it to the finish line. For sugar to work, however, you *must* be exercising. Otherwise it may leave you sidelined with no more energy than the next spectator. The reason? Whenever you eat sugar, your body releases insulin. This hormone ordinarily puts the brakes on energy. When you are exercising, explains California exercise physiologist and dietitian Ellen Coleman, insulin is

And the surprising news is: Candy is just dandy—sometimes.

suppressed. And that means your body is given the green light to use the sugar for an instant fuel fix. So, to help make it up that mountain, candy can be dandy.

Jump, Jack, Jump

After driving downtown to meet your client and sitting through a seminar and a drawn-out dinner with coworkers, all you want to do is crash on the couch and become one with the cushion. Yet that's exactly what you don't need. The reason why you are too pooped to participate is not because of all that you did, but because of all that you *didn't* do. Like exercising. If this scenario describes your life-style rather than an occasional tiring day, you may be in for chronic fatigue—and other problems.

"The sedentary body must work harder because the heart and lungs are less efficient, poor circulation deprives various body tissues of oxygen and muscles deteriorate," explains D. W. Edington, Ph.D., director of the University of Michigan Fitness Research Center, in Ann Arbor. Your body begins to burn fewer calories, the pounds pile on and you feel sluggish. Regular, aerobic exercise fights fatigue by reversing this cycle. It increases the flow of oxygen to all parts of the body. And oxygen is the "gas" that gets your motors moving. To rev up your engine when you're groggy from a day of inactivity, take a brisk ten-minute walk. Dash out to your car. Trot up the stairs to the top floor of your building. Or stand up and do 25 jumping jacks. An exercise break takes only a few minutes but the results are marvelous. You'll be forcing your body to nearly double its intake of oxygen, pump about twice as much blood through your veins and convert blood fats into blood sugar. Va, Vroom!

Even a brief exercise break can generate enough energy to get you through the afternoon.

Seek Out People Pep

You were feeling great until you ran into "you know who." Five minutes of listening to old Gloomy Gus and suddenly your smile drops, your shoulders dip, your spirits droop. You feel drained. That's because Gus robbed you of your energy. "Negative

In a social setting, energy is contagious.

relationships produce a sense of turmoil that merely adds to the problems that you already have," says Charles Kuntzleman, Ed.D., author of *Maximum Personal Energy* (Rodale Press).

For optimum energy, seek out people who motivate you, who smile at you, who listen to you, who make you feel great instead of gloomy. One expert suggests you make a list of all the people you know, or would like to get to know, and decide who is positive to be around. Chances are your list will include people who work at keeping in shape, take care of themselves and are sensitive to others. You might also ask yourself if *you're* a pepper. After all, energy attracts energy.

Beat the Drums with Your Feet

That's what Joan Flint, 53, tells her students from 6 to 65, who come to Studio J, her California tap-dancing studio. "It keeps you loose," she says. Psychiatrists have long known that dance is a good antidote for stress. If you try what California composer and music therapist Steven Halpern, Ph.D., calls sole music, you may not even have to move to the music at all to reap its benefits. Just lie down with your feet facing the speakers and let your imagination flow.

Long called "the food of love," music also fuels the body.

Which platters to spin? For quiet renewal, try calm, unhurried music with a steady baroque beat, such as works by Vivaldi, Bach and Handel. These are said to lessen fatigue. For a musical shove—one to get you through the mopping and waxing, for example—try some hard-driving rock, like The Rolling Stones. Music is energy. "It's as important to have the right music around the house as the right food and the right vitamins," says Dr. Halpern.

Practice Breath Control

Pay attention to your breathing for a minute or two. Is it slow, regular and deep? Is your tummy moving in and out? Congratulations, you are breathing like a baby. And that's good. What's not good is taking short, shallow breaths that only fill your chest. No wonder you feel tired all the time. Chest breathing can keep your body from getting an adequate

To inhale for energy, your stomach—not just your chest—should expand.

supply of oxygen, and may cause your body to be under stress and you to feel fatigued.

Here's how to breathe easier: One expert suggests you inhale for seven seconds, filling your abdomen, then your rib cage, then your entire lungs. Exhale for eight seconds, slowly and evenly. Once you have the hang of breathing, you might also think about reviving the lost art of sighing, which provides you with a rush of energy-rich oxygen and reduces tension. So, go ahead, have a "whew."

Knock Out Noise

Because noise can drain you of energy, soundproof your environment every way you can.

The sound coming from your son's boombox is blissful—to him. To you, it's noise. Nerve-racking, fingernail-biting, hair-pulling noise. Or maybe it's the neighbor's power saw or airplanes roaring overhead that's adding to your stressload. Almost 15 million people live with a daily din loud enough to permanently damage their hearing, says the Environmental Protection Agency. And another 13.5 million encounter enough noise during transportation to cause possible permanent damage to hearing. In addition, noise can make you annoyed, irritated and just plain tuckered out.

Yet it is possible to protect yourself and keep all quiet on the homefront. Some simple suggestions include moving the TV and stereo away from the wall, soundproofing the house, putting carpet under washers and dishwashers, closing doors quietly, speaking softly and getting family members to wear earphones for radios, stereos, even TVs. The hum of an air conditioner or fan might effectively mask what's going on outside your window.

Press Here for Quick Energy

Shiatsu, an Eastern massage, may invigorate your system by stimulating blood flow.

Wouldn't it be nice if you could press a point on your body and recharge yourself? A massage called shiatsu could do that for you. The word "shiatsu" means finger pressure. Imported from Japan, this form of healing involves stimulating points along lines of energy flow (or "ki") which are believed to be situated throughout the body. No one knows exactly how it works, but some experts claim that by stimulating blood circulation your system brings in more oxygen and efficiently removes waste products from muscles. However it works, the massage is certainly invigorating, claim those treated by shiatsu. To relieve drowsiness or fatigue try this: With the flat of your thumb, press directly in the center of the ball of your foot. Hold for ten counts. Do this three times.

Vacate the Premises

Are we having fun yet? If the answer is no, then maybe it's time for a vacation. "New sights can give us new insights," says Edward Heath, Ph.D., professor in the department of recreation and parks of Texas A & M University, in College Station. Just think of the first time you saw the ocean, the forest, a city that was totally different from your own environs. It may be time for a change of scenery if you are irritable; make more than your fair share of mistakes; live, eat and breathe work or think being stranded on a desert island sounds good.

Vacations can be most revitalizing when you leave everything behind—including camera and expectations.

To make sure your vacation is refreshing and not fatiguing, remember to take the vacation for the sheer enjoyment of it. Don't take a camera, don't send the obligatory postcards, don't shop for souvenirs. "Leisure means 'to let go,'" says Geoffrey Godbey, Ph.D., professor of recreation at Pennsylvania State University, in University Park. And try not to think about getting the most for your money.

Go Soak Yourself

Why perk a pot of coffee when you can pop into a cool bath for energy? Cool baths of 80° to 90°F act like a tonic because they stimulate the nerves, explains Richard Hansen, M.D., medical director of the Poland Spring Health Institute, in Poland Spring, Maine. But if a shower is more your style, you're in luck. Falling water, says one researcher, can promote a sense of well-being because it charges the air with negative ions, which are said to make people feel positive, happier and more energetic. Why do you think Niagara Falls is so popular with honeymooners?

Some believe the most supercharged shower of all is the one that runs hot then cold. Turning the taps to hot, take a shower as hot as you can stand for

When showering, alternate hot and cold temperatures for maximum stimulation.

three minutes. Then, turning the taps to cold, take a shower as cold as you can stand for 15 to 30 seconds. Repeat this procedure three to five times, always ending with cold. This type of shower is said to stimulate the nerve centers and promote circulation. (Note: Anyone with diabetes, heart disease or high blood pressure should avoid temperature extremes. Ask your doctor before trying this hot-cold shower.)

Don't save your showers for the beginning or end of the day. One computer analyst arrives home and hits the shower before he says hello to his family. "It's better than a cocktail," he claims. "I feel charged for the rest of the evening."

Ride the Waves at Work

Reevaluate your job, review your options, explore opportunities.

So much change is going on in the workplace—new departments emerging, old departments dissolving, robots moving in and people moving out. Yet you're stuck in a dead-end job, feeling powerless. And that occupational impotence can sap your energy. Before you change jobs, consider changing the job you already have. You can regain personal power and become energized at work by becoming a change master, suggests Beverly A. Potter, Ph.D., author of *Beating Job Burnout: How to Transform Work Pressure into Productivity* (Ace Books) and *Maverick Career Strategies: The Way of the Ronin* (AMACOM). In ancient Japan, change masters, or Ronins, were not part of the feudal system. They were free agents who learned to ride the cruel waves of change that occurred around them. The more modern name for this is "*intra*preneur." The idea is to work within the corporate system, yet function somewhat like a free agent. Dr. Potter suggests taking a fresh look at your job from directions other than *up* the career ladder (which only has a few rungs anyway and is crowded with others scrambling to the top). Better you should set your sights sideways, expanding into areas that require liaison with other departments. In this way you provide yourself with many options for potential moves.

You also can gain power by defining problems and developing solutions. Know a good way to improve the filing or time in/out problem? Write it up.

You could find yourself with a whole new function, with added interest for you and added value to your company. "Becoming an intrapreneur, riding the waves of change and becoming a master of your job can be regenerating," says Dr. Potter.

Decide When Enough Is Enough

That's what California public relations director Carol Osborn, 38, decided after running her own business, caring for two kids, a large house in the country and driving a 40-minute commute. She founded Superwomen's Anonymous, a self-help group with no meetings and no committees. Like many women, Carol was a victim of overcommitment—not to be confused with commitment—which robs you of energy, enthusiasm and fulfillment. "Superwomen try to be all things to all people and perform all their roles perfectly," says Georgia Witkin-Lanoil, Ph.D., author of *The Female Stress Syndrome* (Berkley).

The first step to reversing the chronic fatigue from overcommitment is to decide what you want. This advice applies equally to overcommitted men. Osborn decided she wanted to spend more peaceful times with her family so she said goodbye to the big house, the long commute and 60-hour workweeks. She learned to say no. You can, too, and feel better and more energized for it. Other ways to beat overcommitment burnout and bring balance to your life include making a daily "to do" list that concentrates on high-priority items, delegating responsibilities and creating time to relax and do nothing. And finally, giving up trying to be perfect.

When overcommitted, set priorities, delegate and learn to say no.

12

Eyes:

A Sharper

Vision

E yes are one of the fussiest, most persnickety, parts of the body. The speck of dirt that causes no trouble when it touches your ear, nose or throat will immediately make the eye tear, blink and squint. And whereas the belly may tolerate an occasional playful poke, the eye will have none of that. Because they're so picky, it's a good idea to take care of your eyes—otherwise, they may get cranky and refuse to see things your way.

On a more serious note, everyone probably feels that vision is the most valuable of the five senses. It's ironic, then, that most people so readily accept decreasing vision as part of growing older. But you can prevent—and even correct—failing vision. Here's how.

Nutrition

Is there a vitamin see? Well, research shows that *many* different vitamins and minerals are important for vision maintenance. And vitamin A is at the top of the list.

A lot of poets have praised the eye in verse, but one—a sixteenth century Dutch poet—wrote prescriptions. He wrote, "He who cannot see at night / Must eat the liver of the goat. / Then he can see all right." The poem is probably better medicine than meter. Liver is a rich source of vitamin A, and without that nutrient, you *can't* see at night. (Or in dim light at any time.)

George Wald, Ph.D., a former professor of biology at Harvard University who won a Nobel Prize for his research into the effects of vitamin A on vision, discovered that vitamin A works to maintain vision. His finding led to the discovery that a major sign of vitamin A deficiency is night blindness. But if a lack creates the problem, a surplus can remedy it: Creig S. Hoyt, M.D., of the department of ophthalmology at the University of California at San Francisco Medical Center, reports that large doses of vitamin A, given to a person who is deficient in that nutrient, can result in improvement of night vision within a few hours. (Of course, don't take more than 5,000 international units of vitamin A without your doctor's approval.)

Vitamin A treatment makes sense: To see in dim light, the eye needs a light-sensitive pigment, known as rhodopsin, or visual purple. And without vitamin A, rhodopsin cannot be formed.

But some research has shown that in order for vitamin A to be effective, you also need zinc. It must be present to convert vitamin A into the precise form in which it's used in the retina—a compound called retinaldehyde.

Broccoli, sweet potatoes, spinach, beef liver and carrots are good sources of vitamin A. And meat is a major source of zinc in the American diet.

Liver is good for the eyes for another reason— it's a great source of B vitamins. So are beef, brewer's yeast, chicken (white meat), sunflower seeds and brown rice. And the optic nerve, which carries images from the eye to the brain, needs B vitamins.

Degenerative changes in the optic nerve can be produced in laboratory animals when they're fed a diet which is deficient only in thiamine (B$_1$). Lack of riboflavin (B$_2$) accelerates the deterioration. Humans don't take kindly to B-deficiencies either. During World War II, malnourished prisoners developed an abnormal optic nerve. Treatment with thia-

Vitamin A is necessary for night vision.

The optic nerve needs B vitamins.

mine alone reportedly halted the progression of this disorder. Lack of B_{12} also may harm the optic nerve.

The retina, the membrane at the back of the eye that receives images, is another spot where things can go wrong. A normal process in the body called oxidation, for instance, produces chemicals called free radicals. Left unchecked, free radicals can initiate reactions that result in unwanted tissue changes. Should these changes take place in the retina, unpleasant eye diseases might develop—some considered to be incurable.

Vitamin E may protect the retina.

That's why vitamin E is so important. It may help protect the eye against damage by free radicals. Laboratory animals have been shown to develop retinal diseases when fed a vitamin E-deficient diet.

Vitamin E, when taken with antioxidants selenium and vitamins C and A, has also been helpful in retarding the progression of diabetic retinopathy, a disease of the retina that frequently leads to blindness, according to Ely J. Crary, M.D., an ophthalmologist in Smyrna, Georgia.

The diseases improved in about 70 percent of the cases.

"I've worked with close to 1,000 patients with diabetic retinopathy and senile macular degeneration," says Dr. Crary, "and have seen the diseases retarded in about 70 percent of the cases. This program of nutritional supplementation has shown no adverse effects, either. If someone has early diabetic retinopathy or senile macular degeneration, he or she should at least consider this program in addition to regular therapy—under a doctor's care, of course."

Several different nutrients have been credited with helping to ward off cataracts, a cloudiness in the eye's lens. Since free radicals can also cause cataracts, vitamins C and E, the antioxidants shown to protect the retina, can be expected to protect the lens as well.

Two researchers at the University of Alabama found that older people without cataracts had good amounts of riboflavin in their system. "Riboflavin might not prevent cataracts, but it may be able to help retard their formation," says Harold W. Skalka, M.D., one of the researchers.

Tryptophan and calcium are the other nutrients that, when removed from the diet of laboratory animals, will result in the formation of cataracts.

One prominent New Orleans ophthalmologist, Robert Azar, M.D., prescribes vitamins C, E and zinc to his cataract patients. They're also urged to eat a diet low in fat and high in complex carbohydrates— a diet that stresses fish, fowl and fresh produce. He says that many people who stay on the diet don't have to undergo surgery, which is the usual treatment for cataracts.

This small sampling of findings add up to one conclusion: No one vitamin will help maintain good vision—it takes a balanced diet. More and more eye doctors are realizing this, and recommending dietary programs for their patients.

Eyes, too, benefit from a balanced diet.

"Malnutrition can lead to drusen, a condition in which the first layer of the retina cannot get rid of waste products quickly enough," says Stuart Clark, O.D., of Reading, Pennsylvania. "It's a deposit that can lead to macular degeneration. I see it in a lot of overweight, old and malnourished people. It's somewhat reversible. My mother had it. I told her to eat more complex carbohydrates and take in more vitamins, and now she has less drusen."

Joseph M. Ortiz, M.D., a Philadelphia ophthalmologist, believes that the most important requirement for healthy eyes is a healthy body. He encourages all of his patients, whether they have an eye problem or not, to include whole grains and fresh produce in their diet, to stop smoking and to get plenty of exercise and rest.

Vision Training

Treatment for myopia (nearsightedness) is pretty standard: The doctor prescribes glasses or contact lenses, and you're on your way.

Can following an imaginary bug reverse nearsightedness?

But if you visited Richard S. Kavner, O.D., an optometrist in New York, and coauthor of *Total Vision* (A & W Publishers), he might have you suspend a string from a cabinet to your nose and look at it. Or maybe you'd look at two pumpkin pictures. And then there's the "ball bunt," "quick wink" and "follow the imaginary bug" tricks.

The exercises sound silly when taken out of context, but the idea behind them is that, because vision is learned, you can train yourself to see better. They not only help to correct a "wandering eye" and develop eye movement skills, they even help improve nearsightedness, he claims.

Dr. Kavner, as well as the members of the International Myopia Prevention Association, believe that the strain of close work causes nearsightedness. The eye was meant to look far away, and reading makes the focusing muscles work overtime. In the words of Dr. Kavner, "Eventually, the eye/brain grows accustomed to the strain, gives up sending pain messages, but grumbles a bit when asked to see afar." And then the eye becomes nearsighted.

He draws his conclusion from studies such as these: Monkeys put in a cage with dim lighting and limited visual field became nearsighted, as did Japanese students who started studying intensely after World War II. And so he prescribes exercises and relaxation techniques to prevent or reverse myopia.

Dr. Clark practices Kavner's and other theorists' techniques of vision training. "In cases of high nearsightedness, there must be some genetic factor, and there's no way to reverse that," he says. "But low-level nearsightedness may be caused by stress or faulty vision habits. And focusing and relaxation exercises can reduce it."

Low-level myopia may be caused by stress.

Adherants to Kavner's theories are considered to be renegades in the eye profession.

"Most ophthalmologists don't accept the theory that strain causes nearsightedness," says Steven G. Cooperman, M.D., an ophthalmologist in Beverly Hills. "Nearsightedness is genetic—if your parents have it, you probably will too. But the exercises that relieve strain can be relaxing."

Tips to prevent eye-strain.

With that in mind, here are some tips to prevent eyestrain when reading: Give your eyes a breather every few hours by closing them for about five minutes. Or if that's not possible, look out the window or at something about 30 feet away for about 30 seconds. Hold a pencil at arm's length, pulling it slowly toward you until you see it double. Or you can give your eyes a mini-sauna by squeezing your hands together for a few minutes to warm them and then cupping your palms over your eyes.

Proper reading posture is also important. Sit up straight when you read, have the material about 18 inches from your face (the distance between your elbow and the set of knuckles closest to it) and try to prop your material at a 20-degree angle from your desk. Kavner does not recommend reading in bed, because it distorts perspective.

When to Visit an Eye Doctor

You'll save money by skipping your regular eye exam, but you might save your vision by showing up for it. And, according to Michael Glasspool, M.D., an ophthalmic surgeon in England, and author of *Eyes: Their Problems and Treatments!* (Arco), the following symptoms should send you running: loss of vision, blurring, double vision, the appearance of flashing lights and spots, discomfort or pain in or around the eye, discharge and altered appearance of the eyelids or eyeballs. Any of these could be symptoms of eye disease.

But even in the absence of these conditions, most doctors recommend that you get a checkup at least once every two years. Some diseases, such as glaucoma, have barely-noticeable symptoms at first, but can cause permanent damage if not detected and treated early.

Some diseases can cause permanent damage if not treated early enough.

What kind of doctor should you see, an optometrist or an ophthalmologist? Well, here's the difference: An optometrist has been trained to examine the eyes for focusing errors, to recognize diseases and to prescribe glasses or contact lenses. He or she can't use drugs or surgery, but can refer someone with an eye disease to an ophthalmologist, a medical doctor who has specialized in diagnosing and treating eye problems.

Which one should you go to? "You can use an optometrist to examine your eyes for glasses or contact lenses. They do a very good job," says Clifford M. Terry, M.D., director of the Southern California Eye Institute at Fullerton and assistant professor of ophthalmology at the University of California at Irvine. "But if you suspect you may have a medical disorder of the eye, then you should consult an ophthalmologist, who can diagnose and treat it."

Sunglasses

Sunglasses are more than a beach party accessory. Indeed, their cool appearance belies their importance to the eye: They might help to prevent cataracts.

Sunglasses might help prevent cataracts.

Light promotes oxidation, a normal process in the body that produces chemicals called "free radicals." And too many free radicals may result in cataracts, according to current research.

"The tricky part is that some light may be good for younger eyes," says Dr. Clark. A study showed that up to the age of 20, people need UV-B light (the longer wavelengths of ultraviolet light). The eyes have cells that are set up to take the energy and use it. But paradoxically, as you age, UV light can speed up the progress of cataracts or macular degeneration." Dr. Terry recommends that his patients have UV filters on their sunglasses *and* prescription glasses. "Nobody knows of any harm they could cause, and they might prevent eye trouble," he says.

Smoking

Since a healthy body is so important for healthy eyes, it should come as no surprise that smoking can adversely affect vision.

"If you stop smoking, you get an improvement in acuity (sharp perception)," says Dr. Clark. "And if you smoke just one cigarette, there will be a measurable decrease in contrast sensitivity four minutes later. It's temporary, but just one cigarette does it, even for a nonsmoker. Just imagine the damage frequent smokers inflict on their eyes."

Smoking can have long-term effects too. Dr. Kavner writes that tar and nicotine in smoke destroy large amounts of vitamin B_{12}. This can dim vision and damage the optic nerve, a condition called tobacco amblyopia.

"When the individual stops smoking, vision often quickly returns to normal," Dr. Kavner writes. "If B_{12} is given early enough and the nerve has not deteriorated, complete recovery is possible."

Stop smoking, and your eyes may recover.

Some studies have linked smoking with high pressure in the eye, a dangerous condition, although other studies have found no such relationship.

Preventing Injuries

Even if you eat the right things, go for regular checkups and act very kindly towards your eyes, none of that will matter if a lawn-mower hurls a stone toward your orbs. The National Society to Prevent Blindness (NSPB) compiled the following tips in their pamphlet, "Eye Safety Is No Accident."

• Wear goggles or safety glasses when doing household chores. Your kids will probably laugh at you, but consider this: More eye injuries—some 42 percent—happen around the house than anywhere else. Cleaning agents, such as ammonia, oven cleaners and lye-containing detergents, especially aerosols, can cause serious injury, even blindness, if they get in contact with the eye. If you have a home workshop, welding sparks, plaster dust or wood chips can fly at your face. Even trimming a bush or mowing a lawn can be a catastrophy when debris is shooting up from the blades.

More eye injuries happen around the house than anywhere else.

• Read all package labels and instruction sheets that go with gardening tools and chemicals. About 35,000 eye injuries occur annually in the home workshop, and more than 5,000 are caused by yard and garden mishaps. Don't become another statistic.

• Before you use an aerosol, be sure the nozzle is directed away from you. It sounds pretty simple, but the problem is common enough for the NSPB to list.

Glaucoma— Don't Let It Sneak Up on You

Glaucoma is a sneaky and insidious disease. You can have it for several months to a year and go about your merry way without feeling a thing. But by the time the symptoms (such as tunnel vision and the appearance of colored halos around lights) creep up on you, it's too late—some of your vision has been permanently vandalized. No wonder the NSPB calls it the "sneak thief of sight."

At least that's the case with chronic (open angle) glaucoma, the most common variety. Acute (narrow angle) glaucoma, a less common form of the disease, is no picnic either. It can develop in a few hours, inflicting severe eye pain and nausea on its victim.

Glaucoma is called "the sneak thief of sight."

Glaucoma is the term for a group of diseases characterized by high eye pressure. To understand eye pressure, think of the eye as a basketball. If you pump too much air into it, the ball will be damaged. The air is like the fluid your eye constantly produces, a fluid that usually drains out through a meshwork and returns to the bloodstream. But when more fluid comes in than goes out, you have high eye pressure.

And like high blood pressure, high eye pressure wreaks havoc. The eye's fluid pushes against the retina, damaging nerve cells and fibers. Since the retina's job is to send images to the brain, the result is decreased vision. Damage usually starts with side vision, and, if untreated, may gradually close in until all vision is gone.

This disease is the single leading cause of blindness in the United States and is most common in people who are over 35 years old.

Sounds pretty ominous, but a simple eye exam at least once every two years will detect it early. And several methods are available for controlling eye pressure, even though damage to the optic nerve cannot be reversed.

A common way to thwart the disease is with prescription eye drops. They'll either increase drainage or decrease production of the fluid, depending on which drug is used. But which is the best? It depends on how you react to the drug—discuss it with your doctor.

Every patient should tell every doctor about every disease he has.

"Every patient should tell every doctor he sees every disease he has," says Dr. Cooperman. The patient may think eye doctors are only interested in eyes, but your background is important. Timolol, for instance, an eye drop used as a treatment for glaucoma, can be dangerous for patients with asthma."

Even if you don't have asthma, these drugs aren't much fun. One reason is that you have to apply them every day—sometimes even four times a day. One device, Ocusert, can free you from this schedule. This small drug-filled disk fits under your lower eyelid, and is kept there for a week. It allows pilocarpine, a drug used to treat glaucoma, to seep into the eye at a steady rate, and you don't have to interrupt your hot date to medicate your baby blues. Since its dose is steady, the Ocusert bypasses two of the major problems with drops: decreasing effectiveness in the hours after the drops are used and nightly increases in high eye pressure.

But medications, even with the Ocusert, can cause unsavory side effects, such as nearsightedness, headaches, bad night vision, allergic reactions or high blood pressure, depending on which drug you use. If drugs cause too much hassle, or simply don't work, lasers may be the answer.

"In most cases ophthalmologists use laser treatment for open angle glaucoma only when eye drops are not effective, but lasers are good for almost everybody who has glaucoma," says Dr. Cooperman.

Laser surgery is an alternative.

A laser is basically focused light which permits a surgeon to alter eye tissue without cutting the eye. To treat open-angle glaucoma, the surgeon aims the laser at the meshwork and makes openings, which increase drainage.

"Many people use medications instead of laser surgery because of the cost," says Dr. Cooperman. "But using eye drops for the rest of your life can become expensive too. After most laser surgery, glaucoma is never a problem again, though in about 25 percent of the cases, treatment has to be repeated."

Narrow-angle glaucoma calls for a different treatment. In this brand of glaucoma, the drainage is plugged up because the iris, the colored part of the eye, has come forward. The treatment of choice is an iridectomy, which means a surgeon makes openings in your iris. Nowadays, this is usually done with a laser.

The laser is just one of the recent innovations which have made glaucoma less formidable. "The past decade has seen a greater number of advances in dealing with glaucoma than any other period since the modern treatment of the disease began well over a century ago," wrote M. Bruce Shields, M.D., a professor of ophthalmology at Duke University Medical Center in Durham, North Carolina, in his book on eyesight.

Among the most recently developed treatments is ultrasound. It works something like a laser—laser is focused light, whereas ultrasound is focused soundwaves. But in addition to creating small openings in the eye, ultrasound slows down the rate of fluid production, says Michael E. Yablonski, M.D., Ph.D., director of glaucoma service at the Cornell Medical Center.

"Ultrasound works on types of glaucoma which are unresponsive to laser," says Dr. Yablonski. "It has been effective in 70 to 80 percent of the patients, but currently, we only use ultrasound when every other method fails. In 1985, the Food and Drug Administration allowed 25 investigators throughout the country to perform this operation, under the condition that we document the results. We're still in the experimental stages, so I can't say how promising it is, or whether it will supplant other therapies."

However, the best way to protect yourself is to know about your condition, follow your doctor's instructions, have regular checkups and ask questions when in doubt.

Cataracts

Cataracts are common consequences of aging.

Cataracts, cloudiness in the eye's lens, can cause blurred and dimmed vision and, in advanced stages, double vision and even blindness. The third leading cause of blindness in the United States, they affect an estimated 16 percent of Americans over 50.

"If you live long enough, it's extremely likely that you'll get cataracts," says David J. Apple, M.D., professor of ophthalmology and pathology at the University of Utah School of Medicine, in Salt Lake City. "Most cataracts are a result of aging."

The only known effective treatment for cataracts is surgical removal of the lens. (If you think that's bad, consider the plight of the cataract patient in ancient times. *He* might have had a mixture of ox dung and honey smeared on his eyelids.)

"Some patients think of cataracts as a disease that has to be fixed," says Dr. Terry. "But the patient makes the decision about whether to have surgery and when. If decreased vision interferes with someone's daily activities, surgery may be necessary. A 90-year-old sedentary person may not need surgery, while a 50-year-old jeweler with the same cataract condition would."

Surgery can be a brief procedure, often taking as little as 15 minutes, and is usually done on an outpatient basis. The patient is given either local or general anesthesia (he has a choice whether or not to be unconscious) and the doctor removes the clouded lens.

Without the lens, a person needs special glasses or contact lenses to see. But the glasses have thick "coke-bottle-bottom" lenses, and can cause visual distortions, what Dr. Apple, founder of the Utah Center for Intraocular Lens Research, at the University of Utah, calls "the carnival funny mirror effect": magnification, distortion and telescopic vision. The contact lenses cause less distortion, but some telescopic effects. Moreover, some people have trouble inserting and removing them.

An increasingly attractive alternative is the intraocular lens (IOL)—it's permanently placed in the patient's eye immediately after removing the lens.

According to some reports, the first lens implantation took place in 1795 in Italy. However, the glass lens immediately sank to the bottom of the recipient's eye and the idea was abandoned for more than a century.

Modern precursors to the IOL-wearers were British pilots who had fragments of Plexiglas (from shattered cockpit canopies) accidentally imbedded in their eyes. Ophthalmologist Harold Ridley noticed that their eyes pretty much ignored the intrusions. So in 1949, he decided to go ahead and try out an artificial lens implant.

Early results were promising, but some complications did occur. The lenses have since been constantly upgraded, and now some doctors estimate that the operation may be as much as 98 percent successful. The implant improves distance vision, though reading glasses are usually necessary.

With such a safe operation, most patients now choose an IOL. But they may not be for everyone.

"The patient with use of one eye may want glasses or contacts, because he may not want to risk the operation," says Dr. Terry. "A younger patient may be put on contacts, because the longevity of the lens hasn't been tested."

If you decide on an operation, you should have some input into which procedures will be used. The standard method is called extracapsular extraction,

Surgery is usually done on an outpatient basis.

The intraocular lens is increasingly popular.

Doctors who don't use these procedures are not up-to-date.

which leaves the outer covering of the eye in place. Called the capsule, this membrane holds the IOL in place behind the iris. In this position, it's called a posterior chamber lens. In the alternative (this used to be the procedure of choice but is now considered outdated), the IOL is placed between the iris and cornea. In this position, it may touch sensitive parts of the eye and cause damage.

"Doctors who don't use standard procedures (extracapsular extraction and posterior chamber lens) are not up-to-date, and don't use the safest procedures," says Dr. Terry.

A patient may even ask his or her doctor about operating equipment. "It used to be that IOL surgery could cause astigmatism, because the stitches could be too loose or too tight," says Dr. Terry. "So I devised an instrument, a keratometer, so the doctor knows how tight the stitches are. It can even cure preexisting astigmatism. Most, but not all, doctors use a keratometer now."

Current research may further improve the outlook for those with cataracts. Ophthalmologists are looking into the possibility of anti-cataract drugs, and reshaping the cornea to restore vision.

Myopia: So Near, Yet So Far

A nearsighted kid can be the laughingstock of his classroom. As he matures, the nickname "four-eyes" may wear off, but face it, glasses and contact lenses can still be a nuisance. Whereas most people accept caring for these vision aids as part of a daily routine that also includes washing behind their ears and flossing their teeth, some people are trying to avenge their childhood bullies by achieving better unaided eyesight. There are a few different ways to go about doing this, though none of them is without controversy.

Corrective Surgery

"Refractive corneal surgery" is surgery on the eye's outer layer to change its focus. And *that* means it can be used to correct myopia. Different types of operations fall under this category.

Surgery can correct myopia.

Radial keratotomy (RK) is the most often used, least expensive method to correct low degrees of myopia. Here's a description of how it works from Robert L. Epstein, M.D., director of the Illinois Center for Corrective Eye Surgery, in Ingleside, Illinois: The surgeon cuts several slits in the cornea (the transparent membrane on the front of the eye) in a spokelike pattern. This approximately ten-minute procedure causes a flattening of the cornea, which is supposed to lead to improved, if not perfect vision.

The operation may not be all bad. The first part of a follow-up survey of more than 400 RK patients showed that 78 percent of them did achieve vision as good as 20/40 or better. (Many of them had had vision of only 20/200.) In general, the operation was most effective for people with moderate amounts of myopia.

But then again, the operation may not be all good. The same study showed that some people suffered a small but uncorrectable loss of vision as a result of RK. And this and other research shows that a few patients may experience permanent disabling glare, infection, cataracts, vision fluctuation, astigmatism—and even blindness.

But RK is not always without problems.

"I read about a survey that asked 21 ophthalmologists who performed RK whether they would let their children have radial keratotomy, or if they'd have it themselves," says Dr. Clark. "Twenty said 'no,' and I think the last one was lying. Because it's a new surgical technique, it's not that good. Twenty years from now, it may be better, but meanwhile, it can botch up healthy eyes."

Keratomileusis is a fancy word which means "carving the cornea." It's also a surgical procedure formulated to correct medium to high levels of nearsightedness as well as farsightedness. In this 45-minute operation, the doctor shaves off a disk from the cornea, reshapes it and sews it back on. Compared to RK, it's more expensive, slightly more accurate, less painful, takes longer to heal and leaves the cornea stronger.

Another type of surgery is *epikeratophakia*, which is supposed to cure extreme levels of nearsightedness or farsightedness. In this one, a contact-lens-like wafer is sewn onto the eye like a tire patch.

A wafer is sewn onto the eye like a tire patch.

Epikeratophakia is less accurate, more painful, takes longer to heal, is more likely to produce a decrease in vision clarity, more reversible and more expensive than keratomileusis. (But it has an equally long and fancy name.)

"You've got to realize that all types of radial keratotomy and refractive [surgery] are in development," writes George O. Waring III, M.D., a professor of ophthalmology at the Emory School of Medicine, in Atlanta, and a leading researcher of refractive surgery. "Right now, the predictability of these operations is not as good as we'd like."

"I have a problem with operating on healthy eyes," says Dr. Clark. "Nearsightedness is not a disease, and contact lenses are getting better and better all the time."

Orthokeratology is a program that reshapes the cornea without surgery. The patient wears a series of hard contact lenses that gradually reshape the cornea—it works something like braces for the teeth. It usually takes one or two years to complete.

A contact lens program can reshape the cornea for better vision.

A study conducted at Pacific University College of Optometry, in Forest Grove, Oregon, indicated that a person on this program could be expected to improve his or her vision by six lines on a standard eye chart.

But an earlier study, which took place over the course of several years, found that orthokeratology (or ortho-K, as it's known in eye biz) is not for everyone. Factors such as blinking patterns, eyelid tension, degree of corneal rigidity, contact lens positioning and curvature characteristics can make someone either a terrific or a terrible candidate for this therapy.

Even those who respond to ortho-K have to wear a retainer lens, or else they're back to square one: nearsightedness. Though the lenses may only be required two hours a day or overnight, the fact remains that even an ortho-K "cured" person is still dependent on lenses.

Retinal Disorders

Textbooks often compare the eye to a camera—the camera's lens focuses an image on film, just as *your* lens focuses an image on your retina.

So to get an idea of what retinal disorders are like, just imagine that your camera is loaded with defective film. The pictures would look *awful.*

The retina doesn't need defective film to impair vision. All it takes is a blocked or leaking blood vessel. This can be a result of circulatory problems, diabetes, high blood pressure, hardening of the arteries or many other diseases. Retinal disorders are nothing to smirk at either—taken together, they're the leading cause of blindness in this country.

"It used to be that if someone had a retinal problem, the doctor would throw up his arms in despair and say, 'Forget it! There's no hope!'" says Dr. Cooperman. "It's true that some types of retinal diseases are irreversible, but others are very, very treatable."

Some types are treatable if caught early.

When the central part of the retina (the macula) is damaged, it's called *macular degeneration*, and it causes loss of central vision. This is annoying because you can't see things when you're looking straight at them—you can only sneak peeks through the corner of your eye.

So far, only a few cases may benefit from laser treatment, and only if diagnosed early enough. The Harvard Medical School Health Letter says that about 10 to 20 percent of those with macular degeneration will respond to laser, though Dr. Cooperman estimates that as many as half of his macular degeneration patients are treatable.

Another common type of retinal disease is *diabetic retinopathy,* in which blood vessels may begin to bulge out, leak, bleed, grow wildly or close down completely. This affects people who have had diabetes for many years—60 percent of those who have had diabetes for 15 or more years have some degree of blood vessel damage, though only about 5 percent develop severe vision impairment or blindness.

The most common treatment is with a laser, which seals the leaking vessels and controls the growth of abnormal blood vessels.

Advanced cases call for a vitrectomy, in which the blood deposits are broken up and removed by suction.

13

On

Your Feet

How would you like to take a whirlwind journey around the world: Fat chance, huh? Such a fantasy is either beyond your budget, conflicts with your responsibilities or would be too taxing on your stamina.

What if someone informed you that you have already circled the world a couple of times?

Just ask your feet.

The American Podiatric Medical Association estimates that the average person will walk 115,000 miles in a lifetime. That's more than four strolls around the equator. If you're between 30 and 45 years old, you're probably working on trip number three. Some of you may be well into trek four, plodding along somewhere near Beijing.

Maybe all you really got to see was Boise. Doesn't matter. Regardless of the scenery, 115,000 miles is 115,000 grueling miles to your feet.

With that kind of wear and tear, it's small wonder that corns, calluses, bunions, ingrown toenails, "hammertoes," plantar warts and dozens of other foot afflictions are household words.

Even if you sidestep these painful reminders of the foot's importance, the general process of aging takes a brutal toll on the feet. Years of hauling the load cause the feet to spread out, especially across the frontal area. In addition, the foot's natural padding in the heel section can flatten over time, making that final worldwide voyage painfully uncushioned.

In your lifetime, you'll walk enough steps to circle the globe four times.

The good news is that many of the hundreds of foot ailments are preventable. The American Podiatric Medical Association cites four culprits: improper foot care; injury, especially that due to wearing ill fitting shoes or socks; the effects of aging and heredity. Problems stemming from the first two causes can be avoided altogether. Those that result from aging and inherited problems can be eased, delayed or reversed.

Many foot problems simply don't have to happen.

Let's start by mapping out a lifetime strategy to protect currently healthy feet against both the ravages of time and the constraints of a modern world. To do so, you can follow the advice of some of the nation's top podiatrists, including Elizabeth H. Roberts, D.P.M., professor emeritus at New York College of Podiatric Medicine and author of *On Your Feet* (Rodale Press); Marc A. Brenner, D.P.M., president of the American Society of Podiatric Dermatology and Dennis F. Augustine, D.P.M., director of the Park Avenue Foot Clinic, in San Jose, California.

Tips and Suggestions

Cleanliness. Dr. Brenner recommends bathing the feet daily, preferably twice, in lukewarm water with a mild or deodorant soap. For hard, dry skin, add a softening agent like Alpha Keri-Oil. Dry your feet and apply a foot powder for protection against perspiration. If the feet remain dry or cracked, smooth on a finishing layer of moisturizing lotion or cream. Dr. Brenner uses a vitamin A cream.

Deodorant. When feet are sweaty and smelly, too, it's often the sign of bacterial-induced health problems. Known as bromhidrosis among the medical set, this problem can generally be avoided by practicing the cleanliness tips. In addition, Dr. Brenner says commercial foot deodorants are effective. In a study he performed, the deodorant brand Lavilin—sold only in health food stores—was found to be successful in 34 out of 35 cases.

Socks. Change them daily. Wear absorbent cotton socks or thick athletic socks. Try to avoid nylon materials, which can irritate the skin, especially in warm weather.

Shoes. "The best thing you can do for your feet is purchase a good pair of running shoes, whether

Whether you run or not, get yourself a pair of running shoes.

you're athletic or not," Dr. Brenner advises. Dr. Roberts suggests that you wear sneakers or running shoes if you have a long walk or commute to work. "Carry your high heels or less comfortable business shoes with you," she recommends. "Or don't wear them at all. In New York, the idea of wearing sneakers and mink coats has caught on. I think it's wonderful. Another very good idea is wearing an open-toed and open-heeled shoe. I even recommend that for men. In Europe it's entirely appropriate for men to wear sandals for business. American men have yet to catch on, and they're often paying for it with painful feet." Dr. Brenner says high heels are O.K. if you alternate them often with running shoes or other specially designed footwear. Tight, cramped, badly fitting, slave-to-fashion shoes can result in corns, calluses, tiredness and even aggravate bunions. "It's a good idea to shop for shoes at the end of the day when your feet are swollen," Dr. Augustine says. "Buy shoes one-quarter to one-half inch longer than your longest toes, because your feet slide forward when you stand."

Steven E. Baff, D.P.M., of New York City, says you should "look for shoes with a wide toe box, good arch support, a strong heel counter and shank and a rubberized bottom that gives some compression. Orthopedic oxfords that lace up are excellent."

Pedicures. Another way to be good to your feet is with a weekly pedicure. Professional pedicures performed by nonmedical but trained and certified professionals allow you to sit back and have your feet bathed, trimmed, massaged, steamed and creamed.

Standing. Those who have to stand all day at the job have special problems. "If you must stand on a hard surface, try bringing a square of carpet to stand on, or anything that gives a little," says Dr. Baff. Rene Cailliet, M.D., director of physical therapy/rehabilitation, at Santa Monica Hospital Medical Center, in California, adds that shifting your weight can ease the burden. "Change your stance as often as possible. Get up and down on your toes, and try to keep your feet facing forward. Arch supports might be some help."

Electrodynogram. If none of these methods do the trick, you may opt for a more high-tech approach.

Podiatrists have a new diagnostic tool, an electrodynogram (EDG). Using sensors placed on the feet, the EDG does a computer analysis of how you walk to identify problems and imbalances. Based on this analysis, a podiatrist can custom-design special shoe inserts to help neutralize the pain. "Many foot problems, including bunions, corns, calluses and to a lesser extent, water retention and swelling, are often due to improper weight bearing and improper gait," says Dr. Roberts.

You can have your foot pain analyzed by computer.

Exercise. The best thing for your feet is to let them do their job, keeping the body moving. Being still can promote varicose veins, thrombophlebitis (inflamed veins due to blood clots) and a loss of natural elasticity and valve function in the veins. As a result, feet can swell, ache, cramp and tire. "Try to get up and down on your feet every 15 to 20 minutes," Dr. Cailliet says.

Reversing the Damage

If you looked at the above list, glanced at your painful feet, then slapped your hand to your head and uttered a version of the "Wow, I could have had a V-8" line, take heart. It's never too late to start reversing the damage from those first two or three hikes around the world. Following the above suggestions should help put you on the road to recovery.

For those presently suffering, kick off the program with a trip to the doctor.

"Your best chance of reversing the problem, no matter what it is, is to see a podiatrist at the first sign of a symptom. Most foot problems are progressive problems, so catching them early is vital," warns Dr. Roberts.

"Even if your feet are problem free, it may be advisable to have a checkup. By the time you are in pain, you're in trouble. And the pain doesn't always show up in the feet. Lower back pain, knee problems, leg and foot cramps and fatigue can all result from foot abnormalities."

Bunions, an enlargement of the fluid-filled cushion on the top of the joint of the big toe and the bone jutting against it, are complicated problems that especially demand professional treatment. If caught

Painful bunions can be prevented or surgically repaired.

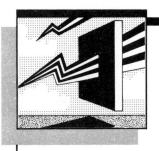

New Horizons in Foot Care

Together, your two feet have 52 bones, 66 joints and more than 100 ligaments, tendons and muscles. With such an intricate structure, it's not hard to see why there are hundreds of surgical procedures involving the foot, including more than 100 for bunions alone. With that many alternatives available, there are sure to be strong feelings among podiatrists and orthopedic surgeons on which method is best.

Two of the newest procedures are also the most controversial. These are minimal incision surgery and laser surgery.

Minimal incision surgery professes to do for the foot what arthroscopic surgery has done for the knee—provide maximum surgical ability through minimum surgical damage. This often results in a shorter recovery period. In the case of bunions, an incision of one-eighth of an inch is made under local anesthesia. The surgeon then uses tiny drills, similar to a dentist's, to realign and smooth down the bone.

"Minimal incision surgery produces better results, is less damaging to the foot, costs less, is extremely less painful and produces a much smaller scar," says Richard Cowin, D.P.M., a Libertyville, Illinois doctor who is board certified in both the traditional and minimal incision techniques.

"Whenever I have a choice, I always opt for the minimal incision technique. When patients come back for a checkup after this sur-

early enough, properly fitted footwear and/or orthotic devices can solve the problem, according to Michael J. Couglin, M.D., chief of the department of orthopedic surgery at St. Alphonsus Regional Medical Center, in Boise, Idaho, and professor of orthopedic surgery at Oregon Health Sciences University School of Medicine, in Portland. If this doesn't work, surgical repair can correct it.

Swollen feet and water retention are another area where self-cures should be avoided. While the symptoms often show up in the feet, the cause could be somewhere else in the body, and could be something serious.

gery, you see a smile on their face instead of the normal painful grimace. To me, that means more than anything else."

Dr. Cowin says podiatrists not trained in this new technique have fought it and in turn discourage their patients from having it.

"If you have been diagnosed as needing foot surgery, I recommend that you at least get a second opinion from a podiatrist certified by the American Board of Ambulatory Foot Surgery. This is a branch of the established American Board of Podiatric Surgery made up of doctors who are trained in minimal incision surgery," Dr. Cowin says.

The Academy of Ambulatory Foot Surgery can refer you to a doctor in your area. Call 314-231-7500.

Concerning laser surgery—a much-publicized technique—many doctors offer a strong caution.

"It sounds high-tech, but its use is limited to soft tissue and is not approved by the Food and Drug Administration for use on bone," says Harold W. Vogler, D.P.M., professor and chairman of the department of surgery at Pennsylvania College of Podiatric Medicine.

To determine which method is appropriate for your case, be it traditional surgery, minimal incision or laser surgery, Thomas DeLauro, D.P.M., vice-president and academic dean of the New York College of Podiatric Medicine, says you should "select a surgeon who has had experience in all techniques. Clinical examination and x-rays will then help determine the type of surgery best for you."

"Go to an internist first to determine the cause, then go to a podiatrist to correct the symptomatic damage to the foot itself," advises Dr. Roberts.

If the natural padding of the feet has worn away over the years, Dr. Roberts says it's usually a result of decades of improper strides. Correcting the stride can ease the discomfort.

As for feet that have widened and spread out over time, Dr. Roberts says changing the width of your shoe can avoid any resulting ailments. If you haven't had your feet measured in a decade or so, she suggests that you may want to have them remeasured during your next visit to the shoe store.

14

Gallstones:

What You Need

to Know

G allstone surgery is the most commonly performed operation in the United States. That should come as no surprise to anyone who has experienced the excruciating pain of a typical gallbladder attack. Who wouldn't willingly, even gratefully, march off to surgery for relief, especially with the knowledge that one agonizing attack may lead to another?

Gallstones afflict over 20 million people in the United States—about 4 percent of the adult population. They are the reason for 500,000 operations each year. Three percent of men and 10 percent of women between the ages of 50 and 62 will have a significant problem with stone disease.

Most gallstones are about the size of a marble, but they can vary from a fine, gravellike substance to a one-inch-diameter boulder. And while many never cause any trouble, others can trigger intense pain, fever, infection, jaundice, peritonitis and pancreatitis—life-threatening conditions.

What determines who will get gallstones? "There seems to be a familial tendency to form gallstones," says Michael S. Gold, M.D., chairman of the department of gastroenterology at Washington Hospital Center and associate professor of medicine at George Washington University School of Medicine, both in Washington, D.C. "Certain ethnic groups have a fairly high incidence—Pima Indians and Latin Americans. In other populations, there are general rules about who gets gallstones. They seem to occur more in women, in middle-aged people, in obese people and in women who've had many children. In medical school we used to call it the four F's: fat, fertile, female and forty."

Casting Stones

Doctors don't know exactly why or how gall-stones form, but they do know that they originate from bile, a thick, yellow liquid that's needed for the digestion of fats. Bile is produced in the liver, then passes into the gallbladder, a teardrop-shaped sac, where it is concentrated and stored until it's needed. When you eat, a hormone stimulates the gallbladder to contract, squirting bile through ducts and into the duodenum, the uppermost part of the small intestine.

"Bile is made up of a number of dissolved substances that have the potential of precipitating out to form stones," explains Dr. Gold, who also serves as vice-president for medical education at the American Digestive Diseases Society. "The three important solids in bile are cholesterol, lecithin and bile salts, which are a derivative of cholesterol and are made in the liver. Those substances exist in little packages called micelles. It's a way of dissolving cholesterol in a water milieu (cholesterol is not readily soluble in water). The lecithin forms layers or plates, and the cholesterol droplets are in between the layers, like a marble sandwich. The bile salts encircle the package like a cellophane bag.

"These substances coexist in a very delicate balance. When the relationship is disturbed, the cholesterol begins to slip out into crystals, and the crystals begin to accumulate in layers—like rolling a snowball."

How do the constituents of bile get out of balance? "If the liver makes fewer bile salts or more cholesterol, that might cause a stone to form," says Dr. Gold. "Obese people may get more gallstones because their cholesterol metabolism may differ. People with diseases of the small intestine, such as Crohn's disease, or those who've had a portion of

Gallstones occur in women, especially those with many children, in middle-aged people, in the obese and in certain ethnic groups.

Gallstones originate from bile, which is produced in the liver, then passes into the gallbladder.

the small bowel called the ileum removed also have a higher incidence of gallstones. That's probably because those areas of the bowel are where bile salts are absorbed to be reused later."

Women who've had many children may get gallstones for another reason. "During pregnancy, a hormone is secreted that causes the gallbladder to contract less than normal," Dr. Gold says. "When the bile is standing still—a condition called stasis—there's a greater chance for cholesterol to crystallize and build up stones. Estrogen use may cause gallstones for the same reason. The point is that there may be several different mechanisms."

Estrogen use may also cause gallstones.

Squeeze Play

Trouble starts when, following a meal, the gallbladder contracts down, pushing a stone into the neck of the gallbladder and blocking the opening pipeline called the cystic duct. That squeezing down behind the obstruction is the pain of gallbladder disease. "The attack may be transient," Dr. Gold says. "If the stone falls back into the gallbladder, the pain will subside and everything will be fine."

If the stone remains in the duct opening, however, the obstructed gallbladder will begin to produce more and more fluid inside until it becomes a big, distended bag. Then there are several possibilities. If the pressure inside is too great, the blood supply may be cut off. Then the gallbladder will rupture. If the blood supply is only partially compromised in the wall of the gallbladder, the stone may fall away and the attack may subside with some fever or infection. Then a scar will form, the gallbladder will become shrunken and won't function normally, and more stones may form.

An obstructed gallbladder can rupture.

But if the stone is small enough, it might be squeezed through the cystic duct into the bile duct, where it will block the bile coming down from the liver. This condition is usually quite painful; the person usually turns yellow with jaundice, and has infection and fever.

"Sometimes the attack is so bad that we have to get the person to surgery right away," Dr. Gold says. But if it's a routine attack, it might be better to wait and do the surgery on an elective basis.

Not all gallstones cause problems, though. In fact, a majority of gallstones are actually painless. "There are a lot of people who never know they're walking around with gallstones in the gallbladder," says Dr. Gold.

So how do you find out that silent stones actually exist? They're discovered during x-rays for some other problems, or they may be found during autopsy.

Until recently, doctors didn't really believe there was such a thing as a silent gallstone. Many doctors felt that eventually all stones caused problems and patients with gallstones were referred for surgery to prevent the "inevitable" future complications.

But a study by William A. Gracie, M.D., and David F. Ransohoff, M.D., respectively of the University of Michigan School of Medicine, in Ann Arbor, Michigan, and Case Western Reserve University School of Medicine, in Cleveland, is changing medical opinion. One crucial finding is that none of the people with untreated silent gallstones in their study died because of their gallstones. Few ever developed problems, so few needed surgery.

Those who did develop pain tended to have no complications, so they were able to have low-risk elective surgery. And when pain did occur, it tended to be soon after the discovery of the stones, permitting elective surgery at a time when the risk was still low. In addition, the doctors found that the yearly risk of developing pain decreased with the passage of time.

"We conclude that innocent gallstones are not a myth, and that in some populations the majority of silent gallstones are inconsequential," say Dr. Gracie and Dr. Ransohoff, writing in the *New England Journal of Medicine*. "We believe that routine prophylactic operation for silent gallstone disease, at least in white American men, is neither necessary nor advisable."

The majority of gallstones cause no pain at all.

The so-called innocent gallstones rarely require preventive surgery.

The Sword and the Stone

When is surgery indicated? "Opinion varies," says Dr. Gold. "It's controversial. But there's probably the beginning of a shift in medical philosophy."

Elective surgery is safer than surgery during complications.

Nearly 80 percent of those with gallstones may never have symptoms.

Sometimes it's wisest to watch and wait.

"Results of a study carried out in the 1940s showed that about 50 percent of people with cholesterol gallstones eventually developed symptoms," points out Thomas Q. Garvey III, M.D., a gastroenterologist from Rockville, Maryland. Eventually, many of these people required surgical intervention. And since elective surgery is much safer than surgery during complications, it used to be if you found gallstones, you'd recommend surgery.

"More recent studies suggest that, in fact, silent gallstones may tend to remain 'silent'—that is, they don't usually cause symptoms. There are several natural histories of gallstones. One of these, and it's pretty common, is a single attack which results in a diagnosis and then nothing—never another attack. It appears that up to 80 percent of people in whom gallstones are found may never have symptoms."

There are, however, several sorts of gallstone patients for whom surgery is still recommended. "If a patient is diabetic, elderly or regularly spends a great deal of time far from adequate medical facilities, there is a relatively strong rationale for preventive gallbladder surgery," Dr. Garvey says. "There is also a rationale for removing a large, solitary gallstone, because such stones tend to cause complications and because there is an association between them and the risk of gallbladder cancer. Whether these large stones cause cancer is unclear, and the risk of cancer is not great, but it's probably enough to recommend surgery. Furthermore, surgery seems appropriate if the patient has intractable pain or has had episodes of inflammation of the gallbladder, bile duct or pancreas.

"If the patient is not having symptoms, does not have a large solitary stone, is not diabetic and has ready access to adequate medical care, it might be wisest to watch and wait."

At this point you might be wondering just how someone goes on living without a gallbladder. "Very easily," says Dr. Gold. "We really don't miss it at all. Bile is still made in the liver, and circulates through the bile duct into the intestine."

One interesting point about gallbladder surgery is that it's only 85 percent effective—15 percent of the patients who have surgery continue to have pain.

"There are several reasons for that," Dr. Gold explains. "First, the pain may not have been due to gallstones in the first place. Maybe the doctor saw the gallstones and decided to take them out, but the pain may have been caused by something else. Second, in the past, doctors didn't always check the ducts when they removed someone's gallbladder, and so they may have left some stones behind. But that happens less than it did in the past, because the ducts are routinely checked today. The third possibility is that years later, the person may re-form a stone in the bile duct. It's rare, but it does happen."

Scope It Out

A new technique can handle precisely that situation—without surgery. It's called (take a deep breath) endoscopic retrograde cholangiopancreatography (ERCP). To locate the stone, the doctor passes an endoscope, a flexible tube, up to the opening of the bile duct. Then the doctor injects a radiopaque dye and observes the filling of the duct under a fluoroscope. Once the doctor has identified the stone, he or she can open up the muscle at the end of the bile duct and remove the stone.

A new technique removes the stone without surgery.

"The procedure is called sphincterotomy," explains Jerome H. Siegel, M.D., assistant clinical professor of medicine at Mount Sinai School of Medicine and chief of gastroenterology and endoscopy at St. Clare's Hospital, both in New York City. "We pass an electrified wire through the endoscope and use it like a knife to open up the sphincter muscle at the end of the bile duct. Then we take out the knife and put in a special catheter to remove the stone. One type of catheter has a balloon at the end. We pass the catheter past the stone, then inflate the balloon and pull it back, gently pulling the stone into the duodenum, where it passes out of the body with the fecal contents.

"People can live with diseased gallbladders," says Dr. Siegel, "but they can't live with an obstructed bile duct. Over half a million people have gallbladder surgery each year. Twenty percent of those people require exploration of the bile duct to

With stones already removed from the bile duct, gallbladder surgery is faster and safer.

take out stones. If we see them first, we can take out the stones in the bile duct and their doctor can deal with the gallbladder later. That's important because morbidity and mortality rise significantly the longer the surgery lasts—the longer they have to explore the bile duct—especially in people age 65 and over. If the surgeon can go in and just remove the gallbladder, the patient's hospital time and complications will be reduced."

To perform the procedure, the patient's throat is sprayed with an anesthetic and they are given a twilight sleep—not general anesthesia. "They're really out of it, though," says Dr. Siegel. "Most patients don't know that the procedure is taking place. The endoscope is passed through the mouth, esophagus and stomach, and into the duodenum. Then the catheter is passed into the opening of the bile duct, the cholangiogram [x-ray] is obtained and the stone is removed.

Etched in Stone

"The procedure is less dangerous than surgery because the belly isn't opened up and there is no general anesthesia. And the convalescence is much shorter—about three to four days in the hospital. And most patients can resume their normal activities when they leave the hospital—they don't have to wait for an incision to heal.

Endoscopy can save about 80 percent of the total cost of surgery.

"We have estimated that the endoscopic procedure costs only about one-fifth as much as the surgical procedure, when you look at time in the hospital and time lost from work," Dr. Siegel points out. Surgery just to remove the gallbladder may entail a hospital stay of one week to ten days. If exploration of the bile duct is done at the same time, the hospital stay may be two to three weeks. "If the gallbladder has stones in it, theoretically it's diseased and most doctors feel that it's going to be a problem," he says. "But we've found that about 90 percent of the people we've treated with the gallbladder intact have not had to have their gallbladder removed."

One of the most important things about the endoscopic procedure is that it's a permanent fix. While stones can be retained after gallbladder surgery, or re-form in the bile duct, that doesn't usually happen after a sphincterotomy. That's because the opening of the bile duct is permanently enlarged. If the duct is open and the bile is flowing freely, there's not enough stasis for the development of stones. "It's the best preventive treatment available against developing further stones in the bile duct," Dr. Siegel says.

Dissolve Your Troubles

A few years ago, a new drug for dissolving gallstones got a lot of press. "Chenodeoxycholic acid is a naturally occurring bile acid that dissolves cholesterol and bile," explains Dr. Garvey. "But unfortunately, when given in the relatively high doses required to dissolve cholesterol gallstones, the drug causes a high incidence of therapy-limiting diarrhea. It can also cause significant liver damage in a not-so-inconsequential proportion of the patients to whom it's given. Furthermore, gallstone dissolution with the drug takes up to two years, and only a small proportion of patients (about 15 percent) will experience dissolution. Chenodeoxycholic acid is on the market now with extremely restrictive labeling and its use is thought appropriate only in patients who are poor candidates for anesthesia or surgery itself, such as an older person with cardiorespiratory disease.

A former "miracle" drug for dissolving gallstones never really panned out.

"In general, if you are dealing with complicated stone disease and you think the patient can tolerate surgery and general anesthesia, you recommend the surgery.

"A closely related drug, ursodeoxycholic acid, is much more promising," Dr. Garvey asserts. "It appears to cause no liver toxicity, and does not cause diarrhea. It is currently on the market in Europe, and a new drug application will soon be submitted to the Food and Drug Administration for approval to market ursodeoxycholic acid in the United States. However, this drug, like chenodeoxycholic acid, dissolves stones slowly, and in considerably less than half the people who receive it."

A European drug is much more promising.

For years the standard therapy for patients with gallstones was to eat a low-fat diet. A meal with a high fat content, doctors reasoned, would make the gallbladder contract more strongly, increasing the chance of it forcing a stone into the ducts. But a study done at Georgetown University School of Medicine, in Washington, D.C., has raised doubts about that approach. The doctors compared how the gallbladder contracted and ejected bile after volunteers ate meals containing differing amounts of fat. The results? "We conclude that the gallbladder dynamics in response to various meals are independent of a meal's fat content," wrote doctors, in the *American Journal of Gastroenterology.* But many doctors have found low-fat diets effective in preventing attacks, and still recommend them.

Diet may prevent gallstones, but evidence is limited.

There is some evidence that diet may have a role in preventing gallstones in the first place, but as yet the information is sketchy. "It seems highly likely that gallstone formation is influenced by diet," says Dr. Garvey. "But just how important dietary factors are and in what ways they exert these influences, nobody knows. Data relevant to this come from Japan, where the prevalence of cholesterol gallstones was very low prior to World War II. Subsequently, however, it has begun to approach the prevalence in Western societies. The only thing anybody can think of to explain this is dietary changes."

One study found that meat-eaters have about twice the incidence of gallstones as vegetarians.

A study done at Oxford University, in England, addressed that issue. The researchers compared the prevalence of gallstone formation in vegetarian women with the prevalence in women who eat meat. They found that the meat-eaters had about twice the incidence of gallstones. "Vegetarians tend to eat less saturated fat, in addition to not eating meat, and have a higher intake of fiber than nonvegetarians," the doctors note. "These data suggest that some dietary factor associated with vegetarianism affords a strong, independent protective effect against this common condition," say English physicians, in the *British Medical Journal.* Further research may bring this factor to light.

15

Freedom from Headache

Sure, there are a few more aches and pains as you grow older. However, "there aren't many headaches that just strike mainly when a person gets older," says Amos Carvel Gipson, M.D., neurologist at the Physicians' Headache Clinic, in Tampa, Florida.

Patricia Solbach, Ph.D., agrees. As codirector of the Menninger Foundation Headache and Internal Medicine Research Center, in Topeka, Kansas, Dr. Solbach knows a lot about headaches. "Fortunately," says Dr. Solbach, "very few headache syndromes develop after age 40. Most migraine and tension headache patterns develop much sooner in life. In fact, some headache syndromes, including migraines, decline as a person ages. If you are over 40 and are suddenly hit with severe, repeated headaches, it is important to seek medical attention. Your headache may be a sign of a more serious illness, like high blood pressure or arteritis (inflammation of an artery)."

Few headache syndromes develop after age 40.

Preventing Headache Pain

Obviously, being older gives you a little bit of an edge. And you can put the odds against suffering headaches as you age even more in your favor by nipping headaches in the bud before they reach their painful and annoying fruition. "Being over 40 doesn't protect you from headaches," says Dr. Gipson. But taking wise preventive measures does.

Through Relaxation

The best thing to do to prevent headaches might be *not* to do some things—like worrying, tensing up and fretting over things you can't control. Should you find yourself feeling tightly wound, relax. Think about the concert you want to see next week, the strides you are making at work or the strides you're going to take on your long Saturday walk. Stress and tension often are an open invitation for a pounding, aggressive headache to begin.

Don't worry about headaches, or you might just worry one into existence.

"Anxiety, tension, depression—eight in ten headaches among older people are caused by one or more of these problems," says Dr. Gipson. The pain of a tension headache feels like a tight band around the head or a weight pressing down on it. Severe tension headaches usually spread upwards from the forehead to the top of the head, and sometimes all the way down to the back of the neck. Other times they'll start in the forehead and the back of the head just above the neck at the same time, with the two pains gradually joining in a torturous band around the head as the day wears on. According to Sampson Lipton, M.D., author of *Conquering Pain* (Arco), the pain is due to scalp muscles that form a sheet over the top and back of the head. When you are stressed, these muscles tighten and stay tightened, causing a tension headache.

While people of all ages are subject to stress and the headaches that often result, many people age 40 and over experience different stressors— some that they may not be prepared for, and that they should circumvent before they become a big headache.

Fear of aging can cause a headache.

"One big stressor is just facing up to aging," says Dr. Solbach. "A lot of people, for instance, have trouble facing the fact that they are celebrating their fortieth birthday." This can cause a "midlife" crisis that is hard to cope with. "But you can't deny the aging process. You can only cope with it. You've got to get active—fitness plays a big role here, by firming up the body and working away stress. Any aerobic exercise, including a brisk walk, will improve your outlook—and your health," says Dr. Solbach. "You should also take the time to be by yourself. Take a walk. And if you are really having trouble adjusting to the aging process, get counseling to reduce your stress—and the possibility of suffering headaches."

Another area of stress which some people aren't prepared for is the way the family situation changes as a person ages. "Perhaps stress will come out of the older people worrying about how the grandchildren are being raised, even though they have little control over it," says Dr. Solbach. Or maybe the presence of grandchildren makes people realize just how old they really are. Either way, stress-induced headaches can be a result of one's reaction to these situations.

The key to preventing this kind of stress and the headaches that result is to "learn to spot the stress before it occurs, and then deal with it," says Kenneth Peters, M.D., of the Northern California Headache Clinic, in Mountainview, and the Stanford University School of Medicine, in Palo Alto, California. Spotting stress mainly involves self-vigilance. Monitor your reactions to different events. If you tense up every time the grandchildren are around, then those kids are a source of stress in your life. If the very prospect of retiring from your job makes you feel out of sorts, the supposedly "golden" years ahead might be fraught with peril for you. Identifying the stressors isn't the whole job, however. You've got to learn to cope with them.

Of course, you could try to avoid every situation that causes you stress. But if that means not seeing your grandchildren, such a tactic might not be easy or wise in terms of your overall happiness. Sure, if the noise and crowds of the shopping mall give you a tension headache every time you make a shopping excursion, then you should by all means avoid the place. But for other problems it might be best to learn how to defuse the tension.

"The first step is cognitive awareness—talking your problems through," says Dr. Solbach. This helps you identify and pinpoint exactly what's bugging you, and gets rid of a lot of tension in the

Family dynamics change with the years, sometimes causing stress.

Pinpoint what's bothering you.

process. Other stress management techniques include biofeedback, in which you use machines to monitor your body's reaction to certain thoughts. The goal is to teach you to consciously and effectively relax in almost any situation, to take the pressure off your head. You must visit a psychologist, a headache clinic or some other health professional to learn biofeedback. But one good relaxation technique you can learn at home from a book is Jacobson's progressive relaxation, a technique that dissipates anxiety through the progressive relaxation of the body's 16 major muscle groups. This can help you clear the stressful thoughts from your head.

One serious source of tension headaches that you should definitely seek professional help for is depression. "Depression can be a serious problem in the elderly," says Dr. Peters. Sometimes headaches can be a result of depression as a person ages. It's a problem more serious than just head pain and should be treated by a physician, he says.

Through Learning about Foods

Simply being hungry can cause a headache.

Not all headaches are due to mental stress. Physical stressors also abound as you age. One of the major physical causes of headaches is food. Or lack of it. "Frequently, older people will miss meals," says Dr. Solbach, "and missing meals will cause problems with tension headaches. Problems you'll feel as pain in various locations of the head." Many people find all sorts of reasons not to eat as well as they should, including diminished sensations of taste, the difficulty of cooking for only one person and boredom. But a big part of staying young as you grow older is eating well *and* enjoying it. Take the time to fix yourself something good. Your head may thank you for it.

Foods containing tyramine can cause headaches.

Just make certain that the foods you eat don't cause headaches. Many people find that their headaches, especially migraine headaches, are triggered by certain foods, especially those that contain a chemical called tyramine, says Dr. Peters. These include ripe avocados, figs, bananas, ripe cheeses, chocolate, beer and red wine. Other common triggers cited by Dr. Peters include nitrate-containing foods, like bacon, hot dogs and other cured meats, and monosodium glutamate (MSG). "Contrary to popular belief, MSG isn't found only in Chinese food," says Dr. Peters, "but also in many prepared foods and frozen dinners. It is important to read the labels." If you often find yourself with a headache after eating one of these foods, try cutting it from your diet.

Another common dietary trigger is caffeine, which Dr. Peters calls a "double-edged sword," because it both cures and causes headaches. A little caffeine (found in many over-the-counter headache remedies) will relieve a headache by constricting dilated blood vessels. But too much can cause a headache. And if you're used to drinking a lot of caffeine, you'll get headaches when you try to withdraw from it. This may account in some cases for the common "weekend" headache, which frequently strikes people on Saturdays when they alter their usual intake of coffee. "Some older people will use caffeine to lift their moods when they are lonely or dissatisfied with getting older. They tend to use more and more caffeine, which indirectly will cause headaches, which will make them use more caffeine," says Joan Miller, Ph.D. Dr. Peters recommends a gradual withdrawal. Limiting your caffeine consumption is a simple and positive step you can take to decrease your risk of headaches. And remember, caffeine is found not only in coffee and tea, but also in chocolate and many soft drinks and medicines.

Weekend headaches can come from caffeine withdrawal.

Another substance, though not considered a food, also is a cause of headaches. The substance is alcohol. Of course, overimbibing can lead to a hangover headache, but even moderate drinking can trigger a headache, which may be due to the tyramine found in some types of liquor. And even if you aren't sensitive to tyramine, your headache may be caused by the accumulation of substances called metabolites that occur as the body burns alcohol. Metabolites cause blood vessels to swell, or become congested or both, resulting in headache pain.

Through Correcting Eyestrain

A frequently overlooked cause of headaches in people over age 40 is eyestrain. And most of these headaches can be eliminated simply with eyeglasses and changes in lighting, says Edward Goodlaw, O.D., emeritus chief of staff at Cedars Sinai Hospital, in Los Angeles, now in private practice. "The relationship between headaches and eyestrain as people age is great. These headaches are most often caused by a maturing change in the relationship between the focusing of the eyes to make seeing clearer and the turning of the eyes to obtain single vision," says Dr. Goodlaw. As a person ages, the focus mechanism gets stiffer and less able to adjust. This leads to muscle tension that gives you a painful headache.

Eyeglasses can relieve a headache problem.

Another problem is just plain old vision. "When you have to strain to see because you have limited vision, that frustration at not being able to see can give you a tension headache," says Dr. Goodlaw. "The right corrective eyeglasses can prevent headaches that are caused by these problems. Therefore, the key to preventing eyestrain headaches is to see your optometrist every year, eat right, exercise and get enough rest. Overall health is one important way to keep your eyes healthy."

Proper lighting is also essential to preventing eyestrain headaches. Dr. Goodlaw advises you to ask your optometrist for specific lighting tips to meet your individual needs, but says that generally there should always be about three times as much light cast on whatever you read as there is in the room in which you're reading. The light should come from behind you on the left side to minimize the chances of shadows falling over what you read.

Sunglasses can help, too.

While most people think that anything natural is always good, Dr. Goodlaw says that too much natural sunlight in your eyes can cause headaches. He recommends that older people wear sunglasses to screen out a kind of ray called "near ultraviolet," which plays a part in cataract formation, and also to reduce the overall intensity of light. He also suggests wearing a good sunhat to prevent glare when at the beach or out for a walk.

Through Sleeping Well

As people age, their sleep needs change. Not only do these changes cause confusion, but they can also cause headaches. "Both too much and too little sleep can cause headaches. Older people should remember that their body may need less sleep," says Dr. Peters. "One should try to maintain regular sleeping hours since large variations (too much or too little sleep) may trigger headaches."

And how you sleep can play a key role in how your head feels. "Turtle headaches" come from sleeping with your head under the covers. When you sleep like this, the blanket acts as a "shell," which shuts out oxygen and gives you a headache. And you shouldn't sleep on your stomach, says Lionel A. Walpin, M.D., of the Walpin Physical Medicine Institute, in Los Angeles. When you do, your head is turned to one side, which can put too much pressure on the side of the jaw and upper neck, causing a headache.

Stopping Headache Pain in Its Tracks

Sometimes all the prevention in the world won't keep you from suffering a headache. For some headaches, like migraines and cluster headaches, there are no foolproof preventive measures. Other headaches just manage to sneak past the defenses you erect. But when the pain strikes, you don't have time to think about where the headache came from; you're more concerned with where you can send it—fast. Here's how to get relief.

When Headaches Strike, Use Your Thumbs

Howard D. Kurland, M.D., author of *Quick Headache Relief without Drugs* (S & S), advises headache sufferers to use acupressure, similar to acupuncture but without the needles. The pressure of a *blunt* thumbnail (not sharpened or reinforced with nail extenders, but well clipped) on certain nerve points seems to relieve pain, says Dr. Kurland. Common headaches respond to pressure on two main points on the head and two accessory points on the hands.

The first main point is by the eye. Find a point halfway between the outer corner of the eye and outer end of the eyebrow. Your finger will be on a ridge of bone, which is the outer edge of your eye socket. Move one finger's breadth back toward the

The pressure of a blunt thumbnail relieves the pain.

ear and you'll be touching a small depression, which is the first main point.

The second main point is at the base of the skull. Find the bony ridge behind the ear known as the mastoid bone. Then find a large muscular groove at midpoint in the back of your neck. Halfway between the two, on each side of the neck, there will be a smaller groove between muscles. Run your thumbnail up the small groove until you come to the base of the skull. Push inward and upward with some force into the groove and against the bone. That's the second main point.

Find the first accessory point by spreading out your hand so the web of the thumb is stretched out. The point is in that triangle of skin between your thumb and index finger on the back of your hand. It's near the bone that runs from the knuckle of your index finger back to the wrist, on the thumb side of the bone and closer to the index finger than to the thumb. You should know you've found it when you press hard. You should feel pain because pressure on any of these points usually hurts, just as if you'd struck your funny bone. Press hard enough to affect the underlying nerves but not so hard that you puncture the skin.

Usually, pressure on these points hurts, just as if you'd struck your funny bone.

The second accessory point is on the wrist. Spread your thumb out and as far back as it will go. Two long tendons will stand out. Where they vanish into the wrist there will be a hollow space. Immediately above this hollow space is a small bone protuberance. Two fingers' width above this is a small depression, which is accessory point two.

Press the two accessory points first, using enough pressure so you actually feel pain. Press each point for 15 to 30 seconds, either with steady pressure or on-off for the full time. Press each pair of head points simultaneously the same way. And always press both points in any given pair, says Dr. Kurland.

Pain Relief Medication

Aspirin is inexpensive and effective.

Aspirin may be your best choice of all the over-the-counter drugs for headaches. Used occasionally, it rarely causes stomach distress and it's usually cheaper than its counterparts, ibuprofen (Advil and

Nuprin) and acetaminophen (Tylenol, Panadol, Anacin-3, Datril). Any of the three are effective for headache pain. Acetaminophen causes less stomach irritation than aspirin, but none of the three is free of potential side effects. Your choice will depend on how you tolerate various types. As for dosage, two regular (325-milligram) tablets of aspirin equal two regular acetaminophen tablets or one 200-milligram ibuprofen tablet.

Steam Heat Away

If your face feels tight, nose full and your headache seems to be enveloping your face as well, you probably have a sinus headache. Steam or moist heat may help. If you can't get to a steam bath, make your own. Sit in the bathroom with the shower running hot and hard. Or try a warm towel across the eyes and cheekbones. Take a fluffy, thick washcloth and soak it in warm water. After you wring it out, apply it to the area that hurts. When it cools off, warm it up and reapply for about ten minutes. A steam vaporizer can be of real value when a sinus headache hits.

Run away from It

According to headache specialist and migraine expert Seymour Diamond, M.D., of Chicago, you may be able to run away from a headache. Running, at least in theory, increases the production of endorphins, the body's natural painkillers. Dr. Diamond, executive director of the National Migraine Foundation and director of the Diamond Headache Clinic, in Chicago, thinks a regular running program could help relieve the pain of a migraine headache. For people who find running relaxing, he says, it could also relieve a muscle tension headache. Before you lace up your sneakers, be aware that your program should be undertaken gradually. Dr. Diamond cautions that individuals respond *individually* to a running program's effects.

Conquering Cluster Headaches

"Cluster headaches usually hit a man in his twenties or thirties, but sometimes they will start to develop when a man is in his forties. They strike six

The Rx is oxygen.

times more men than women, for some reason," says Dr. Solbach. "These are called 'suicidal headaches' because they are so severe that people sometimes want to kill themselves. We can't predict when they will hit, or who they will hit," says Dr. Solbach. However, she has had some success reversing them once they do strike with a prescription for oxygen. Not just air, but oxygen. Dr. Solbach sends her cluster patients home with a tank of pure oxygen. Many can abort their cluster headaches by breathing the oxygen for about a minute.

Reversing Migraines

"I awake with a small, vague ache behind one eye—the prelude to agony. Then light—any kind of light—hurts me, makes me want to crawl under a rock. I pull down the shades and turn away from the slightest glare.

"Then I see dancing, pulsating star bursts in the air, and the pain behind my eye grows sharper, creeping toward the back of my skull. After that, the least scent of perfume or cigarette smoke makes me vomit. The tiniest noise grates against my nerves. I walk like a drunk, bumping into door jambs and the corners of tables.

A migraine is no ordinary headache.

"And worst of all, once the pain begins, nothing can stop it. And when it's going full force, I just want to curl up and die."

So says one migraine sufferer of his misery. This torment can last hours or days, occur every week or twice a year, hurt like a mild toothache or a knife in the brain. Migraines vary from person to person and attack to attack. But migraineurs (migraine sufferers) know this for sure: The discomfort called migraine is no ordinary headache.

Migraines strike mostly women, and they tend to stop occurring after menopause, so aging is often good news for migraineurs. But they can still be a problem at any age. Some women continue to suffer them after menopause, and being male isn't an automatic absolution from the torment of migraine. When the headache finally comes, it usually (but not always) arrives as a dull ache on one side of the head, growing into a deep, throbbing pain that is often punctuated by nausea and vomiting.

Experts say that all this migraine distress is associated with the swelling and narrowing of blood vessels inside and outside the brain. But no one yet knows how or why. While there isn't any cure for the problem, there are ways to get relief when a migraine strikes.

Here's a rundown of some therapies that have helped migraine victims reverse their headaches once they start.

Clinicians report that many migraineurs have great success using biofeedback to head off or curtail migraine attacks.

"We've monitored the symptoms of hundreds of our patients with migraine—both before they received biofeedback training and after," says Jack C. Hartje, Ph.D., director of the Hartje Stress Clinic, in Jacksonville, Florida. "Using what they had learned to forestall attacks, patients with common migraine averaged a 75 to 80 percent reduction in pain. And classical migraine sufferers averaged an 85 to 90 percent reduction."

With biofeedback, migraineurs learn to use their thoughts to raise the temperature of their fingers or hands by increasing the blood flow to them. The theory is that this change in blood flow draws blood from the head, thus shrinking blood vessels there and reducing migraine symptoms.

Since the diameter of your blood vessels can be altered by exposing them to heat and cold, can you use heat and cold to reduce migraine symptoms? There's no scientific evidence that you can, and most headache experts are skeptical. But a few migraineurs claim that they've been able to abort a migraine attack with this kind of therapy.

Augustus S. Rose, M.D., professor emeritus of neurology at the University of California at Los Angeles School of Medicine, advocates hot/cold showers and says that for some patients they work well. He suggests that at the onset of an attack, you take a long hot shower followed by a cold shower that leaves you shivering. Often, he says, this method can actually short-circuit the impending pain. But hot and cold showers aren't for everyone. Elderly people

While there's no cure, there can be relief.

Common migraines were reduced by 75 to 80 percent; classical migraines by 85 to 90 percent.

and others with certain diseases should avoid them. For these people says Dr. Rose, holding crushed ice in the mouth and throat may have the same effect.

Like many headache experts, Joel R. Saper, M.D., and Kenneth R. Magee, M.D., authors of *Freedom from Headaches* (S & S), clearly recognize the two sides of migraine drugs. "Ideally," they say, "it would be safer to treat symptoms without having to resort to medications. But most migraine patients require medicine to achieve the maximum relief."

Most migraine sufferers require medication to achieve maximum relief.

Some medications (like analgesics, sedatives and vasoactive drugs) are used to abort migraine headaches in progress. Others (like antidepressants and tranquilizers) are supposed to prevent migraine attacks from starting. If your headaches come once in a while, your doctor may prescribe the first type of medication. But if your headaches come fast and furious, he may give you preventive drugs to avoid the side effects caused by too frequent use of the abortive agents. At any rate, you should understand that you may not respond to a migraine drug the way another migraineur does. And above all, you and your doctor must weigh the benefits of such medication against its possible side effects.

16

Hearing:

Let's Hear It

for Ears

To you, it's the silvery tinkle of a wind chime. To your ear, it's a pressure that sets tiny hair cells in motion. About 23,000 of them line the cochleas (two small, snail-shaped curls in your inner ears). As they bend—a motion often less than the width of an atom—a chemical reaction sends information along nerve fibers to your brain. You hear a meaningful sound.

But for some, the wind will blow, the pieces of the chime will strike each other, but they will hear nothing. Others will hear, but only faintly. These people have lost some or all of their hearing.

Helen Keller, blind and deaf, and the most famous person with this combination of handicaps to learn full communication with the hearing and sighted world, said that of her two afflictions, her deafness was the worse. It cut her off from other people in ways that her blindness did not.

But even more than the isolation of deafness, some people fear loss of hearing as a sign of advancing age. And in fact, for decades doctors have referred to the most common kind of hearing impairment as presbycusis, which simply means age-related hearing loss.

Old Age Does Not Cause Deafness

But what actually causes presbycusis? "One school of thought is that it's caused by aging. But that's not true," says Ralph R. Rupp, Ph.D., professor of audiology and education at the University of Michigan, in Ann Arbor.

This same kind of hearing impairment also can afflict the young. In groups of incoming freshmen at the University of Tennessee, in Knoxville, David Lipscomb, Ph.D., of the school's famed Noise Research Laboratory, found that more than 50 percent of the students had measurable hearing losses in the high frequency range—the same general pattern shown by old people. These young people were entering their working lives with retirement-age ears.

Some 70-year-olds hear as well as those who are 20.

More proof that age doesn't cause hearing loss was gathered by a scientist studying an isolated tribe in the Sudan. He found that their 70-year-olds had hearing as good as that of American 20-year-olds.

So, if age doesn't cause the problem, why do so many older people have trouble hearing?

"A better name for the condition that some older people get would be 'sociocusis,' " says Dr. Rupp. "It's an accumulation of all the disasters that hit the auditory mechanism during a lifetime."

What's a disaster to your ear? According to Dr. Rupp, any of those things the isolated Sudanese tribe managed to avoid—smoking, a high-fat diet, tension, high blood pressure and, especially, noise. "Anything that interferes with the microcirculation of the blood supply to your ears is going to cause problems with your hearing," he says.

Keep Keen Hearing Forever

But the good news is that this means that deafness in old age is not inevitable. "You can do a lot to offset the damaging environment," claims Dr. Rupp.

Number one on your ears' enemy hit list is noise. It causes more deafness than anything else. And you don't have to operate a jackhammer to be vulnerable.

Protect your ears from loud noise.

Sound, your ears' reason for being, can also be those tender organs' worst enemy. When sound becomes noise or simply grows too loud, even the most delightful strains of music can hurt the tiny hair

President Reagan's Hearing Loss

"What?" is President Reagan's favorite response to questions about his hearing, according to a White House spokesperson.

Suffering a progressive deafness since a gun went off too close to his ears when he was acting in a Western some years ago, Reagan began wearing two hearing aids in 1985.

"He's had a terrific effect," says Ralph R. Rupp, Ph.D., audiology professor at the University of Michigan. "The sales of hearing aid units crossed the million-per-year mark for the first time after he put on that second aid.

"I just wish we could convince everyone that hearing aids are as reasonable, acceptable and appropriate as glasses."

cells that make ears work. Some investigators have found that even symphony orchestra musicians have suffered an occupational loss of part of their hearing. But the cause of hearing loss is usually *not* classical music.

"Shall I tell you about the rock musicians who are sneaking to their otologists to have their hearing tested?" asks Dr. Rupp. In one five-man band, he says, four of the musicians, all still in their twenties, had significantly damaged hearing.

"I don't want to make rock-and-roll the only bad guy," says Dr. Lipscomb. He points out that we live in a noisy world. Power tools, traffic, jet engines, factory noise, drag races, snowmobiles—all of these can gradually take their toll on hearing.

Even screaming babies can exceed a safe decibel count. Dr. Lipscomb, father of an infant son, says, "At my shoulder, I've tested the little guy at 93 decibels. That's a level the Occupational Safety and Health people say is unsafe if it continues for four hours." Other researchers have measured infants at even higher levels—up to 117 ear-maiming decibels.

How Sound Attacks the Ears

"Ear-shattering," "ear-splitting," "so loud it makes my ears hurt"—people use phrases like this all the time, but most people are not aware that they are literally true.

When excessive noise strikes the ear, the tiny hair cells in the snail-shaped cochlea get blown over or knocked down. When healthy, they stand up alertly.

Noise damages hair cells and tiny veins in the ears.

But scientists now believe that it is the effect of noise on the tiny blood vessels that supply the ear that inflicts the most permanent harm.

One of the Catch-22s of hearing loss is that it is the body's effort to *protect* itself from noise that *causes* hearing impairment. Reacting to the stress of noise, veins constrict, reducing the blood supply, which gradually contributes to hearing loss.

"When an autopsy is done on someone in his or her seventies, an almost complete collapse of the

Weird Ear Fixers

Will there be a morning-after pill for noise overdose? Or will people breathe into a bag to heal damage to their ears? These two improbable-sounding methods are under serious investigation by scientists seeking ways to prevent the injury noise can cause the delicate anatomy of hearing.

Both the breathing bag and the noise pill work the same way: They are vasodilators, relaxing veins that too much sound has caused to constrict, which is now thought to be a primary cause of noise-induced hearing loss.

"The trouble with the noise pill," says David Lipscomb, Ph.D., one of the researchers working on the breathing bag, "is finding a chemical vasodilator that doesn't cause heart attacks. Plus you're putting a drug, a foreign substance, into your body."

The rebreathing device he's investigating is more than your everyday brown lunch bag. It uses carbon dioxide to expand clamped down veins. It also slows breathing, exerting an overall relaxing effect. "It's like a big hand reached down and saying, 'Slow down,' " says Dr. Lipscomb.

Just breathing in and out of a paper bag after noise exposure is not recommended, he cautions. The exhalant contains other gases, including carbon monoxide. And that's not good for you.

structure at the base of the cochlea is often seen," says Dr. Lipscomb. And this hearing-damaging collapse is due in part to "a lifetime of exposure to sound," in Dr. Lipscomb's opinion.

How can you know if sound is damaging your ears? Following noise exposure, there are two quick ways to tell, says Dr. Rupp. "If your ears ring for a few hours or a couple of days. Or when you're speaking with someone, and their voices sound muffled."

Ringing in the ears is a warning sign.

The ringing is caused by the injured hair cells firing by themselves, he says. If you're lucky, most of the damage will heal. But if you keep injuring your ears, the damage will be cumulative. You will eventually lose some of your hearing.

That's why the Occupational Safety and Health Administration has established rules governing how much noise workers may be exposed to. When noise exceeds certain levels—more or less the point where people must shout to be heard—workers must wear ear protectors.

But ironically, as the work environment has become quieter, the experts say the home environment has become noisier. You should be wary of the noise made by blenders, vacuum cleaners, dishwashers and power tools. Outdoors, drag races and snowmobiles present extreme dangers. According to one report, deafness and ear disease resulting from snowmobiles is now the biggest public health problem in the Canadian Arctic.

But there's a cheap, easy defense you can mount against noise danger, says Dr. Rupp. "Go to your friendly, local drugstore and get yourself a pair of ear defenders," he advises. "These are soft, flexible little spongelike cylinders that you roll up and put in your ears. I don't even mow my lawn without them."

Use ear protectors.

Take your defenders to concerts, discos, sporting events and other potentially noisy environments. If the noise level doesn't go above a safe 90 decibels (about the level of an alarm clock), you don't need to put them in. But if levels rise, "they provide 30 to 40 decibels of protection for your poor ears," says Dr. Rupp, who found that some Michigan rock concerts registered 120 to 130 literally ear-shattering decibels. Crowds at hockey games have been logged at similar levels.

Special caution should be taken with personal stereos, such as the Walkman says Dr. Lipscomb, because they are such an efficient means of delivering sound to the ear. "But used intelligently, they are a very convenient form of entertainment," he notes.

To Hear Clearly, Feed Your Ears Right

Arteriosclerosis—hardening of the arteries—is another sneak thief of hearing, says Dr. Lipscomb. Painlessly and gradually, it steals your precious sound sense. It may even cause instant deafness if you, as some people do, experience a tiny stroke in the vein structure of the inner ear. In the space of a breath," says Dr. Lipscomb, "you can lose the hearing in one ear."

Eat less saturated fat to help preserve hearing.

Heart attacks, cerebral strokes—these are the well-known risks of hardening of the arteries. But now you have yet another reason to do all the good things for yourself that can help keep plaque from turning your circulatory system into Sludge City.

One way to prevent arteriosclerosis is to reduce the amount of fat in your diet, particularly meat fats like those in beef and pork, and dairy fats like those in whole milk, butter and cheese. If you need to lose a couple of pounds, this reduction should help your weight fall, too. And that's another risk factor subtracted.

A piece of Finnish research compared the hearing of two similar groups over a decade. One group ate a diet high in saturated fat and the other group was given a diet low in saturated fat. No surprise—the low-fat group's hearing was superior. Just to emphasize their point, the researchers then reversed the groups' diets. When they remeasured hearing years later, the group now eating a low saturated fat diet had improved, and the hearing of those now on a diet high in saturated fat had worsened.

Cut down on salt, include fish and fiber in your meal plans and get regular aerobic exercise. And you can double your satisfaction. You're helping your ears stay keen while you're keeping your heart healthy.

One English researcher has discovered a link between progressive deafness and a vitamin D deficiency in certain patients. The *Journal of the Ameri-*

can *Medical Association* reported that some of these patients had improved hearing after treatment with the vitamin. Because older people more often have vitamin D deficits, the English physician who discovered the pattern theorized that a lack of D may be involved in presbycusis. And it certainly can't hurt to make sure you're getting enough. But don't take more than 400 international units of D a day.

Smoke Gets in Your Ears

In 1956, a Commission on Chronic Illnesses said that nicotine might damage hearing. And they noted that this was not a new idea then. Smoking is so toxic to the ear it even hurts the hearing of unborn babies when their mothers smoke, one study has shown.

Some smokers may be familiar with a ringing in their ears following a multi-butt bout. This is the delicate hair cells' cry of protest against a lack of oxygen. And although this form of tinnitus, or ear ringing, will probably stop, you'd do well to take it as a sign to back off from whatever precipitates it. It is, after all, an indication that the hair cells are irritated enough to be firing off on their own. Tinnitus also may result from exposure to noise or drugs, or to certain infections or diseases. Or it may have an origin that's entirely mysterious.

Scientists have had some success in treating tinnitus, a condition that seems to range from the mildly aggravating to the almost maddening. Medication is one way. Some people have found relief wearing a device that masks the sound of the ringing. The masker makes a noise like rushing water. Some severe tinnitus sufferers find this more bearable than their internally generated noise. Sometimes the relief continues for a while even after removing the device. Also under investigation are electrical stimulators which block the ringing temporarily.

You may be able to mask the noise of tinnitus.

"Don't smoke," is Dr. Rupp's simple message to those who would like to reduce their risk of tinnitus and other hazards to the ear. Smoking reduces the amount of oxygen getting to the tiny veins that make your ears work. And a study done in Egypt confirms it: Nonsmokers had better hearing than smokers.

Alcohol also apparently interferes with part of the ears' protective mechanisms—it impedes the muscles in the inner ears that contract the eardrums in the presence of loud noise. Some experts believe alcohol's numbing effect also simply makes you want the music to be louder. The result: You may expose yourself to dangerous levels of sound. And unfortunately, the damage done may be permanent. There is no known method of reversing noise-caused hearing loss.

Alcohol impairs the ears' protective mechanisms.

Facing Up to an Ear Problem

Do people complain that you play the radio and TV too loudly? Do you find yourself muttering that people mumble? Are you missing the punchlines of family jokes and wondering what everybody is laughing about? Do you find yourself making relationship-damaging statements like "I don't listen to the old bat because she doesn't have anything worth saying anyway"?

If so, you may have begun to suspect that you have a hearing impairment. But if you're typical, you're probably involved in a process of denial, trying to convince yourself it isn't true, though deep down in your heart, you know it is. Because hearing loss is generally gradual and physically painless—and extremely unwelcome—almost every victim falls into the denial trap.

Admitting the problem is the beginning of the solution.

But according to Dr. Rupp, people with hearing losses know deep down what their problem is. "These are just psychological ploys they use," he says. "When we get them alone in a testing room, they admit they think they have a hearing problem."

Even though you know in your heart that you have a hearing loss, you may still feel reluctant to seek help. You may see the possibility of having to wear a hearing aid as a sign of old age—though you know it isn't. In fact, doctors now give hearing aids to babies as young as 6 months old when there is early detection of a hearing problem.

A hearing aid is not a badge of old age.

So don't waste years when you could have been enjoying family conversations, listening to TV at normal volume, hearing what the lecturer or minister was saying and not feeling just plain left out.

Glasses that See Sound

"Read my lips!" is a flip way of saying "pay attention." But no matter *how* closely the profoundly deaf may pay attention, it is often impossible to follow a speaker's words. Lipreading simply doesn't offer enough cues to allow full entry to the hearing and speaking world. The word "met," for example, looks exactly like 60 other English words.

But soon there will be a device that helps lipreaders *see* sounds as they are spoken. Eyeglasses, operated by a tiny computer with a microphone, display a phonetic transcription of words spoken to or near the lipreader.

The glasses, which are now being field tested, are the product of 14 years of work by Robert Beadles, director of biomedical engineering at North Carolina's Research Triangle Institute, and Orin Cornett, Ph.D., of Gallaudet College, in Washington, D.C.

The first units may cost about $4,000, but the price could drop to about $1,000, which is approximately the cost of two hearing aids. Not a large price to pay for a device that could revolutionize life for the deaf, giving them full access to the world for the first time.

If you do have a hearing loss, your first step should be in the direction of your doctor's office. The difficulty may be a mechanical one, such as a middle ear problem, which could be medically or surgically reversible. About 5 percent of hearing problems in adults are of this kind. "People are out there walking around who could have their hearing restored in a 25-minute procedure in the surgical suite," says Dr. Rupp.

A lucky few can have hearing restored with a 25-minute operation.

Or your problem may be as simple as impacted ear wax. Impacted ear wax is usually the result of trying to clean your ears yourself with cotton swabs or other implements. Much of the wax is simply pushed up against the drum. Attempts at home removal of wax lead all too often to punctured eardrums. "And this happens more frequently than you might imagine," says one doctor.

Ears clean themselves, say physicians. Little

hairs in your ears face outward and move the wax along to the outer ear. When you use a cotton swab inside the ear, you bend the hairs backwards and push the wax in even further. Moreover, the wax is a protective substance that should be allowed to stay inside your ears, as long as it's not tamped down. It has disease-fighting properties and it also traps dirt.

For the vast majority, the answer to a hearing problem is not surgery or dealing with ear wax. The answer is usually a hearing aid.

How *do* you know what hearing aid is right for you? Should you respond to a newspaper ad placed by a manufacturer? Can you use an aid that's concealed in the earpiece of eyeglasses?

Consult an audiologist.

Hearing aids are expensive and you should get the best help available in choosing the one that will give you top performance. Professional audiologists study for years to be able to do this. Your doctor can recommend one who will be able to help you.

Although hearing aids usually offer the most help with hearing problems, other tools may also make life easier for the hard of hearing and those around them. The deaf will find that many modern theaters and even some churches have listening headsets available. Through an infrared system, the signal—like a radio signal—travels directly to the headset. Similar devices may be used at home, says Dr. Rupp.

Many devices amplify sound, even outside the home.

"For instance, Mrs. Jones does fairly well with her family and friends, but she has trouble with the radio and TV. She can get an infrared unit, occupy her favorite chair and hear the radio and TV as well as if she were 15 inches from the speaker," he says.

A simple microphone and earphones attached to a home stereo can be a terrific boon to the severely deaf and those trying to communicate with them, adds Dr. Rupp. An audiologist can give you more information on this and similar aids, and your local telephone company may have a fairly complete catalog of hearing and listening devices.

If use of a telephone is totally impossible for you, you may also want to see about getting a TDD— a typewriter-like device that transmits over phone wires. The person called must also have a TDD, but more and more offices and businesses do.

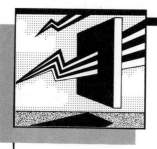

Bionic Hearing

The bionic (or, as the experts like to say, electronic) ear has been born. That's what Karen Berliner, Ph.D., director of clinical research at the famous House Ear Institute, in Los Angeles, says about cochlear implants.

"Medicine, engineering and technology combine to artificially produce stimulation of the auditory system," she says. The implants work by converting sound to electrical stimulation and transmitting it to electrodes surgically implanted in the inner ear. Though the sensing mechanism that feeds the nerve does not function in many deaf people, many nerve fibers often remain healthy.

Intended for use in the profoundly deaf—people with severe to total hearing loss—the implants have been approved by the Food and Drug Administration. About 950 operations have been performed in the United States. Tests of the devices in children are still underway.

Implant recipients who once had normal hearing say the artificial ears are a far cry from a restoration of their lost sense. The implants produce a metallic sound they must work hard to learn to interpret. But the noise does offer enough information to improve their ability to interpret and communicate with the outside world.

Still, Dr. Berliner and others say that the devices' sound quality has already been improved. Newer models offer up to 22 channels. Sometime in the future, they may come far closer to a natural sound. Already, says Dr. Berliner, some star patients have learned to carry on limited telephone conversations. And preliminary results of clinical trials with children from 2 to 18 years old indicate that cochlear implants may help deaf kids learn to communicate more easily with the hearing world.

For more information on cochlear implants, call the National Association for Hearing and Speech Action at 800-638-8255 (301-897-8682 in Maryland) or write to them at 10801 Rockville Pike, MD 20852; or write House Ear Institute, 256 South Lake Street, Los Angeles, CA 90057.

17

The Heart:

New Horizons

for Better Health

Meet Bob and Betty Sloan, a couple in their early fifties, who, between them, average 100 long work hours, a 3-hour commute, two lively teenagers and countless community activities. It's easy to see why they eagerly looked forward to a trip overseas. But news of terrorist activities prompted them to change their plans and opt for what they thought would be a safer summer. They settled in for a season stocked with barbecued steaks, Betty's mouth-watering potato salad, Bob's favorite cigars, frosty pitchers of gin and tonics and hours of sitting comfortably.

Statistically speaking, the Sloans probably would have been safer traveling. For what they failed to do was protect themselves from the nation's number one killer—heart disease—the one that could very well terrorize them in their own home.

"Heart disease lacks the drama associated with other dangers," says James I. Cleeman, M.D, coordinator of the National Cholesterol Education Program, at the National Heart, Lung and Blood Institute, in Bethesda, Maryland. But although heart disease is not sensational, its damage is staggering. Every year it claims 550,000 American lives—or about 1 every *minute*.

Heart disease has grown to be as American as the flag, but that doesn't mean you can't change your stripes when it comes to health. In fact, there has been real progress in reversing this national tragedy. In the past 15 years, there has been nearly a 35 percent reduction in deaths attributed to heart disease. And despite all the fanfare surrounding the awesome artificial hearts, powerful pacemakers and breakthrough bypass surgeries, the truth is, it's not high technology alone that's saving us from our number one enemy. It's us, as well.

According to the results of one study, medical intervention accounted for only 40 percent of the drop in deaths from heart disease, while nearly 55 percent of the lives saved were a result of people adopting healthier habits like eating better, exercising more and smoking less. It appears people are learning that to keep this magnificent muscle functioning well into old age as it was designed to do, they must pay attention to how they live today.

Some people, like Norman Cousins, had to learn this lesson the hard way. Cousins, editor, author and medical faculty member of the University of California at Los Angeles, had a sudden heart attack which scared him sufficiently to examine his life and to later observe: "The human heart is not sealed off from countless processes that take place within the human body. It is a point of culmination, a collection center for all the malfunctions or deficiencies that exist in the body as a whole. It is a zone of infinite vulnerability to all the anguishes and insults and provocations of mind, soul and body."

Cousins began the battle to rearrange his habits in hopes of reconditioning his damaged heart. He began to pay attention to his nutrition, to take long walks and to take time to notice things like ferns unfolding along the way. In the process, he began to notice the heart's ability to "create its own bypass." He marveled at the body's ability to heal and regenerate as the result of "combining diet, exercise and positive attitude." Cousins is a true hero in the struggle against heart disease. Bob and Betty Sloan would do well to follow his shining example, devising their own plan of attack.

Deaths from heart disease have gone down 35 percent in the last 15 years.

One famous author combined diet, exercise and positive attitude to regenerate his heart.

Cholesterol, the Heart of the Matter

The main cause of heart disease is atherosclerosis, a slow buildup of cholesterol and fatty tissue in the arteries. You can compare these arteries to old pipes, which have become encrusted with mineral deposits over the years. A lifetime of abuse can leave the arteries hard and narrow, pinching down on the blood flow. And if blood can't get to the heart, it can mean a heart attack. Or, if blood to the brain is blocked, a stroke may result.

Atherosclerosis can keep blood from flowing freely to the heart and brain.

How do arteries get plugged up? The finger points to fat—the fat found in many of your favorite foods, from cheeseburgers to cherry ice cream cones. Perhaps you think these favorites are just too delicious to give up. If so, try picturing them in a different way.

Picture, for example, the grease left on your plate hours after you've polished off a steak. Now imagine pouring this gunk down your sink. It clogs up your drain, right? Now picture this fat working in a similar fashion in your body.

Fats gum up the bloodstream, robbing your heart of oxygen.

"In the bloodstream, fats gum up the circulation," explains Julian Whitaker, M.D, director of the National Heart and Diabetes Institute and author of *Reversing Heart Disease* (Warner Books). "Just as fat coats your fingers or a frying pan, it coats the red cells and makes them stick together." They clump together and are unable to get through the tiny capillaries single file as they are supposed to do. This clumping reduces the oxygen uptake by as much as 30 percent. And without oxygen, your cells can't live; the heart can't work right.

Fats also play an important role in the manufacture of serum cholesterol—the stuff TV commercials are always talking about. Cholesterol is a waxy, white substance that your liver normally manufactures in just the right amounts to help produce certain hormones and to insulate nerve fibers. You add to your cholesterol cache, though, every time you eat foods rich in cholesterol, like red meat and eggs.

HDL act like blood police—carrying away excess cholesterol.

To make sure that cholesterol is circulated properly throughout the bloodstream, your body wraps it in protein packets. This combination of cholesterol and protein is now called lipoproteins and comes in two types: high density and low density.

The high density lipoproteins (HDL) have been dubbed the good guys, because they take excess cholesterol out of the cells and the lining of the arteries and deliver it to the liver for removal. The low density lipoproteins (LDL) are—you guessed it—the bad guys. They appear to be the culprits that deposit cholesterol on the artery walls.

This process is what prompted the National Institutes of Health (NIH), in Bethesda, Maryland, to conclude that "elevated blood-cholesterol levels is a major cause of coronary-artery disease." This conclusion was the result of a massive study called the Coronary Primary Prevention Trials (CPPT), conducted by the National Heart, Lung and Blood Institute. The study involved following nearly 4,000 men with high cholesterol levels, measured at 265 milligrams (mg) or more per deciliter, for ten years. Some men took cholesterol-lowering drugs while others took placebos, harmless "dummy" pills. It was found that the rate of heart disease among the men who took cholesterol-lowering drugs was nearly 20 percent lower than that of the group that took the placebo.

The equation for a healthy heart is simple: more HDL, less LDL.

Another finding is that you don't need a cholesterol level of 265 to be in trouble. People with cholesterol levels lower than that of the men studied— levels between 210 and 265—experience the most heart attacks. In fact, the risk of heart disease rises significantly when blood cholesterol levels reach a measure of 200. About half of all middle-aged Americans have higher levels and, therefore, are at risk, according to the American Heart Association. To have a healthy heart, says the NIH panel, means a cholesterol reading of not more than 200 mg. You also need to follow one rule: Be careful of the *amount* and *kind* of fat you eat. The proper diet can increase the HDL- and lower the LDL-cholesterol levels in your blood, leading to healthier arteries. Let's look more closely at that heart-saving plan.

Eat for Your Heart's Content

As said, step one is to reduce the amount of fat you eat. There is evidence that a low-fat diet may reverse existing atherosclerosis. Studies with mon-

A low-fat diet may even reverse plaque buildup.

What Sets Off a Heart Attack?

What sparks a sudden heart attack? Researchers are beginning to piece the puzzle together. Based on their findings, if one had to describe the perfect day, here's what it might look like:

Monday Morning. James E. Muller, M.D., Harvard cardiologist, reports that heart attacks seem to have their own sense of timing. Of 847 heart attacks, most occurred between 6 A.M. and noon, the time when arterial pressure and physical activity also increase. Curiously, in one study at the University of Manitoba, 75 percent of all sudden cardiac deaths studied occurred on Monday. Researchers speculated that returning to work after a weekend break might be enough of a psychological stress to touch off an arrhythmia.

The Dead of Winter. Believe it or not, the reason why there are more heart attacks on wintry days isn't because guys are out there shoveling snow. What happens, say some experts, is that while the blood vessels to the skin constrict to conserve body heat, they may also cut off the blood supply to the heart.

A Super Supper. Better make earlier reservations at your favorite restaurant. In one British study, about one-fourth of 100 sudden deaths occurred an hour after eating. What might have happened, says one expert, is that peak digestion probably occurs during deep sleep, when the body is unable to move blood fats through the arteries quickly. If the arteries are already full of fatty deposits, though, these new fats will narrow the arteries even more, and platelets can clump up and clot.

Watching Your Team Lose (or Win). Researchers found that getting emotionally excited can spark erratic rhythms and interfere with your heart's ability to pump blood. Of 117 survivors of arrhythmias, Boston investigators found that nearly one-fourth had some kind of psychological disturbance preceding the attack. But don't sell off your season tickets yet. Stress is usually only acutely dangerous when it's piled on top of years of chronic emotional stress.

keys and other animals have proven that the arterial buildup (plaques) induced by high-cholesterol diets shrinks or disappears when the animals eat less fat and cholesterol.

Does this mean it's time to say farewell to fat? Some experts would strongly suggest it. For most people, though, giving up fats may be easier said than done. A recent survey conducted by the National Health and Nutrition Examination Survey questioned almost 12,000 U.S. adults and found that the leading food offender was hamburger, followed closely by whole milk. That prompted staff nutritionist Bonnie Liebman, of the Center for Science in the Public Interest, to comment: "On a given day, almost 30 percent of the adult population eats a hot dog, ham or lunch meat; 26 percent devours a hamburger, cheeseburger or meat loaf and 23 percent puts away at least one serving of steak or roast beef. No wonder two heart attacks occur each minute in the United States."

Less Is More

When a food pattern is so common, and so much a part of daily life, it may be smart to follow the advice of some experts who suggest reducing, substituting for and alternating—rather than eliminating—certain standard dishes. Hans Fisher, M.D., chairman of the Department of Nutrition at Rutgers University and author of *The Rutgers Guide to Lowering Your Cholesterol* (Warner Books), suggests that you limit eating red meat to three times a week, choose lean cuts and trim away any visible fat before cooking. On alternate days, he says, go for poultry (sans the skin), fish and shellfish, lentils, kidney beans and other protein-rich dried beans and peas. When it comes to dairy products, skim or low-fat milk products, including yogurt, are "much more desirable than those made with whole milk." Try using egg whites or egg substitutes in place of the real thing. Why? Because, says Dr. Fisher, a single large egg contains about 275 mg of cholesterol—and that could blow the recommended daily cholesterol budget of 300 mg.

If you are going to cook with oil, try to use more of the polyunsaturated oils such as safflower, corn and sunflower oil, rather than butter, margarine or lard. Polyunsaturated oils have been proven to lower cholesterol. But don't get carried away. "Fats are fats, regardless of the type, and you should cut back whenever possible," advises Jon Lewis, Ph.D., pathologist at the Bowman Gray School of Medicine, in

Make the dietary conversion by reducing, substituting for and alternating foods high in fat and cholesterol.

Polyunsaturated oils are better than butter or even margarine, because they lower cholesterol.

Winston-Salem, North Carolina. So don't think you can drench your salad with safflower oil just because it's labeled polyunsaturated. And beware of products (like margarine) bearing the term hydrogenated oil. What the manufacturers have done is chemically alter the oil so that it becomes a semisolid. Some research has shown that hydrogenation also may alter the fatty acids into substances which, according to tests on animals, tend to collect in the heart.

A Fish Story

Eat two fish dishes a week.

Perhaps the best thing Bob and Betty Sloan could do to protect their hearts is go easy on the burgers and eat more fish. Researchers have reported that "as little as one or two fish dishes a week" may reduce heart attack risk. Scientists at the Oregon Health Sciences Center, in Portland, have found that fish—especially cold-water fish—contain a class of polyunsaturated fatty acids called omega-3. What these wonder fats do is thin the blood, slow down the potentially dangerous clotting process and inhibit the synthesis of a protein used in the production of fats. In fact, scientists found that adding fish oil to the diet decreased blood cholesterol 27 to 45 percent and triglyceride levels 64 to 79 percent in patients prone to high blood fat levels. Triglycerides are a second type of blood fat, also implicated in heart disease. "No other polyunsaturated oils have been able to get triglycerides to drop in this way," says William S. Harris, Ph.D., an Oregon researcher.

Good sources of this fabulous fat are sardines, salmon, trout, mackerel—and even the lowly canned tuna. In general, ocean fish have more omega-3 than freshwater fish. Shellfish will also provide you with a fair amount. You also can substitute a supplement for fish. Capsules of concentrated marine lipids are available. They supply something called eicosapentaenoic acid (EPA), which is the ingredient in omega-3 fatty acids that makes them heart-savers.

The Magic of Olive Oil

Lovers of Italian food are in for a health treat. The latest word from the lipid labs is that dishes like a Caesar salad (minus the egg yolk) or a plate of spaghetti with clam sauce may be ideal candidates for a healthy-heart cuisine. Why? For one thing, they contain seafood, which is an excellent source of omega-3 fatty acids. But the other ingredient that's causing a stir among scientists is olive oil.

Researcher Scott Grundy, M.D., Ph.D., of the University of Texas Health Science Center, in Dallas, found that monounsaturated fats, which include olive oil, can lower cholesterol in the blood. He devised three liquid diets: a low-fat diet (20 percent fat), a diet high in saturated fat and a third diet high in monounsaturated fat (both containing 40 percent fat). Working with 11 study subjects, he found that the low-fat diet—as expected—lowered cholesterol, and the diet high in saturated fat raised blood fat levels. But the other diet—the one high in monounsaturated fat—did not raise cholesterol levels. It lowered them. In fact, this diet was better in some ways than the low-fat diet. Why? Because the low-fat diet also reduced the amount of "good guy" cholesterol in the blood, whereas the monounsaturated-fat diet did not. Moreover, the low-fat diet raised triglyceride levels whereas the monounsaturated-fat diet did not.

Olive oil has been shown to dramatically lower blood cholesterol levels.

At the end of his study, Dr. Grundy concluded that people may find it easier to live with a diet high in monounsaturated fat than with one that severely restricts fat intake. And that it might be just as beneficial—provided people's weight doesn't change. This former head of the Nutrition Committee of the American Heart Association later told the press, "The kind of very low-fat, high carbohydrate diet favored in the Orient probably just isn't realistic for many Americans." What he suggests instead is a diet where 30 percent of the calories come from fat. Of that, 10 percent or less should come from saturated fat, 10 to 15 percent from monounsaturated fat and the remainder from polyunsaturated fat.

Anti-Cholesterol Cuisine

And so the salmon, it seems, should be sautéed in olive oil. And perhaps served with a side dish of onions. That's right. Studies have shown that onions and garlic contain a sulfurlike compound which stimulates "fibrinolytic activity." That is, they can help break down a fibrous protein that's present in clotting of blood. Or to explain it another way, they

It may not win you friends, but eating onions and garlic can bring you a healthier heart.

make blood platelets less sticky while promoting natural blood chemicals to dissolve clots that have already started to form. What's more, garlic and onions carry off harmful cholesterol. Studies conducted in India showed that people who ate a lot of onion and garlic had healthier levels of blood fats than those who ate just a little. In one of the studies, heart patients fed garlic daily showed significant decreases in cholesterol after eight months. In the United States, studies conducted at St. Elizabeth's Hospital, in Brighton, Massachusetts, uncovered a significant increase in HDL-cholesterol following a daily intake of extract equal to one to two whole onions.

More good news is that you don't have to eat onions or garlic raw. Indian scientist K. K. Sharma reveals that the active substance is not destroyed by heat or water. So next time you hunger for an egg omelet, order yours with plenty of onions.

Here's a rundown of more healthy heart foods:

Fiber for fiber, oats outperform wheat in carrying off cholesterol.

• Our old/new friend fiber. Mama was right. A bellyful of hot oatmeal is healthy. Research shows that oatmeal outperforms other fibers in clearing the blood of cholesterol. That's because oat bran is a water-soluble fiber that surrounds cholesterol molecules in the intestine and carries them out of the body. In a study conducted at the University of Kentucky, when six men ate oat bran muffins every day, their serum cholesterol levels dropped by nearly 10 percent—compared to no drop when they ate wheat bran muffins. Ten percent is more than enough to reduce your risk of heart disease.

• The avocado advantage. If you've been avoiding these buttery-tasting beauties because they contain fat, you may want to reconsider your strategy. You're right, they do contain fat, but 85 percent of their fat content is the *good* kind of fat. In one study, avocados lowered cholesterol levels as much as 43 percent.

• Eggplant anyone? An Austrian scientist found that when he fed some animals eggplant along with cholesterol-rich foods, they appeared to be protected from the buildup of fatty plaques in their blood vessels. Like other kinds of fibrous foods, apparently the eggplant breaks down in the intestine into various components that bind with excess cholesterol and escort it out of the body.

• The promise of magnesium. If you soften drinking water, you may be weakening your ability to overcome a heart attack. Studies have shown that people in hard-water areas have low incidences of sudden death due to an attack. It's believed that magnesium somehow protects the heart muscle from excessive damage after an attack. Magnesium may also dilate the blood vessels. Magnesium works along with calcium for proper muscle functioning, and is best absorbed in the presence of vitamin D and lactose.

If you soften your water you may be removing magnesium, a mineral that strengthens the heart muscle.

• Calcium for a hardy heart. Do you take this mineral to prevent brittle bones? You're in for a bonus—it's probably protecting your heart, too. Studies have found that taking two grams of calcium carbonate daily reduces serum cholesterol and triglycerides.

• Vitamin E will help. Animal studies have shown that vitamin E can inhibit platelet aggregation—the blood cell stickiness that can lead to clots—and also may protect the cells that line the arteries, reducing the risk of arterial buildup.

Eliminating Hurtful Habits

If you've finished your Mediterranean-style mackerel and plan to relax with a glass of chianti and a good smoke—maybe you'd better revise your plan. Heavy drinking (more than two beers, two one-ounce shots of whiskey, etc., a day) and smoking go hand in hand with high blood pressure and being overweight. Separately or combined, these health risks increase the likelihood of developing heart disease.

Ban the Butt

The Marlboro man wouldn't look so tough in the coronary care unit. But that could be his final corral. That little sizzle on the end of a butt is a brand that can mark your heart for slaughter. And if this cowboy comparison seems like a Texan exaggeration, consider these facts: Smoking chokes off the body's supply of prostacyclin, a substance in the

Smoking robs your heart of oxygen and poisons it with carbon monoxide.

blood vessels that prevents artery disease. It also steals the oxygen the heart needs to work, and, in its stead, floods the body with a poisonous gas, carbon monoxide, forcing the heart to beat faster to avoid oxygen starvation.

And that's not all. The arteries begin to degenerate because carbon monoxide prevents the cells lining them from exchanging oxygen.

Fortunately, the damage can be undone. You can reverse your risk of heart attack if you quit now. A report in the *New England Journal of Medicine* included a study by two researchers from the Boston University School of Medicine who found "the risk of myocardial infarction (heart attack) decreases within a few years of quitting to a level similar to that in men who have never smoked."

Watch Your Blood Pressure

It usually has no symptoms. It rarely causes pain. Yet high blood pressure is a serious condition and ranks right up there with high cholesterol and smoking as a leading cause of heart disease. It's estimated that 58 million Americans are hypertensive; that is, their blood pressure measurements are equal to or above 140/90. (The larger figure is the systolic pressure occurring when the heart contracts, while the smaller figure refers to the diastolic pressure when the heart relaxes.) When these increase, you can be at risk for stroke, coronary heart disease or congestive heart failure. High blood pressure also speeds up atherosclerosis and generally overworks the heart. And although it sounds odd, the harder the heart has to work, the weaker it becomes.

If your blood pressure is 140/90 or above, you're at risk for heart disease.

What causes high blood pressure? "For most Americans, an improper diet is the cause and a change in diet is the cure," says Dr. Whitaker. The chief culprits are salt, fat, animal protein and too little potassium. For more information on how to overcome high blood pressure, see chapter 8.

Take Off Pounds

"I can't emphasize enough how important it is to lose weight," says Dr. Grundy, who helped establish the American Heart Association recommendations for preventing heart disease. "Even ten pounds can help in people who are only 20 to 30 percent overweight. Any extra energy [calories] the body has that it doesn't need turns into triglycerides [body fat]. The loose calories floating around in your body that you don't burn up are made into triglycerides."

Where your weight accumulates—either around the beltline or slung around your hips—seems to be a factor in heart attack or stroke. Why? According to Swedish researchers, excess fat cells around the midsection release greater amounts of chemicals harmful to the cardiovascular system than do fat deposits around the hips and thighs. (Yet another good reason to lose the beer belly.)

A beer belly could mean a heart attack is brewing.

Stepping up to Heart Health

Remember Bob Sloan? He was finally convinced that his arteries probably weren't what they should be. So he decided to join the jogging brigade instead of watching them run. He promised himself he'd run a few miles every day, lift weights at night, maybe play a round of tennis on the weekend. But as far as Bob's heart is concerned, he need not work so very hard.

Studies show you don't have to work up a sweat to keep your cholesterol in check.

The latest research is showing that moderate exercise—like walking—may be enough to ease down LDL-cholesterol levels in some people. William P. Follansbee, M.D., of the University of Pittsburgh School of Medicine, studied 30 men exercising at three different rates, ranging from high to low for 20 minutes at a time. Their cholesterol was measured both before and after exercising. Quite unexpectedly, they found that the HDL-cholesterol was raised after low-level exercise just as much as after high-level exercise. Which goes to show that you don't have to get your heart pounding at its peak rate before your body experiences a positive change.

Dr. Follansbee cautions that his study was small and that he only looked at the immediate effects of exercise. More work needs to be done to determine if a regular brisk walk around the neighborhood will prevent heart disease down the road. Still, he believes his findings could be encouraging for those who exercise moderately or haven't yet started.

"The injury rate is low, and it's enjoyable and convenient," says Dr. Follansbee about walking. You can do it throughout the year (try the mall in bad weather), and share the activity with a friend (furry and otherwise). And these are the very keys to sticking to an exercise program for life.

More and more researchers are finding that walking is good for the heart. In one study at Mt. Sinai Medical Center, in New York City, 16 sedentary men were put on a 20-week program, walking four times a week for 40 minutes. At the end of that time, all had lowered resting heart rates. Just how much should you walk? "I advocate walking about 13 miles a week, which is about 4 miles, three times a week," suggests Dr. Follansbee.

Walking isn't the only way to go, though. In a widely reported study, Ralph Paffenbarger, Jr., M.D., of Stanford University, in Stanford, California, has been following nearly 17,000 Harvard alumni from the class of 1920 to 1954. What he has found is that those who had burned 2,500 calories a week throughout their midlife had only about half the risk of a heart attack compared to their sedentary schoolmates.

If the prospect of intense workouts has you breaking out in a cold sweat, cool it. The idea is to adapt an active life-style and find things you can do around the year, rain or shine. Says Steven Blair, P.E.D., of the Institute of Aerobics Research, in Dallas: "Your heart doesn't care how you burn calories, just as long as you burn them."

What if you have had heart disease—is exercise for you? For Ian Martin, a Canadian engineer in his late sixties, running was medicine. About ten years earlier, after undergoing bypass surgery, Ian was told to take it easy, which is often the advice to heart patients. "I wasn't content with having the plumbing fixed—I wanted to better my life," he said. To that end, Martin enrolled in the Toronto Rehabilitation Center headed by renowned cardiologist Terence Kavanagh, M.D., the author of *The Healthy Heart Program* (Rodale Press). It can be said safely that Martin had not only succeeded in his efforts, but triumphed. In 1983 he finished the 26-mile Boston

Walking is no strain, all gain, exercise for your heart.

Regular activities that burn 2,500 calories a week may cut your heart attack risk in half.

marathon, a feat he would have thought impossible before his operation, and one which astonished his doctor even afterwards. " My cholesterol is lowered, my heart rate is lowered, but my all-around health is definitely higher—I don't even get colds much anymore," said Martin at that time.

Ian Martin has passed away. He died, however, of causes other than heart disease. "The autopsy report showed that his coronary arteries were stable, showing no signs of advancing atherosclerosis," says Dr. Kavanagh. "Ian was well liked and respected for his efforts and accomplishments. He devoted himself to everything he did."

Whether exercise will protect against having a heart attack is still unknown. But researchers at the University of Toronto studied more than 600 post-coronary patients who exercised regularly. Compared to heart patients who didn't exercise, they had nearly five times less chance of suffering a second heart attack.

Patients who regularly exercise may greatly improve their chances of avoiding a heart attack.

And what of the horror stories about runners dropping dead in their tracks? It happens, but it's less likely to happen to people who exercise regularly. University of North Carolina investigators found that men who almost never worked out were 56 times more likely to die during vigorous exercise than at other times. Again, the key point is lifelong exercise for a long life.

So Bob is better off starting at a moderate activity, one that suits his life-style and fitness level. And Betty should join him, too. Johns Hopkins Medical Institution researchers found that sedentary women were more likely to have lower HDL-cholesterol and thus more coronary heart disease than women who exercise regularly.

A word of warning: Donning a pair of sweat pants and starting evening strolls are not a license to eat whatever you like or continue smoking. "Exercise is no guarantee against death from sudden heart attacks," reminds Dr. Fisher. It cannot eliminate, only help to mitigate risk factors. But it can be invigorating and possibly life-extending for everybody. Exercise can give a new lease on life even for those whose genes have predestined them for fatal heart attacks.

Exercise is a new lease on life, even for those with a family history of heart disease.

Getting Out of the Stress Mess

Type A. No, that's not an instruction in the Memory Writer owner's manual. It's a *personality* type, a term invented by Meyer Friedman, M.D., who wrote *Type A Behavior and Your Heart* (Fawcett). Type A behavior, explains Dr. Friedman, is "primarily a struggle by an individual who wishes to accomplish too many things in too little time, who exhibits extraordinarily easily aroused anger, irritability when other people do not conform strictly to his ideas of how things should be done." Along with getting your dander up, Type A behavior raises your cholesterol and makes you more vulnerable to heart attacks.

Yet a Type A person is not necessarily doomed to heart disease. In one experiment headed by Dr. Friedman at Mount Zion Hospital and Medical Center, in San Francisco, there was a 50 percent decline in expected repeat attacks among men who changed their Type A ways after having suffered a heart attack.

People who have "hurry sickness" can be cured—and heal their hearts.

"The idea is to change from an AAII to an ASSA," says Dr. Friedman, who is director of the Harold Brunn Institute at Mount Zion Hospital. The first acronym stands for Anger, Aggravation, Impatience and Irritation. The second stands for Acceptance of other people's errors, Self-esteem, Serenity and Affection.

Sounds reasonable enough, but how do you do it? Step one is to recognize Type A behavior in other people. Some examples to watch for are lip clicking, eyes blinking rapidly, deep sighing. Then you can recognize visible signs in yourself. Step two is to substitute pity and compassion for irritation. "In other words," says Dr. Friedman, "if you get stuck behind a slow driver, stop and think instead of getting all worked up. Perhaps he's having car difficulty. Make it a cognitive, not an emotional response." Other tricks include smiling more, eating and talking more slowly, seeking out beautiful things and recalling pleasant memories. Perhaps another component is to change your belief system. Warns Dr. Friedman: "If you believe that Type A behavior is your ticket to the fast track, it will surely lead you down a road of health destruction."

Try to substitute sympathy for irritation.

Hostility Hastens Heart Trouble

But certainly, we've all known hard workers who are not necessarily headed for heart problems. Just exactly what is it about certain personalities that leads to heart disease? Researchers are now closing in on the answer.

Recent evidence suggests that hostility is an even stronger indicator of coronary heart disease than more general Type A behaviors. And this doesn't mean just raging, blow-your-top anger. "Hostility is a general belief that people are more bad than good," explains Redford Williams, M.D., associate professor of medicine at Duke University, in Durham, North Carolina, who evaluated over 400 patients for Type A behavior and hostility and examined their arteries for blockage. His findings? Only half of the patients with low hostility scores had at least one clogged artery, compared with 70 percent of the patients with high hostility scores. Apparently, it's the combination of a hostile attitude and a high level of unexpressed anger—called "anger in"—that more than anything else is seen in people with advanced heart disease.

Some 70 percent of those who were hostile were found to have clogged arteries.

"If you become angry, it mobilizes the free fatty acids, which eventually increases the LDL-cholesterol," explains Theodore Dembroski, Ph.D., professor of psychology and director of the behavioral medicine program at the University of Maryland, in Adelphi. So his solution is to understand *how* you experience anger and short circuit its effects. He suggests that the next time you get angry, evaluate its cause: "Do an instant replay of the situation. Identify just what buttons the other guy pushed." Then reconstruct a healthier response, and try to use that next time.

Learn what pushes your buttons and reconstruct a healthy response.

Tests for the Ticker

How can you tell how much cholesterol you are carrying around? Simple: Get it tested. Better yet, get it tested more than once if necessary. Sometimes there are errors, depending on the method used.

Get two cholesterol readings when necessary to avoid errors.

The latest devices, called finger-stick tests, which measure only total cholesterol at this time, are quick and relatively inexpensive. The tests are still too new for total reliability. But in the future, some may be able to give you a breakdown of your cholesterol count in HDL and LDL levels. What you want to look for is a total cholesterol count that puts you at a low risk for heart disease. Those at a moderate risk for heart disease have a cholesterol count ranging from 170 to 185 for 19- to 20-year-olds; 200 to 220 for 21- to 29-year-olds; 220 to 240 for those age 30 to 39; and 240 to 260 for people 40 years old and older. If your cholesterol count is higher than those found in the ranges that say you are at moderate risk for your age group, you're at high risk. You should have your cholesterol levels evaluated so you can begin a program designed for your health needs.

The following tests can measure your heart health and are recommended, especially if you have a history of heart problems, or if you experience symptoms such as chest pains, shortness of breath or fast or irregular heartbeat.

The ECG. The electrocardiogram, while it can't predict heart disease, can detect damage. It involves attaching metal plates to the skin that amplify the heart's electrical currents, which are then recorded on moving graph paper. The ECG can detect abnormal heart rhythms and warning signals of disease. The ECG is not infallible. Like any other test, it can give false negatives and false positives. But it is helpful in the early evaluation of any heart abnormalities.

Exercise Stress Tests. These are the tests where the patient runs on a treadmill or rides a stationary bike while hooked up to electrodes, which tell if the heart is getting enough oxygen while exercising. If it's not, it may signal blocked arteries. "If you have symptoms of heart disease, it's likely that a positive test (one that shows some sign of heart disease) will be accurate," says one doctor. If you don't have symptoms, there is a higher likelihood that the test will be either false positive or false negative.

The Heredity Check. One of the best predictors of heart disease is heredity. If a scan of your family tree reveals that one of your relatives died of heart problems at an early age, you could be at risk.

A new test developed by Dr. Jennifer Cuthbert, assistant professor in the Department of Internal Medicine, University of Texas Health Science Center, in Dallas, is designed to identify the 1 in 500 persons

Getting up on the treadmill and monitoring your heart can show if it is getting enough oxygen during exercise.

who is born likely to have a heart attack before middle age. The test is based on the discovery that people with inherited high cholesterol (called familial hypercholesterolemia, or FH) have faulty LDL receptors, the substance on the outer membranes of cells that acts as a gatekeeper, removing the cholesterol from blood and pulling it inside cells. What Dr. Cuthbert hopes her test will do is identify people with inherited high blood cholesterol so preventive measures can be started early. But you don't have to wait for the test to pass muster with the Food and Drug Administration (FDA). "If there is a family history of high cholesterol, don't stick your head in the sand," says Dr. Cuthbert.

A new test may identify people with a family history of high cholesterol.

The Chest Medicine in Your Medicine Chest

If you are one of the millions of people with heart problems, an array of drugs is now available to help your heart behave more normally. Some drugs, like digitalis and diuretics, work by draining off the excess fluid that congests and enlarges the heart. Others, like vasodilators, widen the arteries. The beta-blockers can be a blessing to sufferers of angina pectoris because they slow down the heart's rate of contraction, lower its demand for oxygen and widen blood vessels. All heart drugs have some side effects, ranging from headaches to sexual problems. Be sure you get all the information you can about your medication, and make sure your doctor is carefully monitoring you.

An array of drugs help your heart behave normally.

When it comes to the best all-around pill to prevent potentially dangerous blood clots, the award goes to aspirin. Blood cells contain platelets that normally clot or plug holes in broken blood vessels. What aspirin does is keep them from bunching up and sticking to plaques and thus stopping up blood flow. In study after study, such as the one involving over 1,300 men with angina conducted by the Veterans Administration, a daily dose of aspirin reduced their incidence of fatal and nonfatal heart attacks by half.

An aspirin a day may keep blood clots at bay.

That has promoted at least one doctor to prescribe one baby aspirin a day (about 80 mg) for all male patients over 40 whether they have had heart disease or not. Is this safe? Probably not for people with a history of ulcers or an allergy to aspirin.

Heart Repair on the Horizon

Some people have arteries so far gone that, as a last resort, new ones need to be installed. In coronary artery bypass surgery, blood vessels are borrowed from another part of the body, such as the leg, and used to reroute blood around a blocked artery. Still, if your doctor suggests a bypass operation, you should get a second opinion. Experts are now saying

Total Heart Monitoring for the Angina Patient

Thanks to the wonders of technology, scientists have come up with a fashionable way to close in on heart problems. When heart attacks strike suddenly, painlessly and without warning, it's often due to a condition called "silent ischemia," a disruption in blood flow. To stalk this silent killer, a new heart monitor has been designed which alerts patients to problems in blood flow even when no pain is present.

Powered by long-lasting batteries, the monitoring device looks very much like a portable headset radio and is worn in a holster around the shoulder or waist. The monitor is attached to electrode-tipped wires with suction cups that adhere to the chest, and is programmed to record even the slightest disruption in blood flow.

At the onset of abnormal heart activity a soft beep is emitted and written warnings are displayed on a tiny screen indicating that the patient should take medication, stop physical activities or seek a doctor's care.

"Previously, many people might have experienced silent ischemia without knowing it, because there were no visible symptoms," says Carl Pepine, M.D., professor of cardiology at the University of Florida, in Gainesville. "Now that reliable, continuous monitoring is available, treatment for angina patients should be based on eliminating all episodes of ischemia, not just the painful episodes."

that there may be too many of these operations—
and that there's too little evidence that the operation
is worth the risk. Said one doctor recently: "Bypass
surgery has become twentieth-century folk medicine." Investigators at the University of Southern
California School of Medicine found that bypass surgery actually accelerated atherosclerosis in some
cases. "These findings support the view that mini-
mally diseased coronary arteries should not be by-
passed," reported researcher Linda Cashin, M.D.

A safer alternative for choked arteries could
very well be balloon dilatation, or angioplasty
(which means repair of a blood vessel). The procedure involves inserting a tiny catheter tipped with a
balloon into a clogged artery. There, the balloon is
inflated, pushing the sludge of cholesterol, calcium
and blood clots against the walls of the vessel. The
result: A widened artery. Doctors at the University
Hospital, in Zurich, Switzerland (where the technique was first applied in 1977), say that after five
years 20 of their patients remained free of angina
pain. The procedure creates only slight discomfort,
uses local anesthesia and the patient can usually
resume normal activities within a few days. Like all
medical treatments, however, there can be certain
drawbacks. About 5 percent of patients develop
complications which may require more serious surgery. And angina symptoms recur in 25 to 33 percent
of patients. Fortunately, the procedure can be done
again with little additional risk.

Roto-Rooters for Clogged Arteries?

Even more exciting news comes from California
cardiologist John Simpson, M.D., of the Sequoia
Hospital, in Redwood City, California. He has designed a device that shaves the fatty deposits of atherosclerosis from the inner walls of arteries. The
procedure,called transluminal atherectomy, involves
routing a catheter device to the clogged area where,
instead of splitting the plaque and pushing it against
the artery walls, a shaver removes it. Which means,
says a spokesperson for the device, that renarrowing
is less likely to occur. The device awaits clinical trials
and FDA approval, but so far, 43 patients have had
atherectomy with few negative results.

**On the heart repair ho-
rizon: a new device to
scrape away plaque
from narrowed arter-
ies.**

18

Immunity:

Maximum

Power

E very day, every hour, every minute of your life there's a battle for survival going on inside your body. The enemy is an army of invisible germs and viruses that cause colds, flu and any number of other infections and diseases. No matter what your age, you'd have to live in a bubble to avoid being constantly invaded by "bugs" intent on making you miserable. Should you cut your hand, for example, bacteria dive into your body. Shake hands with someone and then touch your nose and some of that person's germs will probably peg you as their new provider. Although these invaders try to set up camp in your body and feed off your tissue, most of the time they are driven off by your immune system.

It sometimes seems that as you get older, the invaders get a little stronger. The fact is, the natural tendency is for the body to get a little weaker with age, requiring you to work harder to keep your immune system in fighting shape.

There are vaccines against a few of the scarier viruses—polio and measles, for example. And it's important for people to continue to have their immunizations as they get older, says William Adler, M.D., of the National Institute on Aging, in Baltimore. These vaccines put the immune system on the alert. But even without vaccines, the body fights back

As you age, you should take steps to keep your immune system in fighting shape.

226

against invasion. Sometimes the white blood cells track down germs and gobble them up. Other times it's the antibodies produced by special cells that destroy the germs. There are even certain proteins called immunoglobulins, complement and interferon, that the cells make just for fighting off viruses, bacteria and other foreign invaders. As if that's not enough, the body is also stocked with fighting white blood cells known as T-cells, B-cells and other cells called—no joke—"killers."

Continue getting immunized as you get older.

"The immune system is strongest during the adolescent stage, and starts deteriorating at about age 30," says Robert Strunk, M.D., an immunologist at the National Jewish Center for Immunology and Respiratory Medicine, in Denver. "It's a gradual deterioration that really starts showing up near age 60, when everything seems to start falling apart."

But not everyone over age 60 experiences a decline in the immune system. "It's not absolutely chronologically related," says Dr. Adler. "That's a good indication that you could reconstitute the immune system if you could capture the factor that keeps certain people's immune system in top shape." Dr. Adler, who heads the clinical immunology section of the Gerontology Research Center at the National Institute on Aging, points to many developments in psychology, immunology, exercise and nutrition that may be the key.

The decline of the immune system can be countered.

The Defensive Diet

One area Dr. Adler is particularly interested in is nutrition. "What you eat is exceedingly important to your immune system," he says. Older people frequently suffer from three main deficits—caloric, vitamin and mineral and protein—that hurt their resistance to disease, says Dr. Adler. He feels that a balanced diet—and simply getting enough food—is essential to keep your body in good enough shape to fight disease.

"The good news," says Robert Edelman, M.D., chief of clinical and epidemiological studies at the National Institute of Allergy and Infectious Diseases, in Bethesda, Maryland, "is that the immune system responds very quickly to adequate nutrition." So, as

You can make dietary changes that have a quick, positive effect.

soon as you start replacing your malnutrition with good nutrition, your immune system will perk up and start defending your body.

The Mineral Zinc

One of the most examined nutritional virus fighters is zinc. It's long been recognized that without zinc, the body's germ-fighting white blood cells malfunction and wounds don't heal. But a group of researchers in Austin, Texas, recently found that zinc may have a positive effect on colds, too.

This story actually began when Austin urban planner George A. Eby gave zinc tablets to his then 3-year-old daughter because he thought it would build her immune system, which was under attack from leukemia. One time the child dissolved a 50-milligram (mg) zinc gluconate tablet in her mouth instead of swallowing it. Within hours, the cold symptoms that also had been plaguing her vanished.

Eby asked his doctor and medical researchers at the Clayton Foundation Biochemical Institute, in Austin, to conduct a test to see whether the lozenges worked on other people. Sixty-five people with colds took part. Thirty-seven were given zinc gluconate tablets every other waking hour, and the rest received a placebo (a fake pill).

The zinc-treated group overcame their symptoms within hours.

The results were almost too good to be true. "In the zinc-treated group, sizable numbers of subjects became asymptomatic within hours," the researchers said. Within a day, one-fifth of the zinc group had recuperated. None of the placebo group recovered that fast. The average length of a cold was 3.9 days in the zinc group, compared to 10.8 days in the placebo group.

But the zinc worked only when it was dissolved like a hard candy instead of swallowed like a pill. That may have been because the zinc ions possibly came into direct contact with the viruses in the respiratory tract.

Zinc seems to keep the virus from multiplying.

"We think that zinc inhibits the cleavage of viral polypeptides," says Donald R. Davis, Ph.D., of the Clayton Foundation, who analyzed the experiment. Zinc ions keep the virus from cloning itself after it hijacks a cell. Whereas this experiment dealt with treating existing colds, not preventing them, Dr. Davis says "it's possible that if your diet is rich in zinc, you would suffer fewer colds."

And there are strong indications that zinc might improve your resistance to other illnesses, too—if your immune system is in a weakened state. At the University of Florida, in Gainesville, Patricia A. Wagner, Ph.D., and her colleagues conducted experiments designed to gauge the impact of zinc on immunity in the elderly.

Dr. Wagner and her associates selected 203 men and women aged 60 to 97, and then checked their zinc status and immune response. They discovered that 22 percent of the subjects were anergic, meaning their immune system was too weak to put up a good fight. And as it turned out, the anergic people were the ones with the lowest zinc levels and the lowest zinc intakes.

After five of the anergic subjects were given 55 mg of zinc per day for four weeks, their resistance rose to standard levels and their immune system rallied to full strength. (Note: Seek your doctor's approval before supplementing your diet with zinc doses this high.)

Other surveys have revealed similar rates of zinc inadequacy, says Dr. Wagner. "Considering such numbers and the positive results we get with zinc supplementation, we should recognize zinc deficiency as a possible cause of immune dysfunction in the elderly," she says.

Vitamin C

Zinc isn't the only nutrient that may help your immunity as you age. According to researchers in Belgium, vitamin C is also essential. Doctors there found that a daily injection of 500 mg of vitamin C significantly bolstered the immune system in a group of people over age 70. The group receiving a placebo shot showed no improvement, say the doctors.

In a similar experiment, the researchers tested a 500-mg oral dose of vitamin C and found that it worked nearly as well as the injected form. They concluded that vitamin C should be considered as a possibly "successful, nontoxic and inexpensive" means of improving the immunity of the elderly.

Vitamin C may beef up the immune system by

Vitamin C increases the speed and efficiency of the defender cells.

boosting the fighting power of lymphocytes that defend the body from invasion. Lymphocytes have a high concentration of vitamin C, and use vitamin C rapidly when fighting infection.

And perhaps vitamin C increases the metabolism of some kinds of lymphocytes, making them react faster, says Benjamin Siegel, Ph.D., a professor of pathology at Oregon Health Sciences University, in Eugene. Or vitamin C may increase the number of what are known as receptor sites on a lymphocyte's membrane, making it easier for the lymphocyte to latch on to a bacterium or virus.

Vitamin C Boosts Interferon. It would be nice to be able to just take injections of interferon, the exotic and terribly expensive chemical that seems to promise so much in the way of immunity—if only scientists could figure out a practical way to produce it. But maybe you don't need to wait for technology to package interferon like insulin. With all the talk about synthesizing interferon and marketing it as a drug, people tend to forget that it is also a natural substance which protects the body against invaders 24 hours a day—for free. Whenever a healthy cell comes under attack by a virus, the cell manufactures interferon and sends it off in all directions to warn neighboring cells to defend themselves.

Once a nearby cell is touched by interferon, it becomes incapable of doing what the virus most wants it to do—convert its nucleus into a virus factory. A cell that's immunized by interferon may still be invaded by a virus, but no new viruses will be born.

Maximize interferon production with vitamin C.

The trick is to maximize the body's production of interferon. All cells are able to produce interferon, but you may be able to give that ability a boost by increasing your intake of vitamin C. Dr. Siegel has found that mice given vitamin C supplements have higher levels of interferon in their blood than mice who receive no extra vitamin C. "It is possible that vitamin C stimulates the increased production of interferon by the affected cell," he says.

The Sunshine Vitamin

Another immune-boosting vitamin is as easy to get as a walk in the sun. A couple of Swedish scientists have confirmed what research first hinted at 50 years ago: Vitamin D deficiency may lead to a deficient immune system. The researchers tested 63 elderly men and women for immune responses and blood levels of vitamin D. By assessing their skin reaction to injections of unfriendly microbes, the researchers determined that 30 percent of the people had weak immune defenses. Blood tests showed that these same people had significantly lower vitamin D levels than the people with normal immunity. In fact, most of the 30 percent were D deficient.

Sunshine can strengthen an aging immune system.

To find out if the lack of vitamin D caused the impaired resistance the scientists chose five of the anergic subjects deficient in vitamin D and gave them daily allotments of either oral vitamin D or ultraviolet radiation. (Ultraviolet light—either from the sun or an artificial source—enables your body to manufacture its own vitamin D.) After two to three months, the five people not only had normal levels of vitamin D but perfectly healthy immune responses as well. A control group of nontreated people, however, wasn't so lucky. Most of the people continued to have a feeble immune response.

If you decide to up your level of vitamin D, just be sure not to spend long periods in the sun. It's been known for a long time that too much exposure to the sun can result in bad burns, premature aging and even skin cancer.

The Mineral Iron

Iron may also help make your immune system as tough as nails. "Researchers have known for a long time that iron is important to our ability to ward off infections. But how it operates is still being worked out," says Jose I. Santos, M.D., assistant professor of pediatrics and pathology at Boston University School of Medicine.

White blood cells called phagocytes, which are the body's primary defense mechanism against bacterial infections, depend on iron-containing enzymes to do their job, says Dr. Santos. These cells engulf bacteria and digest them with corrosive substances called oxidants. "Certainly iron deficiency is going to directly impede this process," says Dr. Santos.

The cells that fight bacteria need iron to do their job.

Other white blood cells, known as lymphocytes, need iron even more. "Lymphocytes need iron for energy metabolism and for the production of enzymes important to their very specialized roles in the immune response," says Dr. Santos. The production of antibodies also requires iron-dependent enzymes, he adds.

And so, it seems, the more iron the better, when it comes to fighting infections. However, life is never so simple. Germs—especially bacteria—benefit from the presence of iron in the body. Paradoxically, low blood levels of iron, therefore, are beneficial in resisting bacterial infections. But the exact opposite is true where viral infections are concerned. Viruses also need iron to multiply, but cannot garner it the way bacteria do. "Most viral diseases, including genital herpes, may become worse with iron deficiency," says Dr. Santos. This is not surprising, since lymphocytes, the major defense against viral infections, also need iron for optimal activity. "Faced with a viral infection, the best thing we can do is keep our iron levels up," Dr. Santos says. Here's how to do it.

Getting Enough Iron. There are two kinds of iron, heme and nonheme. Heme, found only in beef, chicken, fish and other meats, is the easiest to absorb. Liver is the best source of this iron. A three-ounce serving has 7.5 mg iron; sirloin steak, 2.5 mg; chicken, .9 mg and white fish, like flounder, 1.2 mg. About 95 percent of the body's iron comes in nonheme form in vegetables and grains—and also in meats, especially liver.

The availability of nonheme iron is influenced by what you eat along with it. Both the amino acids in meats and the vitamin C in any food can more than double the amount of iron the body can absorb, says James D. Cook, M.D., of the University of Kansas Medical Center, in Kansas City. Consider this unusual fact: The addition of papaya juice containing 66 mg of vitamin C to a meal of corn boosts iron absorption by 500 percent.

Other foods are notoriously unwilling to let you absorb iron. Tea inhibits absorption by 64 percent; coffee by 40 percent. There has been much conflicting information about how badly soy inhibits iron absorption. "Soy protein does inhibit iron absorption by 70 to 80 percent," Dr. Cook says. "But if you're

Those that fight viruses need iron, too.

Vitamin C can double the amount of iron the body absorbs.

adding it to a meal rather than using it to replace meat proteins, it has more than enough of its own iron to offset the inhibiting effect."

Fiber doesn't deserve the bad reputation it's gotten about iron absorption, either. Fiber isn't enough of an iron inhibitor—and has too many other good things going for it—to be concerned about its slight blocking effect, Dr. Cook says.

Calcium tablets should not be taken with iron, Dr. Cook says, since inorganic calcium compounds are potent iron blockers. And taking iron as part of a multivitamin may not be a good idea, because iron will bind with many of the ingredients. The absorbed fraction of a 65-mg iron supplement may drop from 8.1 mg when taken alone to 1.8 mg when taken as part of a multivitamin that contains calcium, reports Gabe Mirkin, M.D., of Georgetown University School of Medicine, in Washington, D.C. For maximum absorption, take iron tablets between meals, with vitamin C.

If you take an iron supplement, take it between meals, with vitamin C.

And get vitamin C with every meal. Tomato sauce that has simmered long in an iron pot is great because it has vitamin C, and iron from the cooking pot. (Simply cooking spaghetti sauce for three hours in an iron pot increases the sauce's iron content to almost 30 times what it would be if it were prepared in glassware.) Mexican cuisine, which uses a little beef with plenty of beans, rice and red chilies, makes the most of each bit of iron.

Fire Power

While it's not the fiery nature of Mexican food that helps you, a little heat doesn't hurt when it comes to helping your immune system fight infection. Body heat is a built-in virus fighter. Both flu viruses and cold viruses flourish when the temperature is between 86° and 95°F, but die quickly at higher temperatures. The body core temperature is too hot for them, but the nasal passages, cooled by inhalation of air, are just right. But when the nostrils are burning with fever, the viruses shrivel up and die.

Here's how the fever works. When viruses or bacteria invade the body, the germ-fighting white blood cells release a protein called pyrogen, which in Greek means "heat-producing." Pyrogen tells the brain to raise the body's temperature from 98.6° to

When your temperature goes up, the number of viruses goes down.

about 102°F. Experiments with animals have shown that when the temperature in the body goes up, the number of live viruses in the nasal passages goes down.

Fever—as lots of wishful truants will tell you—can't be produced on demand. Other methods for heating up the nose and throat will have to be found. A steam bath followed by a hot toddy is one traditional cure. Inhaling warm water vapor is another.

Exercise

And physical exercise is perhaps the most natural warm-up of all. One researcher has suggested that regular exercise promotes the release of pyrogen, which keeps the body temperature high for several hours after the workout is over.

Exercise may be helpful in other ways. Researchers at Purdue University, in Lafayette, Indiana, and the University of Arizona, in Tucson, have examined the twin effects of exercise and vitamin supplements on immunity. They found that vitamins C and E were important in improving immune function, and that exercise strongly augmented these effects.

Exercise, too, can put the heat on "the bug."

The researchers subjected a group of volunteers to a four-month regimen of vitamin C and E, or an 1½-hour workout three times a week, or both vitamins and workouts or neither one. Throughout the study period, they kept tabs on their subjects' immunological strength by measuring infection-fighting T-cells in their blood.

"There was a significant effect of vitamin supplementation with the high-fit group compared to the low-fit group in terms of increase in percent of T-cells," they report. "However, the high-fit group had higher mitogenesis [T-cell production] regardless of supplementation. Apparently both physical conditioning and high intake of vitamins can stimulate cellular immune functions in adults."

Power of the Mind

Here's some news that might improve your social life—and leave you feeling well enough to enjoy it. People who have friends they can turn to in times of stress have more resistance to viral infections than people who are lonely.

A group of psychologists in England wanted to find what effect the emotional events in a person's life have on the severity of colds. So they recruited 52 men and women and gave them a battery of psychological tests and personality inventories.

Then each volunteer was infected with a cold virus and confined to a hospital ward for ten days. The result was that people who were outgoing and extroverted had a milder cold than people who were introverted. And it appeared that people who had recently withdrawn from their friends and hobbies had the worst cold symptoms of all. But the clearest finding was that people who had gone through the most drastic life changes—either for better or for worse—had the highest virus level in their respiratory tract and therefore the worst infection.

Outgoing people seem more resistant to disease.

Another study found that friendships can contribute to a healthy immune system. This study compared dental students' personality with their ability to produce infection-fighting substances called immunoglobulins, and found that warm relationships can be your immune system's best friend. The students who were characterized by a great need to establish and maintain warm personal friendships secreted more of the immunoglobulins than all other students, the study concluded. Those in the study who showed aggressive tendencies, on the other hand, secreted the least of these disease fighters.

The hazards of loneliness can increase when they are combined with stress, according to researchers at Ohio State University, in Columbus. They studied 30 residents of a retirement home. One-third of the people received relaxation training three times a week, one-third received individual "social contact" three times a week and the final third had no contact with the researchers.

Those who learned to relax, it turned out, experienced a 32 percent rise in their white blood cell levels. Those who had social contact enjoyed an 18 percent rise. People in the no-contact group suffered a 6 percent loss of white blood cells, and showed the least resistance to herpes virus infections.

Handling stress also helps to fight disease.

Stress by itself can be harmful, too. Some stress can be good—the kind that challenges and motivates you, for example. But stress that frustrates and limits you can be bad for your immune system. That was the verdict reached by scientists who found that rats subjected to electrical shocks that they could not control wound up with weakened immune systems, whereas rats subjected to shocks that they could control did not suffer impaired resistance. These results led the researchers to speculate that hope is an important ingredient in resisting disease, and that the opposite of hope—hopelessness—can actually weaken the body's ability to fight illness.

The First Line of Defense

Now that you know how to get maximum immunity within your body, you should learn how to prevent the germs and bacteria from getting into your system in the first place. Here are some tips from the experts:

Keep your hands away from your eyes and nose.

• Cold germs are most often spread when someone rubs his nose or eye after touching an infected person's hand, especially if the infected person has just touched his nose. Keep your hands away from your nose to avoid spreading colds. (Coughing and sneezing are definite signs of a cold, but they are much less likely to pass a cold from one person to another. Sneezes and coughs contain very little virus.)

• Taking aspirin reduces the symptoms of a cold, but increases the number of viruses in the nose. If you take aspirin, be extra careful not to touch your nose.

• Wait to show affection to sniffling loved ones. Cold germs are most communicable in their early stages, so if someone you want to hold has a cold, stifle your desire for a few days until the germs have had a chance to lose some of their power.

Rinse your hands to wash away viruses.

• Merely rinsing your hands under water for 30 seconds effectively washes away any viruses that might be on them.

• Don't worry about venturing out into the wintry weather. There's no evidence that cold weather alone will give you a virus infection or even worsen the one you already have.

• Breathe through your nose, not your mouth, so the nasal hairs can filter out some of the 20 billion particles of foreign matter the average person inhales daily.

• Grow a beard. Sexist, but true. "The cold virus is a filterable virus," says Florida physician Sinet M. Simon, M.D., "and the hairs of the beard act as a filter." In 40 years of general practice, Dr. Simon has seen about 70 percent of his bearded patients weather cold and flu seasons without as much as a sniffle.

• Humidify your house. Around 30 to 40 percent humidity is recommended. During the winter many heating systems keep home environments too dry. This can dry out the moist lining of the nose and respiratory passages, your first line of defense, making them more susceptible to viral invasion.

• Avoid tobacco smoke. The nicotine and tars in tobacco smoke dry and irritate the lining of the nose and respiratory passages in much the same way as dry indoor air, and with much the same result.

• Obviously, you shouldn't smoke. Not only can smoking decrease levels of vitamin C in your system, it can also dry and irritate the linings of your respiratory passages, thus cracking them and opening them up to infection.

These guidelines can be a great help. Because no matter how strong your immune system is, it needs the same TLC as the rest of your body. Keeping the invaders out in the first place makes the immune system's job that much easier.

19

Kidney Stones:

Prevention

and Treatment

The pain of kidney stones begins in the back and moves down.

I magine a snake eating a porcupine. Think of the pain as the razor-spiked critter slowly moves through the witless snake's long body.

Not a pretty picture.

But it's a good way to dramatize what it's like to pass a kidney stone.

"The severe pain caused by kidney stones has been described as one of the worst agonies a person can endure," says Peter D. Fugelso, M.D., a urologist who serves as director of kidney stone service at St. Joseph Medical Center, in Burbank, California. "The agonizing pain can last up to several hours. It usually begins in the side and back, in the region of the kidneys, and gradually works its way down as the stone moves from the narrow ureter towards the bladder."

Obviously, this condition is not something you need in your life. For those of you who have never been troubled by kidney stones, but would like to prevent their formation in the future, here are some quick tips: One way to reduce the chance of kidney stones is to follow these simple dietary guidelines. Go light on meat, fat and sugar, and heavy on whole grains, vegetables and fruit. Make a special effort to include foods that are rich in vitamin B$_6$ and magnesium, and always be sure to drink plenty of water.

For those of you who know the pain of kidney stones, have a family history of them or are still reeling from the snake/porcupine analogy and want to make doubly certain that you avoid such misery, here is a lifetime plan for preventing and treating kidney stones.

If kidney stones run in your family, you need a plan to prevent them.

Making Dietary Changes

What's this internal "porcupine" made out of? Mostly calcium and a salt known as oxalate. The problem starts when these two band together and form a crystal. They recruit other calcium oxalate crystals to form a stone, complete with jagged edges. The bonding process often starts when there's not enough body fluid or when the fluid contains so much calcium and oxalate that they cannot dissolve. Instead, they combine. How do you prevent this problem? As Elizabeth Barrett Browning said, "Let me count the ways."

If you can fight fire with fire, you also can fight mineral with mineral. And, for kidney stones, a key mineral may be magnesium—a remedy that's been used for nearly 300 years. More recently, its effectiveness was reconfirmed by Swedish researchers, who found magnesium to be remarkably effective in helping to prevent kidney stones in 55 people prone to forming them. After being treated with magnesium for two to four years, only 8 individuals reported new stones. As a group, the average recurrence rate fell by 90 percent. Scientists speculate that magnesium works because it—like calcium—can bond with oxalate.

Magnesium can be an important weapon against painful kidney stones.

When calcium and magnesium are both present in the urine, they compete with each other to link up with oxalate. The critical difference is that the magnesium/oxalate bond is less likely to form crystals, and more likely to leave the body painlessly in the urine.

Where can you find such a magic mineral? Right in your kitchen. Magnesium is found in soy and buckwheat flour, black-eyed peas, nuts, tofu, kidney beans, lima beans, bananas and shredded wheat.

Three 100-mg doses of magnesium oxide per day have been proven effective in laboratory studies.

Stanley Gershoff, Ph.D., of Tufts University, in Medford, Massachusetts, reported that in his studies, 300 mg of magnesium oxide taken in three doses of 100 mg every day seemed to have a "profound" effect in preventing the formation of calcium oxalate kidney stones.

Another way to counter the one-two of calcium/oxalate, say some doctors, is to increase the amount of vitamin B_6 in your diet. Researchers say B_6 lowers the amount of oxalate in the urine of people who have a disposition toward kidney stones. In India, scientists found that a supplement of only 10 mg a day lowered the oxalate content of urine significantly in test subjects.

Vitamin B_6 is abundant in salmon, beef liver, chicken liver, sunflower seeds, the white meat of chicken, chick-peas, navy beans and brown rice.

Avoid foods high in oxalates, like tea, chocolate and peanuts.

In addition to eating foods high in magnesium and vitamin B_6, also manipulate your diet to decrease the amount of oxalate you put into your body. Foods high in oxalates include spinach, rhubarb, tea, chocolate, parsley and peanuts.

Potassium citrate, a fairly new drug, also prevents kidney stones.

It's also possible to prevent the formation of certain calcium-containing kidney stones by taking a drug, potassium citrate, which was developed at the University of Texas Health Science Center, in Dallas, by noted kidney stone expert Charles Y. C. Pak, M.D. Potassium citrate, a natural component of orange juice, was recently approved as a kidney stone inhibitor by the Food and Drug Administration, and is now available by prescription. Why not just drink orange juice? According to Dr. Pak, you'd have to drink a quart a day to get enough potassium citrate. In that quantity, you'd also be getting a lot of calories and a lot of sugar and calcium—two components of orange juice that can *raise* urinary calcium. Also available are prescription drugs from the thiazide family. They are often the first-choice treatment for kidney stones that don't respond to more conservative therapies. They help prevent kidney stones (and also lower blood pressure) by increasing the output of urine from the body. The trouble is, like many drugs, they have possible side effects, including nausea, dizziness, hives, muscle spasm, weakness and restlessness.

Relief for Stones

If it's too late to talk about preventing stones because you already have one, you are not necessarily between the stone and the hard place. Some options still are available before you submit to the most traumatic one—surgery.

The simplest and most economical thing to try is water. And persevering with this most natural cure often provides the best results.

"Water is the best and safest treatment for most patients," says William D. Kaehny, M.D., of the University of Colorado, in Boulder. Dr. Kaehny says those with kidney stones should drink enough water to produce two to three quarts of urine a day. He also advises patients to set an alarm clock to wake them in the middle of the night so they can pass the water from the day and drink more for the morning.

Urologists recommend that susceptible patients drink plenty of water.

Another option is a new treatment called the "Perc" procedure. It combines microsurgical techniques with an even more advanced form of ultrasonic sound waves. It has made surgical removal of stones from the kidney a thing of the past. "Perc" stands for percutaneous ultrasonic lithotripsy, which is Latin for "pulverization of the stone through the skin." During the operation, a small, three-eighth-inch channel is made through the skin into the kidney. The doctor uses a pencil-sized probe containing fiber-optic lighting and a cystoscope that provides a clear view of the stone. Once located, the stone is broken apart with the high frequency ultrasound vibrations the probe emits. An irrigation system then flushes out the stone fragments.

One new technique eliminates stones in less than one hour.

"The entire procedure usually takes about 45 minutes," says Dr. Fugelso. "The patient feels little postoperative pain and is generally discharged from the hospital in three to five days. By using this simple and almost painless method, patients are saved from considerable discomfort, expense, risk and convalescent time. The ultrasonic stone-crushing technique can be performed at one-third to one-fourth the cost of traditional surgery and at less risk and disability than has previously been possible."

For those close to a major hospital or medical school, the ultrasonic method has been further ad-

The Pulverizing Pool

The President and Congress may debate the need for space-age weaponry, but in the medical world, such space-age techniques are more readily accepted. One of the newest weapons is used to battle kidney stones. German scientists have developed a machine called an "extracorporeal shock wave lithotripter" (ESWL) that uses shock waves to pulverize kidney stones the way ray guns blast apart asteroids. The $2 million device consists of a big immersion tub filled with water, into which the patient, resting in a special body support, is lowered. Shock waves are transmitted through the water and focused on the kidney stones in the patient's body. Doctors watch moving x-ray pictures on monitors as the painful stones are pulverized. The procedure does not involve any incisions, and patients are discharged from the hospital in three days instead of seven to ten.

By 1984, nearly 2,000 patients had been successfully treated by this technique in Munich, Germany, plus an additional 2,000 in the United States. The machines were originally tested in the period of 1983 to 1984 at New York Hospital-Cornell Medical Center, in New York City, as well as at Massachusetts General Hospital, in Boston; Methodist Hospital, in Indianapolis; Methodist Hospital, in Houston; the University of Virginia, in Charlottesville and the University of Florida, in Gainesville. The success of these tests has led to Food and Drug Administration approval.

Another new treatment eliminates surgery altogether.

vanced to include an immersion tank that eliminates the need for any incisions. (See the box above for more information.)

Surgical Removal

"Star Trek"'s doctor, "Bones" McCoy, once described surgery as "the process of cutting and sewing people like garments." He, of course, was speaking from the fictional future, where such "primitive" treatments were completely unknown. Unfortunately, it's still the age of scalpel and suture. Moreover, the cutting and sewing process is especially traumatic when removing stones from the kidneys.

"There are now about 100 of the lithotripters located in the United States," says Peter D. Fugelso, M.D., who uses one at St. Joseph Hospital, in Burbank, California. "They are the absolute state-of-the-art in kidney stone treatment, and will be for years to come."

Birdwell Finlayson, M.D., who headed the team of doctors who tested the lithotripter at the University of Florida, says that about 85 percent of kidney stone patients can be treated with the high energy shock waves, although some people may need more than one treatment to completely disintegrate large or multiple stone formation.

"The good news is that shock wave therapy to the kidney causes no significant damage to the kidneys or to other organs and tissues," Dr. Finlayson says. "However, the location of the stone and its crystalline formation may affect its susceptibility to fracture. We find the more brittle, ceramiclike stones easier to pulverize with shock waves, while uric acid stones and cystine stones are more difficult to disintegrate. And the stones must be located above the bony pelvis in order to be treated with the ESWL."

Dr. Fugelso says those whose stones aren't completely broken up by the ESWL, or whose stones are located below the pelvis, can combine the immersion tub treatment with the percutaneous ultrasonic lithotripsy, a pencil-sized probe that directly pinpoints the ultrasound vibrations onto the stone.

"By combining these techniques, we are able to treat virtually 100 percent of kidney stone patients without resorting to the traumatic effects of open surgery," Dr. Fugelso says.

This surgery involves slicing through the back and into the kidney, then cutting open the organ and plucking out the stone. The operation can cause a growth of scar tissue in the kidney that may cause the organ to fail.

Even without complications, the surgery is no picnic.

"Traditional surgery requires a long (at least ten inches), deep incision across the back, below the patient's rib cage," Dr. Fugelso explains. "Afterwards, in addition to considerable pain, the patient has to be hospitalized for up to 2 weeks and must restrict physical activity for 6 to 12 weeks. Many doctors are still doing this, but with the advances

Today, traditional surgery is almost never called for.

we've made, there are almost no indications for open surgery anymore. I haven't done an open procedure since 1983. I would strongly suggest considering all the alternatives before undergoing this surgery."

Preventing Recurrence

The trouble with kidney stones is that if you've had one, you're likely to have more. Although dietary changes and drinking lots of water can help prevent a recurrence, even these changes may not work for some specific cases.

What to do? Dr. Pak recommends that you find out the type of stone you passed. "Some dietary modifications should not be made universally, but selectively applied according to the cause of the stone. An inappropriate dietary change may be ineffective or may cause harm," he says.

You need to know the chemical makeup of your kidney stone.

Antacids and alcohol may contribute to the production of kidney stones.

Those who are stone-prone also may want to limit the use of magnesium trisilicate antacids and alcohol. John H. Farrer, M.D., and Jacob Rajfer, M.D., of the University of California at Los Angeles School of Medicine, say that a case study has led them to believe that long-term use of antacids containing magnesium trisilicate may cause *silicate* kidney stones. And in Europe, Austrian doctors who studied more than 350 kidney stone patients discovered that a diet high in protein and wheat products together with alcoholic beverages created an imbalance that could lead to kidney stones.

20

Medications

for a Healthy

Life

As you watch Frank, age 77, walking the ten blocks to the market and back, you'd never guess he had congestive heart failure or that bronchitis had made breathing barely possible for many years. "Medications have been a lifesaver for Dad," says his daughter. Frank takes one drug to open up his lungs and another to eliminate the fluid from his chest that was nearly drowning his heart. "The first drug allows Dad to walk around without being winded." As for the second one? Without that, she says, "Dad wouldn't be able to walk around, period."

Without aspirin to free her arthritic fingers, Wanda K. wouldn't be able to create the award-winning quilts she proudly displays in her Florida home. Nor would thousands of adults be able to function in the work world without antibiotics to fight bacterial infection or medications to relieve cold symptoms.

It's easy to see how drugs can be a tremendous health resource. "The whole idea behind most medications is to keep us functioning and independent," says Joseph M. Scavone, Pharm.D., associate professor at Tufts University School of Medicine, in Medford, Massachusetts. That aspect is especially important as you get older, because medications not only

Medications can make you more mobile and keep you functioning independently.

245

control chronic conditions, but also prevent disabling diseases in the first place. The status of the humble aspirin, for example, was recently elevated when the Food and Drug Administration (FDA) approved it as a drug to prevent heart attacks in certain high-risk individuals. What's more, the Centers for Disease Control, in Atlanta, maintain that most people over 65 could be spared the sometimes fatal consequences of the flu just by making sure they get a vaccine when November rolls around each year. The shot is particularly necessary for older people because they are at greater risk for having severe complications following a flu attack, explains nurse/epidemiologist Nancy Arden, R.N., of the Centers for Disease Control, in Atlanta, Georgia.

In fact, you are likely to need—and use—a greater variety of medications as you age. That's why Peter Lamy, Ph.D., director of the Center for Study of Pharmacy and Therapeutics for the Elderly, in Baltimore, says "the time to start learning about these treatment tools is now." *Learning* is the key. Because what you don't know *can* hurt you. Particularly what you don't know about a pill.

Preventing Side Effects

Anyone who takes medication—be it prescription or over-the-counter—can run the risk of having an adverse drug reaction, a "side effect." Drugs might produce a twinge of nausea, a case of diarrhea or a rash on your neck. Medications that treat the heart or the central nervous system may also adversely affect your memory or appetite, or cause your libido to take a dive. And sometimes your adverse reaction might land you in the hospital.

If you don't know how to use them, all drugs are potentially dangerous—even aspirin.

Why do side effects occur? In many cases you can place the blame on the pharmacological makeup of the drug itself: One drug can have many effects on the body. Some of these effects are desirable and some are not. Other times, a quirk or weakness in an individual physical makeup sparks a side effect: A cold tablet may cause drowsiness in some people and not in others.

In other cases, you can blame side effects on your doctor, who may neglect to prescribe drugs according to your individual weight, sex or history of allergic reactions. Many doctors are unaware, for example, of how aging can alter the effects of drugs. "Unfortunately, some physicians choose incorrect medications, prescribe too much of them or combine drugs that are not compatible with each other," reports Jerry Avorn, M.D., associate professor in the Division on Aging at Harvard Medical School, in Cambridge, Massachusetts. What happens then? You can end up with a side effect like depression or confusion, which your doctor may try to cure by prescribing yet another drug. To add insult to injury, doctors may fail to tell you about side effects. In a survey conducted by the American Association of Retired Persons, more than 50 percent of the respondents said their doctors did not always inform them about side effects.

After everything is said and done, though, much of the responsibility for side effects rests with you. Half of all people who take prescription drugs don't use them correctly, according to Craig Burrell, M.D., a vice-president of Sandoz Corporation's Pharmaceuticals Division. They take too much medication or not enough. They take doses at the wrong time of day in the wrong sequence. Sometimes they take someone else's drugs or never get the prescription filled in the first place.

Half of all people who take prescription drugs use them incorrectly.

Who is most prone to making these mistakes? Most notably, people taking drugs for diabetes, hypertension or cardiovascular disease. And it seems the older people get, the riskier it is for them to take medication. Other factors add to the confusion, as well. For example, doctors actually spend less time talking about medications with older patients than with younger patients. A hearing loss may cause misunderstanding of a medication schedule, and poor eyesight can make a label unreadable. The costs of some drugs seem prohibitive for those on a fixed income, leading people to hoard their supply or swap with friends. Then, too, stiffened fingers make struggling with a pill vial nearly impossible. Is it any wonder that taking medications soon becomes more of a bother than a relief?

But a more significant factor, explains Dr. Lamy, is an unwanted side effect that occurs when two drugs are unintentionally mixed. Chances are good that an older person is taking a number of drugs to treat a number of acute and chronic conditions—some experts place the number at four to eight drugs a day, each with its own dosage schedule. Keeping them straight can be confusing.

New Safeguards against Side Effects

Much is being done to protect you from side effects. For one thing, a whole new branch of pharmacology called pharmacokinetics is emerging to help identify how age differences affect absorption, distribution and elimination of drugs. As people get older, explains Dr. Scavone, they have less body water and less muscle and bone, which means drugs don't get distributed as well. And as kidney and liver function decline, the body can't eliminate the drug as quickly as when it was younger. It's the liver and kidney function that determine the half-life of drugs, or the time it takes to clear half of the drug from the body. In a 20-year-old, for example, the half-life of a sedative like Valium is about 20 hours. In someone over 65, it's 90 hours. Following the standard dosage schedule, an older person could be groggy for as long as he or she took the prescription.

Most dosages are based on tests using 30-year-old men, and are hardly tailored to the needs of older people. Testing is about to change, reports Robert Temple, M.D., director of the Office of Drug Research and Review at the Food and Drug Administration. "We have proposed that pharmacokinetic testing for drugs (those affected by a person's age) now include the elderly." Adds Dr. Scavone, "Hopefully, what will emerge from these tests are new drugs with shorter half-lives."

In addition to more sensible testing, you can also expect to see more sensible drugs, developed to have fewer side effects and to be simple and convenient to use. Coming soon to a doctor near you might be medication you can wear. That's right. Small patches left in place on your skin are now being used to deliver nitroglycerin to control angina. The plus for the patches, says Dr. Scavone, is that a patient can receive a constant delivery of the drug but in lower amounts, and therefore with less severe

A new science shows how age affects the way a drug acts.

Expect new drugs that are safer and more effective.

side effects. Another new trend in treatment is to place medication under the tongue. Drug doses delivered "sublingually" go directly into the bloodstream, thereby bypassing the liver and sidestepping side effects.

Charting changes in your personal biological rhythms may be yet another way to make sure you get just the right dose. "Noting what time of day your joints stiffen could provide a clue as to when the best time may be to take an arthritis medication," explains Dr. Lamy.

What's important about these developments is that they are the first step towards customizing drugs based on your body's changes. "Customizing is the key to preventing side effects," says Darrell Abernethy, M.D., Ph.D., associate professor of medicine at Baylor College of Medicine, in Houston, Texas.

Customizing medications can help to prevent side effects.

Safe Drug-Taking Starts in the Doctor's Office

Don't underestimate the importance of your relationship with your doctor for preventing side effects, stresses Dr. Avorn. "If you aren't comfortable with your physician and can't exchange information in a down-to-earth way, you may not feel comfortable about following his or her directions about drugs." Moreover, having faith in your doctor may be a factor in whether you heal or not. "We know that any treatment is likely to be successful if the patient has a great deal of faith in his physician's ability," writes Herbert Benson, M.D., associate professor of medicine, at Harvard Medical School, in *Beyond the Relaxation Response* (Times Books).

Faith in your doctor may boost a drug's effects and help you heal.

To spare yourself from side effects, make sure your doctor offers you information about drugs he prescribes. When your physician pulls out the prescription pad, you pull out your list of questions. At the top of this list, suggests Dr. Benson, should be the question, "Is this drug necessary?" In other words, ask as diplomatically as you can if there might be nondrug approaches. This question is especially important to ask if psychoactive drugs are prescribed. Mind-altering drugs are often given in an attempt to relieve the effects of such life problems as isolation, loneliness or loss. Instead of automatically considering drugs as the only option, says Dr. Avorn, making social contacts or developing new interests should be considered whenever possible.

Learning What You Need to Know

If your doctor says you do need medication, Dr. Benson suggests you then ask, "Might I get along with less of it each time I take it? Or how about taking it for a shorter period of time?" It's also wise to ask for a trial-size dose to try out so you can report the results back to your doctor.

Question number two should always be, "Is the drug right for me?" Is your doctor taking into account your age, weight, and history of allergic reactions? Is your dose the lowest possible? Has your lifestyle been considered? If you have an active life, for example, taking a diuretic several times a day could seriously cramp your style.

Your age, weight, lifestyle and allergies affect the doctor's choice of drugs.

Ask your physician and pharmacist to explain the side effects and interactions for every drug prescribed. How will it react with food and beverages? What will it do to your nutrition? Will the drug interfere with driving or operating machinery? Some drugs produce a reaction with prolonged exposure to sunlight. Other drugs, like diuretics, can dehydrate you in a heat wave. Did your doctor warn you about such unexpected interactions?

Your doctor could help you stick to your medication schedule by choosing drugs that can be taken once or twice a day instead of three times. Or by providing the drug in liquid form if capsules make you choke. You might want to ask for pills that have different shapes and sizes, where possible, to help prevent mix-ups. Be sure also to ask if the doctor can substitute the less costly but FDA-approved generic drug for the brand-name one. If your doctor says you can't go generic, find out why. In some states your druggist can only substitute generic drugs with your physician's approval.

Finally, as extra insurance against side effects, get as much information as you can in writing, so that you will be reminded how to properly take the medication when you get home. In addition to getting written instructions, also check on the doctor's handwritten prescription. In *The New People's Pharmacy: Drug Breakthroughs of the '80s* (Bantam), Joe Graedon, Pharm.D., suggests: "Before you leave your doctor's office, ask the nurse to print or type the words of the prescription right under the chicken scratches. And for double protection, have the generic name (scientific name) of the medicine included along with the brand name."

It's also good practice to tell a doctor who is prescribing medication about any other drugs you take. This system of double checking ensures that you won't repeat the mistake of a woman who landed in the hospital with an overdose, says Dr. Scavone. It seems her general practitioner prescribed the same antidepressant as her psychiatrist, except he called it by its generic name while the psychiatrist prescribed the brand name.

The Importance of Your Pharmacist

Another important member of your treatment team, your pharmacist functions as a kind of interpreter. Having trouble decoding your doctor's scrawls? Your druggist can help you decipher and translate from the Latin "b.i.d." to the English "twice a day," and the "q.i.d." to read "four times a day." And even in English a prescription can pose problems. For example, what exactly does "1 cap 3 × a day " mean? Every eight hours? Do you get up in the middle of the night? Take it with meals? Your pharmacist can answer these questions, help you to space doses and even set up strategies to help you remember to take your medications. And that's not all. You have only to ask for an easy-to-open container or that your instructions be printed in large type, and most pharmacists will eagerly oblige. How do you store your medicine, and when should you get it refilled? These are also questions your pharmacist can answer.

Need help deciding among the dazzling array of over-the-counter drugs? That's what your pharmacist is there for, says Dr. Lamy. Which is good to know,

Pharmacists are patient educators, not just pill dispensers.

Soon, almost half of all medications will not require a prescription.

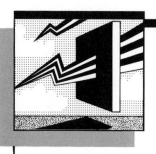

New Card Could Cancel
Medical Mix-ups

Imagine that you've collapsed and are taken, unconscious, to the hospital emergency room. Before the doctors can start treatment, they have to run all kinds of tests: They don't know yet that your blood type is Rh negative, that you're allergic to penicillin, that you are taking insulin for diabetes and that you have a history of heart trouble. At the same time, the admitting desk is trying to find out your social security number and the name of your health insurer. All the while, your life hangs in the balance.

Or say you are staying with your sister in Florida and you get an infection that just won't go away. Your sister's doctor wants to prescribe a new antibiotic for you but first needs to know all the medications you have taken recently. You left most of your prescriptions up North. Your mind goes blank.

Relax. Help might be as near as your wallet. In the next few years you could hold your entire medical record in the palm of your hand, making mix-ups with medications obsolete.

Meet the laser card. Here's a piece of plastic that looks like a credit card but works like a computer diskette. It's able to store up to 800 pages of medical history, including x-rays, EEGs and prescriptions. Present this card to a physician or pharmacist anywhere at any time, and voilà—an instant printout of your medical profile! Called

since it won't be long until nearly half of all medications will be available without prescription. So now you have someone who can tell you if that cold remedy will collide with your antidepressant. (The answer is yes—you'd get a double dose of sedative.)

Pharmacies will also increasingly play a coordinating role, says Richard P. Penna, Pharm.D., associate executive director of the American Association of Colleges of Pharmacy. "If your podiatrist prescribes one drug, your dentist another, your internist another, we can provide a link and intercept potential interactions." To do this, more pharmacies are keeping patient profiles, which might include a list of

the LifeCard by LifeCard International, a subsidiary of Blue Cross/ Blue Shield of Maryland, subscribers in that state are now testing the first laser card of its kind. General usage is expected within the next five years.

Not to be outsmarted, MasterCard will soon offer some of its customers their own kind of computer card. Dubbed a "Smart Card," this little item is actually like a tiny computer. It contains a computer chip with a processor built in so the information is stored right in the card. The card contains not only a medical record but approval for a check as well. Pocket-sized but powerful, this little card could, all at once, simplify medical payments and eliminate diagnostic tests while preventing misuse of medications, explains Arlene Lessin, president of Smart Card International, who is marketing the card under the name "Ulticard."

A comparison of these two new products shows that information in both cards can be updated and changed. The advantage of the laser card, however, is that it holds more information. And that's important as you get older, say many gerontologists, because you are likely to see more doctors and take more medications, and you may not always stick with one pharmacist.

There is one additional disadvantage to the computer cards, however. You still have to remember not to leave home without it!

your allergies, chronic illnesses, frequent over-the-counter drugs, prescription medication, age and general well-being. Put on a computer, this profile can instantly be consulted when filling a prescription.

Another approach is the "Brown Bag" plan. How this works is that you put every container from your medicine chest (and your nightstand, purse or wherever else you stash your pills) into a brown bag and take it to your drugstore. A pharmacist will review your drugs for possible interactions and potential risks, and counsel you as to the right (and wrong ways) to use them.

Bring all your drugs in a bag for your druggist to review.

Becoming the Master of Your Medication

In the end, it's up to you to make the most of your medications. Studies show that given the chance and the right drugs, you can do a pretty good job of it—even in the hospital. In an experiment at the University of Kentucky College of Medicine, in Lexington, surgery patients who administered their own pain relievers actually used less pain medication and reported more relief than the patients who were given medication the standard way. And a new machine, called a Patient Controlled Analgesia (PCA) device, allows patients to push a button and receive small doses of painkillers intravenously as they need them, without the risk of overdosing. A plus for the PCA, says one Stanford University doctor, is that the gradual dosing reduces grogginess. Another advantage is that it puts the patient in charge—and that may speed recovery.

Make the Most of Medications

Here are seven more ways you can enhance the effectiveness of medications and at the same time safeguard against side effects.

Ask for single drug preparations.

Learn to Use Over-the-Counter Medicines Wisely. That's especially important if you take other drugs. Consult with pharmacists and read labels. Look for hidden ingredients you could do without. Some aspirin preparations contain caffeine, and cough medicine frequently contains alcohol. If you are on a low-sodium diet, avoid antacids that have a high salt content. You can avoid extra side effects if you stick to single drug preparations rather than combination ones.

Learn the Warning Signs. Stop taking a drug if you experience confusion, difficulty in urination, dry mouth, blurry vision or any other symptom which began since you started taking the drug, warns Dr. Avorn.

Unless you take all the antibiotics, infection may return.

Follow Directions. That means take *all* your medications. Sounds basic enough, yet it's surprising how many people stop taking pills like antibiotics at the first inkling of recovery. The trouble with this is that the bug could return and hit you with a bigger bout than ever. You may also get yourself in trouble by the opposite kind of thinking: "If one pill makes me feel good, two pills will make me feel great." Wrong. Overdosing makes you feel worse. Remember, too, that pills are personalized, so don't exchange them with your friends. And don't hoard them "just in case," either. Drugs are only guaranteed to be potent up to the expiration date—using them after that time could be dangerous if their chemical composition has changed.

Stick to a Schedule. Set up a system to help you remember to take your medicine. Some experts suggest marking different types of medicine with different colored dots—say, red for your heart medication or green for your antibiotics. Others suggest purchasing a container with compartments, and keeping one day's supply of your various medications in each compartment. Or try one of the newer "computerized" dispensers that light up or beep at dose time. Whatever your system, warns Dr. Scavone, be sure to explain it to someone else—just in case. There are many methods available for addressing the problem of medication mix-ups, reports Judith Brown, health analyst with the American Association of Retired Persons. Pills may come prearranged according to dosage time and days, much the same way most oral contraceptives are packaged.

What if you miss a dose for a few days? Don't double up your dosage. Instead, just get back on the schedule your doctor ordered.

Learn Ways to Make the Medicine Go Down. Unless otherwise directed, advises pharmacist Joe Graedon, author of *The People's Pharmacy* (Avon), your best bet is to take medications with nothing but plain water—a whole glassful, at that. That way you make sure the drug gets into your bloodstream and does what it's supposed to do. From the American Medical Association comes a tip for taking tablets: Put a little water in your mouth and tilt your head back. Tilt your head *forward* when swallowing capsules. Don't take pills lying down—they may dissolve in the esophagus, causing heartburn, nausea or vomiting.

Drinking a whole glass of water helps the medicine go down and get to work.

Don't Drink with Drugs. You're asking for a double dose of drowsiness or even more if you combine alcohol with medications such as antihistamines, insulin, high blood pressure drugs, antibiotics and tranquilizers. That problem may be more pronounced as you age, since alcohol stays in the bloodstream longer. You should also say no to nicotine if you take medications. Smoking can cancel out the effects of some drugs.

Don't Be Misled by Miraculous Claims. "We shouldn't act like sheep and take every drug that comes along," advises Roberta Apfel, M.D., M.P.H., assistant professor of psychiatry at Beth Israel Hospital, Harvard Medical School, in Boston. That's particularly good advice in considering claims for drugs which supposedly extend life or reverse the damage done by aging. "Not all the products associated with anti-aging work or are safe," says Sheldon Hendler, M.D., Ph.D., instructor of medicine at the University of California at San Diego. He's talking about drugs like Gerovital H3, which is a 2 percent procaine solution similar to novocaine. "Claims that it can extend life span, reverse senility, increase sexual potency, overcome arthritis and protect against heart disease have not been supported by scientific research," says Dr. Hendler.

Another substance, Superoxide Dismutase (SOD), often sold in health stores, is a big rip-off, says Dr. Hendler. SOD is an enzyme, produced naturally in the body, which repairs cellular damage. One report by the National Institutes of Health calls SOD "a protein that breaks down during digestion and cannot be reassembled in body cells."

A National Institutes of Health report concludes: "Because aging processes are so complex, it is very unlikely that a single nutrient, hormone or technique will ever stop or reverse all the changes." Aging research is in its infancy. Until more is learned, "scientists urge caution in assessing any claim for a life-extending or rejuvenating agent."

In the meantime, you must learn all you can about the approved drugs available to you now—the ones which may enable you to stay strong as you get older. Whether these tools become your friends or foes depends on what you know and how well you use the information.

Beware of anti-aging and life extension drugs.

It's up to you to learn how to use drugs so they may enable you, not disable you.

21

A Keen
Mind and
a Happy Heart

When a fourth-grader forgets the capital of Montana, does he internalize the experience? Does he wonder whether—now that he's reaching a double-digit birthday—his mind is failing him? Of course not. Quite rightly, he recognizes that he hasn't been paying attention, or didn't spend enough time on his homework assignment to incorporate the name into his memory.

Helena Is the Capital of Montana

In many ways, kids have the right idea. Instead of internalizing and *catastrophizing* things that sometimes go wrong, they shift gears and go on to something else. And that "something else" is usually something that's fun—playing outdoors, spending time with friends, bike riding.

As you grow older, you could benefit from becoming more—not less—like children in these particular ways. So many problems associated with aging—the memory loss, the depression, the occasional confusion—often have absolutely nothing to do with age. Rather, they may have to do with

So many problems associated with aging have absolutely nothing to do with age.

257

boredom, lack of social stimulation, a sedentary lifestyle, a poor diet, side effects of medication or some other factor. And these various problems can be dealt with and solved.

In other words, to retain or recapture youth's mental agility, you need a plan—and one that you can start working on right now. As Fred Astaire once said, "Old age is like anything else. You've got to start early to be good at it."

Step one might be to review your assets, which might be surprisingly greater than you'd assume. Vern Bengtson, Ph.D., director of the Andrus Gerontology Institute, in Washington, D.C., says that as people grow older they gain as well as lose. "Gained is the freedom of increased time, from expectations and for more opportunity for social interactions," he says.

It's very important to have friends.

"Social interactions" is a doctorly way of saying "friends." And it's important to have friends. They're good for you. They pay attention to you, share information with you and also share emotional comfort. Studies at Duke University, in Durham, North Carolina, have shown that people in tense situations have a less harmful physical response when in the presence of a companion. Commenting on these studies, James J. Lynch, Ph.D., author of *The Broken Heart* (Basic Books, Inc., 1977), says that "apparently the emotional support provided by the presence of a friend or companion changes the 'objective stress' inherent in a situation, generally making the situation far less stressful for the heart. One cannot help but conclude that unpleasant life experiences are far more upsetting to humans who lack companionship."

Sociable people have better mental health protection.

There's additional proof, as well. A study of 7,000 residents of Alameda County, California, by researchers from Yale University, in New Haven, Connecticut, found that people with good social support systems were two to five times more likely to outlive people with fewer social involvements. And an investigation by researchers reporting in the *Journal of Health and Social Behavior* found that a strong social support system was a powerful protector of both physical and mental health in 100 men who had been laid off from their jobs. Clearly, having friends is an important element to good mental health. But you've acquired even more than friends during your life.

Other gains include an increased adaptability, objectivity and, contrary to popular belief, an increased tolerance and open-mindedness. Many people become more productive as they age. Perhaps that's why many more seniors are seeking second careers and continuing active employment long past the "usual" retirement age of 65.

People also gain more individuality the older they get. Not everyone will look or act alike. Some will head corporations, while others will head for the golf course. Some will run (and win) marathons, while others run computer printouts.

But perhaps the most surprising gain of age is in the area of intellectual potential. According to researcher John Horn, Ph.D., psychologist at the University of Denver, crystallized intelligence—the ability to use stored information to solve problems—has been shown to increase over the life span of a healthy adult. Sometimes a person's actual intelligence measurably increases with age.

Armed with a list of your personal assets, you are now prepared to take a few potshots at the myths of aging.

You gain tolerance and adaptability as you age.

Crystallized intelligence improves with time.

Fighting Fears with Facts

A major myth is that you're bound to lose mental sharpness as you age. The fear of senility—forgetfulness, confusion, behavior changes—is commonly believed to be a natural part of aging. It's not, says Laurie Barclay, M.D., clinical director of dementia research at Burke Rehabilitation Center, Cornell Medical Center, in New York City. "The truth is that only about 10 percent of the population will show mild to moderate loss of memory, and only 5 percent will exhibit serious mental impairment." Not only is senility *not* a natural part of aging, it isn't even a disease. Rather, it's the name given to any number of conditions which may have more than a hundred causes. (Dementia is the clinical name for these kinds of conditions.)

The good news is that many of these conditions are reversible and often preventable.

Senility is far from the norm.

How Strong Is Your Social Support System?

"Socially Marginal." Is that you? The California Department of Mental Health has put together an enlightening little test to help you find out.

Circle one response for each item. Then add the scores next to each item you circled.

1. At work, how many persons do you talk to about a job hassle?
None (or not employed) .... (0)
One or two .... (3)
Two or three .... (4)
Four or more .... (5)
2. How many neighbors do you trade favors with (lend tools or household items, share rides with, baby-sit for, etc.)?
None .... (0)
One .... (1)
Two or three .... (2)
Four or more .... (3)
3. Do you have a spouse or partner?
No .... (0)
Several different partners .... (2)
One steady partner .... (6)
Married or living with someone .... (10)
4. How often do friends and close family members visit you at home?
Rarely .... (0)
About once a month .... (1)
Several times a month .... (4)
Once a week or more .... (8)

The Mental Effects of Medication

An older person's cloudy thinking is frequently caused by reactions to certain drugs. As people age, their body absorbs, distributes, metabolizes and excretes drugs differently than is the case with younger adults and children. On top of that, many older people visit a number of doctors, all of whom may prescribe different medications, some of which may even be unnecessary. Soon it becomes hard to keep them all straight or even to know if they're affecting the mind. No wonder adverse reactions are twice as

5. How many friends or family members do you talk to about personal matters?

None .... (0)
One or two... (6)
Three to five .... (8)
Six or more .... (10)

6. How often do you participate in a social, community or sports group?

Rarely.. (0)
About once a month .... (1)
Several times a month .... (2)
Once a week or more.. (4)

Total: _____

Scoring:
Less than 15:

Your support network has low strength and probably does not provide much support. You need to consider making more social contacts.

15-29:

Your support network has moderate strength and probably provides enough support, except during periods of high stress.

30 or more:

Your support network has high strength and will probably maintain your well-being even during periods of high stress.

frequent in persons older than 65 as in the younger population.

Those reactions can be reversed, says Canadian gerontologist David Skelton, M.D., of Edmonton General Hospital, in Alberta. Dr. Skelton tells the story of a woman who was taking eight or nine medications and who had been falling, withdrawing and becoming more and more confused. "We simply stopped the medications and she was able to return home in just a few weeks," he says.

The best preventive for that kind of situation is to learn now all you can about the medications you

You may reverse senility by reducing drugs.

take and their potential side effects. Then keep an accurate and detailed record that you can share with your doctor or pharmacist.

The Difference between Depression and Senile Dementia

What else can be disguised as dementia? Depression. In fact, because it so closely mimics senile dementia and is also characterized by forgetfulness, confusion and behavioral changes, it is often called "pseudodementia." Depression in older people is usually caused by some sort of loss—a spouse, self-esteem, status, a job or health. It is fairly common, too. One report indicates that depression is so prevalent among persons aged 65 and over that 13 percent warrant intervention.

That does not mean you are destined for depression in your golden years, though. "Although depressive illness is serious, it is no more a problem in late life than in earlier stages of youth," says Daniel Blazer, M.D., Ph.D., professor of psychiatry and director of the study of affective disorders at Duke University Medical Center. And even if you do bump into the blues down the road, it's good to know that it's possible to take a detour around depression. Dr. Blazer explains that new research has shown that it's possible to reverse depression by such methods as cognitive therapy. Therapists have observed that when older people learn to change their negative self-talk, they can "think" themselves back to mental health, no matter how many years they have been bad-mouthing themselves.

Get a Proper Diagnosis

To depression, drugs and disease as important keys to understanding dementia, add diagnosis. Because many physicians still do not know what to look for, senile dementia is frequently (and tragically) over-diagnosed. Which means you'll need to learn all you can about the symptoms of depression and dementia.

Recognize the difference between depression and dementia.

How do you tell the difference? The clues are subtle but do exist. A depressed person, for example, will anguish over forgetfulness, whereas a senile person will try to hide it. Also, a depressed person will make little effort to perform tasks, whereas a senile person will struggle to perform well.

Once you get your facts straight about what really happens to memory in the aging process, you're less likely to fret about forgetfulness. The truth is, everyone forgets car keys or the name of an acquaintance from time to time. The difference when people age is that they're a bit slower than they were to recall things—especially when they're not concentrating or when they're worried or have the blues. Robin West, Ph.D., gerontologist and author of *Memory Fitness over 40* (Triad Publishing Company), says that it's time to see a doctor if you forget entire experiences, not just details, or if you forget the names of close family members or things like simple math knowledge. Keep in mind too, writes Alex Comfort, M.D., Ph.D., in *A Good Age* (Crown Publishers, Inc.), that "loss of pleasure in life, of appetite, of libido, of sleep and of well-being are not normal features of aging." Don't let anyone tell you (or anyone close to you) that depression is just a normal part of aging. By the same token, if any elderly relative or friend of yours is diagnosed as having "irreversible senile dementia," don't automatically accept the verdict.

New Hope for Alzheimer's

One mental condition, called Alzheimer's disease for the man who discovered it, accounts for half of all cases of dementia. The brain of someone affected by the disease is characterized by tangled nerve fibers and a deficiency of acetylcholine, the neurotransmitter which sends messages from one neuron to the next. Alzheimer's has generally been regarded as irreversible. But recent discoveries about the nervous system and brain cells may be challenging that assumption. "There's reason for optimism," says Robert Butler, M.D., professor of geriatrics and adult development at Mt. Sinai Hospital, in New York. "We're at the juncture of learning how to maintain the nervous system. It's our head that keeps us alive and happy, so anything we can do to keep *it* healthy is good news."

What's got Dr. Butler and other gerontologists excited is the possibility that brain cells (which have long been known to die off with age) have the ability

Brain cells repair themselves, offering the promise of restored mental ability.

to repair themselves. Laboratory studies have shown that active, undamaged cells in healthy elderly people grow more dendrites—the little branchlike structures that receive the body's messages. According to a National Institutes of Health (NIH) report, researchers now hope that because brain cells can repair themselves, they just might be good hosts for transplanted tissues. And that could eventually be the key for reversing damage caused by degenerative brain disorders such as Parkinson's and Alzheimer's disease.

Sound like the stuff of science-fiction? In fact, European and American scientists have successfully tried tissue transplants in lab animals, reports the NIH. What's more, they've been able "to reverse the damage done to the central nervous system that caused . . . changes in learning, memory and other functional impairments that often occur as normal parts of aging."

Transplanted brain cells reverse damage to the central nervous system.

The day of transplanting brain cells into humans is perhaps down the road. Until the neuroscientists reveal the next chapter, it's up to you to do all you can to keep your brain growing and healthy. That means eating well, exercising, keeping mentally stimulated and reducing your reaction to stress.

Brain Food

What does eating liver, soybeans, lecithin, eggs and fish have to do with your brain? Maybe a lot. These foods are rich in choline, a vitaminlike substance. When added to the diets of volunteers in one study, it sparked an increase in acetylcholine, the neurotransmitter in the brain that sends impulses. What happened when the volunteers took 10 grams of choline is that they were able to recall a list of unrelated words more quickly than volunteers who did not take choline. In other studies, patients with Alzheimer's disease had improved memories when treated with choline. Although all the evidence is not in, results of these early studies look encouraging, and it surely wouldn't hurt to put the choline-rich foods mentioned above on your menu.

Liver is also a great source of B_6 and copper, two nutrients which prevent part of your brain cells from shriveling up. So says Elizabeth Root, Ph.D., and John Longenecker, Ph.D., two Texas researchers who found that when rats were deprived of B_6 and copper, the dendrites—branchlike extensions that carry electrical impulses from one brain cell to another—shrivel up and die. The researchers speculate that a mild deficiency of those nutrients over the years could have the same devastating effects on humans.

Eat Right/B-Smart

If you've gotten casual about preparing well-balanced meals, you could be robbing your brain of its power, suggests Dr. Barclay. For one thing, you're setting yourself up for a deficiency of vitamin C and the B vitamins. And without sufficient levels of thiamine, folate and vitamin B_{12}, the brain cannot function properly. As a result, you may have memory problems, inability to concentrate, depression and possibly a misdiagnosis of senility. The solution? Learn which foods are rich in B vitamins. With such a vitamin-rich diet you may even notice a marked improvement in mental functioning. Researchers in New Mexico tested a group of normal volunteers of at least 60 years old on their problem-solving ability and, separately, on their memory. They discovered that those with the lowest B_{12} and C levels did poorly on the memory test. Those with the lowest levels of B_{12}, C, riboflavin and folate scored the worst on problem-solving tests.

Folate and B_{12} are necessary for good brain function.

Think with Zinc

Who would ever imagine that zinc might help you think? The fact is, says Roy Hullin, M.D., more than 80 enzymes, many of them involved in the function of the nervous system, need zinc to work. When Dr. Hullin studied 1,200 patients over 55, he found that the 220 senile people in the group had significantly lower zinc levels than those who were not senile. So, although shellfish and lean meat may be pricey, it may well be worth it to add them to your diet.

And while you're adding good things to your diet, how about subtracting one like alcohol? Long-

A pickled brain ages rapidly.

term alcohol abuse can lead to premature aging of the brain and disruption of memory and abstract reasoning, says Nelson Butters, Ph.D., of the San Diego Veterans Administration Medical Center, in La Jolla, California.

Exercise for a Sound Mind

One way to get your memory in motion is to get your body moving. Researchers in Utah studied out-of-shape people aged 55 to 70 and put them on a four-month program of brisk walking. The results? Across the board, the walkers increased their short-term memory, ability to reason and reaction time. That kind of aerobic exercise makes the body better at transporting oxygen to *all* its organs. "So we are assuming that the brain benefits by receiving more oxygen," says Robert Dustman, Ph.D., of the Salt Lake City Veterans Administration Hospital. Other good aerobic exercises are cycling, swimming, jogging and racquet sports. For best results, you need to perform three 30-minute sessions weekly. See your doctor before starting.

Brisk walking reversed memory loss.

Exercise also gives a boost to your self-image and can energize your emotions. Even if you've been sedentary most of your life, exercise can turn around the way you think of yourself. That's what one study at Duke University discovered. Researchers put half of a group of sedentary people ranging in age from mid-twenties to early sixties on a walking or jogging program three times a week for ten weeks. At the end of the program, when the active group was compared to the nonactive group, the active group reported more mental alertness and vigor.

Exercise to soothe your nerves.

But while exercise can stimulate your brain, it can also serve to soothe it. To ease anxiety and tension, what do 400 doctors surveyed recommend? A regular routine of walking, swimming, golfing or bowling. Try it—you might just like its special side effects. Make sure you get some sunshine while you're at it. Many people neglect to get enough daylight, particularly in winter, and that can make moods plummet, say researchers.

Walking Tall Prevents Forgetfulness

Paying attention to your posture is another way to keep your brain performing at its peak. "Allowing your upper body to sag—with rounded shoulders, head hung over and chin jutting outward—can create kinks in the spine that squeeze the two arteries passing through the spinal column to the brain," says E. Fritz Schmerl, M.D., teacher of gerontology at Chabot College, in Hayward, California. "That causes an inadequate blood supply, which results in fuzzy thinking and forgetfulness, especially as we age." So walk tall—keep your head back and your chin in.

Stand straight to think sharp.

Flexing the Mind Muscle

Exercising your mind is all-important for mental health throughout life. At 65, Grace Young, a part-time teacher and traveler, learned a new trick. She learned how to work a computer. Says Grace, "I was so thrilled I bounced in my chair." Today, at 70, Grace is helping other seniors learn about bytes and booting up. She's already starting on her next endeavor: testing new programs for a book on computer literacy. "If I can't keep learning, I might as well be dead," says Grace.

Learning ability continues into old age.

Grace has nothing to worry about. Studies have found that people continue to learn well into their old age. One study at Duke University Center for the Study of Aging and Human Development found that some individuals have actually increased their IQ with age. Other research indicates similar findings. After studying 4,000 adults for nearly three decades, K. Warner Schaie, Ph.D., professor of human development and psychology at Pennsylvania State University, in University Park, concluded: "When tested for verbal ability, people who led challenging lives showed no deterioration, and some even showed improvement in this area until late in life." You have only to look at some of the world's greatest achievers in the arts and sciences to see that this is so, and to realize that the "old dog/new trick" notion is just another myth about aging.

(continued on page 270)

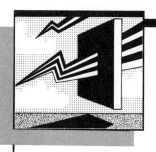

Computers:
A Program for Brain Power

"Any retired person who can afford a personal computer and doesn't buy one is foolish," says K. Warner Schaie, Ph.D., professor of human development and psychology.

What's the reason for the urging? "Computers open up a whole new world to older people, especially those who may be isolated," says Dennis LaBuda, acting director of the Institute of Lifetime Learning. Computers can provide a link to the grandkids, a listing of local services and a look at what menus could be planned on a budget. They can help keep track of your medical records and may even remind you to take a pill.

Perhaps the most intriguing news is that new studies are beginning to show that computers may be able to improve cognitive functioning while providing seniors with a source of mental stimulation. "Computer games offer all sorts of interesting ways to exercise your mind," explains Dr. Schaie. For one thing, they can rev up your recall and retrieval abilities.

In one preliminary study conducted by Shulamith Weisman, M.Ed., director of Human Services at Hebrew Home of Greater Washington, in Rockville, Maryland, 50 nursing home residents in their seventies, eighties and nineties were introduced to video games which had been modified so that the residents would have better chances of success. Except for those with severe mental impairment, the residents were observed to not only be able to play the games, but to enjoy them. What's more heartening is that patients with Alzheimer's and Parkinson's disease also participated in the games. Dr. Weisman hopes that her work will encourage further research into the needs of this ever-growing segment of society, and that psychologists and others who work with the aged will look into the possibilities of using computer games to exercise and sharpen memory, improve hand-eye coordination and increase the ability to concentrate on a task.

Other preliminary work now being conducted by Iseli K. Krauss, Ed.D., former assistant professor of psychology at Syracuse University, in Washington, D.C., could indicate that computer use may improve skills. Why? Dr. Krauss thinks it may be because "computers provide an opportunity for older people to learn at their own pace, and to focus attention without distraction. Both are factors which influence memory and cognition. The achievement of acquiring computer skills is very reinforcing because it lets one know that new skills can still be learned." Dr. Krauss hopes her computer work may one day help individuals with declining memory skills maintain their positions in the work and community environment.

For right now, though, Neal Bellos, Ph.D., director of the Gerontology Center, Syracuse University, says that computers can boost self-esteem for seniors by providing a sense of mastery and control and the chance to be a part of the mainstream. "In traditional societies, it was the seniors who functioned more or less as the computers, the information sources. Now they must learn to use these new tools to be a part of modern society," he says.

That's just why Matt Lehmann, 76, had wanted to learn about them. He needed to use a computer in connection with his research at Stanford University, in Stanford, California. "I was terrified I'd make a fool of myself . . . so I bought a computer and learned to use it at home alone." When asked to teach a course at Little House, a senior center in Menlo Park, California, he elected to teach computer literacy in the belief that other seniors had the same fears he had. "It's kept my mind alive," says Matt, who has just authored a book on basic computer programming and is busy teaching other seniors (average age 65) who seem equally enthused. "I don't have to wait until someone proves computers are good for the mind. I know it," he observes. After a few weeks at the keyboard, he's seen stroke victims speak more clearly and widows become less depressed. "Almost every day you can hear someone shriek with excitement when they get their program to work." Many graduates from the Little House computer class have stayed around to form a computer club, which provides social chatter as much as keyboard clatter.

Matt is now assisting at the University of San Francisco to set up and run a computer network for senior citizens called Senior Net. There are now five locations nationally that communicate through electronic mail and contribute to forums and questionnaires by and for seniors. It's another way for seniors to think—and live—young.

The Elderhostel program allows for low-cost, high-challenge study.

There are lots of ordinary older folks like Grace Young who are flexing their memory muscles and keeping their minds keen, too. In fact, there is at least one learning opportunity open only to those 60 or older. Over the past ten years, 100,000 senior citizens have participated in the studies offered through Elderhostel, a program that combines the low cost of youth-hostel living with the challenge of college courses. The curriculum covers a dazzling array of interest, from war and peace to flora and fauna. To keep up with the growing interest of their adventuresome students, Elderhostel recently added nontraditional classes in some unusual settings. You can learn about nature in a lighthouse, take bagpipe lessons at a music camp or participate in Bible studies at a religious retreat.

"Use it or lose it" goes for the mind, too.

Elderhostel founder Marty Knowlton, now in his mid-sixties, was once quoted as saying: "The mind is a tool, a piece of equipment. The more experienced you are, the better it gets." To carry that analogy one step further, if your mind is like a tool, it'll get rusty if you don't use it. Studies on rats conducted by California neuroanatomist Marian Diamond, M.D., showed that rats raised in an "enriched environment" (in roomy cages with other rats and a variety of playthings) had heavier, more chemically active brains than those of rats raised alone in an "impoverished environment" (a small cage without toys).

Crossword puzzles or Trivial Pursuit can help keep memory sharp.

While enriching your environment can be regenerative for your mind, you don't have to rush off to the classroom. Your brain cells can get a boost by seeing a movie or visiting a museum. Working a crossword puzzle or playing Scrabble or bridge are good activities because they require using memory and verbal skills. Dr. Schaie says that even square dancing is stimulating because "you have to remember the sequences given by the caller and translate them into organized motor behavior." Dr. West considers Trivial Pursuit a good game because it is good practice in retrieving information.

It's this retrieval or recalling that sometimes troubles people as they age, says Dr. West. That's because like everything else, recall time slows down a bit and it takes a little longer to learn something new or to pay attention and ignore distractions. Other than that, though, experts have found no evidence to indicate that memory automatically deteriorates with age. You should be able to remember the name of someone you just met, as well as the names of legendary movie stars or how to ride a bike, assures Dr. West.

Yet when you are older, if you forget where you put the car keys, you blame it on age. Chances are you occasionally forgot them when you were younger, too, but then you put the blame on distraction or not feeling well. Which is exactly where the blame should be put when you're older too, says Dr. West. Ironically, worrying that you're losing your mind can make you even more forgetful.

Keep Your Memory Fit

Instead of panicking, Dr. West suggests you start now to sharpen your memory. "Younger people should get into the practice of using strategies to improve their memory so it becomes automatic later in life. Older people can use these strategies to reverse memory failure and facilitate learning."

Keep your mind fit to reverse forgetfulness.

She suggests you improve concentration by removing yourself from the sights and sounds that distract you. If you're daydreaming out the window, pull the window curtains. Kids clamoring about? Close the doors. Talk yourself through tasks to focus attention. Establish a "memory place" in the house where you put things like glasses, keys, mail. Notes and calendars are good external reminders, but they work best when you also internalize what you need to remember. Give yourself a moment to let your mental notes sink in. If you have trouble remembering, for example, if you turned off the porch light, make a mental note when you flip the light switch. In other words, try not to walk around on automatic pilot—pay attention to your surroundings.

Create a "memory place" where you always put your eyeglasses or car keys.

Try to use visual imagery when you learn names and faces. Dr. West suggests to her students that to remember her name (Robin), they should visualize a robin perched on a weather vane. It's also helpful to repeat the name out loud and rehearse it mentally while the person is still in front of you.

Relax to remember more.

Whatever you are trying to remember, give yourself plenty of time. A sharp memory can be yours if you just learn to become less anxious about recalling things. Memory training specialist Danielle Lapp, of the department of psychiatry at Stanford University School of Medicine, in Palo Alto, California, found that people over 55 showed improved concentration and better success at recalling faces and names after learning relaxation techniques, such as deep breathing and progressive relaxation.

Planning a Richer Route to Retirement

Don't put all your eggs in one basket.

Getting into the habit of learning new things will come in handy once retirement rolls around. One of the factors in determining whether you'll experience retirement as a rut or time of regeneration is if you've learned to *diversify*—that is, to do several different kinds of activity—says Dr. Bengtson.

Diversifying means that you don't put all your eggs in one basket—particularly the work basket. It means you learn to develop a number of activities and secure social ties. By so diversifying yourself, you'll be better prepared to live the estimated 20 years beyond when the work basket is long gone.

Dr. Bengtson tells of a study comparing two groups of retirees: steelworkers and teachers. Which group fared better? Though they were paid less, he says, the teachers fared better because every year they had been faced with the prospect of what to do with three months of unstructured time. Consequently, the teachers learned to develop more interests and plan ahead, which served them quite well once their worklife ended. They had learned the lesson of diversity.

Emotional health ahead depends on diversifying now.

You can think of diversification as a form of emotional insurance. Studies have shown that your happiness in retirement depends just as much on how well you've developed meaningful activities as it does on your marital satisfaction, health or income.

Happily, the majority of people adjust quite well to retirement, reports Erdman Palmore, Ph.D., professor of medical sociology at Duke Center for the Study of Aging and Human Development, in Durham, North Carolina. However, there is a sizable

Pets, Too, Have Future Youth

They say that after a few years a pet begins to look like its owner. Take a look at your dog or cat. Is this the pet of a person undergoing a year of rejuvenation? If your Tabby's flabby or your poodle's paunchy, it's not too late to give him a new lease on life.

Generally speaking, what you may think of as signs of aging may in fact be degeneration, says noted veterinarian Richard H. Pitcairn, D.V.M, Ph.D., author of *Dr. Pitcairn's Complete Guide to Natural Health for Dogs and Cats* (Rodale Press). For example, he explains, it is not a normal sign of old age for dogs to have body odor, or dirty ears or to lose their hair excessively. Nor is it natural for older cats to be less active, to neglect their grooming, to have an eye discharge or to not want to be petted. "These are signs that the pet's health has been compromised," says Dr. Pitcairn.

The good news is that, no matter what your animal's age, most of these changes can be reversed. To start with, have your vet examine your pet every six months to check teeth, heart and kidneys. Then make sure you are paying attention to your pet's special needs. Maintain routines and avoid disruptions. Keep the water bowl full and fresh.

To put spark back into old Spot, you may have to make some dietary adjustments. Older animals need minimal but adequate amounts of protein because their kidneys can't handle it as well. That's why it's important to make sure your pet gets high quality protein—something he may not be getting from the can, says Dr. Pitcairn. He suggests you add lean and organ meats, cooked eggs and maybe some cottage cheese in place of some of the regular food at each meal, and mix in a little bone meal to guard against brittle bones. Vitamins and minerals are important too, so include finely grated, raw vegetables whenever possible.

It's also important that your mature pet exercise regularly. Even a walk around the block can "provide interest and interaction for dogs, which is important because they are social creatures." Get your cat a chew toy or tie a piece of wool or fur to a string and entice it to play. However, don't leave string around an unsupervised cat as the cat may swallow it inadvertently. Daily exposure to sunshine will help stimulate your pet's endocrine system and keep it healthier.

What happens when you put your older pooch or pussycat on a health program of maintenance and prevention? You might just see a return to playfulness and renewed vigor.

group that does experience problems, including psychological and social adjustment. "A lot depends on how much you identify with your work role." Workaholics beware. You'll be doing yourself a favor down the road if you cut back on your hours and start developing activities now you can enjoy all your life.

Plan a Variety of Activities

Dr. Palmore suggests a variety of activities, both indoor and outdoor (how about backgammon and bike riding?), physical and mental (walking and acrostics?), individual and group (reading and folk dancing?), useful and useless (volunteering and daydreaming?). What would your list look like? Write down all the things you'd like to do if only you had the time. File it away. Update it.

A trial retirement is good preparation.

Take stock of your finances. Pre-retirement counselors can help you make sense of health benefits, pension plans, IRAs, social security, etc. Practice living on a retirement budget for a month. Use your next vacation as a trial retirement; develop new interests, new routines. Renegotiate roles with your spouse and discuss what you both have in mind regarding use of leisure time, retirement finances, etc. If you are thinking of moving after retirement, try visiting there for extended periods first.

What's Dr. Palmore's advice for the recent retiree? Don't wait for the doorbell to ring—go out and make social contacts. Build up routines which include time to work, play, socialize, be alone. Find goals that keep you wanting to get up every morning.

Coping Skills for a Lifetime

Retirement is just one of the several turning points in life. Called crises of midlife, they would seem to threaten mental and emotional stability. Yet not everyone is thrown off balance. There is evidence that those who cope most positively with stress consider it natural for things to change. They anticipate changes as a useful stimulus to development. Consequently, they suffer less from the psychological signs of stress.

Midlife changes are not crises for most.

Of all the crises, perhaps none more threatens emotional stability than the loss of a loved one. Yet some experts suggest you can prepare for more serious setbacks if you think about them honestly and plan what to do.

Discuss Anticipated Changes with Your Spouse

A way to prepare yourself for the loss of a loved one is to talk about it beforehand, suggests Dr. Comfort, in *A Good Age.* Far from morbid, this frank discussion about emotions, as well as resources such as finances, may be welcomed. "If these things are indeed faced, and the relationship is deepened by facing them, bereavement is not painless . . . but will lack the elements of guilt, self-deception and role-playing which contribute to making bereavement destructive to the survivor." Planning ahead for loss is especially important for women, because of their increased longevity.

A frank discussion with a loved one helps you adapt later.

Reverse Negative Self-Talk to Beat the Blues

It's not always a major crisis that does someone in. Sometimes it's life's everyday crises that can beat your good spirits into the ground.

To keep yourself from getting down in the dumps on a daily basis, one of the most effective resources you have available is cognitive therapy. This theory suggests that your moods are closely linked to your thinking. If your thoughts turn dark, you'll feel down. By talking back to your internal critic, you'll feel better. "Some depressed elders feel very guilty for things that happened many years ago about which nothing can be done now. Others feel like a failure because of missed opportunities; still others even report that unless things are the way they were at some prior happy period, life is no longer worth living. Cognitive therapy will elicit such thoughts and teach the individual to evaluate the evidence both for and against the truth of that particular thought," explains Larry Thompson, Ph.D., co-director of the Center for the Study of Psychotherapy and Aging at the Veterans Administration Medical Center, in Palo Alto, California. The encour-

Telling off that internal critic can make you feel better.

aging thing about cognitive therapy is that it has been shown to effectively reverse depression in two-thirds of the elderly patients studied after just a few months of treatment.

Of course, this technique is not just for the elderly. You can use cognitive therapy now and throughout your lifetime. All you need learn is what type of negative thinking you have and how to talk back to it. Do you jump to conclusions? Over-generalize? Disqualify the positive? You can learn rational responses and feel mentally healthier.

Readjust your sleep schedule to beat the blues.

Yet another way you might reverse late-life depression is by adjusting your sleep patterns. Dr. Blazer explains: "Older people tend to be less habitual with their sleep habits and depression may disrupt biological rhythms, making them very early risers for instance." The solution can be as simple as forcing the sleep cycle back around to normal time. Studies show this works to reverse mood disorders.

Securing a Support System

Who might be best qualified to help you strengthen coping skills as you get older? Why, someone who is older too, someone who has "come up through the ranks," so to speak. That's just what you might find if you were to stop in the Senior Health and Peer Counseling Center in Santa Monica, California. Here you'd find a cadre of peer counselors, older people who have been trained to work with other older people in emotional distress. You'd be provided with information about mental health services and informed of things you could do yourself to cope with the stresses and strains in later life. You may also be referred to support groups like the Widowed Persons group or Alcoholics Anonymous to help you cope with special crises. Classes and workshops would teach you about stress management techniques as well as educate you about blood pressure control, proper nutrition and exercise to keep you healthy. You'd also learn about medications and how to manage a variety of chronic illnesses that are likely to affect older people.

With peer counseling, older people can learn to cope with stress.

By participating in a mutual aid group like this one, says Harry Moody, Ph.D., deputy director of aging at Hunter College, in New York City, you would be reinforcing a sense of learned resourcefulness and would improve your quality of life. He compares these groups to organic gardening. "Peer counseling groups assist others in tapping their inner resources. They help them grow. You might say they recycle people."

Mutual aid groups reinforce individual resourcefulness.

Participating in mutual self-help groups may restore a sense of self-esteem by fulfilling the need to be needed. Each individual both gives and receives, and that can be healthy, says Dr. Moody. "One of the dangers of aging is . . . we tend to withdraw. These groups help people keep their focus outward, and tied to the outer world. They help us to learn that it's possible to be productive outside of the marketplace."

Strengthen Your Marriage

Chances are that if you have a long and happy life you are probably married. Statistics indicate that married people are more content than single people. In fact, the "golden years" can be a pretty sterling time for marriages. With the children gone and work pressures off, it can be a time of getting reacquainted, of renewal, a time to develop new interests, follow shared dreams and grow in exciting directions. For other couples, it's not such smooth sailing. Changes in health, income and routines can batter a marriage and result in a relationship of "unexcited dependency." Other marriages sink.

Husband and wife are finally free to follow shared dreams.

How can you make sure your marriage will weather the stormy changes that may be ahead? "You must make a conscious decision to commit yourself to intimacy—the closeness of a loving relationship—especially during life's changes and crossroads," says Herbert Zerof, Ph.D., author of *Finding Intimacy* (Harper & Row). The key is in communication. That means openly discussing priorities, needs and expectations—from cleaning chores to retirement plans.

Don't forget the subject of sex. That's the one area that could very well be the deciding factor if your marriage leans to the better or worse side. Try to understand how the changes in aging may affect sexual appetite. That's when it may be important to

Sex can remain satisfying throughout life.

resort to touching, caressing and other forms of sensuality. It's also good to keep in mind that the majority of older people report that sex is about the same as it was when they were younger.

If your marriage doesn't survive to old age, it's never too late to start anew. It may even give you a new lease on life. "Remarriage can be revitalizing," says Holger Stub, Ph.D., a specialist in social gerontology. You may discover that your maturity could make the union you forge in your sixties and seventies the most successful of all.

Start Caring for Something

Caring has a lot to do with mental health in old age. Says psychiatrist Aaron Katcher, M.D., formerly of the University of Pennsylvania, in Philadelphia, it's good to get into a pattern of caring. "Whether it's for a house, a garden, pets or other people, you are protecting yourself against despair."

Whether it's for a house, a pet, others— care.

If you live alone, consider a pet. Gerontologists say that for many older people pets provide a sense of responsibility, usefulness and companionship. Pets can also help you get up in the morning and remind you when to eat. Dogs, for example, can make you get out into the fresh air and even help you meet fellow dog-walkers along the way. Petting the cat or talking to the parakeet can reduce your blood pressure, and gazing at your fish can ease tension.

As you've seen, the ways to resist psychological degeneration and promote regeneration later in life are numerous, and available to you if you only look for them. What you just may discover is that aging itself, as author Ellen Langer believes, is an artifact.

22

The Mouth:

An Owner's

Manual

A beautiful smile can last forever.

"It's a wrong and very dangerous notion that you lose your teeth as you get older," says Krishan Kapur, D.M.D., professor of removable prosthodontics at the University of California at Los Angeles (UCLA) School of Dentistry. "With present preventive and therapeutic measures, there is absolutely no reason people should lose their teeth. It is not inevitable."

Statistics bear that out. Twenty years ago, about a third of the population wore dentures. Today, that figure is at 20 percent and dropping. Why? A combination of simple prevention and amazing technological advances make it possible to save or replace diseased teeth—a combination that's detailed in the following "owner's manual" for healthy teeth and gums.

Stopping Trouble Before It Starts

Your teeth are about the most durable part of your body. They have to be. "Teeth get heavy use," says Jay Watson, D.D.S., a dean of clinical affairs at the UCLA School of Dentistry.

In fact, these miracles of cement, dentin, pulp and enamel are under constant assault. You chew with them at least three times a day, use them as an extra hand, nutcracker, ice crusher and for assorted other tasks that would make your dentist shudder.

But their most dangerous enemy is the platoon of bacteria living in your mouth. There are 200 to 300 different types of germs that call your mouth home. Some of them are beneficial and can help the body produce vitamins, generate enzymes to help you digest food and reduce the level of harmful bacteria in the oral cavity.

Hundreds of types of germs live in your mouth.

Dentists refer to the troublesome bacteria as plaque. Plaque is usually invisible, but you may recognize it as "morning mouth." That's the familiar white film that collects on the teeth overnight when your saliva, turned off while you sleep, can no longer rinse it off. It is actually a sticky colony of bacteria and food debris that not only gives you "the worst breath of the day" but, if it's not removed, will produce acid that dissolves tooth enamel, infects the gums and leads to periodontal disease and bone loss. Let's take a closer look at these two problems individually.

Stopping Tooth Decay in Its Tracks

Ten to 15 minutes after eating, the bacteria in your mouth begin producing acid, which may eat away at the enamel of your teeth.

"The damage is done quite quickly," says Rick Hoard, D.D.S., chairman of the section of operative dentisty at the UCLA School of Dentistry. "In fact, it starts as soon as you stop eating. The physical act of eating is a form of self-cleansing of the teeth. In addition, we produce a gallon of saliva a day, which has a washing effect on our teeth."

The act of eating cleans the teeth.

If a cavity is formed, a cycle starts. The cavity traps food debris, which combines with bacteria to produce the acid that digs even deeper into the tooth. Like most dental diseases, the process can be slow, insidious and painless. "People get a false sense of security if they feel no pain," says Dr. Hoard.

A regular visit to a dentist can detect cavities early and avoid complex and expensive dental procedures. If you experience any tooth sensitivity or discomfort, seek dental care immediately.

Good Mouthkeeping

Cleaning the teeth is an important skill. Here are a few simple suggestions that will help you improve your technique.

• Use a disclosing tablet. A harmless dye available at most drugstores, disclosing tablets reveal invisible plaque colonies. Simply chew the tablet—or, if you're using a solution, swish it around in your mouth. When you spit it out, you'll see a red stain on your teeth. Brush properly until the stain is gone. You may have a residual but temporary stain on your tongue and gums. You don't have to use a tablet all the time, but it might help you to use it occasionally as a spot check after you brush to see if you are missing areas in your mouth when you brush.

• Brush and floss. To clean teeth, angle a soft-bristle brush at about 45 degrees and jiggle or vibrate it in a circular motion. It should intrude into the gum slightly. Scrub chewing surfaces and sides of each tooth. Also, brush the tongue, where bacteria lurk.

Break off about 18 inches of waxed or unwaxed floss and wind it around your middle fingers. Guide it in between teeth with your thumbs and forefingers. Don't snap it between teeth, or you'll damage soft tissues. Use a gentle sawing motion instead.

Wrap it around one tooth and slide it in the space between the gum and the tooth. Hold the floss tightly and scrape the side of the tooth, moving away from the gum.

The simplest tooth repair is a filling of silver amalgam or, occasionally, of tooth-colored plastic that is used for the more visible teeth. Gold may be required in more complex situations. The traditional silver filling is the most common, and may have a life span of many years, but nothing can replace natural teeth.

In fact, in cases where pulp or nerve is injured and the pulp is hopeless, the dentist is likely to refer you to an endodontist, or root canal specialist. The endodontist removes the pulp by drilling into the tooth crown, disinfects the area and hermetically seals it. Though it now has no sensation, the tooth is saved.

Root canal work can save a severely damaged tooth.

However, says Ahmad Fahid, D.D.S., assistant professor of endodontics at the UCLA School of Dentistry, "A lot of pulp could be saved by taking care of cavities before they get deeper into the pulp."

Sealants Team Up with Fluoride to Save Adult Teeth

Even if you brush your teeth with a fluoride toothpaste and use a fluoride mouthwash after every meal, millions of decay-causing bacteria can lurk in the cozy pits and fissures atop your molars. Given enough time, these tough little Ninja warrior germs can jeopardize the health of an entire tooth.

Sealants provide a barricade against destructive bacteria.

Enter sealants: Plastic coatings (usually clear) developed about ten years ago to hermetically seal (an airtight seal) teeth against bacteria, preventing tooth decay on the chewing surfaces of molars, where fluoride is less effective. Once the tooth surface is coated, the sealants act as an impervious barrier between voracious bacteria and nutrients in the saliva. In one study, after two years the number of bacteria on tooth surfaces beneath the sealant dropped 2,000-fold after teeth were sealed. Sealants render teeth virtually immune to decay. That leaves teeth intact and stronger, less prone to fracture and saves you from possible complicated dentistry such as uncomfortable fillings and possible root canal work. And compared to fillings, sealings require no anesthetic or drilling and are easy and painless to apply. While charges vary widely, sealants can cost about the same as simple fillings and last a minimum of five years, depending on individual eating and brushing habits.

So far, surprisingly few dentists apply sealants, which are used primarily to prevent tooth decay in children. When the procedure was first developed, dentists worried that hardy bacteria would inadvertently be trapped beneath the sealant, and would foster tooth decay. But a large number of clinical and laboratory studies have since allayed such fears. In fact, with their food and air supply cut off, the population of trapped bacteria decreased dramatically. Cost, too, contributes to slow adoption. Unlike filling cavities and other restorative dental work, applying sealants is rarely if ever covered by dental insurance. Still, the cost is far exceeded by the benefits, not the least of which are the enhanced self-esteem, aesthetic appearance and peace of mind that come from having a cavity-free mouth.

Other than the expense, there's no reason why many adults can't save their teeth by taking advantage of sealants.

"While sealants are best applied during the first few years after teeth emerge, that doesn't preclude applying a sealant to protect older, established teeth that are prone to decay," says A. John Gwinnett, D.D.S., Ph.D., professor of oral biology and pathology at the dental school of the State University of New York at Stony Brook, and one of the doctors who pioneered the technique.

Sealants can save older teeth, too.

Your dentist may not suggest sealants for your teeth unless you ask about them. One woman whose "cavity-prone years" seemed to be extending well into her thirties spotted a poster advocating sealants for children's teeth on the wall of her dentist's office. She told him, "I plan to keep my teeth for another 35 years. Wouldn't sealants save me a lot of tooth decay?" Her dentist agreed, and applied sealants to the cavity-prone surfaces of her teeth. She hasn't needed a filling since.

"Dentists can determine on a case-by-case basis whether an adult qualifies for sealants, depending on the condition of the teeth and how prone they are to decay," says Dr. Gwinnett. For example, people with teeth that show signs of decay don't qualify. But most others probably would. Age in itself is not a deciding factor. And should you have your teeth sealed, the process will not interfere with any later dental work that may be required, including bonding, crowns, fixed bridgework or any other restorative dental procedures an adult may need.

Sealing does not interfere with bonding, crowns, fixed bridgework or other restorative dentistry.

Having your teeth sealed doesn't give you carte blanche to neglect oral hygiene or quit visiting your dentist. You still have to brush and floss daily. And have regular checkups to help catch dental problems while they're still small. Remember, too, that sealants eventually wear off, and you are protected from bacterial growth only if the sealant remains intact. So you'll need periodic touchups—every year or so, if necessary—to maintain your defense against decay.

Floss and Gloss:
A Guide to Healthy Gums

Millions of Americans have a disease that could affect the way they eat, speak, smile and kiss. It's an infection of the gum and jawbone called periodontal disease. And it accounts for a major proportion of all tooth loss. If you are an adult over 40, chances are you already have some signs of this insidious disease. In its early stages, periodontal disease can be reversed. But unless you see your dentist, you might not even know you have it.

Periodontal disease accounts for most tooth loss.

"Your mouth can be nice and pink and beautiful looking and you may have periodontal disease," says UCLA's Michael Newman, D.D.S.

That's because the real damage is being done under the gum line. Bacterial plaque clinging to the necks of the teeth manages to dig a hole between the tooth and gum, creating a pocket that, safely out of reach, can fill with food debris, plaque and, as the infection advances, pus. At the same time, it eats away at the bone supporting the tooth.

Hardened plaque can lead to erosion of bone and loosened teeth.

If the plaque hardens—which it does when it combines with calcium—this resultant calculus acts "like a dirty splinter," says Dr. Newman, irritating the gums, which then pull away from the teeth, creating more pockets to trap food debris and bacteria. In its advanced stages, this infection—the second most commonly occurring infection—can weaken supporting ligaments as well as bone. Teeth may loosen and even fall out.

If your gums bleed, see your dentist.

Plaque seems to build up faster and in larger quantities as people age, making the elderly more prone to dental problems. So, watch for warning signs: In the early stages of periodontal disease, your gums may bleed when you brush or floss. They may be tender, red and swollen. These are symptoms of a condition called gingivitis. "Bleeding is not a sign of health," says Dr. Newman. "If your gums bleed, it is important to see your dentist."

Your dentist, using a periodontal probe and x-rays, will be able to detect periodontal disease long before you see the first symptoms. In fact, seeing your dental-health professional is the key to prevent-

Sugar Facts for Healthy Teeth

There's no magic involved in maintaining strong, healthy teeth and gums. Common sense tells you that a good diet is important. Common sense also tells you to limit the sugars and carbohydrates in your diet that provide fuel for the bacterial colonies to produce tooth destroying acid. That's why dentists warn against eating too many sweets. But there's more you should know. For instance, all sugars are the same. The bacteria in your mouth can't discriminate between the refined sugar in a candy bar and the fructose in an orange. But don't give up fruit. If you brush and floss your teeth after eating a chocolate bar, brush and floss them after eating an orange, too.

Also, be wary of "sticky" foods. Foods like raisins, dried fruits and even honey stick to the teeth and may even be more harmful than refined sugars. Limit them and brush and floss after eating.

Also, limit the number of times you eat sweets. If you munch on sugary foods all day, your mouth is under constant attack by acid. If you're going to eat sweets, you're better off eating them all at once.

And try to avoid sweets you keep in your mouth for a long time—lollipops, mints and, yes, even cough drops.

ing periodontal disease or arresting it in its earliest, easier-to-treat stages.

One reason is that, although fastidious brushing and flossing can often remedy gingivitis, later stages of the disease can be advanced by well-intentioned home cures. The salt-and-baking-soda remedy, says Dr. Newman, is an effective plaque killer—if you have healthy gums. "But it can make the gum tissue appear healthy at the tip of the gum. The gum tissue acts as a drawstring, causing the bacteria to dig deeper into the bone."

Once periodontal disease has taken hold, the dentist, periodontist and dental hygienist are usually the only ones who can help you. The calculus must be removed (a procedure called scaling) and you may need planing, which smooths tooth surfaces so gums can reattach. You may also need curettage, which is the removal of infected gum tissue.

Advanced cases of periodontal disease, which are usually less responsive to treatment, may call for periodontal surgery, the removal of gum tissue from root surfaces. This works to remove calculus and to reshape diseased gums so they're easier to keep clean. You don't want the disease to advance this far. Once the disease has advanced to this stage, you have already irrevocably lost bone.

Surgery is a last-ditch effort to save your gums.

Without protection of gum tissue, you become more susceptible to cavities that take hold in the tooth root and are extremely difficult to treat. Also, once you've had periodontal disease, you're vulnerable to a repeat performance.

"Like diabetics, you have to be monitored for a lifetime," says Dr. Newman.

New technology has made it possible to replace lost bone with a derivative of natural bone around which the remaining bone grows, strengthening tooth support. You could compare surgery for tooth and gum disease to coronary bypass surgery for heart disease: Like most technology, after-the-fact repair work is more costly than prevention, and the underlying disease may eventually take its toll once again unless you change the unhealthy habits that contributed to the problem in the first place. The experts agree: The best way to beat periodontal disease is never to get it.

New technology can spur growth of the re-maining bone.

What Can You Do?

Luckily, gum disease is nearly 100 percent preventable. Here's how:

• See your dentist usually several times a year, depending on how quickly you build up calculus. Only the dental professional can remove calculus, with dental instruments.

• Brush frequently with a soft toothbrush and floss daily. A hard brush can cause gums to recede and may damage teeth.

• Use a fluoride toothpaste or mouthwash.

• Massage gums frequently to stimulate blood flow and eject plaque from beneath the gum line.

Try using an antiplaque toothpaste.

• Use new antiplaque toothpastes and mouthwashes and irrigating devices as adjuncts to basic care. The irrigating devices are a boon to the handicapped, elderly and retarded, says Dr. Newman.

Dental Crowns:
Beyond the Gold Standard

If a tooth is too decayed to fill—if there's just not enough healthy tooth left to hold a filling securely—your dentist may try to salvage what's left by covering the tooth with a crown (sometimes called a cap). Crowns are also used to restore broken teeth, to splint teeth that wobble due to gum disease, to remodel chipped, stained or misshapen teeth or (when incorporated in fixed bridgework, discussed in the next section) to replace missing teeth.

First, the tooth to be crowned is pared down to a stump. Then the dentist affixes a custom-made crown, conventionally made entirely of gold, or porcelain or plastic fused to a gold core. Once in place, crowns allow you to eat, talk and smile without a second thought. And crowns are getting better all the time. Newer, all-ceramic crowns consist of porcelain fused to a ceramic core. The result is a pearly, translucent crown that more closely resembles neighboring natural teeth than conventional crowns, which tend to have either a flat, opaque look or a slight grayish tint. More importantly, an all-ceramic crown allows your dentist to x-ray your teeth, if necessary, to check for decay or signs of root disease and deal with any such problems before the situation gets out of hand and threatens tooth loss. Metal-based crowns, by comparison, block x-rays. Another bonus: All-ceramic crowns are better insulated than metal-based crowns, so they don't trigger hot or cold flashes in your mouth the way metal-based crowns tend to do when you consume hot tea, ice cream or other hot or cold food or beverages.

All-ceramic crowns look more natural than metal-based crowns.

Overall, all-ceramic crowns are more compatible with your natural teeth and gums. And they're certainly worth asking your dentist about if he or she recommends crowns to repair your dental flaws.

Dentures, Bridgework and Implants

If, despite your best efforts at good dental hygiene, you lose some or all of your teeth, take heart. Artificial teeth have come a long way since George Washington's wooden bridge. And if you want to feel your best, you need the best-fitting, best-per-

Several options are available for artificial teeth.

forming, best-looking new teeth possible. Some of the most nutritious foods—fresh fruits and vegetables, nuts, lean meats and chewy whole grain breads—require strong teeth to chew. And without a full set of properly-fitting teeth, your cheeks will cave in and sag, giving you an older, emaciated appearance. If you've lost any of your teeth, you have at least three options: Dentures, fixed bridgework or implants.

Dentures: Sometimes the Only Answer

If only one or two of your teeth are missing, your dentist may fit you for a partial denture—a removable appliance, sometimes a plastic plate, to which one or two artificial teeth are attached, sometimes anchored to nearby teeth with wire clasps. Full dentures are for people who have no teeth left at all.

To construct the best fitting and trouble-free conventional denture possible, the dentist (or prosthodontist, who specializes in replacing teeth) makes an impression of your mouth, measures your jaw and dental-facial relationship, and chooses new "teeth" in a suitable shape and color for you. Small, delicately shaped teeth, for example, would look out of place on, say, Sly Stallone's face. By the same token, off-white teeth look more natural in older people than stark white teeth, since teeth naturally become somewhat darker later in life.

Custom-made dentures—and most "conventional" dentures are custom-made—require half a dozen or more visits to fine-tune their fit before you can take them home.

Clean your new teeth, but also clean your mouth.

Once you've been properly fitted with dentures, ask your dentist for written instructions explaining how to care for them. Unless you're told otherwise, it's best to remove dentures overnight to allow your mouth to rest. Store them in cool water or denture-cleaning solution to prevent them from warping. To clean your dentures, use a fingernail brush reserved for that purpose. Holding the brush in one hand and your dentures in the other, brush all surfaces gently but thoroughly.

Remember to clean your mouth, too. Plaque doesn't limit itself to natural teeth and can cause sores, infection, discomfort and bone loss in your mouth if it accumulates between your dentures and your mouth. Food also can collect under dentures and around clasps on partial dentures. Gently brush your gums, tongue and the roof of your mouth daily with a soft toothbrush. Rinse your mouth vigorously to remove food debris.

And don't routinely use an adhesive when you replace the teeth, unless your doctor so instructs. If you have to use an adhesive, your dentures probably don't fit properly. Used constantly, denture adhesives can mask oral infections and cause jawbone deterioration, making construction of new, properly fitting dentures more difficult.

If you need adhesive, your dentures probably don't fit properly.

Don't assume that once you have dentures, you no longer need to pay attention to your teeth. Regular dental care is as important as ever.

"The most common misunderstanding about dentures is the impression that when all the teeth are removed, the patient no longer needs dentistry," says Hyman J. V. Goldberg, D.M.D., one coauthor of a dental guide to better health. "Nothing could be farther from the truth."

Dentures do wear out. Dentures can loosen, too, because of structural changes of the underlying bone. Constant friction from poorly fitting dentures can irritate your gums and lead to sores and infection in your mouth. If faulty equipment leads to the tea-and-toast syndrome—avoiding nutritious fare like fresh fruits and vegetables that require chewing—you may risk serious nutritional deficiencies.

Fixed Bridgework: A Better Solution

Fixed bridgework looks, feels and functions like your own teeth. Constructed of any of various materials—porcelain, plastic or a combination of these substances—fixed bridgework consists of a span of teeth anchored to neighboring, natural teeth for support. Once installed, they stay put for ten or more years. And they don't slip. You care for your bridgework just as you care for regular teeth—which means you don't have to take them out at night and soak them in a glass of water.

Dental Implants: Almost Real Teeth

Like prosthetic limbs, dental implants—actual fixed "teeth"—have had their serious drawbacks. But a new implant procedure, taught and practiced by a specially trained team at the UCLA School of Dentistry, may change the lives of those people who have lost their teeth and can't or won't wear removable dentures.

Developed by a Swedish orthopedic surgeon, Per-Ingvar Branemark, M.D., Ph.D., the "osseo-integrated" implant consists of a titanium screw surgically placed in the bone where, because the titanium is able to form biological bonds with living tissue, it actually becomes anchored to the jawbone. Then the dentist can attach the patient's permanent bridgework.

Implants are anchored to your jaw—just like natural teeth.

"Patients tell us it's like having their own teeth again," says Amerian Sones, D.M.D., assistant professor of prosthodontics at UCLA School of Dentistry and a member of the Branemark implant team.

What makes the Swedish technique superior to other implant procedures is that the process causes little bone damage and infection is rare. Once the implant is placed in the bone, it is covered with soft tissue and allowed to heal for four to six months, and it is not exposed to what one expert calls "the bacterial pit of the mouth." After the healing process is completed, a small incision is made and a metal implant post is connected. It is on this post that a fixed denture is secured.

Dental implants have two important functional advantages. First, explains Dr. Sones, they allow the patient to chew more efficiently. There's no problem with ill-fitting dentures or denture slip. Second, there's less bone resorption in the jaw. When you lose teeth, the supporting bone tends to resorb within six months to a year. Some people who wear dentures must have bone grafts to restore enough bone to support the dentures.

"The force of biting travels through the implant, stimulating the bone to be maintained," says Dr. Sones. In that respect, dental implants may have an edge over dentures.

Take an active role in all dental treatments.

Only your dentist can determine which of these options is best for you. But the more you know about the pros and cons of restorative methods, the better able you will be to make an informed choice.

23

Muscles

that Work

B eing strong is like being young. It means you can go where you want to go and do what you want to do. For some, that strength means having the ability to hike in the Grand Canyon, while for others it means being able to heft a 20-pound sack of potatoes from the bottom shelf into the supermarket cart. In either case, being strong allows a person to achieve his or her goals—however grand or modest they may be—without frustration and without a sense of lost ability.

Well-tended muscles, in other words, tend to keep you energetic, optimistic and self-sufficient. Not to mention shapely.

Getting Strong

One way to shape up might be by lifting weights. It's almost never too late to begin. "Many of the best body builders in the business—Boyer Coe, for example—didn't even reach their peak until age 40," says Roger Servin, who at age 50 was a contestant in the Mr. America competition.

On a less glamorous level, researchers at the University of Southern California, in Los Angeles, found that 8 weeks of weight training increased strength in older men. And William J. Evans, Ph.D.,

One doctor discovered great increases in strength.

chief of the physiology laboratory at Tufts University, in Medford, Massachusetts, discovered that people in weight training programs had "a 10 to 20 percent increase in muscle mass in a 12-week period. We also noted great increases in strength."

Dr. Evans is also a great proponent of aerobic exercise, which not only builds muscle, but also a kind of stamina called functional capacity. "When functional capacity is low, a person can't walk upstairs, and can't go to the supermarket alone. This capacity increases substantially as a result of aerobic training." Such training includes activities like walking and swimming.

But medical experts suggest that you don't dive headfirst into an exercise program. It's best to start by getting your feet wet first. "Everybody—young or old—should start to exercise gradually," says Dr. Evans. "Make sure you warm up five to ten minutes before you start the activity, and stretch to cool down afterwards. If you have heart disease or even a family history of heart disease, talk to a doctor before beginning."

Healing Aching Muscles

As you get into your exercise program, you may find yourself so enthusiastic that one day you simply overdo.

A case in point is the Mr. Packer incident. He was impatient with the gradual increases in his weight training program and one day lifted a lot more weight. The result was a snapping sound and a sharp pain in his bicep, followed by a weak arm and a lump the size of a golf ball where his muscle used to be.

Follow your training program carefully.

"This is a common injury," says Stephen Morgan, D.O., of the Sports Medicine Clinic, in Traverse City, Michigan.

"We see injuries like this all the time, and it's usually someone who overestimates his or her own muscular capabilities. The next thing you know that person has strained an arm, calf, groin or hamstring muscle."

Of course it's not always as severe as in Mr. Packer's case. "His was considered a third-degree muscle strain—the worst there is," Dr. Morgan says. With a third-degree strain, muscle fibers have been torn apart completely. It's actually more common to see first- and second-degree strains, which are considerably less severe, since fewer muscle fibers have been disrupted.

"Milder still is a case of plain old sore muscles," adds William A. Grana, M.D., director of the Oklahoma Center for Athletes at the University of Oklahoma Health Sciences Center, in Oklahoma City. "Everybody's had sore muscles at one time or another, whether it's from trimming the hedges, carrying a heavy suitcase or jogging before a proper warm-up. When your muscles become sore, it just means that you've stretched them further than they were prepared to go. But there's been no tearing of the fibers at all."

Muscle soreness develops from stretching too far.

Sore muscles do get better by themselves. "In fact," Dr. Grana says, "most muscle strains do too. But you can aid the process dramatically with some simple home remedies."

RICE Therapy

"Immediately after the injury and for the first 24 to 48 hours, I recommend RICE," says Dr. Morgan. And he doesn't mean the kind that sticks to the bottom of the pan when you cook it. This kind of RICE is an acronym for Rest, Ice, Compression and Elevation.

Rest. "Rest means to stop whatever you're doing," says Frank Bassett III, M.D., professor of orthopedic surgery at Duke University Medical Center, in Durham, North Carolina. "Usually, that's an automatic response because of the severe pain that hits at the moment the injury occurs."

But even if you're not in extreme pain, don't take that as a license to continue using that muscle, advises Dr. Morgan. Once the fibers have torn even a little, as in a first-degree muscle strain, overdoing it can lead to a second- or even third-degree injury.

Ice. As soon as possible after you've strained or pulled a muscle, get ice onto it. "Ice is extremely important in muscle strains because of its ability to stop the internal bleeding and reduce the swelling," explains Dr. Grana.

Ice reduces swelling and stops internal bleeding.

"Ice also helps reduce pain because it has a numbing effect," adds Dr. Bassett. "But be careful about how you apply it. Ice in direct contact with your skin can cause a cold burn or blister. Instead put the ice in a plastic bag and then wrap a towel around the whole thing. Always be sure there is a cloth between the ice and your skin. Apply the cold for 10 to 15 minutes at a time, three or four times a day. The ice therapy should continue for 24 to 48 hours."

Compression. This third component of RICE should also be continued for that period, but only if there's swelling. Wrap the injured muscle with an elastic bandage snugly, but not so tightly that it impedes circulation. To be sure that's not happening, unwrap the area when you remove the ice and check to be sure that all is still rosy.

Elevation. The last part of the self-treatment program gets gravity working for you instead of against you. Of course, some muscles lend themselves to elevation more easily than others, so adjust accordingly.

Heat that Heals

Heat can speed healing after the pain and swelling subside.

Once the muscle is on the road to recovery—that is, the pain and swelling are down—applying heat will increase the blood flow, bringing in nutrients and cells that speed the healing process, according to some doctors.

"What's more," says Dr. Grana, "heat improves the muscle's elasticity and helps get back its range of motion."

To warm up a hurt muscle you can use an electric heating pad or hot-water bottle. If you don't have one handy, soak a towel in warm water and wrap it around the injured muscle. Then cover it with several layers of plastic wrap to hold in the heat and help prevent dripping.

You may also want to try one of the over-the-counter cream rubs advertised to promote local heating. "These rubs dilate blood vessels in the skin," says Dr. Morgan. "This creates a warming effect, which makes the sore muscle feel more comfortable."

"Using these rubs during the time of recovery can also help improve mobility and flexibility," Dr.

Bassett adds. "The important thing is not to use heat therapy too soon. Let your symptoms be the guide. And remember, if you've still got a lot of swelling and pain after a couple of days, it's time to see a doctor. You could be dealing with a much more serious injury, such as torn ligaments or broken bones."

Preventing Soreness

Once your hurt muscles have begun to heal, you should begin some gentle exercising, gradually increasing the load. The object is to strengthen the muscle that was strained so it will be better able to resist reinjury.

In fact, with the proper care you can prevent muscle strains from happening in the first place, according to some doctors. "Most strains occur when you are fatigued or caught off balance," Dr. Bassett says. So don't plan a tennis game after cleaning out the attic, for example.

The best preventive measure is stretching.

"Stretching exercises done before and after a particularly strenuous task can help prevent a muscle pull also," says Dr. Morgan. "Just before a long walk or yard work, stretch the muscles you'll be using. It's the most important preventive measure there is."

Uncramp Your Life

Muscle cramps and injuries often travel together, striking like Bonnie and Clyde. This attack may seem to be a cruel trick of nature, since your pain is doubled. But actually, the cramp serves to protect the body from further injury. The contracted muscles involved in the cramp act as a cast, to immobilize damaged tissue.

We've all had muscle cramps in the calf of a leg, the arch of a foot or just under the ribs. If you were to reach down to rub that recalcitrant calf, you would actually feel a knot or thickening—the contracted muscles. Severe cramps, like those that sometimes occur during convulsive seizures, can be so strong they snap bones.

Many cramps do not result from injuries or convulsions, however. Commonly, cramps seem to come like a bolt from the blue, especially those that strike your legs at night. These can come from assuming an awkward position, says Israel Weiner,

Avoid positions that invite cramps.

M.D., assistant professor of neurological surgery at the University of Maryland School of Medicine, in Baltimore. Perhaps you've let your foot point downward, which automatically contracts the calf muscle somewhat. Then, consciously or unconsciously, you've tensed your calf muscle, contracting it still more. This position is the ideal setup for a cramp.

"When you contract the muscle, if there is nothing counteracting that movement, like another muscle being stretched in opposition, the contracted muscle can shorten beyond its normal limit and go into an uncontrollable shortened state—in other words, a cramp," Dr. Weiner says. In bed, heavy or tucked-in blankets may push your feet down. Then, if you tense your leg muscles, as you inevitably do when you stretch or turn over, it's . . . *gotcha!*

Free Your Feet

Flex the feet upward as you stretch.

Older people, who are particularly prone to nighttime cramps, are sometimes overtreated for this problem, Dr. Weiner says. "It's important for them to know that this problem is usually not serious, and that it can almost always be resolved without drugs." How? By loosening bed covers or using a board or pillow to keep the weight of the covers off your feet. If you sleep on your stomach, hang your feet over the edge of the bed. And keep your feet flexed upward toward your head when you're stretching your legs. That makes the muscles on the front of your legs contract, providing opposition to the calf muscles.

High heels also throw the legs and feet into a cramp-prone position—the plump and shapely calf is actually a contracted muscle. In fact, women who wear high heels constantly may so shorten their calf muscles that when they take the shoes off, they're unable to touch their heels to the ground.

Learn to Stretch

Stand flat-footed and press down hard.

Doctors, athletic coaches and sufferers all agree that the fastest, surest cure for a cramp is to stretch the affected muscles. If your calf cramps, for example, you can simply stand firmly on your flat foot and press down as hard as you can, or you can do more elaborate stretches (see box).

Cramps actually start when the nerves that con-

Stretching Cramps Away

To stop or avoid a cramp, keep your muscles stretched and limber. These three stretching exercises are good for the calves and the arches of the feet, the muscles most likely to cramp.

1. Stand about three to five feet from a wall, and keep your heels flat and your legs straight. Position your feet as far from the wall as possible, lean against the wall directly in front of you and rest on your hands and elbows. Hold this position for 10 to 15 seconds, or longer if you can. Then walk towards the wall and relax. Repeat three or four times.

2. Sit on the floor with your feet about 12 inches apart. Loop a towel around the ball of your foot, holding an end of the towel in each hand. Without locking your knee, lean back until you feel the stretch in the calf muscle. Hold 15 seconds. If your calf is cramped, one doctor suggests that you rhythmically squeeze the calf muscle while you stretch it.

3. Yoga poses provide an excellent way to stretch muscles. For calves and arms, try this position: Stoop on the floor, with feet flat, arms outstretched and hands flat on the floor in front of you. Slowly straighten your legs until your body forms the shape of a triangle, with your hips at the top. Hold this position for as long as it feels comfortable.

trol the muscles are prompted to misfire, for any number of reasons. Stretching, apparently, changes neural impulses, making the nerves change their signal from "contract" to "relax." Usually stretching relieves a cramp within seconds. And staying fit and limber can help prevent cramps.

Monitor the Minerals

But stretching might not be enough if you neglect to eat right. "Cramps that occur when you first start to exercise are usually due to mineral imbalance, such as calcium, sodium or potassium deficiency or excess," says Mona Shangold, M.D., director of Georgetown University's Sports Gynecology Center, in Washington, D.C., and coauthor (with husband Gabe Mirkin, M.D.) of *The Complete Sports*

Medicine Book for Women (Simon and Schuster). "Abnormal blood levels of these minerals usually allow the muscle to contract but prevent it from relaxing."

"Mineral deficiencies can affect blood flow to muscles," says James Knochel, M.D., a researcher with the Veterans Administration Hospital, in Dallas, who has spent many years studying mineral-related muscular disorders. "When you contract a muscle, for instance, it releases potassium into the surrounding tissue, where the potassium acts as a dilator of arteries in the muscle bed. When someone is potassium deficient, it's equivalent to putting a tourniquet around your arm and then attempting to use the arm, which produces a cramp." Perhaps that's one reason Popeye swears by potassium-packed spinach.

Without sufficient dietary potassium, muscles will cramp.

A potassium deficiency also impairs the ability of the muscles to use glycogen, a sugar which is their main source of energy, Dr. Knochel says. This makes them weak and cramp-prone. Potassium and other mineral deficiencies may also affect the "excitability" of nerves—their tendency to fire off a series of muscle-cramping messages. And they may affect the muscles' "fatigue threshold"—their ability to do more work without becoming tired and spasm-prone.

Body mineral levels may be affected by hormonal changes or unusual physical demands. Pregnancy, too, can make women particularly prone to leg cramps.

In one recent study, researchers at Brigham Young University, in Provo, Utah, found that 266 milligrams a day of supplemental magnesium reduced cramping in all their groups of pregnant women. (Of course, expectant mothers should first question their doctors before taking any vitamin or mineral supplement.)

Some clinical studies seem to indicate that additional calcium may reduce muscle cramps in pregnant women and growing children, who may be deficient in these minerals because of increased nutritional needs. Calcium and magnesium work closely together in the muscles, Dr. Knochel says.

If you suspect a mineral deficiency is causing your muscle cramps, it's good to check with a doctor. Mineral imbalances aren't particularly common, Dr. Shangold says. At risk are those taking diuretics or steroids, heavy drinkers, pregnant women and older people who may not be eating well.

Exercise Cramps

Cramps that occur after you have been exercising for a long time are most often due to dehydration, Dr. Shangold says. "When you exercise for a long time, particularly in hot weather, you lose a lot of fluid. During a vigorous tennis match, for instance, a player can lose as much as two quarts of water per hour. Your blood volume is reduced, and there may not be enough blood to supply oxygen to all your exercising muscles. As a result, the most actively exercised muscles may not get enough blood and they can go into spasm and hurt."

You can protect yourself from developing these kinds of cramps by drinking a glass of water before you exercise and at least every 15 minutes while you exercise, Dr. Shangold says.

Drink water before and during exercise.

A stitch, or side sticker, is a cramp in the diaphragm, the large muscle that separates your chest from your gut and controls breathing. The cramp occurs when this muscle doesn't get enough blood during exercise, Dr. Shangold says. "When you run, you lift your knees and contract your belly muscles, so that the pressure inside your belly increases and pushes on the diaphragm from below. At the same time, if you're breathing heavily, you are expanding your lungs, which press down on the diaphragm from above. This dual pressure squeezes the diaphragm and shuts off blood flow to it. The muscle can't get enough oxygen and goes into spasm."

If you develop a stitch, stop exercising, Dr. Shangold says. Push your fingers deep into your belly just below your ribs on the right side to stretch the diaphragm muscle with your hand. At the same time, purse your lips tightly and blow out as hard as you can. This should release the pressure on your diaphragm and stop the stitch.

All this talk of cramps, however, should not scare you away from exercise. Just exercise carefully. Avoid intense, jerky movements. Stretch to warm up and cool down. Don't bounce. Don't exercise beyond the point of fatigue. But do exercise. Sedentary people are prone to cramps, too.

Finally, there are some pains that feel like cramps but are not true cramps.

It's a pain that comes on after a bit of exercise, making the legs feel heavy and weak. It's called intermittent claudication.

This condition is caused by clogged arteries in the leg, and its symptoms are similar to angina in the heart muscle, says Robert Layzer, M.D., professor of neurology at the University of California at San Francisco. It's important to see a doctor if you have such symptoms, or any cramping pain in the legs accompanied by numbness or coldness in the affected leg or foot.

Weak, heavy legs signal the need for a doctor.

Most doctors recommend exercise, quitting smoking, a low-fat diet and medication for this condition when it occurs in the lower leg. In some studies, vitamin E has also relieved symptoms.

A Stiff Neck

Life can give you a real pain in the neck. And guess which part of your body causes the agony? That's right, it's those pesky muscles acting up again. But people do have some blame in the matter. Most people do things every day—at work, at home and at play—that inject tension into the muscles of the neck and shoulders.

But just like back pain, neck pain can be cast off simply by changing a few habits.

A hunched posture causes neck pain.

"One major cause of neck and shoulder pain is a round-shouldered posture," says Susan L. Fish, a registered physical therapist in New York City. "It throws our heads forward and leaves us looking down. But we tend to want to see where we're going. So we arch our heads back. Holding our heads up in that forward-jutting position puts a tremendous amount of stress on the muscles in the back of the neck and upper shoulders. And a muscle that's in a constant state of contraction can become a painful muscle."

That's why neck pain can be an occupational hazard for some professions.

"It's common for typists and people who work at computers to have neck and shoulder pain," says Fish. "Typists should use a book stand to copy from, rather than laying the source flat on the desk. And computer users should have the screen at eye level," she advises. "That will keep them from constantly tiring those neck muscles."

Keep the computer screen at eye level.

Even reading this book might cause pain, especially if you need glasses. "Nearsighted people often jut their heads forward so they can see better," Fish says. "That can also cause neck and shoulder pain."

Reading in bed with your head propped up on a tower of pillows puts a kink in your neck, too. Your chest, it seems, is a poor choice for a chin rest. Fish recommends using angled pillows that hold the head straight but elevate the whole upper body.

Slouching in your easy chair is another way to make your neck and shoulders uneasy. "If you let yourself scoot down in your chair so that you slouch in your lower back, you're going to go into that round-shouldered posture," says Fish. "One of the best ways to avoid that is to support your lower back. When you sit right up on the base of your buttocks with a support in your lower back, it's hard to slouch over. Lumbar-support chairs are helpful for that reason.

"But I don't want to minimize the fact that I give all of my patients with neck and shoulder pain an individualized exercise program geared to strengthening the upper back muscles, stretching the inner chest muscles and maintaining a posture where the spine is straight."

Keeping your spine straight is tough if you carry a large percentage of your possessions wherever you go. "When you carry a heavy shoulder bag or briefcase, you wind up with your body tilted over," explains Fish. "But you hold your head upright so you see straight. So one side of your neck is constantly contracted. The muscle never totally relaxes. If you have to carry heavy things, divide the weight evenly between both of your arms. If you must wear a shoulder bag, switch sides occasionally. And if at all possible, try not to use one at all."

Forgo heavy briefcases and shoulder bags.

Even something as common as talking on the telephone can call up pain in your muscles, if you squeeze the receiver between your ear and your shoulder. So try to avoid that position, says Fish.

The Tense Neck

Once your position has been corrected, you might want to take a look at your temperament. People literally shoulder their burdens, both physical and emotional.

"I call it carrying the weight of the world on your shoulders," says Fish. "It's the second most common problem that I see."

"Every time something upsets you or you feel aggravated, your body tenses up," explains Dennis T. Jaffe, Ph.D., professor of psychology at Saybrook Institute, in San Francisco, and coauthor of *From Burnout to Balance* (McGraw-Hill). "It's part of the body's reaction to anything that's threatening. Your muscles tense up, your breathing gets shallower, you secrete adrenaline and your whole body gets thrown into overdrive. That's what the stress response is.

"If you don't do something to release the muscle tension, it stays there, even after the upset is over. Your body doesn't rebound to normal. And so over the course of a day, muscle tension builds up. Many people have a tendency to hold that tension in their neck and shoulders.

"Physically active people definitely have less trouble with it," Dr. Jaffe points out, "because they're out there releasing their muscles all the time. But people who are sitting all day, especially if they're hunched over, need to find ways to release the tension."

If your shoulders are hiked up to your ears, that's a clue that you're holding tension in them. "I sometimes have patients look in the mirror, then I tell them to drop their shoulders. Some people drop them about three inches," says Fish. "When they see it in the mirror, they become aware of the fact that their shoulders were almost touching their earlobes. Many people don't even know that they're doing it.

"I find the most beneficial thing to recommend is axial extension, or elongating the neck. To do that, look straight ahead, keeping your chin parallel to the floor. Imagine that your head is being pulled straight

Exercise releases tension stored in muscles.

up. When you do axial extension, you're forced to relax the muscles in your shoulders and drop them down. The result is correct posture."

There are many other ways to help relax those muscles. "Letting a hot shower run on the back of your neck is probably one of the most effective ways to relax the neck and shoulder muscles," says Paul J. Rosch, M.D., president of the American Institute of Stress, in Yonkers, New York.

A hot shower can wash away pain.

"Progressive muscle relaxation exercises are also very helpful. To do them, you progressively tense, then relax, the different muscle groups in your body. For example, you may start with your hands, then tense and relax your forearms, then your upper arms, then your shoulders and so on. Deep breathing seems to help, too."

More serious cases may benefit from professional attention. "When a muscle goes into spasm, sometimes it sets up a vicious cycle," Rosch points out. "It may contract down on the nerve that carries the sensation of pain. If it does that, the nerve becomes irritated, which causes continued muscle spasm. In some instances it's possible to break that cycle by injecting an anesthetic to release the spasm. When the spasm is reduced, there's no longer any pressure on the nerve and you break the cycle. Pain-relieving, anti-inflammatory and muscle-relaxant drugs can also be effective if they break the spasm-pain cycle.

Sometimes drugs are needed to break the cycle of pain.

"However," cautions Dr. Rosch, "if you have persistent pain that used to be relieved by simple analgesics like aspirin and no longer is, that's a sign that you should see a physician. You should also seek medical attention if you have numbness or tingling in your arms or fingers, pain down your arms, or changes in the muscle tone in your arms or hands."

"I treat a lot of this muscle spasm with electrical stimulation," says Fish. "That's the use of electricity to stop the muscle spasm. Some people use ultrasound as well. The deep heat it creates increases the circulation."

"When a muscle is tense, the flow of blood can be cut off," says Marilyn Frender, a licensed massage therapist in New York City and editor of the *Ameri-*

can Massage Therapy Association Journal. "Massage can increase circulation, warming the muscles and taking out tension. It can soothe and relax the muscles as well as calm the person. It's good for general body relaxation and stress reduction."

Body and Soul

"The important thing," says Dr. Rosch, "is to recognize where the sources of stress are in your life that might be causing this."

Dr. Jaffe agrees. "Anything that's upsetting or creates conflict in your life can give you tension. It's important to look at the stress in your life and make changes. If you release the tension but keep going back into the same kind of stress, you'll keep creating problems for yourself."

As you can see, there's a close connection between body and soul. If you're distressed, you can cause physical pain. And if you exercise, you can discharge stress, increase your ability to do fun things and mold a firmer body—all of which are bound to improve your spirits.

"The idea that you will become weak as you age is a self-fulfilling prophecy," says Dr. Evans. "People who believe that don't move around much, and they do become incapacitated."

So get moving. Just use your head when you work out your body.

24

Nutrition for

Healthy Aging

Remember the old commercials with those hoary Russian villagers who reached ages beyond 100 years (and still visited their mothers) by eating a particular brand of yogurt?

Well, it turns out that their *real* secret of longevity was to lie about their age. They, and citizens of other remote areas of the world, had fooled the public for years. The jig was up for some "centenarian" Ecuadorians when a scientist met a man who claimed to be 122 years old in 1971, and 134 years old in 1974. Later investigation revealed that nobody there had even reached a 100th birthday, and that village authorities were planning to build a high-rise hotel which would offer a "week of longevity" to rich Americans.

Hoaxes and false leads have not suppressed the search for ways to slow or delay the degeneration which occurs with aging, however. It's estimated that humans have the potential to live up to 115 years, yet life expectancy (the average age at death for a particular population) is now about 74 years in the United States. Researchers working to bridge the gap between reality and potential have found that good nutrition is an important factor in achieving a long, healthy life.

"There is no doubt that life can be shortened by

Human beings have the potential to live 115 years.

Rejuvenators or Just Animal Secretions?

In the 1890s, Charles Edouard Brown-Sequard, a prestigious neurologist, physiologist and endocrinologist did an odd thing. He injected himself with extracts from the testicles of dogs and guinea pigs.

Then something even stranger happened—a cult of followers started doing the same thing.

These injections, meant to rejuvenate the body, eventually lost their popularity when scientists discovered they were ineffective, but they were the basis of many youth cults in the years to come.

There was Dr. Serge Voronoff, for example, who declared that the monkey "most nearly approaches the human species in the highly perfected development of its tissues," and transplanted ape testes into the scrota of many men who were in search of rejuvenation. A Dr. Stanley injected goat, ram, boar and deer teste extract into hundreds of inmates in a California prison in the 1920s. He concluded that his results were excellent. The extract cleared up acne, weakness and senility, but not "impotentia—that might be difficult to determine in jailed patients," he wrote.

Though the work of some of these doctors was questioned by the established medical community, John R. Brinkley, M.D., was the first "goat doctor" to lose his license to practice medicine. He

a variety of forms of malnutrition," writes Alfred E. Harper, Ph.D., of the departments of nutritional sciences and biochemistry at the University of Wisconsin, in Madison, in *The American Journal of Clinical Nutrition.* "There is no doubt that dietary modification can be used to reduce the severity of the signs and symptoms of a variety of genetic and pathological conditions that result in metabolic defects. Application of nutritional knowledge in.these ways can prolong survival—increase longevity—within the biologically determined life span—just as can the application of other therapeutic measures or avoidance of environmental hazards."

In other words, a well-balanced diet won't al-

owned a radio station, from which he broadcasted medical advice. He advised many listeners who were seeking rejuvenation to come to the Brinkley Institute of Health for goat gland implantation.

"To understand properly why there were all these searches for a source of youth, one must be aware of the atmosphere of the times," points out John R. Herman, M.D., clinical professor of urology at Albert Einstein College of Medicine, in New York City, in the *New York State Journal of Medicine.* "In the 1920s, inflation was rampant, 'Jazz was King,' and the entire world was riding high, headed for the great depression in a Cadillac! Let only one or two physicians speak highly of one or another rejuvenation technique, or let a well-known actor claim his permanent youthful bloom was due to such and such, and these methods became popular beyond belief."

But we're smarter than that now, right?

Wrong. Christiaan Barnard, who became famous for performing the first heart transplant operation, and for dating the likes of Gina Lollobrigida and Sophia Loren, has told the press that, whereas he is too scientifically trained to draw any definite conclusions, he believes it is possible that his young-looking skin may result from the fetal-lamb-cell injections he had in a posh Swiss rejuvenating clinic.

Although it's not a stampede, the search for effective animal by-products continues.

low you to live forever, but it may help you live longer than your neighbor. Particular diets can reduce the chances of developing particular diseases, as is discussed throughout this book. But are there any foods which slow the general decline of bodily functions which occurs almost universally in aging?

A well-balanced diet is necessary for optimum health.

Some doctors say "yes!" and that one secret lies in combating free radicals. They base their conclusions on the free-radical theory of aging.

Free Radicals

Electrons are particles that rotate around the nucleus of a molecule. All self-respecting electrons

"Miracle" Drugs: Fountain of Youth, or Mirage?

The preservatives BHA and BHT: Do they cause cancer or prevent it? And Gerovital: Does it rejuvenate the body or cause convulsions? And how about ginseng: Does it make you into a sexual dynamo or a member of the opposite sex?

The answers can be confusing, because claims like these *have* been made. Many people accept the positive claims because they so desperately wish for youth. However, this gullibility can harm the body as well as the wallet.

Take the case of BHA and BHT. Since they are used as antioxidants to extend the shelf-life of foods, scientists began to wonder if they would also extend the shelf-life of human beings. Studies with laboratory animals announced that BHT increases their life span and inhibits the accumulation of "age pigments" in cells. BHA has been shown to stave off cancer in animal studies, and BHT has inactivated herpes simplex virus in a test tube, says Sheldon Hendler, M.D., Ph.D.

However, the best scientific evidence does not support these claims, according to Dr. Hendler. In fact, some evidence suggests that BHT actually can promote the growth of some cancers. The low levels of these chemicals which are used as preservatives are probably harmless, but they should not be taken as supplements, according to Josep G. Llaurado, M.D., Ph.D., of the Nuclear Medicine Service at Jerry L. Pettis Memorial Veterans Hospital and Loma Linda University School of Medicine, in California. He points out that the 2-gram dose recommended in a popular program for longevity is only one notch below the lethal dose, and says that smaller doses must produce some mischief.

And then there's Gerovital H3 (GH3). Famous people such as Mao Tse-Tung, Khrushchev and John F. Kennedy reportedly have

Free radicals are the swinging singles of the molecule scene.

travel in pairs. Molecules with an unpaired electron are called free radicals. They're called free, and act accordingly.

"A free radical is like a convention delegate away from his wife: It's a highly reactive chemical agent that will combine with anything that's around," according to gerontologist Alex Comfort, M.D., Ph.D.

used it. Claims that this drug can reverse just about all the symptoms of old age (including senility, poor hearing, muscle fatigue, depression, heart disease, impotence, graying hair, balding, wrinkles, you name it) have sent people flocking to Rumania for a fix. (According to the Food and Drug Administration, GH3 is a new and unapproved drug.)

Doctors are not equally thrilled, however. The studies claiming to prove its anti-aging effects were shown to be inadequate. Gerovital's "active ingredient" is supposed to be novocaine (the anesthetic you get at the dentist's office), and it breaks down as soon as it hits the bloodstream. Side effects are infrequent but serious. They include allergic reactions, abrupt drop in blood pressure, respiratory difficulty and convulsions, according to Dr. Hendler, who concludes, "GH3 is not recommended under any circumstances."

Ginseng has a more venerable past, having been an ancient Chinese cure-all for centuries. It's right up there with the modern panaceas when it comes to claims—it can increase sexual potency, combat stress, "expel evil effluvia," prolong life, reduce cholesterol levels and stimulate and rejuvenate the entire body, according to its disciples.

Dr. Hendler does not recommend this root in any form, for any reason. He states that there have been reports that, with heavy use, side effects may include a masculinizing effect in women, a feminizing effect in men and a so-called ginseng abuse syndrome, which inflicts high blood pressure, nervousness, sleeplessness, skin eruptions and morning diarrhea on ginseng junkies.

Unfortunately, it seems that the only miracle involved in miracle drugs is that so many people pay so much money for such ineffective treatments.

"Free radicals are produced in your body every day, as by-products of normal body processes, including metabolism, oxidation and detoxification of dangerous chemicals. And they're not complete ne'er-do-wells. White blood cells set them against harmful bacteria.

"Unleash a free radical in the body, and it steals an electron from the first molecule it bumps into.

They steal electrons from other molecules, damaging the body's tissues.

Now *that* molecule needs another electron, and *it* steals an electron from the next guy, and the process continues, like a wild game of tag. This rampage can destroy cell walls, making chromosome damage, and hence, cell death or mutation (which may lead to cancer), more likely to occur."

Most of these reactions are nonlethal, according to Sheldon Hendler, M.D., Ph.D., of the University of California at San Diego, and author of *The Complete Guide to Anti-Aging Nutrients* (S & S). If they were lethal, you wouldn't last more than a few minutes. But the damage from uncontrolled free radicals accumulates, and can cause more problems as time goes by. In fact, some scientists blame free radicals for much of the degeneration which occurs with aging.

Free radicals do their dirty work outside the body too. Have you ever cut apple slices and saved them for later, only to find that they had turned an ugly brown? Or forgotten to put away the butter, which became rancid? Or left your bike out in the rain, where it rusted? Free radicals strike again.

Antioxidants

Mankind has created ways to control free radical production in nature. You can limit contact of food with oxygen, for instance, by tightly wrapping it in plastic wraps which "lock in freshness." Cars are rustproofed, certain kinds of paper are specially treated to keep them from yellowing and special materials are applied to leather and rubber products to prevent them from deteriorating; in each example, an antioxidant compound is what holds the free radicals at bay.

Vitamins can work on the same principle as a rustproofing treatment on your car.

Your body needs antioxidants too, since controlling oxidation also controls the production of free radicals. "We know that animals deficient in antioxidants like vitamins E, C and A and selenium develop cell damage similar to that seen with aging," says Jeffrey B. Blumberg, Ph.D., associate professor of nutrition at Tufts University, in Medford, Massachusetts, and acting associate director of the Human Nutrition Research Center on Aging at Tufts.

"Most people do not take in amounts of antioxidants that are optimal for combating free radicals," says Dr. Hendler.

Vitamin E. Vitamin E has an especially good reputation for foiling free radicals. Research by Jeffrey Bland, Ph.D., of the Linus Pauling Institute of Science and Medicine, in Palo Alto, California, has shown that vitamin E is attracted to cell membranes because they contain large amounts of fatty acids and vitamin E is fat soluble. "The cell membrane," Dr. Bland explains, "is like a sandwich of fatty layers, with vitamin E in the middle, protecting the fats from oxidation. The vitamin E oxidizes instead, soaking up free radicals."

Preventing oxidation of the cell membrane can actually extend the life of a cell. Dr. Bland found that vitamin E prolonged the life of red blood cells exposed to harmful ultraviolet light, which normally accelerates the cells' aging process.

Vitamin E extended the life of blood cells exposed to harmful light.

A group of researchers from the Institute of Food and Nutrition, in Poland, investigated 100 healthy subjects, aged 60 to 100 years. They found that people with higher blood serum levels of vitamin E had lower levels of lipid peroxides (a source of free peroxide radicals). They gave the people daily doses of vitamin E (200 milligrams [mg]), or vitamin C (400 mg) or both, for a year. All groups experienced decline in peroxide levels (which means fewer free radicals), especially the group taking both vitamins.

Vitamin E has attained an almost superhero status—one study has even shown that it lengthens the mean life span (although not the maximum life span) in mice. However, Dr. Hendler cautions against assuming that *more* vitamin E will make you even healthier. It may lead to adverse effects if taken in megadoses. He recommends a daily dosage of 200 international units (I.U.) of vitamin E, and cautions that you should take no more than 600 I.U. per day.

You can get some extra vitamin E from food sources such as wheat germ, sunflower seeds, nuts and lobster.

Vitamin C. This nutrient is a water-soluble mimic of vitamin E. But vitamin C's potent antioxidizing effect takes place *inside* the cell, in its watery fluid. When vitamin C soaks up free radicals, it forms two compounds that researchers speculate may have their own anticancer properties.

Vitamin C soaks up free radicals and forms two potential anticancer compounds simultaneously.

"The National Research Council has recommended 60 mg of vitamin C daily," says Dr. Hendler.

"Most nutritional researchers now regard that as too little for optimal health ... Need for ascorbic acid (vitamin C) varies considerably from one individual to another. Exposure to infection, tobacco smoke, environmental pollutants, various drugs, surgery, burns, trauma, alcohol and other 'stresses' may increase the need for vitamin C. So may pregnancy (but consult your doctor first) and advancing age."

He suggests a daily intake of 500 mg. Or, if you prefer to get vitamin C only from foods, you can find this nutrient in oranges, brussels sprouts, broccoli, strawberries and tomatoes.

Beta-Carotene. Beta-carotene is an enemy to free radicals. It probably protects the body's tissues by serving as a trap for a very toxic free radical called singlet oxygen, says Dr. Hendler.

Beta-carotene may work as a trap for toxic free radicals.

A researcher from Boston University School of Medicine grew human skin cells in culture, some with and some without beta-carotene. Then, she exposed the cells to increasingly strong amounts of harmful sunlight. At the first two exposures, the cells receiving the beta-carotene showed significantly fewer signs of damage than the cells without beta-carotene.

If you want to increase the amount of beta-carotene in your diet, look for certain specific fruits and vegetables. Carrots, sweet potatoes, cantaloupes, parsley, apricots, endive and kale are some of the foods rich in this nutrient.

Selenium. Selenium also works as an antioxidant, but in a more roundabout way. It helps to produce a special enzyme, which turns peroxides into harmless water.

Selenium helps to produce an enzyme that can turn toxic substances into water.

"There is sufficient reason to supplement the diet with 100 to 200 micrograms of selenium daily," says Dr. Hendler. The best natural sources of selenium include grains, fish and the vegetables broccoli, mushrooms, cabbage, celery and cucumbers, although selenium content can vary according to where the vegetables were grown.

Zinc. Not only is zinc a part of an enzyme which protects cells against oxidant damage, but it also may act as an antioxidant when working alone. "Our ability to absorb zinc decreases with age," says Dr. Hendler. "I recommend between 15 to 30 mg daily for adults."

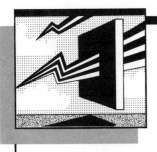

Regenerate Red Blood Cells with Iron

Red blood cells lead a hectic life. They constantly patrol your blood vessels, passing out energy-giving oxygen to every part of your body. After only about four months, they expire—as though from exhaustion.

Your body relentlessly replaces these essential cells—at a rate of two and a half million each *second*. At such a rate, your body had better have the necessary "ingredients" on hand at all times to manufacture such a quantity.

Hemoglobin, an iron-containing protein, is one of the most important of these components, since it is the element which permits the transfer of oxygen and carbon dioxide from one tissue to another. Lack of dietary iron can lead to anemia, a condition in which the amount or quality of red blood cells is inadequate. Symptoms may include fatigue, dizziness, nausea, loss of appetite and a shortened attention span.

You need approximately 20 milligrams of iron a day to unite with the hemoglobin of your new blood cells. It would be impossible to eat enough food to take in that much iron. So your body recycles the mineral—before dead blood cells are removed from the body, the spleen, liver and bone marrow snatch up their iron, which can be used for new red blood cells.

Even though your body is efficient at conserving iron, there is a small loss that needs to be replaced. Liver is the best source of this mineral. You can also get iron from other meats and poultry, green vegetables and nuts. Consult your doctor if you suspect you have a deficiency.

Liver, beef, poultry, nuts and cheese are good sources of zinc.

Limit Fats. Fats can be breeding grounds for free radicals—before and after they have been ingested, points out Dr. Hendler. And he's not just talking about saturated fats, which have received a lot of bad press for being linked with high cholesterol and heart disease.

Cooking with unsaturated oils produces free radicals.

Unsaturated fats in their natural form, as in seeds and grains, are the kind that can lower cholesterol. But unsaturated fat is more likely than saturated fat to react with oxygen and form free radicals when cooked.

In fact, laboratory animals that are fed oxidized fat develop symptoms such as depressed growth or even death of several tissues. One experiment, conducted at the University of Guelph, in Ontario, showed that heated corn oil induced unhealthy fat accumulation in cultures of rat heart cells, and that vitamin E counteracted its adverse effects.

Whether or not you take sufficient vitamin E, Dr. Hendler suggests that you avoid frying if possible. But if you must fry, he recommends quick frying with minimal oil, as opposed to deep frying.

In addition, Dr. Hendler suggests cutting down fats to no more than 30 or preferably 20 percent of total calorie intake.

Special Considerations

There is one type of dogfood that has different formulas for each stage of the pooch's life. Should your diet do the same for you?

The answer depends on which doctor you ask. One reason for the controversy is that there is no "prototypical" person—babies look more or less the same, but each baby's body becomes more unique as it grows. Factors such as drug usage, lower activity levels, reduced basal metabolism and a less efficient gastrointestinal tract can change the nutritional needs of certain people.

"There has been little research on the changing nutritional needs of older people," says Michael L. Freedman, M.D., professor of medicine and director of the division of geriatrics at New York University Medical Center, in New York City. "Many researchers who claim to investigate older people actually study diseased people."

Many bodily imperfections that are blamed on aging may actually be signs of malnutrition.

But doctors know quite a few facts about nutrition. For instance, some of the bodily imperfections that are blamed on getting old—thinning hair, dry skin, loose or missing teeth, muscle weakness, constipation and mental confusion—may actually be signs of malnutrition.

Here are some nutritional requirements that may change as you age:

Protein. If an older person ate huge amounts of protein, that person's kidneys would probably be unable to handle the extra load, according to noted nutritionist Helen A. Guthrie, Ph.D, of Pennsylvania State University, in University Park, author of *Introductory Nutrition* (Mosby). On the other hand, evidence suggests that protein enhances calcium absorption. Also, various illnesses in the elderly result in a decrease in the amount of nutrition absorbed from the food eaten, and can increase losses of protein. So Dr. Guthrie concludes that older people should eat a little extra protein.

"It is not yet possible to prescribe the perfect protein diet, but one can recommend limiting red meat and animal protein intake and increasing plant protein intake," says Dr. Freedman in the medical journal *Geriatrics*, with coauthor Judith C. Ahronheim, M.D. He suggests that protein comprise about 13 percent of the total calorie intake, though some conditions, such as surgery, chronic diseases or skin ulcerations may increase the requirement.

Carbohydrates. Sugar and refined carbohydrates are less than healthful for everyone, but they may be particularly bothersome to older people. "Refined carbohydrates may also increase glucose intolerance, which occurs to an extent in normal aging," writes Dr. Freedman.

That's why he recommends increasing the amount of fruits, vegetables and fiber you eat in lieu of sugary foods. And the fibery foods pack in an extra benefit: They ease constipation, another common complaint in older people.

Vitamin B_{12}. "Several investigators have shown that when vitamin B_{12} is given to the elderly, symptoms of fatigue disappear and the sense of disorientation and confusion may be alleviated," says Dr. Guthrie. "The lack of hydrochloric acid (a stomach secretion) in many older people results in a failure to split vitamin B_{12} from its carrier protein. As a result, very little dietary B_{12} is absorbed."

Some people can get around this problem by taking large amounts of B_{12} in tablets or injections. See your doctor if you suspect a deficiency.

As you age, your body may be less able to tolerate sugar.

Alcohol and certain medications can have an adverse effect on B_{12} absorption. So even though your body needs only tiny amounts of this vitamin, eat foods such as eggs, liver, beef and dairy products to be sure you're getting all the B_{12} you need.

Calcium. The average elderly American has an inadequate calcium intake, according to a study at the University of Massachusetts Medical Center, in Worcester. To make things worse, calcium absorption is blunted with aging, particularly in women. These factors can contribute to osteoporosis, or bone degeneration. For these reasons, some doctors recommend 1,000 to 1,500 mg of calcium per day for older people, which is more than the Recommended Dietary Allowance of 800 mg per day.

Calcium absorption is often impaired with age.

Vitamin D. Vitamin D is another enemy to osteoporosis, since it is required for active intestinal absorption of calcium. Unfortunately, it is another nutrient that is frequently deficient in older people, according to Dr. Freedman. The deficiency might be partly due to lack of sunlight exposure and poor dietary intake.

"All elderly persons should receive at least 400 I.U. of vitamin D a day, preferably from dietary sources," says Dr. Freedman.

Water. Older people are at a greater risk of dehydration than younger adults, according to Annette B. Natow, Ph.D., R.D., and Jo-Ann Heslin, M.A., R.D., authors of a study on the nutritional care of the older adult. And what makes things worse, they may be less sensitive to the normal sensation of thirst.

Drink plenty of water, whether you feel thirsty or not.

Some doctors suggest you consume from one to one and one-half quarts of liquid a day to help flush out waste and take care of other biological jobs dependent on water.

There is no miracle food that will instantly erase the extra pounds from your body, strip the wrinkles from your face and give you the muscle tone of an athlete. However, making a healthy, balanced diet a way of life may minimize the damage with which time afflicts certain people. Research has yet to pinpoint the exact cause of aging or the optimum balance of nutrients, but scientists have been coming up with enough new discoveries to put you on the right track.

25

The

Prostate

T he prostate is the body's equivalent of an unemployed brother-in-law. Its potential for trouble far outweighs its usefulness.

About the size of a Ping-Pong ball, the prostate gland is inconveniently located just below the bladder, adjacent to the rectum. Its single chore is to produce the bulk of the fluid that combines with sperm to make semen—not the sperm, mind you, just the fluid it travels in. It deserves the same amount of credit for aiding the reproductive system as the swimming pool water deserved for helping Mark Spitz win seven Olympic gold medals. It's necessary, but it's far from the most important ingredient.

Look at it this way. Compared to all the complicated and near miraculous tasks done by the body's other parts—pumping blood, digesting and processing food, distributing oxygen—the prostate gland's job is pretty elementary.

Yet, when it comes to whining, squawking and moaning, in the form of disease, discomfort and dysfunction, the prostate jumps to the head of the class. An estimated 12 million American men are suffering from some form of prostate trouble right now. A staggering 95 percent of men who live to age 85 will have to cope with an enlarged prostate. One in every 10 men will have to go under a surgeon's knife for relief from a debilitating prostate problem.

Statistics show that prostate enlargement is one of the leading medical problems in older men.

317

While singular in duty, the prostate is a party animal when it comes to problems. Everyone's invited to come and dance—bacteria, cancer, blockages, congestion, mystery ailments, you name it. Even its location gives doctors fits. When it goes bad, it can also damage the urinary tract, the digestive system and even the back.

The prostate's open-arms welcome of cancer gives that insidious killer a foothold to attack and destroy the entire body. And here's the ultimate insult: Even though it can kill you, the gland is totally unnecessary to maintain a happy, healthy life. New surgical techniques even can remove the prostate without causing impotence.

Still, don't condemn your urologist if he's having trouble giving you relief. Prostate trouble can be an ordeal to detect and treat.

New techniques enable doctors to remove the gland without affecting the patient's sexual ability.

A Triple Threat

The prostate is especially fond of three specific problems—prostatitis, benign prostatic hypertrophy (enlargement) and cancer.

Prostatitis

This condition is simply inflammation of the prostate, but the simplicity ends there. The symptoms include low back pain, fever, pain on defecation and cloudy urine. The specific types of prostatitis include:

• Acute bacterial prostatitis, an infection that usually starts in the urinary tract.
• Chronic bacterial prostatitis, a symptom of which is recurrent bladder infection.
• Chronic nonbacterial prostatitis and prostatodynia, two similar ailments with a cause difficult to determine and therefore difficult to treat. (Prostatodynia means "pain in the prostate.")

Antibiotics can generally combat the two bacterial problems, although the process can take months. Chronic nonbacterial prostatitis has been treated with a variety of methods, including the antibiotic tetracycline, aspirin and ibuprofen, sitz baths and even stress reduction programs.

Ira Sharlip, M.D., assistant clinical professor of

Antibiotics can clear up most cases of prostatitis.

urology at the University of California at San Francisco, goes as far as sending nonbacterial prostate patients to psychologists to learn stress management techniques. "Often, just understanding the problem is enough to keep the man from being so uptight," Dr. Sharlip says. "Muscle relaxants like Valium also help sometimes."

Jay S. Cohen, M.D., of San Diego, himself a sufferer of prostatodynia, used a slant board to elevate his feet above his head in an attempt to relieve gravity pressure.

One doctor used a slant board to lessen symptoms.

"My symptoms gradually but steadily disappeared," Dr. Cohen says of the unusual method. "Now, over a year later, I am virtually without symptoms."

As they say on TV after the knife throwing act, don't try to do this at home yourself. You should consult a urologist immediately if you suspect any prostatitis problems.

Benign Prostatic Hypertrophy (BPH)

This term is a fancy way of describing a gland that grew. The Ping-Pong ball decides it would rather be a baseball, and too bad if it crowds out other, more important body parts, especially the urethra. When that squeeze happens, a person will find it difficult, or impossible, to urinate. Surgery is often necessary to cut away the excess prostate. Doctors aren't sure why the prostate grows, but some experts suggest the cause might be hormonal changes. Whatever the reason, "it's an inevitable result of aging," according to Patrick C. Walsh, M.D., of Johns Hopkins Medical Center, in Baltimore.

The prostate often begins to enlarge when men reach their sixties.

Slight swellings can also mean trouble. Small, undetected prostate enlargements can quietly cause kidney failure. Richard Berger, M.D., head of urology at Harborview Medical Center, in Seattle, recommends that all men with BPH—and that means most men over sixty—get a blood test once a year to determine kidney function.

Cancer

Prostate cancer develops slowly over time. The American Cancer Society estimates that 26,100 men in the United States will die from prostate cancer each year, while another 90,000 will have it diag-

Frequent checkups will enable you to get a lifesaving jump on prostate cancer.

nosed. That level of frequency places the prostate second only to the lung in incidence of cancer. Frequent checkups are the best defense. Doctors recommend that all men over 40 have an annual rectal prostate exam to test for cancer. The exam is a simple, relatively painless procedure in which the doctor actually feels the prostate for enlargement or growths.

Regenerating the Prostate

As stated previously, the best way to deal with all the problems caused by this troublesome organ is to have regular prostate exams. The National Institute on Aging, in Washington, D.C., advises men to see a doctor promptly if any unusual symptoms occur, including frequent urge to urinate, difficulty in urinating or dribbling: "Waiting until severe symptoms appear may result in serious and sometimes life-threatening complications."

See a doctor at the first sign of trouble. Don't wait for the symptoms to become severe.

Diet

With all the trouble it causes, one would envision the prostate as an obese, belching, slovenly creature in a stained T-shirt reaching for a beer. Ironically, new studies aimed at defending the prostate have found that the gland would rather be a dietician. Studies in Asia and South Africa show that in areas where people eat low-fat diets, they have a lower risk of developing prostate enlargement and cancer. Where high-fat diets prevail, the frequency soars. Researchers at Loma Linda University, in California, were able to further pinpoint the results of diet. They studied male Seventh-Day Adventists, most of whom are vegetarians. The men who ate a lot of fatty foods like cheese and eggs, and those who did eat meat, were 3.6 times more likely to have fatal prostate cancer than Adventist men who stuck to a vegetarian diet. The same study showed that obese men were 2.5 times more likely to have fatal prostate cancer than their slimmer counterparts.

Zinc

Using zinc as a prostate aid is fairly controversial.

The question of zinc's effect on the prostate continues to be controversial. While some research touts zinc as important in the prevention and treatment of prostate troubles, other research suggests that zinc taken in supplemental form does not penetrate the prostate, and too much zinc may even impede the body's defense mechanisms.

What started the zinc debate was the unquestioned fact that a healthy prostate contains more zinc than any other organ. Researchers then discovered that men with chronic prostatitis have a diminished amount of zinc in their prostate fluid or semen. Because of this, some experts, such as the late Monroe E. Greenberger, M.D., author of *What Every Man Should Know about His Prostate* (Walker), and Irving M. Bush, M.D., clinical professor of urology at the Chicago Medical School, believe that, in general, patients suffering from prostatic infection tend to do better with zinc supplementation. Additional research determined that zinc may also relieve the symptoms of enlarged prostate and decrease its size. Some studies show that the zinc in supplements doesn't even reach the prostate. But the pro-zinc doctors can explain this seemingly contradictory finding. They say that when zinc is low, the body steals it from the prostate, which is a zinc storage area. By taking supplements, you don't add zinc to the prostate, but you keep the body from raiding the prostate for zinc.

Dr. Greenberger said diabetics and heavy drinkers are especially vulnerable to zinc shortages. Foods rich in zinc include pumpkin seeds, sunflower seeds, oysters, nuts, wheat germ, low-fat milk, chicken, peas, lentils and beef liver. According to Dr. Greenberger, however, some of these foods obtain their zinc from the soil, and in some areas of the country the soil has been severely depleted. For that reason, he says, most pro-zinc doctors prescribe a therapeutic dose of between 50 and 150 milligrams (mg) of zinc a day for prostate disorders, depending on the individual case. Consult your physician before taking more than 30 mg of zinc a day.

Because of the controversy and ongoing research, you should consult your doctor for the latest findings before undergoing zinc therapy.

Consult your doctor for the most up-to-date research on zinc.

26

Sex: What's
in the Future

A ging and sex have never been the best bedfellows. Famed sex researcher Helen S. Kaplan, M.D., Ph.D., director of the human sexuality program at New York Hospital-Cornell Medical Center, in New York City, clarified much of the conflict when she identified the peak age of sexual desire in men and women. Trouble is, it turned out that males peak at 17 years old and women peak at 38.

If that isn't enough to shake up your libido, doomsayers, including many doctors, have long viewed the elderly as asexual. This society perpetuates that belief. In the hit movie *Cocoon*, it took the miracle of a swimming pool crackling with a mysterious alien life force to regenerate the sex drive of a trio of male retirees.

Under this assumption, the big question is, when is that frightful year when sexuality catches the next flight to Florida and calls it a career?

Never.

While Dr. Kaplan's peak age theory grabbed the headlines, her subsequent comments were lost in the media shuffle.

Sexual function, Dr. Kaplan assured, is one of the last functions to decline with age. Men and

Sexual ability can last well into your nineties—and beyond.

women can live sexually fulfilled lives well into their nineties and beyond.

All you need are a few guidelines to help keep the fires going, along with some practical tips to restore the flame to those who feel their internal fires are no match for the growing inferno on their birthday cakes.

Desire

One of the keys to sexual fulfillment is desire. When the desire wanes, so does the sex life. Often if the desire lessens in one marital partner and not the other, the result can be a literal, figurative or often fabricated headache for the relationship.

If you currently have a sex life that rings bells, and you'd like to keep it that way, here are some ways to keep things on the proper course.

Diet. While the subject of sex-enhancing foods remains controversial, there are some factors that you might want to consider. These involve what *not* to eat more than what to eat. Overdosing on caffeine can drain thiamine from the body—a deficiency that may lead to depression. And depressed people aren't exactly super-eager for sex. Alcohol, the alleged aphrodisiac, may reduce male hormone production or raise estrogen levels, which may eventually inhibit desire.

On the what-to-eat side, some doctors believe that nutritional deficiencies may be linked indirectly to lack of sexual desire. They can contribute to an underactive thyroid, which can lead to decreased desire and chronic fatigue. So make sure you're getting a balanced diet.

Exercise. According to Art Mollen, D.O., founder of the Southwest Health Institute, in Phoenix, Arizona, and author of *The Mollen Method* (Rodale Press), a study of fit men showed that they had more sexual desire and a better attitude about sex than men who were out of shape. What's more, the study found that physically active men in their late forties and fifties had sex as frequently as the younger men in the study. In fact, the author of the study, Lawrence Katzman, Ph.D., believes that exercise is the

A key to good sex is keeping desire strong.

Exercise can increase testosterone, a male hormone vital to normal sexual function.

best prescription for problems like impotence, lack of desire, premature ejaculation or an inability to achieve orgasm.

Stress. "Even people with normal sexual appetites can psychologically turn themselves off with overwhelming problems," says Wanda Sadoughi, Ph.D., director of the sexual dysfunction clinic at Cook County Hospital, in Chicago. Dr. Kaplan agrees. "Even moderately depressed people lose interest in pursuing sexual activity and are very difficult to seduce and arouse."

In addition to depression, stress can cause chronic fatigue and adverse hormonal changes, encourage poor diet and induce heavy drinking, all killers of sexual desire.

High blood pressure drugs are sometimes anti-aphrodisiacs.

Drugs. Some prescription drugs can deaden desire (and even cause impotence). Medications used to treat high blood pressure are acknowledged to be one of the worst offenders. (The antihypertension drug guanethidine [Esimil and Ismelin] probably has the worst reputation.) Drugs to combat depression and anxiety can also be trouble. If you are currently taking any medications for the above problems and have noticed your sex life sliding downhill, consult your doctor. Perhaps he or she will be able to prescribe an equally effective drug with less serious side effects.

In addition, even common drug side effects like depression, drowsiness, mental confusion and nausea can indirectly interfere with sexual desire.

The Pill. Shakespeare would love the irony here. Women take the Pill to feel more secure about having sex, then the Pill turns around and cools their desire. One step forward, two backward. Alice Rothchild, M.D., instructor of obstetrics and gynecology at Harvard Medical School, in Cambridge, Massachusetts, confirms that some women suffer libido losses while on the Pill. If this is a problem, doctors suggest consulting your gynecologist for a change of prescription or an alternative method of birth control.

Fan the Fires

If you are already knee-deep in problems caused by factors mentioned above, the obvious way to restore your sexual desire is to avoid the problems, lessen them or find alternative ways to accomplish the original purpose without the devastating sexual side effects. Your doctor should be able to advise you on the best route to follow.

Lack of desire has multiple causes.

For problems where the causes aren't that easy to pinpoint, Waguih R. Guirguis, M.D., head of the psychosexual clinic at St. Clement's Hospital, in Ipswich, England, has some advice.

A Loaf of Bread, a Strip of Bark and Thou . . .

Love potions advertised in the backs of comic books are a giggle for youngsters. But when they're sold through men's magazines to adults, they sometimes become less amusing. While people have probably pushed aphrodisiacs as long as there has been sex, the truth is that love potions, from ground rhino horn to Spanish fly, have traditionally promised a lot and delivered little but an empty wallet.

However, a form of bark from an African tree, yohimbine, has been given some credence as a sex stimulator—at least for rats. While studying something else, researchers at Stanford University, in Stanford, California, led by Julian M. Davidson, Ph.D., professor of physiology, found that yohimbine caused male rats to increase their rate of copulation. Curious about their incidental findings, the researchers did a more controlled study where they injected thirty male rats with yohimbine and exposed them to female rats who were in the mood for love. The rats "exhibited about twice as much mounting behavior" as is normal, noted the researchers, adding that "yohimbine thus appears to be a potent stimulator of sexual arousal in the intact, sexually vigorous male rat."

Further tests on rats that were known to be sexually inhibited showed that yohimbine even revs rats up who normally aren't interested. This prompted the researchers to conclude that "yohimbine may be a true aphrodisiac."

But be careful—yohimbine can interfere with certain medications and may also be toxic in large amounts.

Hypothyroidism can depress sexual desire.

"Lack of desire is not one single condition, but a group of illnesses with different causes that share common symptoms. The only hope of achieving better treatment results is by identifying these different conditions and the methods of treatment that are best for each one."

One condition—a real desire drainer—is a poorly functioning thyroid gland. Hypothyroidism slows down the body's metabolism. This causes depression, which in turn can blunt sexual desire in both men and women, according to Sheldon S. Stoffer, M.D., a Southfield, Michigan, endocrinologist specializing in thyroid and sexual function. Dr. Stoffer says those suspecting trouble should have a thyroid test. If your thyroid is found to be sluggish, proper medication can replace the energy hormones it isn't generating—and give you energy for sex.

Finally, here's a less clinical and more fun way to try to boost desire. Read steamy romance novels! No kidding. Psychologists Claire D. Coles, Ph.D., of the Emory School of Medicine, in Atlanta, and M. Johnna Shamp, Ph.D., studied women who read romance novels with the theory that they were filling a void caused by a lack of sex. Instead, they discovered that readers over 35 made love an average of 3.04 times a week, compared to just 1.75 for nonreaders. The experts concluded that women may use the books as fodder for sexual fantasies and to enhance desire!

The Problem of Impotence

If you've got the desire, but can't get the parts working, don't let it get you down. Although finding the exact cause of your own personal problem is sometimes difficult, curing it once you've discovered the culprit is often simple.

First, let's determine what impotence is. Generally, when people refer to impotence they are speaking specifically about men. (Women have their own forms of impotence, which are discussed later.) The vast majority of impotence cases deal with the male inability to have or maintain an erection.

By age 40, at least 90 percent of men will at least once have had an experience of not being able to get or maintain an erection, according to Barry McCarthy, Ph.D., a sex therapist at the Washington Psychological Center, in Washington, D.C. "Man's most feared experience is, in fact, an almost universal one," he says.

One bad night doesn't turn a man into a sexual wimp. In fact, sex researchers Masters and Johnson say even if you're only hitting .250, that is, you can maintain an erection only once in four attempts at intercourse, you're still not impotent. (The woman in your life may beg to differ, but medical science doesn't.)

"An occasional erection failure is nothing to be concerned about," adds Bruce Forman, Ph.D., director of marriage and family therapy training at the University of Miami. "If you are having chronic problems, and by that I mean a pattern of total inability or multiple misfires over a period of six months, then you should get a physical exam and a psychological life-style check to determine if the problem is physical or mental."

The best way to determine whether it's physical or psychological impotence is this: If you can become erect any time outside attempts at intercourse, including while sleeping, that strongly suggests the problem is psychological, explains E. Douglas Whitehead, M.D., a urologist with the Association for Male Sexual Dysfunction, in New York City.

If you don't wake up with an erection and are therefore unsure if you are having them, there's a simple home test available that consists of wrapping a Velcro band around the penis before sleeping. If the specially designed snaps break apart during the night, that indicates that an erection occurred. These tests cost $41.95 and are available from Dacomed Corporation, 1701 East 79th Street, Minneapolis, MN 55420 (800-328-1103). The more frugal among you can use a ring made from a strip of postage stamps and check to see if any perforations have burst by morning. However, Dr. Whitehead warns that this method simply isn't accurate enough to be of much value.

Nearly all men experience erection problems at some point in their lives.

Differentiate between physical and psychological impotence.

Further Testing

Following are some additional ways to determine if you are psychologically or physically impotent. The cause is likely to be psychological if:

- The problem appeared suddenly without any physical trauma like prostate surgery.
- You're having problems in a relationship.
- You've had sexual problems at other times in your life.
- You are impotent only in certain situations, possibly with one partner but not another, or during intercourse but not masturbation. Dr. Forman says this could mean you just aren't attracted to your partner anymore.

"We become turned on or turned off by our interpretation of things around us," Dr. Forman says. "Your wife may have gained weight, had a mastectomy or aged and no longer seems attractive. These factors, and others like them, can be manifested as a severe lack of desire. You may think you are impotent, or even use impotence as an excuse, but in truth, there is nothing wrong."

Dr. Forman says in these cases, a psychologist can provide techniques that will enable you to "recondition yourself to the changes," by accepting the aging process, dealing with surgery or even fantasizing you are with another partner, a device that may seem controversial but is an accepted practice in medical and therapeutic circles.

The cause of impotence is likely to be physical if:

Physical problems are a signal for immediate medical attention.

- You have problems urinating, and/or numbness, tingling or burning sensations in your legs or genital area. If this is the case, see a doctor.
- You are taking a prescribed drug for an unrelated medical problem. Be especially alert for sex-related problems caused by blood pressure medications, tranquilizers, antidepressants, sleeping pills, the ulcer drug Tagamet, the cholesterol-reducing drug Atromid, estrogen-containing drugs like DES (often prescribed in the treatment of prostate cancer), the heartburn medication Reglan and prescription eye drops containing Timolol. Even some over-the-

counter drugs containing antihistamines, like cold remedies, can interfere with your sexual performance. If problems arise, ask your doctor to change your prescription.

- You smoke. Smoking may constrict blood vessels, which can inhibit erections.
- You have diabetes.

Smoking can weaken erections.

Diabetes is thought to be one of the most common physical causes of impotence. Controlling the diabetes by managing your diet to level off your blood sugar may restore your sex ability. Studies have shown that a diet high in fiber-rich carbohydrates and low in fat is effective in treating people with diabetes. This means starchy foods like vegetables, whole grain breads and cereals and fresh fruits. (Diabetics, however, shouldn't make major changes in their diet without a doctor's approval.)

Undiagnosed diabetes can render you impotent without revealing the cause. Dr. Whitehead says 10 percent of the men who come to the Association for Male Sexual Dysfunction for help turn out to have undiagnosed diabetes. Warning symptoms are excessive urination, thirst, hunger or general fatigue and weakness.

If your problems warrant seeing a doctor, Dr. Whitehead recommends starting with a urologist.

Don't Think about It

How do you prevent impotence? Psychologists like Dr. Forman say don't think about it. Once it gets in your head, you often compound the problem with excessive worry.

The best psychological tip is to realize that one or two failures during a lifetime, or even a week, does not mean you are impotent. Be aware that periods of failure due to stress, fatigue or anxieties of life are routine. Deal with the outside factor and you'll almost always solve the related sexual performance problem.

"Any kind of anxiety can drain the penis of blood instantly," explains Dr. Kaplan. "If you are frightened, the emergency reflexes will cause your blood to rush to your arms and legs so you can fight tigers, not to your penis so you can make love."

Sexual function declines slightly after 50, but should not interfere with enjoyment or reproduction.

Older men should be aware that sexual function does decline somewhat after you've reached 50. These men often require more stimulation to achieve erection and require a longer "rest period" between erections. Just don't get a "lost youth" complex and let this depress you. Doctors say you should be able to continue to have sex well into your nineties and beyond.

On the physical side of the matter, there are some new thoughts on the subject that you might find surprising.

"I've come to think that atherosclerosis is probably the most common cause of impotence in men," says urologist Albert McBride, M.D., founder of the Sexual Impotence Center of San Diego. "Often there are two or three factors involved—medication, depression, diabetes—but the problem is usually primarily cardiovascular."

This evaluation is logical. Since an erection is achieved by blood rushing to the penis, any narrowing or hardening of the blood vessels would hamper the blood's ability to get there.

The obvious preventive measures to avoid cardiovascular impotence are the same as those you should already be doing to prevent a heart attack:

A heart disease prevention plan can also benefit your sexual ability.

- Cut down on fat and cholesterol in your diet.
- Boost your intake of complex carbohydrates (beans, grains, unprocessed fruit and vegetables).
- Exercise.

Future Success

O.K., let's be realistic. Few people give the slightest thought to impotence until it strikes. In fact, if you maintain good health, doctors feel that's probably the best attitude. If you are reading this section, chances are you are looking for help. And help, be assured, is available. In fact, medical science is working overtime to come to the aid of impotent men. Consider these new methods of restoration.

An African love potion cured impotence in some scientific studies.

Papaverine. Although doctors are stopping short of calling it an aphrodisiac, a derivative of a once scorned African love potion made from the bark of the yohimb tree has produced dramatic results in scientific laboratories. The African substance is yohimbine. Previous animal studies were interesting, but inconclusive when applied to humans. While still investigating yohimbine, American researchers turned to a related compound called papaverine, tested it on humans and reported positive results. Although papaverine has been used since 1937 to improve circulation in the extremities, its use to counter impotence has only recently been studied.

According to Lowell Parsons, M.D., a urologist at the University of California at San Diego, it's been discovered that taking papaverine by mouth seemed to have no significant effect on erectile function, but injecting it directly into the penis produced powerful erections that lasted up to two hours in about half of the men tested. Tom F. Lue, M.D., of the University of California at San Francisco, says his research team began giving men with erection problems a series of shots—an average of four over a two-month period—and discovered that half the men had significant, lasting improvement in their erection ability. The drawbacks are that the research is new, so few doctors now let patients inject themselves, and that 2 to 5 percent of the treated men end up with erections that won't quit. When that happens, the doctors can easily deflate the penis with another drug or by flushing the penis with salt water.

Implants. For men whose impotence has not responded to treatment, surgical implants may be the answer. "They are probably the very best treatment we have today," says Dr. McBride. Another alternative, vascular surgery to restore blood flow to the genitals, has a much lower success rate. The implant method is simple in theory. A rigid device is surgically planted inside the penis. One form of the operation merely plugs in a stiff implant that leaves you with a permanent erection. But another treatment is an operation that mirrors the body's natural system. Hollow cylinders are implanted in the penis. These are connected to a reservoir containing a fluid and operated by a golf-ball-size pump, usually tucked inside the scrotum. A few squeezes of the pump and you become erect. Dr. McBride says that the Mentor model is generally regarded as the best of these devices. For information, consult your urologist or call the Mentor toll-free number 800-235-5731.

Implants are viewed as the best treatment available for impotence.

Patient satisfaction with this unusual operation is high. Canadian researchers surveyed 26 men who had undergone the operation and had tested it for an average of two years. The researchers found that 24 of the men said their sexual relations with their wives had improved. Twenty of the men added that non-sexual relations with their partner had also improved. Only 3 of the 26 men said they wouldn't repeat the procedure.

The vast majority report satisfaction.

Sexual Changes in Women

Two common physical problems women have with sex are insufficient lubrication and vaginal atrophy. Insufficient lubrication can be a problem at any age, while vaginal atrophy occurs in varying degrees in postmenopausal women. The two problems are sometimes related, since vaginal atrophy may result in lack of lubrication. Like male impotence, once the cause is discovered, the cure is sometimes simple.

Lubrication problems and vaginal atrophy usually can be rectified.

Lubrication. Earlier you learned that a man's "impotence" can actually be nothing more than the fact that his partner doesn't excite him anymore. This road goes both ways. Famed sex researchers William Masters, M.D., and Virginia Johnson refer to a woman's inability to produce the proper lubrication needed for painless intercourse as "as near as any woman can come to paralleling a man's lack of effective erection." They attribute the cause in some cases to psychological factors, the most frequent being a lack of interest in their partner or the setting. The researchers also attribute the problem to fear, including anxiety over sexual inadequacy, pain, pregnancy and social compromise.

Masters and Johnson say therapeutic counseling can help overcome fear. But it has little to offer a woman who doesn't like her partner—who has, in their words, "little or no personal identification, understanding, affection or even sexual respect" for the partner.

Vaginal Atrophy. After menopause, the reduced levels of estrogen in a woman's body can cause certain changes. One such change is vaginal atrophy—a condition where the vagina thins and is easily injured. In fact, about 15 percent of all cases of postmenopausal bleeding result from this thinning. In addition, the labia become smaller and less elastic, the uterus shrinks and secretions lessen, and the fallopian tubes also become smaller.

For women who want to continue an active and satisfying sexual relationship, the postmenopausal picture may appear pretty grim. But, in fact, it is not. Researchers at the University of Medicine and Dentistry of New Jersey, Rutgers Medical School, in Piscataway, determined that there is some support for the old adage "use it or lose it" when applied to women's sexuality. In their study of 52 postmenopausal women, ages 50 through 65, they determined that "significantly less overall vaginal atrophy was noted in sexually active women."

A Masters and Johnson study of 54 women older than 60 found that only 3 had remained sexually active throughout and subsequent to menopause. These were the only women to physically respond to sexual stimulation in the same manner as younger women, with the production of "considerable" vaginal lubrication.

Taken together, the studies agree with prior studies, which concluded that regular postmenopausal sexual activity increases lubrication, and lessens vaginal atrophy.

"Use it or lose it" sounds like simple enough advice, but some women may not be willing to follow it. Why? Because with vaginal atrophy, intercourse can be painful. While added lubrication may be helpful, a woman's doctor also may suggest ERT—estrogen replacement therapy. Estrogen can, indeed, reduce vaginal dryness and soreness. It also can prevent osteoporosis and reduce or eliminate hot flashes. But ERT is relatively new and controversial. It is not essential, yet it can be quite helpful for some women. The benefits and risks of taking estrogen—and not taking it—vary from woman to woman.

If you are considering ERT, be aware that recent studies indicate that women on ERT should also take progestin to protect against any increased risk of uterine cancer. But progestin may have its own risks. For instance, it may increase the risk of high blood pressure, heart disease or stroke in some women.

An active sex life prevents age-related problems.

Inability to Reach Orgasm. Here, again, the "use it or lose it" adage applies. Writing in the medical journal *Postgraduate Medicine*, Daniel H. Labby, M.D., says, "The orgasmic response of women who receive regular sexual stimulation does not appear to diminish with advancing age. Indeed, older wives with younger husbands are more sexually active than younger wives with older husbands." In fact, Dr. Labby notes that with menopause comes the freedom from risk of pregnancy, a factor that intensifies some women's interest in sex.

Loss of Sexual Desire. Ill health, fatigue and stress all take their toll on the libido. A woman with diabetes, for example, may find sex less satisfying because of degenerative changes in nerve fibers. Additionally, medications can affect sexual desire. Many of these problems lend themselves to common-sense solutions.

Fatigue is a major enemy of good sex.

Tips for Health

Here are some facts, figures and tips on sexual health:

• Rest. "Fatigue is an important element in male sexuality and exerts an ever-increasing influence during and beyond middle age," assert Masters and Johnson. Surprisingly, the researchers report that physical fatigue from recreational activities deflates the sex drive more than job-related fatigue. Mental fatigue, such as occupational, financial, personal and family emergencies, takes an even greater toll.
• Communicate. "If a woman in a two-paycheck marriage is liberated the way women are liberated in Russia—they go to work and then come home and take care of all the household chores—then resentment over that can come out in the bedroom," warns James O'Hagan, Ph.D., a psychoanalyst from New York City.
• Don't drink. Heavy drinking is not a mixed blessing—it can totally sabotage sexuality in both men and women. In men, it can lower testosterone and increase estrogen, hormone changes that can undercut sexuality. It can also have the ghastly effect of causing the development of feminine characteristics, including enlarged breasts. As for women, studies

conclude that alcohol may inhibit a woman's ability to become sexually aroused and reach orgasm. And some male alcoholics risk losing their sex ability altogether.

• Respect each other. Sexual therapist Joseph Waxberg, M.D., of Stamford, Connecticut, says that variations in desire are normal. If one person's desire outweighs the other's, the couple can be taught to take care of and respect their mutual wants and needs.

• Maintain perspective. How important is sex? In an NBC television survey of 1,007 American adults, conducted for an NBC executive, 80 percent of the men said sex was necessary to lead a happy life, but only 59 percent of the women concurred. Only 47 percent of the women over 50 felt it was necessary, compared to 78 percent of the men. Women of all ages put sex at the bottom of a list of five suggested ingredients for happiness, placing it behind health, family, religion and money.

Women do not rank sex above other important things in life.

27

The Skin:

Keeping It

Healthy

"**W**hat's your skin secret?" That's the first question Robert Taylor, M.D, author of his guide to healthy skin, asked of the woman he met, who, although she was many moons past 60, had skin as smooth, soft and clear as a young woman's. She answered: "Since childhood, I've taken the advice of my mother, who had healthy skin until the day she died. I've treated my skin like a fine silk garment that had to last a lifetime."

Mother was right. You don't wash silk too often, or soak it in hot water, rub it with harsh soaps or leave it sitting in the sun. To do so would break down its delicate fibers, wear it thin, fade its colors and leave it blotchy and full of tiny rips. Handle with care, though, and silk will remain nearly as good as the day you got it.

This is not to suggest that the skin will stay "new," but it can look nearly so. "The skin, like all other organs, is subject to physiological changes as it ages," explains Barbara Gilchrest, M.D., professor and chairman of the department of dermatology at Boston University School of Medicine. What's more, these changes can leave you more vulnerable to skin diseases. As you age, explains Dr. Gilchrest, your skin contains fewer pigmented cells, which means you have less natural protection from the searing rays of the sun. And because your skin thins over time, you may become more sensitive to irritants and develop reactions to substances you've been using all your life. Moreover, time takes its toll on the immunity cells near the skin's surface, rendering it less resistant to the invasion of infections and slower to heal after an injury. Ever hear of "Grandfather's Itch?" Perhaps one-third of all elders are bothered by persistently dry, itchy skin. Researchers now believe that this maddening malady is due to some degree of degeneration in the skin's barrier layer or nerve endings, although subtle irritant reactions may also contribute.

Healing Dry Skin

These changes are slow and gradual and you may not even be aware of them, says Dr. Gilchrest. Yet, she is quick to add, "there's no doubt that you can speed up the aging process and invite damage to the skin by what you expose it to." And the good news? You can also slow skin aging down and even reverse the damage. You begin this process by changing your reckless ways.

"As far as your skin is concerned, you may not be able to get away with the same things as when you were a young adult," says Dr. Gilchrest. To prevent or treat dry skin, for example, take shorter or less frequent showers or baths. Overbathing is a prime contributor to dry skin. And keep a jar of petroleum jelly or thick emollient cream handy near the tub. After a short soak, slather some on to prevent cracks which could otherwise be an easy entry for irritants.

Shorter, less frequent showers can prevent dry skin.

Speaking of irritants, unless you use only the mildest soaps and cleaning agents, you may be setting yourself up for an acute inflammatory reaction and not even know it. That's because, as you get older, your threshold of sensitivity for experiencing skin sensations is higher. You might not realize that the household cleaner you are using to scrub the tub is also scouring your skin.

If you're spending more time in warmer climates, make sure your skin is well ventilated and free from moisture-loving infections. Wear looser, nonsynthetic underwear and dust your creases and crannies with nonmedicated powder to absorb excess water.

Northerners, on the other hand, might do well to invest in a warm, woolen lap blanket or two. Why? It's awfully cozy to snuggle close to the woodstove on wintry nights or warm your toes next to a space heater under your desk, but you could be damaging your dermis. The same goes for catching up on your reading under the hair dryer or heat lamps. "Heat penetrates the skin and destroys the elasticity," warns Lorraine H. Kligman, Ph.D., assistant professor of dermatology at the University of Pennsylvania, in Philadelphia. "It damages the connective tissues and fibers." Heat can also contribute to tumors and skin cancers. So keep your skin cool and healthy—set your shower taps toward the "C" side, wrap up in nonelectric blankets and use a hand-held hair dryer.

Too much heat destroys the skin's elasticity.

Diets for Stronger Skin

Are there ways you can spruce up your diet to keep your skin healthy? A "yes" answer may depend on vitamin A, say researchers. Studies now being conducted with natural and synthetic derivatives of this nutrient may soon show that vitamin A holds the key to everything from bolstering the skin's immune system to preventing pimples and even skin cancer. "Dermatology is entering the age of vitamin A derivatives, called retinoids," says James Leyden, M.D., professor of dermatology at the University of Pennsylvania. "It will be to skin diseases what antibiotics are to infections. Eventually," says Dr. Gilchrest, "research may show exactly how diet influences behavior of the skin." Right now, though, the general rule of thumb for healthy skin is, "a diet that's good for your insides is good for your outsides."

A diet that's good for your insides is good for your outsides.

Put another way, what you eat—or don't eat—may be written all over your face. Some B-complex deficiencies cause scaling and redness, especially around the mouth and nose. Zinc deficiencies can cause similar conditions. Both zinc and vitamin C are important in the production of collagen, the main supportive protein of skin, bone and cartilage. And vitamin A is also important for healthy, normal

Scaling and redness can result from a diet too low in B complex or zinc.

growth of skin cells. "You are what you eat, and that goes more than skin deep," says Kenneth H. Neldner, M.D., professor and chairman of the department of dermatology at Texas Technical University Health Sciences Center, in Lubbock.

Preventing Skin Cancer

It won't matter much what you eat if your skin is repeatedly exposed to its number one enemy—the sun. Why is the sun so sinister to the skin? Simply put, it's a form of radiation that penetrates the skin and disorganizes the cells. The shorter ultraviolet B rays (UVB) can burn you, scientists think, while the longer ultraviolet A rays (UVA) can age your skin. Both rays damage. What happens is your cells produce pigment (popularly known as a tan), which is designed to disperse and block further sun damage. Fair-haired and older people produce less pigment, and the result often is a sunburn. Whether you burn or tan, though, ultraviolet light could still disarrange the skin cells, damage the DNA and start the cancer formation process. Darrell Rigel, M.D., clinical instructor of dermatology at New York University School of Medicine, in New York City, warns: "Over the years, sun damage builds up and leaves the skin with brown spots, precancerous changes and possibly skin cancer."

If that's not enough, there's now indirect evidence that ultraviolet light alters the immune system, leaving you more susceptible to everything from allergies to skin cancer in parts of the body that never even see the light of day!

Does that mean you have to lead a shady life? Of course not, says Dr. Rigel. "It just means learning new ways to enjoy the outdoors." One woman learned this lesson the hard way. After having a skin cancer removed from her leg, she completely changed her habits. She began swimming early and late in the day to avoid the most burning rays. She started wearing what she called "attic attire," complete with a parasol. She exchanged her seashore vacation for one in the mountains. This lady was probably doing her skin a favor. One renowned dermatologist notes that when some older people with

As you age, your skin produces less pigment to protect against sunburn.

lots of precancerous skin tumors live indoor lives in a residential home, their skin repairs itself over a period of years. The tumors disappear. Their skin looks "younger than it did ten years ago."

Use a Sunscreen

There's no need to go to such extremes, especially since protection is as near as a bottle of sunscreen. "Sunscreens are the best preventive, anti-aging measure we have," says Dr. Rigel. And they allow you to have a lot more fun and freedom in life.

It's never too late to start wearing these super-shields, even if you've been a sun worshipper all your life. Studies have shown that a sunscreen can help reverse damage by protecting the skin from further harm from the sun while the normal repair process goes to work. In one experiment, when a sunscreen was applied to hairless mice, their previously damaged skin began to repair itself even while it was exposed to continued radiation. "What happens is that sunscreens allow the skin to heal itself, to lay down a new layer of collagen and elastin fibers and to produce new blood vessels," says Dr. Kligman. "It gives you a second chance by preventing further damage."

For ultimate protection, purchase products with a sun protection factor of 15 to 20, which will block more of the sun's rays.

"No tanning occurs without cell damage," says Dr. Rigel. "There's just nothing healthy about a tan." And skip the trip to the tropics to get that fast tan, or to the seashore for your weekend sunburn. There is some evidence that these kinds of short bursts in radiation may contribute to the less common, but dangerous melanoma-type skin cancer. On the other hand, reminds Dr. Rigel, the more common basal and squamous skin cancers are likely to befall people who spend most of their time out in the sun, people like sailors, farmers, even outdoorsy rancher U.S. presidents. "Either way, the sun'll get ya," says Dr. Rigel. Don't *let* it get you! Use your sunscreen whenever you step outside in the daytime, no matter what the season, sunny skies or not.

"If you can't tan, don't try," is a wise rule to follow, especially if you are fair-haired, freckled,

Sunscreens protect the skin while it repairs itself.

That "fast tan" has been associated with melanoma.

blue-eyed, blond, of Irish, Welsh or Scottish descent or take medications, like tetracycline, that make you sensitive to sunshine. For double protection, wear a hat and long-sleeved shirts.

Examine the Skin

Your second line of defense against skin cancer is early detection and diagnosis. "Most skin cancer could be prevented by a regular self-exam," says Dr. Rigel. He suggests you get in the habit of examining your birthday suit on your birthday. All it takes is five minutes, a full-length mirror, a handheld mirror and perhaps a partner to help you scan those hard-to-see areas. First, look for pink/tan or gray/tan spots usually sprinkled on the face and hands. Called keratoses, these precancerous blotches often develop in your fifties or sixties, especially if you are fair or have enjoyed a lot of sun. They are easily scraped off after being painted with a drug called 5-fluorouracil or frozen with liquid nitrogen. Next, look for pale, pearl-colored waxy bumps that are usually 1/4 inch thick and are found on the face, neck, or backs of the legs or hands. These are likely to be basal or squamous cell carcinomas. They may develop scabs or become rough, scaly red spots that may bleed, crust or just never quite heal. This form of cancer is rarely deadly and can be surgically removed. However, it's important to remove these spots when they are small, before they do damage to surrounding tissue.

Finally, to check for melanoma, you'll need to take a minute to measure your moles. Reckless sun-worshipping ways, along with deterioration of the earth's protective ozone layers, has meant an alarming rise in this deadly disease. In fact, 1 in 150 Americans will develop it. "These figures can be reversed," claims Dr. Rigel. "Melanoma is almost 100 percent curable, if detected early." You can keep track of your moles on a figure drawing. And you can check your scalp by lifting your hair away from it with a hair dryer. Finally, use the following guide to distinguish early possible dangerous melanomas from other harmless moles. It could be a melanoma if:

• The mole is asymmetrical in shape—melanomas cannot be divided in half the way normal moles can.

Examine your skin thoroughly for odd bumps or changing moles.

If a mole is bigger around than the top of a pencil eraser, see a doctor.

- Its borders are uneven or notched, not smooth, and fade off into surrounding skin.
- The color is varied, usually a mixture of tan, brown, black or reddish pink.
- Its diameter is wider than a pencil eraser (more than 5 millimeters).

Mole-monitoring should be a monthly ritual if you are light skinned, someone in your family has had melanoma, you have more than 100 moles (mostly located on your back) or you have any new spot that develops after age 40. Any change in any spot should be immediately reported to your dermatologist. Remember, skin tumors were once small spots. Early diagnosis plus prompt treatment equals cure.

Check out any new spot appearing after age 40.

Seek Permanent Protection

If melanoma is diagnosed, the course of treatment is usually surgery. The latest procedures use microscopically controlled excision techniques which get at the root of the cancer, spare the surrounding tissue and have the highest cure rate.

Even more exciting work is being done with melanoma vaccines. Studies have shown that vaccinating mice with dead melanoma cells prevents melanoma from appearing. Jean-Claude Bystryn, M.D., director of the melanoma immunotherapy clinic at New York University Medical Center, in New York City, reports: "We've treated about 50 patients with the vaccines and many of them have developed an increase in their immune response to melanoma." It's encouraging news which indicates the possibility that melanoma can be slowed or prevented altogether by immunization. But don't expect that you will soon be getting a melanoma shot along with your polio vaccine. "This is still very experimental and requires testing," cautions Dr. Bystryn.

A new vaccine could wipe out melanoma for good.

On another research front, hope for reversing skin cancer and perhaps preventing it is coming from work being done with vitamin A by researchers such as Norman Levine, M.D., chief of dermatology at the University of Arizona Health Sciences Center, in Tucson. In one study, Dr. Levine treated a small group of melanoma patients with a topical vitamin A and found that their lesions regressed. He is also looking at oral vitamin A as a potential agent in the prevention of skin cancer in patients with a precancerous skin condition. What's the secret to vitamin A? "No one knows," says Dr. Levine. "It could be that it works on the individual cells and makes them behave more like normal cells or that it works on the skin's immune system."

New Help for Psoriasis Sufferers

Vitamin A derivatives could save the day if you suffer from psoriasis. Those red itchy patches on your elbows and knees are the result of a process in which skin cells multiply at a much faster rate than normal and don't shed like nondiseased cells. Instead, they build up and result in raised "plaques," which are often covered with a silvery scale that peels off like sheets of mica. The cause of psoriasis is anyone's guess, but inheritance seems to play a part.

A vitamin A derivative may clear the skin of psoriasis.

In earlier times, psoriasis sufferers were socially shunned, like lepers. But if you have psoriasis, you know this condition is no less heartbreaking today. That's because psoriasis is persistent—it's a lifelong problem that requires lifelong care. Here's where vitamin A comes in. Etretinate, a vitamin A derivative, awaits Food and Drug Administration approval, but many dermatologists are already singing its praises for psoriasis treatment. What's got them enthused is that etretinate and other vitamin A retinoids may act to correct abnormal skin cells. They also lengthen the time between psoriatic episodes and are devoid of the skin-thinning effects of steroids. The down side of some of these derivatives is that they do not clear from the body and can cause serious side effects, like birth defects.

Thanks to laser technology, an effective alternative treatment may soon be in sight. In one Swedish experiment, doctors used laser beams to destroy psoriatic plaque on three patients. The treated areas healed in three to six weeks, and remained free of psoriasis for the follow-up period of three to five years.

Laser treatment can keep treated areas free of psoriasis plaque for as long as five years.

Strategies and Treatments

Until the bugs are worked out of these treatments, there is much you can do to protect against psoriasis outbreaks. Keep your skin safe from sunburn, dryness, scrapes, stress, irritation, chemicals and excessive drinking.

If you start developing psoriatic plaque, sitting in the sun for a half hour can give you great relief, provided you don't burn. Make your motto, "Keep your skin cool and smooth." Avoid hot baths and keep your skin well lubricated.

Sufferers with severe psoriasis may find help at a psoriasis treatment center. Here you'll find the latest treatment techniques. One is called PUVA, a procedure which uses ultraviolet light combined with a drug such as psoralen, which boosts the healing effects of the ultraviolet rays and clears the skin in two to three months with periodic treatments. "The beauty of the centers is that they allow psoriasis sufferers to be treated on an outpatient basis so they can go to work and function normally," says one center's director, Peter Heald, M.D., of the Yale University School of Medicine, in New Haven, Connecticut. "Special support groups provide help dealing with the emotional side of the disease, which can be pretty traumatic."

What to Do When Shingles Strike

Keeping your skin safe from trauma, both the physical and the emotional kind, just might spare you from shingles, a skin disease that strikes about half of all adults before age 85. You may be a candidate too, if you've had chicken pox as a child. The same virus (herpes zoster) that caused the pox may not have really left your body when your blisters scabbed over and healed. Rather, the virus hid in your spinal nerves. There it remains until a cold, sunburn, stress or just the passage of time lowers your resistance, weakens your natural immunity and triggers the virus to travel down the nerve endings and erupt on your skin—usually in a band around one side of the chest, the neck, lower back or the forehead and eyes.

Unlike lightning, shingles can strike more than once in your life, given the right conditions. Fortunately, an antiviral drug called acyclovir can now help a beleaguered body strike back. It has been dubbed a "suicide promoter" because it causes the virus-infected cell to cooperate in its own demise.

New drugs may search out and destroy the shingles virus.

Allies against Shingles Pain

In addition to drugs, there are other allies to help you fight *postherpetic neuralgia*, the scientific name for the shingles pain, which may linger for years after an outbreak.

In a recent study, 15 of 17 patients who were given a metabolism by-product called adenosine monophosphate (AMP), reportedly felt no pain within two weeks. And when questioned two years later, the patients were still free of pain. This treatment has no side effects, notes S. Harvey Sklar, M.D., consultant with the former shingles clinic at Englewood Hospital, in Englewood, New Jersey. It works best within the first few months of pain, when the nerve endings have undergone minimal damage.

Until AMP or something like it becomes available, at least one doctor suggests that vitamins B and C could help control your pain. Dermatologist John G. McConahy, M.D., of New Castle, Pennsylvania, routinely gives his shingles patients vitamins C and B complex and a multivitamin and mineral tablet, along with corticosteroid drugs. "With that regimen, I've never had a patient whose pain lasted longer than six weeks," says Dr. McConahy. He believes that vitamins C and B complex work by helping regenerate and rebuild nerve cells. Before using these or any other supplements, get your doctor's advice and approval.

Vitamins C and B complex can help to control pain and regenerate nerve cells.

Acne Attackers for Youthful Skin

Think "acne" and you probably think "adolescent." Yet for thousands of adults, severe acne continues long after graduation day is left behind. If this describes you, chin up. Clear skin can be yours at last. Once again, vitamin A comes to the rescue, this time in a synthetic formulation called 13-cis retinoic

Accutane clears the complexion but can cause birth defects.

acid, or Accutane. A single course of therapy has been shown to result in complete and prolonged remission of cystic acne, reducing the production of sebum, a fatty secretion of the sebaceous glands, as well as inflamed lesions. And that's not all. Accutane has even been shown to keep preventing acne for 12 to 20 months after people stop taking it.

Any drug that strong, however, is likely to have side effects and Accutane is no exception. This drug can cause birth defects. That's why its manufacturer has issued a strict warning about the risk to women in their reproductive years, and why many dermatologists reserve Accutane for only severe cases of cystic acne.

Zinc Smooths Out the Skin

Add zinc, subtract iodine and keep your skin safe from eruptions.

One treatment that doesn't have side effects is plain old zinc. Gerd Michaelsson, M.D., a Swedish researcher, theorizes that zinc releases vitamin A in the body, which may normalize cells. Or perhaps zinc has an anti-inflammatory effect. Whatever the reason, it may be wise to add zinc-rich foods to your diet, such as lean beef, cheese and chicken. At the same time, though, certain foods can aggravate acne and should be avoided, advises a Los Angeles dermatologist. These are foods high in iodine such as iodized salt, kelp, turkey and broccoli.

Rx for Repeat Rashes

Find the cause, then consider treating the rash with hydrocortisone.

The phrase "itches like crazy" must have been invented by someone suffering from chronic dermatitis. If it has special meaning for you, you are not alone. Chronic dermatitis, which is the catch-all term for inflamed skin, affects millions of people and is the number one ailment seen by dermatologists. How did this red, scaly, irritated skin happen to you—and why does the maddening itch still persist? Probably you inherited unusually sensitive skin. Then somewhere along the line you ran into something— a cleaner, soap, clothing—that irritated your skin and caused it to become red and cracked or perhaps blistered. So you scratched and scratched until your skin became thick, discolored and scaly. Relief becomes harder . . . but luckily, not impossible.

(continued on page 350)

A Mind/Body Program for Healthy Skin

Part of the problem with chronic skin diseases is feeling out of control, a slave to salves, a prisoner of the persistent itch. Now there may be a chance to put yourself back in the driver's seat, according to Ted Grossbart, Ph.D., a clinical psychologist in the department of psychiatry at Harvard Medical School, in Cambridge, Massachusetts, and author of *Skin Deep: A Mind/Body Program for Healthy Skin* (Morrow).

What's your mind got to do with your skin? Plenty, says Dr. Grossbart. "The skin is an exquisitely sensitive responder to emotions." After all, anger can make the skin turn red as a beet, fear turns it white as a ghost, joy makes it glow. What's more, says Dr. Grossbart, emotions play a role in all skin diseases, whether their cause is physical or not. "Emotional factors sometimes cause, and very frequently can reduce or intensify itching and pain, even when the physical disease itself remains unchanged," says Dr. Grossbart.

And that's not all. Your skin is a gauge of your emotions and it has a language all its own. Take the case of Fred M. When his business went bankrupt, his skin erupted with psoriasis patches. The next time it happened was when he caught his bridge partner cheating. "Those who don't express their feelings might find their skin doing it for them in some way," says Dr. Grossbart. What you're feeling inside might be expressed outside by angry red rashes, or devilishly itchy hives.

Dr. Grossbart believes you can learn to harness your mind so it will become your skin's ally, not its enemy.

Even though your psoriasis is hereditary or your shingles caused by a virus, your emotions can tip the balance from suffering towards relief. "If you have recurrent genital herpes, for example, you're probably free from symptoms most of the time," he explains. "The balance is towards health, with the disease-causing virus held in check by the body's immune system. An emotional upheaval causes a temporary dip in defenses, allowing the virus to come out of hiding and cause an outbreak."

Dr. Grossbart has developed a treatment plan that gives you the edge towards health. The first step is to determine how emotions trigger skin flareups. Chances are you will find, as did one researcher, that when pressure is intense at work or quarrels erupt at home, your skin erupts too.

In 1978, Robert Griesman, M.D., studied more than 4,500 pa-

A Mind/Body Program for Healthy Skin—*Continued*

tients to determine the link between emotional stress and skin disorder, as well as the time it took for the stressful event to trigger the disorder. What he found was that emotions had a triggering role in itching almost 100 percent of the time, in hives 68 percent of the time and in psoriasis 62 percent of the time.

So, to determine the cause of your skin problems, start by keeping a daily chart of your skin flareups and what emotions appear to make them better or worse. Look for patterns. Do your pimples appear after Mother visits? Keep in mind that the period between emotion and reaction can range from a few seconds to days or even weeks.

Step two is to enter a healing state using a technique like relaxation or self-hypnosis. Briefly, it involves sitting quietly for 10 to 15 minutes, with your eyes closed. Begin relaxing each muscle group from your feet all the way to your scalp. Take deep breaths, repeating the word "one" with each inhalation.

Step three involves imagining conditions and situations that will make your skin feel better, make the itching stop and ease the burning and pain, says Dr. Grossbart. "The small but real bodily changes that accompany this ideal imaginary environment can make life that much harder for the viruses, bacteria or inflammatory processes that are bedeviling your skin." What will make your skin feel better? If your dermatitis feels better cooled, imagine swimming in a pool of yogurt. If you use medications along with your imagination, you may find you get more relief out of using less, suggests Dr. Grossbart.

To give your imagery skills a boost, help you relax and alter your physiology, you might want to try biofeedback. It works like this: A sensor device is attached to your body and monitors your heart rate, skin moisture and muscle tension. In one experiment, investigators tried to slow cell growth by lowering skin temperature in psoriasis patients. (Rapid cell growth is a factor in psoriasis.) The results were slight but significant. Temperatures dropped, cell production decreased and the psoriasis improved. Biofeedback may work for you. "If warmth is a part of your ideal skin environment, biofeedback could tell you if your skin is actually getting warmer."

Will Dr. Grossbart's treatment work for you? He lists examples of his own and those of other people working in the field where psychological techniques have provided relief. Among them:

Shingles. A 56-year-old man went through years of drug therapy without lasting relief. Then he learned a technique whereby his therapist had him focus on his pain, gradually imagining it becoming worse until an imagined brush with cotton was unbearable. The suggestion was made that the reverse was equally possible. After the second hypnotic session, the patient could resume his golf games.

Allergies. Often an allergic reaction can be conditioned, linking a particular substance to an emotional issue. One girl developed a strong allergic reaction to wood and wood products. When hypnotherapy allowed her to connect this to her difficult relationship with her father, who was a carpenter, her allergy vanished.

Itching. This is not a disease, but an experience. "While the *cause* of your itch may be either psychological or physical, the experience of itching is psychological," contends Dr. Grossbart. That's why you don't feel a mosquito bite itch while you're watching an exciting ball game. The game prevents you from focusing on your itch. By the same token, you can learn how to focus your imagination to stop the itching.

Here's one example of how to unlink the chain of itching and learn to scratch a little bit without falling into total scratching. (But, remember, it is just one part of an entire program. Don't expect it to bring total relief all by itself.) First, imagine a chain with separate links which move independently. Imagine "unlinking" the itch from, say, the side of your arm, and from other parts of your arm and body. Scratch it a little, but separate this scratch from all other parts of your body. Now unlink today's itch from all other itches. Unlink the urge to scratch from action—let it remain an urge. Finally, unlink yourself from the itchy part of your skin—pretend you are floating across the room.

Dr. Grossbart has this reminder about his treatment plan: Regardless of the role of emotional factors, techniques like relaxation and unlinking the itch/scratch chain will make it easier to live inside your troubled skin. And the best part? You need no prescription, there are no side effects and it puts *you* in charge of your skin. No matter what skin symptoms you have, though, see a doctor first. Find one who takes into account the emotional, as well as the physical, side of the problem.

Enter hydrocortisone, one of the large family of cortisone medications. You can now purchase hydrocortisone without prescription under trade names like Cortaid. What this man-made adrenal hormone does is give you relief from itchiness, redness, scaliness, swelling and inflammation.

Some experts worry, however, that long-term use of cortisone creams for conditions like dermatitis might make your rash more tolerable so you could go right on exposing yourself to offending irritants. Then maybe you'd overuse your cortisone preparation and wind up with thinned skin and possible impairment of your collagen production.

The key to safely using these substances is to follow directions—then they can work wonders for mildly itchy, inflamed skin. "Over-the-counter cortisones are fine for chapped or dishpan hands, sunburn, poison ivy or mosquito bites," suggests Dr. Leyden. "For long-term treatment of scaly, cracked, itchy or dry skin, it's not only risky but costly. You would need a tube a day for effective relief."

Safe, Instant Itch Relief

To reverse recurrent redness and inflammation, start with time-tested anti-itch treatments like this anti-itch slush: Fill a plastic bag with crushed ice and cold water. Wrap it in a towel and apply to the irritated skin.

Uncovering Clues to Chronic Skin Blues

For absolutely total and lasting relief, you need to stay away from the triggers that irritate your skin. That might take a bit of sleuthing. Ask yourself when your skin problems began. After your bubble bath? When you changed the oil in your car? Painted the porch? Went hiking in the woods? Used that new dish detergent? Here are a few of the common skin allergens that might provide further clues to your skin blues:

• Fragrances. Perfumes can be found not just in colognes but in soaps, detergents, fabric softeners, even scented toilet tissue. Products labeled "unscented" may still contain masking perfumes. Look for fragrance-free labels instead.

- Nickel and nickel compounds. If your earlobes, midback or thighs are itchy and red, suspect nickel in your earring, bra clasps or keys in your pockets.
- Formaldehyde. This chemical is commonly found in permanent-press and no-iron clothing as well as deodorants and insecticides.
- Aspirin, penicillin, shellfish, FD&C yellow dye no. 5. If you can't match up an irritant with a rash of red welts, it may mean your body is reacting to something you ate, breathed or swallowed. These notorious offenders cause certain cells to set off histamine chemicals which leave a trail of raised red spots, better known as hives or urticaria, on your skin. There's usually a time lag between exposure and the onset of hives. Using antihistamines, vitamin C and relaxation techniques may help bring relief, and hives usually disappear altogether once you eliminate the suspected food or drug.

Aspirin, shellfish and yellow food dye are common causes of hives.

28

Sleep:

Sound Advice

for Snoozers

Ninety-eight, 99, 100 sheep and not only are you awake, you're getting fed up with the fleecy little critters.

Sleeplessness can be irritating—you may thrash about like a fish out of water, fretfully awaiting much-needed rest. Or you may fall asleep all right, but awaken at the slightest provocation, as though every little household sound has been amplified.

Lying there with wide open eyes, you may nervously recall what sleeplessness can do to otherwise healthy beings. Sleep deprivation in laboratory animals, for example, leads to death through deterioration of body tissue. And in war camps, sleeplessness is enforced as a form of torture, to break down the wills of strong men.

Sleep speeds healing.

Why is sleep so important to physical, mental and emotional well-being? Because sleep refreshes the mind and body. Bedtime is prime time for healing and tissue renewal, since that's when cell division and protein synthesis are fastest, researchers found at the Royal Edinburgh Hospital, in Scotland. Other studies have shown that the body's immune system is most efficient during sleep.

Sleep appears to aid memory, too. In a University of Colorado experiment, subjects were asked to memorize long lists of words 14 hours after studying them. The subjects who stayed awake during those 14 hours remembered less than those who slept for 7 hours.

"During sleep, the mind sorts and sifts recent impulses, assimilates them with past experience and stores them in memory," says Fred B. Rogers, M.D., professor of family practice and community health at Temple University School of Medicine, in Philadelphia. "Dreams seem to have something to do with this process. They also appear to maintain emotional health. Research shows that when people are kept from dreaming they can develop psychological disturbances, ranging from simple irritability to hallucinations."

When radio disc jockey Peter Tripp stayed awake for almost ten days, for example, he saw flames blazing in a desk drawer, clocks with human faces and specks that turned into bugs, reports Dianne Hales, author of a book about sleep.

But losing an hour's sleep each night will hardly drive you to your ruin, says Jon Sassin, M.D., director of the sleep disorders center at the University of California at Irvine Medical Center. "It's not uncommon for elderly patients to come to me worried about their so-called insomnia. It turns out they don't have a sleep disorder at all. They're merely showing typical sleeping patterns for their age."

You may need less sleep as you grow older.

Instead of getting up at 7:00, they might find themselves wide awake at 5:30. The point is not to lose sleep over it. If you feel awake and refreshed throughout the day, then you've had enough sleep regardless of what the clock may say.

"Some people do well on four hours of sleep a night," says Elliot Richard Phillips, M.D., medical director of the sleep disorders center at Holy Cross Hospital, in Mission Hills, California. "Others need ten. Recognize and accept individual sleeping patterns. Remember, too, that as you get older you may require even less sleep."

On the other hand, if sleep or the lack thereof is zapping your daytime energy, you may be able to improve it. "Many people don't even realize their sleep can be improved," says Stuart Rawlings, administrator of the sleep disorders center at Stanford University School of Medicine, in Palo Alto, Califor-

If sleep isn't leaving you refreshed in the morning, you can improve the situation.

nia, and the Association of Sleep Disorders Centers, also in California. "They accept daytime sleepiness as a way of life. Their poor sleep may be the consequence of a serious sleep disorder."

"Increased daytime drowsiness, lighter sleep and frequent awakenings during the night are accepted as common conditions of older people," says Sonia Ancoli-Israel, Ph.D., assistant professor of psychiatry at the University of California at San Diego and assistant director of the sleep disorders clinic at the Veterans Administration Medical Center, in San Diego. "But overall, sleep shouldn't change that much as you age. You should take a look at your sleeping and waking patterns if they're affecting your daytime functioning."

Design Your Bedroom

There's more to sleep than just closing your eyes. Your everyday activities and your bedtime preparations can make or break your sleep. This interdependence can create a vicious circle: poor sleep can ruin your day, and a difficult day can disrupt sleep. But it's a cycle that can be broken, and the bedroom is a good place to start.

First check the thermostat. Room temperature between 64° and 66°F is most conducive to sound sleep, says Dr. Phillips. Too cold and you'll be fumbling for covers. Too hot and you have restless, light sleep.

Room temperature should be between 64° and 66°F.

In addition to controlling temperature, also do what you can about controlling other disrupting environmental factors, particularly light and sound. "The higher proportion of light sleep makes older individuals more liable to be disturbed by lights and noise," point out researchers with Project Sleep, a national program on insomnia and sleep disorders launched by the Surgeon General of the United States. "So try to make your bedroom as dark and quiet as you can."

"Eyeshades may help if bright street lights shine into the room," says Dr. Phillips. "Heavy draperies may reduce both light and sound."

Mask noise with a "white noise" machine or a fan.

Solving sound problems can be difficult if you live near an airport or a superhighway, but you can mask the sound with another noise. A "white noise" generator (which produces soothing background sounds such as simulated rain, surf or waterfalls) or a mere electric fan can do the trick, some doctors have found. Comfortable earplugs may also help.

Now for the actual bed. If the mattress is saggy or lumpy, replace it. You might want to try something different, such as an air mattress or a water bed. Get rid of overly soft, fluffy pillows. They can cause neck stiffness, which disrupts sleep. And consider using wool blankets. They're better able to regulate skin and body temperature than their acrylic counterparts, so they help create a more comfortable sleeping environment.

Associate Your Bedroom with Relaxation and Sleep

The idea behind this advice is that if you worry, work and whine in the bedroom, you will continue to do so come bedtime.

"One woman I counseled used her bedroom as an office," says Thomas J. Coates, Ph.D., codirector of the behavioral medicine unit at the University of California at San Francisco School of Medicine. "She had just reentered the job market and had placed her desk in her bedroom. Every time she saw it there she would get uptight and depressed. When she placed her desk in another room—away from her bedroom—her insomnia disappeared."

Don't use your bedroom as an office.

The same problem can arise from domestic fighting. Another patient of Dr. Coates's said that the bedroom was the only room where she and her husband could argue without the children hearing. "Now they use the garage and she is sleeping again," says Dr. Coates.

If you're the worrying type, schedule a "worry time" for *early* in the evening, suggests Project Sleep. And if you still haven't fallen asleep after 20 to 30 minutes, get up and leave the bedroom. This way you won't associate your bed with sleeplessness.

Instead, your bedroom should be a comforting, relaxing haven. Decorate it in your favorite colors and fabrics. Bring in objects (like photographs and souvenirs) that help you recall the most pleasant times in your life. Practice relaxation techniques or self-hypnosis in the bedroom.

Handling a Nightmare . . . and Other Dream Secrets

Odds are, you will never be consumed by a herd of mutant zombies. Nor will you ever encounter a hideous monster. But that doesn't make nightmares about such things any less frightening.

"The fear in a nightmare is real, even when you know it's only a dream," says Stephen LaBerge, Ph.D., researcher with Stanford University's Sleep Research Center, in California, and author of *Lucid Dreaming* (Ballantine). "And if nightmares are frequent and terrifying, they can interfere with a good night's sleep."

But you can turn a nightmare into a positive experience if you learn to control your reactions to your dreams, says Dr. LaBerge. "You don't have to frighten yourself with your own images. Next time you have a lucid nightmare (one in which you realize you're dreaming), don't just wake up and try to forget it. Visualize a better ending. If you're running away, face the pursuer. If you dream you're crushed in a small room, find a way to get out of it. Make friends with the dragon. Because if you face fear in your dreams, it's easier to do so when awake."

Dreams don't have to be scary to benefit you, says Dr. LaBerge. "Dreams can be a time for self-exploration, adventure and growth."

Dr. LaBerge has found that dream control has seemed to work for many individuals. "I knew a woman who was extremely depressed after the death of her grandmother. So I told her to talk to

How Diet Can Affect Sleep

The warm glass of milk has received quite a bit of good press. And well it should, since it contains L-tryptophan. This amino acid has been shown to stimulate a brain compound called serotonin, which may fight depression, kill pain and yes, aid sleep.

L-tryptophan may relieve chronic insomnia for some people.

A study from Switzerland has shown that even chronic insomniacs can benefit from this nutrient. The 40 patients who participated in the experiment took L-tryptophan for about four months. By the end of the study, half the patients said that their sleep patterns were "much improved." Even at a two-year follow-up, most of the patients were still sleeping well even though they were no longer taking the L-tryptophan.

her grandmother in her dreams—to say the things she wished she had said and to work out unfinished business. She did, and it helped her to come to terms with the loss, to let go and to resolve conflicts."

Even if you don't take control of your dreams, they might teach you something about yourself, says Dr. LaBerge. "Some dream theorists believe that dreams are just random images generated by your mind. I believe that may be true, but you do interpret the random activity—it's something like an inkblot test. So look at a dream as a story you told. The feelings and impressions say something about how you see the world and how you feel about life."

Much of these theories about dreams are based on speculation and clinical observation, says Dr. LaBerge. But research continues to shed rays of light onto this foggy subject. "Scientific experiments show that the brain actually reacts as though dreams were real," says Dr. LaBerge. "If you hold your breath in a dream, you really hold your breath. And if you look to the left in a dream, your eyes really go to the left. The brain sends signals to correspond to everything you're doing in a dream, but another part of your brain paralyzes most of your body. If you were not paralyzed, you would actually do these things. We plan to study whether this has any implications for health: Can you speed healing if you heal a body in a dream? So far this is just wild speculation, but it's a possibility."

This amino acid doesn't work for everyone, found researchers from Tufts University School of Medicine, in Medford, Massachusetts, but it's most likely to aid subjects who complain of frequent nighttime awakenings.

It works best for those who waken during the night.

Along with milk, cheddar cheese, peanuts, turkey and tuna are good sources of L-tryptophan. The best option, however, is tablets, says Ernest Hartmann, M.D., a professor of psychiatry at Tufts University School of Medicine and director of the sleep disorders center at Newton Wellesley Hospital, in Boston, who researched tryptophan. He suggests taking 1 to 2 grams of tryptophan tablets (1 gram is the equivalent of two 500-milligram tablets, the usual commercially available dose) about 45 to 60 minutes before bed. Many people don't see effects for two to three weeks after starting the amino acid. When it does take effect, you can cut your dosage to three to four days on, then three days off, says Dr. Hartmann.

As for side effects, they're virtually nonexistent, found researchers from the University of California at Los Angeles. Even so, they caution that there are some people who should not take L-tryptophan—those with liver disease and those on certain medications. In fact, anyone who is undergoing any medical treatment should check with his or her doctor first before using the amino acid.

Carbohydrates may help L-tryptophan to work.

Eating carbohydrates along with the L-tryptophan may increase the effectiveness of the nutrient, according to Richard Wurtman, Ph.D., scientific director of the Center for Brain Sciences and Metabolism at the Massachusetts Institute of Technology, in Cambridge. After a high-carbohydrate meal is eaten, insulin is released. This hormone helps clear the way for tryptophan to be carried to the brain.

But make those carbohydrates complex. Simple sugars (such as candy bars or cookies) can keep you awake, says Michael Stevenson, Ph.D., director of the insomnia clinic at Holy Cross Hospital. "They often make people feel 'hyped-up.' Instead have a piece of whole wheat toast."

Eating too much or too little also can disrupt sleep.

Whatever you eat, don't eat too much of it. "Digesting a large meal stimulates the body, lightens sleep and arouses the sleeper," says Jerrold S. Maxmen, M.D., author of *A Good Night's Sleep* (Warner Books). On the other hand, don't go to bed hungry either. Gnawing hunger pains and the feelings of emptiness in the stomach can lead to restlessness and a poor night's sleep. Dr. Stevenson suggests eating a banana and milk or even a small tuna sandwich, which contains both complex carbohydrates and L-tryptophan.

Review All Drugs and Medications

Cigarettes and alcohol also can interfere with sleep.

This includes cigarettes. Studies have shown that the nicotine found in cigarettes can adversely affect your sleep. In one study, researchers found that nonsmokers fell asleep after about 30 minutes, while it took smokers an average of 44 minutes. In a separate experiment, heavy smokers, who agreed to quit all at once, decreased the total time spent awake by 45 percent in the first three nights alone.

And forget your "nightcap"—it can ruin your night. "Initially, alcohol does induce sleepiness," says Dr. Stevenson. "But about two to three hours after drinking, you go through alcohol withdrawal, which actually arouses the nervous system to a higher level than before. Too much wine with dinner, and you may be unable to fall asleep at bedtime. If the wine is at bedtime, you may fall asleep easily, only to find yourself wide awake in the middle of the night."

Antibiotics, or any prescription for that matter, have the potential to disturb sleep. If your sleep problems seem to coincide with taking a new medication, consult your doctor or pharmacist about this side effect.

If insomnia coincides with a new prescription, call your doctor.

And sleeping pills can harm your sleep. "Sleeping pills such as Valium or Dalmane produce poor sleep quality while you take them," says Dr. Phillips. "But you get into even more trouble if you try to quit. There's a physiological withdrawal your system must go through which causes insomnia. You can see how people get hooked."

Over-the-counter (OTC) sleeping medications are equally frowned upon. "There's a withdrawal problem from these preparations as well," Dr. Phillips says. "What's more, the main ingredient in the OTCs is actually an antihistamine, which may produce some potentially serious side effects if used for prolonged periods. It can cause glaucoma to worsen, produce irregular heartbeats and urinary problems. These medications should not be used casually."

Refine Your Sleep Routine

Many older people try to increase sleep time by going to bed earlier and staying in bed longer, says Mary A. Carskadon, Ph.D., associate professor with the department of psychiatry and human behavior at Brown University, in Providence, Rhode Island. But this strategy is not only ineffective, it can make things worse—it disrupts the normal daily or circadian rhythm function, and actually can cause insomnia.

So don't go to bed until you are sleepy. Do something relaxing until you feel tired. Read a mildly interesting book, watch a dull late-night TV show or listen to relaxing music, advises Peter Hauri, Ph.D., codirector of the Sleep Disorders Center, Dartmouth Medical Center, in New Hampshire. The key here is not to do anything too exciting. "Keep going until you're falling asleep at what you're doing," says Dr. Hauri. "For example, when you have to read a paragraph twice because you can't remember what you read."

Develop your own sleep ritual if you don't already have one. Do you close all the windows, check that all the doors are locked, wash up, read before bed? Sleep rituals prepare you for bed psychologically as well as physically and should be continued even when you're away from home.

Wake-up time should be consistent as well. You should get up at the same time each morning, every day of the week, regardless of when you went to bed, when you fell asleep or how many hours of sleep you've gotten. "This is one of the most important rules of all," points out Dr. Phillips. "By getting up at the same time every morning, no matter how poor the night's sleep has been, you accomplish two things. The body's circadian rhythm is reset, so that it expects to get up from sleep at the same time tomorrow, and all other sleep and wake cycles are synchronized."

In other words, oversleeping on weekends is a sure way to mess up your body clock. You not only feel groggy after too much sleep, but you make it more difficult to fall asleep the next night.

Taking naps is another way to confuse your body's rhythms. For most people, a daytime snooze will decrease the quality and quantity of sleep at night. But if you must nap, follow a regular schedule, says Dr. Carskadon. Keep it short—about 30 minutes—and plan it for the late morning or early afternoon. "If the nap is taken late in the afternoon or if it is unusually prolonged (over an hour long), it may have the unwanted effect of interfering with nocturnal sleep," she warns.

Watch the late movie, read a dull book—stay awake till you're sleepy.

Waking up at the same time every day may be the most important measure for better sleep.

If you take a nap, schedule it early.

Working on the Night Shift

Circadian rhythms usually work in a benevolent fashion. The body's temperature, hormones and biochemistry apparently fluctuate regularly, making you more energetic, and more tired, at certain times of the day.

But if you disrupt these rhythms by traveling across time zones, working variable shifts or otherwise changing normal sleep time, your body may get its revenge. Poor sleep, digestive problems, decreased performance and a general groggy feeling may be the result. In the week following the switch to daylight saving time, when people have to wake up just one hour earlier, there are 10 percent more traffic accidents than usual.

Biannual time changes can be overcome, but rotating shift work poses a persistent problem. How much of a problem it is, however, depends on how the shifts change, found Charles A. Czeisler, Ph.D., M.D., of Harvard Medical School, in Cambridge, Massachusetts, and Boston Brigham and Women's Hospital. A study he conducted at a Utah chemical plant showed that workers adjust best to shift changes that move forward—morning shift followed by evening and night—because this conforms more easily to the biological clock. He says that workers are more efficient if their shifts are not rotated too frequently—three- or four-week shifts instead of one-week shifts. This improved work schedule, along with a worker education program, improved job satisfaction, health, personnel turnover and worker productivity in his study.

Some shift workers unwittingly make their sleep worse, found Michael Frese, Ph.D., and Claudia Harwich, psychologists with the University of Pennsylvania, in Philadelphia. "Two frequently used coping strategies that have a physiological effect are smoking more and drinking coffee during the night," they point out. And such methods only make the problem worse. Avoid that trap.

Daytime Activity Affects Sleep

It's true that many elderly people complain that they don't sleep as soundly as they used to, are easily awakened and don't feel well rested in the morning. But poor sleep isn't necessarily a burden of aging. Dr. Carskadon believes these changes are more probably due to a sedentary life-style.

Exercise during the day can make sleep more restful at night.

Research conducted at the University of California at Santa Barbara backs her up. In this study of 14 healthy people, aged 57 to 72 years, recordings of sleep patterns showed when they took a brisk, one-hour walk in the afternoon, they all slept better at night. Total sleep time wasn't changed, but sleep was more restful because less time was spent in "light sleep," the researchers say.

But even exercise is a matter of timing. Strenuous exercise can stimulate the cardiovascular and nervous systems for hours, making it difficult for you to unwind and relax, says Dr. Phillips. Dr. Maxmen advises exercising in the late afternoon or early evening. And exercise in moderation, or you'll find yourself kept awake with the aches and pains caused by overexertion.

Increasing mental activity also improves chances of good sleep. Dr. Coates found that boredom, more than overstimulation, can disrupt sleep. His study found that poor sleepers spent more time shopping, relaxing and watching TV, and thought more about going to bed. The good sleepers were more active mentally and physically. They spent more time working, talking and doing chores.

Isolation and boredom can ruin sleep.

So get involved in a project or do volunteer work. "Often," says Dr. Stevenson, "insomnia can be traced back to within one week of retirement. Isolation, boredom, loss of social contacts and preoccupation with self all hit at once. Sleep goes right out the window. Sometimes we have to get the person to go back to work."

And increase social contacts. Isolated people are poor sleepers, says Dr. Coates. Those with a social support system sleep better and are also less depressed, which in itself helps relieve insomnia.

Snuff That Snore

"The loudest snore recorded so far has been 80 decibels," says Dale Rice, M.D., of the University of Southern California, in Los Angeles. "That's about the equivalent of a jackhammer ten feet away. Some have been the equivalent of a 747 taking off or the sound of a diesel bus at close range."

And he's not talking about an occasional snore here and there during the night. A researcher at the University of Florida, in Gainesville, monitored a group of habitual snorers and found that their average output was not less than 1,015 snores per individual per night.

Habitual snorers average 1,015 snores a night.

It's hardly surprising that snoring provokes such marital discord. "We know of a woman in Texas who actually shot her boyfriend because he snored so loudly," says David N. F. Fairbanks, M.D., an otolaryngologist at George Washington University, in Washington, D.C.

Snoring Can Be Hazardous to Your Health

Snoring can be more than just annoying. It can sometimes be the first symptom or the earliest stage of a serious respiratory disorder called sleep apnea, in which the sleeper stops breathing for ten seconds or more in episodes that occur seven or more times an hour. Apnea, which occurs in roughly 30 percent of heavy snorers, can be fatal, but in most cases a vigilant section of the brain has the presence of mind to change gears at the last moment and jolt the body into a lighter phase of sleep. The sleeper half-awakes, gulps in fresh air and saves his own life.

But apnea doesn't have to be fatal to be harmful. It prevents restful sleep, which may cause "disruptive and potentially dangerous physical and psychological side effects, such as personality change, sexual dysfunction, intellectual deterioration and hypertension," says Thomas A. McCabe, M.D., of Arlington, Virginia.

And there seems to be a link between hypertension (high blood pressure) and the kind of chronic low-level oxygen deprivation that accompanies both snoring and apnea. "People who snore every day, who snore loudly enough to make their spouses sleep in another room, put a tremendous amount of strain on their heart," says Dr. Rice. "It can create high blood pressure in the heart, and if it goes on long enough it might cause general high blood pressure."

Snoring and apnea may cause high blood pressure.

This puts a double whammy on older men who may already be afflicted with circulatory problems. "Snoring in most cases gets progressively worse with

A Night in the Sleep Lab

"They taped electrodes all over my body," says Jennifer. "Wires were coming out of my face, chest and legs—I felt like Frankenstein's monster! I don't know *how* I fell asleep, but I did."

The first night in a sleep disorder clinic may feel a little strange, but most people fall asleep anyway, says Stuart Rawlings, administrator for the Association of Sleep Disorders Centers. "Often, it's easier to get to sleep in a lab, because it's less disruptive than the home environment. It's quiet—no screaming kids—and there's nothing else to do but sleep."

Not long ago, no one seemed to know (or care) much about sleep disorders. But new findings on apnea, which began in the 1960s, woke up the medical community to the importance of sleep research and sleep disorder medicine. In 1976 the Association of Sleep Disorders Centers (ASDC) was established, and sleep disorders centers started popping up all over the country.

"A clinic will give you a physical examination, and ask several hundred questions to find out your medical history, life-style, and psychological state," says Rawlings. "Then, if we suspect a serious sleep disorder, such as apnea, we'll conduct an overnight evaluation in the sleep lab. Different machines measure body functions such as brain waves, eye movement, breathing, oxygen saturation, heartbeat and leg movement.

"It is expensive. It might cost $500 to $1,500 for a full sleep evaluation. But we are also developing home monitors, which may be cheaper. I think that in the future, these will become widely available."

Some of the symptoms of disordered sleep that occur in elderly patients during wakefulness are excessive daytime sleepiness, sudden sleep attacks, fatigue, blackouts, memory defects and change in personality. If you suspect you have a sleep disorder, you might consider visiting a sleep center. But see your regular doctor first, suggests Rawlings. Most centers require a doctor's referral.

For a list of sleep laboratories around the country write to the Association of Sleep Disorders Centers, 604 Second Street S.W., Rochester, MN 55902.

age," Dr. Rice says, "so that the strain on the person's heart and lungs gets worse just at the time when he doesn't want any extra stress."

High-Tech Remedies

The most common symptoms of sleep apnea are snoring and excessive daytime sleepiness, says Bernard deBerry, M.D., a Laguna Hills, California sleep specialist. Sometimes this chronic tiredness gets to the point where sufferers actually fall asleep on the job or while driving to work. Other common symptoms include: morning headaches, sexual impotence, personality changes, memory lapses, chronic depression and snoring that's remarkable because of its loud strangling sound (this, of course, is reported by family members).

If you suspect you have apnea, visit a sleep clinic, advises Rawlings. Here are some high-tech remedies a doctor might suggest for treatment of apnea or snoring:

Mask. CPAP ("continuous positive airway pressure") solves the problem of airway blockage by feeding the sleeper a stream of pressurized air through a nose mask, from a bedside tank. "These devices are still kind of cumbersome, but I have no doubt they'll get it down to a neat little space-age package in the next few years," Dr. deBerry says. According to one University of Florida study, CPAP reduced the average number of snores per night from 1,000 to 23.

A special mask reduced snores to 23.

Tongue Retaining Device (TRD). Similar to an athletic mouthguard, it forces you to breathe through your nose. In nonobese patients whose nasal passages are clear (sometimes this requires surgical repair of a deviated septum or other blockage), the TRD is effective in 89 percent of the cases, says Charles F. Samelson, M.D., of Rush-Presbyterian-St. Luke's Medical Center, in Chicago. The TRD is available only through sleep centers.

Surgery. UPPP (uvulopalatopharyngoplasty) is the surgical treatment of choice for apnea, says Dr. Rawlings. Described as a "facelift for the throat," it calls for the surgical removal of the extra tissue that is blocking the airway. UPPP was first meant for the

Throat surgery is used in cases of severe snoring and apnea.

treatment of sleep apnea, but turned out to be a remarkably effective treatment for plain old snoring.

Self-Care Remedies

More than 300 "snoring cures" are registered in the U.S. Patent and Trademark Office. One is a music box, meant to be clamped onto the pajamas, that coos "roll over, darling" when you lie on your back. Fortunately, there are some simpler approaches that doctors have found may be effective in some cases:

Lose Weight. If you're overweight, shedding some pounds may be enough to solve the problem. For the average snorer, who is only slightly overweight, losing as little as 10 percent of body weight can make a dramatic difference, says Philip Smith, M.D., of the sleep disorders center of the Johns Hopkins University Medical School, in Baltimore.

Avoid Depressants. Avoid central nervous system depressants such as tranquilizers, antihistamines, sleeping pills and alcohol within two hours of retiring. In one study, men who had one milliliter of 100-proof vodka per pound of body weight (for a 200-pound man, that's about two drinks) before going to bed had five times as many apneic episodes as they did when they retired sober, says A. Jay Block, M.D., of the University of Florida College of Medicine, in Gainesville.

Prop Up the Head of Your Bed. Put a brick or two under the forward bedposts, Dr. Fairbanks suggests. This elevates the head and helps keep the airway open. Don't use extra pillows—they'll only kink the airway.

Wear a Cervical Collar. It's a device that's usually prescribed for people with sprained necks. Most snoring occurs when the sleeper lies on his or her back with the chin resting on the chest. That position narrows the windpipe. The collar keeps the chin up and the windpipe open.

Wear a "Snore Ball." Since sleeping on your back increases the likelihood that you'll snore, one old-fashioned remedy is to sew a marble into a pocket on the back of your pajama top to encourage sleeping on your side or stomach. Or make a bigger pocket and put in a tennis ball.

Don't Take Poor Sleeping Habits Lying Down

You can stop losing sleep over your sleeping problems. Persistent sleep disorders that had been accepted as normal consequences of aging are now being researched and diagnosed in the many sleep clinics throughout the nation.

Insomnia is a problem you can lick.

People should no longer accept the "common view of the average older person as someone who sits in front of a television set, on a park bench or at a church gathering, and falls asleep," says Dr. Carskadon. "Daytime sleepiness in older persons may be caused by too little sleep at night due to circadian rhythm disturbance, adverse effects of medication or reduction of activity. Physiological sleep tendency may not necessarily be greater in the elderly than in younger adults."

29

Taste and Smell:

Sharpening

the Senses

I t's a smelly world. Gift stores sell piña-colada scented watches and plastic shoes with a fruity bouquet. One can hardly read a magazine without being assaulted by the powerful scent of an advertisement for cologne.

But these aromas mean little to a large part of the older population—those with a diminished ability to detect odors. A study of nearly two thousand people ranging in age from 5 to 99 years old was done to see how well they could identify various smells. More than 80 percent of those over 80 had major impairment in their ability to smell, with nearly 50 percent having no sense of smell at all, reports Richard L. Doty, Ph.D., director of the Smell and Taste Center at the University of Pennsylvania School of Medicine, in Philadelphia. And the problem affects younger people as well. The same study revealed that those between 65 and 80 also showed a major loss of sense of smell, with nearly one-fourth having no sense of smell.

Losing the ability to smell is more than four times as common as losing the ability to taste, according to Robert I. Henkin, M.D., director of the Center for Molecular Nutrition and Sensory Disorders at Georgetown University Medical Center, in Washington, D.C. But since the smell of a food constitutes a large part of its flavor, the end result is the same: A slice of hot apple pie isn't as delicious as it used to be.

The research on this topic is still in the early stages, so the condition can't always be remedied, according to Dr. Doty. But there are some things you can do, and here they are:

See a Doctor

"Diminished taste or smell is not itself a disease," says Dr. Henkin. "It's a set of symptoms that occurs in a wide range of diseases."

Diminished taste or smell may signal the presence of a disease.

The illness may not be serious. "The most common cause of smell loss is upper respiratory viral infections," says Dr. Doty. "The virus can cause permanent damage to the cells of the olfactory region in the top of the nose."

"If you have a significant loss of taste or smell, you should see a doctor to rule out the possibility of a serious disease, especially if the symptom is sudden," suggests Dr. Henkin.

If your smell and taste have just about vanished, and the condition continues nonstop for at least two weeks—and your doctors just shrug their shoulders—think seriously about an appointment with a smell and taste research center. That's the advice of James B. Snow, Jr., M.D., chairman of the otorhinolaryngology and human communications department at the University of Pennsylvania. Such centers are located mainly in the East: the Hospital of the University of Pennsylvania, in Philadelphia; the S.U.N.Y. Health Science Center, in Syracuse, New York; the University of Connecticut Health Center at Farmington; the University of Colorado Health Sciences Center, in Denver; and Georgetown University Medical Center, in Washington, D.C.

A handful of clinics specialize in helping those with failing senses of taste and smell.

"We might not be able to reverse the condition," says Maxwell Mozell, Ph.D., project director of the S.U.N.Y. Upstate Clinical Olfactory Research Center. "But a large percentage of people lose smell because of an obstruction, such as nasal polyps (soft growths in the nasal cavity). These can be removed surgically by an otolaryngologist. However, this surgery is best done through a smell and taste clinic where the sensory loss and reversal probably will be more systematically investigated."

The Zinc Factor

New Jersey smells bad to some people, but not as bad as it did to Rudy Coniglio, a pizza maker from Closter, New Jersey.

"Did you ever when you're a kid burn a plastic comb?" he told the *New Yorker* magazine. "Everything smelled like that." Most food tasted like decaying garbage. He had to take refuge in the woods to escape the rancid odors that he alone could smell.

Doctors and psychiatrists alike were baffled by his disease—except for Dr. Henkin, who was chief of neuroendocrinology at the National Institutes of Health, in Bethesda, Maryland, at that time. He cured Coniglio by prescribing zinc sulphate. This success with one of the earliest cases convinced Dr. Henkin of the importance of zinc in taste and smell.

He found that when laboratory animals (or people) did not get sufficient zinc in their diets, the very first sign of deficiency was loss of appetite. "Further zinc loss results in loss of taste and smell acuity, and onset of unpleasant taste and smell sensations," he says.

Zinc deficiency can lead to defects in taste and smell.

Important as it is, zinc is no panacea for those who have lost their sense of taste. "People who are zinc deficient almost uniformly have taste problems, but there are a lot of people who have taste loss who don't have any problem with zinc. About one-fourth of my patients respond to zinc."

He believes that the lack of zinc changes the chemistry of the saliva proteins that control taste buds—less zinc means less taste sensitivity. And he says there are probably other zinc sensitive proteins in the nasal mucus that control smell receptors.

Good sources of zinc include nuts, meat, eggs, grain and seafood. If you feel you need supplemental zinc, take note: Dr. Henkin feels that you shouldn't take more than 15 milligrams a day without medical supervision.

Other research suggests that zinc may not be the only nutrient necessary for keen senses. Dr. Henkin has found that copper and vitamins A, B_6 and

B_{12} can also influence taste. Susan S. Schiffman, Ph.D., from the department of psychiatry at Duke Medical Center, in Durham, North Carolina, who researches the loss of taste and smell in the elderly, says that since taste buds and olfactory receptors undergo continuous renewal, nutritional states can affect these areas.

Mouth Care

Since the tongue and mouth are inseparable, the condition of the mouth is bound to affect taste. "Reduction in flow of saliva can lead to diminishing of taste, since food has to be in solution for you to taste it," says Vernon J. Brightman, D.M.D., Ph.D., professor of oral medicine at the University of Pennsylvania School of Dental Medicine. "Medication such as antidepressants, antihistamines and antispasmotics can cause dry mouth. The medications may be necessary, but try to avoid them if possible. You can help keep the mouth moist and stimulate saliva by chewing gum or drinking water or tea with lemon."

A dry mouth has trouble tasting.

"Some types of bad taste in the mouth can be corrected by better oral hygiene," says Linda Bartoshuk, Ph.D., co-principle investigator of the Connecticut Chemosensory Clinical Research Center at Farmington, and professor of epidemiology and public health at the Yale University School of Medicine, in New Haven, Connecticut. (See chapter 22 for more information about mouth care.)

Risk Factors

There's no sure-fire way to preserve your sense of smell. But certain things may increase your risk of losing it.

Smoking. One study suggests that smoking may diminish the taste sensation of sweetness. The researcher at Cornell Medical College, in Ithaca, New York, who conducted the study theorizes that the nicotine in cigarettes raises blood sugar, reducing sensitivity to sweet tastes.

Pollution. Breathing can be hazardous to the nose—in certain environments. Exposure to pollution can damage the nose's lining, according to Dr.

Doty. So can working with certain chemicals. "Formaldehyde may cause smell disorders," says Dr. Mozell. "I know some morticians who can't smell a thing anymore." Workers in a chemical and plastic company brought a multi-million dollar lawsuit against their employers because they said they lost their senses of taste and smell as a result of exposure to chlorine and related chemicals.

Even chemicals meant for the nose can be harmful if overused. "There is some suggestion in the medical literature that overuse of nose spray can, in some cases, permanently injure smell receptors," says Dr. Doty.

Flavor Enhancers

People who have lost their ability to taste respond to food in a variety of ways. For some, loss of taste and smell is a ticket to obesity. Dr. Schiffman points out that some people try to make up for lost sensory stimulation by eating more. Others may pour on the salt and sugar. And still others may stop eating, resulting in weight loss and malnutrition, Dr. Schiffman found.

Even if nutrition is good, emotions may suffer. "The loss of pleasure in eating can be distressing," says Dr. Bartoshuk. "If a person's life is centered around food, depression may result."

In addition to sharpening your senses, you also can make your food taste better. Dr. Schiffman encourages people with diminished acuity of taste and smell to chew food thoroughly. "Chewing breaks down the food, allowing more molecules to interact with taste and smell receptors," she explains.

Another trick she recommends is to alternate among foods as you eat. "If one eats only potatoes, the first bite may taste strong, but successive bites become less intense until one can barely taste them," she says. "Alternating from potatoes to meat to vegetables minimizes adaptation and maximizes the amount of taste and odor in a meal. In addition, textural variety can partially compensate for losses in taste and smell acuity."

"One of the most important things is to enhance the beauty of food, so it will compensate for lost

Eating a variety of foods with a variety of textures enhances flavor.

pleasure," says Randy Lee Breslin, R.N., director of
dietetics at the Connecticut Hospice, in Branford,
and author of *Food Services and Hospice*, a video
shown in hospitals, nursing homes and colleges. (A
hospice is a live-in facility for the terminally ill.)
"Many of our cancer patients can't taste anything,
but they say that if the food looks good, they can
remember how it tastes. I try to create an attractive
atmosphere, with nice settings, too.

Prepare food to look beautiful.

"Some people need a pureed diet because of
dental problems, digestability or difficulty in chewing," she continues. "Nursing homes might use baby
food, but that doesn't taste too good, and it's mentally degrading. But you can make such food cre-
atively. Mousses, souffles, creams and pâtés are all
elegant ways to serve soft food."

Adding extra flavor can also help. Schiffman
suggests experimenting with seasonings such as
minced onion, paprika, oregano, ginger, allspice,
cinnamon, vinegar, lemon and dill weed. "Try to use
fresh herbs—they have more flavor than dried
spices," recommends Breslin.

**Experiment with inten-
sifying of spices and
flavors.**

Another way to strengthen the taste of food is
with simulated odors, says Schiffman. Formulated
flavor drops of butter, beef, green bean and other
foods make food easier to taste and smell for older
people though they're unpleasantly strong for people with normal senses.

Future Directions

That's about all modern science can offer you,
nose and tongue-wise. *So far.* Research continues to
suggest new possibilities.

"The most exciting finding in current research is
that an olfactory nerve fiber can die out and grow
back in 30 to 40 days," says Dr. Mozell. "Other nerve
fibers generally don't regenerate that fast—it can
take years. And it is currently believed that in adults
central nerves *never* regenerate. Studying the olfactory nerve might give us a clue about how to regenerate other nerves. And we may also find out how to
preserve the sense of smell if we learn more about
the nature of this regeneration."

**An olfactory nerve fi-
ber can grow back
quickly, researchers
found.**

30

Varicose Veins:

Prevention

and Care

Many people might think of varicose veins as simply a cosmetic problem, particularly troubling in the summer months when the legs are more exposed in shorts, swimwear and dresses. For some that's the case. For others, however, varicose veins cause fatigue, dull aches in the legs, swelling and sleep-inhibiting cramps. And in a small percentage of cases, complications set in that could be life-threatening, like phlebitis, the development of clots in deeper veins and ulceration.

"People who think of varicose veins as only a nuisance are severely underestimating the disease," says Howard Baron, M.D., attending vascular surgeon at Cabrini Medical Center, in New York City.

A varicose vein is a healthy vein gone awry. It didn't start as a varicose vein. It became one. Here's how.

The veins transport blood from the legs back to the heart and lungs, where the blood is cleansed of its impurities (carbon dioxide mostly) and refueled with oxygen for another trip through the body.

The blood has a more difficult journey from the lower extremities because it's fighting gravity. Fortunately, the leg muscles act like a second heart. As the muscles contract, blood is pumped through the veins. The veins in turn are equipped with valves that

The veins are equipped, like a canal, with "locks."

act like locks on a canal. The valves allow the blood to flow upward, then snap shut to prevent backward seepage. When the valves are too weak to prevent this gravitational backward flow, blood begins to collect in the vein, stretching the vein wall out of shape and producing pain and the often unsightly varicosity.

Almost all varicosities occur in the veins near the surface of the leg. Deeper veins are rarely affected because they have sufficient support from muscle and fat.

"We inherit a defect in the venous valve or we inherit a vein with a weak or absent wall," Dr. Baron says. "Then there must be an aggravating factor in our life-style for the problem to develop. If we avoid aggravating factors, the problem might be delayed or blunted, and it might not develop at all."

Varicose veins are somewhat hereditary. But you *can* prevent them.

Five Ways to Prevent Varicose Veins

The aggravating factors in varicose veins are severe obesity, constipation, standing for prolonged periods, sitting for prolonged periods with your legs crossed and lack of exercise. A common thread runs through all of these factors: They all place added pressure on the surface veins of the legs, increasing the likelihood that varicosities will develop and progress.

Overweight and constipation are just two factors that aggravate varicose veins.

Both constipation and straining at stool increase intra-abdominal pressure, which is transferred to the veins of the legs. Think of the body as a totem pole with the veins of the lower legs and ankles being the ultimate recipient of pressure from above. To avoid constipation, eat more high-fiber foods such as vegetables, fruits and whole grains. And don't strain at stool.

Exercise, too, can head off varicose veins. The flip side, of course, is that lack of exercise exacerbates the problem. "We're a sitting society," Dr. Baron says. "My advice is to walk, run, jog, anything to keep the leg muscles working. Don't sit still. Don't stand still."

Walking and other forms of exercise help varicose veins; prolonged sitting makes them worse.

Prolonged standing in one place and sitting (particularly with the legs crossed, since that further impedes circulation) allows blood to pool in the lower extremities. That puts added pressure on a weak valve and can further dilate a vein with a weak wall. Either will hasten the onset of varicose veins. Exercise keeps the body's "second heart," the muscles of the lower legs, contracting and the valves clicking.

The best exercise regimen is to do some activity more often, rather than a lot at one shot. This presents no problem for people who are sedentary at work or who are temporarily captive in a place, such as a theater. Those people can simply press the balls of their feet to the floor to make the calf muscles contract and transport blood. Nothing more elaborate is necessary.

If you have a job that requires that you be on your feet—bartender, beautician, retail clerk—take an elevation break. That is, prop your legs up above your heart several times during the day to allow gravity to speed the blood to the heart.

If your boss won't agree to the break, support hosiery could be the answer. "Support hosiery is very helpful," says Victor Pellicano, M.D., an internist in Lewiston, New York. "Not only does it give comfort to those who already have varicose veins, it could delay the onset of the problem for many years."

Support stockings can delay varicose veins for many years.

Support hosiery exerts graduated pressure on the leg and facilitates blood flow, thus reducing pressure in the veins. Mass-produced stockings will be fine for most people, but research has shown that for those with great calf-ankle disproportion, hosiery will have to be custom-made to be helpful. For those people the larger calf means that the hose will have a tourniquet effect and the graduated pressure will be lost.

A few more preventive tips:

• Stop reading on the toilet. The shape of the hard wood or plastic seat puts undue pressure on the abdominal veins, which, in turn, put pressure on the leg veins.
• Don't wear any tight garment. Particularly harmful are calf-length boots, pantyhose too snug at the groin, girdles, corsets and binding belts. All of those tend to constrict venous blood flow.
• Be sure your diet contains oranges, tangerines or other citrus fruits. They are a good source of

bioflavonoids, which may delay the onset of varicose veins. Bioflavonoids may do that, according to Dr. Pellicano, by strengthening the vein wall, preventing dilation and allowing the valves to work more easily.

The beauty of those doctors' recommendations is that they might stop varicose veins from appearing entirely, or, if they have appeared already, might make discomfort less acute.

Covering Up

If appearance is your main concern, you can try a cover cream. Vanish (available only through mail-order), Covermark, Dermablend (both available in stores) and other non-water-soluble makeups cover distended veins as well as threadlike "spider" veins (enlarged capillaries that sometimes appear on the face or legs).

Cover creams camouflage unsightly veins—even when you swim.

"Many of these products are formulated so that they don't run, even if you spend all day in the pool," says Louis Navarro, M.D., a general surgeon specializing in varicose veins at the Vein Treatment Center, in New York City. "My patients use cover creams either in place of treatment, if their veins aren't too bad, or to tide them over until they have their veins treated permanently."

To camouflage unsightly veins, match the cover makeup as closely as possible to your skin tone. To apply, warm a small dab on the back of your hand so that the makeup is easier to spread, then put a thin layer on the veins and surrounding skin. Feather the edges, to avoid an abrupt line of demarcation. If you don't have time to apply cover cream in the morning before you go out for the day, smooth it on the night before and sleep in pantyhose to prevent it from rubbing off on the bedsheets.

Reverse the Trend

If your condition has deteriorated to the point where the varicose veins are large and the pain is becoming harder and harder to bear, you might want to consider getting them removed.

Three effective treatments are available.

"If you have varicose veins and they're not treated, you're ten times more likely to get phlebitis, clots and ulceration," says Robert Nabatoff, M.D., clinical professor of vascular surgery at Mt. Sinai School of Medicine, in New York City. "The veins that stick out are susceptible to trauma, irritation and bleeding at the ankle. Almost all ulceration occurs at the ankles."

If your veins are bad news, you have three options for treatment:

Surgical Removal. This procedure is commonly called "ligation and stripping." It eliminates the varicosities by tying off and removing the main vein to which they're connected. Years ago, people undergoing stripping were left with dozens of unsightly scars all over their legs. Today, a skillful surgeon can strip the vein by making a single one-inch cut above the groin and another half-inch incision on the foot, so no trace of surgery remains. Some small spider or varicose veins can recur.

Customarily, vein stripping involves an overnight stay in the hospital and several days' rest afterwards. But Dr. Navarro says it's now possible to undergo the procedure on a walk-in surgery basis. "Many people have their veins stripped in the morning and are home walking around the same day—or back at work the next day," says Dr. Navarro.

New "stripping" techniques leave virtually no scars.

The drawbacks to stripping?

"Any time you undergo anesthesia, there's a greater risk, and sometimes there's bleeding that can't be controlled without going back in to tie it off," says James DeWeese, M.D., cardiovascular surgeon at the University of Rochester Medical Center, in New York.

"The operation is a simple one for any competent vascular surgeon," Dr. Baron says. "And there's a 96 percent cure rate. That means that three years after the operation there is no reappearance of the varicosity in 96 percent of the cases."

Injection Therapy. Done as an office procedure, a chemical solution is injected into the affected vein, causing it to harden and wither away over a period of several months. This procedure works best on smaller varicose veins. "Large varicose veins with high backward pressure don't respond to injection therapy," Dr. Nabatoff says. "If you inject that type, they just recur. The heavy ones you have to tie and strip." With both procedures the patient should be seen again on a yearly basis.

Occasionally, injection therapy leaves pigment changes at the injection site. But overall, the procedure has improved greatly in recent years, according to Dr. Navarro. Doctors use smaller needles and milder solutions, tailored to the individual patient. Much, too, depends on the skill of the doctor doing the procedure, says Dr. Navarro. "The more experienced the doctor is, the more procedures of this type he or she has done, the better the results are apt to be," he says.

Dr. Baron, however, feels that injection therapy can be dangerous. "What you're doing is forming a chemical phlebitis, and if you're unlucky the clot could extend and make its way into a large vein," he says.

Argon Laser Treatment. This is a relatively new therapy, developed within the past couple of years or so.

"A powerful beam of high energy light is directed into the veins and absorbed by the red pigment cells of the blood," explains Dr. Navarro. "As the blood cells overheat, the vessel walls are damaged, causing the vein to disappear in a few weeks or months.

"Argon laser therapy is used for superficial varicose veins (of half a millimeter or less in diameter), for spider veins on the face, nose, cheeks and around the eyes. It can be used in conjunction with surgery or injection therapy."

Argon laser therapy zaps spider veins.

Part
Two
Looking
Better

31

What's Age Got to Do with It?

N ow in her late forties, Tina Turner has the legs of a showgirl, the face of a Nubian cherub and the energy of a high school cheerleader. Middle age finds some people in a rocking chair—and others into rock 'n' roll. Tina is a stellar example of a new breed of adults who look, feel and act younger than did their parents and grandparents at the same age. Cosmetic science is part of the secret.

Hair coloring and styling methods, protective skin care products and makeup, a wide choice of figure-flattering clothing styles, restorative dentistry—such products and services can mold people into younger versions of themselves. At the same time, cosmetics can prevent some of the deterioration associated with age. Moisturizers, for example, prevent dryness, while sunscreens help stop the sun damage that is largely responsible for wrinkles and age spots. People who use moisturizers and sunscreens can have genuinely younger-looking skin. By the same token, lipsticks and lip glosses keep the lips smooth, moist and younger looking.

But the youthifying effect of cosmetics and other grooming aids runs more than skin deep. One study shows that older women who were given a "makeover" and then continued to use the new cosmetic techniques on their own felt healthier, more

Cosmetics can prevent some of the outward deterioration associated with age.

Good grooming can promote satisfaction and health.

383

sociable and had a more positive outlook on life. (More about this in a moment.)

"Aging is inevitably associated with deterioration in attractiveness," say psychologist Jean Ann Graham, Ph.D., and Albert M. Kligman, M.D., Ph.D., a professor of dermatology from the University of Pennsylvania, in Philadelphia. But, they add, this association is probably wrong.

If people *assume* that nothing can be done about wrinkles, saggy jowls, missing teeth, thinning hair, thickening physique and sagging energy levels, nothing *will* be done about them. That's no less unfortunate than the assumption that loss of memory, creaky joints and heart disease are inevitable facets of aging.

"I'm a strong believer in the reversal of the appearance of aging," says Robert Kotler, M.D., a cosmetic surgeon practicing in Los Angeles and a clinical instructor of surgery at the University of California at Los Angeles. "We *can* control our own fate—and our own face."

Cosmetics and Your Inner Beauty

Nothing illustrates the power of good grooming to regenerate the appearance more than the popular "magazine makeover." In the "before" pictures, the subjects usually look lackluster and unapproachable. In the "after" pictures, the same people look fresh, vivacious and outgoing—thanks to the wizardry of makeup and hairstyling. Drs. Graham and Kligman wondered, do older women feel better about themselves after a cosmetic makeover? And how does a makeover affect those women who are considered unattractive?

To find out, they chose 32 women, age 59 and older—some considered highly attractive, others considered less so. Both groups were treated to a professional makeover—skin treatment with cleansers, toners, moisturizers; makeup with foundation, blusher, powder, eyebrow pencil, eye shadow and liner, mascara and lipstick. As expected, the women felt they looked better after the makeover.

But they also felt better *inside*. A questionnaire completed by each of the women before and after

Women who wore makeup looked better and *felt* more optimistic and outgoing.

the makeover revealed that the cosmetic treatment left them feeling more confident about their appearance, eager to go out and mingle with others and more optimistic in general. They even felt they looked *healthier.* And the women considered the least attractive felt they benefited the most.

A Longer, More Fulfilling Life

Looking younger than your age may bring more than health and happiness—it may actually add years to your life. So suggests a unique study sponsored by the Gerontology Research Center, in Baltimore, Maryland. Doctors were asked to guess the ages of 1,086 men ranging from 17 to 102 years old, based on outward appearance. Biological age was assessed by 24 medical tests such as vision, hearing, blood pressure and lung function. The men who looked older than others of the same chronological age were biologically older in 19 out of the 24 tests. And the more youthful-looking men lived longer than the men who looked old before their time.

People who looked young for their age *were* biologically younger.

You're never too old to reap the physical and psychic benefits of good grooming, according to Drs. Graham and Kligman.

"The improvement in self-esteem applies regardless of a person's age," Dr. Graham says. "And many resources are available to project an up-to-date image."

Dr. Kotler adds that people are aware of prejudice against older people in the workplace and are reluctant to be considered part of that group. So they use those resources—cosmetics and so forth—to remain youthful looking in order to get a job, promotion and so on. As a result, older people are more youthful, active and socially engaged, and more concerned with self-fulfillment than ever.

Self-fulfillment. Being the best you can be. A touch of vanity and a healthy dose of self-esteem go a long way toward leading a more satisfying life. Just ask Tina.

32

Cosmetic

Surgery and

Its Alternatives

"My oldest facelift patient was a 79-year-old woman who wanted to look good for her wedding," says Joseph Feinberg, M.D., assistant professor of plastic surgery at New York Hospital-Cornell Medical Center, in New York City, and plastic surgeon practicing in Manhattan. Surprisingly, the woman he's talking about isn't all that exceptional. Each year, hundreds of thousands of men and women put guilt and self-consciousness aside and knock on the doors of surgeons' offices in hopes of finding a way to lift sags and bags and erase wrinkles. They refuse to accept the "inevitable" signs of aging, and instead use vacation days and credit cards to do something about them.

Is such surgery a waste of time and money, or is it an investment in yourself? Done for the right reasons, it's an investment—and one that pays off. A "new" face can help you successfully compete against younger (or younger-*looking*) people in the job market. Others—like the December bride-to-be—gain by enhancing their appeal to members of the opposite sex. Most people benefit by simply matching their physical appearance to the mental image they carry of themselves.

Time favors such an investment. Because of a number of factors, from preventive immunization

It's an investment in yourself.

against disease to lifesaving procedures such as coronary bypass surgery, people now can expect to live longer than ever before. Yet, though the body may still be strong and full of zest, the facade changes. Taut, firm skin grows one size too large. Worry lines furrow the brow. Sitting in front of the mirror pressing back the jowls of time, many people who still feel 35 are surprised to find themselves looking tired and old.

"How frequently we hear facelift patients (prior to surgery) say, 'I look in the mirror and what I see isn't me,'" say John M. Goin, M.D., a plastic surgeon, and Marcia Kraft Goin, M.D., a psychiatrist, both at the University of Southern California School of Medicine, in Los Angeles. "They say, 'I feel young inside. I just want to look as young as I feel.'"

Other doctors echo those sentiments.

"The best reason for choosing plastic surgery is to make your mirror image match your self-image," says Mark Gorney, M.D., of San Francisco. The best candidates are not necessarily people who want to look like teenagers again, but men and women who want to look better—less tired, more refreshed.

Cosmetic surgery (one aspect of plastic surgery) has an emotional component absent in, say, gallbladder surgery. Let's face it: Your face is, in many ways, your *identity*. When your features are altered, so is your self-image.

Plastic surgery has a strong emotional component because it affects your self-image.

And who wants to end up with a self they didn't bargain for? That's why it's important to know *all* the facts about cosmetic surgery—because the more you know about what to expect from a procedure, the happier you'll be with the results. Which, if any, procedure might be best for you? How much younger can you expect to look afterwards? How can you find a doctor you trust? What are the possible risks and complications? Most of all, will it be worth the discomfort, cost and inconvenience?

What Are Your Options?

Many people are surprised to learn there's more to cosmetic surgery than facelifts.

"A youthful appearance depends on more than just taut skin," says Richard B. Stark, M.D., clinical

Just lifting up the tip of the nose can make you look younger.

professor of surgery at Columbia University and founder of the plastic surgery service at St. Luke's-Roosevelt Hospital Center, both in New York City. "For example, the tip of the nose often droops with age. Tipping up the nose surgically often restores a youthful appearance."

If bags under your eyes are what haunt you when you gaze in the mirror, you may not need a facelift (rhytidectomy) at all—an eyelid lift (or blepharoplasty) might do just fine. Dermabrasion and chemical peeling (chemabrasion) may remove fine wrinkles (like crow's-feet around the eyes or whistle lines around the mouth) better than a facelift, which is great for jowls and other major folds but doesn't do much to erase smaller irregularities.

Together, you and your surgeon can decide which, if any, of the following procedures—or what combination of procedures—can best suit your needs. (The accompanying chart, Cosmetic Surgery and Other Aesthetic Procedures, provides further details.)

What Surgery Has to Offer

As the years pass, your skin stretches due to a loss of elasticity, growing a size or so too big for your body. The result? Bags, sags and creases. A skilled surgeon can tighten and tuck your skin to eliminate (or greatly diminish) those reminders of age.

Facelift (Rhytidectomy). Years ago, cosmetic surgery left the face as expressionless as a porcelain mask. But surgeons have perfected the craft of facelifting, so you'll end up with a relaxed, natural-looking face, as expressive as ever.

Exactly how the surgeon executes a facelift will depend on the unique features of your face and the individual surgeon's methods. Basically, though, he or she makes an incision inside the hairline of the scalp at the temples, and continues downward, following the natural line around the earlobe and extending into the back of the scalp or the nape of the neck. The surgeon then separates the skin from underlying fat and muscles, much as you might remove skin from a chicken breast, and pulls the skin up and backward, trimming away the excess.

Several new techniques that alter the layers of tissue under the skin improve the facelift and help it to last longer, according to Gerald Imber, M.D., director of plastic surgery at the Institute for the Control of Facial Aging, in New York City. "Most important is the use of suction to remove fatty deposits in the jowls and under the skin that some people develop in middle age," says Dr. Imber. "It's a wonderful advance because, as those who have these deposits will tell you, no amount of dieting is going to remove them. Done in conjunction with a facelift, fat suction makes the skin fit more gracefully and gives the face a leaner look."

Improperly done, though, fat suction can produce a lumpy look, as will be discussed later.

How much younger will you look after a facelift? Five years younger? Ten years? That depends on several factors—your bone structure, your age and how much you coddled your skin through the years. If you've been a sunworshipper, your surgeon may not be able to achieve as good a result with you as with someone who has protected his or her skin from the aging effects of sunlight.

"We're born with only so many fibrils of elastin in our skin," explains Dr. Stark. "Elastin is the springy material that helps skin to look smooth and tight. The sun breaks down elastin—and it never regenerates. When elastin is gone, it's gone, leaving the skin loose and lined like leather."

Tobacco smoke seems to reduce the skin's elasticity in much the same way sun exposure does, according to Dr. Feinberg. "If skin is less elastic, it's harder to do plastic surgery. Skin that's lost its elasticity to the sun and tobacco smoke is like a linen sheet—you have to pull it board tight to get out all the wrinkles." So if you smoke, try to quit.

In other words, the better the condition of your skin before the operation, the better it will look afterwards.

But there are factors you don't have any control over—your genes rather than your life-style—that also influence the outcome of a facelift. "Fair-skinned people are better candidates for facelifts than dark-skinned people," says Dr. Feinberg. "They heal with less redness in the scar, and their skin is

New techniques help facelifts last longer.

The sun breaks down the "elastic" in your skin. Those fibers never regenerate.

easier to stretch tightly, since dark-skinned individuals generally have thicker skin."

How long does a facelift last? That depends on what you do to prevent further aging of the skin. Aside from protecting against overexposure to the sun, using a moisturizer can help, says Dr. Stark.

Using a moisturizer can help.

"After age 40, the sebaceous glands slow production of sebum and oil that lubricate the skin. Lost sebum needs to be supplemented by a moisturizing lotion.

"Drinking too much alcohol, as a rule, is also deleterious to a facelift," adds Dr. Stark. "And squinting can cause crow's-feet and those vertical furrows about the nose."

Maintaining your weight also helps prolong the life of your facelift, because fluctuations produce sags and jowls.

If despite great care your face falls again (eventually, it will) you can have another facelift—and another and another, until you run out of time, money or motivation.

Eyelid Lift (Blepharoplasty). Baggy eyelids are as much a factor of heredity as age. If your mother had them, you could develop them in your teens. Because pouches and droopy lids make people look old and tired even if they feel young and energetic, many people feel they're better off without these misleading bags.

For some, an eyelid lift may do more to restore a youthful appearance than more extensive surgery.

An eyelid lift can make older workers employable longer, says a surgeon.

"Eyelid surgery is popular among older people who have to compete in the job market," says Dr. Stark. "The eyelid lift makes people employable for a longer period of time. I probably do more eyelid lifts than any other rejuvenative procedure."

The surgeon works first on the upper lid, then the lower. Incisions in the upper and lower eyelids follow the natural lines and creases generally extending into the fine wrinkles, or crow's-feet, at the eyes' outer edges. Working through these incisions, the surgeon separates the skin from muscles and fatty tissue underneath and removes excess fat deposits and skin folds.

Nose Repair (Rhinoplasty). In addition to lifting the nose upward, surgeons also can whittle down your nose if it's too big, or chip away an unsightly bump you've lived with grudgingly for years.

The surgeon makes an incision inside the nostrils, giving him access to cartilage and bone, which he or she can cut, trim and manipulate according to plan. "The operation is not like carving a new nose from a block of soap," say John and Marcia Goin in a book they coauthored. "Much depends on the healing of your tissues and no surgeon can make a nose precisely to your order."

Very often, only minor alterations are needed to improve appearance greatly.

"It is common after some types of rhinoplasty for relatives or friends to remark, 'I don't see any big difference,' says a patient information booklet published by the American Society of Plastic and Reconstructive Surgeons, Inc. "Don't consider such a reaction an indication of failure. On the contrary, if your nose looks *better* and *natural*, it may go unnoticed. The idea after all, is not to create a 'new' nose that draws attention to itself, but rather one that blends subtly into the overall features of the face in the proper proportions."

If your new nose looks natural, people may not notice the change.

Breast Lift (Mastopexy). After pregnancy, breastfeeding or considerable weight loss, a woman's breasts may sag. If you wish, surgery can restore both lift and volume to breasts that have lost their youthful tilt and curves.

Three reasons to have a breast lift.

In this operation, explains Dr. Feinberg, the surgeon removes stretched skin and forms a new "skin brassiere" to lift breast tissue. The nipple and the areola around it are also moved upward to match the new positioning.

If you want your breasts plumped up to their youthful volume, a surgeon can give you a breast implant, a flexible envelope containing silicone gel, saline solution or a combination of both. In fact, about 100,000 women have their breasts enlarged this way every year.

The Food and Drug Administration (FDA), however, has serious misgivings about the safety of breast implants, says Paul Tilton, of the FDA Division of Surgical and Rehabilitation Devices. Possible risks include hardening of the tissue around the implants, which may be uncomfortable, painful and, ironically, disfiguring. The gel-filled implants have semipermeable membranes that can slowly leak silicone into the surrounding tissues which, according to evidence from animal studies, may migrate to your liver, kidneys and other vital organs. And saline-filled implants have a potential problem of their own: spontaneous deflation. As a result, the FDA has not approved of breast implants.

That hasn't stopped doctors from using them, however. For one thing, the implants were developed before 1976, when the FDA first began to regulate medical devices, so the government can't legally remove them from the market. For another, many doctors don't share the government's low opinion of implants.

Dr. Feinberg, for example, admits that the success rate of the surgery isn't 100 percent, and that there are occasional problems with the implants, but he also says that they have proved themselves safe: "They have been used in this country since 1961, and they have not been linked to breast cancer or any other physical disorder."

Provided an older woman is in good health, there's no reason why she shouldn't have such surgery, according to another surgeon, Richard B. Bloomenstein, M.D., coauthor of *One Day Plastic Surgery: A Consumer's Guide to Savings and Safety* (Todd & Honeywell). "The surgeon also sees women in their mid- to late-fifties who say they've always wanted to have breast enlargement surgery but have never had the time before," says Dr. Bloomenstein. "Now that their children are grown, and perhaps they've recently been widowed or divorced, they decide it's time to 'do something for myself.'"

Suction Lipectomy. At first, this procedure sounds like the perennial dieter's dream come true—fat disappearing into thin air. And indeed it does. The surgeon makes a half-inch incision in the skin, inserts a foot-long metal tube (called a cannula) the thickness of a pencil and sucks up fat from your thighs, hips and waist. Goodbye saddle bags, love handles and other fatty deposits that cling tenaciously to your figure, no matter how hard you diet or exercise. (And the older you are, the harder it seems to get rid

Suction lipectomy vacuums up love handles, saddle bags and other stubborn fat deposits.

of these stubborn bumps and bulges.)

Unfortunately, suction lipectomy by its very nature is safest and most effective for those who need it the least: people under 35 who are not overweight.

"The candidate must have excellent skin tone," says Joseph Agris, M.D., a Houston plastic surgeon. "When the fat is suctioned away, the skin has to shrink to the body's new contours." Without good elasticity, the treated area could resemble a fallen soufflé.

Even if you qualify for suction lipectomy, the operation isn't risk-free. The surgeon who performs it must be very skilled in order to avoid serious problems. "This seemingly simple procedure is not simple at all," says Dr. Agris. "The surgeon has to make sure that he maneuvers the instrument in the proper plane. He must have good eye-finger coordination to avoid severing blood vessels and nerves. And he has to remove just the right amount of fat from all areas to ensure a symmetrical appearance. If he suctions away too much fat at any given spot, he risks creating a hollow that is impossible to fill and may cause an unsightly indentation in the skin."

Sometimes, even with the right patient and the right surgeon things can go wrong. This procedure, like any other surgery, has risks. (See accompanying table.) And while most people who have the operation are generally satisfied with the results and have few complications, some wish they had left well enough alone. Possible unfavorable results include skin dimpling (a "cottage cheese-textured" surface), asymmetrical fat removal, pigmentation problems, scarring, skin peeling away and permanent numbness in the operation area.

> **Suction lipectomy works best for people who need it least—the young and thin.**

> **Some people who have had suction lipectomy wish they'd left well enough alone.**

Regenerating the Skin without Surgery

If minor wrinkles, crinkles and age spots are your problem, you may not need surgery at all, just surface repairs. Or perhaps you've had a facelift, but need an additional surface treatment to put the finishing touches on the job. Here's what surgeons and dermatologists have to offer.

Chemical Peel (Chemabrasion). When you go in for this procedure, invite the fire department along. And before you go in, stock up on sympathy cards—

Chemical peels regenerate your skin, leaving it free of wrinkles and blemishes.

you'll probably want to send them to yourself. "A chemical peel is a deep, controlled second-degree burn," explains Dr. Feinberg. "A thick crust lasts for a week after the procedure, and the purple-red color of the skin may take six months to fade away. It's hell to go through—and that's probably an understatement."

But some people are willing to pay a visit to the devil if they can get beautiful skin in the bargain—and that's what you're left with when the peel heals.

"A chemical peel is the only means of regenerating elastin and collagen (the skin's supportive tissue) lost to age and sun exposure," says Robert Kotler, M.D., a clinical instructor of surgery at the University of California at Los Angeles and private practitioner in Los Angeles. The new skin, he says, is pinker, tighter, smoother and relatively free of wrinkles and blemishes. It may remain young-looking for 15 to 20 years or longer.

But Dr. Kotler's enthusiasm is tempered by some warnings. "A chemical peel is not for everyone," he says. "If you have dark or olive skin you may end up with a blotchy appearance. And be sure to have a thorough physical examination before having a peel. Phenol, the chemical solution that strips away the upper layers of skin, is absorbed into the bloodstream and may be hazardous to someone with poor liver or kidney function, or someone with a heart problem."

Dr. Kotler also recommends finding out if your surgeon has a lot of notches on his belt. "It takes a lot of expertise to do a good chemical peel. A consumer should look for a skilled doctor and ask the right questions. Is this procedure a big part of his or her practice, one of the two or three most frequently performed? How many chemical peels does the doctor do each week? How did the doctor learn the procedure?"

Dermabrasion. Vigorous friction, too, regenerates skin by stripping off its upper layer and promoting growth of new cells from below. (Shaving with a razor does the same thing, to a lesser degree.) Instead of applying a chemical solution to the skin, the doctor buffs it with a high-speed electrical tool (a rotating wire brush or sander). The result resembles

Dermabrasion regenerates skin by sanding off the old to make way for the new.

a very bad sunburn at first, which turns pink and lightens as healing progresses. You may experience itching or tingling as the skin regenerates. Discomfort can be relieved with medication. Your individual skin condition and your doctor's opinion of how to achieve the best results will determine which of the two, chemical peel or dermabrasion, may be best for you. In general, chemical peel is best for fine wrinkles and dermabrasion is best for acne.

Collagen Injections. This is the least painful, least expensive and least radical way to get rid of wrinkles. Tiny drops of thick, milky collagen, purified from cow hides, are injected just underneath the skin to replace lost collagen and plump up wrinkles and scars. The FDA says collagen injections are safe—and the least likely of the wrinkle-removal methods to develop complications. They're particularly good for brow lines, smile lines and the vertical furrows that often appear above the nose. But the results last less than a year.

"I am convinced you can get better, longer-lasting results with a chemical peel," says Dr. Kotler.

Collagen injections plump out browlines, smile lines and worry lines.

Keys to Success

Cosmetic surgery is *real* surgery. While the criteria for success and satisfaction differ from that of, say, a bypass operation, you still want the same level of surgical skill and expertise. To achieve your goal, you must consider your choice of surgeon, your physical condition, your mental attitude and your ability to afford the procedure.

Choosing a Surgeon

A cosmetic surgeon must be three professionals in one: a medical doctor, an artist and a psychologist. How will you find this virtuoso? Not by flipping randomly through the yellow pages. But do make a call—to a friend who's had cosmetic surgery.

"Word of mouth is best," says Dr. Feinberg. "If you have one or more friends who had good results from a doctor, chances are he does a good job."

He also recommends choosing a doctor who is on the staff of a university hospital or a regional (as opposed to a local) hospital. "These types of institu-

Be sure your doctor is certified by the American Board of Plastic Surgery.

tions tend to be more discriminating about who they allow to practice in their hospital."

And be sure the doctor or doctors you are considering are certified by the American Board of Plastic Surgery. Certification indicates that they've graduated from an accredited medical school, served a three-year residency in surgery, plus two additional years in a Plastic Surgery residency and passed rigorous oral and written examinations. Diplomas are usually displayed prominently in a doctor's office. Don't hesitate to ask the surgeon about credentials, though. A reputable doctor will welcome your questions and be pleased that you are concerned enough to ask.

Finally, Dr. Feinberg urges you to take your time—and your doctor's. "Shop around," he says. "And if the doctor you decide on doesn't spend at least 45 minutes talking to you at the initial consultation, or if you don't develop a rapport with him, go somewhere else. This is *very* elective surgery. Ask questions. Know exactly what you're getting into."

Also, be prepared for your doctor to reject *you.* No surgeon can responsibly operate on just anyone who walks through the door. Because certain medical conditions, such as severe diabetes or emphysema, may rule out the possibility of surgery, be prepared to provide answers to questions about your medical history. While cosmetic surgery is not as serious as, say, a kidney transplant, make no mistake: These are not minor procedures. A facelift, for example, involves cutting close to facial nerves and major blood vessels, so there's always the risk of nerve damage or hemorrhaging. It's not like having a few tucks taken in an outgrown dress or suit. The accompanying table mentions the possible risks and complications of most cosmetic procedures. Some are minor and inevitable (such as swelling after dermabrasion or discoloration after a facelift); others are serious but rare (such as loss of sight after an eyelid lift).

Whether or not you experience complications depends not only on the skill of the surgeon but on your personal health. "The healthier you are going into surgery, the better you will do," says Dr. Feinberg. People who bruise easily, for example, are apt to have more swelling and black-and-blue marks after a facelift than those who don't. People who smoke (and cough) or have high blood pressure are more likely to experience hematoma (bleeding under the skin) than nonsmokers or those with normal blood pressure. Your doctor should review all these factors when he makes the decision to operate—or *not* to operate.

"I flatly refuse to perform a facelift on anyone who smokes," says Dr. Kotler. "The presence of nicotine and other toxic substances from tobacco smoke constricts blood vessels, reduces circulation and delays healing. And smoking increases the risks of anesthesia. So smokers have to quit at least two weeks before and after surgery."

Some doctors refuse to perform facelifts on anyone who smokes.

Assessing Your Hopes and Fears

Don't be insulted if your surgeon asks, however diplomatically, about your mental health—your moods, how you handle family troubles, perhaps even if you are seeing a psychologist or psychiatrist. A responsible surgeon needs to be certain that you are psychologically as well as physically fit for cosmetic surgery.

"Operations that change the size and shape of the body have all sorts of psychological effects— many that are beneficial but some that can be quite disturbing," say Drs. John and Marcia Goin. You can't expect a facelift—or any other cosmetic procedure—to cure depression or other emotional difficulty.

If you're depressed, it may be better to wait.

"After all, you wouldn't decide to have a facelift while you were sick in bed with pneumonia or a ruptured disk," say the Goins. So perhaps you shouldn't have cosmetic surgery during a period of grief or distress. For example, if you're distraught over a failed marriage or the death of a spouse, it could be better to wait until you've adjusted to your new circumstances.

Are You Too Old? As long as you're in good physical and mental health, there's practically no age limit for cosmetic surgery.

"We recently did a fourth facelift on an 85-year-old woman whose duties as chairman of the board of a large corporation made it necessary for her to fly in from Phoenix, Seattle and Salt Lake City for her postoperative visits," say Drs. John and Marcia Goin.

Can You Afford It? Cost is yet another major consideration. Health insurance rarely covers cosmetic procedures. Medically necessary procedures are covered, including breast reconstruction after mastectomy. Otherwise, you have to foot the bill yourself. And surgeons expect full payment in advance. Unless you have heart disease or some other medical condition that increases your risk of serious complications, cosmetic surgery can usually be performed on an outpatient basis, reducing total cost by eliminating overnight hospitalization.

Tips for a Speedy Recovery

In the movies, when a character has plastic surgery, the bandages unwind to reveal a flawless face, complete with makeup. Gazing into a hand mirror, the lovely, charming patient admires the results and smiles appreciatively at the doctor.

In real life, things are different. Bruised and swollen, you'll emerge from cosmetic surgery looking not like the romantic lead in a Hollywood film, but more like a prizefighter who just went 15 rounds with the heavyweight champ—and lost. In short, you will look *worse* than you did before the operation. Even though your doctor warned you that you'd probably look bad for a few days, and even though he assures you that you look just like other postoperative patients, your immediate reaction may be to burst into tears and cry, "*Aak*! What have I done?"

As the days slip by, however, the swelling subsides, the black-and-blue marks fade and stitches are removed. A newer, fresher "you" emerges. How quickly you heal and how well you weather any cosmetic procedure may depend, in part, on health habits. James B. Johnson, M.D., a board-certified plastic and reconstructive surgeon with a special interest in nutrition, has several recommendations for his patients.

Dr. Johnson asks his patients to stop smoking for six weeks before surgery. Like so many other doctors, Dr. Johnson says that smokers take longer to heal and are more likely to have serious complica-

Until you heal, you'll look worse than you did before surgery.

Proper nutrition speeds healing.

tions following plastic surgery. He also asks his patients to exercise three or four times a week to increase surface blood flow and boost immune function.

Two weeks before surgery, Dr. Johnson recommends daily supplements of zinc and vitamin C with bioflavonoids. He also prescribes a multivitamin and mineral supplement with B complex.

Dr. Stark, too, relies on vitamin C to speed healing. "Vitamin C seems to help diminish postoperative discoloration in persons who have a tendency to bruise easily," says Dr. Stark. "I suggest 500 milligrams of vitamin C twice daily for a week prior to surgery. Also during this week the patient should avoid aspirin (acetylsalicylic acid) or any products containing it, because it encourages bleeding."

Vitamin C can minimize bruises.

For a few days before and after surgery, Dr. Johnson adds vitamin A to the program of nutrients mentioned. He adds vitamin E for several weeks after surgery. (Note: Don't take vitamin E *before* surgery, says Dr. Feinberg; it can cause excess bleeding.)

"My impression is that people who do this supplementation heal faster, with less bruising and scar formation," Dr. Johnson says. And he finds that many are motivated to continue taking better care of themselves long after their incisions have healed.

(Discuss with your doctor any nutritional supplementation and medications you're taking so he or she can monitor your progress and, if necessary, adjust your dosages.)

Here's another tip: Dr. Stark suggests people undergoing a facelift or other cosmetic procedure take a large pair of attractive sunglasses and a head scarf to the hospital on the day of the procedure. No, not to help you to slip into the hospital incognito. Wear them when you *leave*, to cover any swelling, stitches and bruises. That way, you won't frighten your doorman—or Doberman—when you arrive home.

Beating the Postsurgical Blues

After the black-and-blue marks fade, don't be alarmed if you still feel blue on the *inside*. This is quite normal. Many people go through a period of slight depression after cosmetic surgery. It's not

(continued on page 404)

Cosmetic Surgery and Other Aesthetic Procedures

Procedure	Problem(s) to Correct	Possible Risks and Complications
Breast lift (mastopexy) May be combined with breast enlargement through implant.	Drooping, sagging breasts.	With lift: Soreness, discomfort, discoloration, swelling. Temporary loss of sensitivity in nipples and breast skin. With implant: Fibrous capsular contracture (breast tissue hardens into a softball-like mass). Silicone may slowly leak into surrounding tissue. Saline implants may deflate. Unacceptable scarring. Hematoma (hemorrhage under the skin). Infection. Breasts may be asymmetric.
Chemical peel (chemabrasion)	Age spots; fine wrinkles and lines on cheeks and around mouth and eyes; wrinkles unaffected by a facelift.	Lighter or darker pigmentation, particularly for people with dark skin. Darkening of moles or spider veins. Increased size of pores. Prolonged redness. Possible scarring. Milia (tiny white cysts). Aggravation of any existing skin conditions. Possibly hazardous for people with poor liver, kidney or heart function.
Collagen injections May be combined with chemical peel, dermabrasion or facelift.	Forehead furrows; wrinkles above nose; folds between cheeks and mouth.	Local redness (allergic reaction).
Dermabrasion	Age spots; "whistle lines" around lips; fine wrinkles on cheeks and around eyes; acne scars; freckles.	Swelling. Pigment changes. Milia (tiny white cysts). Infection (rare). People with dark skin may not get good results.

Average Fee*	Recovery Period	Additional Comments
$2,000 to $2,300	Most people can resume activities, including sports, within 1 month.	Wear a bra day and night until your doctor advises otherwise. Sleep on your back, propped up by pillows. If breast implants are used, you may have to massage the breasts (for 2 minutes, twice a day) to prevent them from hardening. However, implants are very controversial and should be considered with extreme caution—if at all—until further study, according to the Food and Drug Administration.
$700 to $1,100	Tape mask removed after 48 hours. Swelling recedes in 2 to 3 days; some swelling, however, lasts for 3 to 4 weeks. Crust shows signs of loosening after 4 days.	Avoid talking during first few days, so tape doesn't wiggle off. Avoid sun and wear a sunscreen outdoors for a minimum of 4 months. More effective in thin-skinned fair-complected people than in those with olive or dark skin. Should not be used on the hands because of potential scarring.
$300 to $800 for initial series; $150 to $200 for yearly touchups.	Immediate.	All candidates should be tested for allergy to collagen (derived from beef protein) 1 month beforehand. People with arthritis or other autoimmune disease, or a family history of these problems, may not be eligible. Generally, 2 to 6 treatments spaced 2 weeks apart are needed. You may need touchups every few months.
$700 to $1,100	Crust that forms seals off wound and falls off after 5 to 8 days to reveal red or pink skin.	Stay out of sun or use a sunscreen after procedure, to prevent blotchy pigmentation from developing.

* Does not include hospitalization and other peripheral costs.

(continued)

Cosmetic Surgery and Other Aesthetic Procedures— *Continued*

Procedure	Problem(s) to Correct	Possible Risks and Complications
Eyelid lift (blepharoplasty)	Bags under the eyes; drooping, hooded or "crepey" lids.	Swelling. Black-and-blue marks. Hematoma (hemorrhage under the skin). Temporary blurred vision. Excessive tearing. Scarring. Soreness, discomfort and numbness. Dry eyes. Tiny white spots along the incision.
Facelift (rhytidectomy) May be combined with chemical peel, collagen injections, dermabrasion, eyelid lift or nose work.	Crow's-feet; jowls; wattles; double chin; nose-to-lip folds.	Hematoma (hemorrhage under the skin). Swelling. Black-and-blue marks (especially in people who bruise easily). Nausea and vomiting. Temporary loss of feeling in cheeks and neck. Nerve damage and partial facial paralysis. Hair loss. Scarring. Infection.
Rhinoplasty	Drooping, hooked, crooked or large nose.	Black-and-blue marks. Hemorrhages. Infection. Operation not successful in correcting problem. Nosebleeds (rare).
Suction lipectomy	Love handles; pot belly; saddle; other localized fat deposits resistant to diet and exercise.	Rippled or dimpled surface on skin. Pigmentation. Permanent numbness. Uneven (asymmetric) fat loss. Blood loss. Fluid loss. Scarring. Peeling skin. Hematoma (hemorrhage under the skin). Infection. Perforation of the abdomen.

Average Fee*	Recovery Period	Additional Comments
$1,500 to $1,800	Most discoloration disappears in 2 to 3 weeks, although further healing continues for months.	Cold compresses help to reduce swelling immediately after surgery. Warm compresses reduce swelling and discoloration after stitches are removed. Lids may not close completely or blink freely for a month or more, leaving eyes dry. Ask your doctor when you can wear makeup or contact lenses again. Procedure cannot remove second bags on cheek, below first bags.
$2,700 to $3,100	Depends on complications, if any. Discoloration usually lasts from 2 weeks to 1 month. People who bruise easily can expect to stay in seclusion longer. Many return to work in 2 weeks or less.	Stay out of sun until normal facial sensations return; then use a sunscreen on your face and neck. How long the lift lasts depends on how fast you age, how much time you spend in the sun, whether or not you smoke and if your weight is stable. Results are best in people who are not extremely overweight; otherwise, the surgeon may refuse to operate. Fair-skinned people are better candidates than those with olive or dark skin.
$1,700 to $2,000	Recovery takes 2 weeks to 1 month. Breathing may be difficult for several months. Final results not totally apparent for 6 months.	Apply cold washcloth to your eyes to reduce swelling and bruising. Daily doses of vitamin C (500 mg twice daily, the week before surgery) may reduce black-and-blue discoloration. Best done on people with thin (not thick or oily) skin and delicate facial bones.
$300 to $4,000 (Depends on areas treated.)	10 to 14 days.	Not suitable for people over age 45 (or over 35, according to some doctors).

* Does not include hospitalization and other peripheral costs.

pleasant to look bruised and swollen, especially when you've just paid thousands to look more beautiful. Doctors compare this mood to the mild postpartum depression commonly experienced by many women after childbirth, another joyous event.

To bolster your spirits, try wearing makeup. (Ask your doctor first.) By covering any residual redness, scars or discoloration, makeup can shorten your self-imposed isolation and allow you to return to work or your social life as soon as possible. Light, water-based, alcohol-free, hypoallergenic cosmetics are best for recently treated skin. If you're not accustomed to wearing makeup or don't feel confident enough to apply cosmetics artistically, get professional assistance, perhaps someone recommended by your surgeon or dermatologist. Don't underestimate the power of up-to-date makeup and a contemporary hairstyle to make the most of your facelift or other cosmetic procedure.

Makeup can help you return to work sooner.

Was It Worth It?

Is that a new hairdo?... Did you get new glasses?... You look thinner... Have you been dieting?... How was your vacation?... You look so rested!

It's not unusual to hear comments like these. In fact, don't be disappointed if no one guesses you've had surgery. A skillful surgeon knows how to hide his or her tracks. Ears, eyes, chin and breasts all provide natural fold lines where, with careful planning, the surgeon can hide tiny scars. And all of these cosmetic procedures are designed not to alter your identity, but to simply leave you looking like yourself, only better.

Don't be surprised if no one guesses you've had surgery.

How do people who've had cosmetic surgery really feel afterwards? Let two women tell you, in their own words.

Ingrid, a good-humored, confident and articulate woman of 53, says:

"My problem wasn't wrinkles so much as I felt my whole face had slipped down to my collarbone. And I had pouches over my eyes that made me look tired and depressed. I thought I looked awful with or

A firsthand report on facelifts.

without makeup, and aging really began to depress me. So I decided it was time for a facelift.

"I had an eyelid lift at the same time. I was very calm and relaxed about the operations themselves. *Paying* for them made me anxious, since I am self-supporting. But I had confidence in the surgeon and staff—I had checked out their references.

"I had the surgery Friday morning and went home on Saturday. I was swollen and bandaged, and nauseous from the anesthesia. So I *was* uncomfortable. I won't say it was nothing—that would be misleading. But I wasn't miserable, either. By Tuesday, the discomfort began to subside. On Friday, I went to the supermarket, even though I was still swollen and black-and-blue. In fact, someone gave me a card from a shelter for battered women.

"All in all, it took three weeks to recover totally.

"But it made a tremendous difference in my looks—and my life. I began to act younger, to dress differently. Before, I dressed very conservatively; I hesitated to wear anything the least bit provocative. Now I began to wear more fashionable clothes. And I switched from eyeglasses to contact lenses. And of course I began to wear makeup again. I guess the operation gave me the confidence to make additional changes.

The operation gave her confidence.

"People who hadn't seen me for a while and didn't know I'd had cosmetic surgery would say things like, 'You look softer, younger.' But mostly, I did it for me. It's fun to look good."

Margaret, age 52, had a facelift, eyelid lift and a chemical peel nearly three years ago. She, too, feels the procedures improved her outlook on life.

"I was particularly concerned with the appearance of my neck—it was beginning to look like the typical 'turkey neck.' And the chemical peel removed the wrinkles around my mouth.

"I was admitted Friday morning and scheduled for release on Saturday. But I had to stay until Sunday because painkillers given to me for the discomfort prevented me from walking around without help.

"I was well-informed about the procedures. But I wasn't really prepared for how grotesque I would look afterwards. It took real courage to look in the mirror. But fortunately, I heal fast, and as the days passed, I could look at myself more frequently. Once you can wash your hair, you begin to feel more human.

"The problem with a chemical peel is that the treated area remains a brilliant tomato red—like a really bad sunburn—for six to seven weeks. But I covered it with a green-tinted cover cream that I applied underneath my foundation makeup.

"I went back to work in two weeks, and the only comments people made were that I looked rested, or I looked slimmer. And I *had* lost 15 pounds, because I wasn't running to the refrigerator every 15 minutes. I do have telltale scars behind my ears, but my hairdo covers them. So as far as anyone was concerned, I'd been away on vacation.

"I've never regretted having it done. If you really want it, as I did, the discomfort and temporary disfigurement are secondary. It's not easy, but it's to be expected.

This surgery can inspire someone to diet, exercise and continue to improve his or her looks.

"I have more confidence now. The procedure prompted me to do other things, like upgrade my wardrobe, start exercising to get in shape and so on.

"My motivation? To look as good as I can for as long as I can. Was it worth it? Definitely. I'm 52 and I don't look my age. I feel more like 45. This was my way of equalizing the difference between the age I looked and the age I felt."

33

Eyes: Big, Bright and Beautiful

Look into a mirror. Is the face you see there really your face—the face of the *true* you? Does it look as young as you feel? Are your eyes lovely and expressive? Clear and bright?

If you think your baby blues can use a little sparkle, makeup can help you.

Here are some tips from the pros:

• Use eye shadow. It can transform ordinary eyes into outstanding eyes. Soft, muted shades in brown, gray, plum, violet or blue tend to be more flattering than neon-bright frosted shades, because too much iridescence tends to collect in creases. To avoid "crease collection," use a foundation or an eye shadow base (which is a combination of talc, beeswax and other ingredients) to provide an invisible protective shield that prevents your eye shadow from mixing with skin oils.

Matte (not frosted) eye shadow is more flattering.

Dab a little shadow onto the center of each lid, using a sponge applicator or soft pencil. Then brush up and out toward your brow and in toward your nose with an eye shadow brush. For extraordinary eyes, apply an intense shade of color in the crease of your lid and a lighter shade of the same color on the brow bone as a highlighter. Blend all these colors with your fingers.

• Try eyeliner. Just as a frame can set off a fine painting, eyeliners can define the eye. Creative

Use a pencil eyeliner rather than liquid.

beauty director Glenn Roberts, of Elizabeth Arden, Inc., suggests you use a pencil eyeliner. "It is more contemporary than liquid, easier to apply, harder to make mistakes with, makes it easier to correct mistakes and doesn't work against the slackness of the lid." Make sure the pencil's point is slightly blunt and wipe it with a tissue to remove wood particles. Then, holding the pencil parallel to the eye, draw a line from the inner corner of your upper eyelid to the midpoint, then from the outer corner to the center. Smudge the line with your fingers. Do the same thing on the bottom lid, keeping in mind that, for safety's sake, the liner should be applied outside the lashes—that is—above the upper lashes and below the bottom ones. For crinkling lids or unsteady hands, apply a series of closely spaced dots along the lash line, then smudge them, working from corner to corner, with a sponge-tipped applicator.

• Tweeze. Eyebrows, too, accent the eyes. To shape and refine brows, tweeze unwanted strays, one hair at a time. Pluck out any hair growing between the brows over the bridge of the nose, and any growing beneath the natural arch. "If your eyebrows are overtweezed, you won't look right," says Roberts. "On the other hand, if you let your brows extend too low on the outer points, you'll add ten years to your appearance. Holding a pencil horizontally from the inside corner to the outside end, make sure that the outer end of the brow is not lower than the inside corner. If as few as three hairs extend below that line, tweeze them."

• Use fill-in techniques. To make skimpy brows look more attractive, draw short, feathery lines in the direction of hair growth, using powdered eye shadow just a shade lighter than your natural brow color. Lightly smudge the lines into your brows with a brow brush.

• Emphasize lashes. Mascara turns your lashes into a fabulous eye fringe. Apply it by stroking each lash separately, from root to tip, holding the wand parallel to the eye, moving upwards on the upper lash and downwards on the lower lash.

Reserve waterproof mascara for special occasions, for swimming, smoky rooms and steamy days. Although waterproof mascara clumps less easily and resists smudges better than water-based products, it is more difficult to remove. It takes a tissue soaked in oily remover and some pretty serious elbow grease to get the stuff off. And that's just one more irritation the delicate undereye area could do without. To make sure the non-waterproof mascara doesn't leave you looking like a raccoon, skip foundation on the upper and lower eyelids. Instead, pat a narrow streak of eye shadow base just beneath your lower lashes before applying mascara.

Non-waterproof mascara is gentler for the lashes and requires no extra rubbing to remove.

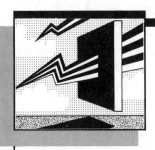

Eyeing Permanent Eyeliner

Imagine waking up every morning looking like Sophia Loren or Liz Taylor—at least around the eyes. All it takes is about $1,200 and access to one of the handful of ophthalmological surgeons who perform the new tattoo-like lining procedure. One such surgeon is Robert Fenzl, M.D., of Garden Grove, California, whose patients include women who have difficulty applying eyeliner because of vision problems or arthritis, athletes tired of sweat-streaked makeup and executive women who desire the always-fresh look the permanent liner provides. And, let's face it, his patients also include women who want the magic of makeup without the daily hassle.

Dr. Fenzl explains that the lining procedure, also called dyelining, works like this: First a local anesthetic is injected into the lids, and then tiny dots of pigment are implanted between the eyelashes. It sounds simple enough but permanent lining is not without risks—such as eyelash loss. The operation is delicate and patients should understand that they will experience temporary bruising and swelling of the eyelid as part of the healing process.

The other problem, explains Mary Stefanyszyn, M.D., is that tattoo dyes tend to turn greenish over time, and may move around a bit. With time, she says, the tattooed line can mottle and become diffused. And should the person with such a tattoo ever want a lid lift, the tattoo could be displaced from the lash line to a less attractive location. So if you would like to wake up and find yourself with eyes lined like Liz's, just make sure your eyes are open to the risks. For more information, contact a board-certified ophthalmologist.

If you are farsighted and wear glasses, the lenses will magnify your eyes, so avoid harsh lines and bright colors. On the other hand, lenses for nearsighted eyes tend to make eyes look smaller. That's where an eyeliner can be especially helpful to emphasize the eyes.

If you wear soft contact lenses, apply makeup after inserting them. But if you wear hard lenses, put on your makeup before inserting them. Use sponge-tipped applicators, removing excess powder flakes before applying. Avoid lash lengtheners; they contain tiny lash-building fibers than can flake into your eyes and lodge underneath your lenses. If you wear hard or daily-wear soft lenses, remove your lenses before removing your makeup. If you wear extended lenses, avoid using waterproof mascara, which requires oily removers.

If you wear contacts, avoid using lash lengtheners.

Safeguarding Your Eye Makeup

A little eye makeup goes a long way, so it's easy to keep it around for months, even years. But age can invite spoilage or contamination. Most of the time, the makeup has added preservatives to keep bacteria at bay. But preservatives can only go so far in protecting you. It's the way cosmetics are used or stored that causes most problems, like eye infections. "Using the same applicator day after day reintroduces bacteria from your eye to the product," says Gail Bucher, past president of the Society of Cosmetic Chemists and corporate quality analyst for the Gillette company.

Keeping old cosmetics invites contamination.

Here are some dos and don'ts for safe eye-dressing:

Label makeup with its date of purchase.

- Do wash your hands before applying makeup.
- Do use disposable eye shadow applicators, cotton swabs or washable sponge applicators.
- Do label shadows, pencils and mascara with the purchase dates and replace mascara every three and shadows and pencils every six months.
- Do discard eye makeup if it has an off color or smell.
- Do keep cosmetic containers clean and covered.
- Don't apply makeup in a moving vehicle—you

could inadvertently scratch your cornea and invite bacterial infection.

- Don't moisten mascara with saliva.

You'd be wise to stop using eye cosmetics if your eyes become swollen, red or itchy. Try switching brands, perhaps trying gentler, non-waterproof makeup. If you suspect that a certain cosmetic is the culprit, stop using all of your makeup, then begin reintroducing each cosmetic until you can determine which one is causing the trouble.

If you've ruled out your makeup or hair products, suspect your nail polish. "Believe it or not, the fumes from applying nail polish are powerful enough to produce a reaction all the way up to your eyelids," says Barbara Braunstein, M.D., assistant professor of dermatology at Johns Hopkins University, in Baltimore. "You can also irritate your eyes if you rub them with polished nails, which can happen when you're asleep." If switching brands doesn't help, you may have to learn to love natural nails for the sake of your eyes.

Your nail polish may be reddening your eyes.

Banishing Bags, Sags and Circles

"The skin around our eyes is especially thin and vulnerable," explains Albert Kligman, M.D., a dermatologist with the University of Pennsylvania, in Philadelphia. "And because your eyes are opening and closing, it's under a lot of mechanical stress."

Use sunscreen, wear sunglasses, don't squint and don't smoke.

So what's the cure for crow's-feet? "It would be great for the eyes if we could take a lesson from women of the past like the French aristocrats who spent hours taking long baths in the afternoon, with their eyes closed, just relaxing and literally not moving a muscle in their faces," says Dr. Kligman. Obviously, precious few people have time to languish in long baths for the sake of a smooth face. What you can do, though, is relax your facial muscles as often as possible.

In addition to rest, using a moisturizer regularly can minimize fine eye lines. "A simple, nonirritating product should be used on the eye area at all times to help slow down the appearance of wrinkles," advises Dr. Kligman. Creams and lotions should be

Nonsurgical Lid Lift—
An Instant Boost

What can you do for eyes that droop? Well, if you have a few spare hours and $2,000 to $3,000, you can have a blepharoplasty done. That's a surgical procedure that cuts out excess skin drooping over the eyes and takes care of the pouches of accumulated fat and loose skin under the eyes as well. Or, you can go to Neiman Marcus and buy some special adhesive for about $35, which instantly lifts up your lids. Developed by Harold D. Clavin, M.D., a plastic surgeon in Santa Monica, these small pieces of hypoallergenic adhesive tuck inconspicuously into the crease of the upper lid, holding up heavy lids and giving you a wider, youthful, less puffy look. Makeup supposedly glides on. There is no problem removing it, and it does not harm the eyelid.

The adhesive is temporary, though, as it is recommended that it be replaced daily (refills cost about $17). Still, for that class reunion or special appearance or night on the town, it may be well worth the price, and will give you an idea of what permanent surgery could do for you—without the risks. "You'd have to wear the adhesives every day for seven years to equal the cost of a surgical eyelid lift," claims Dr. Clavin. Another bonus is that "people can actually see better once all that saggy skin is lifted out of the way."

patted on gently, using your ring finger for a light touch.

"The key word is *gentle*," according to Patricia Engasser, M.D., clinical assistant professor of dermatology at Stanford University, in Stanford, California. "It's important to remember that the skin around the eye is thinner and absorbs things more easily. Therefore this area is more easily irritated." So go easy on your eyes. For example, avoid rubbing them, which stretches the skin.

Other ways you can counteract crow's-feet is to wear a good pair of sunglasses year-round to prevent squinting, and use a sunscreen. And stop smoking—

cigarettes are a sure way to get stampeded with crow's-feet.

Putting the Pinch on Puffy Eyes

If you wake up with little puffy bags you didn't have the night before, it probably means the tissues in your eyelids are filled with fluid. The cause may be eating salty food, which can cause you to retain water. Or if you've been in a position where your head is lower than your heart—such as laying tile or weeding the garden—blood has to move "uphill" and can lead to swelling near the eyes. Sitting upright may reverse swelling.

Puffy eyes can also make their appearance as you get older. "Skin tends to lose elasticity so the tissue around the eyes becomes all the more susceptible to tugs from swelling or the pull of gravity," explains Mary Stefanyszyn, M.D., ophthalmologist and ocular plastic surgeon with the Wills Eye Hospital, in Philadelphia. Fatigue, sinus infection, a cold coming on or a late night—all can aggravate the condition.

A cool washcloth can deflate puffy eyes.

To reduce swelling caused by fluid retention, try placing a cool, wet washcloth on your eyes for several minutes. Raising the head of the bed a bit also may prevent excess fluid from accumulating around the eyes.

Dark Circles

Dark circles could mean too many late nights, or more likely, that your genes are showing. Dark circles often are a family legacy—a result of an inherited type of skin or pigmentation. For these folks, the condition may be present more often than not. But for most, it's occasional. The crux of the problem is that the skin around the eyes is very thin with comparatively little fatty tissue or muscle tone. So when blood passes through this delicate area, it shows through the skin as "dark circles." Certain things can make circles darker, says Adrian Connolly, M.D., clinical assistant professor at the New York University School of Medicine, in New York City. "The eye irritation and subsequent rubbing that accompany some allergies make the area darker." And when you are tired or pale for whatever reason, the circles will seem darker in comparison.

The good news is that dark circles can be concealed. Choose a concealer that's just a shade or two lighter than your natural skin tone. (Yellow-toned concealers are especially good at camouflaging bluish circles.) Dot the dark area with concealer and blend it just under the lower lid. But don't overdo. Too much makeup accentuates any wrinkles or puffiness you may have and gives you odd, pale patches under your eyes. Wearing glasses with tinted lenses is another way to make circles less noticeable.

A touch of concealing cream makes dark circles disappear.

Red Eyes

But maybe it's not the color *under* your eyes that bothers you as much as the color that's *in* them. "Nobody wants to see red—either in the checkbook or in the eyes," says one cosmetologist. For red, bleary eyes, one solution may be a solution. These solutions contain decongestants and/or vasoconstrictors, which shrink dilated blood vessels. And they do get the red out. But they could get you in trouble if you overuse them. That's because after temporary shrinkage, the blood vessels may come back, bigger and redder than ever. So use these products sparingly.

Overusing eye drops can give you rebound redness.

Or refresh your eyes with tear substitutes marketed as "artificial tears." These products contain fluid that moisturizes and lubricates the eye.

Usually, though, bloodshot eyes will go away by themselves once you get some sleep or remove yourself from whatever is bothering them, like glare, air pollution or smoke. If the red doesn't come out, says Dr. Stefanyszyn, it could signal an allergy, infection or something called dry eyes, a condition especially common among older people.

Dry Eyes

This problem can commonly occur when there is a deficiency of tears from the lacrimal glands. With decreased tear production and lubrication, a gritty, sandy, foreign-body sensation is felt in the eye. The sensation usually feels worse later in the day. Relief comes in the form of artificial tears. These products

Artificial tears can relieve dry eyes.

are formulated to mimic the normal functioning of tears. If you find that the preservatives contained in these solutions irritate your eyes, try one of the newer single dose artificial tears without the preservatives, suggests Peter R. Laibson, M.D., director of the cornea service at Wills Eye Hospital and professor of ophthalmology at Thomas Jefferson University School of Medicine, in Philadelphia.

You might also try increasing moisture in the air by using a humidifier at home and work. And although it may sound strange, use a sleep mask to keep your eyes from drying out at night by making sure your eyelids stay closed while you sleep. Wearing sunglasses regularly also helps shield your eyes from wind, sun and swirling debris.

34

Hair:

The Crowning

Glory

H air means nothing to your survival, and virtually nothing to your health, yet many people pay more attention to it—much more—than they do to their heart, lungs, stomach or other life-generating body parts.

Hair. If there's a part of the body that people absolutely coddle and anguish over, that's it.

Even when viewing humanity from a historical perspective, through both fact and fiction, the relentless concern with the slender threads of protein that adorn the head has been, well, hair raising. In fiction, Rapunzel was saved from the loneliness of her towering prison because her heroic prince was able to hoist himself up her incredibly long hair. (Must have been a nightmare to shampoo!)

In history, the secret of Samson's superhuman strength was his hair. King David's rebellious son, Absalom, had such a splendid growth that even the Bible took time out just to marvel at its abundance and beauty (2 Sam. 14:26). It is said that when Prince Absalom had his annual haircut, the shorn locks weighed three pounds!

The tradition continues. Back in the 1960s, the Beatles had an influence of near-Biblical proportions upon the world's hairstyles. The influence—and hair—grew and grew, resulting in a Broadway musical, a movie and a near global obsession. A generation later, "new wave" youths—still hair-obsessed—made their statements by shaving off their hair, or dying it pink, green or blue.

It seems that people of any age, in every age, have tried to show the world who they are, to enhance both appearance and identity, by the way they wear their hair. As a result, Americans, for example, spend billions of dollars a year at hair salons and on hair care products.

Hair care is a multi-billion-dollar industry in America.

How to Wash, Condition and Dry

The most important and frequently used of these products are shampoos, conditioners and hair dryers. Here's what the experts have to say about the basic hair grooming routine that employs these products.

The Complete Shampoo

If you have an active life-style, you may find yourself frequently shampooing your hair. Philip Kingsley, renowned author on hair care, says you have nothing to worry about. Common fears that washing the hair daily will dry it out have proven to be unfounded—unless you're using improper shampoos or washing techniques.

Washing your hair every day will not hurt it.

"Washing the hair daily is O.K.," agrees Jack Myers, director of the National Cosmetology Association. "Those who wear blow-dry styles usually look best, in fact, when they wash and dry their hair every day."

Kingsley recommends the following program for proper shampooing.

Dry Run. To avoid tangles, run a wide-tooth, saw-cut comb through your hair before wetting it. To prepare for shampooing in the shower, comb the hair straight back from the hairline and around the ears. If you're leaning over a tub or sink, bend over and comb the hair forward from the nape of the neck.

Presoaking. Shampoo will lather best in thoroughly wet hair. Spend about 30 seconds wetting the hair with warm water. Draw your fingers through your hair from the scalp to the ends.

Dilute your shampoo with distilled water.

Shampooing. After testing scores of different shampoos in his laboratories, Kingsley concluded that brands don't matter as long as you dilute the shampoo with distilled water. A half shampoo/half water mix works best, while some of the thicker shampoos perform best when diluted to 90 percent water. By the way, here's some good news for your budget. Kingsley's experiments determined that the more expensive shampoos were actually less effective than the cheaper brands, mainly because the expensive brands contain perfumes and unnecessary additives like protein, placenta, etc. The rule of thumb is, the fewer the additives in the shampoo, the better. (The next time you see a fabulously maned Hollywood star extolling some bargain shampoo, don't laugh. She may actually use the stuff!)

You still might want to choose a shampoo formulated for your hair type. The exception is shampoos made for oily hair, which Kingsley feels are too harsh for any hair. If you have oily hair, use a "no-oil" mild shampoo.

When applying the shampoo to your wet hair, don't slosh it directly onto your noggin. Instead, pour the diluted shampoo into the palm of your hand and rub your hands together. Gently smooth the shampoo over your hair.

Don't use regular soap on your hair. It's much too harsh.

Don't think you can save money by using regular body soap on your hair. You won't save much and it will do a poor job.

Lathering. Massage and knead the head with your fingertips; don't scratch or dig in your nails, and avoid massage brushes. Be gentle. Ease out tangles by drawing your fingers though your hair from scalp to ends. Lather for about three minutes. Don't worry about the lack of thick suds. They're only for the television ads.

Rinsing. No need for restraint here. It's better to overrinse than under. Hair should be "squeaky clean." It's not necessary to lather a second time if you wash your hair every day.

Conditioning: Before and After

Conditioners contain substances, usually protein, that smooth over the hair shafts, polishing rough edges and filling in nicks and chips. They restore luster to lifeless hair, seal in moisture, maintain the hair's elasticity and strength, reduce static electricity, prevent tangles and leave hair more manageable. By clinging to the hair shaft, conditioners also can add body and help prevent damage.

Conditioners are especially recommended for people with dry, permed, straightened or color-treated hair, swimmers and those who use hot rollers, curling irons or blow dryers. Kingsley says that those with oily hair should choose a conditioner which contains no oil whatsoever.

For others there are various conditioning agents available to complete an overall hair program.

Hair Reconstructors. These specially formulated conditioners are recommended for extremely damaged hair. Although numerous commercial and salon products are available, Kingsley says a simple hot oil treatment applied once a week works well. Use corn, sunflower, almond or olive oil. Warm the oil. Completely coat each hair shaft and massage the oil into the scalp. Cover your hair with a plastic bag and keep it on overnight if possible. Wash out the oil completely the next day.

Shampoo/Conditioner Combinations. Skip these, Kingsley suggests, since shampoos and conditioners have opposite actions and don't work well together.

Post-Shampoo Conditioners. A dizzying array of popular brands exists, but as a general rule, the thicker the conditioner, the better it will work, says Kingsley. If you feel that your hair needs a conditioner or creme rinse, pour a small amount in your palm, rub your hands together and smooth the conditioner across the ends of your hair. Don't apply it to the scalp which should be clean and free of superficial oils. Leave the conditioner on the hair for just a minute or so. Rinse thoroughly.

If you prefer not to condition, you still can achieve a high sheen. Leaving your hair in its natural state—undyed, unpermed, undamaged—is one approach. Natural hair shines. Hair that's been roughed up by teasing, careless brushing, sun damage or chemical treatments can end up dull. Even shampoo can leave a soapy film on the hair that dims the shine. A good shine restorer is a post-shampoo rinse using a slightly acidic solution. Two tablespoons of white vinegar, lemon juice or camomile tea diluted in

Conditioners are recommended for people with dry, permed, straightened or color-treated hair.

Allow a post-shampoo conditioner to work for just a minute before rinsing it out.

A vinegar rinse produces real luster.

a quart of water will remove all traces of shampoo and leave hair shiny.

Blowing in the Wind

In the past two decades, blow dryers have become standard equipment in most homes. Yet Kingsley says leave the hot-air pistols in their holsters. Letting the hair air dry slowly and naturally is the ideal way.

For those who don't have the time to sit around waiting for their hair to dry, or whose hairstyle is dependent upon the blasts of arid air, here's how to dry without broiling your hair.

Power. You need a hair dryer, not a flame thrower. Blow dryers pack a lot of power—over 1,200 watts for many models. Kingsley recommends stopping at 1,000. Diffuser attachments deflect the air and add additional protection.

Technique. Hold the dryer six inches away. Dry the back and side of your head and work toward the crown and front. Start with a high, warm setting, then cut back the heat and power as the hair dries. If you use a brush, choose one with long, smooth, blunt bristles made of soft, pliable plastic. Brush with light, stroking movements. Never use a brush when hair is wet, as wet hair is damage prone, and can easily snap. Wide-tooth combs are preferred.

Quitting Time. If you can, stop using the blow dryer when hair is still damp, then let it dry naturally. If this is not practical for styling reasons (curly hair can twist back to its natural shape if left even a slight bit damp), Denise Buntin, M.D., of the department of dermatology at Tulane University, in New Orleans, suggests setting the dryer on a cool setting; then it probably will not damage the hair. Don't linger. Even drying for a few extra seconds can lead to brittleness, dullness, splitting and breakage. Commercial conditioners to be used with blow dryers can help protect the hair from this kind of damage.

"These blow-dry conditioners are the new generation of hair conditioners," says Jack Myers. "When you're subjecting your hair to thermal dryers, you need a conditioner that stays in so it can protect it. Leave-in products are superior to the old wash-out conditioners."

If you must blow dry, reduce both temperature and power level as the hair dries.

Specially formulated "leave-in" conditioners will fight the damaging effects of hair dryers.

A Doctor Defines Hair

So what is hair anyway? Here's what a doctor sees: In the words of R. Jeffrey Herten, M.D., clinical professor of dermatology at the University of California College of Medicine at Irvine, "Hair is an extension of the epidermis, sunk into the dermis. It is composed of compact strands of sulfur-rich keratin, produced by primitive epidermal cells at a rate of about four-tenths of a millimeter per day. The normal diameter of the hair shaft is about eight-hundredths of a millimeter. The hair shaft is covered by a delicate cuticle composed of platelike scales staggered like roof tiles. Hair growth is controlled by a growth hormone, a thyroid hormone and, in certain locations on the body, by sex hormones."

A past problem associated with blow dryers appears to have been rectified. In the late 1970s, consumers were warned that many brands contained asbestos, a material used to insulate parts of a hair dryer that has been linked to cancer. In the interim, manufacturers have switched to other materials. If you have an old dryer lying around, or picked one up cheap at a flea market, beware. The Consumer Product Safety Commission, in Washington, D.C., can provide you with a list of all the brands and models that contained asbestos or answer your questions about specific models.

Combs and Brushes

Surprisingly, many doctors and hair specialists are anti-brush.

"Use the brush only to finish a hairstyle, or when a comb just won't do the job," says Vera Price, M.D., clinical professor of dermatology at the University of California at San Francisco. "Otherwise, frequent, vigorous brushing can actually damage the hair, causing splitting and breaking."

Frequent, vigorous brushing damages the hair.

If you must use a brush, choose a style with smooth, rounded bristle tips to prevent scratching. Many brushes today have ball-tipped bristles for extra protection.

As for the combs, use a wide-tooth or saw-tooth type. Choose rubber over plastic, and avoid metal combs altogether. Wash brushes and combs once a month.

Keep combing and brushing to a minimum. The old wives' tale about brushing your hair 100 strokes a day will actually leave you with split ends and battered hair instead of beauty.

Treating Dandruff

If combing or brushing your hair tends to shower your shoulders with white flakes, you have a common problem known as dandruff. More socially annoying than physically harmful, dandruff is nothing more than skin being shed from your scalp.

Regular shampooing can combat light dandruff.

Everybody's scalp flakes somewhat. It's the scalp's way of shedding dead cells. This light dandruff can be easily controlled with regular shampoos. How regular? Enough to keep the dandruff from reappearing. For example, if the dandruff begins appearing on the third day after your last shampoo, then shampoo every two days.

Chronic dandruff can be more difficult to control. It results from having a very scaly scalp that is either too dry or too oily. It's often accompanied by an itch. Causes include scalp bacteria, hormone production, oil gland malfunction, infrequent shampooing, improper rinsing, overconditioning and sunburned scalp. Here are some successful treatments for dandruff: frequent shampoos; thorough rinses; dabbing the scalp with cotton balls soaked with a dilute solution of 1 part witch hazel or lemon juice to 4 parts water or wearing a hat or scarf outdoors.

If that doesn't work, try using one of the specially formulated dandruff shampoos. They contain sulfur, tar, salicylic acid, selenium, zinc pyrithione or a combination of these compounds. Experiment to find the brands that work best for you. These shampoos can lose their effectiveness after two or three months as the skin cells build a resistance, so switching to a brand with a different compound is recommended.

Stress, hormonal changes related to pregnancy or the menstrual cycle and a diet high in animal or dairy fats, salt and sugar, and low in raw fruits, vegetables, whole grains and water, can result in temporary dandruff. Altering your diet, life-style or shampooing patterns may help prevent flareups.

Severe cases of dandruff, psoriasis and a form of dandruff coupled with a rash known as seborrhea, warrant a visit to a dermatologist.

Seasonal Hair

Changes in temperature, humidity and environment can take their toll on hair. As the seasons change, your hair care needs also may change. Here are some tips to help you through the two extreme seasons, winter and summer:

Drink six eight-ounce glasses of water a day.

In Winter:

• Keep drinking water even though you might prefer a warm beverage instead. Try to down at least six eight-ounce glasses a day.
• Shampoo and condition often. Many people think they can get away with less cleansing in the winter because they don't sweat as much. Unfortunately, scarves, hats and overheated buildings increase the production of sweat and oil on the scalp.
• Use a creme rinse after washing to reduce static electricity.

In Summer:

• Limit the time you spend in direct sunlight. Those blond streaks look sharp, but the price is high. The sun makes your hair dry and brittle, and if it's color treated, the sun can alter its color to an undesirable shade. If you're out in the sun, wear a hat or plan ahead and after you shampoo comb a conditioner that contains a sunscreen through your hair. Don't rinse it out until you get home, being sure to remove it completely. In a pinch, you can rub your sunscreen on your hair.
• Highly active individuals who must wash their hair often should switch to a mild shampoo with a pH of about 4.5 to prevent the hair shaft from absorbing too much water. Monthly hot oil or deep conditioning treatments are recommended for damaged hair.

In a pinch, you can protect your hair with a sunscreen made for the skin.

- Blot your hair dry instead of rubbing it with a towel.
- Use a wide-tooth comb, starting from the end and working to the scalp so you don't pull the comb through and tear the snarls out.
- Coloring, perming or straightening the hair weakens it. If you can, postpone the process until the fall.
- Both chlorinated pool water and natural salt water batter the hair. Protect it with a rubber swim cap, which is more water proof than fabric ones and leaks less. Caps also protect blonds from the greenish tint that taints the hair after bathing in chlorinated pools. Coating your hair with a heavy, water-repellent sunscreen lotion before swimming can help, and mixing the lotion with baby oil works even better. New shampoos like UltraSwim have recently been developed to beat the greens.

Coping with Humidity

"If you have naturally curly hair and live in a humid climate like Florida or Louisiana, just cut your hair short," laughs Myers. "If you have naturally curly hair or a perm, humidity will make your hair frizz and lose its shape. In all honesty, there's not much even the best hairdressers can do. Hair sprays and mousses can help, but when you try to fight humidity, you usually lose."

Myers says those particularly tormented by humidity can try one of the heavily oiled or moisturized "wet-look" styles popularized by singer Michael Jackson. "These styles flood the hair with its own moisture and therefore protect it from the effects of humidity."

"Wet-look" styles fight the frizz caused by humidity.

Changing Your Hair Color

You can add a little sparkle to your looks by brightening your hair. Options range from adding highlights to completely changing a wan and fading color to a vibrant new shade, or covering up gray. Various jobs require various dyes. You can select from temporary rinses or permanent dyes.

Regardless of the type of dye you choose, be careful with the process.

Temporary Colors. These are rinses and high-intensity coloring agents that generally last until your next shampoo. Rinses wash through the hair leaving a slight tint of color that comes out in your next shampoo. With a rinse you can add gold, copper or a variety of more vibrant glints. High-intensity or "leave-in" colors coat the hair and give deeper, darker shades. They can change brown hair to auburn, or darken it to near black. Rinses don't damage the hair but they might damage your ego. Temporary dyes can come off anywhere, on your clothes, pillows or lover's shoulder. If you sweat, there's potential for a grand mess, especially if you have long hair.

Semipermanent Colors. Applied like shampoo, the color lasts through five to six washings. Some advantages of semipermanent dyes are that they rarely rub off from your hair onto your clothes, are less allergenic than permanent dyes and offer a wide variety of shades. Choosing a shade lighter than your original color will create a highlighted effect, rather than a complete color change.

Vegetable Dyes. In the distant past there were many of these dyes, made from vegetation—henna, indigo, camomile and even walnuts. Today, only the henna plant remains in wide use. The advantage of henna is that it causes less hair damage than chemical dyes. The disadvantage is that natural henna color will make you see red—too much red—regardless of the color you choose. The color itself tends to be harsh, and repeated use can make hair stiff and brittle. New henna products aimed at countering these drawbacks are now available on the market. Consult your hairdresser for an update.

Vegetable dyes cause less hair damage than chemical dyes.

Metallic Dyes. Widely promoted as a "youth restorer" that slowly covers gray hair, metallic or "progressive" dyes trade ease of application (you just comb it in), and shade control for an often unnatural result. And once used, you're pretty much stuck with it. They are incompatible with other coloring products, and make the hair brittle.

Aside from this, questions have risen about the product's safety because the main ingredient is lead acetate, a potentially harmful substance. However, the Food and Drug Administration continues to give these products the O.K., saying the safety risk has not been proven.

Oxidation Dyes and Tints. These are the most popular permanent dyes, the ones that fill the long shelves

Oxidation dyes are the most popular but can cause allergic reactions.

at the local drugstore. They offer a wide variety of colors, good results and ease of application. Mostly a shampoo-in product, coloration is achieved by mixing the dye with a cream peroxide developer and leaving it on the hair for about 20 minutes. Totally cream formulations are also available, and these are said to cover gray a little better.

Disadvantages of oxidation dyes are mostly relegated to the small percentage of people who may be allergic to the chemicals—a percentage said to be only about 1 in 100,000 applications, according to the American Medical Association and the American Academy of Dermatology.

Some research has suggested that there could be a link between oxidation dyes (and other dyes) and cancer. Recent medical studies cleared the dyes, but research is ongoing. Consult your dermatologist for the latest findings.

Bleaching. To obtain lighter shades, bleaching strips the hair of its natural color, usually with a 6 percent hydrogen peroxide solution. Bleaching the hair past the yellow shade damages the hair and can limit the way you style it. For example, using hot combs, curlers or curling irons can increase the damage, as would teasing the hair.

Bleaching batters the hair so badly you may not be able to use some curling techniques.

Mild bleaches, which slightly lighten the hair, are available, and are less damaging. Most bleaches are used in conjunction with a color toner to create a new color and neutralize the "brassy" red tones. Thus the peroxide removes the hair's original color and the toner replaces it with a shade like "champagne" or "honey" blonde.

Frosting, Tipping, Streaking, Hair Painting. All are creative ways of enhancing your looks by dying sections of the hair instead of the whole head. The bleaching agents used are strong, so be careful. The process also can be difficult to do on yourself, depending on your own creative abilities, painting skills and patience. Having a friend or hairdresser do it may be best for those less nimble of hand.

Regardless of which type of dye you choose, it's imperative that you follow the directions exactly and heed all warnings. Most products call for a patch test on the skin and a strand test on the hair a day before applying, and these steps should not be overlooked.

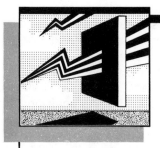

Hate That Gray? Read This

With 75,000 to 120,000 hairs on the average human head, a few gray strands mixed in with the dark shouldn't be all that significant. But many people view gray hair as a sign of age and deterioration. As soon as the gray strikes, they start looking for a way to stop it.

What they really want is to restore a pigment called melanin. The denser the melanin in a hair shaft, the darker the hair. And gray hair (if you look closely at a gray hair, you'll see that it's really white) is hair that has lost all its melanin. While no one really knows why some hairs lose their melanin and become gray, many people purport to have cures.

Irwin Lubowe, M.D., professor emeritus and dermatologist at New York Medical College, in New York City, says an amino acid called para-aminobenzoic acid (PABA) will halt the graying process. While it won't restore color to already gray hairs, says Dr. Lubowe, oral doses of PABA tablets will change the physiology of the hair shafts so they'll retain melanin—and therefore their color.

According to Dr. Lubowe, you have to be in good health and must get your doctor's permission before you use PABA. The only problem, he says, is that not too many doctors prescribe PABA internally for gray hair.

In fact, Dr. Lubowe seems to be a lone wolf when it comes to using PABA. According to one noted trichologist, the only way to stay the gray is with hair dye. "People say many things reverse gray hair—zinc, tyrosine, etc.—but nothing I know of will cure it; there are only things that will cover it up," he explains.

Curling and Straightening

It's a tribute to the ingenuity of cosmetic marketing that people with naturally straight hair spend a fortune having their hair curled, while people with naturally curly hair spend equal amounts straightening it. Depending upon the latest whims of style and fashion, you'll probably do battle with a permanent or straightener at some time in your life. And the term "doing battle" is appropriate. Both permanents

Permanents and straighteners chemically alter the hair and can lead to severe damage if not used correctly.

and straighteners alter the chemical alignment of the hair shaft and can lead to severe damage if used incorrectly. Even if these products are used correctly, the hair loses some of its strength and texture.

There are currently two types of permanents—cold waves and heat-activated acid perms. The odorous cold wave lotion soaks into the hair shaft and chemically alters the hair, so that it takes a shape determined by curlers. A neutralizing agent must be used to stop the process before the hair disintegrates. Heat-activated acid perms work essentially the same way, with an additional step. Heat from a dryer or lamp helps set the curls. Heat perms are gentler on your hair, but tougher on your skin.

Philip Kingsley offers these tips to counter the damage done by perms and straighteners.

- Never use them more than once every four months, and then only on hair that is in excellent condition.
- Deep condition your hair two or three times a week for two weeks prior to any chemical treatment.
- Never perm or straighten hair if the surrounding skin is inflamed or broken.
- Wait at least a week (and a shampoo) between perming or straightening and coloring your hair.
- Stop the perm process a few minutes earlier than suggested during hot weather, when warm temperatures can make the chemical solutions work faster.

Other experts suggest that you protect your skin with a barrier of petroleum jelly around the hairline, then wrap absorbent cotton over the barrier. Place a thick terrycloth towel around your neck to catch drips.

Protect your skin from permanent wave lotions by creating a barrier of petroleum jelly and absorbent cotton around the hairline.

Wesley Wilborn, M.D., an Atlanta dermatologist, adds that you should remove straightening solutions immediately if you feel burning or stinging on your scalp. People with scalp conditions such as dandruff, seborrhea or psoriasis should not use a straightener until the condition clears.

Selecting a Hairstyle

Hairstyles change fast, but the guidelines for selecting a style are unchanging. One basic decision is whether to wear the hair long or short.

"Almost all hair types can go short," says John Chadwick, hair consultant and coauthor (with Suzanne Chadwick) of *The Chadwick System, Discovering the Perfect Hairstyle for You* (S & S). "Short hair accentuates good bone structures, small noses, big eyes, pretty necks and tiny ears. It can also hide irregular hairlines and low foreheads, as well as less-than-perfect profiles and head shapes."

Who shouldn't go short?

"Very large, big-boned people should steer clear of very short hair," Chadwick says. "People with wide necks, double chins, receding chins or jaws should not wear very short hair. Also, extremely damaged hair and ultrafine, thin straight hair doesn't do well very short."

Before you take the big step toward a new style, evaluate your features and your hair type.

A short hairstyle shows off good bone structure.

Styling Aids

Cosmetic company researchers are working diligently to create the perfect hair spray, the magic mist that cements your hair perfectly in place, yet allows it to feel free and natural. While the concept seems contradictory, the advent of modern hair sprays, mousses and gels has brought us closer to that goal.

It's also brought us safer products. Nonaerosol hair sprays function as well as aerosol products. Aerosol products spray a fine mist and are more easily inhaled into the lungs, possibly causing health problems. A study at the Medical College of Wisconsin, in Milwaukee, found that people with asthma, hay fever or respiratory infections should avoid using hair sprays. If you're healthy, you should use them in a well-ventilated area, hold your breath while spraying or breathe through your nose and limit the length of exposure.

Nonaerosol hair sprays are as effective as aerosol products.

Similar to hair spray in results, mousse is a foam that looks and feels like shaving cream. You use the mousse before styling and set the style in place with total hair holding power, rather than spritzing on a surface holding agent when you finish. To use, just lather the mousse through your hair and sculpt waves, peaks or whatever you please. Some brands

Mousse allows you to mold your hair into many styles.

also contain dye, conditioners, dandruff medications, moisturizers and sunscreens for variety and vitality.

Another useful product is setting gel. Today's gels are glorified versions of the setting gels of the 1950s and 1960s. They look wet when first applied, then stiffen as they dry. Left in place, gel makes the hair so shiny it appears wet. Brushed out, it gives body, volume and lift.

The Bald Facts

Minoxidil may produce hair growth in some people.

If you have no use for sprays, mousse and gel because your hair is only a fond memory, cheer up. Help may be on the way. Quite by accident it was discovered that the blood pressure drug, Minoxidil, made by the UpJohn company, can produce regenerative hair growth in some bald people. That discovery was followed by three years of intensive study by Upjohn researchers, along with application to the Food and Drug Administration for approval. One researcher, Ronald C. Wester, Ph.D., of the department of dermatology at the University of California at San Francisco School of Medicine, reports that the studies have been promising. Minoxidil, taken internally, produced "general and unpredictable" excess hair growth in 30 to 50 percent of men and 50 to 80 percent of women, Dr. Wester says. Further studies using Minoxidil applied directly on the head have produced promising, although less successful results. Dr. Wester speculates that the blood pressure drug increases blood flow to dying hair follicles, sparking a rebirth. If you'd like to give this drug a try, check with your dermatologist for availability, or to see if it's appropriate for you.

Another product, Nutriol, has garnered considerable attention in the hair-growing business. Foltene, similar to Nutriol, is an Italian-made substance sold in Europe as a hair restorer. In this country Nutriol is sold as a "hair fitness preparation." Can it help a balding pate? Wilma Bergfeld, M.D., head of dermatopathology at the Cleveland Clinic Foundation, remains skeptical. Consult a dermatologist before signing up for the expensive series of treatments.

If you are balding, it's possible that you may not even need a miracle product. There are many other causes outside the presently incurable hereditary pattern baldness (androgenetic alopecia) that is responsible for most cases of baldness in men and thinness of hair in women. A pamphlet by the American Academy of Dermatology explains that childbirth, fever, infections, flu, thyroid disease, inadequate protein in the diet, drugs, birth control pills, low serum iron, surgery, debilitating chronic illness, ringworm, improper hair cosmetic use and improper hair care can result in hair loss. Some of these problems don't cause permanent baldness. In these cases hair will regrow spontaneously, or hair loss can be treated successfully by a dermatologist.

Some cases of baldness are temporary.

Most hair shedding is due to the normal hair growth cycle. Losing 50 to 100 hairs per day is no cause for alarm. Deborah Spitz, M.D., says this normal loss pattern is seasonal. Like trees, hair seems to shed more in autumn. "At any given time, 85 percent of the hair follicles are in an active growing state, 14 percent are in a resting stage and 1 percent are in a shedding phase," Dr. Spitz says.

For those unwilling to wait for the Minoxidil verdict, surgical techniques to correct baldness exist. The most popular is the hair transplant, a procedure in which small, pencil-eraser-size grafts of skin are dug out of the side of the head where hair remains and plugged into the bald area. The result is hair, but also an irregular tufted "doll's hair" appearance noticeable at the hairline. The texture of the hair often changes as well, becoming more wiry or kinky, leading to styling problems.

Some surgical transplant techniques give more attractive results than others.

An alternative technique is to have entire sections or "flaps" in strips one and a half inches wide transferred from abundant areas. Toby G. Mayer, M.D., and Richard W. Fleming, M.D., both associate clinical professors and chairmen of the division of facial plastic and reconstructive surgery at the University of Southern California, in Los Angeles, say this procedure offers more thickness, eliminates the tufting and texture changes and creates a more natural hairline than transplants. More importantly, the results are immediate. However, complications from flap surgery are slightly higher than transplants (both are minimal). Costs of either procedure range from $5,000 to $10,000 depending upon the doctor, the area of the country and the extent of baldness.

Hair that thins slightly is a normal consequence of aging. "Progressive hair loss begins in both sexes at about age 50 and accelerates in the seventh and eighth decades," says R. Jeffrey Herten, M.D., assistant clinical professor of dermatology at the University of California at Irvine College of Medicine.

If you are "cursed" with fast-falling hair, don't feel alone. It's estimated that nearly two out of every three men suffer from some form of balding while an even higher percentage of men and women have some form of hair loss during their life.

It is normal for hair to thin slightly as you age.

35

Beautiful

Hands

L et's play a little Trivial Pursuit. What do you think is the most common plastic surgery operation?

a. Nose job
b. Facelift
c. Breast enlargement
d. Hand operation

Like many of the popular game's queries, this is a trick question. The correct answer is the one you probably least expected.

And what a trick. According to the American Society of Plastic and Reconstructive Surgeons, plastic surgeons perform 166,300 hand operations per year—thousands more than any other operation.

One of the obvious reasons is that the hand is extremely prone to damage. "Injury to the hand is one of the most common in the workplace," says Garry Brody, M.D., clinical professor of plastic surgery at the University of Southern California, in Los Angeles.

That's because people stick it places, at home and work, where it gets maimed—in machinery, ovens, stoves, heaters, fireplaces, cooking pots, fanbelts, around cigarette lighters, cigars, matches, etc.—places where they never risk other body parts.

The hand is extremely injury prone.

433

Plastic surgery techniques are used in most hand surgery, including reconstructive operations.

There's a catch to this trivia answer, too. The bulk of the hand operations are not cosmetic, unlike the other three operations. Rather, they are done to restore the hand's function. Dr. Brody explains that the same technology plastic surgeons use to minimize disfiguring scars is necessary on the hand because scars can result in restricted motion. Since plastic surgeons are experts in these surgical skills, it was a natural progression for them to take on a large portion of hand operations.

"Most hand surgery is functional, not cosmetic, but we have no objection to trying to improve the appearance of the hand," Dr. Brody says. "Some burns are unsightly, and we will take special steps to correct those scars."

The reason is obvious. Your hand is also a part of the body that is rarely covered. Social custom requires presenting the hand to friends and strangers. Business associates shake hands. A man may kiss a woman's hand. He asks for her "hand" in marriage. The first intimate moment between lovers is usually holding hands. It's not hard to understand why people are so concerned with how their hands look.

Correcting problems may be easier and more economical than you imagine.

If you have a scar, burn or birth defect that makes you hide your hand in embarrassment, you may want to consult a plastic surgeon. Correcting the damage and erasing blemishes may be easier and more economical than you imagined. If you have a disease, deformity or functional problem with your hand that requires surgery, you should consult a specialist in hand surgery.

Handling Wear and Tear

Routine wear and tear can diminish the hand's natural beauty.

Despite the strong desire for presentable hands, people still put them through the toughest ordeal of all body parts. Aside from using the hands in situations that have the potential to injure them, people also routinely subject their hands to hot water, detergents, solvents, polishes, waxes, cleaning fluids and scores of other chemicals. These chemicals can remove the skin's protective oils, permitting the hands to become dehydrated.

Winter is an especially bad time for hands. Cold, dry outside air, along with even drier indoor heat, literally sucks the water out of the skin.

Sweet Creams

Dermatologists start every discussion of hand care by talking about hand protection. They report that almost all economical, commercial hand lotions work well in protecting the skin from damaging air, so hand-wringing about which brands or ingredients are best is unnecessary. The differences that are important are those that might keep a person from using it as often as five times a day. These factors—fragrance, feel, tackiness and drying time—are individual preferences. Experts recommend sampling the various brands until you find one you like. Or you may decide to use several—a quick drying, nonscented type for work and a creamier product for home. The best method yet is to bathe your hands in the richest brand before going to bed and cover them with soft cotton gloves available at most pharmacies.

Inexpensive hand creams work as well as the fancier brands.

These suggestions are offered to both men and women. Men often overlook rough, dry, cracked "work" hands that are in far worse shape than any self-respecting woman would tolerate. Macho types are advised that "masculine" hand creams with appropriately manly names like Corn Huskers Lotion are readily available. Those with less fragile egos can save money and use their wife's lotion, or purchase the basic house brand found in any drug or department store.

Men should use hand creams too.

Application is simple. Just rub it on. Both men and women should be generous in applying the lotions, covering all areas of the hand, paying particular attention to the crevices around the fingernails.

And go easy when washing the hands, avoiding hot water and harsh soap. A creamy soap like Dove, baby soaps or superfatted soaps like Basis are recommended, even for men.

Rashes and Dermatitis

Sometimes hand problems can become so bad they require medical treatment. Terms like "derma-

Dermatitis may have multiple causes.

Hand eczema and rashes can be caused by allergies.

titis," "hand eczema" and "rash" replace the simple description "yeccch." These three terms, often interchanged, describe general skin problems marked by inflammation, itching, redness, crustiness, blisters, watery discharges, fissures or other unpleasantness. Often the cause is unknown. "The most common type of hand dermatitis is housewives' eczema, usually aggravated by irritating materials such as chemicals or detergents. Another common form is allergic contact dermatitis, which is caused by an allergic reaction to some substance your hands have touched," according to Stephen M. Schleicher, M.D., codirector of the Dermatology Center of Philadelphia.

The best response is to go to a dermatologist to find out what the culprit is. If no one substance can be identified and eliminated, then protecting the hands is the best idea. Here are some suggestions.

• Check ingredients. While hand creams and creamy soaps are of possible benefit, people with dermatitis should be careful. Fragrances, coloring agents, deodorants, paraben preservatives and even lanolin may aggravate the problem. Watch out for medications containing neomycin, ethylenediamine or benzocaine. These can be irritants. Doctors recommend using plain white petroleum jelly as a moisturizing agent.

• Baby your hands. Norman Levine, M.D., of the University Medical Center, in Tucson, says women with babies are vulnerable to dermatitis. Protect your hands when touching soiled diapers, harsh detergents and the usual run of household chemicals, and also during extensive handling of food, especially fruits.

• Wear gloves. Rubber gloves can irritate hands. Dr. Schleicher recommends a combination of plastic and cotton gloves, using the cotton gloves as a liner under the plastic gloves for added protection. Don't wear plastic gloves for more than 15 to 20 minutes at a time. If water enters the glove, immediately remove it. Wash the insides of the gloves several times a week by turning them inside out and rinsing them under hot water. Allow them to dry thoroughly, and sprinkle them with talc.

• Avoid contact. When you handle shampoo, hair lotion, hair cream and hair dye, says Dr. Schleicher, wear plastic gloves.

• Ban the band. Don't wear rings when doing housework, even after the problem has cleared, advises Dr. Schleicher. Take off your rings before washing your hands to avoid soap caking under them. Clean your rings frequently on the inside with a brush.

• Cheer up! "Frustration and emotional stress often express themselves in hand dermatitis," says Bernard A. Kirshbaum, M.D., chief of dermatology at the Medical College of Pennsylvania, in Philadelphia. "Housewives' eczema is not just detergent dermatitis. It is usually caused by stress and aggravated by detergents."

Rashes can be a sign of emotional unrest.

Here's something to cheer up about. Regardless of how lizardlike your hands may look, the damage isn't permanent and can be quickly repaired. The skin on the hand completely regenerates, so with proper care, it can become as soft and lovely as a baby's.

• See a doctor. Severe or stubborn cases may warrant a visit to a dermatologist. "Patients who don't respond to topical medications may require oral corticosteroids," says Dr. Schleicher. "Oral antibiotics can be effective when a bacterial infection is present or suspected."

Sweaty Palms

This affliction is steeped in bitter irony. Because you care so much, you come across as uncaring, a cold fish. You are meeting someone new and want to make a good impression. You're nervous. Your palms are oozing sweat. The person you are supposed to meet comes in. He motions for the traditional handshake. Terrified, you offer up your soggy paw. You see his face cringe as flesh meets fish. One good impression down the drain.

The above scenario happens all too often to people cursed with sweaty hands. Known as hyperhydrosis, it can be a tough problem to solve. Dermatologists usually treat it with solutions containing the antiperspirant aluminum chlorhydroxide, which usually works temporarily. Tranquilizers and

Sweaty palms are difficult, but not impossible, to correct.

drugs that block nerve impulses (anticholinergic drugs) have had minor results, while some doctors have had success with a drastic procedure in which water is driven into the sweat glands electrically, making them swell up and stop working. For the really desperate, an operation exists that severs the nerves which control the sweat glands. Biofeedback and relaxation training may offer some nonsurgical hope.

Writer's Bumps and Calluses

Writer's bumps are harmless. They can be removed if you find them ugly.

Bumps and calluses are your body's natural defense against pressure and friction. They are harmless. If you find them unattractive, a dermatologist can plane them off, that is, gently slice down the skin. However, if you maintain the same writing grip, they'll just grow right back. Varying your hold on the pen or pencil will shift the pressure and enable the bumps and calluses to disappear by themselves. Better yet, learn to type or operate a computer.

36
Young and
Healthy Lips

L ips. Like skin, but also like the mucous lining of your mouth, there's nothing quite like them anywhere else on your body. And as with other body parts, young-looking lips and rough, chapped, old-looking lips are partly a genetic, partly an environmental matter.

"Dry skin is more of a problem as people get older—and chapped lips are another aspect of dry skin," says Solange Beauregard, M.D., a geriatric dermatologist at Boston University School of Medicine. "Exposure to cold, dry air is one cause of chapped lips. So is sun exposure. And with time, sun damage will 'age' the lips just as it 'ages' the skin."

Aside from causing otherwise lovely lips to chap and peel, sun exposure can trigger brown spots called labial lentigo—"age spots of the lips"—which are not only unattractive blemishes but can develop into cancer.

"The lower lip takes a particular beating because it protrudes and, unlike the upper lip, isn't shaded by the nose," says Hillard H. Pearlstein, M.D., assistant clinical professor of dermatology at Mt. Sinai School of Medicine, in New York.

You can make that beating worse by trying to ease the discomfort with licking. But licking your lips only makes chapping worse. It moistens lips at first

Sunlight can age your lips.

439

but eventually dries them even further as the saliva evaporates.

Protection—in the form of a greasy film of some sort—is the key to keeping lips looking healthy and beautiful for life, according to Drs. Beauregard and Pearlstein. Lipstick earns high marks because it protects your lips from sun and wind damage while enhancing their appearance.

"Lip problems occur more frequently in men because they tend to spend more time outdoors— although that's not the case now as much as it used to be," says Dr. Beauregard. "And men don't often take care of their lips—nor do they wear lipstick."

Dr. Pearlstein agrees.

"Women have far fewer problems with their lips because they usually wear lipstick," he says. "I actually encourage women to wear lipstick. And there are cosmetically acceptable alternatives for men *and* women—petroleum jelly, or better yet, greasy, non-pigmented lip creams with a built-in sunscreen ingredient that blocks out damaging sunlight by chemical means."

Lipstick and protective lip creams may also prevent painful, unsightly attacks of herpes simplex— cold sores—that often crop up on or around the lips, according to Dr. Pearlstein. "The herpes simplex virus responsible for cold sores lurks beneath the surface of the skin and lips and can be activated by sun exposure."

Lipstick protects your lips from sun and wind.

Men need lip cream or petroleum jelly.

Wetting Your Lips from the Inside Out

A dry *internal* environment can chap your lips, too, according to dermatology professor Bernard A. Kirshbaum, M.D., of the Medical College of Pennsylvania, in Philadelphia. Many people do not drink enough water and other liquids during the winter because they don't sweat as much so they don't get as thirsty. So to keep lips soft, make a concerted effort to drink more liquids (even if you're not thirsty). And cut back on caffeine-containing beverages such as coffee, tea and cola: You'll lose more fluid than you've gained, because caffeine acts as a diuretic.

In addition to simple chapping, your lips may become split or inflamed if your diet is short on B vitamins—particularly B_2 (riboflavin) and B_6, says Dr. Beauregard, adding that studies show B-vitamin deficiencies are not uncommon in people over age 60. (Almonds and wheat germ are good sources of vitamin B_2; salmon, sunflower seeds, brown rice and bananas are good sources of B_6 and liver and broccoli are rich sources of both.)

If your lips are inflamed but not cracked, perhaps you're not eating enough citrus fruit, green pepper, broccoli, cantaloupe or other rich sources of vitamin C.

Are your lips dry or cracked even if you coat them with lip balm? That's a possible sign of too much vitamin A—or too little. (Five thousand to 25,000 international units [I.U.] per day of vitamin A is plenty to prevent a deficiency.) And few people realize that too much vitamin E—more than 300 I.U. a day—can cause chapped lips in some people, according to Dr. Beauregard.

In a roundabout way, getting enough calcium might help to prevent another problem commonly associated with (but not caused by) aging: thin lips.

"The illusion that lips become thinner in older people is just that—an illusion," says Dr. Pearlstein. "What's really happening is that the configuration of the whole face may be changing. Bones may thin, due to osteoporosis, which affects the entire skeleton. Or people lose their teeth and get dentures, which changes their bite. Either way, the lips may invert, or turn inward, and appear thinner. Also the corners of the mouth may become more angular."

Consequently, preventing osteoporosis and tooth loss—and getting good bridgework, if you need it—can keep your lips looking plump and youthful.

Often, lips not only thin, but also wrinkle. "Whistle lines"—tiny vertical lines around the lips—are almost the exclusive property of older lips. Whistle lines are most pronounced in smokers. Years of pursing the lips to inhale cigarettes accelerates the wrinkling process.

But facial exercises aren't the way to smooth out these lines, no matter what you've heard.

Split or inflamed lips can be signs of vitamin deficiency.

Preventing tooth loss prevents thin lips.

Facial exercises make "whistle lines" worse.

"Facial exercises do not lessen wrinkles around the mouth," says Dr. Pearlstein. "If anything, stretching the mouth—grimacing or otherwise contorting the skin—makes wrinkles *worse.* The only way to erase whistle lines are dermabrasion, chemical peel, collagen injections or silicone injections." (Safe and effective methods of removing wrinkles are discussed in chapter 32.)

A Makeup Artist's Tips for Smoother, Fuller Lips

Whistle lines can be particularly annoying because they act as little canals, allowing lip color to escape from the lips so that it feathers beyond their border. How can you get your lipstick to stay put?

Cosmetics minimize the lines and keep them from worsening.

• Avoid supermoist, glossy lipsticks. So advises Glenn Roberts, creative beauty director for Elizabeth Arden, Inc. "Older women do need moisturizing lipstick—to a point," says Roberts. "The moisturizing ingredients in all lipsticks plump out the tiny dry lines that can cause the 'bleeding' effect. But very moist, wet-look lipsticks can promote feathering."

• Use a lip color base. Lip color bases, such as Lip Fix Creme by Elizabeth Arden (the first of its kind) helps to prevent lipstick from feathering and, used over a period of time, can minimize the tiny vertical lines and prevent them from getting worse, according to Roberts. (Lip Fix Creme prevents feathering by coating the lips with Primilin II, a "secret" ingredient.)

• Look for featherproof lipstick. Another major cosmetic company has addressed the problem of feathering lip color by developing a lipstick that's designed not to bleed. Appropriately enough, it's called Featherproof Lipstick, by Estée Lauder.

• Don't blot your lips. "Today's lipstick formulas do not require blotting to set the color," says Roberts.

Learn new application techniques.

"It's a waste, and can sabotage an otherwise perfect lip color job."

If your makeup, including your lipstick, is poorly applied or out-of-date, it will make you look older, says Roberts.

Other tips for keeping your lips looking attractive and contemporary:

• Outline your lips with a pencil, then fill in lip color with a brush. "This method gives you much more control than applying lip color directly from a lipstick tube," says Roberts. "Start with your lips closed—they will be steadier and firmer."

"This can improve the shape of a less than perfect mouth. Don't try to make your lips much thicker or thinner than they are, though," warns Roberts. "For best results follow the natural lines of your lips."

• Update your color choices. Don't try to hang on to lip colors you wore when you were in your twenties. Skin tone changes over the years and chances are your old favorites are neither up-to-date nor flattering now.

Select flattering new colors.

"In general, brighter, clearer shades of lipstick are most flattering for older complexions," says Roberts. "Least flattering are hot neons and—at the opposite side of the palette—browns. Bright reds are fine, but avoid the dark reds typically worn in the fifties. As for frosted shades, some sheen is flattering. But you don't want to look like you're wearing birthday cake frosting."

Defuzzing Your Upper Lip

Some women feel self-conscious or unfeminine with soft fuzz on their upper lips. Facial hair isn't unusual in women of Mediterranean or Middle Eastern ancestry. But women past menopause often develop a darker or denser growth of hair on their upper lip for the first time in their lives, regardless of their ethnic heritage.

This growth is usually related to hormone changes that accompany menopause. It works like this: From puberty on, men and women alike produce androgens, male hormones responsible for "male pattern" hair growth on the face, chest and lower abdomen. Until menopause, women's ovaries usually produce enough estrogen, the primary "female" hormone, to offset the influence of androgens on hair growth. With the drop in estrogen that heralds menopause (or with the removal of the ovaries

Facial hair growth is related to menopause.

in a total hysterectomy), hair growth on the upper lip may increase. (A *dramatic* increase in facial hair in women at any age calls for a medical evaluation, especially if accompanied by a spurt in hair growth on the breasts or lower abdomen.)

Ways to Remove Unwanted Hair

You don't have to live with a fuzzy upper lip if you don't want to. Here are your options:

Shaving. Technically, there's no reason why women can't shave their faces just as men do. In Japan, women routinely shave their faces once a month, starting in their teens, to keep their faces smooth as a geisha's. It's quick and easy, and contrary to what people believe, shaving will *not* cause hair to grow back darker, thicker or coarser. No, the *real* reason most women think nothing of shaving their legs but don't even consider shaving their faces is probably purely psychological: Shaving the face is a sexually charged grooming ritual—for men. As such, a woman is just as likely to feel unfeminine taking a blade to her upper lip as she would wearing her moustache. And that's a valid reason for choosing another option.

Bleaching. If your hair is very fine and your skin fair, bleaching the hair on your upper lip will solve the problem. If you have dark hair or dark skin, however, you may find that bleaches make hair even more noticeable.

Depilatories. Hair-removing creams or lotions dissolve hair just below skin level. Applied about once a month, depilatories will remove unwanted hair and keep the regrowth tapered and soft. However, even products designed for use on the face contain strong chemicals and can irritate sensitive skin. To avoid problems, try the product on a small patch of skin, preferably at a tender spot like the inside of one elbow the day before you use it. If you are sensitive to it, don't use it. And follow the directions exactly to avoid an unsightly chemical burn. Retest the depilatory each time you use it.

Waxing. Hair-stripping wax has its pros and cons. First dust-on cornstarch, then liquified wax—specially formulated for the job—is applied to the skin.

Shaving could be the answer.

Chemical depilatories require a skin patch test.

When it cools, the wax is stripped off Band-Aid-style, pulling off hairs with it. (Yes, it stings!) While waxing may work well for removing hair on the legs, it may not be the best way to eliminate upper lip hair—mainly because you must let hair regrow to about one-fourth inch before you can repeat the procedure.

Electrolysis. This is the only really permanent hair removal technique. The process involves inserting an extremely fine wire into the hair follicle (the pore from which a hair grows) and zapping it with a tiny charge of electricity to destroy the root. You can expect to feel anything from a slight tingle to enough pain to warrant a shot of Novocaine. Since a certain percentage of hair is dormant at any given time, you may have to return for a follow-up treatment later to destroy that growth.

Electrolysis is the only way to get rid of unwanted hair permanently.

"The results of electrolysis depend much on the skill of the person doing the procedures," says Frank L. Schwartz, M.D., an endocrinologist (specialist in hormone disorders) who published an article on excessive hair growth. Don't use a do-it-yourself home electrolysis kit. You can write to the International Guild of Professional Electrologists, 3209 Premier Drive, Suite 124, Plano, TX 75075. Enclose a stamped, self-addressed return envelope. They will send names of reputable (and sometimes certified) professional electrologists in your area.

The effort expended in upgrading your nutrition, updating your cosmetics and removing unwanted hair will be rewarded. Small improvements in your lips may make a surprisingly big difference in your appearance.

Smoother, plumper lips and a lack of wrinkles contribute to attractiveness and make your whole face look younger.

"We judge the beauty of the face by subtle things," comments Dr. Pearlstein. "In other words, when you look at a larger structure of the body, such as the torso, you notice the overall size and shape. But you look at the face more closely. It's the details—smooth surface, smooth lips and lack of wrinkles, scars or other distractions—that contribute to attractiveness."

37

Caring for

Your Nails

People of all races, creeds and religions share similar problems when it comes to their nails.

I n Miami, Florida, a sprawling metropolis teeming with new settlers representing a dizzying array of races, creeds and religions, there are few common threads that enable residents to interact across the wide ethnic barriers.

One thread that exists is their fingernails. Whether they are voodoo priests from Haiti, dreadlock-crowned Rastafarians from Jamaica, refugees from any number of politically unstable South American countries or Russian Jews, they all share the same mass of hard protein on the tips of their fingers.

Concern for their nails brings many of them to the same house in South Miami where master cosmetologist Zobe Peon and her colleague Laudelina Prieto hold court. The attraction is a secret nail hardener that enables working women from all economic backgrounds to grow sturdy, catlike nails that can withstand everything from the chemical assault of cleaning fluids to the bangs and clicks of typewriters, computers and adding machines, not to mention the scrapes and bumps of a postwork game of racquetball or beachfront volleyball.

Unfortunately, these two Cuban nail specialists (Peon is also a much sought after beautician) won't

Nail Down These Facts

Kenneth Arndt, M.D., chief of the dermatology department at Beth Israel Hospital, in Boston, and a professor at Harvard Medical School, offers these insights into the nail.

"A nail grows constantly, unlike a hair, which tends to rest for a while. On the average, a fingernail grows one-tenth of a millimeter each day, which adds up to one-eighth of an inch a month or one inch in eight months. Nobody knows why, but the longer the finger, the faster its nail will grow. Thus, the middle fingernail grows fastest, whereas nails on the thumb and pinkie are slower. Toenails grow only one-third to one-half as fast as fingernails.

"The nail itself is about half a millimeter thick. It is made up of tough protein, known as keratin, which is also the main component of hair and the outer layer of skin. The nail is not alive, in the sense that it does not contain living cells."

reveal their "secret formula." But they have agreed to unveil their overall nail care program, one that they admit plays a greater role in maintaining beautiful nails than their secret hardening lotion.

The "Miami Nice" Nail Formula

Here are some specific tips from the pros:

Filing. "The most important aspect of good nail care is the way you file your nails," Peon says. "File nails square, not round, so if they chip or break, you can save the nail. Square nails will grow in correctly, and they won't turn in at the edges. File gently across, in a line. Use an emery board. Don't use a metal file. You want to sculpt your nails, not saw them off!"

Correct filing techniques are the most important key to beautiful and healthy nails.

Hardeners. "The key here is restraint," Prieto says. "Hardeners or other nail strengtheners should not be used weekly. If your nails are really brittle, apply a hardener every other week until they become stronger. Good nails need a hardener only once a month."

Hardeners should be used only once a month.

Commercial hardeners are readily available, including hypoallergenic nail products which use an alkyl-polyester resin in place of the more common formaldehyde ingredient.

Polish. "Small touch-ups are O.K., but never repaint your nails by putting new nail polish over old nail polish. That strains your nails," Peon says. "Women with hard nails don't need to use clear base first, a common mistake. A double layer of polish places an unnecessary burden on the nails. The exception is if you use a frosted type of nail polish. These are the polishes which have a pearly consistency rather than a slick shine, and can include glittery metallic flakes. Frosted polishes are tougher on the nails and can dry them, so they should never be applied directly to the nail."

Kenneth Arndt, M.D., chief of the dermatology department at Beth Israel Hospital, in Boston, explains why.

Nails are permeable to fluids and can easily be damaged by them.

"Although nails look tough and are physically hard, they are extremely permeable to water or solvents. Water can move through a fingernail 100 times faster than it can penetrate the outer layer of skin. Because nails are so porous, they can be injured by fluid."

Long-lasting Polish. If you want the polish to last and remain free of chips, Peon says you should leave unpolished a minute strip along the edge of each nail. Do this by delicately using a cotton-tipped orange stick and nail polish remover to wipe away the polish while it's still wet. You can also do this by gently rubbing the inside of your thumb across the edge of the wet nail. This uncovered edge will not only prevent chips, but also looks pretty.

Another expert recommends touching up chipped nail polish instead of removing it to save the beating of polish removers on your nails.

Rest. "You should leave your nails completely polish-free for two or three days a month," Prieto says. "This allows your nails to breathe. If you use polish all the time, the nails will turn yellow."

Washing Dishes. Never wash dishes in very hot water, the Cuban experts say. Hot water dries out the nails. Wear cotton-lined plastic gloves when doing the dishes and when using any household cleaners, especially scouring cleaners.

Buy a dishwasher or wear cotton-lined plastic gloves.

Dr. Arndt explains that extreme nail permeability is the problem again, and this is why bartenders, surgeons, cooks, swimmers, homemakers and others whose hands are moist a good deal of the time are very likely to complain of nails that split or break near the end.

Cream. "Use lots of hand cream around the nails and cuticles, especially after your nails have been subjected to water and other liquids," Peon says.

Split Nails. This clothes-snagging affliction is caused by dryness or trauma. Gently file out the split as soon as possible. "Both men and women should carry an emery board at all times for emergencies," Peon says. "A split can catch on something and rip the nail. If your nails are prone to splits, warm some baby oil or olive oil and rub it gently into the nail and cuticle area."

Arnold W. Klein, M.D., and James H. Sternberg, M.D., coauthors with Paul Bernstein of *The Skin Book* (MacMillan) agree that olive oil is a good overall nail treatment.

"If you do not use nail polish (listen up men), care for your nails by soaking them first in warm water and then in warm olive oil. After soaking them in the olive oil, pat the nails dry and apply a moisturizer," the authors advise.

Keep an emery board handy to immediately file out splits.

Aging Nails

"As you age, your nails either get very weak or very hard," Peon says. "Either way, you need to use hand creams three or four times a day to moisturize them and enable them to return to their former condition."

Dr. Arndt adds that nails grow more slowly as you age, and almost stop growing altogether during periods of major illness. The result of such slow growth often is a groove running crossways on all ten fingernails. Only camouflage will help. Polish the nails and wait until the grooves grow out. Pregnancy and excessive thyroid hormone can make nails grow faster, Dr. Arndt says.

To cut your toenails, "first soak your feet for about 15 minutes in warm water," Peon says. "Then pat dry, and while the nails are soft, clip them straight across. Wait a few minutes to allow the nails

Nails grow more slowly as you age, and can stop altogether during periods of illness.

Soak your feet in warm water before cutting your toenails.

to reharden, then file down the sharp edges. You should have a professional pedicure once a month to keep your toenails looking their best."

"Manicures are vital to beautiful nails," Peon stresses. "You should have a manicure once a week, one that includes soaking your nails in heated oil."

The Beverly Hills Manicure

While Prieto charges only $4 for a manicure and $10 for a pedicure, some ritzy salons in Beverly Hills charge as much as $40 and $100. If you don't live near an economical master cosmetologist, here's how to give yourself a Beverly Hills-style manicure.

1. Remove old polish with a conditioning non-acetone polish remover and cotton balls. Don't do this more than once a week because polish remover dries out the nails.

Don't overuse polish removers. They can dry out your nails.

2. File to shape using the proper techniques mentioned above.

3. Put a teaspoon of baby shampoo into a bowl of lukewarm water and soak your fingertips for about two minutes. Scrub lightly with a nailbrush, rinse, pat dry, then gently push each cuticle back with a towel. Afterwards, massage hand cream into the cuticle, sides and base of each nail. Next, with a cloth or orange stick wrapped in cotton, gently push back your cuticles again.

4. Lightly buff diagonally across the nail with a chamois buffer. Buff in one direction only, using long, even strokes. You can use cream while buffing, but make sure it's completely nonabrasive. If your nails heat up, you are buffing too hard and creating friction. Lighten up.

Buff in one direction only, using long, even strokes.

5. If your nails tend to split at the ends, polish them to provide a bit of added protection.

Nutrition and Nails

Will protein gelatin supplements make your nails grow stronger? That popular belief has spurred arguments in medical circles for years.

"No particular food or nutrient you consume will force your nails to grow differently from their usual way," Dr. Arndt states. "Of course, if you have been badly malnourished your nails will have suffered right along with the rest of your body. Resuming a normal diet will correct that, but adding supplements to an otherwise healthy diet won't make any difference."

Herbert A. Luscombe, M.D., professor and chairman of the department of dermatology at Jefferson Medical College, Thomas Jefferson University, in Philadelphia, disagrees. He says different people have different reactions.

The question of nutrition remains controversial.

"Gelatin does work for some people," Dr. Luscombe says. "Usually, if the nails are going to respond, they will do so within six months. Otherwise, the gelatin is probably not going to have any effect."

The Technicolor Nightmare

If you notice that your unpainted nails seem to be producing a color of their own, beware. The nails mirror the condition of the body. Discolorations can signal trouble. Here are some things to look out for.

Discoloration can signal problems in other areas of the body.

• Unusually white nails. "This may indicate that the person is anemic," warns Dr. Luscombe. An opaque nail could indicate cirrhosis of the liver, adds Dr. Arndt.
• Blue-tinted nails. "This can indicate that a person's lungs or heart are not working properly," says Dr. Luscombe. Dr. Arndt says poisoning with excess copper or silver can also make the nails bluish.
• Nails that are red near the tip, white across the base. Chronic kidney disease can be telegraphed by these colors, according to Dr. Arndt.

In addition, the doctors say iron deficiency can cause concave, spoonshaped nails; psoriasis can cause round pits to appear in the nails; an overactive thyroid may cause the nails to separate from the underlying skin; prolonged oxygen deficiency due to lung or heart disease often causes the nails to get a "clubbed" shape and feel squishy when you press the base and prolonged use of the antibiotic tetracycline can cause the ends of the nails to become detached.

If you notice any unusual colorations or structure problems in your nails, see a doctor at once. Don't try and cover it up with polish.

38

Skin: Its Care and Feeding

How you treat yourself shows on your skin.

I t is the largest organ in the human body, and it weighs twice as much as the brain. It weighs in at around six pounds and stretches over 18 square feet. It's involved in keeping your body warm and in cooling it off. It takes in oxygen and it excretes waste. It manufactures hair, nails and vitamin D. It's how you stay in touch with the world. Through it you communicate love, caring, sexuality. And its appearance tells the world a lot about you. We're talking, of course, about the skin. *Your* skin. Hopefully, your *beautiful* skin.

"Glowing" is the word most frequently used to describe beautiful skin. Provoking an image of an ember, it suggests the radiation of warmth, light and color from within. And that's a wonderful way to think about the way your skin works. Because the beauty of your skin does radiate from within. What you eat, what you do, how and how much you sleep determine how your skin looks. Your skin becomes a letter to the world that communicates how you treat yourself.

Do you survive on a diet of potato chips and soft drinks? Did the tequila sunrises cause *you* to set last night? Is your idea of a workout walking from the car to the doughnut store? Do you have to consult the dictionary to learn the meaning of the verb "to sleep?" Your skin knows all about it.

But before you read about all the good things you can do to make your skin more attractive—from the inside out and the outside in—you should recall a warning about the one thing you *mustn't* do.

Sun Worshipping

If you haven't heeded the warnings about the harm the sun can do the skin, start now. Here's why: The sun is the number one cause of wrinkling, pigment changes and skin cancer. That's the opinion of many skin experts.

"But until I was 20, I spent every moment I could at the beach soaking up sun . . . Had I gone on this way, I could have passed for a century-old peasant woman by the time I reached 30," says Jane Ogle, a former Vogue editor and the author of *Ageproofing* (New American Library), now in her practically wrinkle-free sixth decade.

When you are in the sun, your skin produces melanin—the color that gives you a tan in an effort to protect itself. And melanin does provide some protection from sun damage. That's the reason dark, thick, oily skin gets fewer wrinkles than badly sun-damaged fair skin.

A tan is the way the skin tries to protect itself.

When melanin patches are found in clumps, one result of sunning may be freckles. In older people, exposure to the sun too often yields those brown patches known as age or liver spots. These are the result of shifts in melanin production and have nothing to do with the liver. Once acquired, they can be a real nuisance to get rid of, so it's best to avoid them—by avoiding too much sun—from the beginning.

The sun's rays also penetrate deep into your skin and play havoc with the collagen network, the usually springy web of fibers that give support and strength to skin. This damage may be difficult, if not impossible, to heal. And don't forget the link between the sun and skin cancer.

The sun can damage the internal structure of your skin.

Does this mean happy days at the beach are behind you? It need not. But it certainly does mean that you have strong motivation to avoid sunburns and deep tans. And that may not be as difficult as you might imagine.

Modern sunscreen products are easy to apply, nonmessy and provide protection for hours. PABA is one of the active ingredients to look for. It's offered in different concentrations that earn various sun protection factor (SPF) ratings. An SPF of 15 provides an almost total sun block and might be just right for your delicate facial skin.

Cosmetic companies are also offering makeup, like foundation liquids, with built-in sunscreens. So at the same time that you are smoothing out your facial tones, you are helping your skin stay young. What better excuse to look glamorous at the beach!

Smoking is another major no-no for young-looking skin. One plastic surgeon says that women who smoke get more and deeper wrinkles all over their faces than do nonsmokers.

The Basics of Younger Skin

How does Johnny Carson, now in his sixties, stay so youthful? Ask his makeup man, Harry Blake, formerly NBC's chief makeup man on the West coast for 15 years and now the artist who prepares Carson and some of his guests for the "Tonight" show. "He keeps in good physical condition. He plays tennis. He has an active life-style. An active life-style and a good physical appearance go hand in hand," says the man who has been counseling the stars on their looks for decades.

Physical activity helps keep you young. It's as simple as that. Your skin can only be as handsome as what's within. It's bound to look more attractive draped across a lean, well-defined body than it is outlining some lumpy souvenirs on your hips of too many roast beef and gravy dinners and too few long walks. Don't rush to lose weight, though. Take it off slowly. Yo-yo dieting is one of the worst wrongs you can do your skin.

Everyone knows that exercise gives you a glow. And scientists say they have evidence that exercise has especially important benefits for the skin. Comparing middle-aged athletes with a matched group of sedentary people, they found the athletes' skin denser, thicker and stronger, with a significantly better elastic quality. That's not surprising when you

Athletes' skin is thicker and stronger, with better elastic quality.

consider that exercise flushes the skin, bringing blood rich in oxygen just where you'd most like it to go. And it may be that collagen production is enhanced by internally generated heat—an effect you can't get by applying heat from the outside. Movement itself seems also to send messages to the fibroblast cells, manufacturing plants for the skin's elastic fibers, that they need to make more.

Your skin color should improve as you follow an exercise plan, and one study shows working out may even eliminate the bags under your eyes.

Your Skin's Nourishment Needs

A baby's skin is soft, tender and dewy—it has a quality of moistness. (And not just when the baby needs to be changed!) And it is a lack of this moistness, aggravated by the repeated drying out of your skin year after year by indoor heating, too-hot baths, icy winds and sun exposure that is one principle reason your skin differs from that of a baby. To illustrate the impact of the sun on the skin, one dermatologist points to the skin in the protected areas on the inside of the upper arm or on the bottom of a woman's breast.

Your skin needs protection and moisture.

Taking Care of the Outside

Every person walks around in a little cloud of the discarded skin cells the body is constantly shedding. Though this may not create an enticing image, it is accurate, and graphically illustrates part of the way skin works. Constantly renewing itself, the lower, living levels of skin multiply and push older, dead cells toward the surface to form the outer skin. Medical people call this the *stratum corneum*. That's Latin for "horny layer."

Your skin renews itself every 30 days or so.

Your skin entirely renews itself every 30 days or so. But one of the things that happens as you age is that this renewal rate slows. This is one of the reasons the skin may lose its fresh look as the years add up. Another thing that happens to aging skin is that it secretes less oil. While this generally means fewer pimples, it also means skin loses internally generated moisture faster.

Water is the source of skin's moistness, and oilier younger skin holds on to it better. Thus all the conditions that are drying to the skin—excessive exposure to the sun, hot baths, desert climates, contact with detergents and dry indoor air—dry out older skin faster than younger.

Dried-out skin looks dull and flat and is prone to wrinkling. Just like a dry piece of paper, it will form a thousand creases when crumpled, while moist paper (or skin) will not easily retain a fold.

What this comes down to is that a major challenge of dealing with older skin is to balance keeping its surface clean and well scrubbed, removing damaged skin cells and stimulating blood circulation, without depleting its ability to retain moistness.

> **The trick is to scrub the skin without impairing its ability to hold moisture.**

When she turned 40, Jane Ogle visited a dermatologist popular with the fashionable set. She thought it time to arm herself against the ravages of age on skin.

After examining her, the fancy dermatologist asked her what she used on her face. "Just soap and water," she replied sheepishly.

"No wonder you have such good skin," was his response.

Ms. Ogle offers the story to illustrate her opinion that the best things for your skin are also the simplest. After you have done your best for your skin internally by exercising and eating right, skin care should be easy. Cleanse, exfoliate, moisturize—those are the three magic words for skin care.

> **Cleanse, exfoliate, moisturize—those are the three magic words.**

Rub-a-Dub-Dub

Whether it's 100 percent pure, hard milled and lavender scented or translucent, some people choose soap to clean their skin. But be alert to the reaction of your skin to your soap of choice. Some people find heavily perfumed soaps irritating. Deodorant soaps may also be bothersome to sensitive skin. Since soap is supposed to be completely rinsed off your skin—a residue can dry the skin—the question is, why add these ingredients to soap at all, only to send them down the drain?

At least one beauty expert warns against the use of any soap, no matter how mild and pure, on the face. They can be drying, cautions makeup artist

Jeffrey Bruce, author of *About Face: An Hour a Week to Radiant Skin and Flawless Make-Up* (Putnam). He advocates the use of a nonsoapy cosmetic cleanser containing no alcohol or grains, followed by a toner or astringent.

To follow the Bruce method you would apply the cleanser to your face. Let it stay on for a minute or two while you brush your teeth or do some other small chore. Then wipe it off with a tissue. Follow up with a warm wash cloth. Then pat on an astringent or toner with a cotton ball.

Tonics like astringents, toners and fresheners remove the last traces of dirt, soap or cleansing cream. But astringents can contain large proportions of witch hazel or alcohol, which may be harmful to dry or sensitive skin. A clarifying lotion is a tonic which dissolves dry, dead cells from the skin's surface. If you want to follow this routine, just be sure to choose a product designed for your skin type; mild for normal skin, stronger for oily skin. You are taking care of your one and only face, after all.

If, on the other hand, you choose to stay with plain (or fancy) soap, take the extra few seconds necessary to be sure you've rinsed thoroughly. Three rinses is not enough. Count ten rinses to be sure you've freed your face of residue. Of course, use a toner or astringent after cleansing with soap, too.

When rinsing, count to ten.

If you follow the Bruce method, exfoliation should be part of your facial cleansing routine, two or three times a week. Exfoliation is a long word for removing some of the dead cells on the surface of your skin. It can be accomplished with a cosmetic buffing sponge or a grainy cleanser. (Take care not to scrub too briskly—you could buff your skin to glowing rawness.) This procedure can give skin newer, fresher, plumper, younger-looking characteristics. And it's possible that it may encourage faster cell renewal.

Exfoliation can give skin a younger, fresher look.

Masques are a fun way to accomplish some of these good things for your skin. You can use either a masque which rinses off or one that peels off. A masque is the heart of the salon facial, a procedure which may set you back $35. By putting on your own masque you can save almost all that money to spend on other indulgences.

Besides helping your skin to exfoliate—shed its dead outer cells in an orderly manner, a process that keeps it looking fresh and vital—masques also stimulate your skin's circulation. And some masques seem to help the skin hold moisture better, at least temporarily.

But unplug the phone before you put one on, suggests Jeffrey Bruce. Not only do you want your time with the masque to be relaxing—you don't want to upset callers, who'll assume you have an advanced case of lockjaw as you try to form words.

Last, but far from least, is moisturizing. "Rub lotions on yourself constantly" is the advice of a stunningly beautiful model in her early forties who has kept her skin flawless. Of course, not even she can follow her own advice perfectly, but you get the point. But remember, *over*-moisturizing your face can clog pores, and people with oily skin only need to moisturize areas that are dry.

Use a moisturizer to help seal wetness into the skin.

Many moisturizers are available on the market. They contain mineral oil, lanolin or other forms of oil to help seal wetness into the skin. The drier your skin, the thicker the cream should be. And if you have sensitive skin, you may wish to avoid products containing perfumes.

Don't neglect your body. Soothe dry skin on the arms, legs, neck or wherever it feels tight. Right after you step out of your shower is the best time to apply moisturizers. Then you can seal in a little bonus wetness from the bath.

No Skin Miracles

People want so fervently to look younger that even the most sophisticated will occasionally fall for an outlandish claim about the rejuvenating, wrinkle-removing effects of some cosmetic product. Common sense should indicate that if the product being touted by the famous doctor really worked, he himself would not look so old and the makeup company president would not still be using photos of herself taken in 1955. But the will to believe is so strong, common sense often goes out the window.

In sophisticated, knowing New York, people pay more than $50 for a "chicken placenta" masque!

Skin Scams

The buzz words in the beauty biz these days are *anti-aging, rejuvenation* and *cellular renewal.* And what the products bearing these words have in common, commented one cosmetic expert, is that they all represent the concept of "hope in a jar."

The truth is that these so-called state-of-the-art skin products simply moisturize the skin, plumping it up so lines and creases are less noticeable. But removing or reversing the tracks of time is something no skin cream can do, no matter how high-tech sounding its name.

What about all those special wrinkle-fighting ingredients in the supercream formulas? Many skin creams claim to make skin behave like younger skin because they contain a substance normally found in the skin which, supposedly, can penetrate it and rejuvenate it. One such ingredient is collagen, the connective tissue that holds your skin taut but breaks down over time, causing the skin to sag.

Collagen is commercially manufactured from animal protein and included in skin creams with the idea that it will enhance the production of your own collagen. The trouble is, collagen molecules are simply too large to be absorbed topically by your skin. "It's like trying to get an elephant into a house," explains New York dermatologist Norman Orentreich, M.D.

Other anti-aging skin formulas include the genetic coding material, RNA and DNA, superoxide dismutase and the latest, glycosphingolipid (GSL), which one cosmetic company claims can rejuvenate cells. None of them have any effect on your body's internal chemistry. "It's like rubbing blood on your skin if you need a blood transfusion," says Dr. Orentreich.

And what does the government think about the latest line removers? According to the Food and Drug Administration, if they alter the structure or function of the skin, they become regarded as drugs, not cosmetics. Manufacturers would then have to submit data to demonstrate that these products were safe and performed their intended function—something not now required of cosmetics.

So it seems the only line these products can really improve is the bottom line of cosmetic companies.

**Bees, minks, quail—
people try anything.**

Equally exorbitant prices are regularly shelled out for such silliness as quail egg omelettes for the face, seaweed cleansers, moisturizers containing bee jelly and oils squeezed from turtles, sharks and minks. Do these products perform the age-retarding, wrinkle-stopping miracles their ads hint at? You probably know the answer.

Again and again, beauty experts with nothing to sell say there are no miracle creams, lotions or potions. But there is something that can work a near miracle with skin. And that something is makeup.

"I've seen Sophia Loren without her makeup, and believe me, she doesn't look so hot," states Jeffrey Bruce. He offers that opinion in support of his argument that as you age, you need more, not less, makeup, more artfully applied.

**Makeup improves on
nature.**

But what if you prefer a natural, unmade-up look? It takes a lot of makeup to create that look on the magazine models you see wearing it, counters Bruce. They pack ten-pound makeup cases, he says. What you'll achieve if you leave your looks to nature is too often simply a dull look.

"Makeup can create the illusion of youth," affirms Harry Blake. You can use makeup to narrow a nose, remove a double chin and hide skin blemishes, he says.

You may be able to wear more makeup and get more benefit from it—without looking "made up"—than you may have guessed, the experts say.

And increasingly, it is not just women who want to know how to make their skin beautiful. "If appearance matters in a man's job, it behooves him to look his best," says Blake, who has provided the makeup for such masculine stars as Dean Martin, Bob Hope and Gene Kelly. A bit of concealer under the eyes to hide dark circles is a bit of makeup more and more men choose to use, he says.

Both sexes turn to makeup to look more youthful. But you do not have to be young to look young.

**Mature women can be
gorgeous.**

In the words of Jeffrey Bruce, "There is nothing more gorgeous, more appealing, than a ripened woman who has grown accustomed to her face. She isn't trying to compete with starlets when she skillfully brings out the seasoned sensuality she's earned." And the artist adds, "Beauty does *not* belong to the young. Pretty paint and wise skin care can transform dull maturity into *great* sophistication."

If you are a seasoned woman, how can you know what kinds and amounts of makeup to wear? Many experts will tell you firmly that mature skin and features should follow the "less is more" rule. Innovator Jeffrey Bruce advises older women to wear *more* makeup. And one well-known artist would like to see businessmen wear dark gray eyeliner underneath the top eyelashes to make their eyes look brighter, sharper and larger!

The bottom line is that it is a matter of personal style, and the best look for you can only be arrived at by bold experimentation. Most makeup professionals warn older women away from heavy eyeliner, for instance. But Sophia Loren, now in her fifties, wears tons of it and her beauty is recognized around the world.

If you're not Sophia, heavy eyeliner may not be for you.

Another 50-plus beauty, Joan Collins of "Dynasty" fame, also wears heavy eye makeup. "She has a look," says Blake. "But that look might not work for everyone."

The only way to really know if something will work for you is to try it. Of course, you can do this in the privacy of your makeup mirror. Here's how to start:

If your skin is oily, you may want to use a water-based foundation near your own skin color which gives a matte finish and helps avoid shine. But dry skin may look more beautiful smoothed out with an oil-based makeup. Or you can try a liquid that promises a satin finish, somewhere between flat and shiny.

If you find that your foundation collects in and accentuates lines in your face, particularly after a few hours of wear, you can try several remedies. The first would be to use slightly less. Sometimes you can get a thin, even application with a makeup sponge, an inexpensive item available in any dimestore. Switching brands is also worth trying. And some women, including some over forty, prefer to use only a light application of a pressed foundation put on with a slightly damp sponge.

Try a makeup sponge to smooth foundation.

The second step in creating a glamorous face is to apply concealer. A concealing makeup provides a heavier cover for dark circles under your eyes, dark skin patches, freckles or blemishes. Concealer will stay in place better and look less obvious if you put it on after your liquid foundation, says Jeffrey Bruce.

Next comes the step which makes you the Van Gogh of the makeup table. It is the placement of highlights and shadows. And it is the technique which makeup artists agree is the very heart of their art. The tools you need are a foundation a shade or two lighter than your own and a foundation a shade or two darker, or a darker contouring powder and brush—and patience and good lighting.

Learn the art of contouring.

Although you will be able to see what exciting and dramatic difference contour shadowing and highlighting can make in your face the first time you try them, it takes a while to build the skill to make your results look natural.

To begin, first examine your face closely. What is the best spot to highlight on your cheekbone? Does a too wide forehead need to be narrowed by some shading at the sides? Can highlighter make the creases from nose to mouth less obvious? Will dark contouring along the bottom of your jawline erase sags and make double chins vanish? Apply the makeup, being sure to blend it well so no lines are obvious.

"You want people to say, 'That's a pretty face,' not 'That's pretty makeup,' " says Blake.

If your results are good in one area, bad in another or too uneven, blotchy, obvious or undramatic, there's a simple remedy: Wash it off and begin again. Even once you think you've got it down, it pays to repeat the whole process a few times so that putting on your makeup becomes almost second nature. Through practice, you will learn to do it quickly and expertly.

Critique your makeup with an eye to keeping it up to date.

But don't let it become too rote. If you're not in the habit of giving your makeup a critical scrutiny at regular intervals, find a way of reminding yourself to do so. Keeping your makeup up to date is an important way of keeping your look young.

After you've styled your face with foundation, concealer, highlights and shadows, put on your eye makeup, lipliner, lipstick and blush. (Helpful directions for making up eyes and lips are found in chapters 33 and 36.)

Blush can add life and interest to a face of any age. But don't overdo it. Avoid clown circles in the middle of the cheeks.

You can apply blush discreetly on any of several areas on your face. A light coating across the tops of the cheeks can give a natural, sun-warmed look. A lamb chop shape under cheekbones and rising onto cheeks may add sophistication. As you work on achieving your special look, try a small amount of blush in several different areas. Even a tiny amount on the chin or forehead may help bring your face alive.

You'll also want to experiment with different formulas—creams versus brush-ons, for instance, and with various colors. But older women will do best to stick to colors like soft burgundy, rust and coral to avoid calling attention to any increased sallowness in their skin. A dusting of translucent powder applied with a sable brush sets and finishes your artistry.

Mature women look best in shades of burgundy, rust or coral.

Again, try not to fall into an unvarying routine with your makeup. Almost everyone's complexion changes, depending on weather, health, exercise, sleep and fresh air. Try to assess what looks best today, instead of just wearing what looked good yesterday.

Solving Skin Dilemmas

You can't fool Mother Nature, and you can't fool your skin. It knows if you've been worrying too much or holding a grudge—*angry* red blotches aren't called that for nothing, you know. And your skin knows if you've been living on sour cream and onion potato chips, skimping on sleep, skipping aerobics class, neglecting to remove makeup at night and forgetting the sunscreen when outdoors.

Worse, your skin not only knows all your sins, it tells the world. But you don't have to sit back passively while your skin blabs away about you. While you're taking vows about changing your ways, here are some solutions to common skin problems:

• Dry skin. Regular moisturizing with creams and lotions is the answer. Upping your water intake will help, too. If these methods still leave you flaking, see chapter 27 for more tips.

- Wrinkles. No, there aren't any miracles. But the wrinkle sticks sold by some cosmetic companies can help obscure fine lines by temporarily irritating the tissues, causing them to swell and puff out minor wrinkles.
- Age or liver spots. Bleach creams work so slowly, often taking a period of months to show any results—you'll wonder if they're working at all. Another solution is to use a concealer to hide them if you find them disfiguring. Do take care to avoid sun, which probably helped them form in the first place. If the spots trouble you a great deal, see chapter 32 to read about cosmetic surgery techniques which may give more permanent results.

39

Teeth:

Beauty Restored

A re you still flashing that broken front tooth you chipped when you fell off your bike as a kid? Your gap-toothed grin may have looked cute when you were 12, but now that you're all grown up, it may no longer look quite so adorable.

Perhaps your teeth are intact but losing their sparkle. Like ivories on a not-so-new piano, older teeth can yellow and darken over time, especially if you smoke or drink a lot of coffee or tea.

Or maybe your teeth have slowly drifted out of line. As the skeleton ages, imperceptible changes in the jawbone can cause teeth to tilt or stray. One pivots a bit. The other juts out. Gradual drifting can also leave noticeable spaces between teeth that once abutted each other snugly.

Even if you've taken good care of your teeth and gums over the years and have an essentially healthy mouth, unsightly dental flaws can turn your otherwise warm and winning smile into a scowl. A mouth full of worn, mottled, crooked or chipped teeth can make *anyone* look older than they really are.

Your teeth can make you look older than you are.

But there's a solution to this problem: cosmetic dentistry. No, that doesn't mean mascara on your molars. It means polishing and repositioning, special plastics for braces and coatings—a wide variety of techniques that can restore your mouth to its youthful sheen. And even make you feel and look younger.

465

Many people are surprised to learn that certain dental procedures performed entirely inside the mouth can make their face look younger.

"Did you know, for example, that the loss of back teeth can contribute to an aging face?" asks Ronald E. Goldstein, D.D.S., in his book, *Change Your Smile* (Quintessence). "It's true. The teeth and bone structure form the underpinnings for the mouth and surrounding tissue. When that framework is not completely aligned and the bottom teeth do not meet with the top teeth with exact precision, then the area around the mouth can lose its tone and therefore its shape. This causes a drooping effect that can give an aged appearance.

"During 28 years in cosmetic dentistry, I have seen how more attractive smiles have dramatically improved my patients' self-images. They feel like smiling, and stained or crooked teeth won't stop them anymore."

Wizardry the Tooth Fairy Never Knew

All but the worst teeth can be restored or re-modeled.

Many people with badly stained or chipped teeth incorrectly assume that pulling them out is the only answer. People with crooked teeth may not consider having them straightened because they think braces are for kids alone. Both notions are incorrect. Dentists can restore or remodel all but the most delinquent teeth, sometimes in one inexpensive, painless appointment.

Cleaning, Polishing and Bleaching

All toothpastes are abrasive and some can remove minor stains. However only professional cleaning, usually done by a dental hygienist, can remove stains caused by coffee, tea or smoking—stubborn stains that tend to accumulate near the gum line. Dr. Goldstein cautions against using commercial abrasives such as smoker's toothpastes without the guidance of your dentist. Even though smoker's toothpastes may be no more abrasive than regular toothpaste, scrubbing too aggressively with commercial abrasives can wear down the enamel, especially if you've already lost considerable enamel

Seven Steps to a More Youthful Smile

Ronald E. Goldstein, D.D.S., cofounder of the American Academy of Esthetic Dentistry, offers these tips for preventing your teeth from growing old before their time.

1. Don't clench or grind your teeth. These habits accelerate natural wear and tear, prematurely aging the smile.

2. Avoid bone and gum loss. Spaces between the teeth can give an older look to the smile. Take proper oral hygiene seriously and request frequent periodontal evaluation from your dentist.

3. Replace fillings when necessary.

4. Don't let your crowns or bridges age you. If they are worn down, replace them.

5. Have any discolored teeth corrected. Staining makes you look older.

6. Replace any missing teeth as soon as possible. Missing teeth can cause your bite to collapse and tissues to sag.

7. Correct your bad bite. As you age, the bad bite tends to become more pronounced. It's never too late to have it corrected!

Adapted with permission from *Change Your Smile* by Ronald E. Goldstein, D.D.S. (copyright 1984 by Quintessence Publishing Co., Inc.)

---

through wear and tear, exposing the dentin or cementum underneath and jeopardizing the health of the tooth.

Dental professionals scrub away stains and plaque with either powdered pumice stone or a device known as the Prophy Jet, which sandblasts the tooth surface with baking soda. Teeth are then polished to a high gloss to discourage deposits and reflect light, giving them a pearly appearance.

Polished teeth look pearly—and may resist stains.

Don't worry that professional cleaning and polishing will harm your teeth.

"We remove only a few microns' depth of enamel," Dr. Goldstein says reassuringly. "I've never seen tooth enamel damaged by judicious polishings by either the hygienist or dentist."

Some people's teeth stain more easily than others' and may need three or four professional

Some people may need their teeth cleaned three or four times a year.

cleanings a year instead of two, as usually recommended. Eating habits play a big role.

"Consuming too many oranges, too much grapefruit juice or other highly acidic foods and beverages can erode enamel, leaving tiny pits or grooves that accumulate deposits," says Dr. Goldstein. "So can hairline fractures caused by chewing ice or hard candy."

Bleaching is a quick way to whiten yellow teeth.

Stains that can't be scrubbed away can sometimes be bleached. The dentist applies a strong oxidizing agent, activated by heat or light. Bleaching can whiten as many as 10 to 12 teeth at one time, without anesthesia.

"Teeth that have yellowed with age can many times be whitened with bleaching," says Dr. Goldstein. "Why bond or put crowns on ten discolored teeth when you can bleach them for a fraction of the time and money?" He advises to first try bleaching if your dentist suggests it might work and if after three treatments it is not working, then you can always elect to bond or crown the teeth.

Bonding can cover unsightly stains left by antibiotics taken in childhood.

Teeth that are blue-gray due to extensive silver fillings or darkened by stains ingrained in the tooth (such as those caused by taking tetracycline or other drugs during childhood) may not respond as well to bleaching. And extensive stubborn stains call for close investigation. A darker-than-usual tooth could be caused by an injured or dead nerve, in which case root canal treatment (discussed in chapter 22) may be necessary to save the tooth before the dentist can consider bleaching or other cosmetic treatment.

Bonding: A Facelift for Your Teeth

If a tooth is badly discolored, pitted or chipped, composit resin bonding may be the answer. To bond teeth, the dentist first etches the surface with a mild acid gel or liquid, then applies a plastic veneer that covers the flaws. Skilled dentists can apply the veneer in thin layers of subtle, varying shades, to look like natural tooth enamel. Newer, stronger bonding materials can also be used to reconstruct missing tooth structure and fill in large chips, deep grooves or gaps between teeth.

Bonding may last anywhere from about three to

eight years, depending on how well you take care of your teeth. Don't bite your nails, chew on ice, crack nuts with your teeth or otherwise use your teeth as a tool. The force can crack the bonded surface.

Treated with care, bonding may last for several years.

"You can still eat apples and other chewy foods after your teeth are bonded," says Dr. Goldstein. "But pamper your teeth. Instead of biting into an apple with your front teeth, cut it up and chew with your back teeth, to avoid unnecessary strain."

Bonded teeth stain more easily than enamel or porcelain does, so you should probably have your teeth cleaned three or four times a year. "Try to avoid or keep to a minimum coffee, tea, soy sauce, cola drinks, blueberries and fresh cherries," says Dr. Goldstein. "And don't smoke!"

Needless to say, you should also brush your teeth thoroughly and floss regularly to prevent cavities and gum disease, just as you would with unbonded teeth.

Contouring Can "Straighten" Some Teeth

If your teeth are only slightly crooked, or if some are considerably longer than others, cosmetic contouring may "straighten the fence" by minimizing irregularities.

"Cosmetic contouring reshapes teeth to achieve the illusion that they're straight," explains Dr. Goldstein. "If one tooth juts out a bit or overlaps its neighbor, artistically filing it can give the illusion that the teeth are straight."

Cosmetic contouring can make teeth appear straight and properly aligned.

"Ninety percent of the people who come into my office could benefit from some kind of straightening technique," says Dr. Goldstein. "If their teeth are only slightly out of line, cosmetic contouring may be all that's required. Sometimes we combine contouring with bonding, depending on what other improvements the person wants."

Cosmetic contouring takes very little time—less than 30 minutes or so per tooth, with no anesthesia needed. Not all teeth are good candidates for cosmetic contouring, however. If your two center front teeth are too long, for example, shortening them to conform to their neighbors could leave too little tooth surface showing, which could make you look

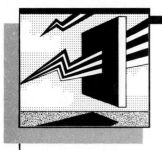

Look! No Cavities!

The mouthwash of the not-so-distant future will do more than make your breath socially acceptable. One swish a day will keep the dentist away—by preventing and even repairing tooth decay. Older adults as well as youngsters will have stronger, healthier teeth.

Scientists are hard at work developing this painless method of tooth repair, and they're basing their formulas on nature's own way of controlling decay: fluoride. This mineral, naturally present in saliva, fights tooth decay by helping calcium and phosphate to recrystallize in regions of early decay near the tooth surface (a process called remineralization). One way to accelerate remineralization—and thus prevent cavities—is to supply extra fluoride. Enter "super salivas."

These specially formulated mouth rinses prompt the growth of mineral crystals that are larger, stronger, more acid-resistant and more tenacious than natural tooth enamel, making the rinses five to ten times as effective as natural saliva in fighting decay. And these synthetic salivas can actually strengthen teeth and *repair* developing cavities. Remineralizing rinses, as these fluids are also called, are about as close to a cure for cavities as you can get—and constitute the biggest breakthrough in dental care since the discovery of fluoride itself.

How do they work?

"We start with calcium and phosphate, the building blocks of tooth enamel normally present and at work to remineralize teeth," explains John Featherstone, Ph.D., head of the oral biology department of the Eastman Dental Center, in Rochester, New York, and one of the pioneers in cavity control research. "By adding fluoride to this mixture, we can speed up the process of remineralization. Ex-

older. So your dentist should consider your lip line when deciding whether or not cosmetic contouring is the correct option for you. Perhaps bonding, laminating or crowns—discussed later—would be better choices.

Brace Yourself

Cosmetic contouring can only do so much to fool the eye. If your teeth are seriously out of line,

perimentally, we are also trying to go yet one step farther by including small amounts of strontium (a harmless form of the mineral occurring naturally in drinking water) which, when accompanying fluoride, works with calcium to rebuild tooth enamel and enhance resistance to decay.

"We've also added tartrate, a naturally occurring substance that forms a water-soluble complex of calcium and strontium in solution. Altogether, the combination mimics the action of saliva," says Dr. Featherstone.

"A rinse of this type will result in a tremendous decline in tooth decay in future generations," says Leon M. Silverstone, D.D.S., Ph.D., director of the Oral Sciences Research Center, University of Colorado, whose work is also considered to be on the cutting edge of tooth decay research. Most exciting, you're never too old to rinse away decay, according to both Dr. Silverstone and Dr. Featherstone.

"As the population ages and people retain more teeth than ever due to good dental care, their gums will recede and expose root-level enamel—enamel that's still vulnerable to decay," says Dr. Silverstone.

"Nearly all older people have receding gums and exposed tooth roots which are prone to decay and more difficult to restore once decay has set in," adds Dr. Featherstone. "That's partly because the tooth is softer at the root surface level and more susceptible to abrasion."

You don't have to wait for the experimental rinses to be available to save your teeth, though.

"For many people, the fluoridated rinses that are now available are 100 percent effective in preventing and reversing early decay, especially when used with a fluoridated toothpaste," says Dr. Featherstone.

repositioning them may be the only solution. Poorly aligned teeth can make you look completely toothless. Or your face may appear to have collapsed. Missing back teeth, too, can lead to shifts in the front teeth, giving your mouth an elderly, shrunken look. Consequently, straightening wayward teeth can take years off your appearance. But if you think wearing a "tin grin" is the only way to straighten teeth, you're in for a pleasant surprise.

Today even adults can benefit from wearing braces.

**Clear plastic braces
are almost invisible.**

"Many adults have preconceived notions about repositioning teeth and assume that metal braces are the only option," says Dr. Goldstein. "But other options exist. Modern dentistry can now apply clear plastic 'see-through' braces, removable braces (worn overnight or in the privacy of your home) or sometimes even 'invisible' braces. Inside braces do take longer to straighten teeth than exterior braces but are quite inconspicuous. A young man, for example, came to my office to have his crooked teeth cosmetically contoured. Afterwards, I turned to his mother, who'd accompanied him, and said, 'So when are you going to have your teeth straightened?' She said, 'I'm wearing an appliance right now.' She had a removable inside brace, and I, a dentist no less, hadn't noticed."

Crowns: Royal Treatment for Run-down Teeth

If you have too little tooth structure left to bond, contour or straighten, crowns (also called caps) may be the answer. Crowns can also close spaces. As explained in chapter 22, most crowns are plastic, all-porcelain, porcelain fused to metal or all-metal and can be used to restore what's left of a tooth that's worn down over time or partially destroyed due to disease or injury. Crowns can also anchor a bridge of one or more artificial teeth onto existing, adjacent teeth.

**Crowns are a long-
term solution to prob-
lem teeth.**

Crowns take considerably more time and money than contouring or other conservative remodeling techniques—often two appointments of one to two hours per tooth. But crowns can look and feel much like real teeth. Take good care of your crowns and they'll last for years. The most beautiful crowns will deteriorate, however, if the teeth underneath begin to decay or if your gums recede. So remember to brush, floss and take other steps to avoid tooth decay and gum disease. And be careful not to bite down hard on chewy foods or chew ice!

Deciding if a New Smile Is for You

"Cosmetic dentistry should not be started until all your basic dental work has been completed," says Melvin Denholtz, D.D.S., in his book about dental "facelifts." "It is only then that the cosmetic aspects of your treatment should be considered."

Dr. Goldstein encourages potential patients to find out all they can when considering cosmetic dentistry, and then to help decide what technique will best restore the teeth's original beauty.

"A person with crooked teeth, for example, should be aware that he or she may be able to choose a compromise treatment such as cosmetic contouring, or the ideal solution, orthodontics," says Dr. Goldstein. To learn more about the choices available through cosmetic dentistry, Dr. Goldstein encourages people to ask the following questions:

If considering cosmetic dentistry, ask the right questions.

• What will the results look like? Your dentist may be able to make "before" and "after" wax models of your teeth to show exactly how they will change.
• Will the restoration match my natural teeth?
• How long will the results last? Will the treatment need to be touched up or replaced eventually?
• What type of maintenance will be required?
• Will my eating habits change?
• What other options are possible to achieve the same results?
• How much will it cost? Insurance plans rarely cover purely cosmetic work. Be frank about your finances. Everyone—orthodontists included—lives on a budget. You may be able to work out an installment plan.

After considering all your options, you may decide your smile is good enough just the way it is.

"Not everyone should have a new smile," says Dr. Goldstein. "I see many people with crooked or spaced teeth who are perfectly happy with their appearance. The self-confidence that many people have regardless of their appearance is admirable. We should all like ourselves. But if we don't like ourselves with the smile we have, then let's get a new one."

Don't feel guilty about fixing your smile.

40

Revitalize

Your Wardrobe

C lothing can be a nonverbal way of communicating how you feel about yourself. Take the
case of one 95-year-old gentleman, a regular
customer at Barneys New York, a quality clothing
store in Manhattan.

"He came in the other day and bought three
new sports jackets, four pairs of slacks to go with
them and I can't remember what else," says Christo-
pher Ryan, corporate program director of Barneys.

Clearly, this particular customer doesn't consider himself too old to look good. Like many other
mature men and women, his attitude toward clothes
bespeaks his attitude toward himself, life and living.

"Age should not be a limitation to style," says
Renee Weiss Chase, an assistant professor of clothing design at Drexel University, in Phildelphia. "I
think that many women feel they have to stick to a
certain 'look' that identifies their age: They don't
want to wear anything that may be considered too
'young' or 'bright' or 'avant garde.' They think such
clothes are inappropriate for their age. But the way
clothes are designed these days, with such versatility
of style, many suit people from 20 to 80 or older."

"I have a grandmother who's totally fearless
when it comes to clothes," says Chase. "It's wonderful, because somehow wearing what's current and

**The right clothes can
make you feel more
confident.**

wearing color and taking chances with her wardrobe make her look young and feel young."

Just as 20-year-olds are not all "clothes horses," so older people, too, differ in how much importance they place on their wardrobe. Their reasons vary.

"Some people give up on fashion the minute they retire," says Linda A. Snyder, Ph.D., assistant professor of clothing and textiles at Queens College, in New York City. "They accept a stereotyped image of what they think is expected of someone who's older, that they should be sedate, wear darker colors and dress in more conservative styles, supposedly in keeping with their more conservative political leanings and so forth."

"For these people, retirement means, 'I quit,' " says John T. Molloy, nonverbal communications researcher and author of the best-selling book, *Dress for Success* (Warner Books).

"Retiring from your job doesn't mean you're going to slip into your jeans or Saturday khakis and never dress up again," says Ryan. "You may not need as much business clothing, but you're still going out to social functions, meeting people and so forth. If you're at a party and dressed poorly, people may be less apt to come over and introduce themselves to you than if you look well dressed and confident. That's important when you no longer have the business world to rely on for social contacts."

"In fact, some people become *more* active after they retire," says Dr. Snyder. "With no young children or job responsibilities to worry about any longer, they develop new pastimes. Their clothing has to accommodate these new interests. And other people who've raised families may have simply put their wardrobes second to their children's needs for years, making do with whatever clothes they could afford. Suddenly they may want to revitalize their wardrobe even if they don't have a lot of money to spend."

At this point, some older people—particularly men—go overboard.

"For many people one of the signs of being retired is looking up-to-date and fashionable— flashy," says Molloy. "They say to themselves, 'Oh boy, now I can wear all those things I've always

Dressing well is *more* important as you get older.

Clothing can reflect a variety of interests.

wanted to wear.' If you go to Florida you see former executives wearing things you would never have seen them wear before in their lives—Hawaiian shirts, bow ties. Or they'll revert to elements of style, like ascots, that were in vogue when they were young—elements that went *out* of style years ago."

Not everyone who retires *stays* retired, adds Molloy. And launching a second career demands careful attention to clothing if one is to succeed.

"Some people retire for six months and say, 'What am I doing? I want to do something.' But they find they are unemployable. Very talented, very skilled, but unemployable—or employable only in their own business. So they'll start their own business or act as a consultant or buy a little business that's floundering. Many of these people have run a major corporation for years and have seen the gaps in the system and know how to fill these gaps. And many become very successful at their second career."

"As a matter of fact," interjects Molloy, "most millionaires become millionaires *after* age 65. Why? Because they can afford to gamble now. Yet all of these people tell me that to be taken seriously, they had to dress themselves up.

"The men who were more successful than others their age were the ones who spent the most time putting themselves together in the morning," says Molloy. "Vanity is considered a sin, but after 65, it's a virtue. The most successful older people are vain."

Dress Well to Be Treated Well

Taking pride in what you wear diffuses some of the bias that exists against older people, says Molloy.

"If older people want to be taken seriously, if they want to be treated well, they have to pay attention to their image. In fact, dress becomes *more* important as you get older. There's no reason you shouldn't look as good at 65 as you did when you were 25. In fact, you should try to dress *better* because prejudice against older people does exist." Molloy's advice applies whether you're holding down a job or not.

"One of the problems that women in particular have when they reach fifty is they tend to lose their authority," says Molloy. "I call it the 'little old lady syndrome'—looking helpless no matter how capable they may be.

Women, especially, need a clothing strategy.

"My mother is a good example. She was brilliant, a statistician. One day when my father was ill she left work to visit him in the hospital. When she read the directions on his respirator, she discovered it was hooked up wrong. She immediately reported this to the doctor and nurses, but they gave her a hard time. They figured, 'What does a little old lady know?' So she fixed it herself. But when they checked the respirator themselves, they discovered she was right."

The same attitude prevails in business, says Molloy.

"We get complaints from many women executives who say they have to dress extremely well to look effective—wearing clothing that's conservative yet shows wealth and success. Relaxing her standard of dress is the last thing a woman should do as she gets older."

"The image one presents affects relationships with other people no matter what your age," says Dr. Snyder. "It affects the kind of response you get from service people, waiters, mechanics who work on your car, store attendants, taxi drivers, doormen and so forth. And the larger your community, the more critical your dress, because people who don't know you have nothing else to go on *but* your appearance."

Dressing better can mean better service.

Your clothing may affect how your family treats you, too. "Dress so that your children and grandchildren regard you as someone who has skills and ideas to contribute, who's capable of handling situations and communicating with younger people as well as with people your own age, rather than looking like someone who needs constant care and attention," says Dr. Snyder.

In other words, if you wear clothes that label you as old, people may treat you as an old person.

Most importantly, clothing affects how you feel about yourself. Think about it: How did you feel the last time you bought a new sweater? You probably couldn't wait to wear it. Or think about the last social affair you attended. If your outfit was just right, you

A new outfit can boost your spirits.

probably felt happy and confident and had a great time. But if you sensed that your clothes were all wrong, you probably felt awkward or self-conscious, much as a teenager in the 1950s would have felt if she arrived at high school on the first day wearing bobby socks when all the other girls had graduated to nylons.

"The feeling you get when you buy a new outfit—how great it feels and how eager you are to wear it to a special occasion—is how people should feel about their wardrobe 24 hours a day," says Ryan.

The Fashion Formula

If your hair has turned gray, reevaluate the colors of your clothing.

Dressing well means wearing good quality clothing that fits well and is appropriate for the occasion. But you can't expect to throw on any old thing you find and look your best. For one thing, your body may have changed over the years. Even if you weigh the same now as you did when you were 20 years old, your proportions may have changed. Men tend to lose mass from their shoulders and gain at their midsection. Many women have trouble keeping their tummy from bulging, no matter how many sit-ups they do. So you'll need to choose clothing cut for your figure and proportions. Color can be an asset, too. If you've let your hair turn gray, the same colors you looked great in when you were a brunette may not be as flattering now. You may need something brighter to wear. And you may have an entirely different set of hobbies, friends and responsibilities now than you did 10 or 20 years ago. To help you reevaluate your present wardrobe and select clothing that's best for your age, build and life-style, the Fashion Formula is divided into four simple elements: style, fit, fabric and color.

Style vs. Trend

Don't dress like a teenager to look up-to-date.

"Dressing youthfully doesn't necessarily mean wearing youthful clothing," says Ryan. "I know so many men who, once they retire, say, 'I'm going to get a younger girlfriend' or 'I'm going to find a young wife' and then decide they have to dress like a 20-year-old to attract women," he says. "But that's all wrong: They'll just look silly. They can look attractive and up-to-date just by buying good quality clothing that fits well."

"I recently saw an older woman in skintight stirrup pants and a great big shirt with shoulder pads," says Zäzel Wilde Loven, fashion and beauty director of *McCall's* magazine. "I admired her intentions—not wanting to look like a 'little old lady'—but in all honesty, she looked ridiculous. She could have achieved the same silhouette and looked as up to date with slender pants and a slightly oversized sweater instead of a top with shoulder pads out to here."

That's the difference between a trend and style. Trends are clothes that are hot one day and cold as yesterday's mashed potatoes the next. Style is a longer-lasting look.

"Anyone who's interested in longevity of their wardrobe should look for style, not trendiness, in clothes," says Chase. "To understand the effect of style versus trend, simply recall the Nehru jacket or the leisure suit. Nothing looks more dated than a jacket that went out of style 18 months earlier—or 18 years earlier," says Ryan. "Buying more traditional styles prevents older men from getting caught unawares and looking out of date. The traditional style lapel hasn't varied more than a quarter of an inch in the past 10 years. And *no one* can detect a quarter of an inch difference."

The traditional lapel hasn't changed much in ten years.

For women, too, this is the best time in fashion history to be buying clothes, because styles are so diverse that you're sure to find something flattering. Take hemlines, for example.

"For years, women were obsessed with how many inches above or below the knee their skirts should fall," says Chase. "Everyone had to run to the tailor and get their whole wardrobe altered every season. Now it doesn't matter—hemlines range from somewhere around the knees to just a few inches above the ankles. You can wear the skirt length that best suits you and still look up-to-date."

Shopping in the juniors' department or trendy boutiques is tempting because the clothing fairly pulses with energy—everything is new, hot, exciting. But you have to temper your enthusiasm with good judgment.

Adapt styles to your individual image.

"There are a lot of terrific clothes out there, but you have to analyze what you see and interpret it for your image," says Loven. "Train yourself to look at what may appear to be a totally crazy assortment of clothes on a mannequin and say, 'There's a great pair of knit pants with a long jacket that falls below the hips—I could wear that.' Or, 'That oversized sweater would look great with my long pleated skirt.' "

The secret, says Loven, is editing what you see and adapting it to yourself. (For tips on how to choose flattering clothing, see the accompanying box.)

A Proper Fit

"No matter how expensive your clothing, if it fits poorly, you won't look good," says Ryan.

Molloy agrees. "Wearing a garment that's too big or too small will make anyone look dated."

"The first thing we tell anyone, whether they're

How to Choose Clothes that Flatter Your Figure

The right clothing—style, color and pattern—minimizes your figure problems. To achieve a more pleasing silhouette, Renee Weiss Chase, assistant professor of clothing design at Drexel University, in Philadelphia, offers these tips:

Look for styles that balance your proportions. If you have heavy hips or thighs, for example, counterbalance them with jackets, shirts or sweaters that are broad in the shoulders, adding volume to your upper torso.

If you're short waisted (and especially if you also have an ample bosom), avoid clothes that are belted at the waist. Instead, wear slightly longer jackets, tunics and sweaters that create a horizontal line well below your midriff.

If your neck is chubby, avoid crew neck or boat neck tops and round collars. Instead look for V-neck sweaters and open collared shirts—sweaters and blouses that draw the line of sight vertically and downward from your chin, not horizontally. V-necks also help to minimize broad shoulders or other upper torso figure problems.

19 or 69, is fit the suit to your body, not your body to the suit," says Ryan. "To do that, a man has to be honest with himself and not let vanity stand in the way of proper fit. Middle-aged or older men, for example, often come into our store and ask for pants with a 34-inch waist when they really need a size 36. Their immediate reaction is, 'Oh-oh, I've gained ten pounds.' But what may have happened is that their body may have changed proportions. Say you weighed 165 pounds when you were 23 years old. You may still weigh 165, but you need a different size suit because as men get older, they lose weight from their shoulders and chest and gain it in their waistline and seat. If your body has changed proportions, so should your clothes.

"In a traditional cut suit there is a six-inch difference between the chest measurement and the waist—a size 40 jacket and size 34 pants," says Ryan. "The same style suit in a 'portly' or 'executive' cut will have a size 40 jacket and a size 38 waist.

Proper fit is as important as your selection.

Contrast light colors with dark to further balance your proportions. If you're small-busted and heavy hipped—the classic pear shape—wear a light colored top with a deeper colored shirt or slacks. (Light colors reflect light and create the illusion of more space.) If your proportions are the opposite—slim hips with a full bust—reverse the contrast: Wear the darker color on top and the light color below your waist.

Use patterns to create the illusion of volume where you need it most. If you're pear-shaped, wear a floral blouse with a solid skirt or pants to create visual interest on your upper torso and counterbalance your hips. If you're the opposite—T-shaped—wear a solid top with striped pants or a floral skirt to minimize your upper torso and "expand" your hips and thighs.

Keeping these few simple principles in mind will enable you to sort through a rack full of clothes and select figure-flattering styles in minutes, saving you hours of frustration and avoiding costly wardrobe mistakes.

Be aware that the same size can vary from one designer to another.

"The size you wear can also vary from one designer to the next. Someone may wear a 42 regular in a European suit and a 40 regular—or even a 39 regular—in an American suit. In order to get a suit that fits you properly you have to be aware of these size fluctuations and not insist on one particular size out of vanity.

Regardless of age, if you're thin buy tapered shirts.

"If you've gained weight around your middle, buy a fuller cut shirt," says Ryan. "But by the same token, if you're slim, buy a tapered shirt. Nothing makes a thin person look weak and sickly more than a full cut shirt. It just hangs on him."

"Many older men don't even consider buying tapered shirts," says Molloy, "because they think such shirts are for young guys. I say, if you have a tapered body, wear a tapered shirt."

"Remeasure yourself for shirts from time to time," says Molloy. "Men tend to buy the same size throughout their life. I see men in their forties and fifties whose shirt collars are too tight. They then hit sixty and lose weight, yet they continue to wear the same size shirt, which is too loose—especially if their neck is beginning to wrinkle."

Even a suit that's the correct size will probably need to be altered, because no two people are built exactly alike. A tuck here and a little more room there can make the difference between a good- and a great-looking suit. One big mistake people make is allowing too little time—or none at all—for alterations. Everyone knows someone who waited until the day before an important date—like a wedding— to buy a suit and had to settle for something he didn't really like or that didn't fit well. Maybe you've done it yourself. *Plan ahead.*

"And by all means, when you shop, bring in the shirt and shoes you're planning to wear with the suit," says Ryan. "Otherwise, you can only guess if the sleeves and trousers are the right length. Bring in the accessories, and you'll make your life easier."

Fabrics that Work for You

Polyester clothing is practical, affordable and wrinkle-resistant.

Polyester fabric can be perfect for busy people who want to dress neatly but who don't want to bother ironing or dry cleaning cotton, linen, silk, wool and other natural fibers. Throw it in the washer and dryer and polyester emerges wrinkle-free. You're all set to go. You can sit in polyester clothing for hours and it won't wrinkle. Sleep in it, roll it into a ball and run over it with a fleet of golf carts, it still resists wrinkling. And it's less expensive than natural fibers. Not surprisingly, the apparel industry sells millions of dollars worth of polyester clothing every year, much of it to people who enjoy its wash-and-wear properties.

Trouble is, polyester isn't perfect. Modern polyester may look and drape more like natural fibers than early polyester did, but many people insist they can spot the difference between polyester and the more expensive natural fibers at 20 paces. Aside from its appearance, polyester doesn't "breathe" the way natural fibers do. Instead, it traps body heat against your skin. That's a problem in warm weather—or for women who suffer hot flashes during menopause. Blends (polyester combined with a hefty proportion of cotton, wool, rayon or other natural fibers) give you the best of both worlds: relative ease of care combined with rich, good looks.

Blends of natural and synthetic fibers are more comfortable to wear.

"There are some cottons now with a permanent press finish that makes them easier to take care of," says Chase. "And rayon (made of wood cellulose fibers) is making a big comeback. It's comfortable to wear and has a beautiful feel. Also, lightweight, tropical wool feels great for spring and fall—and it looks wonderful," adds Chase.

Be careful about clingy, body-revealing fabrics, he cautions. "Even if they're roomy, they can reveal every body contour when you move. Unless you have a perfect figure, choose fabrics that are crisp, that have some substance, that don't accentuate imperfections.

Crisp fabrics can disguise figure flaws.

"The finish of a fabric, too, can help play down figure problems," adds Chase. "For example, if you have a small bust and heavy hips, wear a shiny top and dull, matte-textured skirt or pants. If you're the opposite—broad-shouldered or large-busted with slim hips—wear a matte-finish top with a skirt or pants in shiny fabric."

Incidentally, bulky knits may actually be better than lightweight, clingy knits for overweight people because lightweights cling and show every bulge or roll, whereas bulky knits have more substance and fall away from your contours.

Colors that Flatter

Black is sophisticated and chic—it makes people look worldly and wise. That's great if you're 19 and want to look grown up. It's *not* so great when you look as grown up as you want to. If your skin has lost its rosy glow, wearing black can leave it looking wan.

"Basically, older people need to wear brighter, deeper colors to perk up their skin tones," says Loven. "If you want to wear black, wear a black skirt or trousers and a brighter colored article closer to your face—a pastel shirt or blouse or sweater, a rich-colored jacket or a bright scarf."

Deep jewellike colors (sapphire, emerald, ruby) perk up your skin tone.

"Color can be one of your most valuable assets," says Chase. "It can brighten a sallow complexion and add sparkle to your eyes if positioned next to your face. Don't be afraid of color. You don't have to undergo wholesale color analysis, either. Experiment on your own. Hold a garment up to your face and ask yourself whether or not it enhances your appearance."

Gray hair calls for a revised color scheme.

If your hair has become gray, the colors you wore when you were a blonde, brunette or redhead may no longer be the most flattering. Beige, brown, yellow, gold or orange probably won't be nearly as flattering as blue-green, pink or other rich colors.

By all means, don't try to rely on your memory to coordinate new purchases with the color of clothes you already own. If you're shopping for a sweater, bring in the skirt you plan to wear it with. If you're buying a tie, bring in the shirt and jacket it will accessorize.

Shoes: Looks vs. Comfort

In a rerun of an old "Bob Newhart Show" episode, Bob and Jerry arrive at the office to find their substitute receptionist, Gail, with her leg in a cast. Gail says she broke her leg "falling off her shoes," and Bob and Jerry both laugh.

"Why do men always laugh when women fall off their shoes?" Gail asks.

Indeed. In real life, such injuries are no laughing matter. The reason Gail fell off her shoes is that high heels compromise stability and create an abnormal stance and gait.

That's a podiatrist's way of saying, "high-heeled pumps prevent you from walking naturally," says Nancy Lu Conrad, D.P.M., footwear editor of the *Journal of the American Podiatric Medical Association*. Walking in heels for any length of time strains your feet, toes, ankles, knees, legs and back. Not surprisingly, the litany of disorders this can cause keeps foot doctors everywhere well heeled for life: Ailments range form simple corns, calluses and bunions to hammertoes, misaligned joints, circulatory problems and benign but painful nerve tumors, some of which may require surgery to correct.

It's not only the height of dress pumps that causes problems. Their shape, too, is downright unnatural.

"Take a dress shoe and place it on the floor beside your bare foot," says Dr. Conrad. "Now, try to visualize crowding your whole foot into that shoe. Your foot is a firmly packed organ to begin with, with little if any excess internal space. If you try to squeeze it into a tight pump, it's like wearing a corset on your feet."

Wearing high heels full-time will strain more than your feet.

Compromise with Your Feet

"People with foot problems come to me and say, 'But I *like* these shoes,' " says Dr. Conrad. "And I say, 'I know, but your feet don't like them. You're not arguing with me, you're arguing with nature.' As you get older, the soft tissues of the feet—the ligaments, muscles and tendons—lose their resiliency. They are no longer able to adapt as they could when you were 21 or so. Therefore, you have to make allowances."

By "make allowances," Dr. Conrad means you should:

• Wear pumps on a part-time basis only. "I realize everyone wants to look nice, particularly if they're wearing a dress or a skirt. But change into sneakers, flats or oxford-type shoes whenever you can," says Dr. Conrad. "I admit you probably don't want to

Here are several ways to minimize the discomfort of wearing dress pumps.

wear 'sensible shoes' when you go out to dinner. I don't either. But wear them when you come home from work. A trend which proves my point is the habit of women going to work with athletic shoes, carrying their pumps to wear at the office.''

• Exercise your feet. "Whenever you have a chance, sit down, take off your shoes and wiggle your toes," says Dr. Conrad. "Five minutes of walking in your bare feet, wiggling your toes and massaging the balls of your feet in the evening really helps."

• Shop for shoes in the afternoon or evening. "If your feet are going to swell, they'll be larger then, and the shoes you buy won't feel tight later," says Dr. Conrad.

• Don't take your shoe size for granted. "As you get older, your feet do not grow," says Dr. Conrad. "But the soft tissues weaken and elongate, enlarging your foot." So you probably need a shoe a half-size or even a full size larger.

You may need shoes a half or full size larger as you get older.

Also, shoes are not sized uniformly, says Dr. Conrad. As with dresses, size is only a rough guide to fit. "Even in the best of shoes, you can buy two pairs of the same style shoe, supposedly the same size, and one pair may feel different. Wear what feels comfortable, regardless of the size."

• Ask the salesperson to bring out more than one size of each style shoe. That way, you won't have to send the sales help back to the stockroom if the first pair you try doesn't fit.

Take your time really walking around while trying on shoes.

• Wearing both shoes, walk around. Take more than a few dainty steps down the carpeted aisle. Walk around on a hard surface, if possible, long enough to overcome your love-at-first-sight of the shoes. How do the shoes *really* feel? Will they feel comfortable after you've worn them all day—or late into the evening?

• Don't crowd your toes. The very front of the shoe—the toe box—should have ample room for your toes. Because pumps pitch your feet into the front of the shoe, you may have to buy pumps one-half size larger than the size you wear in flats or oxfords.

• Avoid too-high heels and stiletto heels. "Stay with 1¾-inch heels at the highest," says Dr. Conrad. "And look for heels that aren't so narrow that you wobble when you walk."

• Customize your shoes. Dr. Conrad advises people to ask a shoe repair shop to replace their shoes' leather heels with rubber ones, or to affix a nonskid sole to the bottom of the shoe.

• Consider inner soles. Even the best dress shoes may have soles as thin as one-sixteenth of an inch, leaving very little cushion between you and the pavement. To alleviate discomfort, you can buy inner soles and tuck them into your new shoes. Be sure they're positioned correctly and that the shoe is large enough to accommodate the inner sole.

Inner soles add comfort.

Dr. Conrad adds that inner soles do the most good in practical everyday shoes, but do little to improve the overall design of dress pumps—which need the most help. Still, every bit of added comfort helps. So inserts are certainly worth a try if you're going out dancing.

Compared with women, men have few problems finding footwear that looks good without compromising their health. Still, men's feet age, too, and men are equally entitled to comfort.

"The most important thing is support for your feet," says Ryan. "A man can have a hair transplant or a facelift, but he can't get new feet, so he has to take care of them. And shoes with laces give more support than loafers."

Shoes with laces support your feet better than loafers.

Look for Quality, Not Quantity

One of the first steps to revitalizing your wardrobe is to accept the fact that clothes, including footwear, have a life span. Then decide what to keep and what to throw out (or give away).

"If your overcoat is old and ratty, you'll look old and, well, mousey," says Ryan. "We all have things in our closet that are screaming for burial. Put them out of their misery."

"Women are much better at revitalizing their wardrobe than men are," says Ryan. "Go into a man's closet and look at the suits he hasn't worn in five years but has yet to throw away. Men hang on to things much more than women do."

When reviewing your wardrobe, force yourself to weed out what no longer looks good.

A full closet lulls you into a false sense of security about your wardrobe. You may ask yourself, "Why should I buy more clothes when I have a closet full?'' when in fact only half your clothes may be presentable. If clothing doesn't fit or it's worn out or out of style, give it away. Then buy the best clothing and footware you can afford.

"The idea isn't to look like you have a million dollars or like you're up on the very latest styles, but that you care enough about yourself to put some thought into how you look," says Loven.

"It's better to have fewer articles of good quality than to have a closet full of clothes that don't look rich," says Chase. "Take my grandmother, for example. She doesn't have a lot of clothes. But those she does have are well made and a little on the expensive side, and she looks great every time she wears them, even though we've seen them before."

Buying good quality clothing in classic styles may cost a bit initially, but actually save you money in the long run. Amortizing the cost of your clothes over their lifetime will help you determine their actual cost.

"Say you spend $500 on a traditional suit," says Ryan. "Properly cared for, it can last up to ten years, or the equivalent of $50 a year. That begins to look reasonable when compared to buying a bargain brand suit for $100 that doesn't fit nearly as well, looks cheap and is out of style in two years.

Keep an open mind. Try things on. Experiment.

"Also, don't be afraid to try several things on before you buy," says Ryan. "You may end up buying the first thing you selected anyway, but you'll feel more confident about your final choice. Twenty years ago, men had much fewer choices—there weren't nearly as many designers, you didn't have the Italian, European and American cuts to choose from. It's a whole new world of clothing out there. Take advantage of it.

"One thing I always tell my customers is 'You don't get a second chance to make a good first impression,' " says Ryan. "Think of how you judge others—by the way they look when you first meet, by how they act. Later, you either say to yourself, 'Boy, was I wrong' or 'Boy, was I right.' So if your clothes are sending the wrong signals about you, you're doing yourself a disservice. Everyone likes to be treated well, and much of that depends on appearance."

41

Overweight:

Slimming Down,

Firming Up

"**A**ctive people who exercise and eat properly look younger than their age," says Art Mollen, D.O., founder and medical director of the Southwest Health Institute, in Phoenix, Arizona. "I've watched my patients seemingly grow younger as they've lost weight. Some say, 'I look better than I've looked in my life.'"

Unfortunately, Dr. Mollen's patients are not typical of most Americans. Statistics show that weight tends to creep upward with age. In fact, middle-age spread is accepted as a natural and inevitable part of aging—right along with gray hair and the need for bifocals. Dr. Mollen, however, says, "Sorry, getting older is no excuse for getting fatter. Metabolism does start to slow down after the age of 30, but that only means that there's more reason to exercise and eat less as you grow older.

"And you're never too old to tone your body. I have a patient who ran the Honolulu marathon when he was 70. Yet when he was 69, he was sedentary and overweight!"

Certainly most people—at any age!—never will run a marathon, but it is inspiring to see how dramatically slimming down can improve health and vitality. Medical researchers know, for example, that obese laboratory animals suffer an increased incidence of all diseases associated with aging. And a series of medical studies on animals suggests that restricted food intake could extend longevity even if restriction does not occur until maturity. In fact, a National Institutes of Health panel of experts declared obesity to be such a killer that it deserves as much medical attention as high blood pressure or smoking.

Fitness boosts your energy level.

And besides, being fat doesn't feel good. "I was five feet, seven inches tall and weighed 241 pounds—any way you look at it, that's fat," says Sandi Nowe, who has since lost 106 pounds. "But looking awful was not the worst of it. I didn't know it at the time, but all those extra pounds were taking a big chunk out of my enjoyment of life. For one thing, I felt tired, almost lifeless, day in and day out, and I actually thought that was normal."

And being thin feels good. "My patients who lose weight become more buoyant and energetic," says Dr. Mollen. "Self-image, confidence and relationships are enhanced for many of them."

Should You Lose Weight?

If you're not sure, take Dr. Mollen's advice: Pay a visit to your mirror. Look at yourself honestly—without holding in your stomach. If you don't like what you see, you may have to slim down.

While this method of evaluation sounds straightforward, it may not work for everyone. Some slim people look in the mirror only to see a fat person staring back at them. "People starving from anorexia nervosa think they're fat," says Reubin Andres, M.D., clinical director of the National Institute on Aging, in Baltimore, Maryland. "There is almost universal anxiety about weight. Too many people think they should look like lean models. I wish models had somewhat fleshier bodies. You don't want to be able to count your ribs."

A caliper measures your fat-to-muscle ratio.

For a more objective evaluation, find someplace (a doctor's office or health club maybe) where you can be measured with a caliper. This little tool helps to measure how much of your body is fat and how much is made of lean tissue. It pinches you in various areas of the body—the abdomen, the upper arm, the thigh and so forth. Generally, the bigger the pinch, the more fat you have. To play a home version of this game, Dr. Mollen suggests you pinch your waist. If you can grab more than an inch, it may be time to lose weight.

If you've tried and failed, you're not alone. But that doesn't mean you won't succeed this time.

Making Your Diet Work

Some people believe the road to damnation is paved with Twinkies. In their minds, HoHos and Cheez Doodles are sinful and sinister, and dieting is a way of repenting for yielding to their call. If you believe that, your diet may be ill-fated.

"The labeling of obesity as a disease, sin or crime [hence the idea that you can 'cheat' on your diet] leads quite naturally to a labeling of means of control," says Henry A. Jordan, M.D., coeditor of *Evaluation and Treatment of Obesity* (SP Medical & Scientific Books). "The traditional diet then becomes either a cure for the disease, a part of repentance and atonement for the sin or a punishment to fit the crime. Little wonder that obese individuals are so ambivalent in their feelings toward dieting."

In other words, if you think of a diet as a kind of punishment rather than what it really is—a way of reaching a desirable goal—you will not want to stay on it. Nobody, after all, enjoys being punished. Some studies even suggest that a diet often increases the likelihood of binges. One researcher induced a group of volunteers to starve themselves down to an average of 76 percent of their initial weight with a low-cal diet. When food was later made available in unlimited quantities, they had a tendency to binge—intakes as high as 11,000 calories were observed.

The first step in successful dieting, then, is developing the *right attitude*. A diet is a way of limiting the number of calories you consume each day. It is simply a tool that assists you in reaching your desired weight, and not a matter of crime and punishment.

The second step in successful dieting is choosing the *right diet*. Some people who want to shed

A strict diet may actually lead to binges.

Too few calories cause the metabolism to rebel.

You lose muscle but re-gain fat.

pounds quickly opt for a very low-calorie diet. And, indeed, they do lose some weight quickly, but then they run into trouble. They starve and they starve but they stop losing weight. Why? Some doctors believe that when you drastically cut down on food, your metabolism goes on strike—or at least calls for a work slow-down. As a result, the body doesn't burn those few calories you feed it. Your weight loss stalls and you become frustrated.

Worse yet, the weight already lost is often the wrong *kind* of weight. During severe dieting you tend to lose muscle rather than fat. But if you go off the diet and gain weight back, do you regain muscle? No. You gain even more fat. As a result, you're worse off than when you started.

And not only are you fatter, you may also look older.

"The loss of skin elasticity becomes visible as wrinkles and fine lines after the age of 40 or 50," says

Diet Pills

Open most any women's magazine and you see the ads.

"The pill to end all diet pills!" they say. "Now you can eat more and weigh less! Shed 10, 20 or 50 pounds—the easy way!"

Can it be true? Yes and no, say some researchers. "Phenylpropanolamine (PPA), the drug used in most over-the-counter diet pills, cut down lunchtime intake in a double-blind study I conducted," says Bartley G. Hoebel, Ph.D., of the psychology department at Princeton University, in New Jersey. "On the average, the pill counted for an extra pound or two of weight loss. There's some evidence that it works by stimulating the part of the hypothalamus which suppresses feeding." But it's common knowledge that the lost weight often comes back after the pill is discontinued.

Fenfluramine, a prescription diet drug, has been shown to have a rebound effect. One study compared the success of three groups attempting to lose weight. One group employed behavioral modification, another used fenfluramine therapy and the third used a com-

Joseph Feinberg, M.D., FACS, assistant professor of plastic surgery at the New York Hospital-Cornell Medical Center, in New York City, and North Shore University Hospital, in Manhasset, Long Island. "Extreme weight fluctuations caused by alternate binging and crash dieting exhaust elasticity even more, and accelerate the aging process.

"When excess pounds are shed abruptly, the skin responds like a rapidly deflating balloon, becoming slack and flaccid, and never quite resuming its natural tone. But skin can adapt to gradual weight loss, especially when accompanied by exercise. A good goal is about a pound a week."

Losing one or two pounds a week is healthy.

The right diet, then, allows for slow and gradual weight loss. And the results of such a diet tend to be permanent, according to Dr. Mollen. "One or two pounds a week is reasonable and healthy," he says. The best approach to losing weight is based on two activities: eating sensibly and exercising.

bination of the two. Rita Yopp Cohen, Ph.D., of the department of psychiatry at the University of Pennsylvania, in Philadelphia, found that both drug groups lost a few more pounds during treatment, but regained more weight afterwards, as compared with the first group. The drug seemed to compromise the long-term effects of behavior therapy.

Though she conducted this experiment with just one particular drug, Dr. Cohen attributes the results to the very nature of what she calls "pharmacotherapy. Psychological theories suggest that those who received combined treatment may have attributed their weight loss to the pharmacological agent rather than to their own behavior," she says. Thus, the trust in your own ability that develops with increased self-control would not develop in those individuals who gave credit to the drug for their success.

Whether they work or not, many doctors advise against diet pills. "Behavior therapy is superior to pharmacotherapy not only in better maintenance of weight loss but also in terms of cost effectiveness and the physical side of treatment," says Dr. Cohen.

Food Guidelines

"Going on a diet" implies that you will later "go off" it. A diet lasts until you rue the day cottage cheese was invented and long for more chocolatey pastures. In place of this on-and-off approach, simply try eating better. Make *permanent* changes in your diet that you can live with, emphasizes Dr. Mollen.

Foods to Limit:

Fats. "It's ironic that we work so hard to find a good sugar substitute when what we really need is a fat substitute," says Dr. Mollen. "Fats are the highest source of calories available. Every ounce of fat contains more than twice the calories you'll find in an ounce of protein or an ounce of carbohydrates.

Fats are the highest source of calories available.

"I try to limit the number of calories from fat to 20 percent of total intake. That's about half of what the average American consumes. Percentage may not mean much to most people, but if you follow these suggestions, you'll reduce the amount of fat you eat: Cut down on red meat, dairy products, creamy sauces and pastries."

Sugar. You're probably aware that sweets are fattening. *Too* aware. But the drawbacks of sugar come not only in the number of calories, but in the quality thereof.

Sugary foods "are a poor source of nutrition, hence the term 'empty calories'," says Kelly Brownell, Ph.D., codirector of the Obesity Research Clinic and associate professor of the department of psychiatry at the University of Pennsylvania School of Medicine, in Philadelphia, in his program for weight control. "These simple sugars stimulate insulin release. Since insulin is related to hunger, you will feel hungry in less time."

Alcohol. Not only is it high in calories (just one scotch and soda has close to 100 calories), but it can also stimulate the appetite. Enough said.

Protein. The protein issue can be confusing, but Dr. Mollen believes most Americans eat too much of it. "Our bodies need protein to build and repair tissue," he says. But the average person doesn't need as much protein as he thinks. Protein that isn't used becomes fat. I limit protein to 15 percent of total intake."

Americans tend to eat too much protein.

Eat More of These:

Fiber. Fiber has become something of a superhero, food-wise. Doctors have found that it can fight heart disease, some types of cancer, diabetes, tooth decay, varicose veins and yes, constipation, in a single bound. And it turns out that it also combats the arch-rival, obesity.

The battle starts in the mouth. Fiber-rich foods take longer to chew, giving your stomach the time it needs to register "full." As a result, you eat fewer calories.

That's what University of Alabama researchers found when they allowed people to "pig out" on high fiber "low energy-density" foods. While the selection included chicken, it also offered plenty of fresh fruits, vegetables, whole grains and beans. Another group had free access to low-fiber foods such as ham, roast beef, french fries and desserts. The first group spent more time eating but took in half the calories (1,570 versus 3,000) compared to the second set of diners.

Fiber lets you eat longer, for fewer calories.

Once eaten, fiber continues combating hunger in the stomach. The type of fiber in whole wheat products tends to expand by absorbing water, which contributes to feelings of fullness. What's more, fiber can help prevent sugar-induced hunger by slowing absorption of glucose. These findings may explain why people who took part in an experiment conducted in Stockholm reported reduced hunger hours after eating fiber with their lunch.

This undigestible roughage won't give up, even in the intestines. Fiber actually erases some of the calories eaten by helping to escort certain dietary fats out of the intestines before they've had a chance to be absorbed. It's been estimated, in fact, that a diet rich in fiber could reduce the number of available calories one eats by about 5 percent, enough to dispose of about 100 extra calories a day.

A high fiber diet can "erase" 100 calories a day.

If you want to add more fiber to your diet, here are ten foods that are delicious, readily available and high in fiber: 100 percent bran cereal, prunes, apples, lima beans, pears, nectarines, shredded wheat, peas, brown rice and unpeeled potatoes.

Fruit. Not all sugars are created equal.

Yale University researchers compared what effects fructose (fruit sugar), glucose (table sugar) and water had on hunger and food intake.

Those who took the glucose ate nearly 500 calories per day more than those who took fructose. And those who drank water ate an average of 225 calories more than the fructose group.

So satisfy your cravings for sweetness with fruits and other foods that are naturally sweet. Not only are they lower in calories and higher in nutrition, they also may curb your appetite better than pastries and candy.

Soup. What is usually served to whet the appetite may actually suppress it. Because hot soup is difficult to consume with the same speed as a cool ham-and-cheese on rye, it can be an effective food for losing weight, says Dr. Jordan. During the time it takes to finish a bowl of soup, the brain recognizes that you are eating and turns off the hunger pangs. As a result, you're no longer ravenous when the main course arrives, and you probably will eat less. When Dr. Jordan fed 1,056 obese people varying lunches, he found that those who were given soup wound up ingesting an average of 54.5 fewer calories per meal.

"Lite" Foods. Though blatantly misspelled and often expensive, these products can indeed help you become "lite," too.

Advertising claims have been backed up by a study conducted by the Health, Weight and Stress Program at the Johns Hopkins Medical Institutions, in Baltimore. The researchers divided more than 100 overweight people into two groups. One group followed a standard low-calorie reducing diet, and the other group was asked to cut calories by eating lite foods. Over a four-month period, the people who ate the lite foods each lost five to seven pounds *more* than the people on the standard reducing diet.

"Lite" foods provide variety and help you stay on your diet.

The appealing flavor of the lite foods seemed to help people stay on this nutritionally balanced, low-calorie diet without the usual feelings of boredom or deprivation, the researchers found. Variety, too, appeared to be very important. "The successful dieters in our study used a wide variety of lite food products, including fruit, cheese, margarine, bread, soup and even beer," says Janet Gailey-Phipps, Ph.D., a researcher on the study.

A word of warning: Some lite foods are packaged as a complete meal for one person. Its portion size can work for or against you. It may help your diet because there's no option for seconds. But if bulk is important to you, check the size—it might be rather small.

Also, the words "lite" or "light" don't always mean fewer calories. Manufacturers also use the words to indicate reductions in other things, such as salt, sugar or cholesterol. So read the labels carefully.

Learn Low-fat Cooking

Lite foods can be good alternatives to fast-food palaces when you have neither time nor inclination to cook, but you can make your own recipes "lite" if you practice the following "lo" fat, "hi" flavor cooking methods.

Cut away visible fat, and cut down on cooking oil.

• Trim fat. Cut away the visible fat from all roasts, steaks and chops, and remove the skin and visible fat from chicken and other poultry before cooking. This simple step can cut content by up to one-half.
• Cut cooking oil. With a nonstick pan or a nonstick vegetable spray, you can bypass cooking oil. Or, instead of sautéing meat, poultry and fish in oil or butter, poach it in seasoned stock, flavored vinegars or water mixed with lemon juice or soy sauce. Instead of frying chopped onions, steam them. And if you absolutely *must* use oil or butter to sauté, don't use more than one-half to one teaspoon per serving.
• Roast meat. Cook roasts, chops, steaks, chicken parts, meatballs, hamburgers and other meat patties on a raised broiler pan in the oven. Excess fat will drip into the lower pan, away from the food.
• Lighten up gravy. If you want to make gravy with the meat dripping from the bottom of the broiler pan, degrease it first. Here's a quick method: Place the drippings in a heat-proof measuring cup. Then submerge the cup in ice water three-quarters of the way up. The fat will rise to the top and begin to thicken so you can skim it off easily.

Cool drippings to skim off fat.

Then, for a thin gravy, simply reheat the remaining juices and season them with bouillon or herbs and spices. For a thicker gravy, blend two tablespoons of flour and one cup of water, stock or skim milk and add to the skimmed meat juices. Stir over medium heat until mixture has thickened.

• Devise low-fat substitutes. Use stock, herb tea or juice instead of oil in marinades. Replace at least two-thirds of the oil in a basic vinaigrette salad dressing with pureed cucumber or plain low-fat yogurt. In recipes that call for ricotta cheese, use 1 percent low-fat or dry curd cottage cheese instead—it can reduce the calories by as much as 50 percent.

By incorporating the above tips and making them a part of your everyday eating style, you'll naturally be cutting calories without feeling deprived or exerting willpower.

Change Your Eating Behavior

If it were *easy* to exercise and eat less, perhaps everyone could wear a bathing suit with pride. Human nature being what it is, however, and cheesecakes being what *they* are, weight rarely comes off easily.

Identify what triggers your desire to eat.

"Hunger is one of the most powerful drives," says Mark Bricklin, editor of *Prevention* and author of *Lose Weight Naturally* (Rodale Press). "It is essential for survival. But in modern America, more than anywhere else, instant food is always readily available. It's hard to resist overeating."

And many people don't. The environment, your own physiology and even your emotions may figure into overeating more than true hunger. But behavioral psychologists agree that you can develop better responses to these factors than eating.

Custom-Tailor Your Own Plan

"We can view eating as a chain of events which contains many links," says Dr. Brownell in his weight control program.

Devouring an entire box of cookies, for example, has several links before and after the actual eating, such as buying cookies, leaving them on the counter, being bored, wandering into the kitchen, eating rapidly, feeling guilty and eating more. "Once you identify the links in your chain, you can spot the best link to break, and how to break it," explains Dr. Brownell. "The more links you break, and the earlier in the chain you break them, the easier it will be to control eating."

A food diary can help you identify your links. Use a small spiral notebook or something convenient to carry with you. Make columns for food, time, place, feelings, activity and calories.

A food diary pinpoints the troublesome times, places and emotions.

The food diary is the holy book of Dr. Brownell's program. "Awareness is a key step in changing habits," he says. One benefit of record keeping is that you learn about calories. Dr. Brownell's program warns, "There are calories lurking where you least suspect." One cup of fruit yogurt has almost as many calories as an ice cream cone. Ten innocent potato chips contain 105 calories, more calories than are found in four cups of plain popcorn. Becoming a calorie expert insures that you won't be derailed by calorie surprises.

"You are aware of what you eat. You might be thinking, 'Of course I know what I eat.' However, one does not always recall the exact number of Doritos consumed at happy hour or the ounces of milk poured into the bowl of Wheaties. These are 'forgotten' calories, sometimes because we like to forget them!" says Dr. Brownell.

The food diary not only reveals *what* you eat, but *when*. You may discover that you're likely to eat when you're bored or worried. Or you may learn that certain activities (like watching TV) or certain times of day (before going to bed) awaken the urge to eat. Knowing your patterns is a big help in changing habits. In fact, research has shown a food diary to be one of the most important parts, if not *the* most important part, of habit change.

Once you've kept a diary for at least a week, you can start looking for problem areas. Then go through the following tips, recommended by behavioral therapists, and select the ones which correspond to your particular eating habits.

Weakened restraint does little harm if you don't buy fattening foods.

• Shop with care. "Having problem foods available in the house, office, car, briefcase, purse or pocket can be asking for trouble, even if you vow to 'eat only a little,' " explains Dr. Brownell. "On the other hand, if your refrigerator resembles a salad bar because of wise shopping, weakened restraint can inflict only minor damage.''

Never shop when you are hungry. Everything will look appetizing, and you'll buy too much. Use a list, and don't carry more cash than you need for the listed items.

And buy foods that require preparation. If a food has to be cooked before it can be eaten, you can't impulsively just pop it into your mouth.

• Store foods. "Out of sight, out of mouth!" as Dr. Brownell puts it. Which means, if you've been foolish enough to buy peanuts, at least don't leave them on the coffee table.

Out of sight, out of mouth.

• Avoid seconds. And thirds. The out-of-sight principle applies here, too. Remove serving dishes from the table, where they won't beckon to you. Moving them prevents the absentminded or automatic refilling of your dinner plate. If you are really still hungry, you'll have to get up from the table to get a second helping.

Remove serving dishes from the table.

Or go one step further and wait five minutes before going back for extra helpings. This slows eating and gives you time to decide if you really want it. And throw away leftovers. Eating them may seem penny-wise, but it's pound-foolish.

• Find your high-risk situations. Flip through your diary and look for patterns in your snacking. Do you eat more in certain situations? It may be when you're bored at home, your spouse is eating ice cream or your best friend is over for a gab fest.

Whatever it is, learn to be prepared. If, for instance, you eat when you're home alone on a Saturday afternoon, leave the house or invite someone over.

Once you have identified your high-risk situations, you can plan ahead to control the cravings that so often come with them. Some dieters believe that a craving grows and grows and will wreak havoc unless it's extinguished with food. Balderdash, says Alan Marlatt, Ph.D., psychologist and director of the Addictive Behavior Research Center at the University of Washington, in Seattle, and author of *Relapse Prevention* (Guilford Press). He points out that gratifying an urge makes it stronger and more frequent. But if you ignore it, you'll weaken it. If cravings appear at the first sign of loneliness, for example, eating will just reinforce the associations between emotions and food.

So make new associations. Walk the dog. Go shopping. Play the saxophone. Make a list of fun things to do for times when you *think* you need food.

• Eat in one place. You might have heard this advice already—several therapists recommend eating in one place. And you might have wondered why. After all, eating while sitting on a couch instead of at the kitchen table adds no calories to food.

The problem comes from association. If you frequently eat in one chair, you'll feel hungry whenever you sit there, according to Dr. Brownell. So select one spot in your home where you will eat. Do *all* your eating there.

• Do nothing else while eating. This is the same principle: If you often eat while watching TV, then "Dynasty" will make you head straight for the refrigerator. The same goes for reading, talking on the telephone and any other activity. Remember, such activities distract you from eating, subtracting from your eating pleasure.

• Slow down. The faster you wolf down your food, the more you can eat before your stomach registers "full," or so the theory goes. Slow eating may even make food taste better—it gives your taste buds a fighting chance to experience the food before it zooms into your stomach. Ted L. Edward, Jr., M.D., in his handbook, *Weight Loss to Super Wellness* (Hills Medical), put together some strategies meant to prolong eating while eating less:

Put your fork, spoon or finger food (sandwich, fruit, etc.) down after every bite. Don't add food to your mouth before you have swallowed the previous bite. Use a delay tactic; take a two-minute break in mid-meal. Take very small bites and chew longer.

• Don't clean your plate. "It is nice to avoid wasting food, but think for a minute of the folly in cleaning your plate," states Dr. Brownell. "When you eat everything on the plate, you are at the mercy of the person doing the serving. You will usually be served more than enough. If you clean your plate, you are responding to the *sight* of food, and eating stops only when no more food is in sight."

When you're "just dying" for ice cream, go for a walk.

A Little Help from Your Friends

In addition to simple diet and behavior tips, many people find real incentive when they participate in a weight-loss program. It was the battle of the bulge, for example, at competitions set up by researchers from the University of Pennsylvania School of Medicine, and the County Health Improvement Program, in Williamsport, Pennsylvania. The war against fat was raging in business and industrial workplaces, where each participant paid five dollars to compete. The team that achieved the greatest percentage of its goal won the pool of money.

Weekly weigh-ins spur weight loss.

As it turns out, participants from all teams lost weight—a mean of 12 pounds each during the 12 to 15 week program. Most of the subjects reported that team support and weekly weigh-ins were the most effective components of the program. The study elicited more than just weight loss, too—the managers reported improvements in employees' morale, energy level and relations with coworkers.

Studies have found similar benefits in groups such as Weight Watchers. A survey of 151 Weight Watchers members who had reached their goal weights showed that though food-and-behavior-change plans were useful, social monitoring (which consists of a weekly weigh-in and discussion of progress) and the peer-help dimension of the program were most important to the participants.

If belonging to a group of dieting people sounds overwhelming, maybe a dieting partnership is more your style.

A supportive partner can help, too.

"A spouse (or mate) can be a tremendous help if he or she knows what to do," says Randy Black, Ph.D., the psychologist who ran the Stanford University Medical School study on dieting couples. "The spouse's place is to offer verbal positive support, not to be a policeman, and to ignore the negatives. For example, the spouse should not reprimand his or her mate for eating a piece of cake. The dieter already knows that it's bad. Bringing it up makes the spouse the bad guy and the one dishing out punishments. Instead we teach the spouse to compliment the dieter when he or she sticks to the diet program."

Dr. Brownell, who conducted several studies on

partnership dieting, suggests you achieve such a supportive relationship through communication. "Tell your partner how to help," he advises. "Do you want to be praised when you do well or scolded when you do poorly? Should the person avoid eating in your presence? Can your partner help by exercising with you?

"The more specific your requests, the easier it will be for your partner to comply. If your request is vague and general, like 'Be nice,' your partner is at a disadvantage. A more specific request is better, such as, 'Please tell me you love me when I lose weight.' Instead of saying, 'Don't eat in front of me,' say, 'It helps me when you eat your evening bowl of ice cream in the other room.' Replace a general statement like 'Exercise with me' with 'Please take a half-hour walk with me each morning.' "

Tell your partner how he or she can help.

"Your spouse can help you along with rewards," says Dr. Mollen. "The promise of new clothing or a money reward for reaching a certain weight can help motivate a dieter. I know someone who took his wife on a romantic vacation when she reached her goal."

But don't forget to reward your partner too. "One-way relationships don't last long," states Dr. Brownell. "Remember that a partner can be draining and that you need to acknowledge their help."

Think Thin

Thoughts can be fattening. That was shown by researchers from the University of West Virginia, in Morgantown, when they allowed subjects to eat as much ice cream as they wanted after drinking a shake. Dieters who were told the drink was high-calorie ate twice as much as the dieters who thought the drink was low in calories. Non-dieters didn't follow this pattern.

If you think you blew your diet, don't follow up by binging.

"It was demonstrated that a restrained person's belief that he or she has overeaten may be sufficient to trigger an eating binge," conclude the researchers. It's important to short-circuit that kind of thinking. Here's how: "Whenever a dieter overeats, instead of thinking, 'It's too late now. I might as well

Surgery for Weight Loss

When a 200-pound person loses 40 pounds the effect is striking and the diet usually ends. But a 300-pound person losing the same amount of weight may still have 100 pounds to go. The seemingly endless dieting is one reason extremely heavy people become discouraged with conservative methods of weight control.

Ironically, people 100 pounds or more over their ideal weight (which is considered to be morbidly obese) can reap the most health benefits from weight loss. Diabetes, cholesterol and triglyceride levels, hypertension, heart condition, respiratory problems, ulcers, life-expectancy and mobility can be improved with weight loss in morbidly obese people, according to Richard E. Symmonds, Jr., M.D., associate professor of surgery at Texas A & M University College of Medicine, in Temple.

Some heavyweights make a last-ditch effort at weight loss with surgery. Intestinal (jejunoileal) bypass was the first obesity operation, but has been all but abandoned because of the long-term complications, such as liver failure, chronic diarrhea, vitamin and mineral deficiencies and gallstones.

"Most surgeons use stomach stapling (gastroplasty) nowadays," says Edward R. Woodward, M.D., a surgeon with the University of Florida College of Medicine, in Gainesville. The stomach is literally stapled, so that it holds less food. Any attempt to eat more leads to discomfort and vomiting, and will put an end to that.

"Stomach stapling works for many of my patients," says Dr. Woodward. "But it's still possible to cheat. Liquid calories, such as alcohol, and ice cream, which melts immediately, run right through

enjoy myself,' dieters could be trained to make coping self-statements such as, 'O.K., I've overeaten. I'm not going to make it worse,' " researchers recommend.

Dr. Brownell also deals with the importance of attitudes in weight loss. And contrary to what one might expect, the findings suggest that being extremely ambitious about losing weight can actually hinder progress.

Above all set realistic goals.

According to Dr. Brownell, dieters tend to set out-of-reach goals for themselves, often uncon-

the stomach. And some patients develop complications such as infections, hernias, undernutrition and scarring.

Some doctors say this operation may be too risky for people over 50, but Dr. Woodward reports success with older patients.

If the idea of surgery seems too drastic, maybe a balloon will help you deflate. Gastric balloons, which were approved by the Food and Drug Administration in 1985, are inserted into the stomach with a tube and inflated to a round cylinder two inches in diameter and three and a half inches long.

"New procedures call for removal of the balloon after three to four months because of the apparent high incidence of premature deflation between the third and fourth month," says W. Edward Keach, director of the balloon program at Grand View Hospital, in Sellersville, Pennsylvania.

"The balloon basically helps a diet by decreasing feelings of hunger," says Walter L. Percival, M.D., a pioneer in the field and a surgeon with a private practice in Windsor, Ontario.

"This procedure can cause gastric erosion, but I have seen no major complications," says Keach. "It is less risky than stomach stapling, which is major surgery, and requires a four- to ten-day hospital stay."

But both methods are useless without behavior modification, better eating habits and exercise. "I like to compare balloon implants to training wheels on a bicycle," says Keach. "They give a good boost at first, but when they're off, you should be able to continue riding the bike, or following the thinner life-style."

sciously. "When the goals are not met, the negative emotional response can send your diet into a tailspin."

Begin to Exercise

Exercise. People love it or hate it.

Participants in a health conference at Lehigh University, in Bethlehem, Pennsylvania, indicated that they thought most joggers are masochists who

Exercise is a major element in losing weight.

hate what they're doing. Some participants in a weight-loss clinic hesitated to take up walking "because their neighbors would think they were out looking for action."

These two groups—sharing a negative attitude—are composed of people who do not regularly exercise. Would their attitudes change if they began?

"When I tell my clients to start exercising, they expect hard, grueling work," says Dr. Mollen. "They're surprised when they find out how good it feels."

And not only does exercise make you feel good, it makes you *look* good. It helps you to lose weight in several ways. First, it revs up your metabolism. Metabolism, in a cruel trick of nature, slows down as you age, and sometimes even as you diet. But you want your metabolic rate to be *high*—like those people who can polish off entire buffet platters and remain skinny while *you* gain weight on the salad. Routine exercise can do it for you. It can boost a dieter's sluggish 40-calorie-an-hour metabolic rate to 70 or 80 calories an hour, says Gabe Mirkin, M.D., the author of *Getting Thin* (Little, Brown and Company). "Just a half hour a day will keep you burning calories at a faster rate all day long."

And they may keep burning away all *night* long too. Scientists have found that aerobic exercise can stimulate metabolism for up to 24 hours after you've stopped exercising.

Exercise also can reverse another bad consequence of dieting—muscle loss. One study reported by the President's Council on Physical Fitness and Sports compared what effects diet, exercise and a combination of the two had on middle-aged women. All groups lost weight, but both exercise groups lost more fat and gained muscle. The diet group *lost* muscle.

And muscle is much better than fat. Muscles are firm and attractive, of course, but did you know they burn up more calories than fat?

"But if I exercise, won't I just work up an appetite?" you may ask. No, say the experts.

Scientists found this out by counting the calories eaten by a group of obese women during a two-

It helps you burn more calories even after you stop exercising.

And it does not increase the appetite.

month experiment. Each underwent three 19-day treatments—a sedentary period, a period of mild daily exercise and a period of moderate exercise. Each woman was allowed to eat as much as she wanted, and although all of them gradually became more active, their caloric intake did not increase.

Some experiments suggest exercise may even help *suppress* appetite, according to Dr. Brownell. "If you exercise and feel like hunger increases, your mind is at work rather than your body," he says. And while exercise is doing wonders for your body, it's also improving your spirits. When you meet a challenge and overcome it, you begin to feel more positive about yourself. If you're overweight, surely you don't relish the thought of putting on running shorts, leotard or bathing suit. Thus, such a challenge may be found in exercising. The positive outcome provides a sense of accomplishment and self-control."

Exercise provides the tools you need for long-term success. It helps counter the emotional triggers to overeating, for example. "When my patients eat as a reaction to emotional distress, I tell them to exercise instead," says Dr. Mollen.

Evidence suggests that exercisers can lose weight without even dieting. A Dutch research team found that overweight people actually eat *less* (in terms of energy intake per pound of body weight) than their thinner counterparts. It's just that the heavier people were less physically active and therefore needed less fuel to burn.

Exercise may be as important to weight loss as dieting.

"The major implication of these results may be that in weight-reduction programs and health strategies more emphasis needs to be placed on increased physical activity (exercising) than on reduced energy intake (dieting) because obese people are already eating less than their lean counterparts," the group concludes.

And, of course, the most obvious benefit of exercise is that it burns calories. But don't depend too much on this benefit. As Dr. Brownell advises, "Be careful to avoid feeling that a modest amount of exercise entitles you to more calories at the table. You will probably eat more calories than the exercise expended."

Choosing an Exercise

You don't need expensive equipment. You don't have to join a health club. And you don't have to jog. Not if you don't want to. One exercise anyone can try is walking. Mile for mile it burns up about as many calories as jogging and it can really help you lose weight too. Walking's effectiveness was proven in an experiment involving a group of overweight Californians, who each lost an average of 22 pounds in one year simply by adding a walk to their daily routine.

All 11 women in the experiment were chronic dieters who were never successful at keeping off any of the weight they had lost on repeated calorie-cutting regimens. For this test, there were no dietary restrictions, but a daily walk was a must. Weight loss didn't start until walks routinely exceeded 30 minutes a day.

Any aerobic exercise will produce results.

The importance of walking was demonstrated even better by two women in the group who started to regain weight after they became ill and stopped exercising. But once walking resumed, weight loss started all over again.

If you would like to begin a walking program, see Dr. Mollen's 26-week plan in Part Three.

If walking isn't your thing, try cycling. Or dancing. Or swimming. "It doesn't matter which exercise you choose, as long as it's aerobic," says Dr. Mollen. "That means it should keep your pulse rate elevated. Pick a program that's fun and easy to fit into your lifestyle and daily schedule."

Impossible? You're booked up as it is? Well, do you have ten minutes? "I start my patients at ten minutes of exercise a day because that's the minimum addictive dose," says Dr. Mollen. "Eventually, you should build up to at least 30 minutes a day, but most people are put off by that much at first. If you start gradually, you'll realize how good it feels and want to do more."

Another way to get more exercise is to make it part of your routine activities. Take the stairs instead of the escalator, park at the far end of the lot, go for a walk at lunchtime, ride your bike to work, take your dog for a run. You get the idea.

Keeping It Off

Myra stands in front of a full-length mirror. For the first time in 20 years, she can accomplish this without flinching. Months of effort have paid off to the tune of 50 lost pounds. Then why does she feel down?

"Losing weight can open up a Pandora's box of problems," says Dr. Marlatt. "Overeating often functions to reduce anxiety. Some people may have subconsciously wanted to be fat, to avoid having to deal with dating. If they believe that becoming thin will magically cure all problems, they'll end up frustrated, angry and disappointed."

Such a letdown might undermine even the best maintenance program. Unless you deal with these problems constructively. "If you lost weight with the help of a spouse or a weight-loss program, make sure you take advantage of their continued support after you've reached your goal," says Dr. Marlatt.

To stay thin, maintain your support system.

As for the exercise, food and behavior changes necessary for weight loss, they should continue to be a part of your life-style in order to keep those pounds off, says Dr. Marlatt. Once the substantially overweight person has reduced, he or she—to stay at the new, lower weight—must often either exercise more or eat less than a person the same size who was never fat.

But that doesn't necessitate a life of deprivation. "Schedule a treat day every one or two weeks," suggests Dr. Marlatt. "That way, you can eat foods you like and still maintain control over your eating habits."

Plan an occasional treat.

And for Sandi Nowe, control was an important part of weight loss. "When I went somewhere, I'd wear the jacket with candy in the pocket," she says. "I'd always know that the candy was there and that I was making a choice not to eat it. Being in charge was a real kick.

"Now I don't even think of what I'm doing as weight control, even though I've lost 106 pounds. It's my way of living a healthy life. After all that I've been through, after seeing how much happier and healthier I am now, I know I'll never be fat again."

Part
Three
A Year of
Rejuvenation

Introduction

A Year of Growth

Welcome to your Year of Rejuvenation! This program is designed to help you turn the scientific research that you've read about in this book into a way of life. One year from today, you can be *younger* in tangible ways.

Sound like a pipe dream? It's not. But "turning back the clock" does require consistent effort: exercise, proper nutrition and stress reduction. Small changes in your lifestyle can add up to many years of feeling and looking great. Each week, you'll focus on a different aspect of nutrition, physical or mental health, relaxation and fun.

The most important part of this program is exercise. If you're not sure what kind of exercise to do, you can try the simple walking program, designed by a doctor, which begins in Week 1.

Maybe you've already begun eating a diet that emphasizes fruits, vegetables and whole grains, with a minimum of calories from fat. If not, this program can show you how to make the switch, gradually and deliciously.

And speaking of diets, if you're a weight-watcher, this program can help you shed those extra pounds. You'll find specific suggestions to reach your target weight.

Along with the exercise and nutrition weeks, there are weeks devoted to psychological well-being. Disturbances of the mind can make you sick; stress, for example, is a major coronary heart disease risk factor. Conversely, a positive attitude may protect you from disease. The techniques you'll sample this year have proven health benefits.

How the Program Works

In Week 1, you'll start your exercise program and 'Take Inventory' of your current health habits. Every three months, there will be another inventory. These quarterly inventories will help you become aware of what you're doing right—and show you where there's room for improvement. They'll allow you to chart your progress as you become healthier.

Each week, continue with your exercise program, plus focus on the ideas and behaviors presented that week. Behavioral scientists say it takes the body 21 days to accept new behavior. Try to make each week's most important changes permanent.

You won't have to wait a year to start seeing results. A scientific study indicates that just six weeks of regular exercise and better eating will have you feeling and looking much better.

Have a great year!

Goal: *Start Moving*

Date: _____

Walk: 7 days, 5 minutes, ¼ mile

If you could do only one thing this year to renew your mind, body and spirit, what would you choose?

There's no single operation that can make you young. No drug or vitamin. No particular food.

But there is one *activity* that benefits you from head to toe, muscle and bone, heart and spirit, that may increase your life span and even *reverse* some of the damage that bad habits have caused to your health.

That activity, of course, is exercise.

In chapter after chapter, you've read about the regenerating "miracles" that exercise performs. You don't have to be an Olympic athlete to reap all those dramatic benefits. In fact, the easier you take it in the beginning, the more likely you will be to stick with it—increasing the odds that you'll be physiologically *younger* at the end of this year than you are now.

So this week, set some easy goals:

If you've been sedentary for a long time, do a *little* exercise. If you join our walking program, you'll see that we *really* mean *little*. Just five minutes of brisk walking a day to start! Start slowly, and stay at a comfortable level for two weeks before attempting small increases.

If you're already well into your own exercise program, just keep up the good work! Studies show that exercise three times a week, for 20 minutes each time, is required to maintain cardiovascular fitness, so be sure you're achieving this minimum level. If you're an enthusiastic exerciser, be sure to check your pulse to see that you're moving vigorously, but not overexerting yourself.

The Walking Program

If all your past attempts at fitness have floundered, consider that walking is one of the easiest, most pleasant and least injury-causing exercises around.

And it *is* a good aerobic activity, providing you do it briskly and often. "Walking is a great exercise," says Art Mollen, D.O., author of *The Mollen Method* (Rodale Press) and founder of the Southwest Health Institute, in Phoenix, Arizona. "It would work for most people. And it burns as many calories as jogging. If you walk at a moderate pace seven times a week, you'll get a good cardiovascular workout and lose weight." Here's how the walking program, designed by Dr. Mollen, works. You'll find each week's goal in the heading at the top of the page.

This week's suggested goal is easy: Simply walk five minutes a day or one-fourth mile a day.

How to Take Your Pulse

It's important to monitor your heart rate because you don't want it to go too high, which is dangerous, or too low, which means you're not getting enough of a heart-strengthening workout.

How to do it: Start with the number 220. Subtract your age. Multiply by 70 percent (.70). That's the minimum number of heart beats per minute that you should aim for during the most active part of exercise to ensure cardiovascular benefits (unless your doctor says otherwise). Now, do it again, but multiply by .85 instead of .70. That's the maximum target pulse during exercise. Higher than that may not be safe. Take your pulse during and immediately after exercise to ensure that you're in the right range.

Art Mollen, D.O., notes that if you're on certain medication, particularly a blood pressure medication, you may not be able to get your pulse that high. You'll benefit anyway, he says, at a lower pace. Be sure to consult your doctor first.

Sound slow? It is. This level won't give you cardiovascular fitness. But it will get you on the right path, mentally and physically. Gradually, you can try the recommended distance in the recommended time.

Dr. Mollen says you're better off with a moderate level of exercise done frequently rather than overly vigorous exercise only three days a week. "I think exercising moderately, to your target pulse, seven times a week, is the only way to control obesity, a major risk factor for disease," says Dr. Mollen.

You won't have to wait a year to start feeling the difference. "You'll definitely feel better in two weeks. Also, friends will tell you how much better you look!"

What You Need to Start

Not much! Walking is one of the least expensive "sports" around. You don't have to buy special walking shoes if you've already got a perfectly good pair of running shoes. Just don't use tennis or racquet ball shoes, which have a lot of twist in them.

Also, try not to let the weather get in the way of your walks. In extremely hot or cold weather, walk in a shopping mall, a museum, the hall of your apartment building or around a track in a gym.

Attention All Exercisers

Whether you're doing your own program or doing the walking program outlined here, it's important to consult your doctor first, especially if you have health problems or haven't had a checkup in some time.

Inventory 1

Part I: Diary. In Part I, you'll record everything you eat and drink during the week (including water). Also, write down a brief summary of your moods and activities. In the same chart, jot down the amount of exercise you did each day (length of time, and/or distance, if applicable), and any stretching you may have done. Finally, write down what kind of relaxation you did.

Part II: Vital Statistics. Sometime during the week, record your

I. Diary

	Sunday	Monday	Tuesday	
Food and Drink A.M. P.M.				
Moods and Activities Summary				
Exercise and Stretching				
Relaxation				

II. Vital Statistics

1. Weight _____ 2. Resting pulse _____ beats/minute

weight, your resting pulse, your blood pressure and, if possible, your cholesterol level (optional).

Ideals to aim for: Over the year, you want to bring your blood pressure to a safe level. If you're 30, that's around 105/60 to 105/70. For those who are older, it ranges from 110/70 to 120/80. Blood cholesterol levels should be 200 milligrams or less per deciliter. And your resting pulse rate* should be below 70 beats per minute.

*Take your resting pulse first thing in the morning, for ten seconds. Multiply the result by six for beats per minute.

	Wednesday	Thursday	Friday	Saturday

3. Blood pressure_____   4. Cholesterol _____ mg/deciliter

Goal: *Trim the Fat*

Date: _____

Walk: 7 days, 5 minutes, ¼ mile

Fat. It slows you down and clogs you up. It's a blot—or rather a blob—on your figure. And far worse, dietary fat can reduce your life expectancy by increasing the risk of heart disease, cancer and stroke. Though there may be a strong genetic factor at work, for the most part these conditions are preventable. And if caught early enough, arteriosclerosis—which can lead to heart disease and stroke—can even be reversed. Exercising regularly is a big step in the right direction. Step two is to begin trimming the extra fat off your body and out of your food.

A Tour of the Fat Farm

Actually, not all fats are equally bad. The most important kind to cut back on is saturated fat, the type found in red meat and whole-milk dairy products. It tends to increase the levels of harmful low density lipoprotein (LDL) cholesterol in the blood, even more than cholesterol-rich foods raise these levels. And it's the LDL cholesterol that is linked to increased risk of developing problems in the arteries that nourish the heart (coronary artery disease) and to increased risk of heart attack.

There are also "good" fats—polyunsaturated fats. Unlike saturated fats, which almost always come from land animals, unsatu-rated fats tend to come from plants and fish. Corn oil, for example, is an unsaturated fat. (Exceptions: coconut and palm oil, frequently added to processed foods, are saturated fats.) The polyunsaturated fats can help lower the levels of the bad, LDL cholesterol while maintaining high levels of beneficial high density lipoprotein (HDL) cholesterol, the kind that may escort cholesterol out of the cells. But this is true *only* if the amount of polyunsaturates is equal to the amount of saturated fats—which is not the case for most burger-eating Americans.

So the trick here is to try to keep intake of both kinds of fat roughly equal. But that doesn't mean that if your boss insists on buying a steak dinner, you should run home and guzzle a bottle of sunflower oil to make up for it! Intake of *both* kinds of fat should be kept moderate, ideally to fewer than 30 percent of total calories.

How Much Fat Do You Eat?

How can you tell what percentage of your calories are from fat? That's what the Superfoods chart on page 608 of this section is for. Pick at least two days from Week 1—a day on which you were good, and maybe one on which you weren't so good—and look on the chart for the foods you ate.

Check the two columns marked "Calories (KCAL)" and "Percent of Calories from Fat." For each food, multiply the *number of calories* by the *percent of calories from fat*. For example, if you had eaten three fresh apricots, the number of calories would be 51. The percentage of calories from fat would be .07 (7 percent). Multiply 51 × .07, which comes out to 3.57 calories from fat. Do this for all the foods you ate that day. Add up the total number of *calories* and the total number of *calories from fat*. Divide calories from fat by total calories. Say, for example, you ate 2,200 calories, and 880 of those were calories from fat. Divide 880 by 2,200. The result is .40 (40 percent)—telling you that 40 percent of the calories you ate that day came from fat.

For a quick guesstimate, look back on your four-day diary. Chances are, if your overall number of servings a week of red meat, ice cream, whole-fat cheese, whole-milk dairy products, egg yolks* and fast foods is greater than eight, you're getting more than 25 percent of your calories from fat. Make it your goal for the coming months to cut in half the amount of these foods you eat. If you're already eating eight servings a week or less of bad fats, you may choose to cut back to five servings or remain where you are.

Use the Fat Substitution table (below) to help you balance and moderate fat intake.

*The fitter you are, and the lower your total fat intake, the better your body removes cholesterol—such as that in egg yolks—from your body.

Fat Substitutions

Category	Go for the Good Foods (Substitute for bad fats when possible; eat in moderation)	Avoid the Bad Fats (Don't exceed 8 servings per week)
Dairy	Low-fat cheeses (cottage cheese, feta, part-skim mozzarella, ricotta); low-fat yogurt; 1%, 2% or skim milk (or, if you're not quite ready for skim, try cutting whole milk with 25% skim—later raise to 50%); tofu ice cream	High-fat cheeses (Brie, cheddar, Neufchâtel, Swiss, etc.); whole-fat yogurt; whole-fat milk; cream; ice cream
Meat and protein	Poultry, skinned and visible fat removed; fish; shellfish; dried beans and peas; egg substitutes and egg whites; tofu and tempeh	Red meat, all visible fat trimmed before cooking; organ meats; egg yolks; processed meats
Oils and frying mediums	Corn, cottonseed, safflower, soybean, sunflower	Bacon fat, lard, shortening
Spreads	Margarine, peanut butter without hydrogenated fat	Butter, "regular" peanut butter

Goal: *Fiber Up*

Date: _____

Walk: 7 days, 10 minutes, ½ mile

Last week, you worked on eating *less,* less of the nasty fats that clog the arteries and dimple the thighs. The good news this week is that you'll be eating *more,* munching and crunching on delicious foods every day. This is the week to add *fiber* to your diet. You don't have to face a small mountain of bran and tree bark every morning. We're talking about raspberries. Pasta. Potatoes, blueberries, baked beans, bananas, granola . . . *more* of the good things!

We guarantee you that this lipsmacking kind of eating isn't going to add pounds (if you play by the rules and stick to your exercise and low-fat ways). On the contrary, you may well shed pounds without ever having counted a calorie. Bulky high-fiber foods, like apples, are ideal for weight-watchers, because they satisfy the appetite, but contain relatively few calories. Research even indicates that calories from high-fiber foods "count less"—are less likely to be stored as fat—than calories from fat. There have been studies in which overweight people lost pounds *only* by adding fiber to their diets—with no other dietary changes!

Yet fiber does much, much more than ease the dieters' path. It may help prevent and/or provide some relief from many chronic illnesses, ranging from hemorrhoids and varicose veins to heart disease, appendicitis, diverticulosis (an intestinal disorder) and colon cancer. A Dutch study that followed 871 middle-aged men for ten years found that "men with a low intake of dietary fiber had a three times higher risk of death from all causes than men with a high intake." The researchers concluded that "a diet containing at least 37 grams [of] dietary fiber per day may be protective against chronic diseases in Western societies."

Pretty impressive. How does fiber do it? The first thing to understand is that whereas fiber is not a nutrient, it affects the way the body absorbs nutrients. It can add bulk to the diet, relieving constipation. It may bind to cholesterol and flush it from the body, which in the long run means lower risk of heart disease. It speeds up the digestive process, possibly minimizing exposure to harmful wastes in the intestinal tract, which means protection against colon cancer. And it may slow the release of sugars into the bloodstream, which is a boon for diabetics.

If you're an average American, you're probably consuming about 15 grams of fiber a day—roughly half the protective amount. (Consult the Superfoods chart and your food diary to compute the amount you're actually eating.)

520

- It really isn't all that difficult to get enough fiber. A cup of 100 percent bran cereal, one apple, one potato with skin, a nectarine, half a cup of split peas and half a cup of cooked spinach a day supply about 37 grams.
- Your dietary fiber should come from a variety of sources, like whole-grain foods, vegetables, fruits, nuts and dried beans. Variety is the key word here because all fibers are *not* alike. Wheat bran, for example, relieves constipation, but it's a matter of some controversy as to whether it can lower cholesterol levels. On the other hand, oat and corn bran can lower blood cholesterol levels. So can pectin, one of the forms of fiber found in produce like pears, bananas, apples, tomatoes and carrots. But neither oat bran nor pectin can relieve constipation. That's why variety is so important.
- Snack on fresh fruit. It's light, energizing and high in vitamins *and* you-know-what. Top ranking fruits, fiber-wise, are dried prunes, pears, nectarines and blackberries.
- Legumes—peas, soybeans, lentils and chick-peas—are super-high in fiber, outdoing most fruits and vegetables. A can of baked beans provides more than 7 grams of dietary fiber per 100 grams (3½ ounces) of beans, outdoing raw broccoli, which provides just 1.4 grams per 100 grams.
- Eat whole-grain breads and muffins. Use brown rice instead of white.

If you determine that you need more fiber, the increase should be gradual, since your system needs time to adjust. Go slowly. Increase your intake of dietary fiber in easy stages. If you suddenly blitz your body with bran, you'll experience intestinal distress. It will take a while for the helpful bacteria that live in your intestine to learn how to break down whole wheat, for example. The products of bacterial fermentation build up, causing bloating and gas. So prepare a sensible plan for adding fiber to your meals.

Goal: *Try a New Start*

Date: _____

Walk: 7 days, 10 minutes, ½ mile

What better way to get your year off to a good start than by getting your days off to a good start? That's what you'll be doing for the next two weeks: improving your morning *foods* and *moods*.

Start at the beginning, with wake-up. When you open your eyes in the morning, do you take a few moments to celebrate the new day?

Or is awakening the signal for little starting gates in your mind to swing open; your list of things "To Do" gallops out and you spend the rest of the day chasing after it?

If your money's on the To Do List, then you probably need help to relax. Sure, you just spent the night sleeping, but that's not the kind of relaxation we're talking about. We're referring to the stress management techniques that can

How to Meditate

There are many different schools of meditation in the United States, ranging from centers that practice Korean Zen Buddhist techniques, like the Cambridge Zen Center, to the Transcendental Meditation (TM) organization, which promotes a simplified form of yoga. The latter is the best-documented scientifically in terms of physiological changes and benefits, but unfortunately can be a relatively expensive activity.

Herbert Benson, M.D., a cardiologist and associate professor of medicine at the Harvard Medical School, in Cambridge, Massachusetts, was one of the first to study the physiological benefits of TM, and he adapted that technique for his bestselling book, *The Relaxation Response* (Avon).

Here is Dr. Benson's eight-step method to relaxation. Before you begin the doctor's technique, find a quiet environment free of distractions. If you must, hang a "Do Not Disturb" sign on the door.

1. Choose a word or phrase—a "mantra"— to focus on. Dr. Benson recommends "one," but you may prefer something else, like "love" or "peace." The word should have a soothing sound. Once you pick

help you be more optimistic, self-confident and productive on a day-to-day basis, and that in the long run may help lengthen your life by countering the cumulative impact of stress on your health.

These techniques induce a state of consciousness that's different from waking or sleeping. Practitioners have described it as profound rest combined with heightened awareness. You need to practice this kind of relaxation regularly to reap the benefits.

The technique you're going to learn this week is a kind of meditation, which involves sitting quietly and being aware of your breathing.

Morning is a very good time to meditate. "For two reasons," says George Bowman, Zen teacher at the Cambridge Zen Center, in Cambridge, Massachusetts. "First, it's usually quiet in the morning, so you don't have as many distractions." The other reason, says Bowman, is that it goes a long way toward getting your day off to the right kind of start. I can easily slip into a frustrated, anxiety-ridden way of thinking in the morning. What I usually do instead, first thing when I wake up, is watch my breathing. Even when I'm still in bed. It's nice to start the day from a quiet, centered place.

the word, you should stick with it, because you'll come to associate the word with calming effects.

2. Sit upright in a comfortable position, with your hands resting naturally in your lap.

3. Let your eyes close gently.

4. Take a few moments to relax your muscles.

5. Now, breathing normally, become aware of each breath. Working with the slow, natural rhythm of your breathing, repeat your focus word silently on every exhale.

6. Disregard distractions. Thoughts, imagery and feelings may drift into your awareness. "One should not concentrate on these perceptions, but allow them to pass on," says Dr. Benson.

7. Continue the technique for 10 to 20 minutes. Use your judgment, or sneak an occasional peek at a wristwatch. Don't use a timer or alarm clock, because the noise can be too jarring. When your time is up, remain quiet, with your eyes closed for a few minutes, to allow your thoughts to adjust to wakefulness.

8. Do this twice a day. Before breakfast and dinner are good times.

Good Morning.

Goal: *Go for a Better Breakfast*

Date: _____

Walk: 7 days, 15 minutes, ¾ mile

Sid feels nauseous when faced with food before 10:00 A.M. Irma's the opposite—she feels queasy all morning if she doesn't eat. Breakfast: Some people can't live with it, others can't live without it. Should those like Sid be urged to overcome their dislike of the morning meal? Maybe.

"By late morning, people who skip breakfast are likely to feel sluggish and dull. After going without food from 8:00 P.M. on, energy levels will dip at around 11:00 A.M. the next day, as blood sugar levels drop," says Brian L. G. Morgan, Ph.D., assistant professor of human nutrition at Columbia University College of Physicians and Surgeons, in New York City. "But studies also have shown that high-carbohydrate meals make people sleepy. A high-carbohydrate meal elevates levels of serotonin, a neurotransmitter in the brain that makes you feel sleepy.

"The sedating effect of a high-carbohydrate breakfast is more noticeable past the age of 40," says Dr. Morgan. "For some reason, many people in their twenties and thirties seem to be able to compensate and concentrate despite poor breakfast habits.

"Protein seems to counteract the sedating effect of carbohydrates. So the ideal breakfast is a combination of carbohydrates and protein," says Dr. Morgan.

So-called larks—people who do their best in the morning—may withstand skipping breakfast better than others, because their energy levels are on the upswing. "But by and large, skipping breakfast deprives your brain of the energy it needs to function at its best," says Dr. Morgan.

"If you don't perform well in the morning, try eating breakfast," says Judith J. Wurtman, Ph.D., research scientist at the Massachusetts Institute of Technology, in Cambridge. "It's that simple."

Skipping breakfast to forgo the calories—as many dieters do—is doubly defeating, according to Dr. Morgan. "Cutting calories in general often makes dieters feel lousy. Skipping breakfast will only make them feel worse. People who are trying to lose weight are better off consuming, say, 1,000 calories in three meals instead of two, because their metabolism revs up to digest each meal, burning extra calories in the process. So weight-watchers will lose more quickly if they eat part of their daily calories at breakfast."

Experts offer the following strategies to overcome the most common reasons for skipping—or skimping on—breakfast:

Have a midmorning snack—or an early lunch. If you have neither the time nor the appetite for an early-bird breakfast, brown bag it—or buy something nourishing on the way—and eat at your workplace.

"If you wait until 10:00 A.M. to eat breakfast, that's O.K.," says Dr. Morgan. "Or you can take an early lunch, as they do in Scandinavia. People there eat lunch at around 11:00 A.M."

Don't typecast your breakfast. If you're bored with conventional breakfast choices (cereal, toast, eggs, juice) or breakfast foods simply don't appeal to you at all—eat something you do like. A turkey sandwich, suggests Dr. Morgan, is a perfect example of a combination of protein and carbohydrates that can keep your energy levels from flagging before midday. So is a grilled cheese sandwich.

"Look to other cultures for ideas for interesting, nutritious breakfasts," suggests Dr. Wurtman. "In Japan, breakfast typically includes fish, seaweed and cooked rice. A typical Israeli breakfast may include cucumbers, tomatoes, low-fat cheese, smoked fish and fruit."

And in Holland and other parts of Europe, cheese and bread are standard breakfast fare.

Thinking beyond stereotypical breakfast food also helps if you're allergic to eggs, wheat and milk, three common food allergens that happen to be the mainstay of many breakfasts.

Nothing in the fridge? Improvise! Say you have plenty of cereal but the milk's gone sour. Or all that remains of the loaf of bread are two stale ends. If breakfast pickings are slim, look at what you *do* have. Leftover roast chicken and an apple; low-fat cottage cheese or yogurt with cantaloupe; crackers and tuna or cold salmon sprinkled with lemon juice—all make great breakfasts (and perk up jaded taste buds, too!).

Prepare your breakfast the night before. "I just can't make food decisions in the morning," says one woman. "It's hard enough to decide what to wear to work."

If that sounds like you on a typical weekday morning, make your breakfast—or part of it—the night before. Set out your cereal bowl and spoon. Select a piece of fruit and wash it—and place the paring knife where you'll be able to find it quickly in the morning. Then you can eat breakfast on automatic pilot.

If you're not used to eating breakfast, start with small portions. "If the thought of eating breakfast disgusts you, try small amounts to begin with, even if it's only a slice of toast or a little cereal with milk," says Dr. Morgan.

Too big a breakfast can leave you groggy, especially if you're not used to it, adds Dr. Morgan. "The effect on performance is the equivalent of not getting a good night's sleep. So whatever you do about breakfast, be consistent. If you eat a light breakfast most days, a big breakfast will make you feel groggy and dull."

Goal: *Stretch Yourself*

Date: _____

Walk: 7 days, 15 minutes, ¾ mile

A good stretching program can increase flexibility regardless of your age, says Jeri Katz, president of the Fitness Barn, a New York City consulting group that provides exercise programs for employees at the Beth Israel Hospital, in Manhattan, and other New York City hospitals and corporations.

"People can definitely become more flexible as they get older instead of less," says Katz. "But, like everything else, it takes consistent practice. You don't have to stretch every single day if you don't want. But do stretch before you exercise, and try to do a full stretching routine two or three times a week. Don't skip a week."

This stretching routine was developed by Katz. Before you start, a few rules:

- Before you begin stretching, take a few controlled deep breaths, to relax and expand your lungs and rib cage, and create a deeper awareness of your body. Try to count to 15 as you inhale, and 15 as you exhale. Repeat ten times.
- Use gentle, slow, deliberate movements. Go to the point where you feel the muscle stretch—but no pain—and hold that position.
- Remember to breathe as you stretch. And exhale as you release the tension from your muscles.
- Repeat the movement until you feel the stretch again. Don't bounce.

- Never lock your joints, especially your knees.

You'll find that these exercises stretch with you—that is, over time you'll be able to do more and more. It's a very basic routine. You may want to supplement it with stretches to suit your particular needs.

From a Standing Position

Legs should be shoulder-width apart, arms at your side.

Full Body Stretch. Inhale slowly, and as you do, bring your arms above your head, go up on your toes and reach up as high as you can. Hold a second or two, then exhale, bringing arms down and heels back to the floor. Repeat three times.

Reach-Overs. Drop your right hand down so it touches and trails down the side of your right thigh to your knee, as you lean from your waist to your right. Your left upper arm should be raised close to your ear, left hand pointing to the right. Stretch by moving your left arm a little further to the right. Stretch eight times to your right. Then, drop your left arm, curl slightly forward and over to the left side, bring up the right arm, and stretch eight times to the left side. This stretches the waist and side of the body.

526

Neck Stretches. Stand upright again. Facing forward, tilt your head to the right, so your right ear approaches your right shoulder, and hold a second. Repeat to the left. Do slowly three times on each side. Then, bring your head forward and down, so chin approaches chest. Hold, then tilt your head back so you're looking straight up. Repeat three times, slowly.

Now, swivel your head so you're looking out over your right shoulder. (Keep shoulders facing forward.) Hold. Then turn head slowly to left. Hold. Repeat three times in each direction, remembering to breathe.

Calf Stretch. Especially good for walkers. Stand about two feet from a wall, facing it. Put your palms against the wall, at about shoulder height and shoulder-width apart. Step forward with your right foot so it's only about a foot from the wall. Both heels should be on the ground. Bend your right knee and bring your hips gently toward the wall, so you feel a stretch in the back of your left calf. Hold for five breaths. Repeat five times. Reverse legs and repeat.

Sitting Stretches

Sit on the floor, with your legs together, straight out in front of you.

Spine Stretch. Lean forward and grasp your legs as far down as you can without straining—at your lower calfs, ankles or toes. Gently drop your head and stretch yourself forward. Your elbows should naturally bend and go outside of your legs. Your head should approach your knees, and your back should be rounded. Hold. This stretches thighs, legs and gluteals. Stretch forward eight times. You should feel the stretch in your upper back as you relax the spine.

Side to Side. Sit up and spread your legs as far apart as is comfortable. Then, bring your right heel in to your inner thigh. Your left leg should be out straight. Gently, stretch out over your left leg, reaching both arms forward. Put both hands as far down on your left leg as you comfortably can. Bend elbows, drop head, round your back, relax shoulders and gently stretch downward eight times. This stretches your spine and leg muscles. Come up, and reverse, so your left heel is in to your thigh and your right leg is out. Stretch right eight times.

Then, with both legs straightened and spread out, put your hands in front of your thighs on the floor and stretch forward, relaxing your shoulders and bending your elbows. This stretches your inner thighs.

If you experience any pain as the result of performing these exercises, be sure to check with your doctor. And always be sure to warm up before you stretch.

Goal: *Check Your Calcium*

Date: _____

Walk: 7 days, 20 minutes, 1 mile

This is the week to hug a farmer: Because the milk they squeeze from cows and the greens they pull from the earth are among the best sources of a nutrient that's vital to staying healthy and active: calcium.

Women, pay special attention. You're most susceptible to a disease called osteoporosis, thinning and weakening of the bones, a problem which some experts say is virtually an epidemic among older American females. Calcium may help prevent the disease. And even if you've already started to lose bone density, adequate amounts of calcium plus regular exercise can help stop the loss and strengthen the bones you have left.

But this milk's for you too, Bud! It's not just women who should keep calcium intake up. Studies suggest that calcium may help prevent high blood pressure, and that it may help lower blood pressure significantly in some hypertensives. Other studies report that calcium has been used successfully to treat gum disease and to lower blood fats. Some people even claim that taking extra calcium has relieved their muscle cramps and spasms.

Just how much calcium do you need? The current Recommended Dietary Allowance is 800 milligrams (mg) per day for adults. But experts generally agree that some people need more, possibly 1,200 mg per day for teenagers, 1,000 mg for women aged 20 until the onset of menopause, and from 1,000 to 1,500 mg after menopause.

Add It Up

Are you getting enough calcium? A federal survey shows that up to 50 percent of men aged 18 to 34 don't get enough calcium in their diet, and *two-thirds* of women between 18 and 74 are falling short!

So use the Superfoods chart to estimate your calcium intake for at least two days in Week 1. How did you do?

Getting enough calcium isn't always easy. Unfortunately, many of the foods that are calcium-rich tend to contain a fair amount of fat and sodium too, like some cheeses and milk. Many Americans—like people of Eastern European, Asian and African descent—can't digest lactose, the form of sugar in milk (although lactose-free milk is available in many stores). In addition, milk triggers food allergies for many people.

If you're definitely down on dairy products, it is possible to get enough calcium from other sources. It gets into cow milk, after all, from the green they graze on. In fact, a study which appeared in the *New England Journal of Medicine* concluded that the calcium intake of today's hunter-gatherer tribes who eat no dairy products is more than 1,500 mg per day! Consult the Superfoods chart to see which foods to hunt and gather for your daily fare. Fish with soft bones that you can eat—like sardines and salmon—are good bets. So are green, leafy vegetables; chick-peas; figs; black-strap molasses; oranges; broccoli; navy beans; soy products like tofu; shellfish like scallops and shrimp; and nuts like brazil nuts, almonds and filberts.

Annemarie Colbin, director of the Natural Gourmet Cookery School, in New York City, and author of *The Book of Whole Meals* (Ballantine), recommends that people eat greens like kale, collards and mustard greens to maximize calcium intake. "People don't eat them enough, because they cook them wrong and then these kinds of greens can taste too bitter." Colbin maintains that steaming the "bitter" greens for a few minutes isn't enough. "I boil them for 10 minutes, uncovered so they don't turn brown. Then I scoop them out, chop them up, sauté in olive oil with garlic, and dust with a tiny bit of nutmeg. Delicious!"

If you do love milk, the calcium requirement will be a snap. A glass of low-fat milk contains about 300 mg of calcium, so several eight-ounce glasses would meet the Recommended Dietary Allowance. Another plus: Milk is rich in other vitamins and minerals which may enhance calcium's effectiveness. Research indicates that milk may also protect against colon and rectal cancer, because the calcium with the assistance of vitamin D may form compounds that flush harmful fatty acids from the body. Low-fat yogurts and cheeses are fine ways to meet your calcium requirement too, though they don't contain much vitamin D.

If your diet is irregular, or you can see that you're not getting enough calcium from food alone, you may wish to take a calcium supplement. Chapter 5 explains what to look for in a supplement.

If hypertension is a problem, think potassium when you think calcium. Together, these minerals may work even more effectively to pull down blood pressure. Foods that are high in both potassium and calcium include yogurt, sardines, milk, buttermilk, salmon, broccoli, almonds and soybeans. Other potassium-rich foods to indulge in: apricots, avocados, bananas, potatoes, cantaloupe and turkey.

And remember to keep walking. Calcium will do its job best if you're getting regular exercise.

Goal: *Meet a Friend*

Date: _____

Walk: 7 days, 20 minutes, 1 mile

A faithful friend is the medicine of life.

> (Ecclus. 6:16)

That biblical wisdom is also medical fact. Researchers are finding that people with social ties live longer than isolated people, *regardless* of cigarette smoking, alcohol consumption, obesity, sleeping and eating habits or even medical care. Which is not to say that your program this week requires nightly beer bashes! It *does* mean that if you scored low on the quiz on pages 260–261, this is the week to start bringing that score up. If you do, you're in for a powerfully rejuvenating year!

Ten Ways to Start Meeting and Greeting

Leave home. Go looking. The only people who come looking for you buried in your house are burglars and intruders.

Look at yourself in the mirror and ask yourself honestly, "What do I have to offer?" One woman said she invited more people to her house than invited her back. Sometimes you have to do that.

Sit down and write a resume—not for a job but for a friendship. If you have nothing but blank spaces on the sheet, you can start now and work on it.

Start with acquaintances—don't ask for friends. They might turn into friends, but if they don't, acquaintances might be all you need.

Make a list of all the clubs, groups and organizations in your community—then ask yourself, "What's in it for me?" It's O.K. to ask that. It sounds crass, but in the long run it works for you and the organization.

Put a star near the *doing* types of organizations. Making small talk while sitting with your hands folded is a bore. You will do better hiking or stuffing envelopes for a political campaign or delivering meals-on-wheels with a partner.

The same is true of taking a course. Pick one that's a workshop, so you don't sit and listen to a professor lecture. You meet people by *doing things together.* (Be leery of applying this rule to bar-hopping—ahem.) A very basic interaction between two people is to teach someone something. You can teach for a little money in a not-for-credit evening course. Or, you can volunteer.

What can I teach?

- Bridge
- Chess
- Computer skills
- Cooking
- Gardening
- How to insulate a house
- How to paint a house

530

- Math
- Oil painting
- Reading, to a child
- Skiing
- Spanish
- Tennis

Put up with nonsense. To have friends, you have to do that. Committee meetings can drive you crazy, but loneliness can too. You simply have to put up with bother.

Don't fight with all your relatives. Relatives can be friends. And they'll hold your hand when you have been deserted by the world—and maybe even deserved it.

Don't fight with your neighbors. Once you start a fight, it can turn into a real Hatfield-McCoy feud, with your grandchildren still fighting when your bones are phosphorus ash.

Live someplace where things are going on. You don't have to go as far as one woman, who described her apartment complex as "a regular Peyton Place," and said the words with pride. But you certainly don't want to hibernate in a cellar, either.

Excerpted and condensed from *Kim Williams' Book of Uncommon Sense; A Practical Guide with 10 Rules for Nearly Everything* (HP Books). The late Kim Williams was a writer, amateur naturalist, teacher, lecturer, hiker and traveler. For ten years, she was a guest commentator on National Public Radio's award-winning "All Things Considered." She met her husband in a nightclub.

Important Reminder

Have you done at least one cancer self-examination since you began this program eight weeks ago?

Women should be doing breast self-exams, and men, testicular self-exams, once a month. While the chances are you'll find nothing, breast and testicular cancers are much more treatable if they're caught early.

For instructions, refer to page 86 for the breast self-exam, and page 87 for the testicular self-exam.

Goal: *Shake Your Salt Habit*

Date: _____

Walk: 7 days, 25 minutes, 1¼ miles

You know that your body needs salt—but did you know that it needs only a quarter teaspoon a day? The average American's daily consumption is 20 times that amount!

There's no doubt whatever that salt, a guest at almost every kitchen table in America, can contribute to high blood pressure. Even moderate cutbacks in salt can help bring a person's blood pressure down to healthier levels.

But unfortunately, salt, like fat, can be hard to avoid because so much of it is *invisible*—tucked into processed foods, commercial baked goods and fast foods. Soft drinks can be notoriously high in the stuff: So even if you've virtuously replaced the salt in your shaker with an herbal mixture, you could still be overdosing on salt from that chicken soup you bought in the deli, the tomato paste you used in your homemade pasta recipe, the cheese you're eating to boost calcium levels. A little vigilance is in order!

The other problem is that salt is a little bit "addictive." If you try to go cold turkey, foods may taste flavorless at first. There are several ways around this dilemma. One is a little creative herbcraft, which puts even better flavor into foods. And the salt cravings usually diminish over time. Scientists at the University of California at Davis School of Medicine illustrated it was so. They restricted the sodium intake of 43 people aged 25 to 49. Another group had no salt reduction. At the end of six months, both groups were served salted and unsalted soups, and were asked to mix the two until the soup reached the desired level of saltiness. The low-sodium subjects reduced their salting level by more than 50 percent, while the other group had virtually unchanged tastes.

A diet moderately low in sodium contains 2,200 to 3,000 milligrams of sodium per day—the equivalent of about 1 to 1½ teaspoons. If your diet is heavy on the prepared and processed foods, and if you eat in restaurants—or friend's houses, for that matter—it's quite likely you're getting too much salt.

Use the Superfoods chart to estimate your sodium intake during at least two days you tracked the first week. If you find that the figure is high, it's time to take action!

At Home

This is where it's easiest to ebb the salt tide. If you haven't already, invest in one of the herbal salt substitutes. By the way, we recommend avoiding potassium chloride, the most common salt substitute and lookalike. The Food and Drug Administration says no one, especially children, should use it without a doctor's O.K. Too much can be dangerous, especially if you're being treated for certain medical conditions, like diabetes or kidney or heart disease.

• Limit yourself to two or three soft drinks a week, or less (unless you buy the sodium-free variety).
• Limit fast foods, processed foods and convenience foods, unless they specifically indicate that they're low in sodium.
• Say "no thanks" to high-salt meats like bacon, ham, sausage, frankfurters and luncheon meats.

Pass up the salted nuts, pickles and sauerkraut.
• Fill your table shaker with herbs, or in the beginning, half herbs and half salt. Cut your use of salt in cooking by two-thirds.
• Go easy on cheese—it tends to be high in salt as well as fat.

At the Market

The front line of your battle against salt is the supermarket aisle. Check labels for sodium content. Everything from soup to nuts is available in low-sodium varieties these days—not to mention low-sodium cheese, crackers, pretzels and pickles.

Herb-and-Spice Salt Substitutes

Product	Taste	Aroma	Comments
Mrs. Dash	Excellent, well-balanced peppery citrus flavor	Peppery and robust	Good low-cal topping for baked potatoes; Low-Pepper and No-Garlic varieties
Deep Roots	Good, herbal flavor; Mexican very hot	Herbal	Mexican, Whole Herb and Italian flavors
Instead of Salt	Good, well-chosen flavors; most should be added before cooking	Good and full, especially Vegetable flavor	All-Purpose, Fish, Chicken, Beef and Vegetable flavors
Mixed Spices for Low-Sodium Diet	Nicely balanced flavors, especially Grill flavor	Full	Meat, Chicken, Herb and Grill flavors
Vegit	Good, slightly yeasty	Herbal and yeasty	Good on popcorn

Goal: *Put Laughter into Your Life*

Date: _____

Walk: 7 days, 25 minutes, 1¼ miles

This week, you should look again at the diary you kept for the first week. What you're looking for this time isn't exactly exercise, though it gets the body moving and turns the cheeks pink. It isn't exactly a nutrient, though it is nourishing. It's laughter.

Do you remember laughing that week? Did you laugh today? If you're not meeting the recommended daily requirement of lots of laughter and joy every single day, then you should make it a priority!

That advice comes from a growing number of doctors, psychologists and "laymen"—like Norman Cousins, former *Saturday Review* editor, who, in his bestselling book *Anatomy of an Illness* (Bantam), describes how he recovered from a debilitating spinal disorder by checking *out* of the hospital ("A hospital is no place to be for a person who is seriously ill," he writes), and into a hotel room. There he entertained himself with humorous books and films like those of the Marx Brothers as well as television show reruns like Candid Camera. "I made the joyous discovery that 10 minutes of genuine belly laughter had an anesthetic effect, and would give me at least two hours of pain-free sleep."

He recovered from the disease, he says, beating 500 to 1 odds. Later, he was appointed a se-nior lecturer at the University of California School of Medicine at Los Angeles. After long years of resistance, the medical establishment has admitted—and proven—the power that thinking has over health.

"Norman Cousins calls laughter an internal jog, and what I like about it is that you don't have to wear a special outfit," says Joyce Anisman-Saltman, a brassy, Brooklyn-bred, certified psychotherapist, assistant professor of Special Education at Southern Connecticut State University, in New Haven, and sometime-standup comedienne, who teaches executives, teachers and clients all over the country how to take responsibility for putting more laughter into their lives. Anisman-Saltman notes that laughter brings on a host of physiological changes, ranging from the release of painkilling endorphins (which accounts for drug-free relief) to a "cleansing" tearing of the eye "so the world looks brighter," to an expansion of the capillaries under the cheeks. "That makes your cheeks pink," she notes. "You'll notice that my cheeks are always pink." (They are.) "I never wear blush or foundation. It's because I laugh hard and often. You'll save a bundle on cosmetics. And it's especially important for men, who look tacky in blush."

534

In an only slightly more serious vein, Anisman-Saltman notes that in addition to the proven physiological benefits, laughter can cut the cycle of psychological negativity that people can fall into. Laughter can renew their perspective. Here is her advice for putting more laughter and joy into your life:

"Make a list of 20 things you like to do. They don't all have to be ambitious things, like taking a trip around the world. My list includes things like, 'Take showers,' 'Get my back scratched,' 'Listen to music while I drive.' Every single day I do 18 of the 20 things on my list, and if my husband's not tired, 19. Don't wait for vacations to nurture yourself—the vacations may never come. Be good to yourself every day.

"Call in Well. If you don't like your job, and you find yourself feeling terrific one day, take the day off. Why should you only stay home when you feel sick?

"If you can afford it, get a VCR. This adjunct to television is a *must* for chronic pain patients. Use it to record programs that tickle you— Buddy Hackett reruns, the Cosby show, whatever. Then you can watch them anytime you want.

"Devote a corner of your home solely to humor. Get funny books, paste up cartoons. (I have cartoons all over the house, even on the front door!) This is not to say that everything can be joyous and happy all the time—but it will help you deal with serious things.

"And surround yourself with positive people!"

Make Your List

Use this space for your list of 20 things you enjoy doing. "It may be harder than you think," says psychotherapist Joyce Anisman-Saltman. "But don't give up. Then, every single day, you make sure you do at least half the things on the list."

1.	11.
2.	12.
3.	13.
4.	14.
5.	15.
6.	16.
7.	17.
8.	18.
9.	19.
10.	20.

Goal: *Color Code Your Diet for Health*

Date: _____

Walk: 7 days, 30 minutes, 1½ miles

Riddle: What's green and yellow and orange-red all over?

Give up?

The answer should be on your plate: fruits and vegetables.

Mom was right, and so was Popeye. It's not simply a matter of vitamins, minerals and fiber—as if those weren't good enough reasons to eat this delicious, low-calorie fare provided fresh by Mother Nature.

Mounting scientific evidence suggests that eating fruits and vegetables has regenerative benefits. Eminent authorities, from the National Academy of Sciences to the American Cancer Society, say orchard and garden fare have specific substances that may prevent disease. There is even evidence that these foods may reduce the risk wrought by years of bad habits, such as reducing the risk of lung cancer for smokers.

Check your food diary. Did you eat at least one serving of fresh fruits or vegetables at every meal? If not, it's time to start. If you can decorate your plate at each meal with shades of green, red, orange and yellow, you'll have a beautiful way of eating that will help put you in the pink!

Green is for leafy vegetables, like Popeye's favorite, spinach, along with kale, parsley, beet greens, lettuce, chard and others.

You've already seen the greens lauded as prime sources of calcium and fiber.

But perhaps most important, these green leaves—along with broccoli and reddish fruits and vegetables—are high in vitamin A and beta-carotene, a specific form of vitamin A which scientific studies strongly indicate has a protective effect against a number of different cancers. In one study, the more carotene-rich vegetables people ate, the less risk they had of developing cancer.

And there's more. The greens are good sources of vitamin C. Studies indicate that people whose diets are rich in vitamin C are less likely to get cancer, particularly of the stomach and esophagus. It may also keep the immune system healthy, enhance absorption of iron for strong blood and help control cholesterol levels.

Another cancer-fighting substance in greens is chlorophyll, the green substance that turns sunlight into plant food. Scientists have found that chlorophyll has certain healing qualities, possibly including the ability to reduce the damage carcinogens wreak on cells. The greens are fair sources of the B vitamins, potassium, magnesium and iron.

Green. This color identifies cabbage and its kin, brussels sprouts,

536

broccoli and their pale cousin cauliflower. This "cruciferous" family may have special cancer-fighting properties, in addition to fiber and vitamins A and C. People who consume these vegetables may have a lower risk of developing cancer; and tests in laboratory animals reveal that the cruciferous vegetables may prevent chemically-induced cancer.

Red and Orange. These are the "Pilgrim" vegetables, like pumpkins, sweet potatoes, squash, red peppers and carrots. They're rich in beta-carotene, the nutrient linked to cancer prevention. They also provide plenty of fiber and other nutrients.

Red and orange are also for fruits like peaches, cherries, apricots, cantaloupes, mangoes and papaya, which are rich in beta-carotene, fiber and vitamins. These fruits also contain potassium.

Orange and Yellow. These colors mark the citrus fruits. A group of Florida researchers note that in Florida colon cancer rates are lower than in the northern states.

Many of the people who live in Florida have backyard citrus trees, and the scientists say that the easy availability of the fruit may be the prime protective factor. They speculate that vitamins A, C and E, as well as the fiber pectin, may have a synergistic effect that helps prevent cancer.

What's more, citrus fruits offer generous amounts of vitamin C and also provide some B vitamins, potassium and bioflavonoids, nutrients that strengthen capillary walls.

It's not really difficult to add these color-coded foods to each and every meal. Breakfast is easy: a half-grapefruit, some orange juice—or, if you're late, an apple to munch on the way to work.

These days, lunch is easy too. Most restaurants, and even some fast-food outlets, present beautiful salad bars.

Dinner can fill out the day if you have soup that contains vegetables, a salad and two vegetables with your entree. Still hungry? Have a piece of fruit!

Goal: *Take Inventory*

Date: _____

Walk: 7 days, 30 minutes, 1½ miles

Inventory 2

I. Diary

	Sunday	Monday	Tuesday	
Food and Drink A.M. P.M.				
Moods and Activities Summary				
Exercise and Stretching				
Relaxation				

II. Vital Statistics

1. Weight _____ 2. Resting pulse _____ beats/minute

	Wednesday	Thursday	Friday	Saturday

3. Blood pressure_____ 4. Cholesterol _____ mg/deciliter

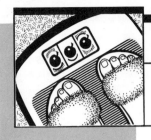

Goal: *Check the Fat*

Date: _____

Walk: 7 days, 35 minutes, 1¾ miles

This week is structured especially for people who want to lose weight. But first, a new goal for *everyone.* In Week 2, servings of high-fat food were cut in half. Starting this week, try to cut back to eight servings a week. To accomplish this may mean saying "no thanks" to butter one night at dinner; frying up onions, mushrooms, and tofu instead of steak; piling your potato with low-fat yogurt instead of sour cream. Keep substituting and finding ways to enjoy!

For weight-watchers only: Have you noticed? To date, there's been no information about weight loss. In fact, over the past months, you've counted everything—fat, fiber, calcium, sodium, laughs—everything *but* calories. So maybe you're wondering when the heavy-duty *dieting* starts.

Believe it or not, your weight-control program began three months ago, and is going strong. If you've been following the suggestions week by week, then you probably *are* shedding fat.

The beauty of the life-style outlined here is that if you need to lose weight—you *will.* Calorie counting does have its place in a weight loss plan—but remember:

• Regular aerobic exercise is one of the most effective diet tricks around. It burns calories, creates muscle, which requires more calories to sustain, and increases metabolism all day long. And contrary to popular mythology, it will not give you Godzilla's appetite!

• A low-fat/high-fiber diet is another effective weight loss tactic; it fills you up with a minimum of calories and reduces the number of calories that your body turns into fat.

Losing weight has been compared to building a house: The longer it takes to do it, the longer it's apt to last.

Suppose you've been following the program faithfully, but still aren't dropping pounds at the pace you'd like? Don't despair. If you are exercising, you're probably building muscle, which weighs more than fat. It also looks much better in a bathing suit!

If that scale just isn't budging, and your clothes aren't getting looser, either, then it's probably time for you to count your calories.

Use the Superfoods chart to estimate your calories for a day in Week 12. Now count up the calories and see if they exceed the levels outlined in the accompanying box.

The good thing about counting calories is that it can make you aware of hidden sources. For example, did you know that eight ounces of orange juice contain 112 calories, more than twice as much as the same amount of tomato juice? If you downed half a pitcher of citrus juice after your last walk in the sun, you're probably hitting your forehead and saying—"Gee! I could've had a V-8!" Or a glass of mineral water, for that matter.

Inner Dieting

Losing weight is a mind/body exercise—you have to change your head to change your body. Here are some suggestions that will help.

- *Don't* get too ambitious and set an unrealistically low ideal weight, or try to starve yourself to levels below the caloric goals outlined in the box. Your body will start to believe it's starving, and eventually will try to protect you by producing *more,* not fewer fat cells. Mentally, deprivation will set you up for a binge.
- Don't forbid your favorite foods, either. Moderate them. The foods to outlaw are the high-calorie staples you may be taking for granted—like oily dressings on salads, or butter on vegetables.

A Trick to Tote Up Calories

Here's an easy way to "guesstimate" the number of calories you can eat each day to maintain your ideal weight. To lose weight, of course, eat fewer calories. If you're on the walking program, you're probably in the "reasonably active" category.

If You Are . . .	And Want to Weigh . . .	Multiply By . . .	For Your Total Daily Calories Limit
very inactive (don't exercise)	_____ ×	13	= _____
mildly active (exercise once in a while)	_____ ×	14	= _____
reasonably active (exercise once or twice a week, walk a fair amount and put physical energy into the job)	*139* ×	15	= _____
very active (do aerobic workouts 3 to 4 hours a week and a somewhat physically demanding job)	_____ ×	17	= _____
super-active (training for a marathon and work on a loading dock)	_____ ×	21	= _____

Goal: *Picture the New You*

Date: _____

Walk: 7 days, 35 minutes, 1¾ miles

Week 14

Take a moment right now to think about the not-so-distant future, nine months from today. Turn to the end of your Year of Rejuvenation program and, in your mind, fill out the blanks of the final inventory. Can you see yourself that week, fitter and more energetic, eating right and exercising regularly?

If this picture is clearly focused, you may have come a long way toward making it a reality. A technique called "visualization," playing out positive images in your mind, can benefit your well-being in many ways. Psychologists have used visualization to help people change their behaviors, their bodies and even their lives.

Peter Miller, Ph.D., executive director of Hilton Head Institute, in Hilton Head, South Carolina, uses visualization to motivate overweight people to trim down. "We tell them to imagine that they are about 20 pounds lighter . . . Then we ask them to imagine how it would feel to be shopping for flattering clothes, or to be working in an office or to be in certain family situations. It's important for them to visualize themselves behaving differently rather than just appearing different."

The power of visualization has been used for other kinds of physical improvement, too. Suki Rappaport, Ph.D., movement educator, fitness consultant and director of the Transformations Institute, in Corte Madera, California, has studied and interviewed 25 people who have accomplished remarkable physical transformations, like overcoming disfiguring accidents, in some way slowing the aging process and conditioning their body to an extraordinary degree. "All these people told me the same thing," says Dr. Rappaport. "They all had an image in their minds of who and what they wanted to be. And they literally grew their physical body into that imagined form."

Everyone has the ability to transform himself or herself, says Dr. Rappaport, but, "We must not only learn to create positive images and hold them in our mind, but to act upon them . . . The image guides and reinforces those acts, and vice versa."

One super-athlete who has used visualization to motivate and change himself is bodybuilder Arnold Schwarzenegger. "When I train the biceps, I picture huge mountains, much bigger than biceps can ever be," says Schwarzenegger. "My wanting to be Mr. Universe came about because I saw myself so clearly being up there on the stage and winning."

So this week, begin painting a brighter picture of the *future* you!

Take a Free Vacation

Here's a way you can enjoy the relaxing benefits of an ocean, lake or wilderness vacation without spending a cent on airfare: visualization. Sharon Fried-Buchalter, a behavior modification therapist and stress management consultant to major hospitals and corporations in Manhattan, teaches her clients to imagine themselves in an idyllic setting, for effective stress control. One widely held theory explaining the effect of this kind of concentrated "imagining" is that it apparently fools the subconscious mind, which can't always differentiate between an actual experience and a vivid image. It calms the body down.

"If you're imagining a relaxing scene, you have a feeling of actually being there," says Fried-Buchalter. "It relieves stress. Like other good relaxation techniques, that means it can reduce blood pressure, and may reduce the risk of stress-related disease."

Fried-Buchalter suggests using this realization technique several times a week, or as needed. Do it at home, in a room free of distracting sounds. Make sure you're wearing loose-fitting clothing, and lying down or sitting in a comfortable chair. Take a few deep, controlled breaths before you start. Visualize a scenario that goes something like this:

"You're going to take a mental journey. You can go alone, or bring your favorite people, whatever's most comfortable. It starts as you step into a forest. You can smell the trees, the scent of pine is all around you. You can see the blue sky above you and feel the sun shining warm on your skin. There's a warm breeze blowing.

"You come to a clearing, and there's a field of flowers. Smell all the beautiful wild flowers. Now you approach a small lake. Dip your hand into the water. Feel it running down your hands and your arms, soft on your skin.

"Now you're going past a pond, and you reach the beach. There's an ocean of blue water. The temperature is just right. Walk into the water and start to float. Feel the sun on your body.

"Now come out of the water, dry yourself off, lie down on a blanket on the sand. Maybe your friends are there with you. You can feel the breeze, see the palm trees swaying."

Whenever you want to end the journey—say after 15 minutes—return slowly by becoming aware of your breathing. "Now you should feel very relaxed," says Fried-Buchalter.

She adds that you don't have to take this precise journey. You can linger at the place you like most—be it forest, lake or seashore. Of course, you can make your imaginary journey a visit to any paradise you like.

Goal: *Go on a Shopping Spree*

Date: _____

Walk: 7 days, 40 minutes, 2 miles

You've worked hard over the past 14 weeks, exercising and eating right. It's definitely time for a reward. A tangible reward. Something you can touch. Something you can hang in your closet. Something you can wear and feel great in.

It's time for a shopping spree! Tell your neighbor, your accountant or your spouse that it's not just frivolity. This kind of splurge can have important and lasting benefits.

But before you start spending, it's important to do a little thinking first.

You want a wardrobe that will help you grow and explore your potential. Think about some of the things you'd like to do this year: start a new class, meet more people, join a health spa or just feel better in your daily activities. Look for clothing that will give you confidence in both new—and familiar—situations and if you're still at a loss for what to buy, check the following shopping lists of worthwhile wardrobe investments. You can also refer back to chapter 40.

Hold on one more second! Before you dash out the door waving that credit card, a last word of advice from psychotherapist Joyce Anisman-Saltman, M.S. "Try it on. Look at yourself in the mirror. If your reflection doesn't make you smile—don't buy it!"

For anyone who hates shopping—man or woman—it's a good idea when you do shop to buy several items that match. That way, you won't have to shop again for a long time, and clothes you pull out of the closet every morning will always go together. How about:

Wardrobe Shopping List

Women:

• A richly colored scarf. Buying one is the *minimum* splurge for this week. A simple scarf can go a long way. It brightens a dark outfit—and a sallow complexion—and can bring out the color of your eyes.

• A versatile, quality dress. One, for example, made of cotton jersey. It drapes nicely, resists wrinkling, can be worn to the office or dressed up with heels and jewelry to wear out to dinner or even to an afternoon wedding. It's good for summer, or with a jacket, to wear in an overheated office in winter.

• A neat jacket. Wear it anywhere from the office to your literature class. You may be surprised to find that people listen to you more when you dress with authority. So don't make this purchase lightly. Invest in a figure-flattering, comfortable jacket that you really like. Maybe one that matches the new dress and scarf. Material? The nubby linens are nice; or a silk/

544

linen/polyester blend, with an open weave.

- Smart-looking, well-made slacks. That doesn't mean polyester pull-ons or silk pajamas. Try a pleated pair, made of summer-weight wool, or wool gabardine. Choose a color that's neutral but not boring, like a muted brick, which goes with teal, green, camel brown or navy.
- Good shoes. Shoes can make or break your outfit—not to mention your mood. Fortunately, comfortable flats can be just as fashionable as heels. Flats are, of course, better for your feet, but when you need heels, try to find the most comfortable ones you can. Consider having your feet measured the next time you're in a shoe store. One of the ironies of growing older is that while most of the skeleton shrinks, the feet, alas, spread.

Men:

- A good sports jacket, perhaps in a lightweight wool, and a conservative (but not drab) color and cut. To protect your investment, avoid extremes in lapel size and cut, so the jacket doesn't become out-dated in a year.
- A few shirts that match the jacket. Choose a full-cut shirt if you're large; a tapered-cut if you're slender. While you're at it, get some matching slacks.
- If you don't have one already, a quality overcoat or suit. They are expensive, but this kind of invest-ment will pay off for many years. Be sure to have it fitted to your figure.
- A variety of shoes. Those wing-top oxfords look awful with any-thing but a business suit, and loaf-ers aren't suitable for work. You need a good pair (black) or two (black and brown) for business, and a pair of casual shoes like loaf-ers or top-siders for after hours. And keep them polished! For sports, buy the best pair of sneakers you can afford.
- Socks should always be dark in color, except for athletic socks.
- Ties are for fun. Buy a beautiful silk tie that goes with your shirts and suit—but consider something madcap as well.
- For the daring, try a hat. A tweed cap adds the jauntiness of an En-glish sports car, a straw boater shields you from the summer sun. And wearing the hometown team's baseball cap will endear you to all the kids on the block—both big and little.

Goal: *Get Into Grains*

Date: _____

Walk: 7 days, 40 minutes, 2 miles

Grains are probably the least expensive, but richest source of nutritional rejuvenation around. You already know about the importance of eating whole-grain foods for their fiber content. But whole grains provide much more than fiber. Satisfying dishes like mushroom-barley soup, rice pilaf, buckwheat pancakes or Mexican rice-and-beans can restore and protect health in ways you may never have considered.

First, the whole grains that go into these kinds of dishes—like brown rice, buckwheat, barley, corn millet and wheat—are low in fat and free of cholesterol. Second, they're loaded with vitamins, particularly vitamin E and many of the all-important B vitamins. Third, they're crucial sources of minerals: iron, magnesium, zinc, copper, manganese and selenium, good for everything from rapid wound healing to healthy nerves, muscles and kidneys.

And grain has one more sterling quality: *Protein,* which helps muscle tissue to regenerate.

Just what is a grain? Basically, it's a seed—a seed composed of the *germ* (which allows the seed to germinate), the *endosperm* (the starchy part that nourishes the seedling during its early growth) and the *bran* (the protective outer hull). Whole grains have all three

parts, and are delicious.

By eating more grain and less meat and whole-fat dairy foods, you'll help ensure that your eating habits correspond to the nutritious low-fat, high-fiber diet that authorities say helps to prevent disease.

And you needn't worry about gaining weight from grains. In fact, you'll probably *lose* weight, since with grains a little goes a long way.

While you're experimenting with eating more grains, you also may want to experiment with different kinds of grains. There's more in the world than just whole wheat, after all.

Consider barley. It's not only a delicious addition to homemade soup, but also a chewy, nutty substitute for rice or potatoes. Or try bulgur, a satisfying grain that is the mainstay of a delicious cold-grain salad called taboulleh.

Be adventurous when you shop and experimental when you cook. You'll learn to love these grains, and many others as well.

Review your food diary to see if you eat grains daily—on occasion replacing main-course meat with a grain recipe. If not, the chart on the opposite page can help you put more whole grains into your diet.

Six Great Grains

Grain Type	Comments	Recipe
Amaranth	Not yet a household grain, but will be someday. The "mystical grain of the Aztecs" has high quality, more of the amino acid "lysine" than any other grain, plus significant amounts of iron and magnesium. Look for it in new health-food products like cereal and pasta.	Add 1 cup grain to 3 cups water. Bring grain and water to a boil and cook 25 minutes. Yields 2½ cups.
Barley	Rich in B vitamins and minerals, including calcium and iron. Choose unhulled, whole-hulled or flaked barley. Unfortunately, "pearl barley" has the hull removed, taking with it some of the nutrients.	Add 1 cup dry barley to 4 cups boiling water and boil 45 minutes. Yields 4 cups.
Buckwheat	High in protein. Also a good source of iron and B vitamins, especially B_6. And contains rutin, a bioflavanoid, which may help to keep small blood vessels healthy.	Kasha is the most popular form of buckwheat. To make, beat 1 egg with 1 cup fine buckwheat. Put mixture in a skillet and stir constantly over medium heat for 2 to 3 minutes, separating grains and coating them with egg. Add 2 cups boiling water and 1 teaspoon margarine or butter. Cover skillet tightly, lower heat to simmer and cook for 5 minutes or until liquid is absorbed. (Coarser buckwheat grains will take a little longer.)
Bulgur	A traditional food in the Middle East and Asia. Kernels of wheat have been partially dehulled, cooked and cracked, with minimum loss of nutrients: B vitamins, iron, calcium and fiber.	Soak 1 cup of bulgur in 3 cups of water for 2 hours, or overnight. Or, add 1 cup of bulgur to 2 cups of boiling water and boil 15 minutes. Yields 2½ cups.
Rice, brown	Has far more fiber, B vitamins, vitamin E, iron, magnesium and zinc than does white rice.	Add 1 cup of brown rice to 2½ to 3 cups of water. Bring to a boil, then reduce heat and simmer 45 minutes or until water is absorbed.
Wheat	Rich in many of the B vitamins, vitamin E, iron, potassium, magnesium, zinc and protein.	You can cook up a pot of whole wheat breakfast cereal. But normally you'd get your whole wheat in the form of breads and other baked goods.

Note: Using a pressure cooker will cut cooking times in half. In general, use twice as much water as grain in a pressure cooker.

Goal: *Drink More Water*

Date: _____

Walk: 7 days, 45 minutes, 2¼ miles

Are you drinking at least six glasses of water a day? It may sound like folk medicine, but drinking six cups of fluid is a good prescription for health. Your body is more than 50 percent water, after all. And a loss of even one-tenth of your body weight in water can result in death. But fear not. Coffee, tea, milk and juice count toward the total. Six cups of coffee, obviously, are not as healthful as six glasses of pure water! So let's consider our H_2O.

Water can cleanse and rejuvenate the body in a number of ways. It promotes regularity and replenishes lost fluids. By diluting the salt and minerals that pass through the kidneys, drinking plenty of water can also help prevent the formation of kidney stones. And it flushes bacteria from the urinary tract, helping prevent urinary tract infections. For the weight-conscious, it's better than low-cal—it's no-cal!

Will *any* water do? Tap water may have problems, depending on where you live. Sometimes, it's softened to make it suitable for sudsing; that means good minerals like calcium may have been sacrificed for bad minerals like sodium. Then there's the problem of substances either added to water or left in it: chlorine, pollutants, bacteria, lead, mercury or other toxic wastes. Ugh.

One option is to filter water, reducing chlorine and some pollutants. Some filters work better than others, however, and most of the good brands tend to be expensive.

No wonder bottled water has become downright trendy! A cool bottle of mineral water, like Perrier, Poland Spring, Evian, Vichy and many more, can contain important minerals, like calcium and potassium. For anybody trying to avoid excess calories, sugar, alcohol, caffeine or additives, it's simply a pure and delicious way to quench thirst.

Easy Ways to Get Wet

- Start with one glass of water before every meal. Have another before you go to bed. Here is a weight-watcher's bonus: A glass of ice water before a meal shrinks the stomach and reduces appetite.
- Sip water while you're doing quiet activities, like reading or watching TV.
- Make those second cups of coffee at break-time glasses of water instead.
- Substitute water for diet soda, which may contain ingredients of dubious value, such as saccharin.

A Quick Guide to Bottled Waters

Here are some brief pointers to help you make a naturally good selection.

548

- If you're on a sodium-restricted diet, look for waters that specifically say low-sodium or no-salt. Some mineral waters are surprisingly high in sodium (see chart).
- Look for waters that say "natural" spring water. If the word "natural" doesn't appear on the label, it means minerals have been added artificially.
- Bottled water can be "still" or "effervescent." Still waters are those without bubbles. Save distilled water for your iron—no minerals or taste are left in the water after processing.
- If you have a good reason for avoiding drinking your tap water, don't forget to use bottled water for ice cubes, too.
- Seltzer is simply tap water that's been filtered and carbonated with bubbles. Club soda has had minerals and mineral salts added, so look for the brands labeled low-sodium or no-salt.

Refreshing your body with high-quality water can help relieve constipation and keep the urinary tract functioning smoothly. It's Mother Nature's original low-calorie drink, and, generally, it's really economical.

Sodium Content of Bottled Waters

Brand	Sodium (mg per 8 oz)	Brand	Sodium (mg per 8 oz)
Still Waters		Sparkling Waters	
Poland Spring	0.32	Perrier	3.04
Deer Park	0.39	San Pellegrino	10.02
Mountain Valley	0.65	Canada Dry Club Soda	44.00
Evian	1.18	Vichy (Celestins)	277.40

Goal: *Have a Safe Week*

Date: _____

Walk: 7 days, 45 minutes, 2¼ miles

- Martha can find time to make her own yogurt and whole-wheat bread, but she can't seem to find time to buckle her seat belt.
- Don can afford $4,000 for a hot tub and exercise bike, but he can't seem to manage $5.95 for a smoke alarm.
- And Bob, who just quit smoking, drives like a bat out of hell!

Anything seem illogical about the health efforts ot these people? Maybe the fitness boom has been making so much noise about good health that it's deafened some people to the importance of good sense. And that's what you should think about this week. Because the "sensible" safety measures—things like wearing a seat belt and having a smoke alarm—are among the most important actions you can take to live a long life!

That's the view of 103 of America's leading health experts, who were polled by Louis Harris on behalf of *Prevention* magazine. The experts were asked to vote on what they thought were the most important things people could do to live long. Of the top 12, fully 50 percent had to do with safety! The point is clear: All the health and fitness in

Get Into the Seat Belt Habit

In chapter 2, you read about the importance of using a seat belt, and why it's far safer to be strapped into a car than not. The National Highway Traffic Safety Administration estimates that 17,000 lives could be saved *every year* if everyone used seat belts. And 4 million injuries would be minimized dramatically.

Seat belts *work*. So why doesn't everyone buckle up? Studies suggest that the biggest reason is simply that people haven't developed the habit. For most drivers of today, the idea of strapping in is quite alien.

But the seat belt habit can be learned! All it takes is a concerted effort. *The next time you get in the car this week, make a point of using your safety belt!* You *will* get used to it. As one recent convert said, "I now feel a little naked if I'm not buckled up!"

the world can't protect you from your own carelessness. Here, in order, are the top 12 ways to live a long life.

1. Don't smoke.
2. Avoid smoking in bed.
3. Wear a seat belt.
4. Don't drive under the influence of alcohol.
5. Live in a home or apartment with a smoke detector.
6. Socialize regularly.
7. Exercise strenuously.
8. Keep alcohol consumption moderate.
9. Avoid home accidents.
10. Restrict dietary fats.
11. Maintain a normal weight.
12. Obey speed limits.

Make this your Personal Safety Week! Study the list, and look back at chapter 2 for ways to accident-proof your home and your life—like buying at least one smoke detector, anchoring that old throw rug, clearing your stairs and *not* driving when upset. And most important, make this the week you start buckling up! (See boxes.)

Guardian against Fire: Your Smoke Detector

If your home isn't equipped with at least one smoke detector, buy one this week. Without a smoke detector, you're doubling your odds of dying in a house fire.

Clearly, alarms work. But they also have to be installed and maintained properly. Here's what the experts suggest:

Proper installation. For maximum protection, you should have at least one smoke detector on each level of your home—basement and attic included. And each bedroom should have its own detector positioned just outside its door. (Consult manufacturer's instructions for more precise placement recommendations.)

Proper maintenance. A smoke detector with a worn battery is useless. Most units make intermittent chirping sounds when their batteries begin to run down, so keep your ears open and be quick about battery replacement. To be doubly safe, it's a good idea to check a detector every couple of months by exposing it to smoke from an extinguished match or candle. If the unit doesn't sound off, either the battery needs to be replaced or the unit itself should be replaced. Most detectors are reliable, but none are infallible.

Goal: *Go Fish*

Date: _____

Walk: 7 days, 45 minutes, 2¼ miles

Remember the child's card game, "Go Fish"? If you were collecting certain cards in your hand, you asked another player, "Got any tens?" If he didn't, he told you to "go fish!" And with any luck, you'd pull a winning card from the undealt deck.

In the "staying young game," "Go Fish" is one of the most winning pieces of advice around. Fish is high in vitamin D to help keep bones, nerves and muscles strong, as well as delicious and easy to prepare. But best of all, fish is a natural heart protector.

Scientists figured that out as they pondered the puzzle of the Greenland Eskimos. These hardy Northerners eat staggering amounts of fat—whale blubber, seal and fatty fish. Yet their rate of heart disease is among the lowest in the world.

Then the researchers discovered that many fish (and shellfish) contain a special class of polyunsaturated fat called omega-3 fatty acids. These acids pull down levels of cholesterol and triglycerides, two heart-larding blood fats.

As few as two servings of fish a week may have the power to cut the risk of heart disease by as much as 50 percent: That was the conclusion of an exciting study by scientists in the Netherlands, who examined the eating habits of 872 men over 20 years. They found a strong connection between fish consumption and protection from heart disease. Men who ate about eight ounces of fish per week were about half as likely to die of heart disease as men who ate none.

Even shellfish like shrimp, lobster and crabs, once shunned for their high levels of cholesterol, have been approved in modest quantities (three- to four-ounce servings) for people who have to watch their cholesterol. That's because they also contain high levels of omega-3 fatty acids, which tend to neutralize the ill effects of cholesterol. (Fish oil even outperforms polyunsaturated vegetable oil when it comes to lowering triglycerides.) Collectively, these protective substances have lowered both cholesterol and triglyceride blood levels, and reduced both the quantity and the adhesiveness of clot-forming blood platelets when consumed in the equivalent of five servings of fish a week. Now *that's* a lot of fish, so you might want to set your sights a little lower.

Go-Fish Tips

Are you eating two or more servings of fish a week? Start this week! When you cook fish at home it's best to bake, broil, poach, steam or pan-fry it. Use a little oil, not butter. Broiled fish retains most of its nutrients; fried fish suffers the greatest nutritional losses. For a taste treat, try dressing it with herb or malt vinegar instead of tartar sauce or butter.

Also, take advantage of the convenience of canned fish like sardines, salmon and tuna. They also contain the healthy omega-3 acids. Whenever possible, pick water-packed canned fish. The nutrients you want are in the fish, not the added oil. Also, beware of tomato-sauce packed fish; it can be salty.

Don't take advantage of pre-breaded and fried fish, which often contain more bread and fat than fish.

Also, use care when dining out. American restaurants all too often serve fish swimming in butter. Tell the waiter you're on a low-fat diet, and ask if the cook can broil the fish in just a little butter—or none.

And if you prefer not to eat fish, a fish-oil supplement can also have beneficial effects, according to scientific studies. But supplements will cost you more!

After you learn to love fish, don't make like the Eskimos and assume you now can indulge in whale blubber, or for that matter, Brie. Remember that neither fish nor fish oils give anyone a safe license to indulge frequently in eggs, fatty meat, butterfat and hard cheese. Unless you trudge around the Arctic in snowshoes all year, it's wise to stick with your low-fat eating plan.

Goal: *Explore a Different Path*

Date: _____

Walk: 7 days, 50 minutes, 2½ miles

Perhaps you think walking is simply a matter of putting one foot in front of the other. Well, it doesn't *have* to be so simple. Walking can stretch your mind, your creativity and your spirit. If your walking program has become routine, consider taking a different path.

The Camera Walk

Ever walk down the street with a photographer? Just as you're explaining some crucial point, you realize your companion isn't next to you anymore—but rather 20 feet back, taking a picture of an unusual shop sign, a flower, an icicle—or maybe of you. Things you've always looked at but maybe never really have *seen*. Bring a camera on your next walk—you'll be amazed how new objects, patterns, colors and ideas come into focus.

The Kid Walk

There's no way to predict what will interest a child. Here's a report filed by a grownup who recently learned a walking lesson from a 14-month-old toddler.

"We were walking through a park, and I was pointing out all the things I thought she'd like—you know, squirrels, dogs, trees. She wasn't too interested. Suddenly, she stopped. She stared downward, with a look of utter fascination. She

reached down to the sidewalk, and picked up—solemnly, with a face full of awe, then holding it up to me like a sacred offering—the itty-bittiest crushed scrap of a fragment of a brown leaf. I looked at small things differently after that."

The Dog Walk

Pets provide company and affection, which is why some therapists recommend them as solutions for depression and loneliness. Dogs have the added advantage of forcing you to get frequent exercise, which is not necessarily the case with a cat or goldfish. Plus, walking a dog is a terrific way to make friends of the canine and even human variety!

The Morning Walk

This kind of walk is in a class by itself. The world is *different* in the morning. Normally busy city streets are tranquil canyons that echo the cries of swooping birds. Meanwhile, country roads shimmer as the sun's rays illuminate the dew. You'll probably find a steady walking partner or two. And the air has that crisp, clear quality—delicious!

The Thoreau Walk

"I frequently tramped eight or ten miles through the deepest snow to keep an appointment with a

554

beech tree, or a yellow birch, or an old acquaintance among the pines," wrote the nineteenth-century naturalist Henry David Thoreau. You, too, can make friends with the trees—and the flowers and the birds—with the help of a good guidebook. "When you identify a tree," says Deborah Brien, a historian and folklorist who teaches workshops on seasonal traditions for the Arnold Arboretum of Harvard University, the Cambridge Center for Adult Education and the Massachusetts Audubon Society, "it really does become your friend. And it gives you something important—oxygen. Every time you pass it, you think, 'Hello! I know you! You're a little different today!'"

What? You say you live in the heart of the city? That doesn't mean you're not surrounded by nature—why do you think they call it an "urban jungle?" The streets and buildings of New York City, for example, are home to—not just pigeons and people—but also sparrows, gulls, falcons and nighthawks, says Starr Saphir, a director of the New York City Audubon Society, who leads nature walks in the Big Apple. What's more, city parks are often teeming with wildlife, says Saphir. In Central Park, an on-the-ball birder could spot some 250 varieties of birds, including the North American songbirds. Not to mention fish, turtles, snakes, raccoons and squirrels. Plus wild flowers. And trees.

The Pure Walk

"In all Buddhist meditation practices, a walking meditation is important," says George Bowman, Zen teacher at the Cambridge Zen Center, in Massachusetts. "It's really a continuation of the sitting meditation." Sitting meditation, of course, involves watching your breathing and being simply "aware," instead of letting your mind wander or worry. Similarly, when you walk, you can focus on breathing and stepping. "Coordinate your breathing with your steps," says Bowman. "When you inhale, take two easy steps. Do the same when you exhale. Be mindful of lifting the foot, striding, placing the foot down, the texture and quality of that. As your thoughts scatter, bring them back to the awareness of the stride, of the breathing. It brings you to a state of 'mindfulness'—simply having a mind that's open and aware of what's going on in the moment, and not rerunning tapes of the past or projecting into the future." Bowman says that he experienced a sort of moving meditation when he used to train as a long-distance runner. "Initially, I was always preoccupied. I'd worry about my training, the upcoming race—continual judgments and comparisons. Then, something happened where the thinking just stopped. My mind was no longer preoccupied. It came to a place 'before thinking,' where I was aware of the birds singing, my breath, maybe an ache in my foot—but without a story line. Pay attention to the rise and fall on the feet, until you reach a place where the mind quiets. Until, in the most fundamental sense, you're just walking."

Goal: *Make Fitness a Habit*

Date: _____

Walk: 7 days, 50 minutes, 2½ miles

Are you hooked on exercise? Is moving your feet as much of a habit as brushing your teeth? If not, you know that it's all too easy to squirm out of regular exercise. Bad weather, a crowded agenda, a case of the blahs—all offer an easy excuse. First one day goes by with no workout, then a week and, if you don't watch out, you're headed for a whole season of hibernation!

Some days you need an extra psychological push out the door. Here's an exercise you can do sitting down to get yourself up and out every single day. All you have to lift is a pencil. Refer back to these pages whenever you need that extra gentle push.

Step One: Remember Your Reasons

What *really* makes you want to exercise? The prospect of losing weight? Fighting fatigue? Meeting more people? To alleviate or prevent a specific problem, like stress, osteoporosis or a heart condition? Write your reasons here in order of importance.

1.

2.

3.

4.

5.

Now, "play your strong suit," says sports psychologist Dorothy Harris, Ph.D., author of *The Athlete's Guide to Sports Psychology: Mental Skills for Physical People* (Leisure Press). "Develop feedback related to your motivations," says Dr. Harris. Read books about exercise, and mark the sections in this book that talk about what exercise can do for you. Compare notes with friends. Consciously use the ideas to get yourself moving again.

One more thing about that list. It's important to separate the "negative" incentives from the positive ones. For example, being fit can make you look younger, slimmer, *better.*

Step Two: Set a Simple Goal

What was your exercise goal last week? If it was something like, "to swim an extra 15 laps," you're heading for problems. Keep your short-term exercise goals simple and achievable. Aim for a small increase, or even "to continue at my present level for two weeks." Write a simple exercise goal for next week here:

_____

Step Three: Make Some Fun

A bored athlete won't be athletic for long. There are dozens of ways to make your exercise program more enjoyable. Who says you have to listen to disco when you do aerobic dance? Switch to Broadway show-tunes, and pretend you're in the chorus line! Read a novel while riding your stationary bike. Go to the library and check out a book on architecture or animal tracks to make your next walk downright *fascinating*. Try a sport—racquetball is a good one, easier to play than tennis. Or simply, find a partner—someone to share the agonies and ecstasies. Write down five ideas for adding fun to your exercise program.

1.
2.
3.
4.
5.

Step Four: Reward Yourself

Heavens, it's been five months; you deserve *at least* a good movie for all that diligence and sweat. Rewards can be spectacular, like getting a professional massage or a new bicycle. But you can reward yourself in little ways, every day,

too. How about a long hot bath? An exotic flavor of tea? A favorite magazine? Even food is a good reward; you can slip in an occasional treat and still lose weight.

Write down eight rewards you can earn over the next month.

1.
2.
3.
4.
5.
6.
7.
8.

Step Five: Reap the Big Rewards

Look back to your first week to see how much you exercised. Now look at your records for recent weeks. If you're doing more—congratulations! Recognize not only your improvement but also the depth of your commitment. You've taken a giant psychological leap toward improving your health!

Now review the other changes. You're feeling better; maybe your pulse is a little slower. Did you make a new friend? Discover something new in your neighborhood? Are you feeling less stressed? Write down the pleasures and rewards of exercise, and the ways you're closer to your goals.

Goal: *Find Some Time*

Date: _____

Walk: 7 days, 50 minutes, 2½ miles

A time to plant
    and a time to uproot . . .
A time to pull down
    and a time to build up . . .
A time to scatter stones,
    and a time to gather them . . .
A time to keep
    and a time to throw away . . .
      (Eccles. 3:2-6)

Those were some of the priorities in biblical days. Today you might as well add a time to exercise, a time to unwind, a time to soak beans, a time to bake bread, a time for family, a time to work overtime . . . wait a minute! Who has all that time?

Time and energy are the subjects of the next two weeks. The topics are combined because it takes both to do all these good things for yourself. Time management, like figure skating, is one of those feats that looks easy enough—"just make a list"—but turns out to be very difficult indeed.

Almost everybody has problems with time management, says Abigail Lipson, Ph.D., a clinical psychologist and senior counselor with Harvard University's Bureau of Study Council, who often consults with students and faculty on issues of procrastination and time management. Dr. Lipson points out that there are objective circumstances that make it difficult to manage time. A crowded agenda, unexpected illness, a friend in need—almost anything can disrupt our best-laid plans. Yet another force also gets in the way of controlling our time and our lives, says Lipson. It is ourselves.

"It can be tremendously difficult to do something if only half of you wants to do it," says Dr. Lipson. "When that happens, all the good intentions and schedules in the world don't work."

What kind of circumstances are at the root of "wasting time?" A lack of self-confidence that stops you from meeting people or trying something new. Guilt. "A woman who wants to go back to school may feel bad that she's abandoning her family by taking time for herself. So she puts it off," says Dr. Lipson. Someone may have to finish a project for work—but keeps delaying because of a feeling that "I'll be damned before I let anyone evaluate me." Result? Procrastination, and even feelings of intense shame. "People get down on themselves instead of recognizing that getting control of your time is really hard," says Dr. Lipson.

"That's why knowing yourself is a critical part of our time management system," she adds. "It helps you acknowledge the things going on in your life, even if that complicates the picture."

Your Time Organizer

If you can't find time for all the things you think you should be doing, and you're concerned about your tendency to procrastinate, try an experiment this week. List what has to be done tomorrow. Be as specific as possible. Don't forget needs besides work and chores—like exercise, socializing, recreation, etc. Break down big jobs into smaller jobs that can be done sequentially and at different times. For example, if you wrote, "Prepare a report," it can be broken down into, "Go to library, prepare an outline, write a rough draft, then rewrite."

Now, on a separate sheet of paper, spread those activities over the periods of the day in a column marked, "What I Plan for Tomorrow." Do they all fit? Does your schedule allow for play, exercise and unstructured time? Are there things you can postpone, rearrange or coordinate?

It's important to look at what you hope to do, what you think you *ought* to do and what you actually do. Those aren't always the same. At the end of the day tomorrow, fill in a second column with an account of what you actually did.

Are you so far off your intentions that you're tempted to give up? Well, hang on. This kind of discrepancy is very common, and there's a lot to be learned from it.

For example, you can figure out when you were most energetic or tired. You may find that things you thought don't take long—like driving to the store—take more time than you expected. This can help you plan a more realistic schedule.

As people look back at the things they did, they often accuse themselves of being lazy or disorganized. But in fact, their choices had reasons. Use your log to discover how you really think and feel about the things you're supposed to do each day.

Remember, schedules are designed to give a sense of what needs to be done, and to spread tasks over time. But they're almost always idealistic—and, as such, unrealistic. The idea is not to feel bad when you can't stick to it. These feelings can drain your energy and even lead to more procrastination.

Understanding the difference between the rigidity of schedules, and the fluidity and expansiveness of human nature and everyday living, can give you a different perspective on what it means to be in charge of your time, and thus, your life.

Adapted and condensed from, "Managing Your Time: Hints on How to Beat Procrastination," prepared by the Bureau of Study Council, copyright 1984, President and Fellows of Harvard College.

Week 22

Goal: *Make Energy*

Date: _____

Walk: 7 days, 55 minutes, 2¾ miles

Last week you made the time—but did you have the energy to enjoy it? What happened at noon? Did you find yourself longing for an after-lunch siesta—or even taking one? Maybe midafternoon was your personal Twilight Zone. How were your evenings? In spite of the best-laid plans, some people simply collapse when they get home from work.

What makes it worse is that everyone knows super-people who Go-Go-*Go!* All day and half the night, they enjoy work, friends, hobbies. The more they do, the more they seem to recharge. How do they do it?

Part of it is inborn. People's energy levels and cycles do vary. There are also physiological reasons for the lags that occur at certain times of day, which you can alleviate to some degree. Not everyone can be a super-person, but regular exercise, weight control and good nutrition can dramatically increase personal energy potential.

Beyond that, the real secret to boundless positive energy is doing things you want to do. Even if you're tired, you usually can muster up the energy to do something that's fun.

At work, that means putting aside the report that's tormenting you, and focusing on some task you prefer. Perhaps you can read a magazine related to your job or make some phone calls. When you're finished, your energy probably will have returned.

At home it means making a positive commitment to setting aside 20 minutes or so every day for something upbeat that you love to do—especially at the times when you're feeling most draggy, like right after work. Draw, paint, throw yourself a pot. Read a thriller. Play lively music and dance. Get involved in some enjoyable volunteer activity with positive people.

Here are some specific ways to bridge your daily energy gaps.

- Know yourself. Schedule your toughest jobs for when you're at your energy peak. If you ignore your natural energy currents, you'll wind up fatigued from all that swimming upstream.
- Get physical. A few minutes of vigorous exercise is one way to recharge during the day. Even 25 jumping jacks can increase your metabolic rate temporarily. And don't forget that an aerobic exercise program will keep you strong, trim and vibrant for the long run!
- Eat something healthy. Among the best energy snacks are nuts and seeds. Though relatively high in calories, when combined they more than make up for it with protein,

polyunsaturated fats, B vitamins, calcium, potassium, iron, zinc and copper. They can replace minerals lost in exercise through sweat, putting the power back into your muscles.

• Eat a "power" lunch. The after-lunch lag is a documented physiological phenomenon, called postprandial (after eating) dip. The South American and Mediterranean countries handle it sensibly, by allowing for a nap, while Americans try to work through it. Experts recommend two ways to deal with the problem: eat a light lunch, with as many raw foods (like fruits and vegetables) as possible. Also, taking a walk after lunch can be a big help. Make fresh air and sunshine your daily luncheon dessert.

• Take a deep breath. Or two or three. Breathing slowly and deeply alleviates stress and provides more energizing oxygen.

• Check your iron level. If you're tired most of the time, it could be due to an iron deficiency. Women of child-bearing age and people over 65 are particularly prone to this problem. Iron is present in meats, especially beef liver, and to a lesser extent in foods like sunflower seeds, broccoli, apricots, almonds and raisins.

• Pace yourself. Now that you've learned not to overschedule your day, but rather to set a reasonable number of tasks, you'll no longer be paralyzed by the "where do I begin" phenomenon.

• If you feel tired, rest. A short nap or a quiet daydream often can recharge run-down batteries.

But in the *long* run, it's doing what you really want to do that will energize your life.

Goal: *Try Bedtime Relaxation*

Date: _____

Walk: 7 days, 55 minutes, 2¾ miles

Did you have a chance to relax today? What about yesterday? If you just can't find the time to de-stress during your busy days, there's still hope! Evening is one of the best times to practice a very effective technique called "progressive relaxation." It can put you to sleep this week—and in the long run, it can help prevent stress from taking a toll on your mind and body.

This simple method involves tightening and relaxing the major muscle groups, explains Manhattan therapist Sharon Fried-Buchalter, M.B.A.

"These are almost isometric exercises," she says. "When muscles are tightened and then relaxed, you learn what tension and relaxation really feel like. You experience a very profound relaxation. The blood flow to each area is increased. This is one of the stress-reduction techniques that can lower blood pressure, meaning it can also reduce the risk of heart disease."

Fried-Buchalter has taught this technique to lawyers in their offices and doctors in classrooms, but she says the best setting is at home, in the evening, in bed, just before you go to sleep. Progressive relaxation is *not* the ideal afternoon pick-me-up. "You're much better off with an aerobic exercise if you're feeling stressed-out during the day. When you're very tense and do progressive relaxation, you can fall asleep. Very often, people in my classes don't get up when the exercise is over!"

Learn to Relax

Here is the technique that therapist Fried-Buchalter uses to relax her clients. ("It also puts my husband to sleep," she adds.) It's best if someone else reads you the instructions. Or you can read them into a tape recorder, counting out the numbers where indicated. Or, read the instructions several times so you can do the relaxation technique without peeking at the book.

Fried-Buchalter combines progressive relaxation with breathing techniques for maximum relaxation. This week, after dinner, try it! It should take about 15 minutes.

Sit in a comfortable chair, or better, lie down. Take off your shoes and loosen your clothing. Relax, and become aware of your breathing. Keep your breathing calm and natural throughout the exercise.

Now, clench your toes as hard as you can. Hold them tight for a slow count of five. Now slowly release the muscles, to a count of five, until they're totally relaxed.

Next, tighten your calves by flexing your feet (pointing your toes upward). If you're lying down, your feet and calves should come up off the bed. Hold for a count of ten. Slowly release them to a count of five by bringing your toes down and lowering your feet.

Now your thigh muscles. Tighten them by tightening your buttocks. If you're lying down, feel your legs lifting slightly off the bed. Hold for a count of ten, then slowly release to a count of five. Feel your legs falling back onto the bed.

Now you're coming to your upper body, where you're more sensitive to stress. Remain aware of your breathing. When you inhale, think about clean, pure air coming into your lungs, expanding them, filling your body. If you feel any tension within the body, visualize it as some ugly color, and imagine it leaving your body as you exhale. Then breathe in a beautiful color to soothe tense places.

Tighten your pelvic muscles by tightening your buttocks and stomach muscles. Hold for a count of ten. Release slowly, to a count of five.

Keep visualizing your slow breathing. Now, your stomach muscles. Tighten your stomach and abdominal muscles as hard as you can by pushing your abdominal muscles down, so the small of your back touches the bed. Hold for a count of ten. Release to a count of five.

Keep breathing in the good air, breathing out the bad, breathing away the tension.

Now you'll tighten your chest and pectoral muscles. Do this by bringing your arms close to your body and your hands up to your shoulders, while pushing your elbows into your sides. Hold for a count of ten. Release slowly.

The neck is next. Tighten it by pushing your head back into your pillow, and clenching your jaw. Hold for a count of ten. Release.

Now, your arms. Hold your hands out in front of you, with your palms upward, and make fists. Tighten them as hard as you can. Hold for ten, then slowly relax.

The mouth. Clench your teeth tightly, with your lips pulled back. Hold for a count of ten. Slowly release for five.

Now, your tongue. This is a yoga exercise, and it's supposedly good for skin tone, too. Open your mouth as wide as you can, and stick out your tongue as far as possible. Hold. Release by slowly bringing the tongue back into the mouth.

Now you'll tighten your eyes by clenching them shut as hard as you can. Your nose should be crinkled. Hold. Slowly release to a count of five.

Finally, your forehead. Make a frown, bringing your brows close to each other. Hold. Relax slowly.

Keep breathing deeply. Feel the calmness, and the pure air filling you up as you breathe out the tension.

When you're finished, get up slowly. Or relax into a peaceful sleep.

Goal: *Positive Thinking*

Date: _____

Walk: 7 days, 55 minutes, 2¾ miles

Take the test below to determine whether you're your own worst critic.

If you are, it's time to start "talking nice" to yourself. The problem with negative thinking is that it's *more* than just talk. People who always see themselves and life in a negative light are often prone to low self-esteem, depression and even physical ailments.

The good news is, you aren't born with a cloudy—or sunny—disposition. It's a *learned* response. And there's a relatively simple and effective technique called "cognitive therapy" that can turn even the most relentless self-critic into a positive thinker.

What cognitive therapists have discovered is that people's negative thoughts often contain gross distortions. Here are some errors they're likely to make, spelled out in detail:

Exaggerating. "I just can't get myself to do any work around the house—everything's falling apart." You overestimate the size of your problems and underestimate your ability to deal with them.

Jumping to Conclusions. This is a two part mistake that combines mind reading with fortune telling. The mind-reader error—"My friend didn't call. She must be angry." How do you know? Maybe she has the flu. The fortune-teller error—you make a mistake at work and

think, "They're going to fire me." You jump to erroneous conclusions without evidence.

Ignoring the Positive. "Sure, the party went all right, but I had a run in my stocking." You tend to remember only negative events, or positive events in a negative way.

Personalizing. "Everybody in the room kept looking at me because of the rip." You tend to think everything revolves around you.

Either/Or Thinking. "Either I get elected to the committee or I'm a complete failure." Surely there are other alternatives.

Overgeneralization. "Nobody likes me . . . Nothing ever turns out right." You focus on one negative detail and let it darken your whole vision of reality.

As you can see, these negative thoughts begin to sound alike after a while. And they *are* alike, says one cognitive therapist—they're generally wrong.

The first step in the therapy is awareness—to become aware of what you're really thinking and feeling. Tune in to your self-talk. Strip away everything except the plain simple facts. You've got to drag your negative thoughts into court, put them on the witness stand and confront them with the facts. Usually they'll wilt under pressure.

The next step is answering

Are You Kind?

1. A friend doesn't call you for several weeks. You would be most likely to assume:

    a. She doesn't like me anymore.

    b. She's probably busy.

2. Your department hires a new manager. Your response is:

    a. Maybe he'll fire me.

    b. Now there's a chance I'll get the promotion I've been waiting for.

3. You get a small tear in your clothing just before a party. You would probably:

    a. Spend some time at the party berating yourself and worrying that people were looking at the rip.

    b. Ignore it and assume most other people were ignoring it.

If you answered "a" to all these questions, it's time to learn to turn your thinking around!

The form below shows you how you can "talk yourself" out of negative thought.

Evaluate Your Responses

Automatic Self-Critical Thought	Cognitive Distortion	Rational Response
"My friend is angry."	Mind reading	"She's been very busy lately."
"I'll probably get fired."	Fortune telling	"I'm an experienced worker, with a good reputation. There is no indication that I'll get fired."
"I'm a careless slob for putting a rip in this shirt. I never do anything right. Everyone was looking at me."	Mind reading, exaggerating, ignoring the positive, personalizing	"I met some wonderful people at the party. People at the party had plenty of things to talk about aside from my ripped clothing."
Your Examples		

"Evaluate Your Responses" adapted from *Feeling Good: The New Mood Therapy*, David D. Burns, M.D. (New York: New American Library, 1980).

those negative thoughts. One way is to ask yourself good questions. Am I exaggerating or overgeneralizing? Am I confusing a mere thought with fact? Am I overlooking my strengths?

Goal: *Quarterly Inventory*

Date: _____

Walk: 7 days, 60 minutes, 3 miles

Inventory 3

I. Diary

	Sunday	Monday	Tuesday	
Food and Drink A.M. P.M.				
Moods and Activities Summary				
Exercise and Stretching				
Relaxation				

II. Vital Statistics

1. Weight _____   2. Resting pulse _____beats/minute

	Wednesday	Thursday	Friday	Saturday

3. Blood pressure_____ 4. Cholesterol _____ mg/deciliter

Spring celebrates *itself*. The trees burst out in green and pink; the scent of earth rises and, even in cities, wins out over car exhaust for a time. And the sun and warmth return.

Some people can hardly resist joining nature's jubilation. Come the first spring day, they adorn their hair with flowers and indulge in outdoor revelry with their friends. Others find that religious observances are part and parcel of the season—the resurrection that Easter represents, the deliverance of Passover. Here are some ideas to help you bring the spirit of renewal to your spring.

Eat Greens

In Week 11 you read about the virtues of greens, which are high in vitamins A and C and the minerals iron and calcium. For folklorist Deborah Brien, a bowl of dandelion greens is a nutritious way of celebrating the arrival of spring. Her recipe: Pick the greens early in spring, before they begin to bloom. Wash them and remove all the roots. Cook the leaves in a large amount of water, rapidly boiling until just tender. Drain and season. They're also good raw when very young, served with vinegar, pepper and oil.

Laugh at the Rain

April showers can be a particular problem if you're on an outdoor exercise program, like walking. Most plastic-coated rain slickers hold perspiration in, so you end up wet anyway. But now there are products that can let you sing *and* sweat in the rain and stay drier than Gene Kelly did. One is Gore-Tex, a material that is both waterproof and breathable. It allows humidity from perspiration out but doesn't allow drops of water from the outside in.

Cope with Spring Fever

Some researchers believe that the lengthening days as winter turns into spring affect people's hormonal system, making them happier, more playful and more likely to fall in love.

But there can be a dark side to this change. Some people become very depressed in early spring and summer. Psychologists speculate, it may have to do with seeing others having fun. In the winter you can blame your troubles on the weather, but you can't in the spring. That's why it's important to find ways to get outside and have fun with others. How about joining a hiking or gardening club?

Grow with the Seasons

"The nice thing about the seasons is that they keep repeating. It's like you keep getting another chance for growth," says folklorist Deborah Brien.

Although the seasons seem to have less significance for life nowadays than they did for our agricultural forebears, scientists know that changes in light do affect people profoundly. Like other animals, humans have seasonal rhythms.

What's more, celebrating the seasons is great fun—and can be good for you. "I don't see the year as a circular rut that we're stuck in, but really as a spiral," says Brien. "Maybe you're not doing what you ought, taking care of your health; maybe you just took a wrong turn, and slid down the spiral—but you can climb back up. The seasons are something that can help you to do that."

Particularly in modern, urban society, Brien says, awareness of nature can enrich lives. "Recognizing and celebrating the seasons make us feel like we're part of something good that makes sense," says Brien.

"So many people are unhappy. They're always looking in the mirror. If they looked outside themselves, at nature, they'd realize they had a good day today."

Celebrate the Seasons

Deborah Brien will help guide you through the traditions and delights of the four seasons. Meanwhile, here's her advice for making an appreciation of the seasons part of your daily life.

- Learn weather lore. "It's fun to play with. Weather lore was created by agricultural people who needed to know when to plant and when to harvest. It gets you outside—and outside of yourself."
- "Every day make a point of eating a food that's in season."
- "Have a seasonal party!"

Do a Spring Cleaning

Says Jeff Cox, in his book *Seasonal Celebrations* (Rodale Press):

These are days to hang the blankets and comforters like bunting from the windows. The winter's dust and dirt is shown to the door. Windows sparkle. Spring cleaning transforms the dim recesses of an overused house into sweet smelling rooms filled with buttery sunlight.

Our personal interiors can always use a sprucing up. Grudges, anxieties, bad habits, worries—toss them out! Leave nothing in the heart that isn't fresh, clean and beautiful. It's spring!

Midyear Break

Summer

Ancient Europeans ushered in the hazy days of summer with a May Basket. "Like trick-or-treating and caroling, a May Basket is one of those rituals of bringing what you love about the season anonymously to your neighbors. You lay the blossoms of summer at peoples' door," explains Deborah Brien.

Brien keeps this tradition alive in her own New England neighborhood. "I'm up before dawn on May Day, hanging a basket of flowers on about 20 doors, including a couple of shops. For ten years now, they've been wondering who's doing this! It gives you the greatest feeling to give someone the things you love about the new season."

Along with the blossoms, there's a lot to love about summer.

Berry Good!

"No other seasonal celebration is quite as sweet and beneficent as the ceremony of berry picking and the sacrament of a raspberry tart," says Jeff Cox. "Because wild berries are sweeter and more flavorful than the cultivated kind, I always go berrying. I like to do this alone, on a sunny July day when it's too hot to do anything else."

Whether you pluck your fresh summer berries from a bush or the produce shelf in your grocery store, you'll also be doing yourself a nutritional favor. Berries are rich in vitamin C and some are sources of fiber as well.

It's Vacation Time!

A summer vacation can be an opportunity to break out of old routines and sample a healthier, more creative way of living. Consider these:

A Spa Vacation. What better way to pamper yourself, relax and get fit than at a health spa? Many offer specialized programs in stress reduction, weight loss and smoking cessation. If you can afford it, you can opt for ritzy spas like the world-famous Golden Door in Escondido, California, but there are also plenty of moderately priced rejuvenating getaways. One example is the Kripalu Center for Yoga and Health, in Lenox, Massachusetts, in the Berkshire Hills. Clients practice yoga, and can take workshops on meditation, stress reduction, improving relationships, holistic health, Danskinetics (their own version of aerobic dance) and changing dependent behaviors. This kind of program can have permanent benefits.

A Fitness Vacation. Walking or bicycling tours, for example—

choose your countryside and there's sure to be a way to pedal, stroll or hike around it. There are bicycling and walking tours from A to Z: the Adirondacks, Barbados, China, Japan, Tanzania, New Zealand and more. Ask your travel agent to order catalogs.

A Learning/Travel/Fitness Vacation. Learn, get fit and go somewhere exotic—all in one vacation. There are universities and organizations that match volunteers with scientific, archeological and cultural projects all over the world. One of the best known is Earthwatch, based in Belmont, Massachusetts. Their volunteers have tracked rhinoceroses in Kenya, scuba dived the coral reefs of the Red Sea and analyzed the architecture of country houses in France. Many tour groups and universities also offer tours led by teachers and Ph.D.s knowledgeable in the culture, natural environment or architecture of the area.

Coping with the Sun

The sun offers many opportunities for delight, but it also has its dangers.

As you read in chapter 27, many age-related changes in the skin are actually the result of sun damage. This summer, be sure to use a good sunscreen. Avoid sun exposure in the blazing hours, 10 A.M. to 2 P.M. (or 11 to 3 during daylight saving time). When you do go out, take the sunshine in small doses. Beware of cloudy days: Harmful rays still get through.

Protect Your Crowning Glory

Buy a tightly-woven broad-brimmed hat to shade your face and hair from the aging effects of the sun. And do get yourself a swim cap, to protect your hair from chlorine and sun. Rubber caps are more waterproof than fabric ones, and they leak less.

Summer

Midyear Break

Autumn

I am grateful for what I am and have. My thanksgiving is perpetual. It is surprising how contented one can be with nothing definite, only a sense of existence. My breath is sweet to me. Oh, how I laugh when I think of my vague indefinite riches! No run on my bank can drain it, for my wealth is not possession but enjoyment!

(Henry David Thoreau)

Since ancient times, autumn has meant gathering in the crops and giving thanks. The age-old harvest rituals, says Deborah Brien, can be updated to enrich our lives today.

"At harvest time in the British Isles, the farmer and all his workers would gather around the last of the grain. The farmer would make a speech thanking the spirit of the grain. It was a solemn moment. Then they would all throw their blades into the grain, so they cut it down communally. Everyone cheered, and the grain was made into a harvest effigy and carried into a harvest feast.

"If you think about it," says Brien, "we do a similar thing today. I talk with my students about our own harvests—for example, a good job. When you get that job after a long search, the natural instinct is to bring together the people who helped you. You make a serious speech—the harvest speech—and then you have a party. If your harvest is that you've earned your degree, you hang it on the wall, just like a harvest effigy."

Brien says that in the autumn, she encourages her students to make their own "harvest effigies," like a wreath or a doll, as an emblem of their personal harvests for the year. "I remember one woman, a widow, who came to my class. After her husband died, she thought her world was coming to an end. But she had lots of health and energy. A friend of hers persuaded her to work in a soup kitchen. It gave her an interest outside her life: She felt needed again. So as her harvest effigy, she made a whole bunch of wreaths for the soup kitchen, and hung fruit on them— but not too much fruit, because she didn't want to seem like she was wasting food!"

In addition to personal harvests, says Brien, she encourages her students at harvest time "to recognize the role that nature plays in giving them happiness."

"If there's a tree I pass every day, I have silently thanked the tree for that beautiful color it gave me every morning for two or three weeks.

"If you have eyes to see, and a nose to smell, you can experience incredible beauty and drama.

572

"At Thanksgiving, that's what I think of. That's what that Thoreau poem means to me. He's so wealthy, not in possessions, but in enjoyment."

Other ways to make your autumn rejuvenating:

Eat an Apple a Day

The apple is a legendary part of the autumn season, says Brien. Traditionally, apple butter, pie, cider and preserves are prepared after the fall harvest; the Jewish New Year, Rosh Hashana, is celebrated with apple slices dipped in honey; on Halloween, a favorite game is bobbing for apples and the early New England settlers even made wrinkled, charming dolls' heads out of leftover dried apples.

Make yourself a healthy seasonal dessert like apple pandowdy, apple cobbler or simply baked apples. Since apples are naturally sweet, you can reduce the amount of sugar in the recipes. And what could be better than a steaming mug of spiced apple cider on a frosty autumn evening?

Apples, by the way, may indeed keep the doctor away. A study at Michigan State University, in East Lansing, found that students who ate an apple a day for three years were healthier and less susceptible to colds than other students.

Have a Healthy Thanksgiving

Here are a few ideas to make your Thanksgiving feast healthy:

- Season the turkey with lemon juice, garlic, thyme and sage. Skip the salt.
- For stuffing, use a whole-grain bread and other flavorful ingredients like chestnuts, apples, garlic, onions and lots of herbs.
- For healthy holiday snacking, pop up some popcorn.

Popcorn is a bona fide Thanksgiving tradition. One of the things that the Indians brought to that first Thanksgiving feast of 1622 was bags made of deerskin hide, filled with popcorn," says Brien. Among many American Indian tribes, she adds, corn was one of the foods used in their own rituals of thanksgiving. Popcorn is also low in calories and high in fiber.

Go Back to School

There's something about the sharp autumn air that makes people want to sharpen their minds. The semester is starting at universities and adult education centers. So sign up!

Midyear Break

Winter

Crackling fires, goose-down comforters, simmering stews, icicles and snowmen: No doubt about it, winter has its wonders.

But on days when you wake up in darkness, and trudge through slushy streets under a dull sky, it's hard to respond to it joyfully.

That dark sky is more than an aesthetic annoyance. Scientists now know that, for a surprisingly large number of people, the blues set in in the winter, and vanish in spring. Like plants and animals, people's seasonal rhythms have a great deal to do with changes in the light.

So if you get the winter blues, the first thing you can do is turn up the lights in your house—or buy some new ones. And there are plenty of other ways to emphasize the positive aspects of winter.

Look Inward

First, consider the joys of the indoors. "I always find summer incredibly demanding," says Deborah Brien. "You have to visit friends, go to big parties, get a suntan; whereas in winter, it's O.K. to do less. You can come inside and be with fewer people, and spend quiet time in front of a fire. I love it."

"Use winter to assess and maybe redirect your life," says Frederick Flach, M.D., author of

The Secret Strength of Depression (J. B. Lippincott). Winter is, in fact, an ideal time to read self-improvement books, learn new skills, take up a new hobby or go back to school.

Another indoor delight is socializing. That's how some North American Indians made it through winter. It was a time for dancing, telling stories and fulfilling social obligations.

"Progressive dinners or weekly suppers in your neighborhood or apartment building are a good way to be with others," says Milton N. Silva, Ph.D., psychiatry professor at the Medical College of Wisconsin, in Milwaukee. "Organize book clubs or card nights."

Push Yourself out the Door

But maybe it's being indoors that gets you down. "The phenomenon of cabin fever is a reality. People become restricted during winter by their environment," says Dr. Silva. Rather than hiding from nature, adapt to it. Exercise is perhaps the best way to change your attitude about winter. First, because exercise is a natural antidepressant. Second, because exercise improves circulation, so you'll be warmer all the time, indoors and out.

Along with walking, there are all those delightful winter sports like skating and skiing. One of the best is cross-country skiing. While this sport can be super-challenging, it can also be done at a walking pace. Rent skis and take an easy glide through a silent white forest. (And if you live in a warm climate, a cross-country-skiing vacation is worth a trip up north.)

Over the weeks, the more time you spend outside in the cold, the more acclimatized you will become. Begin with a few minutes a day, and work up to an hour a day. Be sure to dress warmly, wear a sunscreen and sunglasses, drink fluids and keep moving. Don't forget to do some warmup stretches and movements before you step outside. A word of caution: Extreme cold is a risk factor for heart attacks.

Don't Be a Fall Guy

Proper shoes are important to avoid falls. For packed snow, wear a substantial shoe with a tread that looks like a snow tire. On smooth ice, you'll need metal cleats you can strap to your shoes.

Dressing for Warmth

If it's bitter cold outside and your main form of exercise is walking, you'll want very warm insulation in your coat, such as goose down, or Quallofil (a synthetic made by du Pont which is less expensive than down and insulates better when wet), because you may not be generating much body heat.

If you want less of the Michelin Man look, and you're very active outdoors, a thin insulation, like Thinsulate (3M) or Thermolite (du Pont) may be more appropriate. They provide about 70 to 75 percent of the warmth of down insulation, and allow more freedom of movement.

Also remember to protect your face and hands from the cold. They are prime frostbite spots.

Midyear Break

Christmas

'Tis the season to be jolly! What makes *you* happy at this time of year? Maybe it's visiting with friends or family, exchanging presents or the joys of your faith, whether you celebrate the birth of a Savior, a miraculous deliverance or the New Year.

But there's something else that you may be happy about at this time of year, without even realizing it; something that has to do literally with your place in the universe. In the northern temperate zones, late December is the time when the light returns.

Since the summer solstice (June 21 or 22), daylight has been waning. "The age-old interpretation is that the sun is dying, ever so slowly," explains Deborah Brien. "By mid-October, people thought, 'I hope it doesn't go away completely.' It was frightening.

"But right after the winter solstice (the day of shortest light in the year), around December 21, the light gets a minute or so longer. People believed the sun must have been reborn. Ancient Romans called the solstice *dies natalis invincti solis,* or 'the birthday of the unconquerable sun.' Hope is reborn!

"There is a mechanism in us—in all cultures—that recognizes and celebrates the return of the sun," Brien explains.

Appropriately, people symbolize their hopes in this season with lights. The "menorah" of Hanukkah, a candelabra lit for eight days; the shining lights on Christmas trees and the burning Yule log.

"When you have hope, you feel wealthy, and more relaxed about sharing with others," says Brien. "That's why at this time there's a feeling of brotherly love and generosity."

Give What You Can

It's the spirit of the season. And there's nothing that feels better than knowing you've helped someone. Get involved with one of the seasonal good causes, like repairing toys and distributing them to needy children. See if you can volunteer at a shelter for the homeless or an old-age home. Bring toys and food to needy families. Get your children or grandchildren to join in. It's a perfect way to teach children a lesson of generosity.

Joy That's Ever Green

"O Christmas tree! O Christmas tree! Your leaves are faithful ever." So goes the old hymn. Deborah Brien notes that nearly all the plants used for Christmas decoration are evergreens. "Evergreens are so defiantly green and alive dur-

Christmas

ing that seeming death that is winter. They're a perfect symbol of hope."

There are other great reasons for bringing some greenery indoors at this time of year (see Week 40). Besides providing the eyeful of color that you're missing in winter, indoor plants can also add valuable moisture to the air, minimizing the drying effect that low wintertime humidity can have on nasal passages and throats. Result: better resistance to colds.

How about dressing up your house with a live indoor tree that can double as a Christmas tree? There are many dwarf species ideal for raising indoors.

Coping with Holiday Blues

Ironically, this season of joy can also be one of anxieties and sorrows. Loneliness, the recent loss of a spouse or loved one, conflict with or isolation from family members, financial or physical fatigue can all contribute to a feeling of letdown around Christmas.

If you are alone during the holidays, says psychotherapist Joyce Anisman-Saltman, a specialist in "laughter therapy," make extra sure you have plenty of entertaining and diverting material at home to get you through the holidays and keep your spirits up. Treat yourself to novels and entertaining records or videos.

The Present Solution

Holiday presents can be great fun, a headache or both. Remember, a gift need not be elaborate or expensive to show your friends and loved ones that you care. How about a gift of health? Give your loved ones presents that will help them feel better. For example:

- A loofah back scrubber.
- An exercise mat.
- An air-filter machine, to filter dust, pollen, tobacco smoke and odors from air.
- A stationary bike.
- Gifts that get people outdoors: a fantastic kite, boomerang, badminton set, star chart to track the constellations or cross-country skis.

A Word to Weight-Watchers

Don't forget to take a brisk walk after a big holiday meal. A University of New Hampshire study suggests that aerobic exercise will cause the body to burn calories faster than usual for up to 24 hours.

Goal: *Stay Fit*

Date: _____
Bike: 7 days, 30 minutes, 8 miles
Swim: 7 days, 10 laps

Congratulations, exercise buffs! Over the past six months, you've discovered a new, healthier way of living. If this is the first time you've stuck with a progressive exercise program, you've seen big changes in your energy, attitude, appearance and maybe even health.

Your Year of Rejuvenation is now at the six-month mark. If you're exercising at least three times a week for 20 minutes, you can keep doing exactly what you're doing for a lifetime of fitness. Or, you may want to try something new. So here are the options:

• You can continue walking at the 55 minute per 2.5- to 3-mile level. "This is a perfect program for someone to maintain for a lifetime," says Art Mollen, D.O., founder of the Southwest Health Institute, in Phoenix, Arizona. "At this level, you would maintain cardiovascular endurance and control your weight."

• If you have been following the walking program, or a different exercise program, and are now fairly fit, you may want to try a different kind of exercise. The two often recommended are swimming and bicycling. Suggested levels will ap-

Exercise Options

Bicycling. At its best, it's an exhilarating sport, a wonderful way to make friends, see the world *and* get fit. At the very least, it's a practical way to exercise while doing something else—like watching TV or reading. A sturdy ten-speed for outdoors, and/or a stationary bike for indoors can provide a lifetime of pleasure and fitness.

Work yourself up gradually, using Dr. Mollen's program, suggested in the heading above.

Depending on where you live, outdoor biking can keep you happy and fit for much of the year. If you do bike outdoors, a helmet is essential. In bicycling accidents, head injury is the most common cause of death. Head injury also occurs frequently in nonfatal accidents. Many of these injuries and deaths would be prevented by

pear in the heading above. If you've been walking an hour a day most days, then you're probably ready to begin at the levels outlined here, says Dr. Mollen. But take it easy—if these goals are too challenging, do less to start.

• If you haven't been able to exercise regularly for the past six months, this is the week to grant yourself a second chance. Begin walking for the time or distance suggested in Week 1. It's only five minutes to start. Or talk to your physician, or a trained exercise professional about starting an exercise program to suit you.

Get Ready

If you're continuing with your own exercise program, remember that the minimum amount of vigorous aerobic activity required to achieve a level of cardiovascular fitness is three times a week, 20 minutes each time.

Get Set

Don't forget warmups and gentle stretches before you work out. And take your pulse during and immediately after exercise.

Before you start any new exercise program—particularly if you're going to make different demands on your body (for example, if you've been walking and want to start aerobic dance), consult your physician.

Go!

But take it easy. Let your body be your guide. Stay under the recommended maximum pulse rate. If you're hurting, stop. And don't forget to cool down gradually afterwards by moving slowly and stretching for five minutes.

wearing a good helmet. Your head is worth the $50 investment.

Swimming. In many ways, it's the ideal exercise. It's no impact, so injuries are minimal. It's ideal for people with back problems or arthritis. Water's buoyancy allows the body to move freely, so muscles can be strengthened, and movement maximized, while the skeleton is buffered against pounding.

If you like, you can follow Dr. Mollen's swimming program suggested above. He notes that swimming may not burn as many calories or trim as much fat as other forms of exercise. The horizontal position of the body means the heart doesn't work as hard, and the cooling effect of water keeps the metabolism slower, so it takes longer to work off fat and strengthen the heart than with other forms of exercise.

Goal: *Cut Fat, Add Flavor*

Date: _____

Bike: 7 days, 30 minutes, 8 miles
Swim: 7 days, 10 laps

Are there times when low-fat eating feels like deprivation? When what you really want to do is fry the chicken, add cream to the sauce, douse the salad with blue cheese dressing?

Then you should know that, with the right preparation techniques and seasonings, it *is* possible to make low-fat fare luscious.

This week, prove it to yourself by trying some of these flavor-up, fat-down ideas.

• Sauté meat, poultry and fish in a little seasoned stock or liquid instead of oil or butter.

• Use stock instead of oil in meat marinades.

• Stewing or braising is an ideal way to cook meat, because the slow cooking allows the meat to give off its fat, which can later be skimmed away.

• Sauté sliced vegetables with plenty of mushrooms, which naturally give off lots of liquid.

• To reduce the fat in salad dressings, replace at least two-thirds of the oil in basic vinaigrette dressing with plain low-fat yogurt.

Fat Check

Time for another fat checkup! Review your last inventory. In Week 26, did you eat no more than eight servings of fatty foods like marbled beef, whole-milk dairy products or oily snack foods?

For a more precise evaluation of your diet, fat-wise, choose at least two days from the last inventory. Use the Superfoods chart to estimate those days' total calories, and then the percentage of calories that came from fat. (For more complete instructions, review Week 2.) See if those calories are about 25 percent of your daily total.

If they are, great! In all likelihood, you could healthfully stay at this level. But if you're trying to lose more weight, or trying to significantly reduce your risk for heart disease and other fat-related disease, some experts believe you should drop your fat intake to a maintenance level of 20 percent of calories. You can do this by counting fat calories; or set a general rule of thumb to limit your weekly intake of high-fat foods to no more than five modest servings.

Goal: *Think Thin*

Date: _____
Bike: 7 days, 32 minutes, 9 miles
Swim: 7 days, 12 laps

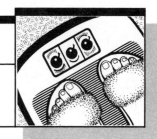

How's it going, weight-watchers? Last week, by adding new flavor to your low-fat fare you've made your diet not only more bearable but also more durable.

But experts are finding that *how you think* about food may be as fundamental to the success of a diet as what you actually eat. Psychology now plays a major role in weight-loss plans. And one of the most effective techniques is called "behavior modification"—changing the patterns of thinking and action that lead people to overeat.

Experts say that it is important to identify your "food cues"—the things that trigger you to overeat—and then plan ways to resist them.

For example, one powerful food cue for many people is the refrigerator. They get the munchies every time they get near it. Fight back by putting the tempting food out of sight or stashed away in the freezer. Keep low-calorie foods toward the front. Stay out of the kitchen as much as possible.

The buffet table at a party is another eating spur. Again, planning can block this food cue. Eat a salad before you go to the party, so you won't be hungry.

A mouth-watering restaurant menu also can undo a diet in the time it takes to yell "Waiter!" So when eating out, scan the menu quickly and direct your vision straight to the poultry and fish entrees.

Another behavior to modify is how fast you eat. Experts believe that eating slowly means eating less. Savor your food. If you're eating with other people, try this ploy: Be the last to start eating, and the last to finish. "Talk, rearrange your napkin, cut your meat into tiny pieces . . . stall any way you can to be the last person to start eating," says Kelly Brownell, Ph.D., codirector of the Obesity Research Clinic at the University of Pennsylvania, in Philadelphia.

Dim the Lights, Switch the Plates

Some fascinating research on what stimulates and reduces the appetite has been conducted at Johns Hopkins University Health, Weight and Stress Program, in Baltimore. One finding is that bright lights and bright colors make you want to eat more. So dim the lights. Plates with patterns on the face also encourage people to eat more. "Just like a kid will drain his cup to see Mickey Mouse on the bottom, we're psychologically stimulated by patterned dishes to clean our plates," says program director Maria Simonson, Ph.D. If you decide to try new plates, use a smaller size so that your portions will look larger.

581

Goal: *Stretch with Yoga*

Date: _____
Bike: 7 days, 32 minutes, 9 miles
Swim: 7 days, 12 laps

"Hey I'm touching my toes! Couldn't do that before!"

Now that your fitness routine is established, regular stretching is more important than ever. If you're using the stretches you learned in Week 6 (or any program of your choosing) several times each week, you no doubt feel more supple and relaxed.

This week, you should not only keep stretching several times a week, but also take advantage of a form of exercise that offers all the benefits of an excellent stretching program—*and much, much more.*

Yoga isn't a vigorous aerobic exercise. It's meditative and careful. Breathing is an important part of yoga—not huffing and puffing, but slow, controlled breathing, which is said to balance mind and body.

At the very minimum, yoga dramatically increases flexibility. What's more, it can be an effective stress reduction technique. People report that yoga cleared up their stress-related health problems, and gave them new energy.

If there's a yoga program at your local health club, community center, etc., you may want to check it out this week. There are, of course, dozens of books on yoga—find one that you can work with.

Meanwhile, here's a yoga stretch to start with. You can add it to your stretching program for improved flexibility.

The Cobra

Yoga postures should be preceded by relaxation and deep breathing. Never force or strain. The posture should be performed slowly and deliberately.

Lie on your stomach, with your toes extended. Place your hands, palms down, under your shoulders on the floor. Then, inhaling, raise the chest and head, arching the back, and bringing your head back so you're looking straight up. Do this without lifting the navel from the floor. Retain the breath, then exhale while lowering slowly to the floor. Repeat one to six times.

This exercise limbers the spine. It's not recommended, however, for people with a peptic ulcer, hernia, or hyperthyroid problem.

582

Goal: *Shop for Beauty*

Date: _____
Bike: 7 days, 34 minutes, 10 miles
Swim: 7 days, 14 laps

This is another shopping spree week! But instead of clothing, this week concentrate on skin care products, and, if you choose, cosmetics. These products not only help your skin look younger and healthier, but some contain sunscreens which can help to prevent sun damage that causes wrinkling, and even skin cancer.

Women, if you're putting on the same makeup you wore five years ago, it's definitely time for a change. With a few new products and techniques, you can have a more polished, attractive, up-to-date look—and protect your skin better.

Here's a shopping list of skin care and cosmetic basics. Their use is explained further in chapter 38.

Shopping List for Women

• Non-soapy cosmetic cleanser.
• Cosmetic buffing sponge and grainy cleanser. They really can give skin a fresher, younger look and may speed cell renewal.
• Moisturizer. An ordinary fragrance-free moisturizer will be as effective as the expensive kind that promises wrinkle removal. One requirement, though: Be sure to get one that contains a sun protection factor.
• Water-based foundation, if you have oily skin. For dry skin, an oil-based foundation.
• Concealer for dark circles and blemishes.
• Cosmetic brushes for applying powders. Not a luxury—they're a necessity. Today's powdered cosmetics are made to be applied with brushes, or they'll go on too thick, giving you a clown-face.

Shopping List for Men

We won't tell you that you have to buy that expensive line of men's skin care products and bronzers, if that's not to your taste. Like women, you can find inexpensive products that will revitalize your look. Here's the minimum:

• A moisturizer. Be sure to get one with a sun protection factor. Use it not only on your face, but on the back of your neck, earlobes and hands.
• An unpigmented lip balm that contains a sunscreen.
• Concealer to lighten dark circles under your eyes.

And for both sexes, indulge in a full line of hair-care products—not only shampoo and conditioner, but also styling mousse or gel, hair spray and a once-a-month deep conditioner.

The result of all these products? A you who looks healthier and younger.

Goal: *Steam Your Food*

Date: _____

Bike: 7 days, 34 minutes, 10 miles
Swim: 7 days, 14 laps

Ponce de Leon not withstanding, our bet is that if there is a Fountain of Youth, it isn't in Florida. It's probably in the Orient.

The Asians are generally slender. Their skin hardly shows a wrinkle until well into middle age. Japanese women live longer than any others in the world, and are renowned for their beauty.

What's their secret? Diet may have much to do with it. The Japanese diet has less than half the fat of the typical American diet. Also, the Japanese consume a great deal of fish, which has unique regenerating powers (see Week 19).

There is also much to learn from the ancient healing arts and exercises of the Orient. If you ever have the opportunity to take an early morning stroll in a Chinese city, you may be amazed to see, everywhere, groups of people—especially older people—standing in parks, on sidewalks, even in traffic circles, dancing the slow, graceful movements of t'ai chi.

So break out the rice, the fan and the kimono—you're going for a four-week oriental interlude.

You'll send your stomach to the Orient first, via a simple cooking technique that's ideal for vegetables and fish—steaming.

The secret of steaming is that food cooks above, not in, water. Vegetables look better because they're not soaked and churned into soggy oblivion.

And steaming means a big difference in the vitamin department, too. Boiling can cut the iron content of spinach by more than half. Steaming can save you 25 percent more. In addition, steaming can save you up to twice the B vitamins, vitamin C, calcium, magnesium and phosphorus. The reason? Those nutrients, along with iron, are water soluble. Steamed vegetables don't touch the water. Steaming should be brief, so the vegetables are still crunchy. The longer they cook, the more vitamins they lose.

Easy to Do

The steaming procedure is simple. Pour an inch or so of water into a pot, and place your steamer inside. Make sure the water level is below the floor of the steamer. Bring the water to a boil, then put the food into the steamer. Be sure to cover the pot with a tight lid.

Steaming won't cost you big bucks in kitchenware. You can use a colander or mesh frying basket. For a very few dollars you can buy a folding steamer, an aluminum rack with side petals to fit different pot widths. Or you can buy a beautiful and inexpensive set of Chinese tiered bamboo steaming baskets.

584

They fit into one another, so you can cook several different courses over the one pot of boiling water.

Great for Main Dishes

But don't forget that steaming isn't just for veggies. It also adds moisture to dry inexpensive cuts of meat, without adding any fat. You can whip up a quick, oriental-style meal with thinly sliced meat, like chicken or beef, and chopped vegetables. Throw the meat into the steamer first, and the vegetables later.

Steamed fish is luscious! The easiest way to try it is at a good Chinese restaurant. The second easiest way is at home. Wrap seasoned fish in cheesecloth to prevent it from falling apart. Then wrap it in brown paper, parchment or foil so it steams in its own juices—yum!

Steamed Vegetable Timetable

Asparagus
   whole: 10–15 minutes
   2-inch pieces: 5–10 minutes
Beans, snap
   whole: 10–15 minutes
   cut: 7–12 minutes
Broccoli
   stalks: 10–20 minutes
   cut: 5–15 minutes
Brussels sprouts
   whole: 10–15 minutes
Carrots
   whole: 20–30 minutes
   ¼-inch slices: 10–15 minutes
Cauliflower
   florets: 10–15 minutes

Corn
   on cob: 7–10 minutes
   cut: 4–5 minutes
Peas
   whole: 5–8 minutes
Potatoes, white
   whole: 15–25 minutes
   ½-inch slices: 5–10 minutes
Spinach leaves
   leaves: 3–5 minutes
Zucchini
   whole: 10–15 minutes
   cubed: 5–10 minutes

Goal: *Warm Up to a Bath*

Date: _____

Bike: 7 days, 36 minutes, 11 miles
Swim: 7 days, 16 laps

The Japanese don't soak their vegetables, but one thing they do soak is themselves. At home, they never miss their evening's alternately vigorous-and-meditative scrub-and-soak. If their apartments don't have a tub, they just wrap up in a robe and head for the nearest public bath, where grandmas gossip as they wash each other's backs, children frolic and everyone gasps as they climb into a clean (no soap allowed) hot tub and take a few minutes to contemplate a lovely mosaic of Mt. Fuji.

A nighttime soak can relax and rejuvenate you, too. For an authentic Japanese-style bath, first take a shower, scrubbing with a loofah or facecloth (go easy on your face) to stimulate your skin. Then, fill the tub with hot water, and soak. Keep a picture of your favorite mountain pinned to the wall, so you'll have something to contemplate. Bliss! If you do this in the evening, you'll be warm and cozy, your skin will glow and you'll tumble into a sweet sleep.

You'll reap all kinds of other benefits, too. "There is probably nothing in the world better for relaxing the muscles than a hot bath," says D. L. Moore, M.D., medical director at the Living Springs Retreat, in Putnam Valley, New York. "Whether muscle tightness is from disease, fatigue or strain, peo-

ple often find great relief soaking in a hot tub."

Bath water should be about 100° to 110°F with 102° to 104° the ideal. Anything above 110° is not recommended.

Baths are particularly good for people with arthritis. Gentle joint movement and gentle, simple stretching are easier in the bath, and you can improve your mobility and range of motion. Hot baths can also relieve many other pains, like back pain or menstrual cramps.

Probably the only bad thing that could come from so much soaking is dry skin. Take precautions—use bath oil or a post-bath skin cream. If you use bath oil be sure to also use a bath mat.

Some other safety reminders: Don't soak in a very hot bath for more than 30 minutes. It can stimulate the heart, and be exhausting. If you have high blood pressure, a heart condition or diabetes, it is best to stay away from any extreme temperatures unless you get your doctor's permission. Don't soak if you've been drinking alcohol. And never leave a plugged-in appliance, like a hair dryer or a radio, near a tub full of water.

When you've finished your hot bath, you may enjoy a quick cool down. A splash of cold water restores oxygen flow to the brain to normal.

586

Goal: *Try Li Shou*

Date: _____
Bike: 7 days, 36 minutes, 11 miles
Swim: 7 days, 16 laps

Li Shou means "hand-swinging," and that's exactly what it is. It can relieve a headache, relax you, provide your heart with a freshly oxygenated supply of blood, and induce the euphoria associated with vigorous exercise.

Do these claims sound far-fetched? How, you may ask, can the simple act of swinging your hands relieve a headache? Consider: Your head throbs when the cranial blood vessels are swollen. When you swing your arms, you shunt the flow of blood to your limbs, thus reducing the flow of blood to your head. Result? No more headache.

To perform Li Shou, first warm up by rubbing your palms together for a few seconds, creating a pleasant warmth. Now, using both palms, massage your face from forehead to chin as if you were washing it. Repeat 30 times, always moving your hands up and down. Then, consciously relax your entire body, put on a happy face and begin.

First, stand with your feet shoulder-width apart, toes pointing forward. Keeping the upper part of your body upright, let your arms and elbows sink naturally downward, spreading your fingers slightly. Close your eyes partially, your lids not quite meeting. Without bending your head, mentally focus downward to your toes.

Second, raise both hands, extending them frontward only to navel level.

Finally, swing your arms to the back, raising your hands no higher than the buttocks, but moving them with sufficient force so that your arms bounce back effortlessly. Keep swinging your hands back and forth rhythmically, like a pendulum, for 100 swings. Be aware of your hand movement while focusing attention passively on your toes. If your mind should wander or worry, get it back on track by paying attention to toes and fingers.

When you swing back, feel tenseness in the muscles of both hands and feet; when you swing frontward, experience a lovely relaxation in your whole body.

Gradually increase your swings to 1,000. Reduce the number if you experience nausea, chest pain, dizziness or extreme fatigue. Also, it may be wise not to perform Li Shou after a heavy meal or when you're really hungry.

After a few weeks, says Dr. Chang, you will discover a sensation like a mild but pleasant "electric current" drizzling down your fingers and toes even when your hands are not in motion. This is like the "in control" feeling you get from biofeedback.

Goal: *Taste Tofu*

Date: _____

Bike: 7 days, 38 minutes, 12 miles
Swim: 7 days, 18 laps

Your oriental interlude concludes with an ode to tofu. If you haven't tried soy-based food yet, this is your week to discover how delicious it really can be. And if you're already a fan, you'll find a new way to prepare tofu or introduce it to a friend.

Soy-based foods have been staples in Asian cuisine for nearly 3,000 years. In this country, vegetarians have eaten soyfoods—like tofu, tempeh and soy milk—for a long time. But only over the last few years has tofu become readily available to most people. Today, more than a million pounds of tofu are eaten in the United States every week. Several trendy new tofu-based products have appeared on the market, ranging from frozen tofu lasagna to Tofutti, the tofu-based "ice cream."

The popularity is hardly surprising, given that tofu is free of cholesterol, and high in protein, iron and calcium. It has a mild taste, like bland cheese. In cooking, it's incredibly versatile, and can star in its own dishes, or extend and/or substitute for dairy and meat products.

You can cut fat and calories significantly by using tofu in place of meat or cheese. A typical four-ounce serving of tofu contains 82 calories, one-third the calories of a quarter-pound of cheese. That same serving provides about 9 grams of protein, which is 15 to 25 percent of an adult's Recommended Dietary Allowance (RDA), and over 2 milligrams of iron, 20 percent of an adult male's RDA.

Tofu can also contribute calcium to your diet, if you use tofu made by the processing method that uses calcium compounds instead of magnesium salts (check the label). Tofu made this way contains 145 milligrams of calcium per four ounces.

If you've never tasted tofu, you can try it at an oriental restaurant, where it's often listed on the menu as "bean curd." You'll find it nestled among the water chestnuts and snow peas, and wonder, "What is this? Cheese? A mushroom? Yum!" If it's sliced or cubed, white and yummy, it's probably tofu.

If you've bought tofu yourself and didn't like it, it may be because you bought the supermarket kind, which comes vacuum-packed in plastic. This type often has a less delicate flavor than fresh, loose cakes available in health food stores. It's worth trying the fresh variety, because it really is different. When you bring your tofu home, immerse the contents you don't use immediately in water, and change the water daily.

The Twain Shall Meet

Below are two wonderful tofu recipes—one Eastern, the other Western. Try them both to convince yourself of tofu's adaptability.

Tofu Strips and Snow Peas in Chinese Restaurant Sauce

3 cups rich chicken stock
2 teaspoons minced, peeled ginger root
2 large cloves garlic, minced
1 tablespoon soy sauce
3 tablespoons cornstarch
1½ pounds tofu, cut into 2 × ½ × ½-inch strips
2 cups fresh snow peas

Pour 2½ cups of the stock into a saucepan and add the ginger and garlic. Place over medium heat and bring to a boil. Reduce heat and simmer 5 minutes.

In a bowl, combine the remaining stock with the soy sauce and the cornstarch. Stir until combined. Stir into the stock mixture. Cook, at a simmering heat, stirring, until the sauce has thickened slightly. Add the tofu and snow peas and continue to cook until they are heated through. (Fresh snow peas should still be bright green in color after cooking.) Serve over hot, cooked rice.

Yield: 6 servings

Chili con Tofu

2 tablespoons olive oil
1 large onion, chopped
1 green pepper, chopped
2 cloves garlic, pressed or minced
2 teaspoons chili powder
¼ teaspoon ground cumin
1½ cups mashed tofu
2 teaspoons soy sauce
2 cups tomatoes, canned or fresh
1 cup corn, fresh or frozen
½ teaspoon dried oregano
2 cups drained, cooked pinto beans

Heat the oil in a large Dutch oven and sauté the onion, green pepper and garlic until just tender. Stir in the chili powder, cumin and tofu. Sprinkle the mixture with soy sauce and add the tomatoes, corn and oregano. Simmer gently, uncovered, for 30 minutes, stirring occasionally.

Add the pinto beans and cook 10 minutes more. Taste for seasonings.

Yield: 4–6 servings

Goal: *Turn Off the Noise*

Date: _____
Bike: 7 days, 38 minutes, 12 miles
Swim: 7 days, 18 laps

Did you know that noise is the leading cause of deafness? In chapter 16, you learned about the toll that loud living can take on your hearing. There's the din outside: jackhammers, traffic, jet engines, factories, sirens. But even inside your home may be no haven for your poor ears. Assaulted by blenders, vacuum cleaners, dishwashers and power tools, the tiny hair cells in your ears may just fall over and surrender!

And deafness isn't the only consequence. For many problems considered stress-related—like anxiety, insomnia and indigestion—the stress in question may be noise. Steven Halpern, Ph.D., composer and coauthor of *Sound Health* (Harper & Row), who has researched the physiological effects of sound, believes that stress caused by too much noise may even cause alcoholism, or tobacco and drug abuse.

This week, try turning down the din in your life!

Do you really need that brain-rattling alarm clock to awaken you in the morning? How about a clock radio that comes on quietly, with soothing music? Better yet, sleep near a window and let the sunlight awaken you—softly, gently and in silence!

Before you buy any appliance, check its noise level. In the kitchen, noise from countertop appliances can be greatly reduced with the use of foam pads.

Be sure your home is well insulated and/or decorated with carpets and drapes that cut down noise levels.

Buy yourself some earplugs made from silicone putty or foam. Those are the kind designed to protect against noise, not water. Use them when you operate power tools, ride a subway—any time you're subjected to continuous, loud noise. If your job environment is noisy, try the plugs there, too. Bliss!

"Rings on her fingers and bells on her toes and she shall have music wherever she goes." That's all well and good, but what about those headphones on her ears? Even if they're delivering soothing music, keep them at a low volume, and use in moderation. Unlike ground-level bells, these deliver sound straight to your delicate ear.

Goal: *Turn On the Music*

Date: _____
Bike: 7 days, 40 minutes, 13 miles
Swim: 7 days, 18 laps

Music alone with sudden charms
    can bind
The wand'ring sense,
      and calm the troubled mind.
        (William Congrove)

Three hundred years after the seventeenth-century poet penned that tribute to harmony, it's been scientifically verified. Certain kinds of music can actually relax you on a physiological level. Music can bring on a relaxation response similar to the one you might achieve by practicing meditation!

Not all music, of course, induces such profound tranquility. Steven Halpern, Ph.D., "New Age" composer and noted authority on music and relaxation, says that music that reflects your own heartbeat and breathing tends to be more relaxing. That's music with a rhythm of about one beat per second. Parts of certain classical pieces come closest to fitting that description, particularly the slow second movements of some baroque pieces by Bach, Handel and Telemann, according to Dr. Halpern.

The final determination of whether music is relaxing to you is *yours*. Treat yourself to a relaxing music break this week. Choose some soothing music, stretch out in a comfortable space, and—don't read, don't knit, just *unwind*. "Just watch your body and see how you

feel . . . You'll know if you've picked the right music. If the music helps you breathe slower and deeper, it is relaxing you," says Dr. Halpern.

Selecting Soothing Sounds

What if your entire record and tape collection was built around the recommendations of an aerobic dance teacher? Then you'll need something new and different. Here's some music many people find helps to "Stop the World."

- Ball, Patrick. *From a Distant Time* (Fortuna); Celtic harp music.
- Halpern, Steven. *Comfort Zone, Eventide* and others (Anti-Frantic Alternative); creates unworldly reveries on grand piano, electric piano and string synthesizers.
- Horn, Paul. *Inside* (Epic); improvisational flute recorded in the dome of the Taj Mahal.
- Jarrett, Keith. *The Koln Concert* (ECM); 70 minutes of brilliant improvisational piano.
- Kitaro. *Silk Road 1 & 2; Tunhuang* (Oasis); incredibly soothing electronic reveries (one of the most popular New Age musicians).
- Pachelbel, Johann. *Canon in D Major* (many recordings); a classical canon that calms with the restfulness of pure form.

591

Goal: *Quarterly Inventory*

Date: _____

Bike: 7 days, 40 minutes, 13 miles

Swim: 7 days, 20 laps

Inventory 4

Now that you're an expert in taking inventory, you can do it for only four days a week. Choose any four days, and write in the dates in the chart.

I. Diary	Day 1 _____	Day 2 _____	Day 3 _____	Day 4 _____
Food and Drink A.M. P.M.				
Moods and Activities Summary				
Exercise and Stretching				
Relaxation				

II. Vital Statistics

1. Weight _____

2. Resting pulse _____ beats/minute

3. Blood pressure _____

4. Cholesterol _____ mg/deciliter

Goal: *Jog Your Mind*

Date: _____
Bike: 7 days, 40 minutes, 13 miles
Swim: 7 days, 20 laps

"People who lead active lives, take advantage of education and have hobbies that are mentally stimulating will have an advantage in later life," says K. Warner Schaie, Ph.D., professor of human development and psychology, at Pennsylvania State University, in University Park.

Dr. Schaie questioned about 3,000 people over many years about their occupations, leisure activities, and incomes. He also tested their word recognition and usage skills and their ability to solve problems and adjust to unfamiliar situations, initially and then again when they were in their sixties. Those who led active, challenging lives showed no deterioration in those areas, whereas people whose lives were less stimulating showed a marked decline.

Keeping yourself mentally stimulated is a lifetime pursuit. But this week, you can begin with just a little extra brainwork: Try the quiz below.

A Little Mental Exercise

The following questions in logic, reasoning and mathematics are from *The Mensa Genius Quiz Book 2* (Addison-Wesley), by Marvin Grosswirth, Abbie Salny and the members of Mensa.

1. You have 24 socks in a drawer, 6 each of brown, black, white and red. How many socks must you take out of the drawer, without looking, to be sure of having a matched pair (of any color)?

2. Which of the lettered words could logically come next in the following sequence?

APE BIRD CAN DIG EAT
a. MAN b. HAT c. CAR d. SEA e. FIG

3. Sally goes out on a shopping expedition for some new clothes. She buys a coat, a skirt and a scarf. The coat costs twice as much as the skirt, and ten times as much as the scarf. She starts out with $180 and comes back with $20. What was the cost of each item of clothing?

Answers:
1. Five—one more than the number of colors.
2. e. FIG (alphabetical order)
3. Coat, $100; skirt, $50; scarf, $10.

Goal: *Take Nature for Nerves*

Date: _____

Bike: 7 days, 40 minutes, 13 miles
Swim: 7 days, 20 laps

You already know that you need greens inside your body for proper nutrition. But did you also know that greenery outside your body—on your windowsill, in your backyard, in the corner of your office—also can contribute to better health?

A full-scale flower garden—or even a lone, pampered avocado plant—gives you something to care about outside yourself. Plants can soften modern high-tech environments. And raising flora can provide stress relief.

If you're already a gardener, you're undoubtedly familiar with the tranquility that comes with tending plants. Physiological data confirm that gardening can have calming effects, such as slowing the pulse rate. It relieves tension in other ways, too: Hoeing and weeding are better ways to deal with stress than hollering and worrying.

Plants Are Calming

You don't have to cultivate a prize-winning garden to benefit from plants. Merely looking at greenery—via a stroll in the park or a gaze out the window—may enhance your health. A few years back, a study showed that hospital patients whose rooms overlooked trees and grass left the hospital sooner and needed fewer potent painkillers than patients whose windows overlooked a brick wall.

For many, contemplation of plants has an almost spiritual aspect. Charles Lewis, horticulturist and administrator of the collections program at the Morton Arboretum, in Lisle, Illinois, believes that plants' growth cycles reveal an innate intelligence. "You have to work with plants according to *nature's* rules," he says. At the same time, you have a certain amount of control. "[Plants] can't talk back, they can't bite you, but they *will* respond to what you do for them."

Meet Fellow Gardeners

Plants are also a good way to get involved with another life form, neighbors. The neighbor growing gorgeous tomatoes down the street may clue you in to what's eating yours.

So this week, buy a plant. Your local plant shop will help you choose one that's easy to care for.

If you want to get into gardening more seriously, the extension services of land grant colleges and universities are a great resource.

At the very least, if you're feeling deficient in greenery, make a point of visiting a park or botanical gardens.

Goal: *Treat Your Feet*

Date: _____

Bike: 7 days, 42 minutes, 14 miles
Swim: 7 days, 20 laps

You've asked a lot of your feet on this program. First, there was all that walking. Now you may be running, bicycling, gardening, park-strolling—with your feet doing much of the dirty work.

So declare this "Be Sweet to Your Feet Week." Review chapter 13 for information on daily foot care and hygiene. If you have a nagging problem—like pain from a bunion or a plantar's wart—call a podiatrist this week to make an appointment. Don't delay any longer; you don't want things to worsen.

And as a special reward for all the pleasures they've brought you, give your feet the treatment this week.

Exercise Them. Slip off your shoes and sit with your feet dangling above the floor. Point your toes down hard, then in, then up, then out, so they draw circles in the air. Simultaneously flex and extend the toes. This exercise strengthens leg and foot muscles.

Beautify Them. That's enough footwork. Now for the pampering, beginning with a beauty treatment. The basic cleaning procedure is explained in chapter 13. Or, if you can afford it, get a professional pedicure.

Massage Them. Bliss! A good foot-massage can prevent soreness, relieve tiredness and keep muscles flexible. Try this technique.

1. Sit on a chair and place one foot on top of the opposite thigh. Rub some massage oil or lotion on your foot. Using your thumbs, apply pressure to the sole of your foot, working from the bottom of the arch to the top, near the big toe. Repeat five times.
2. Make a fist, and use your knuckles to move from the heel area up to the toes. Repeat five times.
3. Massage each toe by holding it firmly and moving it from side to side. Apply pressure to the areas between the toes.
4. Hold all your toes with one hand and bend them backward. Hold for five to ten seconds. Move the toes forward. Hold. Repeat three times.

Buy Them a Present. Or two! Comfortable shoes are always at the top of your feet's wish list. Runner up: a pair of shock-absorbing full-shoe inserts. These are *not* the foam inserts you buy on racks in the drugstore, explains Barry Block, D.P.M., a Manhattan podiatrist, marathon runner and author of *Foot Talk* (Zebra). These special inserts cushion and absorb shock, and prevent friction and blistering on the bottom of the feet.

One of the most highly recommended brands is Spenco Insoles, made of nitrogen-impregnated foam, by the Spenco Medical Corp. You can find them at shoe and sporting-goods stores.

Goal: *Remember to Laugh*

Date: _____
Bike: 7 days, 42 minutes, 14 miles
Swim: 7 days, 22 laps

This is serious: Are you remembering to laugh? Each and every day? Now, don't say you're too busy getting fit. Even fitness can be funny, as demonstrated by humor writer Dave Barry in this excerpt from his tongue-in-cheek fitness guide.

The Basic Fitness Fashion Look for Women

This is, of course, the leotard and tights, which is the preferred outfit because it shows every bodily flaw a woman has, no matter how minute, so that a woman who, disguised in her street clothes, looks like Victoria Principal will, when she puts on her leotard, transform herself into Bertha the Amazing Land Whale. This encourages her to exercise vigorously and watch what she eats. She cannot, of course, drink anything, as there is no way to go to the bathroom in a leotard and tights.

Many a woman who suffers an exercise-related injury during an aerobic workout is forced to lie in great pain for hours on her exercise mat, trapped, while frustrated rescue personnel wait for the helicopter to bring various specialized torches, saws, and other equipment they need to free her from her tights and leotard so they can render medical treatment.

Fitness Fashion for Men

What you want, men, is a fashion look that gives you freedom of movement but at the same time displays, in large letters, the names of at least three major manufacturers of sporting equipment. Also, you want to wear a headband and wristbands to absorb the tremendous outpourings of sweat that we males emit when we are engaged in strenuous masculine physical activity. (If you are one of those unfortunate males who does not emit tremendous outpourings of sweat, you should purchase, from the Nike corporation, a container of "Pro-spiration" spray-on sweat droplets, which you apply discreetly in the locker room before you begin your workout.)

Excerpted from *Stay Fit and Healthy Until You're Dead*, by Dave Barry, illustrated by Jerry O'Brien, Rodale Press, 1985.

Goal: *Try an Ice Cream Alternative*

Date: _____

Bike: 7 days, 42 minutes, 14 miles

Swim: 7 days, 22 laps

Americans eat a *lot* of ice cream. If you put the 1.8 *billion* half-gallons consumed in one year side by side, you'd have a global sundae big enough to wrap around the earth eight times!

And speaking of wrapping, all that ice cream isn't making people's belts any easier to fasten. Federal standards require that ice cream be at least 10 percent butterfat even to be *called* ice cream. In terms of percent of total calories from fat, that translates to 45 percent, a hefty amount considering that the American Heart Association advises keeping fat consumption down to 30 percent of total calories or less.

So this week, look for new ways to "hit the spot." You need something sweet, something cold, something creamy smooth—like a *banana.* Simply peel small, really ripe bananas, put them on wooden sticks, wrap in foil or plastic wrap and freeze.

Low-fat yogurt is another good substitute. Top it with fruit, nuts or granola to make a "sundae," or mix it in the blender with fruit for a shake.

If you really must have something more ice-creamesque, try this superhealthy alternative, "Nice Cream."

Nice Cream

1½ cups low-fat cottage cheese

½ cup pureed fruit (cherries, bananas, peaches)

10 packs Equal (granular NutraSweet)

2 teaspoons vanilla

1½ cups water

In a blender or processor, combine cottage cheese, fruit, Equal and vanilla. Blend until color is uniform. Continue to blend while slowly adding water.

Process mixture in an ice-cream maker according to manufacturer's directions, and serve immediately.

Note: To make Vanilla Nice Cream, simply omit pureed fruit.

Ice Cream vs. Nice Cream*

	Regular Ice Cream	Banana Nice Cream
Calories	181	48
Fat percent of calories	46	7

*Nutrient values per half-cup serving.

Goal: *Grains in a Hurry*

Date: _____

Bike: 7 days, 44 minutes, 15 miles
Swim: 7 days, 22 laps

What's your grain count? Are you eating whole grains, like brown rice, barley and oats, several times a week? As explained in Week 16, whole grains are one of the best ways to swallow the good things—vitamins, minerals, fiber and protein—without the bad things, like lots of fat.

But cooking whole grains can take a lot of time. If the time-crunch sometimes gets in the way of your grain-munch, try these super-fast ways to harvest the benefits of whole grains.

• Stock up on whole-grain breads. Try whole-wheat pita bread, rich in B vitamins and minerals. Keep pita pockets in the freezer. When you need one, pull it out, toast and stuff the pocket with anything: Tuna, cheese, chick-peas, tomato, lettuce, bean sprouts.

Have you tried crunchy rice cakes, made of puffed brown rice? They taste like popcorn and make a great base for grilled cheese or spreads. They keep well, too. No need to freeze—seal tightly and store in a dry place.

Sample sprouted grain bread—the sprouts are super-high in nutrients, and this kind of bread is baked at low temperatures to conserve vitamins. It also freezes well.

• Try a pasta of a different color. *Udon,* an oriental pasta, is flat, light tan and made of 100-percent whole wheat. *Soba* is light brown, and made of rutin-rich buckwheat. The dark brown *ramen* noodles sold in health food stores are usually composed of whole-wheat flour, buckwheat flour and sea salt. There's also Superoni, a soy-fortified American pasta; brown whole-wheat spaghetti; green spinach noodles and even golden-colored corn spaghetti. All are quick and easy. Experiment!

• Add wheat germ. To almost anything. It deserves its reputation as a health food superstar. Compared with enriched white flour, wheat germ has 76 times more niacin, more than 3 times as much riboflavin and 8 times more thiamine than enriched white bread. Also, 3 times more protein, 4 times as much iron and 8 times more potassium! It can be kept in the freezer, and used without thawing. The toasted variety keeps longer than untoasted.

Goal: *Eat Like a Cowboy*

Date: _____
Bike: 7 days, 44 minutes, 15 miles
Swim: 7 days, 22 laps

Chuckwagon cooks knew the value of beans: They were compact and easy to transport to the range, they didn't spoil and they provided the cowpokes with filling, nutritious meals.

Today's cooks should still hold beans in high esteem—if not for their ability to travel well, then for their top-notch nutrition. Beans are high in protein but low in fat. Beans also offer goodly amounts of some B vitamins, as well as iron, calcium, magnesium and fiber.

And of all the high-fiber foods that scour cholesterol from the system, probably none is more effective than beans. Scientific tests have shown that beans can lower blood-fat levels significantly.

Many of the world's cultures make regular use of beans. Consider the Mexican staple *frijoles refritos* or refried beans, using pinto beans. In the Middle East, cooks rely on chick-peas for standard dishes such as falafel, while in the Orient they use soybeans as the basis of tofu and miso as well as mung bean sprouts, which provide crunch to a variety of cooked dishes.

Easy Beans

There are probably two reasons people avoid beans. One is convenience. Beans usually require a long time to soak and/or cook.

If you're in a rush, you can buy canned beans. Or you can try this "no-tend" method:

- The night before, place a pound of beans into a large bowl with about two or three quarts of water. You'll need enough water to cover the beans as they expand.
- The next day, drain the beans and put them into a very large casserole dish or small roasting pan. Then, re-cover the beans with a generous amount of water, cover the pan and bake until tender.

The other problem with beans is that they can generate intestinal gas. To get around this problem, change the water after the beans' overnight soak. After a half-hour of cooking, again discard the water and replace with fresh water, cooking the beans until they are tender.

Goal: *Cope with Anger*

Date: _____

Bike: 7 days, 44 minutes, 15 miles
Swim: 7 days, 24 laps

Anger. The question is whether it's healthier to let it all out, or lock it all up? Some studies indicate that suppressed hostility may be a factor contributing to breast and heart disease.

Surely the alternative—igniting at every annoyance—is not the answer, either. "I notice that people who are most prone to give vent to their rages get angrier, not less angry," notes Carol Tavris, Ph.D., author of *Anger, the Misunderstood Emotion* (S & S).

One study found that people who take steps to *resolve* their anger have the lowest blood pressure. How is anger resolved? The following techniques can help.

Make a List. Write down all the things you're angry about. Next to each complaint, list the reasons why you think the problem is someone else's fault. In a third column, write down the aspects of the problem that are your fault. "Then you can take steps to either change your behavior or speak to the person whom you see as the source of your anger," says Michael L. Silverman, Ed.D., a stress specialist in private practice in Philadelphia.

Learn to Rethink. If someone blows up at you unjustly, rather than exploding in return, try to understand where they're coming from, says Dr. Tavris.

Drop the "Shoulds." Anger is of-ten based on what you think other people *should* be doing. Stop and ask yourself if your "should" is reasonable. Don't become obsessed with other people's failure to live up to your standards.

Express Anger the Right Way

There are times when expressing anger is justified and necessary. But still, some people will hold it inside, says Dr. Hendrie Weisinger, Ph.D., author of *Dr. Weisinger's Anger Workout Book* (Morrow).

"People who don't express their anger are usually afraid of the consequences: 'She won't love me anymore,' or 'He'll fire me,'" says Dr. Weisinger. But you can learn to express anger in the way that's least likely to make the other person angry. Express your anger in "I feel," emotional statements, instead of "I think" intellectual statements. If someone you're supposed to meet stands you up, don't say, "I think you're unfair." Instead say, "I feel hurt that you didn't call."

The next step is to tell the person you're angry at what you'd like him to do. For example, "I would like you to call me in the future if you can't make an appointment." That way, Dr. Weisinger explains, the other person will understand exactly what you want and will be less likely to get angry back.

600

Goal: *Adopt an Animal*

Date: _____

Bike: 7 days, 46 minutes, 16 miles
Swim: 7 days, 24 laps

It's been discovered that animals provide both emotional and physical help so effectively that, in some cases, they may even increase their owners' life spans.

The most convincing evidence of the health benefits of having a pet appeared in 1980, when University of Pennsylvania researchers interviewing heart attack survivors unexpectedly found that people with pets lived longer after their attacks than people without them. Soon after, they discovered a link between pet ownership and blood pressure.

Why are pets so good for us? Veterinarian Richard H. Pitcairn, D.V.M., Ph.D., says he thinks the most important reason is this: "The animal provides a relationship which is totally without judgment or criticism. The effect of such an easy relationship is a sense of deep relaxation."

So this week, think about getting more love and friendship in your life. Think about getting a pet.

Buy a Friend

Affectionate, intelligent, loyal, playful—dogs deserve their reputation as man's (and woman's) best friend. But before you rush out to buy a puppy, consider a few basic facts. A dog must fit into both your living situation and your life. If you are a city dweller, for example, Richard H. Pitcairn, D.V.M., Ph.D., suggests getting a breed of dog that will remain small even when fully grown.

Working an animal into your life-style may be somewhat trickier. "Dogs need people who have time for them," explains Dr. Pitcairn. "They like to interact a lot. If someone doesn't really have a schedule that allows time to take the dog out to play, that's hard on the animal. That kind of person should have a pet other than a dog.

"If you work and are not home much during the day, a cat or other animal is a good pet," explains the doctor. Even people who live in apartments can provide a cat with a happy home. "Cats can be happy indoors if they are raised that way from the beginning, and if they're given several sources of stimulation. And now and then, bring home new things of interest—like a cardboard box with a hole in it."

Goal: *Guess...*

Date: _____

Bike: 7 days, 46 minutes, 16 miles
Swim: 7 days, 24 laps

One syllable. Sounds like "clay" . . .

If you know the game of charades you may have guessed the word is *play*. And it's one of those things, as a songwriter once wrote of new math, which is "so easy that only a child can do it!" But experts say that adults need the release of joy and play, too.

The benefits of play aren't to be taken lightly. "I try to get patients to rediscover the sense of play and fun that they had as children," says E. T. "Cy" Eberhart, a certified hospital chaplain, in Salem, Oregon, who has used humor with patients for years. "I encourage them to get involved in a game or hobby they enjoyed in childhood, and often the experience is enough to rekindle their innate playfulness. Frequently, the result is a lifting of depression, and an increased feeling of well-being."

Fun isn't optional—it's a must for good health. So forget all your goals for a while, and "waste" some time on play—for the sheer fun of it!

Try "This Is My Nose"

How should you respond when someone approaches you, sticks his finger in his ear and says, "This is my nose"? Chances are, he's not attempting to transmit an obscure message, but merely extending an invitation to play the New Game.

Someone could quite properly respond to him by tugging her chin and saying, "This is my ear." Then he could continue the game by scratching his head and claiming, "This is my chin." And then she might pat her butt and insist, "This is my head."

Undoubtedly some onlooker will wisecrack that these two can't tell one end from the other. You should explain that the object of this ultimate test of hand-eye-mouth coordination is to say the body part the other person has just pointed to, while pointing to another body part. Then you should challenge him to a game and see how long he can keep the chain going before his tongue gets twisted with his anatomy.

Adapted from *More New Games* (The Headlands Press, Inc., 1981).

Goal: *Throw a Party*

Date: _____
Bike: 7 days, 46 minutes, 16 miles
Swim: 7 days, 24 laps

Throw a party to your health! Make it an event that proves to yourself and your friends that you can still eat, drink and be merry—without dying tomorrow.

• Look for low-sodium or no-salt potato chips, pretzels and corn chips in the health food store.
• High-fiber, no-salt and low-salt crackers abound. Choose wheat wafers, bran wafers, rye wafers, sesame crackers, whole-wheat pita and sesame bread sticks, to name a few.
• Serve crudites—raw carrot sticks, green pepper strips, cauliflower florets, broccoli spears. Team them with healthy dips.
• Try this avocado dip: Mash some avocado. Add a bit of lemon or lime juice and grated onion. Spread on crackers or vegetables and top with chopped tomatoes.
• For vegetable pâté: Blend together steamed spinach, carrots and cauliflower. Stuff into celery or spread on slices of cucumber. Your weight-watching friends will bless you.
• Season yogurt with herbs, like garlic, dill and savory, for a flavorful, low-fat dip.

A Word on Social Drinking

Drinking alcohol can relax people in a social situation. But as everyone knows, excessive drinking means problems. Drivers, alcoholics and pregnant women should steer clear of alcohol on any occasion. Others can drink safely in moderation. To keep yourself from overdoing, follow these rules:

Dilute. Lowering the concentration of alcohol in your glass means slowing its entrance into your bloodstream. It's not the carbonated mixers that have this slowing effect—it's the sweet mixers, like orange juice. So choose a fruit juice drink, like a screwdriver.

Pace yourself. Drink slowly, and alternate alcoholic beverages with nonalcoholic ones. Wait until the effect of the first drink settles before you reach for a second.

Don't forget about alternatives. Light beers and wines have reduced alcohol content, and there are also alcohol-free beers and wines, for the festive flavor without any side effects at all.

Goal: *Open Your Heart*

Date: _____

Bike: 7 days, 48 minutes, 17 miles

Swim: 7 days, 26 laps

These things I command you,
that ye love one another.
(John 15:17)

And that was *truly* a prescription for happiness and health. This week, celebrate the love in your life—and if you're feeling a lack, consider these two simple ways to enrich your life with love.

Be an Altruist. Helping others is a life-enhancing form of love.

"Altruism is what we call prosocial behavior," says Perry W. Buffington, Ph.D., an Atlanta psychologist. "It's a way of putting others before your own ego, of reaching out to people around you. And that can only increase well-being, because without some connections to others, life doesn't have much meaning."

There are many organizations that need volunteers: hospitals, senior citizen centers, shelters for the homeless, schools.

Give a Hug/Get a Hug. Educator and bestselling author Leo F. Buscaglia, Ph.D., has written eloquently of the power of love to transform lives. Here's his advice about learning the art of the loving touch.

We shake hands, we pat each other on the back, we playfully mess each other's hair . . . . These all represent common, physical, nonsexual expressions of affection. They are very human ways of bringing others closer, expressing our love and understanding or conveying our warmth . . . . Still, for some of us they present monumental barriers.

If we are strangers to the physical show of affection, it is natural that it will create anxiety and discomfort in us. But if we feel touch-starved and a need to change our physically intimate behavior, then it is well to know that it can be done. But as with all behavioral change, we should not expect that it will happen overnight. To start embracing, after years of standing aloof, would be unnatural. We may want to start making contact within the safety of family and caring, understanding friends. . . . We may want to start with a handshake, a pat on the back, a touch of the fingers, and move to other more intimate, nonsexual behavior. . . . The results are often immediate and dramatic. . . .

Excerpted from *Loving Each Other: The Challenge of Human Relationships* by Leo F. Buscaglia Inc. Published by Slack Inc., 1984, used by permission.

604

Goal: *Help a Friend to Health*

Date: _____
Bike: 7 days, 48 minutes, 17 miles
Swim: 7 days, 26 laps

In this next-to-last week of your Year of Rejuvenation, we're going to talk about beginning the cycle again—with someone you love.

Is your husband overweight? Is your daughter thin, but not very fit? Naturally, you're worried about them. You would like to see them revitalize *their* lives, too.

But as much as you want the best for them, you've probably found that lecturing gets you—and them—nowhere. There *are* ways to help your loved ones drop bad habits.

Do It Together

Most of the activities we've talked about this year can be done together. Bring your family on your walks. Some evening, read your stressed-out friend the instructions for progressive relaxation (Week 24). Or give him or her a tape of relaxing music (Week 37). "People are often very receptive to being taken by the hand and shown an interesting thing," says Dr. Barry Sultanoff, M.D., a psychiatrist in Bethesda, Maryland. Should your husband order fried steak, don't nag him about his weight or predict he'll have a heart attack. Instead, be positive when [people] do something right, says Lewis Losoncy, Ph.D., author of *Turning People On: How to Be an Encouraging Person* (Prentice-Hall). Praise them when they order a salad instead of a heavy meal. You should be a role model for the good life you're pushing. So think about starting the cycle again in the new year—eating even better, exercising right, taking time for relaxation and fun. And in your next Year of Rejuvenation, bring along someone you love.

To Your Health

Here's a health to all those that we love,
Here's a health to all those that love us,
Here's a health to all those that love them that love those
That love them that love those that love us.

(Old Toasting Song)

Goal: *Final Inventory*

Date: _____
Bike: 7 days, 48 minutes, 17 miles
Swim: 7 days, 26 laps

Inventory 5

Compare: To see how far you've come, write your "vital statistics" from the first inventory next to the vital statistics for this week. Congratulations!

I. Diary

	Sunday	Monday	Tuesday	
Food and Drink A.M. P.M.				
Moods and Activities Summary				
Exercise and Stretching				
Relaxation				

II. Vital Statistics

1. Weight _____   2. Resting pulse _____ beats/minute

	Wednesday	Thursday	Friday	Saturday

3. Blood pressure_____ 4. Cholesterol_____ mg/deciliter

Superfoods Chart

Foods	Serving Size	Calories (kcal)	Percent of Calories from Fat	Major Nutrient	Calcium (mg)	Sodium (g)	Fiber
Alfalfa sprouts	1 tbs	1	17	C	1	0	0.1
Almonds, dried, unblanched	¼ cup	209	74	E	94	4	1.7
Apple, raw w/skin	1	81	5	C	10	1	2.8
Apple juice, canned or bottled	½ cup	58	2	Potassium	8	4	—
Applesauce, canned, unsweetened	½ cup	53	1	Potassium	4	2	1.0
Apricots:							
Dried, sulfured, uncooked	½ cup	155	2	A	30	7	15.6
Raw	3	51	7	A	15	1	1.4
Asparagus, cooked	4	15	11	C	15	3	0.6
Avocado	1	324	80	Potassium	22	21	4.7
Bacon	3 strips	109	77	B_{12}	2	303	0
Banana	1	105	4	Potassium	7	1	1.6
Bass, striped, ovenfried	3 oz	170	39	—	—	76	0
Beans:							
Lima	½ cup	104	2	Potassium	27	14	3.6
Pinto	½ cup	167	2	—	54	2	4.8
Snap, (Italian, green and yellow)	½ cup	22	7	C	29	2	1.1
Soybeans, green	½ cup	127	38	—	131	2	2.5
Beef:							
Chuck rib roast, choice grade, braised	3 oz	212	50	B_{12}	11	43	0
Chuck steak, choice grade, braised	3 oz	164	33	B_{12}	12	45	0
Club steak, choice grade, broiled	3 oz	207	48	B_{12}	10	62	0
Flank steak, choice grade, braised	3 oz	167	33	B_{12}	12	45	0
Ground, lean, broiled	3 oz	186	47	B_{12}	10	57	0
Liver, fried	3 oz	195	42	B_{12}	9	156	0
Plate beef	3 oz	169	35	B_{12}	11	45	0
Porterhouse steak, choice grade, broiled	3 oz	190	42	B_{12}	10	63	0
Rump roast, choice grade, roasted	3 oz	177	40	B_{12}	10	61	0
Sirloin steak, choice grade, broiled	3 oz	188	40	B_{12}	10	64	0
Stewing beef, braised	3 oz	182	40	B_{12}	11	45	0
T-bone, choice, broiled	3 oz	189	42	B_{12}	10	63	0
Tongue, braised	3 oz	207	62	—	6	52	0
Beef broth	1 cup	16	30	—	15	782	Trace
Beef gravy	1 tbs	8	40	Zinc	0.9	7	—
Beets, cooked	½ cup	26	1	Potassium	9	42	0.7
Blackberries	½ cup	37	6	C	23	0	3.3
Blueberries	½ cup	41	6	C	5	5	2.2

Superfoods Chart

Foods	Serving Size	Calories (kcal)	Percent of Calories from Fat	Major Nutrient	Calcium (mg)	Sodium (g)	Fiber
Blue cheese dressing	1 tbs	77	92	—	12	153	0
Bluefish, baked w/butter	3 oz	137	30	—	24	88	0
Brazil nuts	¼ cup	230	84	Thiamine	62	0.5	2.7
Bread:							
French	1 slice	102	9	Thiamine	15	203	1.0
Italian	1 slice	83	2	Thiamine	5	176	1.1
Pumpernickel	1 slice	79	4	Potassium	27	182	2.4
Raisin	1 slice	66	9	Potassium	18	91	0.7
Rye	1 slice	61	4	Thiamine	19	139	1.2
Whole wheat, firm crumb	1 slice	61	11	Magnesium	25	132	2.2
Broccoli, cooked	½ cup	23	8	C	89	8	0.6
Brussels sprouts, cooked	4	32	12	C	28	16	1.2
Butter	1 tbs	102	99	A	3	116	0
Cabbage, cooked	½ cup	16	9	C	25	14	0.4
Cantaloupe	¼	47	7	C	14	12	0.4
Carrots, cooked	½ cup	35	3	A	24	52	1.5
Catsup	1 tsp	5	5	—	1	52	0.01
Cauliflower, cooked	½ cup	15	6	C	17	4	1.0
Celery stalk, raw	1	6	7	Potassium	14	35	0.4
Cheese:							
Blue	1 oz	100	72	Calcium	150	396	0
Brie	1 oz	95	73	B_{12}	52	178	0
Cheddar	1 oz	114	72	Calcium	204	176	0
Colby	1 oz	112	71	Calcium	194	171	0
Cottage, low-fat, 1%	½ cup	82	12	B_{12}	69	459	0
Cream	1 oz	99	88	A	23	84	0
Edam	1 oz	101	69	Calcium	207	274	0
Feta	1 oz	75	71	—	140	316	0
Gruyère	1 oz	117	69	Calcium	287	95	0
Monterey	1 oz	106	71	Calcium	212	152	0
Mozzarella, part-skim	1 oz	72	55	Calcium	183	132	0
Muenster	1 oz	104	72	Calcium	203	178	0
Neufchâtel	1 oz	74	79	Riboflavin	21	113	0
Parmesan	1 tbs	23	57	Calcium	69	93	0
Provolone	1 oz	100	66	Calcium	214	248	0
Ricotta, part-skim	½ cup	171	50	Calcium	337	155	0
Roquefort	1 oz	105	73	Calcium	188	513	0
Swiss	1 oz	107	64	Calcium	272	74	0
Cherry stone (raw) clams	6	84	10	B_{12}	72	216	0

(continued)

Superfoods Chart—*Continued*

Foods	Serving Size	Calories (kcal)	Percent of Calories from Fat	Major Nutrient	Calcium (mg)	Sodium (g)	Fiber
Chicken:							
Breast, roasted	3 oz	140	20	Niacin	13	62	0
Drumstick, roasted	3 oz	147	30	Niacin	10	81	0
Liver, simmered	3 oz	133	31	B_{12}	12	43	0
Thigh, roasted	3 oz	178	47	Niacin	10	75	0
Wing, roasted	3 oz	174	36	Niacin	12	77	0
Chicken broth, canned	1 cup	39	32	Niacin	9	776	Trace
Chicken gravy, canned	1 tbs	12	64	Zinc	3	86	—
Cod, broiled with butter or margarine	3 oz	144	28	B_{12}	27	93	0
Cola	12 oz	159	0	—	11	20	0
Corn, cooked	½ cup	89	10	C	2	14	1.3
Crab:							
Deviled	3 oz	160	45	B_{12}	40	736	0
King, steamed	3 oz	79	18	B_{12}	37	314	0
Crackers:							
Cheese	10	52	37	Riboflavin	36	112	0.4
Graham, plain	1 large	55	20	Potassium	6	95	1.4
Oyster	10	33	25	Iron	2	83	0.3
Saltine	10	123	23	Iron	6	312	1.1
Whole wheat	10	161	29	—	9	219	5.5
Cranberries, whole	½ cup	23	3	C	4	0.5	2.0
Cream:							
Half and half	1 tbs	20	76	B_{12}	16	6	0
Heavy whipping	1 tbs	52	94	A	10	6	0
Light, coffee or table	1 tbs	29	88	Riboflavin	14	6	0
Cucumber, sliced	½ cup	7	8	C	7	1	0.3
Dates, chopped	¼ cup	122	1	Potassium	15	1	2.3
Duck, domesticated, roasted	3 oz	171	50	Niacin	10	55	0
Egg:							
Fried	1	83	70	B_{12}	26	144	0
Raw or hard-cooked	1	79	64	B_{12}	28	69	0
Scrambled	1	95	67	B_{12}	47	155	0
Eggplant, cooked	½ cup	13	7	Potassium	3	2	0.6
Endive	1 cup	8	10	A	26	12	1.1
Figs, dried	¼ cup	127	4	Potassium	72	6	8.0
Filberts	¼ cup	213	83	E	63	1	2.1
Fish cakes, fried	5 bite-size	103	42	B_{12}	6	—	—
Flounder	3 oz	171	37	B_{12}	19	201	0
Frankfurter, beef	1	184	82	B_{12}	7	584	0

Superfoods Chart

Foods	Serving Size	Calories (kcal)	Percent of Calories from Fat	Major Nutrient	Calcium (mg)	Sodium (g)	Fiber
French dressing	1 tbs	67	84	—	2	214	0
Fruit punch drink	1 cup	132	0	—	8	36	0
Ginger ale	12 oz	113	0	—	11	30	0
Goose, domesticated, roasted	3 oz	202	48	Niacin	12	64	0
Granola, homemade	½ cup	298	48	Thiamine	38	6	2.9
Grapefruit	½	38	3	C	14	0	0.2
Grapefruit juice, fresh	½ cup	48	2	C	11	1	0
Grape juice, bottled	½ cup	78	1	Potassium	11	4	—
Grapes	10	15	4	Potassium	3	0	0.07
Haddock, fried	3 oz	140	35	B_{12}	34	150	0
Halibut, broiled w/buttter or margarine	3 oz	145	37	B_{12}	14	114	0
Ham, chopped	1 oz	65	68	Thiamine	2	389	0
Herring, plain, canned	3 oz	177	59	B_{12}	125	—	0
Honeydew	⅛	58	2	C	10	16	1.5
Italian dressing	1 tbs	69	91	—	1	116	0
Kiwi fruit	1 medium	46	6	C	20	4	—
Kohlrabi, cooked	½ cup	24	3	C	20	17	0.9
Lamb:							
Leg	3 oz	158	34	B_{12}	11	60	0
Loin chops	3 oz	160	36	B_{12}	10	59	0
Lemonade	1 cup	105	Trace	—	2	—	0
Lettuce:							
Boston	1 cup	7	14	C	19	3	0.4
Iceberg	1 cup	7	12	C	10	5	0.5
Romaine	1 cup	8	13	C	20	4	0.5
Liverwurst	3 oz	276	79	B_{12}	21	—	0
Lobster, cooked	3 oz	81	14	B_{12}	55	178	0
Mackerel, broiled w/butter	3 oz	200	60	B_{12}	5	53	0
Milk:							
Buttermilk	1 cup	99	19	Calcium	285	257	0
Condensed, sweetened	¼ cup	246	24	Riboflavin	217	97	0
Evaporated, whole	¼ cup	85	50	Calcium	165	67	0
1% low-fat	1 cup	102	22	B_{12}	300	123	0
Skim	1 cup	86	4	B_{12}	302	126	0
Whole, 3.3% fat	1 cup	150	48	B_{12}	291	120	0
Muffin:							
Bran	1	104	31	—	57	179	2.5
Plain	1	118	28	Riboflavin	42	176	—

(continued)

Superfoods Chart—*Continued*

Foods	Serving Size	Calories (kcal)	Percent of Calories from Fat	Major Nutrient	Calcium (mg)	Sodium (g)	Fiber
Mushrooms, raw	4	20	13	Potassium	4	4	1.4
Nectarine	1	67	8	C	6	0	3.3
Noodles, egg	1 oz	35	10	Thiamine	3	0.6	0.3
Oatmeal, cooked w/o salt	½ cup	73	14	Thiamine	10	0.5	1.3
Ocean perch, fried	3 oz	193	53	B_{12}	28	130	0
Okra, cooked	½ cup	25	5	C	50	4	1.6
Onions:							
Cooked	¼ cup	15	5	C	15	4	0.4
Raw	¼ cup	14	7	C	10	1	0.3
Orange	1	62	2	C	52	0	0.6
Orange juice, fresh	½ cup	56	4	C	14	1	0
Oysters, fried	6	162	53	B_{12}	102	140	0
Pancakes, plain or buttermilk	1	164	27	Riboflavin	157	412	1.0
Papaya	½	59	3	C	36	4	1.4
Parsley sprigs	10	3	8	C	13	4	0.4
Peach	1	37	2	C	5	0	0.5
Peanut butter, w/o added salt	1 tbs	95	72	E	5	3	1.2
Peanuts, unroasted	¼ cup	207	73	E	21	6	3.4
Pear	1	98	6	C	19	1	4.1
Peas:							
Green, cooked	½ cup	67	2	C	22	2	3.0
Split, cooked	½ cup	115	2	Potassium	11	13	5.1
Pecans, dried	¼ cup	180	85	Thiamine	10	0.3	1.4
Peppers, sweet, raw	1	18	15	C	4	2	0.8
Pickle:							
Dill	1 medium	7	12	—	17	928	1.1
Sweet, gherkins	1 large	51	2	—	4	299	0.6
Pineapple, raw	1 slice	42	7	C	6	1	1.3
Pineapple juice, canned	½ cup	70	1	C	21	1	0
Pistachio nuts, unroasted	10	35	70	E	8	0.4	0.6
Pizza, w/cheese topping	1 slice	153	31	—	144	456	—
Plums	3	108	10	C	6	0	1.5
Popcorn, plain	1 cup	23	11	—	1	Trace	—
Pork:							
Boston blade, fresh, broiled	3 oz	233	61	Thiamine	5	71	0
Ham, cured, roasted	3 oz	140	42	Thiamine	7	1177	0
Ham, fresh, roasted	3 oz	187	45	Thiamine	6	55	0
Loin	3 oz	208	51	Thiamine	9	39	0
Spareribs	3 oz	338	69	B_{12}	40	79	0
Potato chips	10	105	56	—	5	94	2.5

Superfoods Chart

Foods	Serving Size	Calories (kcal)	Percent of Calories from Fat	Major Nutrient	Calcium (mg)	Sodium (g)	Fiber
Potatoes:							
Baked, w/skin	1	220	0.8	C	20	16	3.7
Boiled, cooked w/o skin	1	116	1	Potassium	10	7	1.4
French fried, frozen, home prepared, heated in the oven	10 strips	111	35	C	4	15	0.8
French fried, restaurant prepared	10 strips	158	46	Potassium	10	108	1.1
Hash brown	½ cup	163	56	Potassium	6	19	1.0
Mashed, w/milk added	½ cup	81	6	Potassium	28	318	0.9
Potato salad	½ cup	179	51	C	24	661	—
Pretzel, rod	1	55	9	—	3	235	—
Prune juice, canned	½ cup	91	0.3	Potassium	15	6	—
Prunes, dried, uncooked	½ cup	193	2	Potassium	41	3	13.0
Rabbit, stewed	3 oz	184	42	—	18	35	0
Radishes	3	2	29	C	3	3	0.1
Raisins, seedless	¼ cup	124	1	Potassium	20	5	2.8
Raspberries	¼ cup	15	9	C	7	0	1.4
Rhubarb, raw	½ cup	13	8	C	52	2	1.1
Rice:							
Brown, long grain, cooked	½ cup	116	4	Magnesium	12	275	5.4
White, long grain, cooked	½ cup	112	1	Thiamine	11	384	2.2
Russian dressing	1 tbs	76	91	—	3	133	0
Salami:							
Beef, cooked	1 oz	72	71	B_{12}	2	328	0
Hard, pork	1 oz	115	75	B_{12}	4	633	0
Salmon, pink, canned	3 oz	120	38	B_{12}	167	329	0
Sardines, canned in oil	3 oz	172	49	B_{12}	371	699	0
Sauerkraut	½ cup	22	6	C	36	780	1.6
Sausage:							
Bratwurst, cooked	3 oz	256	77	Thiamine	38	473	0
Italian, cooked	3 oz	274	72	B_{12}	20	783	0
Pork, cooked	3 oz	315	76	B_{12}	28	1099	0
Scallops, steamed	6	67	11	B_{12}	69	159	0
Shad, baked w/butter	3 oz	171	51	—	20	67	0
Shrimp, canned	6	22	8	B_{12}	22	429	0
Spinach, cooked	½ cup	21	9	A	122	63	1.7
Spinach, raw	1 cup	12	14	A	56	44	1.8
Squash:							
Acorn, cooked, baked	½ cup	41	2	C	32	3	1.5
Zucchini, raw	½ cup	9	8	C	10	2	0.3

(continued)

Superfoods Chart—*Continued*

Foods	Serving Size	Calories (kcal)	Percent of Calories from Fat	Major Nutrient	Calcium (mg)	Sodium (g)	Fiber
Strawberries	¼ cup	11	10	C	5	0.5	0.7
Tangerine	1	37	4	C	12	1	1.8
Thousand Island dressing	1 tbs	59	84	—	2	109	—
Tomato, raw	1	24	9	C	8	10	1.0
Tomato juice, canned w/added salt	½ cup	21	3	C	10	441	—
Tuna:							
In oil	3 oz	245	38	B$_{12}$	5	679	0
In water	3 oz	108	6	B$_{12}$	14	35	0
Turkey:							
Breast, roasted	3 oz	115	5	Niacin	11	44	0
Leg, roasted	3 oz	135	21	Zinc	19	69	0
Turkey gravy, canned	1 tbs	8	37	—	0.6	—	—
Turnips, cooked	½ cup	21	4	C	26	58	1.1
Veal:							
Boneless veal for stew	3 oz	200	49	B$_{12}$	10	41	0
Loin cut	3 oz	199	52	B$_{12}$	9	55	0
Waffle	1	138	32	Riboflavin	120	343	0.8
Watermelon	1 slice	152	11	C	38	10	1.0
Yogurt:							
Low-fat, fruit varieties	8 oz	225	10	B$_{12}$	314	121	—
Low-fat, plain	8 oz	144	21	B$_{12}$	415	159	0

Sources:

Adapted from *Nutritive Value of American Foods in Common Units*, Agriculture Handbook No. 456, by Catherine F. Adams (Washington, D.C.: Agricultural Research Service, U.S. Department of Agriculture, 1975)

Composition of Foods: Vegetables and Vegetable Products, Agriculture Handbook No. 8-11, by Nutrition Monitoring Division (Washington, D.C.: Human Nutrition Information Service, U.S. Department of Agriculture, 1984)

Composition of Foods: Fruits and Fruit Juices, Agriculture Handbook No. 8-9, by Consumer Nutrition Center (Washington, D.C.: Human Nutrition Information Service, U.S. Department of Agriculture, 1982)

Composition of Foods: Dairy and Egg Products, Agriculture Handbook No. 8-1, by Consumer and Food Economics Institute (Washington, D.C.: Agricultural Research Service, U.S. Department of Agriculture, 1976)

Pantothenic Acid, Vitamin B$_6$ and Vitamin B$_{12}$, Home Economics Research Report No. 36, by Martha Louise Orr (Washington, D.C.: Agricultural Research Service, U.S. Department of Agriculture, 1969)

"Provisional Tables on the Zinc Content of Foods," by Elizabeth W. Murphy, Barbara Wells Willis and Bernice K. Watt, *Journal of the American Dietetic Association*, April 1975

Recommended Dietary Allowances, by Committee on Dietary Allowances, Food and Nutrition Board (Washington, D.C.: National Academy of Sciences, 1980)

Composition of Foods: Poultry Products, Agriculture Handbook No. 8-5, by Consumer and Food Economics Institute (Washington, D.C.: Science and Education Administration, U.S. Department of Agriculture, 1979)

McCance and Widdowson's The Composition of Foods, by A. A. Paul and D. A. T. Southgate (New York: Elsevier/North-Holland Biomedical, 1978)

Composition of Foods: Sausages and Luncheon Meats, Agriculture Handbook No. 8-7, by Consumer Nutrition Center (Washington, D.C.: Science and Education Administration, U.S. Department of Agriculture, 1980)

Bowes and Church's Food Values of Portions Commonly Used, by Jean A. T. Pennington and Helen Nichols Church (New York: Harper & Row, 1980)

Composition of Foods, Agriculture Handbook No. 8, by Bernice K. Watt and Annabel L. Merrill (Washington, D.C.: Agricultural Research Service, U.S. Department of Agriculture, 1975)

Composition of Foods: Nut and Seed Products, Agriculture Handbook No. 8-12, by Nutrition Monitoring Division (Washington, D.C.: Human Nutrition Information Service, U.S. Department of Agriculture, 1984)

The Sodium Content of Your Food, Home and Garden Bulletin No. 233, by Science and Education Administration in cooperation with Northeast Cooperative Extension Services (Washington, D.C.: U.S. Department of Agriculture, 1980)

Composition of Foods: Pork Products, Agriculture Handbook No. 8-10, by Consumer Nutrition Division (Washington, D.C.: Human Nutrition Information Service, U.S. Department of Agriculture, 1983)

Nutritive Value of Foods, Home and Garden Bulletin No. 72, by Science and Education Administration (Washington, D.C.: U.S. Department of Agriculture, 1978)

"Vitamin E Content of Foods," by P. J. McLaughlin and John L. Weihrauch, *Journal of the American Dietetic Association*, December 1979

Composition of Foods: Fats and Oils, Agriculture Handbook No. 8-4, by Consumer and Food Economics Institute (Washington, D.C.: Science and Education Administration, U.S. Department of Agriculture, 1979)

Composition of Foods: Soups, Sauces and Gravies, Agriculture Handbook No. 8-6, by Consumer and Food Economics Institute (Washington, D.C.: Science and Education Administration, U.S. Department of Agriculture, 1980)

"Fiber Analysis Tables," by D. A. T. Southgate and P. J. Van Soest, *The American Journal of Clinical Nutrition*, October 1978

"Folacin in Selected Foods," by Betty P. Perloff and R. R. Burtum, *Journal of the American Dietetic Association*, February 1977

Composition of Foods: Breakfast Cereals, Agriculture Handbook No. 8-8, by Consumer Nutrition Center (Washington, D.C.: Human Nutrition Information Service, 1982)

Composition of Foods Commonly Used in Diets for Persons with Diabetes, by James W. Anderson, Wen-Ju Lin and Kyleen Ward, *Diabetes Care*, September/October 1978

Introductory Nutrition, fifth ed., by Helen A. Guthrie (St. Louis: C. V. Mosby, 1983)

Provisional Table on the Nutrient Content of Beverages, by Nutrient Data Research Group, Consumer Nutrition Center (Washington, D.C.: Human Nutrition Information Service, U.S. Department of Agriculture, 1982)

Information provided by Peter J. Horvath and James B. Robertson, Department of Animal Science, Division of Nutritional Sciences, Cornell University.

Index

Rodale Press, Inc., publishes PREVENTION®, the better health magazine.
For information on how to order your subscription,
write to PREVENTION®, Emmaus, PA 18049.